Contents

ELLIO

The Ohi

Real Estate Education Compan
a division of Longman Financial Services In

Preface

This book is written for the nonlawyer, real estate student or professional. A knowledge of law in the real estate business is probably more important than in any other nonlaw business. Survival and success in the real estate business require an awareness of the possible impact of the law on the particular undertaking. This is particularly true in brokerage, where the day-to-day activities of the broker require that he or she understands basic principles of contract law, agency and zoning, to name a few.

The law has a significant impact on the real estate business for several reasons. First, the business revolves around the single most precious commodity on earth, the land itself. Land has been and continues to be an important resource for mankind. Second, purchases and development of land involve large sums of money; consequently, the participants have a significant economic stake in the land. Because the function of law is to regulate and define rights, it is appropriate for the law to be significantly involved in the rights associated with such an expensive and precious resource.

This textbook, which is an adaptation of *Real Estate Law* by Gibson, Karp and Klayman, focuses on the law in Texas with respect to real estate. In adapting the text we had several goals in mind. First, we wanted it accurately and clearly to explain the fundamental concepts of law as they pertain to real estate. Second, we tried to provide historical background to explain why the law is as it is and its purposes. Third, we wanted the student to be able to recognize a transaction or business problem that contains questions of law that should be considered in structuring the transaction or solving the problem. We believe that some problems and disputes can be avoided if the parties understand the legal environment in which they operate. Fourth, we wanted the student to have a better understanding of the role of the legal system and law in American society. Finally, we wanted the book to be a handy reference in the day-to-day operations of a real estate broker.

The first twelve chapters cover some of the fundamental principles of law. These chapters include topics such as the different interests in land, limitations on land use, transferring of interest in land, title assurance and involuntary liens. Chapter 7 discusses three forms of real estate ownership: condominiums, cooperatives and time-shares. Each of these has specific legislation that controls the rights and responsibilities associated with it. Chapters 13–25 focus on transactions involving real estate. The topics here include licensing requirements for those who represent others in real estate transactions, agency, contracts, mortgages and leases.

Pedagogically the textbook offers several features that should be helpful to both the instructor and the student. We believe that reading cases increases the student's comprehension and retention of legal principles. We, therefore, have included three different approaches to placing the law in a factual context. These approaches are case examples, case briefs and case excerpts. The case examples are hypothetical situations that provide a setting in which to illustrate a particular legal principle. The case examples are generally very simple. Case briefs are the authors' summaries of actual cases. The case briefs usually include a summary of the facts, the court's decision and a summary of some of the reasons for the decision. If any portion of the court's opinion appears in a case brief it is indicated by quotation marks. Case excerpts are the actual opinion rendered by the court. We have deleted portions of the opinion that we believed were unnecessary for an understanding of the legal principle illustrated. On a few occasions, we have summarized the facts, but where this has been done we have so indicated. Our purpose in including the longer cases is to provide the instructor who wishes to include case studies a basis from which to teach. We also believe that part of knowing the law is understanding legal reasoning and determining why a court has made a particular decision.

As appropriate throughout the textbook, we have included citations to statutes that are discussed in the chapter. These citations provide the reader with the source of the law in the event he or she wishes to read further. Within the chapters we have created tables, logic charts, comparison charts and visual graphics to assist the student in learning the basic principles in some of the more complex areas. Also included are illustrations of legal documents that are discussed in the text and that the real estate professional is likely to encounter in the real estate business. Finally, at the end of each chapter there are questions for discussion. Each chapter contains two types of questions. The first type checks the student's knowledge of the legal principles covered in the chapter. The second type of question, called case problems, tests the student's ability to apply the law to specific facts. Most of these case problems are based upon actual court cases.

We conclude by thanking those persons who assisted in the preparation of this book. First, we thank Frank Gibson, James Karp and Elliot Klayman, who provided us with an excellent foundation on which to base *Texas Real Estate Law*. Second, we thank the following reviewers for their suggestions and recommendations for improving the text: Sam Lanham, associate professor, Schreiner College, Kerrville, Texas; Barbara A. Eubanks, GRI, DREI, Collin County Community College, McKinney, Texas; Paul Metzger, Houston Community College System, Houston, Texas; Thomas G. Naler, board attorney, Lewisville Board of REALTORS®, Lewisville, Texas, and John B. Garrett, American College of Real Estate.

1

Introduction to Law and the Texas Legal System

LAW AND THE REAL ESTATE BUSINESS

Many aspects of the real estate business are closely associated with law. In fact, only the world of finance may be more closely controlled by law. Almost any professional activity of a broker, salesperson, appraiser or investor involves certain legal restrictions. For this reason, people employed to do these jobs, as well as people employed to do many other jobs in real estate, have a genuine need to know about the law and legal systems. The more extensive their knowledge, the more effectively will they be able to do their jobs.

Real estate professionals deal not only with lawyers but also with lenders, title companies, recording clerks, building inspectors, tax officials, zoning board employees and personnel from state and federal housing agencies. All of these people have specialized functions in the legal system. Understanding what they do and some of the responsibilities of their jobs increases the real estate professional's ability to work effectively with them. Many private individuals with whom salespeople and brokers come in contact also have specialized knowledge of the law; loan officers and appraisers are examples. Real estate professionals who have similar knowledge will be able to work more effectively with other specialists and improve their professional image at the same time.

Legal knowledge is especially important to people who sell real estate. They are involved in the real estate transaction at a critical point as far as legal input is concerned. Clients and customers will often question them about legal matters or the advisability of consulting an attorney. Although sales personnel should never give legal advice, a knowledge of law will help them develop an awareness of situations in which a lawyer should be consulted. Because legal knowledge is considered so important, some states require salespeople and brokers engaged in selling real estate to complete a formal course in real estate law. In Texas, real estate law is one of the courses described in the Real Estate License Act and recommended by the Texas Real Estate Commission for licensees.

Although this book is devoted to a study of real estate law, to some extent that designation is misleading. Real estate law cannot really be separated from other types of law. A famous jurist once said, "Law is a seamless web"; nevertheless, because of the complexity of law, people who want to understand it often consider it in small segments. The boundaries of these segments are never exact, nor is there general agreement on what they include. So, initially, the reader must realize that, although much of what is said about real estate law applies to law in general, some strands of the "seamless web" are more important to the real estate business than others. This book deals primarily with these strands.

Most of this book discusses specific rules important to real estate people. In this first chapter, however, the book takes a broader look at law and the legal system. This chapter attempts to clarify the law by looking at some of its functions, where it is found and the structure in which it operates.

FUNCTIONS OF LAW

Defining law has been a challenge to thoughtful men and women throughout the ages. Although numerous definitions have been proposed, no single one is satisfactory. Each civilization, each age, each segment of society has different ideas about what law is. This fact is readily understandable; ideas about the law reflect the way people think about such things as religion, ethics, economics and morality. Some people contend that nothing can be law unless it is also moral. Others argue that law is merely the command of the sovereign or that law is anything the courts will enforce as law.

In the absence of general agreement of what law is, one way to understand it better is not to define it but to look at some of the things it does. Law is one of a number of institutions that people have developed to solve some of the difficult problems that arise out of societal life. Although other institutions direct their resources to the same difficult questions, in the Western world legal solutions generally provide the ultimate answer.

Consider, for example, a dispute between a brother and a sister over ownership of certain property. Ordinarily the dispute will be solved in consultation with other members of the family. If the dispute is really serious, perhaps neighbors, the church or even an employer will become involved. If the dispute remains unsettled, however, eventually the parties will take their problems to a court. What then are some of the major purposes of law and the legal system?

Provides Order

Order is a need fundamental to every society. Without order no society can survive. Where there is chaos, men and women must spend inordinate amounts of their time protecting themselves, their families and their possessions. This leaves them with little time to obtain from a hostile natural world those items that are necessary for enjoyable, productive lives. The first task of law then is to provide conditions that are conducive to an orderly society so that people can devote their time to winning their livelihoods and trying to live fulfilling lives.

Settles Disputes

Order is difficult to maintain. To maintain order, parties who have a dispute must have a reasonable expectation that it can be settled. In addition, for resolution of the dispute to be satisfactory, the parties must be confident that their controversy will be settled fairly and within a reasonable time. The legal system provides a forum for settling many disputes between individuals. Local, state and federal courts as well as administrative tribunals offer the facilities and supervise the processes that resolve many problems. The courts also indirectly support individuals who use means such as mediation and arbitration to settle problems.

If public facilities were not available, the parties in many instances would resort to self-help. Threats and eventually violence would be involved in the resolution of disputes. Both of these would lead to retaliation and the consequent disruption of society.

Protects Expectations

The kind of order that is necessary for a society to function effectively extends beyond the elimination of violence and strife. People need the assurance of reliability in their dealings with others. In the modern world, planning is vital in almost everything that we do. Unless we can depend upon promises and commitments that are made to us, our efforts to plan are futile. Law protects reasonable expectations of the future. The legal system provides compensation if anticipations based upon promises are not met. Protection of expectations is especially necessary to the real estate business. The legal relationships and objectives of leases, land contracts, insurance policies, listing agreements and employment all depend upon the protection of expectations.

Prevents Exploitation ·

One of the significant contributions that law can make is to prevent exploitation. Many laws that are important to real estate people have this as their primary purpose. Laws allowing a remedy for victims of false advertising, fraud and misrepresentation are among those that prevent the exploitation of one individual by another. In a democracy, laws also prevent the exploitation of an individual by government. An illustration would be those constitutional provisions that require the government to provide just compensation when it takes private property. Although the state does have the right of eminent domain, this right cannot be exercised unless the individual's property is to be used for public purpose. In addition, an owner who feels that the compensation offered by the state is insufficient has a right to a judicial determination of a fair price.

Ensures Equality

Justice is an integral part of what we have come to call "the good life"—an ordered society. Although the concept of justice differs from one society to another, the promotion of justice is usually considered a major responsibility of law. In the United States, one significant contribution that law makes in promoting justice is to ensure that equality of treatment exists for all Americans. In a democracy, government should not permit different treatment of people because of their race, nationality, religion or sex. A number of laws important to the daily work of real estate personnel are intended to ensure equal treatment for all people.

SOURCES OF LAW

The answer to many legal questions comes from life's experiences. As a person learns in school, on the job or through daily living, laws important to that person become part of his or her knowledge of the manner in which things operate. Sometimes legal questions arise that are not answerable from experience. How does one find the answers to these questions? To what source does the student, the real estate professional, the lawyer or the judge turn to find out what the law is?

One of the prevailing myths about law is that all laws are found in nicely indexed, officially published volumes of statutes enacted by a legislative body. According to this belief, all a person has to do to answer a legal question is to locate the correct page in the right book, and the law will be there in clear black letters. Unfortunately, few legal questions are answered this simply.

There are several different sources of law. In Texas, as elsewhere, the four principal sources are court decisions, constitutions, statutes and regulations promulgated by administrative bodies. All four sources must be consulted because each can influence the outcome of a specific legal problem. Typically, several different books must be read before all the sources have been considered. For example, court decisions are reported in books called *Reporters*, while federal administrative regulations are reported in a series of books called the *Code of Federal Regulations*.

Appellate Court Decisions

A distinctive feature of English and American law is its reliance upon cases decided by appellate courts as a source of law. Reports of these cases are published in opinions. The opinions of the Texas appellate courts are reported in a series of books called the *Southwestern Reporter*. These decisions are important because they serve as precedents. A ***precedent*** is a previously decided case that serves as authority for determining a legal question in a later case with similar facts.

In the legal system of English-speaking countries, judges are obligated to follow principles established by prior cases. This obligation is ingrained in our system. The extent to which a court is governed by precedent is difficult to assess. Although the practice of following precedent is not a legal duty, it is definitely more than a tradition. A judge who failed to follow precedent would not be convicted of a crime, but he or she ordinarily would be reversed and in extreme cases censured or possibly impeached. People trained in our system generally consider reliance upon precedent an effective and fair way to reach a decision, and the concept is fundamental to American law.

The obligation to follow precedent is limited by a number of factors. A court need not follow precedent established in another state, although in reaching decisions courts sometimes consider precedent from other states when their own state has no case law on the subject. Lower courts are bound to follow decisions rendered by higher courts of their state. Again, failure to do so may result merely in the lower court's decision being reversed. The highest appellate court in a state can overrule its own precedent. Although this occurs on occasion, most state appellate courts overrule reluctantly because they believe that certainty is a desirable characteristic of law. The reluctance to overrule is often seen in private areas such as real estate law, for certainty is deemed very important where property rights are involved. A court will overrule a prior decision when the rule of law was applied incorrectly in the first place or when the rule is not considered applicable because of a change in circumstances.

Courts and attorneys frequently avoid the effect of a previous case by distinguishing it from the case under consideration. A case is distinguished when a significant factual difference can be pointed out between the two situations. For example, in the case of *Humber v. Morton*, which is included in this section, Claude Morton was held to be liable to Ernestine Humber for damages she suffered when her new house was partially destroyed by fire. The fire was caused by an improperly constructed fireplace and chimney. Claude Morton, who was in the business of building houses, had sold the house to Mrs. Humber. This case would serve as a precedent for other cases in which a builder-seller had defectively constructed a new house and as a result the purchaser was damaged. However, the case would not be a precedent for holding a seller who was *not* the builder of the house liable for poor workmanship in the construction of the house. For example, assume that Mrs. Humber bought the house from Mrs. Lincoln, who had lived in the house for three years. Mrs. Lincoln was not aware of the faulty construction performed by the builder, Mr. Morton. Is Mrs. Lincoln liable to Mrs. Humber when the house is destroyed by fire? The facts in this hypothetical case are significantly different from the facts in the case of *Humber v. Morton;* therefore, that case would not control the outcome of the hypothetical.

Law that evolves from cases is often called *judge-made* or *decisional law.* In England, reliance upon previous decisions and upon customs and tradition created a law that was common to the entire country. Because of this, reliance upon cases is often referred to as common law. Sometimes people have difficulty accepting the idea that in these opinions statutes are not involved in any manner. In fact, often no statute exists that can be used to settle the dispute.

The increasing responsibility of builders for defective homes is a current example of judge-made law involving real estate. Prior to World War II, the builder of a defective home had little legal responsibility after the purchase. The purchaser was required to make his or her own inspection of the premises. On the basis of this inspection, the purchaser accepted responsibility for all defects; the builder was no longer responsible for defective construction. The courts were applying the ancient doctrine of caveat emptor—"let the buyer beware."

During the 1950s and the 1960s, courts began to recognize the inequities of this rule. In 1968 the Texas Supreme Court in a landmark case changed this rule and held that buyers of new homes could recover for personal injuries and property damage resulting from defective construction. The following is an excerpt from the court's opinion in that case. Throughout this book portions of appellate court opinions will be included to illustrate points of law and their application to particular facts.

CASE EXCERPT   *Humber v. Morton, 426 S.W.2d 554 (Supreme Court of Texas 1968)*   NORVELL, Justice.   The widow Humber brought suit against Claude Morton, alleging that Morton was in the business of building and selling new houses; that she purchased a house from him which was not suitable for human habitation in that the fireplace and chimney were not properly constructed and because of such defect, the house caught fire and partially burned the first time a fire was lighted in the fireplace. Morton defended upon two grounds: that an independent contractor, Johnny F. Mays, had constructed the fireplace and he, Morton, was not liable for the work done by Mays, and that the doctrine of "caveat emptor" applied to all sales of real estate. . . .

It conclusively appears that defendant Morton was a "builder-vendor." The summary judgment proofs disclose that he was in the business of building or assembling houses designed for dwelling purposes upon land owned by him. He would then sell the completed houses together with the tracts of land upon which they were situated to members of the house-buying public. . . .

Mrs. Humber entered into a contract when she bought the house from Morton in

May of 1964 and such house, together with the lot upon which it was situated, was conveyed to her. According to Morton, the only warranty contained in the deed was the warranty of title, i.e. "to warrant and forever defend, all and singular, the said premises unto the said Ernestine Humber, her heirs and assigns, * * *." and that he made no other warranty, written or oral, in connection with the sale. . . . However, it is undisputed that Morton built the house and then sold it as a new house. Did he thereby impliedly warrant that such house was constructed in a good workmanlike manner and was suitable for human habitation? We hold that he did. Under such circumstances, the law raises an implied warranty. . . .

Originally, the two great systems of jurisprudence applied different doctrines to sales of both real and personal property. The rule of the common law—caveat emptor—was fundamentally based upon the premise that the buyer and seller dealt at arm's length, and that the purchaser had means and opportunity to gain information concerning the subject matter of the sale which were equal to those of the seller. On the other hand, the civil law doctrine—caveat venditor—was based upon the premise that a sound price calls for a sound article; that when one sells an article, he implies that it has value. . . .

The purchase of a home is not an everyday transaction for the average family, and in many instances is the most important transaction of a lifetime. To apply the rule of caveat emptor to an inexperienced buyer, and in favor of a builder who is daily engaged in the business of building and selling houses, is manifestly a denial of justice. . . .

If at one time in Texas the rule of caveat emptor had application to the sale of a new house by a vendor-builder, that time is now past. The decisions and legal writings herein referred to afford numerous examples and situations illustrating the harshness and injustice of the rule when applied to the sale of new houses by a builder-vendor, and we need not repeat them here. Obviously, the ordinary purchaser is not in a position to ascertain when there is a defect in a chimney flue, or vent of a heating apparatus, or whether the plumbing work covered by a concrete slab foundation is faulty. It is also highly irrational to make a distinction between the liability of a vendor-builder who employs servants and one who uses independent contractors. . . .

The caveat emptor rule as applied to new houses is an anachronism patently out of harmony with modern home buying practices. It does a disservice not only to the ordinary prudent purchaser but to the industry itself by lending encouragement to the unscrupulous, fly-by-night operator and purveyor of shoddy work.

The judgment of the courts below are reversed and the cause remanded for trial in accordance with this opinion.

Constitutions

A basic source of law, constitutions provide the framework within which the federal and state governments must operate. Governments have inherent powers that are limited by constitutions. Two important powers inherent to governments are eminent domain and the police power. Both the United States Constitution and the Texas constitution place limitations on these two inherent powers.

Eminent domain is the power of governments to take private property for a necessary public purpose. It is the authority by which the state can acquire private land for streets, parks, public buildings and other uses. Both the federal and the state constitutions require that owners be justly compensated for any property taken by a government.

The police power of government is the power to adopt and enforce laws and regulations that promote the public health, safety and welfare. It is from its police power that city government can enact zoning codes. This power, though, is also limited. Excessive regulation of property resulting in substantial destruction of its value constitutes a taking of property without just compensation and therefore is unconstitutional.

The Constitution of the United States allocates power between the states and the federal government. The Tenth Amendment provides that "powers not delegated to the United States by the Constitution, nor prohibited by it to the States, are reserved to the States respectively." Because the states generally have retained power over local matters, most real estate law is state law. On the other hand, inasmuch as the states have given the federal government power to regulate businesses affecting interstate commerce, numerous federal statutes apply to the real estate business. At present, many people in the field are concerned with the application to real estate of federal statutes such as the Sherman and Clayton acts. Bankruptcy statutes and consumer protection laws like "Truth-in-Lending," the Real Estate Settlement Procedures Act and environmental protection legislation are other examples of federal law that apply to real estate.

Constitutions also create and protect individual rights, including property rights. For example, the Texas constitution protects a person's homestead from a forced sale by a general creditor. Another important individual right created in the Texas constitution is the mechanic's or materialman's lien. This constitutional lien provides a person who has improved another person's land with a method for guaranteeing payment.

The federal and state constitutions also protect individuals by requiring that the law be applied equally to all and by prohibiting government from depriving a person of life, liberty or property without due process. This means that an individual's property can be taken by government only under limited circumstances.

Due process, required by the U.S. Constitution and the Texas constitution, is a fundamental concept of American jurisprudence. There are two types of due process. **Procedural due process** requires government to use methods that are fair and just when taking private property. Minimally, procedural due process requires that the individual be provided with notice of the government action and an opportunity to defend before a fair, competent tribunal. In eminent domain cases, the opportunity to defend necessitates that the individual be allowed to establish the fair market value of the property or that the property is not being acquired for a public purpose.

Substantive due process, a broader concept, guarantees that legislation and governmental regulations that deprive a person of life, liberty or property will not be unreasonable or arbitrary. In addition, the method the government selects to accomplish its purpose must have a real and substantial relationship to the objective sought.

Statutory Law

The term statutory law refers to laws enacted by local and state legislative bodies and by Congress. Although for many years the opinions of courts were the chief source of real estate law in English-speaking countries and for the legal system generally, during the past 100 years statutes have gradually assumed this role. Among the numerous reasons for this trend to statutory law are these: statutes are more comprehensive; statutes can modify the law more rapidly; statutes can treat an entire problem rather than just a part and statutes are usually more understandable than cases.

During the past 75 years, statutes have been used to bring greater uniformity to state law. Economic expansion after the Civil War has been characterized by the growth of regional and national markets. States, however, have often adopted different laws to solve common problems occurring in these markets. This practice has increased the cost of doing business as well as causing confusion and uncertainty.

In 1890, the National Conference of Commissioners on Uniform State Law was established to alleviate this problem. The commission is charged with determining what uniform laws are necessary, drafting a uniform statute and trying to get states to adopt it. More than 100 uniform laws have been recommended, although few have been adopted by all or even a majority of the states.

The commission has recently proposed a number of laws that deal with real estate. These include a uniform condominium act, a uniform residential landlord-tenant act, a uniform simplification of land transfers act and a uniform eminent domain code. As of 1987, however, the impact of these uniform laws on real estate has been negligible.

Despite the growing importance of statutes as a source of law, court opinions continue to play a significant role in determining what the law is. Many statutes are broadly written. Often their meaning is not clear until they have been interpreted by a court. It is probably safe to say that, in a majority of instances, a lawyer looking for the answer to a legal question will first check for an appropriate statute and then review relevant court opinions interpreting that statute.

Several statutes deal specifically with some aspect of real estate or the real estate business. For example, the Texas Real Estate License Act regulates the qualifications and activities of persons who represent others in real property transactions, inspections and appraisals. These statutes will be cited and discussed in this book as appropriate.

Much of Texas law has been codified, or gathered and indexed into related topical codes. The Texas Property Code includes laws pertaining to condominiums, recording, landlord-tenant rights and a host of other laws relating to real property. The Texas Natural Resources Code includes laws relating to the development of natural resources in Texas. The Texas Water Code deals with laws relating to the private and public use of water. Property tax laws are included in the Texas Tax Code. These codes as well as others greatly simplify topical research since the statutes were passed over 150 years. Each of these codes has an index organized by subject matter that usually appears in the last volume of the code.

In addition to these specific laws, others, spread throughout the civil statutes, regulate real estate and the transactions pertaining to it as well as other types of transactions. Unfortunately, no single book can be consulted that would comprehensively cover real estate law. One of the main works containing the Texas constitution, the various codes described above and the miscellaneous statutes is Vernon's. This series of books is divided into *Vernon's Texas Constitution, Vernon's Texas Civil Statutes, Vernon's Texas Property Codes* and so on. There is a general subject matter index for the civil statutes as well as an index for each of the separate codes. All public libraries in Texas have a copy of the Texas constitution and statutes.

Administrative Rules and Regulations

In our dynamic, complex society, much of the work of government is done by administrative agencies such as the Environmental Protection Agency, the Interstate Commerce Commission and others. Many boards, commissions and departments make up the bureaucracy. Often these bodies have been given the authority to settle disputes. Their function in this process is similar to that of the courts and is called *administrative adjudication.* Many agencies also have the power to make rules and regulations that have the force of law. The combination of rule making and adjudicative powers is a distinguishing feature of the administrative process.

Administrative rules and regulations are so pervasive that they influence almost every aspect of American life. Administrative agencies have a far-reaching influence on the real estate business. They are the source of rules pertaining to such diverse problems as licensing sales personnel, zoning, safeguarding the environment, financing and protecting landlord and tenant rights.

An agency's authority to make rules and regulations is granted to it by the legislature. If the rule is constitutional and the proper procedures are followed, agency rules based upon a grant of power from the legislature may not be modified by the courts. Other types of agency rules interpret statutes that the agency was created to enforce. These interpretations are subject to judicial review. Ordinarily the courts give the interpretations by the agency considerable respect because the agency is the expert body charged by the legislature with enforcing the statute.

It is helpful to be familiar with the Texas state agencies that deal specifically with aspects of the real estate business and real estate transactions. These agencies and a general description of their roles are as follows:

Texas Real Estate Commission: licenses and regulates real estate salespeople and brokers

Texas Railroad Commission: regulates the production, transportation and conservation of oil and gas

Texas Department of Water Resources: regulates use and development of Texas water and waterways; issues water permits

General Land Office: registers all land titles emanating from the state of Texas

Figure 1.1: SOURCES OF LAW BY RANK*

1. The United States Constitution
2. The Texas Constitution
3. Statutes enacted by the U.S. Congress
4. Statutes enacted by the Texas Legislature
5. Precedents or common law
6. Administrative regulations

*All of the above laws are subject to interpretation by the appellate courts. These interpretations become precedents for similar cases.

The general publication for regulations promulgated by the state administrative bodies is the *Texas Administrative Code*. This publication can be found at law libraries and at some public libraries in the state. Proposals to change administrative regulations are published in a weekly magazine called the *Texas Register*. Specific regulations also can be obtained by writing to the appropriate state agency.

COURT STRUCTURE

Judicial systems in the United States consist of different levels and types of courts. These systems reflect the existing amount of litigation, the existence of federal and state governments and the specialized personnel and procedures needed to solve certain types of legal problems most effectively and fairly.

Federal and State Courts

The federal government and each of the states has its own structure of trial and appellate courts. Federal courts do not have authority over state courts except for questions that involve the U.S. Constitution. Each of the systems —state and federal—is the final authority within its own area of jurisdiction. Cases that involve federal statutes such as the Civil Rights Acts, Environmental Protection Acts and bankruptcy statutes are heard in federal courts.

Federal courts may also hear cases that involve citizens of different states. This practice of *diversity jurisdiction* is based upon the Constitution. In order to limit the number of diversity cases that the federal courts will have to decide, Congress has passed a statute requiring that the amount in controversy be more than $10,000.

CASE EXAMPLE

Able was a resident of New Hampshire and Baker a resident of New York. The two entered into a contract in which Baker agreed to purchase a large resort hotel in New Hampshire from Able. Baker breached the contract, and Able sued her in the New Hampshire courts for $25,000 damages. Baker may transfer the case to the federal district court since the parties are residents of different states and the amount in controversy exceeds $10,000.

Most real estate litigation can be decided in state courts. The problems generally do not come under federal statutes and the parties are usually residents of the same state. Many real estate legal problems concern land located within the state and few questions involving the jurisdiction of state courts ordinarily arise.

Texas Court System

The Texas court system is divided into two levels: the trial level and the appellate level.

Trial Courts

At the trial level the court hears testimony, decides what the facts are and applies the law to the facts. The trial courts in Texas include justice courts (also called *small claims courts*), county courts, county courts at law and district courts. Each of these courts is limited in the type of case it can hear. These limitations on power are called the *jurisdiction* of the court.

Justice courts and small claims courts are presided over by an elected official called a *justice of the peace*. These courts can hear disputes in which the amount of money in dispute is $1,000 or less. The justice courts also have jurisdiction to hear eviction cases and some criminal matters.

County courts are sometimes referred to as *constitutional county courts*. In some counties, the county courts have been completely replaced by a county court at law, which is discussed below. In those counties that retain county courts, the civil jurisdiction of the court overlaps with the justice courts. These courts can hear cases involving an amount in dispute that is greater than $200 but no more than $1,000.

County courts at law have been created by the legislature for the more populous counties. The jurisdictional limits of these courts differ from county to county. In many counties, these courts are limited to cases involving disputes of $5,000 or less. However, in a few counties, such as Harris County, the jurisdictional limit is $20,000. The legislature has also created county courts that hear probate matters and appoint guardianships. Probate matters include determination of heirs, probate of wills and any land disputes related to a probate proceeding. These matters can also be resolved in a district court.

District courts are presided over by a judge and hear most of the cases involving real estate problems. These courts can hear any case in which the amount in dispute is $500 or more. In addition, district courts have exclusive jurisdiction over land title disputes, foreclosure of liens against real estate and divorce proceedings.

In the more populous counties the trial courts may be divided into special areas. For example, in Dallas County there are county courts that hear only probate matters. There are also district courts that hear only divorce matters. This division of duties allows for specialization and facilitates the flow of cases through the judicial system.

Appellate Courts

The second level of the Texas court system is called the *appellate level*. At the appellate level a panel of judges reviews the application of the law by the judge at the trial level. Appellate courts do not hear testimony and do not decide facts. Appellate court review is limited to determining whether the law was properly applied to the facts as found by the judge in a trial court.

At the appellate level two different courts review civil cases: the Texas Court of Civil Appeals and the Texas Supreme Court. The first court to hear a case on appeal is one of the Texas courts of civil appeal. The state is divided into 14 appellate districts with a court of appeals for each district. A party who loses in the trial court can generally appeal the case to one of the courts of appeal. After the Texas Court of Civil Appeals has rendered a decision, the losing party can appeal that decision to the Texas Supreme Court. The Texas Supreme Court is not required to review every decision appealed to it. If the Texas Supreme Court declines to review a case, then the decision of the Court of Appeals is final.

REMEDIES

As stated at the beginning of this chapter, one of the functions of the legal system is to resolve disputes. Courts resolve disputes by ordering a course of action that will correct or counteract the wrong committed. These courses of action are called *remedies*. A **remedy** is the legal means by which the violation of a right is prevented or compensated for. For example, in *Humber v. Morton*, Mrs. Humber wanted the court to order Morton to pay for the repair of the damaged house. This monetary loss is called *damages*. The awarding of damages is one of the remedies a court can order.

Courts are limited in the type of remedy they can order. These limita-

Figure 1.2: **TEXAS COURT JURISDICTION—CIVIL CASES**

Appellate Courts

Texas Supreme Court — Reviews decisions made by the courts of appeals
Texas Courts
 of Appeal — Review the trial courts' application of law to a particular
case

Trial Courts

District Courts — Resolve disputes in which the amount of damages sought is
$500 or more; land title disputes; actions to foreclose liens
against land; and divorces

County Courts
 at Law — Resolve disputes in which the amount of damages sought is
no more than $5,000 (in some counties, no more than
$20,000); probate matters; and guardianships

Constitutional
County Courts — Resolve disputes in which the amount of damages sought is
greater than $200 but no more than $1,000

Justice Courts — Resolve disputes in which the amount of damages sought is
less than $1,000; cases to evict tenants

tions are based upon both public policy and practicality. Generally, the relief that a court orders should be reasonable given the wrong committed. In criminal law it is said that the punishment should fit the crime. The same is true in the area of civil disputes. What is a reasonable remedy given that a builder has not properly constructed a house? Should the court take the builder's first son and give him to the plaintiff? That *is* a remedy, although not a particularly useful or reasonable one. Perhaps a more reasonable course of action would be for the court to order the builder to rebuild the house or repair the defective parts of the house. However, this remedy is fraught with some practical problems. Can the court adequately ensure the quality of the rebuilt house or the repaired section? Another hearing could be held after the repairs were made to determine whether they were adequate to correct the wrong, but this is both time-consuming and costly for all concerned. Consequently, in fashioning a remedy the court considers not only the reasonableness of the relief but also whether the remedy can be administered or enforced practically by the legal system. For these reasons the most frequent remedy granted by courts in resolving disputes is the awarding of money to the injured party. In our example, the builder can simply be ordered to pay the homeowner the cost of making the repairs. The court's sole administrative function is to assist the plaintiff in collecting the money from the builder. This is a much simpler task than supervising the repair work.

Although there are several different means by which a court can correct or prevent a wrong, some of these remedies occur more frequently than others in disputes involving real estate. Throughout this book we will be discussing the legal rights associated with land ownership and use. These various rights will be enforced by the court by the granting of a remedy to an aggrieved party. These remedies will be discussed as appropriate. However, a brief overview of the four major categories of remedies may clarify the role of the legal system in dispute resolution.

Damages

When a party files a lawsuit, he or she is usually seeking compensation for his or her economic loss. The compensation is in the form of money paid to the injured party. For example, assume that Ryan purchased a home that was supposedly free and clear of all liens except a mortgage lien. Five months after the purchase Ryan is notified by Smith that there is a materialman's lien against the property for the cost of a new roof ordered by the former owner, Julliard. Ryan pays Smith, the roofer, $2,750 to avoid losing the house through foreclosure of the materialman's lien. Ryan then contacts Julliard and demands that Julliard reimburse him. Julliard refuses, and Ryan sues. First, Ryan must prove to the court that Julliard has violated some right. The right violated in this case would be Ryan's expectation that there were no other liens. This legal expectation arose because Julliard warranted that there were no liens against the property except the mortgage lien. After Ryan proves to the court that this legal right has been violated, Ryan asks the court to take some action to correct the wrong. In this case a reasonable and practical remedy would be for the court to order Julliard to pay to Ryan the cost of removing the lien, which is $2,750. This money will compensate Ryan for his economic loss and is appropriately called compensatory damages.

However, Ryan is very angry that Julliard deceived him and that he has had to file a lawsuit to collect from Julliard. Ryan wants to punish Julliard and asks the court to award him $150,000 in punitive damages. The remedy of punitive damages is not available in most lawsuits, and therefore the court cannot grant Ryan's request for $150,000. This limitation reflects the court's policy that an injured party should be made whole or put in the position he would otherwise be in but for the wrong committed by the defendant. It is not the purpose of the legal system to award the injured party a windfall.

Restitution

The second major category of remedies is restitution. Restitution means to return or to restore. Occasionally the awarding of damages does not fully compensate a party for his or her loss. For example, a dispute involving a unique item that was taken under false pretenses from the owner can be adequately resolved only if the court orders the defendant to return the item.

Damages would not enable the plaintiff to purchase a substitute since there are no substitutes for a unique item. Courts will also order restitution if neither party has yet performed his or her obligations under a contract and the dispute can best be resolved by canceling or rescinding the agreement. Rescission, though, will be ordered only to protect the party who has been wronged. The courts will not order cancellation of a contract simply because one of the parties has decided it was a bad deal. The remedy of restitution is sometimes referred to as an *equitable remedy*. An equitable remedy is one the court orders for the purpose of preventing the wrongdoer from being unjustly enriched.

Coercive Remedies

The third major category of remedies is called *coercive* because the court is commanding a person to do or not to do something. The two most common coercive remedies are specific performance and injunction. Coercive remedies are also referred to as equitable remedies and are more difficult to obtain than the remedy of damages. Generally, a coercive remedy is awarded only if the plaintiff is ethically, morally and legally right and the traditional remedy of damages is inadequate to protect from injury or correct the wrong committed.

Specific Performance

Specific performance is common in real estate contract disputes. When this remedy is granted, the court is ordering the defendant to perform specifically that which he or she promised to do in the contract. For example, assume that Hughes contracts to buy Blackacre from Ivan. After the contract is signed, Ivan notifies Hughes that he does not intend to transfer title. There may be other land that Hughes could buy, but it would not be exactly the same. Blackacre is a unique tract of land. In this situation the court could order Ivan to sell Blackacre to Hughes (specifically perform as promised in the contract).

Injunction

The injunction is another coercive remedy that can be very effective in certain types of real estate disputes. The purpose of an injunction is to stop the offending party from engaging in a certain activity. For example, assume that Jim's neighbor has begun operating a computer repair service company in his home. All of the lots in the subdivision are subject to a deed restriction limiting property use to residential purposes. In this situation Jim is not interested in receiving money from his neighbor; he wants his neighbor to stop operating a business in the neighborhood. Furthermore, it would be very difficult for Jim to prove an economic loss caused by his neighbor's computer repair business. In this situation Jim wants the court to enforce the deed restrictions of the subdivision.

Declaratory Remedies

The final category of remedies is called *declaratory* because the plaintiff is asking the court to interpret a contract or a statute and state what his or her rights are under the contract or statute. The courts are reluctant to declare what a person's rights are unless there is a real cause for concern. Should a court interpret a contract provision if there is no dispute between the parties to the contract concerning the meaning of the contract term? The answer is simply no. It would be a waste of the court's time.

Statutory Remedies

Statutory remedies includes all remedies created by a statute to redress a particular wrong. It has become common practice for Congress and the state legislatures to create rights or prohibit certain conduct and establish a mechanism for enforcing those rights. For example, in Chapter 16, a state law known as the Deceptive Trade Practices Act is discussed in some detail. The law prohibits certain types of deceptive or misleading business conduct. The act also sets out that the party who has been wronged by a deceptive act has a remedy that can include the awarding of three times the amount of compensatory damages. A statutory remedy may include one or more of the remedies discussed previously. For example, the deceptive trade practices act provides for damages and one of the coercive remedies, the injunction. Therefore, if the plaintiff is relying upon a particular statute for the creation of a right, it is advisable that the statute be consulted regarding the possible remedy for violation of the right.

SUMMARY

People employed in the real estate field have a genuine need to know about the law and the legal systems that regulate the profession. In fact, licensing requirements in Texas include a course in real estate law.

The law of any society reflects the way its leaders think about basic social and moral questions. In Western society the functions of law are to provide order, to settle disputes between parties, to protect citizens' expectations about the actions of others, to prevent exploitation by means of force or fraud and to ensure equality of all persons under the law.

Law has several sources: precedents or prior court opinions, constitutions, statutes and administrative regulations. All four of these sources should be consulted in resolving a legal dispute.

Much law today results from appellate courts' interpretation of statutes' and the body of law called *common law*. These interpretations become precedents that judges have a fundamental obligation to follow.

The constitutions of the United States and of Texas provide the framework within which government operates. The constitutions also protect and create individual rights, including property rights.

Several statutes in Texas regulate aspects of real property ownership and the real estate business. These include the Texas Real Estate License Act and the Texas Property Code. There are also federal statutes that control aspects of real estate. For example, the Clayton Antitrust Act and the Real Estate Settlement Procedures Act directly impact on brokers' activities.

Rules and regulations promulgated by the various federal and state administrative agencies have become so numerous that almost every aspect of American life has been affected. In Texas, several agencies directly concern themselves with real property. These include the Texas Real Estate Commission, the Texas Railroad Commission and the Texas Department of Water Resources.

An important component of the legal system is the court structure. There are both federal and state courts. Most of the disputes relating to land and the real estate business are resolved in the state courts. In Texas there are trial courts that hear testimony, decide the facts and apply the law. The trial courts are justice of the peace courts, county courts and district courts. Each trial court is limited by its jurisdiction as to the type of case it can hear. There is also an appellate court level in Texas. At the appellate level a panel of judges reviews the application of the law by the trial courts and corrects any errors. The appellate courts in Texas are the Texas Courts of Civil Appeal and the Texas Supreme Court.

When a person files a lawsuit in a court, he or she is seeking a court order correcting a wrong he or she has suffered. The relief that can be granted by a court is called a *remedy.* There are four main categories of remedies: damages, restitution, coercive remedies and declaratory remedies. In addition, the state legislatures and Congress frequently create remedies when they enact new laws. These are called *statutory remedies.* The most common remedy granted by a court is the awarding of damages to compensate a party for his or her economic loss. Two other remedies useful in real estate disputes are specific performance and injunction.

QUESTIONS AND CASE PROBLEMS

1. (a) Define the *doctrine of precedent.* (b) Indicate limitations on the use of precedents.
2. Name the courts in Texas and define their jurisdiction.
3. In what publications are the following sources of Texas law found? (a) precedents (b) constitution (c) statutes (d) administrative regulations
4. During the past 50 years, statutory law has gradually replaced judge-made or decisional law. Explain the reasons for this.
5. Sorensen, a licensed real estate broker, entered into a listing agreement with Schomas. Sorensen located a buyer who submitted a purchase offer. Schomas refused to accept the offer or to pay Sorensen the commission that was clearly owed. Enraged, Sorensen

threatened to "take the case to the United States Supreme Court, if necessary." Explain why Sorensen probably would be unable to do this.

6. The City of Lubbock, Texas, under the Texas Urban Renewal Act, designated a particular area for slum clearance. The land was to be cleared and sold for private development. The sales would be subject to restrictions to prevent the future growth of slums. Johnson owned property within the designated area. Although his structures met all requirements of the city's building code, they were to be demolished along with substandard buildings. What arguments might Johnson raise against the condemnation? Would he be successful?

2
Land and Related Concerns

LAND

Land is a commodity limited in supply that, along with elements associated with it (water and minerals), is both an essential agent in production and a desirable consumer good. Until recently the idea that people could exist for any length of time apart from land was inconceivable. Even today, when the idea of human beings living out their lives on islands in space is a possibility accepted by serious scientists, human destiny remains linked with land. Whenever humans have survived, they have taken their living directly or indirectly from the land. Because land and people have always been inseparable, the ways in which land has been viewed are as diverse as the world's communities.

Much of the conflict between the American Indians and Europeans who settled this hemisphere resulted from attitudes toward land. The Indians regarded land differently than did the Europeans who settled North and South America after 1500. Land, to the Indians, was a resource possessed by the tribe. It was not subject to individual ownership. Some native groups in Africa, Australia and South America hold similar views today. In western Europe during the late Middle Ages the idea of community ownership in some lands existed, but by the time major colonization occurred in North America, the concept of individual property rights prevailed. Most settlers who came to this country after 1700 wanted to own their own land. Although themes other than individual ownership can be discerned in the way Americans regard land, a majority, especially those living in the United States, continue to consider it a commodity to be owned individually.

A number of factors account for this view. Probably the most important is historic. Our pioneer ancestors were individualistic in economic matters. The men and women who wrested the land from the great forests of the East and from the prairies of the West were acquiring wealth for themselves and their families. They saw land, like any commodity, as something that could be bought and sold or passed on to their children. These people also believed in personal freedom. They regarded private ownership of land as a bulwark against both the intrusion of the state and the inquisitiveness of their neighbors. Finally, traditional economic theory in the Western world includes land as an important factor of production. Although land—like labor and capital—is not productive alone, a price has to be paid for it because it is both necessary and scarce. Land is an important good that, with labor and capital, can be put to work to provide profit for the owner.

The treatment of land is traditionally within the control of the state where the land is located. This basic tenet of law has been recognized since the beginning of this country. As states were formed out of the wilderness, control over land transfers and use became the realm of the individual states.

CASE EXAMPLE

The Martins live in Ohio and own a condominium on Padre Island in Texas. Does the law of Ohio or the law of Texas govern the ownership and use of that condominium? The answer is the law of Texas.

The United States government has chosen to enter some fields of regulation with respect to real estate. These are regulations based upon the interstate commerce clause of the United States Constitution. The federal government also controls the federal lands it has acquired. However, the bulk of law pertaining to real property and land is derived from the individual states.

Although there are 50 different states with the potential for 50 different sets of laws relating to real estate, there is great similarity in the treatment of real estate in many areas. There are several reasons for this development. First, the source of much law in the United States is the English common law. There are other sources, such as Spanish and French law, but the English common law is the most prevalent and influential. For example, many of the land laws in Texas have their roots in both Spanish and English law. A second reason for similarities in the laws is the reliance courts and legislatures place upon another state's handling of a particular problem. The states borrow from, improve upon and adapt laws from other states to meet their needs.

In spite of generalities and similarities among the states, there are sufficient variations and distinctions to require some additional study of the state law in which the land in question is located. For example, a deed as an instrument by which land can be conveyed is fairly universal. However, the components that make a deed valid or the warranties that arise under a particular deed may depend upon the law of the state in which the land is located.

TRESPASS

The right of a person to occupy land peacefully and exclusively is of paramount importance. Over the centuries both the civil and criminal laws in England and the United States have provided remedies to secure this right. *Trespass* is the act of entering or remaining upon land in the possession of another without authority from the owner or lawful occupant. A person injured by another's trespass may recover damages even if the injury is inconsequential. An injunction, which is a court order forbidding the trespass, can be obtained if the occupant establishes that the trespass is repetitious and that irreparable injury will occur if the act continues.

In Texas the criminal trespass statute is found in §30.05 of the Texas Penal Code. A person commits an offense if he or she enters or remains on property or in a building without the consent of the owner and he or she had noticed that entry was forbidden or was asked to leave the property. Notice includes the posting of a sign or the enclosure of property by a fence.

In civil cases, the invasion or trespass can be either intentional or negligent. Negligence is the failure to act as a reasonable person would act. For example, a reasonable person would take precautions to avoid cutting trees on a neighbor's property. Therefore, a person who does not carefully ascertain the boundaries of his property and, as a result, removes three live oak trees on his neighbor's property would be liable for trespass, even though he did not *intend* to interfere with his neighbor's use of his land. Trespass occurs when a person interferes with the owner's or lawful occupant's exclusive possession. That definition includes the setting in motion of a thing that invades another's property, such as air pollutants, water or animals. Failure to take precautions against the discharge of air pollutants is negligence, and the injured property owner can sue the offending party for trespass.

Most trespass cases involve interference with possession of surface property, but trespass may occur either above or below the earth's surface as well. Unpermitted excavating beneath another's land constitutes a trespass, as does excavating solely beneath one's own lands if material is removed in sufficient quantities to cause injury to a neighbor's property by removing lateral support. Unpermitted flight over another's land is also a trespass. Because of the importance of air transportation, this problem has been solved by allowing flight at levels that do not interfere with an occupant's use of the property. Air rights are discussed later in the chapter.

Actual invasion of the premises of another is not necessary in a trespass action. If a person initiates a force that violates an occupant's exclusive right to possession, a remedy is available to the occupant. The following case illustrates this principle of law.

CASE EXCERPT *A. W. Gregg v. Delhi-Taylor Oil Corp.,* 344 S.W. 2d 411 (Supreme Court of Texas 1961) GREENHILL, Justice. A. W. Gregg is the owner of an oil and gas lease on .42 acres in the City of Pharr, Hidalgo County, Texas. The tract is approximately 75 feet wide. Delhi-Taylor Oil Corporation and Mayfair Minerals Inc. (herein called Delhi-Taylor), own the mineral estates in land surrounding Gregg's lease. Gregg is drilling or has drilled a well 37½ feet from Delhi-Taylor's lease on the east and 80 feet from its south line. He plans to increase the productivity of his well by fracturing the gas-producing formation, a process by which sand is mixed with liquid and forced into the structure under great hydraulic pressure. Veins or cracks are thus opened so that the gas may flow from the producing rock or sand into Gregg's well. Delhi-Taylor brought this suit to enjoin Gregg from fracturing the common formation beyond Gregg's own property lines into Delhi-Taylor's lease. It is a suit by Delhi-Taylor to enjoin a subsurface trespass by Gregg. . . .

We think the allegations are sufficient to raise an issue as to whether there is a trespass. The invasion alleged is direct and the action taken is intentional. Gregg's well would be, for practical purposes, extended to and partially completed in Delhi-Taylor's land. The pleadings allege a physical entrance into Delhi-Taylor's leasehold. While the drilling bit of Gregg's well is not alleged to have extended into Delhi-Taylor's land, the same result is reached if in fact the cracks or veins extend into its land and gas is produced therefrom by Gregg. To constitute a trespass, "entry upon another's land need not be in person, but may be made by causing or permitting a thing to cross the boundary of the premises." . . .

The judgment of the Court of Civil Appeals is affirmed.

LAND AS A NATURAL RESOURCE

Although the view of land as a commodity has been dominant in the United States, this is but one view of land. Especially during this century, the idea that land is a social resource that must be preserved for future generations has gained credence. As a result of this trend, vast areas of our nation have been set aside as a public domain, and governments at all levels have adopted legislation to control land use for the benefit of society. Because of these different views, and because of its importance to society, land has become the subject of a large body of law as our nation tries to cope with the problems involved with its use and disposition.

As traditionally defined by courts and commentators, land encompasses the surface of the earth, everything above that surface and all that is below. Land has been described as an inverted pyramid extending upward indefinitely into space and downward to the center of the earth (*see* Figure 2.1). Many items such as water, minerals, oil and gas can be separated from the land. Because these things are both scarce and desirable, they, along with space, are often severed and treated as independent commodities. The result has been that detailed laws regulating their use have developed throughout the United States. These laws differ from place to place as they reflect the needs of people in a particular area.

Figure 2.1: **LAND OWNERSHIP: THE INVERTED PYRAMID**

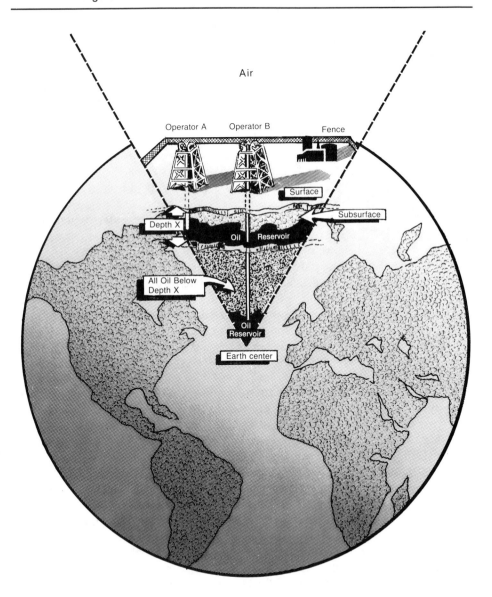

WATER RIGHTS

Water is one of the earth's most precious resources. This simple statement explains why water rights are so very important. The competition for water continually increases. Farmers, ranchers, manufacturers, developers, cities and all of us need water. Unfortunately, there is a limited supply of usable water. In Texas the existence of a water supply directly affects the value of land. Therefore, a basic understanding of individual rights to use water is important to land ownership.

Ownership and use of water depend in part upon the source of the water. Traditionally, water sources have been divided into three categories: water from a river, stream, natural lake or bay; water from an underground reservoir or stream; and water that accumulates on the earth's surface not in a stream- or riverbed. The most complex water rights are those associated with water from a river, stream, lake or bay.

Rivers, Streams, Lakes and Bays

The water in a river, stream, natural lake or bay is owned by the state. If the river is classified as "navigable," the state also owns the riverbed. Water rights with respect to these water sources are rights of use. In law these are called *usufructuary rights*. A **usufruct** is the right to use, enjoy and receive the profits of property that belongs to another. Since water rights with respect to rivers, streams, lakes and bays are rights to use the property owned by the state, they are usufructs.

The rights associated with these bodies of water are complex because Texas recognizes two different and inconsistent theories of use. As a matter of fact, the Texas Supreme Court has described water law in Texas as chaotic. The two theories of water rights that cause much of this chaos are called *riparian rights* and *appropriation rights*. To understand water rights in Texas you must first understand these two theories.

Riparian Rights

The term **Riparian rights** refers to the water rights doctrine that is based upon the idea that all owners of riparian lands are entitled to share equally in the use of water for domestic purposes. Riparian lands are those that border on a stream or watercourse. Riparian lands extend away from the stream, including the stream's drainage area or watershed, although all of the drainage area is not necessarily riparian land. The riparian area of the watershed is only that portion under ownership of a person whose property fronts on the waterway. A landowner's property might be in the watershed of a stream, but the landowner is not a riparian owner unless his or her property fronts on the stream.

In Texas, riparian rights exist for any landowner who can trace title to the land back to a grant from either the state or a sovereignty before July 1, 1895. It was on that date that the first appropriation statute was enacted. Grants of land from the state after July 1, 1895, don't carry riparian rights.

Where they do exist, riparian rights are considered to be property rights and pass with title to the land.

Riparianism has two basic principles. First, ownership of the land bordering water establishes a right to use the water equally. Second, as the abutting land owner has no proprietary right in the water itself, any control over flowing water is lost once it passes the riparian tract. Specifically, riparian rights include:

1. the right to operate a ferry with a permit;
2. the right to have the body of water flow, uninterrupted, in its accustomed channel;
3. the right to free access to the body of water;
4. the right to a reasonable use of the water for domestic purposes, provided the use does not interfere with other riparian owners' use of the same water; and
5. in some cases the right to a reasonable use for irrigation purposes.

One of the rights of a riparian owner is the right to the uninterrupted flow of water in the river, stream, lake or bay. This means that a riparian owner cannot interfere with the natural flow of the river or stream. A riparian owner cannot use so much of the water or divert the water so that it diminishes the flow in quantity or quality. For example, an upper riparian owner cannot construct a dam right across the channel. Another important right is the right to make reasonable use of the water. At common law the right of reasonable use was interpreted as a requirement that the use be beneficial. In 1967 the right to reasonable use was modified by the Texas Legislature. In that year it passed the Water Rights Adjudication Act. (Tex. Water Code §11.301 et seq.)

This statute required all claimants to riparian rights to file sworn statements with the Texas Water Commission by September 1, 1969. The claim to water would be recognized only if it was valid under existing law and only to the extent of the maximum actual application of water to beneficial use without waste. To determine how much water each riparian owner had a claim to, the highest beneficial use during any one year from 1963 to 1967 could be used. As a result of this law, a riparian owner's right to use water has been limited to the amount for which he or she has a state permit.

Appropriation Rights

Appropriation is a water rights doctrine giving primary rights to the first users of water. The right of prior appropriation is limited to the extent that the water can be used beneficially. There is no requirement that the appropriator own land adjacent or contiguous to the river, stream or lake. Like the riparian system, prior appropriation creates a right to use water that can become vested and exists as a property right. Since land acquired from the state after July 1, 1895, did not carry riparian rights, the right to use the water had to be acquired by appropriation.

The law in Texas after 1895 provided that "water of the ordinary flow, underflow, and tides of every flowing river, natural stream, and lake, and of every bay or arm of the Gulf of Mexico, and the stormwater, floodwater, and rainwater of every river, natural stream, canyon, ravine, depression and watershed in the state is the property of the state." (Tex. Water Code§5.021) The right to use this water can be acquired by permit from the state. The law limits appropriation of water for domestic and municipal uses, industrial uses, irrigation, mining, hydroelectric power, navigation, recreation, stock raising, public parks and game preserves, with the priority among uses in the same order as enumerated. Domestic and municipal purposes always take priority over other uses.

A person desiring to appropriate water files an application with the Texas Water Commission. In the application, the applicant discloses the purposes for which he or she intends to use the water and how much water is requested. The commission then notifies other permit holders in the same watershed, giving them an opportunity to object. If the commission grants the request, the individual then has the right of appropriation. When an appropriator has used water under the terms of the permit for three years, he or she acquires a vested right of use against any other claimant of water from the same source. The appropriator's use is limited to the amount of water stipulated in the permit or the amount he or she can use beneficially, whichever is less. Between appropriators, first in time is first in right.

Although the right of appropriation can vest after three years of use, it can be lost by forfeiture. Wasting of the water, defined as any nonbeneficial use, is one ground for forfeiture. Appropriation rights can also be forfeited by nonuse. An appropriator who willfully abandons the right to use the water for three successive years forfeits his or her permit. Nonuse of the water for ten successive years results in an automatic termination of appropriation rights.

Many of the conflicts in Texas regarding water rights arise between a landowner with riparian rights and a person who has acquired appropriation rights by permit from the state. The case that follows illustrates the type of dispute that can arise.

• CASE BRIEF •

Adams is a stock farmer who owns 1,700 acres of land, with approximately seven miles of river frontage along the Leon River. The original grants of this land were issued by the state of Texas in 1847, 1848 and 1853. Adams has riparian rights to use the water from the Leon River. North Leon River Irrigation Corporation is a nonprofit organization of 46 members who are peanut farmers and own land on or near the river. The corporation has a permit to use water and purchases from the Brazos River Authority 2,800 acre-feet of water per year. Upon request by the corporation the Brazos River Authority releases water stored in the Proctor Dam Reservoir into the Leon River. Adams has been intercepting and diverting a portion of this water for irrigating his farm land. The corporation seeks to enjoin Adams from pumping this released water from the Leon River. Adams claims that he has the right as a riparian landowner to pump water from the Leon River at any time. The court held that Adams's riparian rights extended only to use of water that occurs from the ordinary flow of the river and that he should be enjoined from using the water released by the Brazos River Authority. *Adams v. North Leon River Irrigation Corporation*, 475 S.W.2d 873 (Tex. Civ. App.—Eastland 1972).

Groundwater

Groundwater is water in the earth below the saturation point. There are two main sources for groundwater: underground streams and percolating waters. Underground streams are subterranean waters that flow in a clearly defined channel. Underground streams are governed by the same rules of law that govern rivers and streams on the earth's surface. Water rights in underground streams are relatively less important than water rights in percolating waters for two reasons. First, establishing that an underground stream exists is difficult. The person asserting that water is flowing in an underground stream must establish without excavation that the stream has a definite bed, bank and current. Second, in Texas it is presumed that groundwater is percolating water.

Percolating water is water that passes through the ground beneath the surface, not flowing in an underground stream or supplied by streams flowing on the surface. Percolating waters belong absolutely to the owners of land in which they are found. The individual landowner can use as much of this water as he or she chooses. This is true even if the use depletes the reservoir, denying an adjoining property owner of his or her supply of water.

There are two limitations on the use of groundwater. First, the landowner cannot be willfully wasteful of the water. Second, the landowner cannot use the water or divert the water in such a way as to intentionally or wantonly harm an adjoining property owner.

One of the problems associated with withdrawal of groundwater is subsidence of the surface. In 1973 a class action suit was brought by several property owners who alleged that severe subsidence of their land was caused by withdrawals of vast quantities of underground water from wells on neighboring land. The subsidence increased the risk of flooding. This case finally reached the Texas Supreme Court in 1978. The case is included at length below because it modified the long-established rule in Texas with respect to withdrawal of groundwater. It is an example of a court's creating a new precedent.

CASE EXCERPT   *Friendswood Development Company v. Smith-Southwest Industries, Inc.*, 576 S.W.2d 21 (Supreme Court of Texas 1978)   DANIEL, Justice.   The question in this case is whether landowners who withdrew percolating ground waters from wells located on their own land are liable for subsidence which resulted on lands of others in the same general area.

Smith-Southwest Industries and other landowners located in the Seabrook and Clear Lake area of Harris County brought this class action in 1973 against Friendswood Development Company and its corporate parent, Exxon Corporation, alleging that severe subsidence of their lands was caused by the defendants' past and continuing withdrawals of vast quantities of underground water from wells on defendants' nearby lands. . . .

The trial court had before it depositions, interrogatories, affidavits and exhibits which showed rather clearly that Friendswood had pumped large amounts of sub-surface waters from its own property for sale primarily to industrial users in the Bay-port industrial area developed by Friendswood and Exxon. These wells were drilled from 1964 through 1971, even though previous engineering reports to defendants showed that production therefrom would result in a certain amount of land subsi-dence in the area. . . .

The English rule of so-called "absolute ownership" was applied by this Court in . . ., which held that a landowner has the absolute right to sell percolating ground water for industrial purposes off the land. . . .

We agree that some aspects of the English or common law rule as to under-ground waters are harsh and outmoded, and the rule has been severely criticized since its reaffirmation by this Court in 1955. Most of the critics, however, recognize that it has become an established rule of property law in this State, under which many citizens own land and water rights. The rule has been relied upon by thou-sands of farmers, industries, and municipalities in purchasing and developing vast tracts of land overlying aquifers of underground water. . . .

As heretofore mentioned, the Legislature has entered the field of regulation of ground water withdrawals and subsidence. . . . The legislative policy contained in Chapter 52 of the Texas Water Code is designed to limit the exercise of that portion of the English rule which has been interpreted as giving each landowner the right to take all the water he pleases without regard to the effect on other lands in the same area. . . .

This case, however, gives the Court its first opportunity to recognize, and to en-courage compliance with, the policy set forth by the Legislature and its regulatory agencies in an effort to curb excessive underground water withdrawals and result-ing land subsidence. It also affords us the opportunity to discard an objectionable aspect of the court-made English rule as it relates to subsidence by stating a rule for the future which is more in harmony with expressed legislative policy. We refer to the past immunity from negligence which heretofore has been afforded ground water producers solely because of their "absolute" ownership of the water. . . .

Therefore, if the landowner's manner of withdrawing ground water from his land is negligent, willfully wasteful, or for the purpose of malicious injury, and such con-duct is a proximate cause of the subsidence of the land of others, he will be liable for the consequences of his conduct. The addition of negligence as a ground of recov-ery shall apply only to future subsidence proximately caused by future withdrawals of ground water from wells which are either produced or drilled in a negligent man-ner after the date this opinion becomes final.

While this addition of negligence as a ground of recovery in subsidence cases applies to future negligence in producing water from existing wells and those drilled or produced in a negligent manner in the future, it has been suggested that this new ground of recovery should be applied in the present cause of action. This is often done when a court writes or adds a new rule applicable to personal injury cases, but seldom when rules of property law are involved. This is because precedent is necessarily a highly important factor when problems regarding land or contracts are concerned. In deeds, property transactions, and land developments, the parties should be able to rely on the law which existed at the time of their actions. . . .

Accordingly, the judgment of the Court of Civil Appeals is reversed and the judgment of the trial court is affirmed.

Surface Waters

Surface waters are waters that collect on the land's surface not in a naturally occurring channel or riverbed. Surface water that is trapped in a manmade lake, pond or tank belongs to the owner of the land. The landowner can use this water in any way, provided he or she does not harm adjoining property. For example, a landowner cannot divert surface waters from his or her property in such a way that it would cause flooding on an adjoining tract. However, if the natural terrain of the land causes a flow of surface waters that produces flooding, the landowner is not liable. Landowners are not required to alter the natural flow of surface waters.

Figure 2.2: **WATER RIGHTS IN TEXAS**

Water Source	Rights	Limitations
Rivers, Streams, Natural Lakes and Bays: (pre–1895 grant from sovereignty)	Riparian rights: 1. reasonable use for domestic and occasionally irrigation purposes 2. free access to water 3. natural flow in the water channel	Quantity and use stated in permit from Texas Water Commission
(post–1895 grant from sovereignty)	Appropriation Rights: 1. beneficial use 2. first in time first in right	Quantity and use stated in permit from Texas Water Commission
Underground Water: flowing in subterrarean riverbed	Treated the same as rivers, streams, natural lakes and bays as summarized above	
percolating waters	Reasonable use for any nonwasteful purpose	Negligent withdrawal resulting in subsidence or withdrawal with intention to harm neighbor
Surface Water	Can collect and use in any manner	Cannot divert so as to harm neighbor

Administrative Regulation of Water Use

Water usage in Texas is heavily regulated; therefore, some familiarity with the agencies responsible for water use regulation can be helpful. The Texas Water Commission has the primary responsibility for implementing the laws in this state relating to water. This agency issues water permits, adjudicates water right disputes, supervises the various water districts, enforces the water quality programs, monitors hazardous waste disposal and is responsible for coastal water management.

The Texas Water Development Board has primary responsibility for water planning and administration of water financing assistance in the state. In addition to these two state agencies there are various water districts throughout the state that regulate certain aspects of water use. Figure 2.3 lists the various types of water districts and a general description of their authority. Most of these water districts have the power to assess water charges for users, assess taxes against real property in the district, borrow money to finance their programs and acquire property by eminent domain.

MINERAL RIGHTS

The common law envisioned the surface owner's rights as extending upward indefinitely into the sky and downward to the center of the earth. Until the industrial revolution, this definition was adequate to solve most legal questions. Except for a limited number of metals such as gold and silver, minerals were not of great concern to society. Consequently, problems involving subsurface rights were rare. The industrial and technological revolutions changed this situation. The demand expanded for many minerals found below the surface. This led to an increase in the value of these minerals and the subsurface in which they are found.

Early industrialization depended upon coal as a source of energy. Metals such as iron, copper, tin and lead also contributed to commercial growth. Technological developments of the 20th century have further increased dependence upon these and other minerals as well as gas and oil. As these resources become more valuable, real property law adapted to provide solutions for legal problems created by their increased use.

Land was recognized as a commodity that could be divided horizontally for the purposes of ownership. One person could own the surface while others had rights in the subsurface. An owner could grant the right to extract minerals, lease land with the right to take minerals or convey title to the subsurface in which valuable resources were located. American law clearly allows a surface estate and one or more subsurface estates to be separately carved out of a single tract and held in entirely separate ownership. However, in the absence of a reservation or conveyance of mineral rights, these rights remain with the land ownership.

Mineral rights are acquired in a number of ways. One is a mineral deed. This instrument is similar to the deed, discussed in Chapter 10, used to

Figure 2.3: **WATER DISTRICTS IN TEXAS AND THEIR MAJOR FUNCTIONS**

Municipal Utility Districts

1. control, storage, preservation and distribution of stormwater, floodwater and the water of rivers and streams for irrigation, hydroelectric power and all other useful purposes
2. solid waste disposal
3. water purity enforcement
4. reclamation, conservation and preservation of water resources
5. distribution of treated water

Water Control and Improvement Districts

1. improvement of rivers, creeks, and streams to prevent overflows
2. construction and maintenance of pool, lakes, reservoirs, dams, canals and waterways for irrigation, drainage or navigation
3. water purity enforcement
4. navigation of coastal and inland waterways

Underground Water Conservation Districts

conservation, preservation, protection, recharging and prevention of waste of underground water reservoirs

Fresh Water Supply Districts

conservation, transportation and distribution of fresh water from any source in the district for domestic and commercial purposes

Water Improvement Districts

1. irrigation of land
2. furnishing water for domestic, power or commercial purposes

Drainage Districts

control and supervision of construction and maintenance of canals, drains, ditches and levees

Levee Improvement Districts

construction and maintenance of levees; reclamation of lands from overflow and provision for proper drainage of reclaimed land

Navigation Districts

1. improvement of rivers, bays, creeks, streams and canals
2. construction and maintenance of canals and waterways to permit or improve navigation

transfer title to surface estates. Although the mineral deed transfers only title to mineral rights, the law relating to the two has many of the same features. The person acquiring mineral rights by deed ordinarily acquires absolute title just as one would who acquired a surface estate. The deed grants in express terms a mineral estate, describing the size and kinds of minerals acquired. The deed or other document conveying the mineral rights should also grant all rights necessary to conduct a mining operation. These would include rights related to access, development, processing and transportation. Figure 2.4 is an example of a mineral deed.

Absolute title to mineral rights is also often acquired by a mineral reservation in a deed. In this situation the owner, upon disposing of the surface, retains the mineral rights. In each instance, the grant or the reservation, the owner of the mineral rights has an interest that can be conveyed without regard to surface ownership. The following language would reserve the mineral rights for the grantor:

> Save and Except, and there is hereby reserved unto Grantors, their heirs and assigns, the oil, gas and other minerals in and under and that may be produced from the above property, together with the right of ingress and egress at all times for the purpose of mining, drilling, exploring, operating and developing said lands for oil, gas and other minerals and removing the same therefrom.

Finally, mineral rights can be acquired by lease. The lessee obtains an exclusive right to carry out mining operations and title to the ore. Unlike the absolute sale of mineral rights, the lessor usually retains a present or future right in the mineral estate. In a lease arrangement, the owner of the property is compensated by royalty payments. These payments are based on a fixed percentage of the value of extracted minerals. A mineral lease should contain provisions setting forth the duration of the lease, renewal rights of the lessee, any rights to suspend lease provisions and responsibilities of the lessee relative to the surface condition of the property. Figure 2.5 is an example of a mineral lease.

Characteristics of Mineral Ownership

Ownership of the mineral estate, whether it has been severed or not, carries with it certain general rights. The most basic of these rights is the right to explore for and remove the minerals from the land. The owner of the minerals can engage in this activity personally or transfer these rights to someone else through a short- or long-term arrangement. The most common method of transferring exploration and development rights is by the execution of a mineral lease. The mineral estate owner is free to negotiate the lease terms without interference or consultation with the owner of the surface estate. If the mineral estate owner chooses to lease the mineral rights, he or she will receive in exchange a percentage of the mineral extracted, called a *royalty.* A royalty can be paid in kind by giving the owner of the mineral estate a percentage of the oil or uranium or other mineral. However, the more prevalent method of payment of the royalty is in money, the amount of which reflects the value of the percentage of the minerals produced. Different types of royalties can be negotiated in a lease of the

Figure 2.4: **MINERAL DEED**

---

82 MINERAL DEED—Texas Standard

POUND PRINTING & STATIONERY COMPANY
2325 Fannin, Houston, Texas 77002 (713) 659-3159

MINERAL DEED

THE STATE OF TEXAS

COUNTY OF..

    THAT..

KNOW ALL MEN BY THESE PRESENTS:

....hereinafter called Grantor,

of...County, Texas, for and in consideration of the sum of

....Dollars ($....................) cash in hand paid by

....

hereinafter called Grantee, the receipt of which is hereby acknowledged, have granted, sold, conveyed, assigned and delivered, and by these presents do grant, sell, convey, assign and deliver unto the said Grantee, an undivided .... interest in and to all of the oil, gas and other minerals in and under, and that may be produced from the following described land situated in ....

County, Texas, to-wit:

Together with the right of ingress and egress at all times for the purpose of mining, drilling and exploring said land for oil, gas and other minerals, and removing the same therefrom.

    Said land being now under an oil and gas lease executed in favor of ....
.... , it is understood and agreed that this sale is made subject to the terms of said lease and/or any other valid lease covering same, but covers and includes .... of all of the oil royalty and gas rental or royalty due and to be paid under the terms of said lease, in so far as it covers the above described land.

    It is understood and agreed that .... of the money rentals, which may be paid, on the above described land, to extend the term within which a well may be begun under the terms of said lease, is to be paid to the said Grantee; and, in event that the above described lease for any reason becomes canceled or forfeited, then and in that event, Grantee shall own ....

of all oil, gas and other minerals in and under said lands, together with a like   (   ) interest in all bonuses paid, and all royalties and rentals provided for in future oil, gas and mineral leases covering the above described lands.

    TO HAVE AND TO HOLD the above described property, together with all and singular the rights and appurtenances thereto in anywise belonging unto the said Grantee herein, and Grantee's successors, heirs and assigns forever; and Grantor does hereby bind .... successors, heirs, executors and administrators, to warrant and forever defend all and singular the said property unto the said Grantee herein, and Grantee's successors, heirs and assigns, against every person whomsoever lawfully claiming or to claim the same, or any part thereof ....

    WITNESS .... hands this the .... day of .... , 19 ....

Figure 2.4: (continued)

SINGLE ACKNOWLEDGMENT

THE STATE OF TEXAS

COUNTY OF_____

Before me, the undersigned authority, on this day personally appeared _____

known to me to be the person____whose name____is (are) subscribed to the foregoing instrument, and acknowledged to me that ____executed the same as____free act and deed for the purposes and consideration therein expressed.

Given under my hand and seal of office this ____day of_____, 19____

My Commission Expires

_____   Notary Public, in and for the State of Texas

_____   Notary's Printed Name

JOINT ACKNOWLEDGMENT

THE STATE OF TEXAS

COUNTY OF_____

Before me, the undersigned authority, on this day personally appeared_____

and_____husband and wife, known to me to be the persons whose names are subscribed to the foregoing instrument, and acknowledged to me that they executed the same as their free act and deed for the purposes and consideration therein expressed.

Given under my hand and seal of office this ____day of ,19

My Commission Expires

_____   Notary Public, in and for the State of Texas

_____   Notary's Printed Name

CORPORATION ACKNOWLEDGMENT

THE STATE OF TEXAS

COUNTY OF_____   BEFORE ME, the undersigned authority, on this day personally

appeared_____, known to me to be the person whose name is

subscribed to the foregoing instrument, as_____of_____ a corporation, and acknowledged to me that he executed the same for the purposes and consideration therein expressed, in the capacity stated, and as the act and deed of said corporation.

Given under my hand and seal of office this the_____day of_____A. D. 19____

My Commission Expires

_____   Notary Public, in and for the State of Texas

_____   Notary's Printed Name

FORM No. 82

No._____

MINERAL DEED

FROM

TO

_____County, Texas

Dated_____19_____

No. Acres.

Term.

This instrument was filed for record on the_____day of_____19_____at_____o'clock_____M., and duly recorded in

Volume_____Page_____of the records of this office.

_____County Clerk.

By_____Deputy

When recorded return to

POUND PRINTING & STATIONERY COMPANY 2525 Fannin, Houston, Texas 77002 713/659-1150

Figure 2.5: **MINERAL LEASE**

Producers 88 (4/76)   Revised
With 640 Acres Pooling Provision

POUND PRINTING & STATIONERY COMPANY
2325 FANNIN, HOUSTON, TEXAS 77002, (713) 659-3159

OIL, GAS AND MINERAL LEASE

THIS AGREEMENT made this _____ day of _____ 19 ____, between

_____

_____

_____

_____

Lessor (whether one or more), whose address is: _____

and _____ , Lessee, WITNESSETH:

1. Lessor in consideration of _____ Dollars

($ _____), in hand paid, of the royalties herein provided, and of the agreements of Lessee herein contained, hereby grants, leases and lets exclusively unto Lessee for the purpose of investigating, exploring, prospecting, drilling and mining for and producing oil, gas and all other minerals, conducting exploration, geologic and geophysical surveys by seismograph, core test, gravity and magnetic methods, injecting gas, water and other fluids, and air into subsurface strata, laying pipe lines, building roads, tanks, power stations, telephone lines and other structures thereon and on, over and across lands owned or claimed by Lessor adjacent and contiguous thereto, to produce, save, take care of, treat, transport and own said products, and housing its employees, the following described land in _____

_____ County, Texas, to-wit:

This lease also covers and includes all land owned or claimed by Lessor adjacent or contiguous to the land particularly described above, whether the same be in said survey or surveys or in adjacent surveys, although not included within the boundaries of the land particularly described above. For the purpose of calculating the rental payments hereinafter provided for, said land is estimated to comprise _____ acres, whether it actually comprises more or less.

2. Subject to the other provisions herein contained, this lease shall be for a term of _____ years from this date (called ''primary term'') and as long thereafter as oil, gas or other mineral is produced from said land or land with which said land is pooled hereunder.

3. The royalties to be paid by Lessee are: (a) on oil, one-eighth of that produced and saved from said land, the same to be delivered at the wells or to the credit of Lessor into the pipelines to which the wells may be connected; Lessee may from time to time purchase any royalty oil in its possession, paying the market price therefor prevailing for the field where produced on the date of purchase; (b) to pay lessor on gas and casinghead gas produced from said land (1) when sold by lessee, one-eighth of the amount realized by lessee, computed at the mouth of the well, or (2) when used by lessee off said land or in the manufacture of gasoline or other products, one-eighth of the amount realized from the sale of gasoline or other products extracted therefrom and one-eighth of the amount realized from the sale of residue gas after deducting the amount used for plant fuel and/or compression; while there is a gas well on this lease or on acreage pooled therewith but gas is not being sold or used, Lessee may pay as royalty, on or before ninety (90) days after the date on which (1) said well is shut in, or (2) the land covered hereby or any portion thereof is included in a pooled unit on which a well is located, or (3) this lease ceases to be otherwise maintained as provided herein, whichever is the later date, and thereafter at annual intervals on or before the anniversary of the date the first payment is made, a sum equal to the amount of the annual rental payable in lieu of drilling operations during the primary term on the number of acres subject to this lease at the time such payment is made, and if such payment is made or tendered, this lease shall not terminate, and it will be considered that gas is being produced from this lease in paying quantities; and (c) on all other minerals mined and marketed, one-tenth either in kind or value at the well or mine, at Lessee's election, except that on sulphur mined and marketed the royalty shall be fifty cents (50¢) per long ton. Lessee shall have free use of oil, gas, coal, and water from said land, except water from Lessor's wells, for all operations hereunder, and the royalty on oil, gas and coal shall be computed after deducting any so used.

Figure 2.5: (continued)

4. Lessee, at its option, is hereby given the right and power to pool or combine the acreage covered by this lease or any portion thereof as to oil and gas, or either of them, with any other land covered by this lease, and/or with any other land, lease or leases in the immediate vicinity thereof to the extent hereinafter stipulated, when in Lessee's judgment it is necessary or advisable to do so in order properly to explore, or to develop and operate said leased premises in compliance with the spacing rules of the Railroad Commission of Texas, or other lawful authority, or when to do so would, in the judgment of Lessee, promote the conservation of oil and gas in and under and that may be produced from said premises. Units pooled for oil hereunder shall not substantially exceed 40 acres each in area, and units pooled for gas hereunder shall not substantially exceed in area 640 acres each plus a tolerance of ten percent (10%) thereof, provided that should governmental authority having jurisdiction prescribe or permit the creation of units larger than those specified, for the drilling or operation of a well at a regular location or for obtaining maximum allowable from any well to be drilled, drilling or already drilled, units thereafter created may conform substantially in size with those prescribed or permitted by governmental regulations. Lessee under the provisions hereof may pool or combine acreage covered by this lease or any portion thereof as above provided as to oil in any one or more strata and as to gas in any one or more strata. The units formed by pooling as to any stratum or strata need not conform in size or area with the unit or units into which the lease is pooled or combined as to any other stratum or strata, and oil units need not conform as to area with gas units. The pooling in one or more instances shall not exhaust the rights of the Lessee hereunder to pool this lease or portions thereof into other units. Lessee shall file for record in the appropriate records of the county in which the leased premises are situated an instrument describing and designating the pooled acreage as a pooled unit; and upon such recordation the unit shall be effective as to all parties hereto, their heirs, successors, and assigns, irrespective of whether or not the unit is likewise effective as to all other owners of surface, mineral, royalty, or other rights in land included in such unit. Lessee may at its election exercise its pooling option before or after commencing operations for or completing an oil or gas well on the leased premises, and the pooled unit may include, but it is not required to include, land or leases upon which a well capable of producing oil or gas in paying quantities has theretofore been completed or upon which operations for the drilling of a well for oil or gas have theretofore been commenced. In the event of operations for drilling on or production of oil or gas from any part of a pooled unit which includes all or a portion of the land covered by this lease, regardless of whether such operations for drilling were commenced or such production was secured before or after the execution of this instrument or the instrument designating the pooled unit such operations shall be considered as operations for drilling on or production of oil and gas from land covered by this lease whether or not the well or wells be located on the premises covered by this lease and in such event operations for drilling shall be deemed to have been commenced on said land within the meaning of paragraph 5 of this lease; and the entire acreage constituting such unit or units, as to oil and gas, or either of them, as herein provided, shall be treated for all purposes, except the payment of royalties on production from the pooled unit, as if the same were included in this lease. For the purpose of computing the royalties to which owners of royalties and payments out of production and each of them shall be entitled on production of oil and gas, or either of them, from the pooled unit, there shall be allocated to the land covered by this lease and included in said unit (or to each separate tract within the unit if this lease covers separate tracts within the unit) a pro rata portion of the oil and gas, or either of them, produced from the pooled unit after deducting that used for operations on the pooled unit. Such allocation shall be on an acreage basis—that is to say, there shall be allocated to the acreage covered by this lease and included in the pooled unit (or to each separate tract within the unit if this lease covers separate tracts within the unit) that pro rata portion of the oil and gas, or either of them, produced from the pooled unit which the number of surface acres covered by this lease (or in each such separate tract) and included in the pooled unit bears to the total number of surface acres included in the pooled unit. Royalties hereunder shall be computed on the portion of such production, whether it be oil and gas, or either of them, so allocated to the land covered by this lease and included in the unit just as though such production were from such land. The production from an oil well will be considered as production from the lease or oil pooled unit which it is producing and not as production from a gas pooled unit; and production from a gas well will be considered as production from the lease or gas pooled unit from which it is producing and not from an oil pooled unit. The formation of any unit hereunder shall not have the effect of changing the ownership of any delay rental or shut-in production royalty which may become payable under this lease. If this lease now or hereafter covers separate tracts, no pooling or unitization of royalty interest as between any such separate tracts is intended or shall be implied or result merely from the inclusion of such separate tracts within this lease but Lessee shall nevertheless have the right to pool as provided above with consequent allocation of production as above provided. As used in this paragraph 4, the words "separate tract" mean any tract with royalty ownership differing, now or hereafter, either as to parties or amounts, from that as to any other part of the leased premises.

5. If operations for drilling are not commenced on said land or on acreage pooled therewith as above provided on or before one year from this date, the lease shall then terminate as to both parties, unless on or before such anniversary date Lessee shall pay or tender (or shall make a bona fide attempt to pay or tender, as hereinafter

stated) to Lessor or to the credit of Lessor in _____ Bank at _____

Texas, (which bank and its successors are Lessor's agent and shall continue as the depository for all rentals payable hereunder regardless of changes in ownership of

said land or the rentals) the sum of _____

_____ Dollars ($ _____), (therein called rentals), which shall cover the privilege of deferring commencement of drilling operations for a period of twelve (12) months. In like manner and upon like payments or tenders annually, the commencement of drilling operations may be further deferred for successive periods of twelve (12) months each during the primary term. The payment or tender of rental under this paragraph and of royalty under paragraph 3 on any gas well from which gas is not being sold or used may be made by the check or draft of Lessee mailed or delivered to the parties entitled thereto or to said bank on or before the date of payment. If such bank (or any successor bank) should fail, liquidate or be succeeded by another bank, or for any reason fail or refuse to accept rental, Lessee shall not be held in default for failure to make such payment or tender or rental until thirty (30) days after Lessor shall deliver to Lessee a proper recordable instrument naming another bank as agent to receive such payments or tenders. If Lessee shall, on or before any anniversary date, make a bona fide attempt to pay or deposit rental to a Lessor entitled thereto according to Lessee's records or to a Lessor, who, prior to such attempted payment or deposit, has given Lessee notice, in accordance with subsequent provisions of this lease, of his right to receive rental, and if such payment or deposit shall be ineffective or erroneous in any regard, Lessee shall be unconditionally obligated to pay to such Lessor the rental properly payable for the rental period involved, and this lease shall not terminate but shall be maintained in the same manner as if such erroneous or ineffective rental payment or deposit had been properly made, provided that the erroneous or ineffective rental payment or deposit be corrected within 30 days after receipt by Lessee of written notice from such Lessor of such error accompanied by such instruments as are necessary to enable Lessee to make proper payment. The down cash payment is consideration for this lease according to its terms and shall not be allocated as a mere rental for a period. Lessee may at any time or times execute and deliver to Lessor or to the depository above named or place of record a release or releases of this lease as to all or any part of the above-described premises, or of any mineral or horizon under all or any part thereof, and thereby be relieved of all obligations as to the released land or interest. If this lease is released as to all minerals and horizon under a portion of the land covered by this lease, the rentals and other payments computed in accordance therewith shall thereupon be reduced in the proportion that the number of surface acres within such released portion bears to the total number of surface acres which was covered by this lease immediately prior to such release.

Figure 2.5: (continued)

6. If prior to discovery and production of oil, gas or other mineral on said land or on acreage pooled therewith, Lessee should drill a dry hole or holes thereon, or if after discovery and production of oil, gas or other mineral, the production thereof should cease from any cause, this lease shall not terminate if Lessee commences operations for drilling or reworking within sixty (60) days thereafter or if it be within the primary term, commences or resumes the payment or tender of rentals or commences operations for drilling or reworking on or before the rental paying date next ensuing after the expiration of sixty days from date of completion of dry hole or cessation of production. If at any time subsequent to sixty (60) days prior to the beginning of the last year of the primary term and prior to the discovery of oil, gas or other mineral on said land, or on acreage pooled therewith, Lessee should drill a dry hole thereon, no rental payment or operations are necessary in order to keep the lease in force during the remainder of the primary term. If at the expiration of the primary term, oil, gas or other mineral is not being produced on said land, or on acreage pooled therewith, but Lessee is then engaged in drilling or reworking operations thereon or shall have completed a dry hole thereon within sixty (60) days prior to the end of the primary term, the lease shall remain in force so long as operation on said well or for drilling or reworking of any additional well are prosecuted with no cessation of more than sixty (60) consecutive days, and if they result in the production of oil, gas or other mineral, so long thereafter as oil, gas or other mineral is produced from said land or acreage pooled therewith. Any pooled unit designated by Lessee in accordance with the terms hereof may be dissolved by Lessee by instrument filed for record in the appropriate records of the county in which the leased premises are situated at any time after the completion of a dry hole or the cessation of production on said unit. In the event a well or wells producing oil or gas in paying quantities should be brought in on adjacent land and within three hundred thirty (330) feet of and draining the leased premises, or acreage pooled therewith, Lessee agrees to drill such offset wells as a reasonably prudent operator would drill under the same or similar circumstances.

7. Lessee shall have the right at any time during or after the expiration of this lease to remove all property and fixtures placed by Lessee on said land, including the right to draw and remove all casing. When required by Lessor, Lessee will bury all pipe lines below ordinary plow depth, and no well shall be drilled within two hundred (200) feet of any residence or barn now on said land without Lessor's consent.

8. The rights of either party hereunder may be assigned in whole or in part, and the provisions hereof shall extend to their heirs, successors and assigns; but no change or division in ownership of the land, rentals or royalties, however accomplished, shall operate to enlarge the obligations or diminish the rights of Lessee; and no change or division in such ownership shall be binding on Lessee until thirty (30) days after Lessee shall have been furnished by registered U.S. mail at Lessee's principal place of business with a certified copy of recorded instrument or instruments evidencing same. In the event of assignment hereof in whole or in part, liability for breach of any obligation hereunder shall rest exclusively upon the owner of this lease or of a portion thereof who commits such breach. In the event of the death of any person entitled to rentals hereunder, Lessee may pay or tender such rentals to the credit of the deceased or the estate of the deceased until such time as Lessee is furnished with proper evidence of the appointment and qualification of an executor or administrator of the estate, or if there be none, then until Lessee is furnished with evidence satisfactory to it as to the heirs or devisees of the deceased and that all debts of the estate have been paid. If at any time two or more persons be entitled to participate in the rental payable hereunder, Lessee may pay or tender said rental jointly to such persons or to their joint credit in the depository named herein; or, at Lessee's election, the proportionate part of said rentals to which each participant is entitled may be paid or tendered to him separately or to his separate credit in said depository; and payment or tender to any participant of his portion of the rentals hereunder shall maintain this lease as to such participant. In event of assignment of this lease as to a segregated portion of said land, the rentals payable hereunder shall be apportionable as between the several leasehold owners ratably according to the surface area of each, and default in rental payment by one shall not affect the rights of other leasehold owners hereunder. If six or more parties become entitled to royalty hereunder, Lessee may withhold payment thereof unless and until furnished with a recordable instrument executed by all such parties designating an agent to receive payment for all.

9. The breach by Lessee of any obligation arising hereunder shall not work a forfeiture or termination of this lease nor cause a termination or reversion of the estate created hereby nor be grounds for cancellation hereof in whole or in part. In the event Lessor considers that operations are not at any time being conducted in compliance with this lease, Lessor shall notify Lessee in writing of the facts relied upon as constituting a breach hereof, and Lessee, if in default, shall have sixty days after receipt of such notice in which to commence the compliance with the obligations imposed by virtue of this instrument. After the discovery of oil, gas or other mineral in paying quantities on said premises, Lessee shall develop the acreage retained hereunder as a reasonably prudent operator, but in discharging this obligation it shall in no event be required to drill more than one well per forty (40) acres of the area retained hereunder and capable of producing oil in paying quantities and one well per 640 acres plus an acreage tolerance not to exceed 10% of 640 acres of the area retained hereunder and capable of producing gas or other mineral in paying quantities.

10. Lessor hereby warrants and agrees to defend the title to said land and agrees that Lessee at its option may discharge any tax, mortage or other lien upon said land, either in whole or in part, and in event Lessee does so, it shall be subrogated to such lien with right to enforce same and apply rentals and royalties accruing hereunder toward satisfying same. Without impairment of Lessee's rights under the warranty in event of failure of title, it is agreed that if this lease covers a less interest in the oil, gas, sulphur, or other minerals in all or any part of said land than the entire and undivided fee simple estate (whether Lessor's interest is herein specified or not), or no interest therein, then the royalties, delay rental, and other monies accruing from any part as to which this lease covers less than such full interest, shall be paid only in the proportion which the interest therein, if any, covered by this lease, bears to the whole and undivided fee simple estate therein. All royalty interest covered by this lease (whether or not owned by Lessor) shall be paid out of the royalty herein provided. Should any one or more of the parties named above as Lessors fail to execute this lease, it shall nevertheless be binding upon the party or parties executing the same. Failure of Lessee to reduce rental paid hereunder shall not impair the right of Lessee to reduce royalties.

11. Should Lessee be prevented from complying with any express or implied covenant of this lease, from conducting drilling or reworking operations thereon or from producing oil or gas therefrom by reason of scarcity of or inability to obtain or to use equipment or material, or by operation of force majeure, any Federal or state law or any order, rule or regulation of governmental authority, then while so prevented, Lessee's obligation to comply with such covenant shall be suspended, and Lessee shall not be liable in damages for failure to comply therewith; and this lease shall be extended while and so long as Lessee is prevented by any such cause from conducting drilling or reworking operations on or from producing oil or gas from the lease premises; and the time while Lessee is so prevented shall not be counted against Lessee, anything in this lease to the contrary notwithstanding.

Figure 2.5: (continued)

IN WITNESS WHEREOF, this instrument is executed on the date first above written.

_____   _____

_____   _____

_____   _____

STATE OF _____   INDIVIDUAL ACKNOWLEDGMENT

COUNTY OF _____

    Before me, the undersigned authority, on this day personally appeared _____

known to me to be the person ____ whose name ____ is (are) subscribed to the foregoing instrument, and acknowledged to me that _____

executed the same as _____ free act and deed for the purposes and consideration therein expressed.

    Given under my hand and seal of office this _____ day of _____, 19 ____.

My Commission Expires

_____   _____
                                                          Notary Public in and for the State of Texas

                                                          _____
                                                          Notary's Printed Name

STATE OF _____

COUNTY OF _____   HUSBAND AND WIFE ACKNOWLEDGMENT

    Before me, the undersigned authority, on this day personally appeared _____

and _____

husband and wife, known to me to be the persons whose names are subscribed to the forgoing instrument and acknowledged to me that they executed the same as their free act and deed for the purposes and consideration therein expressed.

    Given under my hand and seal of office this _____ day of _____, 19 ____.

My Commission Expires

_____   _____
                                                          Notary Public in and for the State of Texas

                                                          _____
                                                          Notary's Printed Name

Producers 88 (4-76) Revised
with 640 Acres Pooling Provision

No. ____

Oil, Gas and Mineral Lease

FROM

TO

Dated _____, 19 ____

No. Acres _____

_____ County, Texas

Term _____

This instrument was filed for record on the _____ day of _____, 19 ____ at _____ o'clock ____ M., and duly recorded in

Book _____, Page _____ of the _____ records of this office.

By _____ County Clerk

_____, Deputy

When recorded return to

POUND PRINTING & STATIONERY COMPANY
2325 Fannin, Houston, Texas 77002 (713) 659-3159

minerals, such as overriding royalties and shut-in royalties. The amount of the royalty and the types of royalties paid are determined by the lease agreement and therefore should be negotiated carefully by the mineral estate owner.

Frequently, the mineral owner is paid a "bonus" when the mineral lease is executed. The amount of the bonus is also subject to negotiation. In addition to receipt of a bonus and royalties, the owner may also be entitled to a sum of money called a *delay rental*. A delay rental is payment made by the lessee to the owner of the mineral estate because the lessee has failed to commence drilling operations within the original lease period. The payment of the delay rental extends the lease period. The existence of a delay rental provision in a lease as well as the amount of the payment is subject to negotiation.

To summarize, the rights generally associated with ownership of the mineral estate are (1) the power to develop the minerals or lease the development rights, (2) the right to receive any bonus paid, (3) the right to receive any royalties due and (4) the right to receive any delay rental.

The mineral estate can be owned by one or more than one person. If more than one person own the same interest in land at the same time, they are called co-owners. There are different types of co-ownership. These forms are discussed in detail in Chapter 6. The relative rights of the co-owners of the mineral estate are the same as the relative rights of the co-owners of the surface estate. This should be remembered when the material in Chapter 6 is studied.

The owner of minerals is free to contract with two or more different lessees for the exploration and removal of minerals. Such a situation typically involves different depths or strata, as illustrated in Figure 2.1. In that figure, we see that the mineral owner has leased to Operator A the right to explore down to depth X and has leased to Operator B the right to explore only below depth X.

Finally, the relationship between the mineral estate and the surface estate should be discussed since severance of the mineral estate is common in those areas of Texas that are rich in mineral deposits. What happens if the owner of the mineral estate wants to develop his minerals, but the owner of the surface estate refuses to allow him access to the property? The general principle of law is that the mineral estate is the dominant estate and the surface estate is the servient estate. This means that the rights of the mineral estate holder are greater than the rights of the surface estate holder. Thus the owner of the mineral estate is guaranteed access to the property to develop his mineral interest. Mineral development takes precedence over a conflicting use of the surface, provided it is in compliance with the law and there is a reasonable need for the use. The use of the surface for mineral development includes building roads and structures and drilling wells to use groundwater. The case that follows illustrates the court's handling of a dispute between the owner of the surface estate and the owner of the mineral estate.

• CASE BRIEF •

Edward and Jane Ottis are surface owners of a tract of land that is subject to an oil and gas lease. The Ottises had purchased the surface estate from J.L. and Martha Kopecky. In the deed the Kopeckys reserved the mineral estate. The Kopeckys leased the minerals to Charles Haas. Haas installed tank batteries on the property that were approximately 400 feet from the residence of Edward and Jane Ottis. The Ottises sued to enjoin Haas from locating the tank batteries in such close proximity to their residence on the ground that it constituted a nuisance and was unreasonably dangerous. The court held for Haas, citing the rule that "In Texas an oil and gas estate is the dominant estate in the sense that the lessee is impliedly authorized to use as much of the premises as is reasonably necessary to produce and remove the mineral authorized by the lease. . . . These rights, however, are to be exercised with due regard to the rights of the owner or owners of the servient estate." There was no evidence in this case that Haas had acted negligently in choosing the location of the tank batteries. The tank batteries were located 50 feet from the well. Further, there was no evidence that the location of the tank batteries materially interfered with use of the surface estate by the Ottises. *Ottis v. Haas*, 569 S.W.2d 508 (Tex. Civ. App.—Corpus Christi 1978).

Hard Minerals

Mineral law should be divided into two areas by the type of minerals. Minerals such as coal, lignite, uranium and uranium ore fall into one category. These are sometimes called *hard minerals*. Common to this group of minerals is the fact that they are stationary. The other type of minerals is the migratory minerals, such as oil and gas. These will be discussed later in this chapter.

The nonmigratory minerals pose few special legal problems. One problem that has arisen regarding hard minerals involves deposits of minerals that lie on or near the surface of the land and that can be removed only by destroying the surface. An example of this type of problem would be the strip-mining of coal from the land. If the mineral ownership has been separated from the surface ownership, does the owner of the mineral estate have the right to destroy the surface in order to remove his minerals? If he does have that right, is the owner of the surface entitled to any compensation for the loss of his surface rights? Unfortunately, there is no clear standard in Texas for settling this type of dispute. The answers depend on two facts: (1) the date the minerals were leased or severed from the surface estate and (2) the specificity of the description of the mineral in the lease. If the severance of the minerals occurred prior to 1983, then the surface owner owns any minerals that lie within 200 feet of the surface and cannot be removed without destroying the surface. This means that, even if the mineral estate has been severed, the surface estate owner retains ownership of certain minerals that lie close to the earth's surface. Consequently, the owner of the mineral estate has no right to remove those minerals since he does not own them. If the severance of the minerals occurred after 1983, then the mineral estate owner owns all the minerals, regardless of where they lie in relation to the earth's surface. This also means that as owner of those minerals he can remove them, provided the method of removal is reasonable. Therefore, if strip-mining is a reasonable method of extracting coal from the land, then the mineral estate owner is free to use strip-mining.

Let's turn now to the second question. Assuming that the mineral estate owner has the right to remove the coal through strip-mining, is he required to compensate the surface estate owner for the destruction of the surface? The answer to this question depends upon the second fact mentioned earlier. If the document that severed the minerals specifically listed the substance, then no compensation is due the surface estate owner. In the example of coal, the document would have to state "coal" specifically. On the other hand, if the document severing the minerals does not name the substance, then compensation is due to the surface owner for the destruction of the surface. For example, if the document simply refers to "all minerals" or "and other minerals," then the owner of the mineral estate would be required to pay the surface estate owner for his loss.

Oil and Gas

Oil and gas are migratory minerals because they can flow within the earth's strata much as groundwater does. There are a host of special laws relating to the migratory minerals. Texas recognizes ownership of oil and gas in the ground as a part of the land. In the absence of a severance of the mineral estate the owner of the surface owns all oil and gas underneath the surface. Although oil and gas in the ground is part of the realty, the Texas courts have recognized that this interest can be lost if the oil and gas migrates. The fact that the oil and gas may have migrated as a result of man's intervention and application of technology does not matter. This doctrine is called the *rule of capture*. Under the rule of capture the owner of the surface has the right to appropriate all oil and gas from wells on his or her land, including oil and gas that has migrated from the land of another. The landowner who first captures the oil and gas is the owner even if the oil and gas have migrated from adjoining tracts of land. The landowner has the absolute right to recover as much of the oil and gas in the reservoir as is physically possible with legal drilling operations. The landowner who does capture the minerals is not liable to adjoining landowners for the oil or gas removed even though he may have captured oil and gas that was once underneath their property.

The rule of capture is somewhat legally inconsistent with the law of ownership. On the one hand, the Texas law holds that oil and gas in the ground are the property of the person who owns the land on which the oil and gas are located. However, this property right is subject to forfeiture or loss without compensation under the rule of capture.

To avoid the possible inequities that can arise from the rule of capture, landowners can enter into pooling agreements. **Pooling agreements** allocate to the various interests a proportion of the production from a reservoir. A pooling agreement can be either voluntary or involuntary. A voluntary pooling agreement is one in which the owners have consented to the allocation. An involuntary or forced pooling agreement is one in which the Texas Railroad Commission has entered an order allocating production among owners in a defined area. Forced pooling arrangements are very difficult to obtain in Texas. Forced pooling is not available to owners of land that was already in production in 1962. This was the year the Texas Pooling Act was passed. (Tex. Nat. Res. Code §102.001 et seq.) This eliminates from coverage a significant portion of the minerals in Texas. The Railroad Commission has also placed on the person wanting to pool the burden of showing that he or she has exhausted all other remedies. The result is that the law encourages owners to enter into voluntary pooling agreements. Finally, the Texas Railroad Commission has no authority to force pooling arrangements unless it has been petitioned by a landowner to act.

AIR RIGHTS

Until recently, the traditional theory that whoever owns the soil owns to the heavens was sufficient to solve most disputes involving invasion of airspace. Airspace problems, which usually concerned overhanging branches, bushes or eaves, were important to the parties but of little significance to society. With the advent of the airplane as a major means of transportation, courts and legislative bodies had to reconsider the old concept of absolute control of airspace. The early English rule that airspace was an appurtenance to land, giving absolute and exclusive right to the owner "to the highest heavens," was repudiated. In general, the courts recognize that the public interest in efficient transportation outweighs any theoretical trespass in airspace. As long as air flight does not interfere with the owner's right to the effective use of the space above his or her land, airplanes passing through this space are not trespassing. In brief, a landowner's exclusive domain extends at least to a height that makes it possible for the land to be used in a reasonable manner. To this extent the owner of the surface has absolute ownership of the space above his or her land.

Recently some important developments in real estate have been possible because the ownership of airspace may be separated from ownership of the surface. As population has expanded, investors have turned to space above land to satisfy both commercial and residential needs. When an individual purchases a high-rise condominium, that person is acquiring title to airspace. In metropolitan areas such as New York City and Chicago, railroads owning downtown property have separately conveyed airspace above the tracks to be used for commercial buildings. The purchaser acquires that space above the area needed by the railroad for its trains and a surface easement sufficient to support construction and facilities.

SUMMARY

Land is a limited commodity that is fundamental to human survival. Throughout much of history, land was considered a resource of the tribe or social group, to be cultivated for the general good. By the time North America was opened for colonization, individual property rights prevailed. Now land is viewed as wealth—a major factor of production to be controlled according to the prevailing economic and political theory of the nation in which it lies.

In this country, stringent laws prohibit trespass, the unauthorized act of entering land or buildings owned by another. Trespassers are liable to prosecution as criminals in some circumstances.

Of growing significance to environmentalists is the view of land as a social resource to be preserved for future use. This view currently influences the passage of laws affecting land use and development. Large areas have been set aside for public use. Land has become the topic of a large body of environmental law.

The value of land is increased by its closeness to water or by the presence of mineral deposits underneath it. Extensive law serves to resolve disputes and regulate usage when water or mineral rights are at issue.

Ownership and use of water depend in part upon the source of the water. There are three major sources of water in Texas: naturally occurring rivers and lakes, groundwater and surface water.

Water flowing in a river, stream, lake or bay is owned by the state. A landowner in Texas can have either riparian rights or appropriation rights. Both of these water rights doctrines allow usage of state-owned water. However, water usage from this source is regulated extensively by the Texas Water Commission.

Groundwater is water in the earth below the saturation point. Groundwater is presumed to be percolating water and is owned by the person who owns the surface estate. A landowner can use as much of this water as he or she chooses, provided he or she is not wasteful.

Surface waters are waters that collect on the land's surface not in a naturally occurring channel or riverbed. Surface waters belong to the owner of the property on which they collect.

Mineral rights in the land have been very important in Texas. Mineral rights belong to the owner of the surface unless the rights have been severed. Severance of mineral rights can be accomplished by a reservation in a deed, by a grant by mineral deed or by a lease of the mineral rights. When the mineral rights are severed, the mineral estate is the dominant estate.

Ownership of the mineral estate includes the right to develop and extract the minerals. Frequently, the owner will not have the ability to remove the minerals and will transfer the development rights to someone else by mineral lease. In exchange for the lease the mineral estate owner will receive a royalty. The amount of the royalty is subject to negotiation between the mineral owner and the lessee and is included in the lease.

Minerals can be divided into two categories: hard minerals and migratory minerals. The migratory minerals, such as oil and gas, pose the greater problems of ownership because they can migrate within the earth's strata. In Texas, ownership of oil and gas in the ground is part of the land. However, under the rule of capture the landowner who removes the oil and gas becomes the owner even though his drilling may be drawing from a reservoir that lies under his property and adjoining tracts.

Air rights belong to the surface owner. This allows the landowner to use as much of the space above the surface as is reasonably necessary for beneficial use of the surface.

QUESTIONS AND CASE PROBLEMS

1. Explain and distinguish three methods of severing mineral rights in Texas.
2. Explain and distinguish riparian rights and appropriation rights in Texas.
3. Bishop and Harris acquired adjoining parcels of land located in a commercial subdivision on Loop 281 in Longview, Texas. Prior to construction, surface waters created by rainfall ran off from the west to the east across the properties. Bishop owns the "lower" estate lying to the east, and Harris owns the "upper" estate lying to the west. After Harris constructed his building and parking lot on the upper estate, the flow of surface water increased and accelerated. As a result Bishop constructed a concrete block retaining wall to prevent the rainwater from washing out the lower estate. Harris's property now floods during heavy rains. Harris sues Bishop to remove the concrete block retaining wall. Who will prevail and why?
4. Jones sues Tarrant Utility Company in trespass for damages caused by water overflowing from two water storage tanks. Between 1974 and 1979, the tanks had overflowed approximately 60 times a year. Jones alleges that Tarrant Utility Company has a duty to prevent water from continuously overflowing and damaging the property of others. The water tanks were equipped with a sensing unit in the top of the tank. When water reached the top of the tank, the sensing unit would trigger the main control center so that the pumping system would shut off. Does Jones have a cause of action in trespass against Tarrant Utility Company? Why?

5. Robinson owns only the surface estate of an 80-acre tract. Robbins Petroleum Corporation owns the mineral estate and is presently operating three waterflood units on the tracts. Robbins is using salt water from the 80-acre tract to inject and drive the waterflood units. (This is a method for secondary recovery of oil from the tract.) Robinson seeks to deny Robbins Petroleum Corporation use of the salt water. Who owns the salt water? Does Robbins Petroleum have the right to use the salt water in its drilling operations? Why?

6. Gilliam owned an airplane that he used for crop dusting. While flying over Shrock's property to reach a field that was to be sprayed, crop dust was released. Although it was not clear how this occurred, Gilliam clearly was not negligent. At the time the dust was released, Gilliam was flying at a safe altitude. Shrock sued for damages as the poison dust destroyed valuable nursery stock. Would Shrock be successful? Discuss.

3
Land Descriptions and Boundary Disputes

LEGAL DESCRIPTION

This chapter deals primarily with descriptions found in real estate instruments. Boundary disputes are also discussed as an intricate relationship exists between descriptions and boundaries. A description in a real estate instrument indicates the physical dimensions of what is being conveyed. The term *legal description* refers to a description of a parcel of land that will be accepted by courts because it is complete enough to locate and identify the premises. Boundaries are based upon this description. They establish the property on the earth's surface. Often they are imaginary lines, but sometimes they are marked by an object.

With only a few exceptions, American law requires a written instrument to transfer an interest in real estate. To be enforceable the written instrument must contain a valid description of the property involved. The courts will not enforce the written instrument if the description is incorrect or ambiguous. A seller or lessor who has agreed to transfer an interest in real estate is in breach of contract if the instrument executed does not properly describe the property. Even if the physical boundaries of a property are clear, no interest will pass if the property is not described properly.

The chief purpose of the description is to furnish a means for identifying a particular parcel of land. In addition, the description must describe an area that is bounded completely. In other words, the boundaries indicated by the description must close the parcel.

For a deed or other conveyance to be enforceable, the description must make possible positive identification of the land. Courts consider this accomplished if a surveyor or other person familiar with the area can locate the property and determine its boundaries using the description in the conveyance.

There are two rules in Texas that are important to remember when writing and reading legal descriptions. The first rule is that the description of the property that is written in the instrument is given precedence over the intent of the parties. The presumption here is that, if the parties had intended a different parcel or configuration of land, they would have described it. The result is that a misdescription in a deed will control over the parties' intent in most circumstances. However, if both parties agree, a misdescription in a deed can be corrected by reforming the deed. Disputes usually arise when one of the parties cannot be located or simply refuses to reform the instrument. When this happens, the court will honor that which was written.

The second rule that is fundamental to understanding the importance of legal descriptions in Texas is that the description should contain sufficient information to locate the property on the ground with reasonable certainty. The parties do not necessarily have to use a metes-and-bounds description or a lot-and-block description in order to describe the property effectively. In certain instances a very general description, such as "all of my land located in Wharton County, Texas," would be adequate. The lands of the grantor located in Wharton County can be located by reviewing other records, since the description clearly states that it is *all* of the grantor's land within the confines of a certain county. However, determining the boundaries of land conveyed under such a description depends upon the sufficiency of the other records in providing a more precise description. Consequently, if the location of the grantor's land in Wharton County cannot be ascertained by reviewing the other documents of record, the conveyance will fail.

HISTORICAL CONSIDERATIONS

Texas land titles have a somewhat different history from land titles in other states. In researching a land title, the abstractor should always find the conveyance of the property from a sovereign entity. In Texas the sovereign entity could be Spain, Mexico, the Republic of Texas or the state of Texas. The first title to land in Texas was issued in 1731 by Spain. The Spanish government granted land to settlers for colonization in Texas. These grants describe the land by reference to the name of the colonizer. After Mexico gained its independence from Spain, the grants for land settlement were obtained through the individual towns, through the Mexican states and in some cases through empresarios. Again these descriptions will refer to the name of the settler and to the amount of and general configuration of the land. The measurement used in these grants was a *vara,* which is, by Texas statute, equivalent to 33$^1/_3$ inches.

Following establishment of the Republic of Texas, grants were issued by the new sovereign to those persons who had not previously been granted land but were Texas residents. In addition, the Republic of Texas did issue some colonization contracts, which subsequently were the basis for grants from the republic. Following the admission of Texas into the United States of America, the state retained sovereignty over the lands inside its borders and issued patents to persons seeking to acquire title to the land. In reviewing land titles that were derived by patent from the state of Texas, the abstractor must carefully study the document for a mineral reservation. Many of the patents issued involved some type of mineral reservation by the state.

These early documents usually describe the location of the land in relation to other grants or patents, an approximation of the number of acres or leagues conveyed and the configuration of the land by reference to distances and directions. The following is an example of a legal description found in one of these early instruments.

Whereas, said Richard Carter has established that he is married and requisites prescribed by the colonization law of the State of March 24, 1825, are found in his person; in accordance with said law and the instructions governing me dated September 4, 1827, and the additional article date April 25, of the past year of 1830, and in the name of the State, I grant, concede, and put said Richard Carter in real and personal possession of a league of land which tract has been surveyed by the Surveyor Horacio Chreisman previously appointed for the purpose, with the following situation and boundaries:

Situated on the creek called Saline Creek east of the Brazos River and above the Labahia Road, and known as Number 5. And from the north corner of Number 4, which is a landmark 10 varas distant from a Spanish Oak bearing North 49° West, and another bearing South 50° West 12 varas distant, a line was run North 45° West, and at 2020 varas crossed a little creek, at 2460 varas farther crossed said Saline Creek, 240 varas farther crossed the same creek again, 280 varas farther drove another landmark for the north corner of this league, from which a hickory bears South 13° West 4 varas distant, and a Spanish Oak bears South 27° East 5 varas distant; and

Thence South 45° West ran another line, at 40 varas crossed said creek, 1160 varas farther crossed a little creek, at 3300 varas farther crossed another little creek, 500 varas farther drove another landmark for the west corner; and

Thence South 45° East ran another line 5,000 varas until intersecting the west corner of said League No. 4, from which a blackjack bears North 47° West 18 varas distance, and a Spanish Oak bears South 72° East 12 varas distant; and

Thence North 45° East, following the northwest line of said number 4, 5000 varas to the POINT OF BEGINNING.

This league has 5,000 on each side and 25,000,000 varas in plane area. Said tract has four/twenty-fifth parts farming land and twenty-one/twenty-fifth parts grazing land, which serves as a qualification for the price he must pay the State therefor, according to Article 22 of said law under the penalties therein established; it being understood to him that within one year he must construct permanent landmarks at each corner of the tract and that he must settle and cultivate according to the requirements of the law.

Rectangular Survey System

The rectangular survey system is a system of land description that applies to most of the land in the United States. However, due to the unique historical development of Texas leading to its admission into the Union, the rectangular survey system is not used in Texas to locate land.

The rectangular survey system was enacted by the United States Congress in 1785 as part of a plan for disposal of the vast areas of unsettled lands west of the Mississippi River. Surveyors divided this land into townships that were rectangular in shape. A township was approximately six miles square. Townships were then divided into 36 sections. A section was one square mile, consisting of 640 acres of land. All townships and sections were either named or numbered. Land descriptions in these areas usually reference the township and section out of which the land in question was parceled.

METES AND BOUNDS

One of the most common methods of describing land in the early history of the United States was to name the parcel. For example, the property would be described as the Jacktown Plantation or the Ebenezer Smith farm. Usually boundaries were indicated by showing the owners of adjoining property or by natural landmarks called *monuments*. An early 19th-century deed in a trespass case described the property as follows:

A certain tract or parcel of land, including the mill-seat and mill known as the "Jethro R. Franklin Mill," the said tract situated in the county of Gates, embracing as far as the highwater mark, and bounded as follows: on the north by the lands of Richard E. Parker, Reddick Brinkley, and others, on the east by the lands of Harrison Brinkley and others, south by the desert road, west by the lands of Josiah H. Reddick and others. . . .

A description based primarily on adjoiners (names of owners of contiguous property, a road or something similar) and monuments is still used if the costs of a survey are out of proportion to the amount of money involved. Descriptions of this nature may cause problems if some impermanent monuments are selected.

Metes-and-bounds descriptions provide a more sophisticated method of describing real property. *Metes and bounds* is a method of describing land by specifying the exterior boundaries of the property using compass directions, monuments or landmarks where directions change and linear measurement of distances between these points. It is based upon a survey that commences at a beginning point on the boundary of the tract and follows compass directions, called *courses*, and distances around the area to the point of beginning. Monuments are placed at the corners or at points where directions change. Monuments are visible objects, sometimes natural but often artificial. They consist of posts, iron pipes, piles of stone, trees, streams or similar objects. By following the courses and distances, a person should be able to walk the boundaries of the property.

Metes-and-bounds descriptions based upon a survey provide a very accurate method of designating the physical dimensions of a particular tract of land. When the land itself is supplied with permanent markers at each corner or angle, the parcel can be readily located for a long period of time.

This method of describing land is the basis for most legal descriptions in Texas. Outside of incorporated cities in Texas it is the most accurate method of describing the boundaries of a particular parcel. In incorporated cities that require platting of land prior to development, the plat that is required to be approved by the city and filed with the county must contain the metes-and-bounds description of each lot. A similar requirement is found in the development of condominium projects. Although the individual units are not required to have metes-and-bounds descriptions on the plat, the common areas, outside areas and building locations require a metes-and-bounds description. An example of a metes and bounds description follows.

> Being 1.0414 acres of land out of Oakhollow, Section One, proposed Reserve "G," as recorded in Volume 303, Page 94 of the Harris County Map Records, located in the W.K. Hamblin Survey, Abstract No. 317, and being more particularly described as follows:
>
> COMMENCING at a point for intersection of the most Westerly line of Windfern Road (based on a width of 60 feet) with the most Northerly line of Emmott Road, (based on a width of 60 feet);
>
> THENCE S 88° 32' 34" W along the Northerly line Emmott

Road, 10.29 feet to a 5/8" I.R., set for the most Southeasterly corner of the 1.0414 acre tract, and the POINT OF BEGINNING;

THENCE continuing S 88° 32' 34" W, along the Northerly line of Emmott Road 159.29 feet to a 5/8" I.R., set for the Southwest corner of the herein described tract;

THENCE N 02° 12' 00" W, 266.60 feet to a 5/8" I.R. set for the Northwest corner of the herein described tract;

THENCE N 87° 34' 22" E, generally South of the East-West barbed wire fence, 169.32 feet to a 5/8" I.R., found for the Northeast corner of said tract, said corner lies in the Westerly right-of-way line of Windfern Road;

THENCE S 02° 14' 56" E, 259.41 feet along the Westerly right-of-way line of Windfern Road to a 5/8" I.R. found for corner;

THENCE S 43° 47' 32" W, 14.29 feet to the POINT OF BEGINNING and containing 1.0414 acres of land.

Plats

A *plat* is a map designating items such as natural and artificial monuments, lots, blocks and streets in a town or subdivision drawn from a survey. The property to be divided is surveyed and laid out in lots that are numbered in sequence. State law (Tex.Rev.Civ.Stat.Art. 974a) requires that the owner who plans to subdivide a tract of land that lies within the city limits or five miles outside the city limits (the city's extraterritorial jurisdiction) must file a plat with the city. Subdividers of land outside this area must file their plat with the Commissioner's Court (the legislative body for the county) for the county in which the land is located.

The plat must accurately describe by metes and bounds the individual lots, streets, alleys and parks or public areas within the tract. The lots must be located in relation to the original corner of the original survey and must give the dimensions of each lot, street, alley and public area. After approval by the city, these plats are recorded in the office of the county clerk where the land is situated. Thereafter, it is common practice to describe property within the plat by a lot-and-block number with reference to the plat. This is an example of a lot-and-block description:

> Lot 15 in Block 2 of Norwood Meadows, a subdivision in Harris County, Texas, according to the map or plat thereof, recorded in Volume 62, Page 35 of the Map Records of Harris County, Texas.

Condominiums

Developers of condominium projects in Texas are required to prepare and record a condominium declaration that contains the description of the land, the location of each building on the land and the common areas by a metes-and-bounds description. (Tex.Prop.Code §81.102) Each building is denoted by a letter. The declaration must also describe the square footage and location of each apartment within the building. Floors and apartments are assigned numbers. If the project includes garages or carports, these areas must also be located and identified by number if such are to be limited common areas. The declaration must also contain the fractional interest that each apartment shares in the general common areas. Thereafter future descriptions of condominiums must contain the apartment number, floor number and building number with reference to the condominium declaration. In addition, the documents must include the fractional share of that apartment in the general common areas. Ownership of the apartment cannot be separated from the undivided proportional ownership in the general common areas. Here is an example of a legal description of a condominium:

> Unit number 36, Building "F" together with an undivided 1,149/114,542 fractional interest in and to the common elements, and together with 2 garage or parking spaces marked G-36, of Seven Oaks, a condominium project in the City of Houston in Harris County, Texas, all as fully described in and as located, delineated and as defined in the Condominium Declaration for Seven Oaks, and the survey plats, Bylaws, and Exhibits attached thereto, recorded in Volume 62, Page 130, of the Condominium Records of Harris County, Texas; together with all of the rights, titles, appurtenances and hereditaments thereto.

Townhomes

The legal descriptions used for townhomes is very similar to those used for lots within a city. The townhomes are identified by lot-and-block number in reference to a recorded plat. This is an example of a legal description for a townhome:

> Lot 1, Block 2 of Willow Vista Townhouses, Section One, a Subdivision out of the Day Land and Cattle Co., Abstract 1025, of Harris County, Texas, according to the map or plat thereof recorded in Volume 249, Page 20, of the Map Records of Harris County, Texas.

BOUNDARY DISPUTES

One of the problems that can arise in a property description is ambiguity. The Texas courts have consistently held that oral testimony regarding the intent of the parties can be considered in resolving an ambiguity in the legal description. However, enough information must be provided within the written description to provide the framework for locating the property. The

oral testimony or extraneous documents can be used to clarify and comple-
ment the written information regarding the property. For example, the description of the property in the deed reads, "the old Baker homestead in
Austin County." The court will allow oral testimony to aid in locating the
"old Baker homestead." However, if the deed had described the same property simply as "3,000 acres in Austin County," no oral testimony could be
used to aid in locating this property. The written description does not provide a framework within which to work.

Another problem that arises in interpreting legal descriptions is a conflict in the written description. Texas courts use several rules of construction in resolving these types of problems. The first rule is that the more
specific description prevails over the general. Consequently, a general reference in the deed to "the old Baker homestead" followed by a metes-and-
bounds description will convey that parcel of land as established by the
metes-and-bounds description. This is true even if one of the parties alleges
that the metes-and-bounds description does not contain the entire tract.
References to the number of acres being conveyed following a specific description by metes and bounds that does not include that number of acres
are usually considered estimations. However, if the number of acres varies
significantly from that included in the metes-and-bounds description, the
court can either reform or rescind the instrument.

Finally, there can be a conflict within the metes-and-bounds description.
Metes-and-bounds descriptions contain references to monuments, courses
and distances. These different monuments, courses and distances are referred to as *calls*. Sometimes natural monuments used as calls are destroyed; in other instances, conflicting calls are the result of human error.
To solve problems resulting from conflicting calls, courts have established a
general order of preference to be given to calls when the intention of the
parties is not clear. Monuments are preferred because they are considered
more reliable than courses and distances. The general order of preference is
as follows: (1) natural monuments, (2) artificial monuments, (3) courses,
(4) distances and (5) quantity of acreage. Adjoining landowners (adjoiners)
are also important elements in some descriptions and receive a high degree
of priority. Unless the adjoiner is clearly a mistake, it ranks with monuments, prevailing over courses, distances and quantity of acreage.

Sales Personnel and Property Description

Property description is an important element of almost every real estate
transaction. Although it is ordinarily the concern of the real estate lawyer,
all real estate sales personnel should be aware of its important legal aspects.
If problems involving descriptions are discovered early in the proceedings,
before the deed or other document involving the property is prepared, time
and trouble can be saved.

Sometimes real estate personnel obtain information about boundary problems when listing property or drawing up a contract. These should be carefully noted and an effort made to have the owner resolve the problem before entering serious negotiations with prospective buyers. Because boundary disputes may indicate description problems, a sales associate who becomes aware of a boundary controversy when negotiating a sale of real estate should alert the seller's attorney so that the description can be verified.

An incomplete, vague or inaccurate legal description can seriously affect the rights of parties in a real estate transaction. The description must be accurate not only in the deed but also in all contracts relating to the land. Therefore, care and consideration should be taken in preparing and reading legal descriptions. One of the best sources from which to obtain a good description of the property is the seller's deed. If the seller does not have a copy of the deed, then one can be obtained from the county clerk's office. A common mistake is reliance upon the description found in a tax statement. These descriptions are generally incomplete and at times inaccurate.

SUMMARY

In order to be enforceable, a real estate instrument must contain a legal description of the property. The description must be complete enough to locate and identify the premises. The physical boundaries are integral to this description because they locate the property on the earth's surface. The boundaries in a legal description must be complete; they must enclose the parcel. In cases where boundary disputes exist, courts hear testimony of the parties to the dispute, surveyors, neighbors and others to determine what property the parties intended to convey.

In Texas a land title could have been derived from any one of the following sovereign governments: Spain, Mexico, the Republic of Texas or the state of Texas. As a result of this unique historical development, the rectangular survey system found in most of the United States is not present in Texas.

The basic method of describing land in Texas is by metes and bounds. A metes-and-bounds description specifies the exterior boundaries of the property, based on a survey that commences at a beginning point on the boundary and follows courses and distances around the area. By following the description and observing any call or monument (a tree, stream or post, for example) noted in the wording, a person should be able to walk the boundaries of the property. Over time monuments may be destroyed or obliterated. In the case of conflict courts have established an order of priority, with natural monuments taking precedence over artificial ones as well as over courses and distances. Established boundaries of other owners (adjoiners) rank along with natural monuments.

State law requires that property within a city or its extraterritorial jurisdiction must be platted prior to development. These plats are recorded on maps that are filed in the county where the land is located. Plats contain the metes-and-bounds description for individual lots, streets and public areas in the subdivision. After the plat is filed, the individual lots are described by a lot-and-block number. Townhomes and condominiums are described in a similar manner.

The courts have adopted several rules or guidelines to solve the types of boundary disputes that have arisen in the past. Where the language is ambiguous or conflicting, the court will try to determine the intent of the parties by reference to oral testimony or extraneous documents. To reduce the incidence of disputes, however, real estate professionals should be aware of the need for a clearly written description as part of the real estate transaction.

QUESTIONS AND CASE PROBLEMS

1. Explain what is meant by a metes-and-bounds description.
2. Steward and Jones entered into an earnest money contract covering a tract land legally described as follows:

> All that certain tract or parcel of land situated in Bowie County, Texas of the J.H. Bennett headright survey, a part of Tract four described in a deed executed by A.J. Williams to Pauline R. Williams recorded in Volume 560, page 820, Deed Records of Bowie County, Texas, and being more fully described as follows: Being all of said Tract four located on the west side of a county road and being bounded on the West by the J.R. O'Rear tract, on the North by the James E. Pirtle tract described by deed recorded in Volume 632, page 785 Deed Records, of Bowie County, Texas, on the East by the said county road and on the South by a county road and being fourteen acres of land more or less.

After the contract was executed, Jones discovered that the tract actually contained 20.76 acres and therefore refused to convey the land to Steward. Steward filed suit to specifically enforce the contract. Steward claims that the phrase *more or less* made it a sale of land in gross, not by acre. Jones seeks rescission of the contract based on mutual mistake. Who will prevail?

3. E. I. DuPont de Nemours & Company entered into a lease of raw land from Zale Corporation. The lease provided that Zale would erect on the land an office and warehouse building. The parties

also executed an option whereby DuPont could purchase the land and building from Zale at a stipulated price. After completion of the building, DuPont exercised their option. Zale tendered to Du-Pont a deed that conveyed "Lots 4 and 5 and the northeast 44.17 feet of Lot 3, Block 1/6368 of the Expressway Industrial District." This legal description matched the description of the property set out in the lease and option. DuPont refused to accept the deed because it did not convey a good and marketable title to the building and land. DuPont proved that the building had been constructed by Zale on Lots 4 and 5 and the northeast 52 feet of Lot 3. Therefore, in order to gain title to the entire building, the legal description should include the additional 7.83 feet along the northeast side of Lot 3. Should the court order Zale to convey to DuPont the additional 7.83 feet without further consideration?

4
Property and Related Concerns

PROPERTY

In traditional legal usage, **property** generally refers to an aggregate or "bundle" of rights that people have in tangible items. It is the rights in the item that determine the economic value of the article. For example, the right of ownership of a car is more valuable than the right to use a car under a lease. People often refer to the items—the automobile, guitar or home—as their property: from a legal point of view, however, the items themselves are not significant. What is important are the rights the person has in these items. These rights include the right to use the item, sell it or even destroy it if the person wishes (*see* Figure 4.1). In his famous *Commentaries on the Law of England*, Blackstone describes property as an "absolute right, inherent in every Englishman...which consists in the free use, enjoyment, and disposal of all his acquisitions, without any control or diminution, save only by the laws of the land." Today, the term *ownership* is often used as a synonym for *property.*

The concept of property is readily understood when related to something tangible like an automobile or land. A person can, however, own something that is related only indirectly to a tangible item. An example would be a lease. The tenant of a commercial building has a right to occupy space. This right is valuable because of the building's existence, but the right itself is intangible. Property also is used to refer to rights that people possess independent of anything tangible. Contracts, trademarks, copyrights and patents are examples. They are all property in that the owner has something

61

that can be used, sold to others or destroyed through nonuse. An invention or a literary work protected by patent or copyright may be unused. Since no one else can use the item, nonuse destroys the property.

The existence of property depends upon government. State and federal laws provide guarantees and protections creating and maintaining the "bundle of rights" that the legal system refers to as property. For example, in our society property exists in land because numerous laws allow individuals to do certain things with land such as sell it, dispose of it to one's heirs or exclude others from it. On the other hand, although one's right to vote is important, it is not property. The state provides no aggregate of rights related to a person's right to vote. All that the individual can do is vote or refrain from voting. Whether or not something is a property right has important constitutional implications because the Bill of Rights prohibits government from taking property without due process of law.

Property is a dynamic concept that is continually being reshaped to meet new economic and social needs. In the United States today, appreciable legislation and case law is developing that modifies traditional property rights or at least reevaluates them in relation to civil rights. Many good examples can be found in cases and legislation protecting fundamental interests of minorities.

• CASE BRIEF •

Shelly, a black man, purchased real estate from Fitzgerald. The sale violated a recorded restriction upon which former owners of this parcel and a number of other owners had agreed. This restriction prohibited occupancy by "any person not of the Caucasian race." Kramer and others who owned real property subject to the restriction sued to restrain Shelly from taking possession and to divest him of title. When the Missouri courts granted the relief requested, the United States Supreme Court reversed. The court held that state courts cannot enforce a private agreement that deprives a person of a constitutional right. *Shelly v. Kramer*, 334 U.S. 1 (1948).

Although one clearly visible trend in the law is to limit property rights when weighed against civil rights, in other areas property rights have been expanded. In a number of cases, plaintiffs have contended that they have a property interest in their employment or in the facilities necessary to practice a chosen profession and even in their status and reputation. At present the movement of the law in this direction is slow, but the trend is discernible.

• CASE BRIEF •

Roth was hired as an assistant professor at a state university for a term of one year. His contract was not renewed by the university, and he was given no reason for this action. Roth brought an action against the university, arguing that the due process clause of the Constitution, which prohibits government from taking property without due process, required the university to give him reasons for its decision. Since no reasons were given, he contended, the university was taking his property unfairly. The United States Supreme Court ruled against him on the grounds that the terms of his employment accorded him no "property interest" in employment beyond one year. *Board of Regents v. Roth*, 408 U.S. 564 (1972).

Real Property Rights

Legal institutions reflect dominant economic, political and social values. Laws and the legal system sustain the existing order and are used to attain objectives that society considers important. Throughout the history of England and the United States land and law have been closely interwoven. In both countries, as well as in most other nations of the Western world, land has been an important form of wealth. In addition, for many hundreds of years in England not only was land the major source of wealth, but the possession of land, even particular tracts of land, determined an individual's social position. Possession or ownership of land also had important politi-

Figure 4.1: **PROPERTY: A COLLECTION OF RIGHTS**

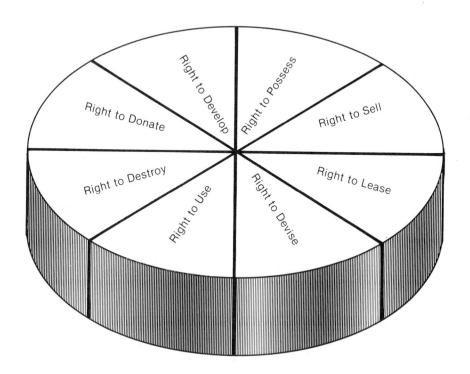

cal connotations in both England and the United States. For many years in England and in most of the United States, only landowners were permitted to vote.

One result of the historic importance of land is a distinction in law of English-speaking countries between it and other forms of wealth. Because of land's economic significance, the early common law provided extensive protection to landowners. A landowner ousted from possession could immediately bring an action to recover the land. This was known as a real action, and it is the reason land is called *real property* or *real estate*. Consequently, ownership or proprietary rights in land or anything permanently affixed to land are called ***real property rights.*** On the other hand, a person who lost control of something of economic value other than land, usually a movable item, initially could sue only for money. This was known as a *personal action* and the items involved as *personal property.* In modern law the distinction between real and personal property continues to be recognized.

Personal property generally is characterized as being movable. Historically, the items of personal property of importance were tangible things such as cattle, farm equipment and the tools of a person's trade. Today, many nontangible forms of wealth exist. An example would be a franchise. These intangible rights are also personal property. Over the centuries these forms of personal property have expanded, and personal property has become more equivalent to real property as wealth. One result has been a narrowing of the legal distinctions between the two, but differences continue to exist and to influence American law.

Real Versus Personal Property: Legal Problems

The fact that real and personal property continue to be treated differently in the law of English-speaking countries causes many problems. For example, a deed, the written document establishing ownership of real estate, conveys only real property, separate from personal property. This sometimes results in confusion when a home or business is sold. The potential buyer of a home, an apartment for investment, a factory or a farm examines the premises from a functional, not a legal, viewpoint. If the real estate is a residence, the buyer is thinking about a place to live, not about the distinction between real and personal property. Items such as the stove, refrigerator, storm windows or perhaps a bar (other than a wet bar with sink) are functionally related to the reason for the purchase. The buyer understandably considers these items integral parts of the building. At the same time the seller, perhaps having purchased the items separately, often thinks of them as independent of the structure. If the law considers these articles part of the real estate, they pass to the buyer by deed unless specifically excluded by agreement. If the items are deemed personalty and hence not part of the real estate, they are not covered by the deed, and the purchaser does not get them.

CASE EXAMPLE

David, by warranty deed, conveyed land to Bessie. A hay barn was located on the land. The barn contained equipment for unloading hay. The equipment consisted of a track, hangers to support the track, a carrier, a hay harpoon, two pulleys and rope. The hangers were bolted to the rafters and the track attached to the hangers. David removed the equipment. Bessie expected to be successful in an action brought against David for the value of the equipment because the courts usually consider the equipment part of a barn.

The distinction between real and personal property is also significant in real estate financing. A debt secured by a mortgage is secured only by the real estate. Personal property is not part of the security. For example, if a bank takes back a mortgage on a motel as security for a debt, the furniture that is integral to successful operation of the business is not covered. Of course, the furniture could also be used as security if designated as such by a separate security agreement.

CASE EXAMPLE

National Bank lent funds to a small manufacturing company and took back a mortgage on property owned by the company. On the premises was a 2,000-gallon tank set on concrete blocks. The tank was used to store gas and was connected to a garage by lines that ran above ground. The bank was forced to foreclose because the debt was not paid. Both the bank and the company claimed the tank. If the court held the tank to be part of the real estate, the tank could be sold at the foreclosure sale.

Whether an item is real or personal property also raises important insurance, tax and inheritance questions. Sometimes state statutes help provide answers to these questions, but most continue to be settled by case law. Contractual terms in sales or mortgage documents should make the distinction explicit.

Fixtures

Fixture is the legal term used to describe an item that was once personal property but has been changed to real property by its use or attachment to land or buildings. Chandeliers, carpeting, hot water heaters and shrubbery are common examples of fixtures associated with residential real estate. All these items are personal property while part of the seller's inventory, but when annexed to land or buildings they are generally considered part of the real estate. On a farm, items such as cattle stanchions, water pumps and fencing would ordinarily be fixtures. Many items associated with industrial or commercial real estate are also classified as fixtures. How would you classify the mirror behind the bar in your favorite nightclub or the overhead track for moving heavy material in a factory? Both could be readily detached without harm to the building, and they appear movable as is personal property, but they, too, are probably fixtures.

The key to determining whether an item is a fixture is the *intent* of the parties. Was the article intended to improve the real property permanently? If it was intended to remain with the land or buildings, then it is a fixture and part of the real property. If it was temporary and intended to be removed, then it remains personal property. Determining a subjective element like intent can be difficult if there is no written or oral communication of the intent. Consequently, the court considers several factors when trying to decide whether or not an article is a fixture.

When there is no clear proof of a party's intention, the court considers the following factors very important:
1. the manner in which the item was annexed or attached
2. the character and use of the item
3. the relationship between the party making the annexation and other claimants of the property

The consideration of the first factor is often referred to as the *annexation test*. The inquiry under the annexation test is whether the item is physically attached to the real estate. The physical attachment must be reasonably permanent. In determining permanency, the courts often look at the amount of damage that the land would sustain if the item was removed. The greater the damage, the more likely it is that the court will find that the attachment was permanent and that the parties intended it to remain with the land.

The second factor considered important by the court is called the *adaptation test*. The question under the adaptation test is whether the article was adapted for use with the land. Even if the item is not physically attached to the land, if it is on the land and was intended to enhance the value of the land, then it is a fixture. The more customized an article is with respect to the real estate, the more likely it is that the court will find that it is a fixture and must remain. Frequently, the adaptation test is used to determine whether an article that merely sits on the land was intended to improve it permanently. Such items as planter boxes, statues, outside lighting and storage sheds could be fixtures if they were adapted for use with the land on which they were placed.

The final factor considered by the court in deciding whether an item is a fixture is the relationship of the parties. Between a buyer and a seller, there is a presumption that improvements are made to enrich the land permanently. Therefore, in the absence of any agreement, things that are permanently affixed to the land are fixtures and are transferred to the buyer upon the sale of the land. The case that follows illustrates the court's handling of this issue between a buyer and seller.

CASE EXCERPT *Herrin v. Bunge*, 336 S.W.2d 281 (Tex. Civ. App.—Houston 1960) BELL, Chief Justice. On March 14, 1956, Herrin and Bunge entered into a

Figure 4.2: **FIXTURE**

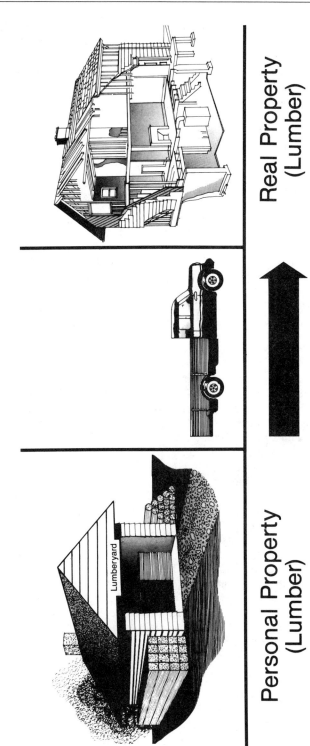

Personal Property (Lumber) → Real Property (Lumber)

written contract, under the terms of which Herrin agreed to sell to Bunge and Bunge agreed to purchase from Herrin for a consideration of $112,500, 1,250 acres of land in Colorado County. The part of the contract material to this appeal is the provision that "large barn to be moved by Seller as his own separate property and not part of this consideration." Also the seller was to, 90 days from the date of the contract, deliver possession of the land to Bunge.

The sale of the property was consummated April 10, 1956, by the payment of the consideration and the delivery of a deed. . . .

The evidence shows that Herrin removed 3 concrete watering troughs and their fittings, 1 steel tank, 277 feet of 2-inch water pipe, and 67½ feet of 2-inch pipe used as sign posts. . . .

The first contention of Herrin is that the 277 feet of 2″ water pipe and the 3 concrete water tanks were a part of the barn which was reserved in the contract of sale. . . .

The evidence shows that the 2-inch line ran from a point near the water tank to a point near the barn. From the 2-inch line 1″ lines led up to each water tank. None of the 3 troughs here involved was connected physically with the barn. . . . The troughs rested on the ground, but soil had been banked up around the bottom part of each, so that you might accurately state that the lower portion was below the surface of the ground. A creosoted fence pole was at the end of each, about the middle of each end, and across the center line of each, two 1″ × 6″ boards were placed and nailed to the pole. The trough would in this manner afford drinking facilities in two separate exercise pens. . . .

Unquestionably all of these items were a part of the realty that would pass with the sale of the land to which they were affixed in the absence of a reservation in favor of the seller. The question is what the parties intended when there was an agreed reservation to the seller of the barn. We think that when reference is made to a "barn" it would undoubtedly be understood to mean the structure where there are stalls for stock, where they are fed and protected from the weather, wash rooms for washing and currying the stock, and where feed is store. . . .

The fact that these structures were built to use in connection with the barn does not make them a part of the barn. . . .

Herrin next contends the trial court erred in holding the 1,000 gallon tank passed under his deed to Bunge because, he contends, it was neither actually nor constructively attached to the land. . . .

The trial court had before him evidence that the tank was bought for and brought to the land for use by Herrin as a water tank. He had 300 yards of concrete poured into the forms to hold the tank. . . .

The tank was sufficiently attached to the land, considering its nature and the use to which it was to be put. No additional act was necessary to hold it in place even when in use. The nature of the concrete columns and the weight of the tank were all that were required to hold it in place for the purpose to which the tank was adapted and for which it was purchased and taken to the ranch.

These factors together with the admission of Herrin of his intention to make it a permanent part of the ranch are sufficient to support the court's finding that it was a fixture that passed to Bunge under the deed. . . .

Between a landlord and tenant there is a greater tendency for the court to find that improvements made by a tenant are not fixtures. Of considerable importance, however, is the intention of the tenant in making the improvement. The objective manifestation of this intent is found in the nature of the estate, the character of the improvement and the circumstances surrounding the annexation. If the fixture is something erected for the purpose of carrying on the tenant's trade, it is always removable by the tenant at the expiration of the lease. The tenant can, however, forfeit this right to remove trade fixtures by failing to do so within a reasonable time after the termination of the lease. The definition of a reasonable time depends upon the type of fixture involved and other individual circumstances of the case. For things that are not trade fixtures, the nature of the estate becomes very important in determining whether the article is removable. A tenancy that can be terminated at the will of either landlord or tenant offers very little security to the tenant, and therefore it is unlikely that the tenant would make permanent improvements to the land. However, a tenant with a long-term lease or a lease with option to purchase is more likely to make permanent improvements to the land. In addition to the nature of the estate, the character of the improvement and attending circumstances are important elements. The case that follows involves a residential tenant who constructed a small house on the landlord's property.

• CASE BRIEF •

In November 1941, Smart began renting a small house and lot from Mrs. Baten. The house was in a poor state of repair. Smart lived on the land under a tenancy at will from 1941 to 1949. Upon Mrs. Baten's death in 1947, her son acquired title to the property and continued renting to Smart until 1949, when he ordered Smart off the property for nonpayment of rent. Sometime between 1941 and 1949, Smart had built another house on the Baten land. Smart and his family lived in this new house. The house was constructed from materials owned by Smart. When Smart vacated the land, he removed the house he had built. Baten sued Smart for the return of this house. The court found that the house was not a fixture. It reasoned that Smart had built the house entirely for his own use and benefit with the implied consent of Baten. When a tenant at will builds a house on his landlord's premises, the legal presumption is that it was the intention of the tenant at will not to enhance the value of the freehold, but to build it for his own use and benefit, and that it should retain its character as personalty. Baten had the burden of proving otherwise; and he had failed to do so. *Baten v. Smart*, 295 S.W.2d 521 (Tex. Civ. App.—Beaumont 1956).

The law as it relates to the determination of fixtures is imprecise and confusing. When parties are involved in a real estate transaction, the best way to prevent problems that may arise is to agree in writing that certain items are included in the sale to the buyer. In insurance, the problem can be solved by agreement between insured and insurer as long as the problem is recognized, and a bank can make certain that its security agreements specifically cover items that might be either fixtures or personal property.

Trade Fixtures

We have seen that items of personal property, annexed to realty with the intention that the item become part of the realty, are fixtures. Fixtures are real estate and usually may not be removed or treated separately unless the parties agree. It is clear, however, that a business firm leasing real estate would be seriously hampered if this rule applied to items needed to operate a plant or shop effectively. Because of this the legal system differentiates between fixtures and trade fixtures. *Trade Fixtures* are items annexed to land or buildings by a tenant to be used in the tenant's trade or business. A tenant may generally remove trade fixtures. Agricultural fixtures have been treated in a similar manner. In order to remove a trade or agricultural fixture, the tenant must restore the premise to its original condition and remove the trade fixture within a reasonable time after termination of the lease.

Allowing tenants to remove trade fixtures has social benefits. It encourages both the use of land and efficiency in business. Tenants will be more apt to invest in new and improved equipment if they can remove these items after they have been attached to the realty. Statutes in a number of states establish tenants' rights to remove trade fixtures.

Although the doctrine of trade fixtures is important to tenants, parties to a commercial lease should include provisions clearly expressing their rights. They might agree that the tenant shall not remove items that ordinarily would be trade fixtures. On the other hand, a lease provision stating the tenant's right to remove items added to carry out the business or trade shows the intention of the parties and lessens possibilities for disagreement and litigation.

Crops

Vegetation that occurs naturally on the land is part of the real property. However, legal disputes can arise with respect to annual crops. Crops grown for harvesting at maturity are generally considered to be personal property. Therefore, the crops can be removed by a tenant at the termination of a lease. Similarly, a lease of real property would not necessarily give the tenant the right to harvest crops in existence at the beginning of the lease. There is an exception in the law for the sale of land on which annual crops are in production. A sale of the land will include annual crops unless the crops are expressly excluded.

SECURED TRANSACTIONS

Lenders use various types of personal property to secure repayment of loans. Sellers, too, often retain an interest in goods being sold on credit to ensure payment of the purchase price. Secured transactions of this nature are very important to the economy of the United States. They range from relatively minor purchases by consumers of appliances and television sets to extensive financing of inventory and equipment by business firms. These secured transactions frequently involve real estate, inasmuch as fixtures are often used as collateral, or security for the loan. Common examples would be air-conditioning equipment and industrial machinery. Even after these are installed in a building, the credit seller attempts to retain a lien until the purchase price is paid.

In law the term *secured transaction* includes any transaction in which the parties agree that personal property or fixtures will secure a loan or the purchase of an item on credit. The law pertaining to secured transactions is found in Section 9 of the Texas Business and Commerce Code. Section 9 applies to all personal property and fixture security interests created by agreement. A *security interest* is a lien against personal property or fixtures to secure repayment of a debt. Section 9 does not apply to real estate mortgages or to other real estate liens created by statute. For Section 9 to protect a creditor effectively, both attachment and perfection must occur.

Attachment

A security interest is not effective between the parties until it has attached to the collateral. *Attachment* is the process by which a security interest in collateral is created. Three events must take place for a security interest to attach. Although these events usually occur in the following order, no particular order is required. The security interest attaches when the last event occurs.

- The debtor and secured party agree that a security interest attaches.
- The secured party gives value to the debtor.
- The debtor has or acquires rights in the collateral.

Of these three requirements, the most important is the agreement; the others usually occur automatically in the normal secured transaction in which personal property is used as collateral.

In most circumstances a security agreement is initiated when the secured party supplies a standard form that is to be completed by the borrower or buyer. This is usually labeled a security agreement, but other terms such as conditional sales contract are also used. Whatever the form is called, if it includes the necessary information, a security agreement exists under the Texas Business and Commerce Code. Figure 4.3 is an example of a security agreement.

Perfection

The purpose of perfection is to notify third parties of the existence of a security agreement. *Perfection* is the process by which notice of the security interest is given to all third parties and priority in the collateral is established among competing claims.

Under general legal principles, when a third party knows or has available information as to the existence of a security interest, the third party's rights are subordinate to the prior security claims. Two principal methods

Figure 4.3: **SECURITY AGREEMENT**

2267
Prepared by the State Bar of Texas for use by lawyers only.
Revised 10-85.
© 1985 by the State Bar of Texas

SECURITY AGREEMENT

Date:

Debtor:

Debtor's Mailing Address (including county):

Secured Party:

Secured Party's Mailing Address (including county):

Classification of Collateral:

Collateral (including all accessions):

Obligation
   Note
      Date:

      Amount:

      Maker:

      Payee:

      Final Maturity Date:

      Terms of Payment (optional):

   Other Obligation:

Debtor's Representation Concerning Location of Collateral (optional):

Subject to the terms of this agreement, Debtor grants to Secured Party a security interest in the collateral and all its proceeds to secure payment and performance of Debtor's obligation in this security agreement and all renewals and extensions of any of the obligation.

This form is reproduced here with the permission of the State Bar of Texas for informational purposes only. Further reproduction is not authorized without permission from the State Bar of Texas.

Figure 4.3: (continued)

Debtor's Warranties

1. Financing Statement. Except for that in favor of Secured Party, no financing statement covering the collateral is filed in any public office.
2. Ownership. Debtor owns the collateral and has the authority to grant this security interest. Ownership is free from any setoff, claim, restriction, lien, security interest, or encumbrance except this security interest and liens for taxes not yet due.
3. Fixtures and Accessions. None of the collateral is affixed to real estate, is an accession to any goods, is commingled with other goods, or will become a fixture, accession, or part of a product or mass with other goods except as expressly provided in this agreement.
4. Financial Statements. All information about Debtor's financial condition provided to Secured Party was accurate when submitted, as will be any information subsequently provided.

Debtor's Covenants

1. Protection of Collateral. Debtor will defend the collateral against all claims and demands adverse to Secured Party's interest in it and will keep it free from all liens except those for taxes not yet due and from all security interests except this one. The collateral will remain in Debtor's possession or control at all times, except as otherwise provided in this agreement. Debtor will maintain the collateral in good condition and protect it against misuse, abuse, waste, and deterioration except for ordinary wear and tear resulting from its intended use.
2. Insurance. Debtor will insure the collateral in accord with Secured Party's reasonable requirements regarding choice of carrier, casualties insured against, and amount of coverage. Policies will be written in favor of Debtor and Secured Party according to their respective interests or according to Secured Party's other requirements. All policies will provide that Secured Party will receive at least ten days' notice before cancellation, and the policies or certificates evidencing them will be provided to Secured Party when issued. Debtor assumes all risk of loss and damage to the collateral to the extent of any deficiency in insurance coverage. Debtor irrevocably appoints Secured Party as attorney-in-fact to collect any return, unearned premiums, and proceeds of any insurance on the collateral and to endorse any draft or check deriving from the policies and made payable to Debtor.
3. Secured Party's Costs. Debtor will pay all expenses incurred by Secured Party in obtaining, preserving, perfecting, defending, and enforcing this security interest or the collateral and in collecting or enforcing the note. Expenses for which Debtor is liable include, but are not limited to, taxes, assessments, reasonable attorney's fees, and other legal expenses. These expenses will bear interest from the dates of payments at the highest rate stated in notes that are part of the obligation, and Debtor will pay Secured Party this interest on demand at a time and place reasonably specified by Secured Party. These expenses and interest will be part of the obligation and will be recoverable as such in all respects.
4. Additional Documents. Debtor will sign any papers that Secured Party considers necessary to obtain, maintain, and perfect this security interest or to comply with any relevant law.
5. Notice of Changes. Debtor will immediately notify Secured Party of any material change in the collateral; change in Debtor's name, address, or location; change in any matter warranted or represented in this agreement; change that may affect this security interest; and any event of default.
6. Use and Removal of Collateral. Debtor will use the collateral primarily according to the stated classification unless Secured Party consents otherwise in writing. Debtor will not permit the collateral to be affixed to any real estate, to become an accession to any goods, to be commingled with other goods, or to become a fixture, accession, or part of a product or mass with other goods except as expressly provided in this agreement.
7. Sale. Debtor will not sell, transfer, or encumber any of the collateral without the prior written consent of Secured Party.

Rights and Remedies of Secured Party

1. Generally. Secured Party may exercise the following rights and remedies either before or after default:
   a. take control of any proceeds of the collateral;
   b. release any collateral in Secured Party's possession to any debtor, temporarily or otherwise;
   c. take control of any funds generated by the collateral, such as refunds from and proceeds of insurance, and reduce any part of the obligation accordingly or permit Debtor to use such funds to repair or replace damaged or destroyed collateral covered by insurance; and
   d. demand, collect, convert, redeem, settle, compromise, receipt for, realize on, adjust, sue for, and foreclose on the collateral either in Secured Party's or Debtor's name, as Secured Party desires.
2. Insurance. If Debtor fails to maintain insurance as required by this agreement or otherwise by Secured Party, then Secured Party may purchase single-interest insurance coverage that will protect only Secured Party. If Secured Party purchases this insurance, its premiums will become part of the obligation.

Figure 4.3: (continued)

Events of Default

Each of the following conditions is an event of default:

1. if Debtor defaults in timely payment or performance of any obligation, covenant, or liability in any written agreement between Debtor and Secured Party or in any other transaction secured by this agreement;

2. if any warranty, covenant, or representation made to Secured Party by or on behalf of Debtor proves to have been false in any material respect when made;

3. if a receiver is appointed for Debtor or any of the collateral;

4. if the collateral is assigned for the benefit of creditors or, to the extent permitted by law, if bankruptcy or insolvency proceedings commence against or by any of these parties: Debtor; any partnership of which Debtor is a general partner; and any maker, drawer, acceptor, endorser, guarantor, surety, accommodation party, or other person liable on or for any part of the obligation;

5. if any financing statement regarding the collateral but not related to this security interest and not favoring Secured Party is filed;

6. if any lien attaches to any of the collateral;

7. if any of the collateral is lost, stolen, damaged, or destroyed, unless it is promptly replaced with collateral of like quality or restored to its former condition.

Remedies of Secured Party on Default

During the existence of any event of default, Secured Party may declare the unpaid principal and earned interest of the obligation immediately due in whole or part, enforce the obligation, and exercise any rights and remedies granted by the Texas Uniform Commercial Code or by this agreement, including the following:

1. require Debtor to deliver to Secured Party all books and records relating to the collateral;

2. require Debtor to assemble the collateral and make it available to Secured Party at a place reasonably convenient to both parties;

3. take possession of any of the collateral and for this purpose enter any premises where it is located if this can be done without breach of the peace;

4. sell, lease, or otherwise dispose of any of the collateral in accord with the rights, remedies, and duties of a secured party under chapters 2 and 9 of the Texas Uniform Commercial Code after giving notice as required by those chapters; unless the collateral threatens to decline speedily in value, is perishable, or would typically be sold on a recognized market, Secured Party will give Debtor reasonable notice of any public sale of the collateral or of a time after which it may be otherwise disposed of without further notice to Debtor; in this event, notice will be deemed reasonable if it is mailed, postage prepaid, to Debtor at the address specified in this agreement at least ten days before any public sale or ten days before the time when the collateral may be otherwise disposed of without further notice to Debtor;

5. surrender any insurance policies covering the collateral and receive the unearned premium;

6. apply any proceeds from disposition of the collateral after default in the manner specified in chapter 9 of the Texas Uniform Commercial Code, including payment of Secured Party's reasonable attorney's fees and court expenses; and

7. if disposition of the collateral leaves the obligation unsatisfied, collect the deficiency from Debtor.

General Provisions

1. Parties Bound. Secured Party's rights under this agreement shall inure to the benefit of its successors and assigns. Assignment of any part of the obligation and delivery by Secured Party of any part of the collateral will fully discharge Secured Party from responsibility for that part of the collateral. If Debtor is more than one, all their representations, warranties, and agreements are joint and several. Debtor's obligations under this agreement shall bind Debtor's personal representatives, successors, and assigns.

2. Waiver. Neither delay in exercise nor partial exercise of any of Secured Party's remedies or rights shall waive further exercise of those remedies or rights. Secured Party's failure to exercise remedies or rights does not waive subsequent exercise of those remedies or rights. Secured Party's waiver of any default does not waive further default. Secured Party's waiver of any right in this agreement or of any default is binding only if it is in writing. Secured Party may remedy any default without waiving it.

3. Reimbursement. If Debtor fails to perform any of Debtor's obligations, Secured Party may perform those obligations and be reimbursed by Debtor on demand at the place where the note is payable for any sums so paid, including attorney's fees and other legal expenses, plus interest on those sums from the dates of payment at the rate stated in the note for matured, unpaid amounts. The sum to be reimbursed shall be secured by this security agreement.

4. Interest Rate. Interest included in the obligation shall not exceed the maximum amount of nonusurious interest that may be contracted for, taken, reserved, charged, or received under law; any interest in excess of that maximum amount shall be credited to the principal of the obligation or, if that has been paid, refunded. On any acceleration or required or permitted prepayment of the obligation, any such excess shall be canceled automatically as of the acceleration or prepayment or, if already paid, credited on the principal amount of the obligation or, if the principal amount has been paid, refunded. This provision overrides other provisions in this and all other instruments concerning the obligation.

5. Modifications. No provisions of this agreement shall be modified or limited except by written agreement.

Figure 4.3: (continued)

6. Severability. The unenforceability of any provision of this agreement will not affect the enforceability or validity of any other provision.

7. After-Acquired Consumer Goods. This security interest shall attach to after-acquired consumer goods only to the extent permitted by law.

8. Applicable Law. This agreement will be construed according to Texas laws.

9. Place of Performance. This agreement is to be performed in the county of Secured Party's mailing address.

10. Financing Statement. A carbon, photographic, or other reproduction of this agreement or any financing statement covering the collateral is sufficient as a financing statement.

11. Presumption of Truth and Validity. If the collateral is sold after default, recitals in the bill of sale or transfer will be prima facie evidence of their truth, and all prerequisites to the sale specified by this agreement and by the Texas Uniform Commercial Code will be presumed satisfied.

12. Singular and Plural. When the context requires, singular nouns and pronouns include the plural.

13. Priority of Security Interest. This security interest shall neither affect nor be affected by any other security for any of the obligation. Neither extensions of any of the obligation nor releases of any of the collateral will affect the priority or validity of this security interest with reference to any third person.

14. Cumulative Remedies. Foreclosure of this security interest by suit does not limit Secured Party's remedies, including the right to sell the collateral under the terms of this agreement. All remedies of Secured Party may be exercised at the same or different times, and no remedy shall be a defense to any other. Secured Party's rights and remedies include all those granted by law or otherwise, in addition to those specified in this agreement.

15. Agency. Debtor's appointment of Secured Party as Debtor's agent is coupled with an interest and will survive any disability of Debtor.

16. Attachments Incorporated. The addendum indicated below is attached to this agreement and incorporated into it for all purposes:

( ) addendum relating to accounts, inventory, documents, chattel paper, and general intangibles

( ) addendum relating to instruments

_____   _____
Secured Party   Debtor

for perfecting a security interest are public filing of the security agreement and possession of the collateral by the secured party. The latter is usually not applicable where fixtures are involved because the debtor almost always is in possession of the real property to which the fixture is attached. Although public filing may be accomplished by recording the signed security agreement, a form containing information from the agreement is used more frequently. This form is called a financing statement. Figure 4.4 is an example of a financing statement.

In Texas, to perfect properly a security interest in a fixture, the creditor must file the financing statement in the county clerk's office with the real estate mortgage records. (Tex. Bus. & Com. Code §9.313). This fixture filing must contain the name of the owner of the real property, the address of the real property, a description of the collateral and a statement that the collateral is to become a fixture.

The county clerks are directed to index these financing statements as if they were mortgages. Sometimes there is a question as to whether an item is a fixture. In this event, the secured party should file twice. The second filing should be made as state law directs for items other than fixtures.

Priority

Because the purpose of a security interest is to protect creditors in the event of default by the debtor, the creditor wants to protect his interest from claims made by other creditors. The secured creditor can preserve his right to remove and sell the collateral if he properly perfects his security interest. Occasionally a conflict will arise between a mortgage lender who has a lien against the real property and the secured creditor who has a security interest in a fixture. The issue between these two creditors then becomes who has priority with respect to the fixture.

The priority rule in Texas is that a secured party who extended credit to the debtor to assist the debtor in purchasing the collateral will have priority over a prior mortgage lender if he perfects his security interest in the fixture within ten days after the article has become a fixture.

CASE EXAMPLE

Fran's Pizza needed a new oven. One was purchased on credit from Only Oven, Inc. The oven was installed in the pizza parlor, which was owned by Fran but heavily mortgaged to the Bank of Durango. Despite the new oven, Fran's business was unsuccessful and she became bankrupt. Only Oven tried to remove the oven, but the bank argued that it was a fixture and should be sold as a part of the building.

Under the law, Only Oven would have priority over the Bank of Durango if it had properly perfected its security interest. Proper perfection requires fixture filing before the goods become fixtures or within ten days thereafter. The ten-day grace period given to the secured party applies only against

Figure 4.4: FINANCING STATEMENT

13450 Uniform Commercial Code—FINANCING STATEMENT—Form UCC-1 (Rev. 9-85)

"Litho Snap" • • • Lithographed by Hart Graphics, Austin, Texas • • •
IMPORTANT—Read instructions on back before filling out form

This Financing Statement is presented to a Filing Officer for filing pursuant to the Uniform Commercial Code

1. Debtor(s) Name and Mailing Address:
(Do not abbreviate)

2. Secured Party(ies) Name and Address:

3. For Filing Officer (Date, Time, Number and Filing Office):

5. Name and Address of Assignee of Secured Party: (Use this space to describe collateral, if needed)

4. This Financing Statement covers the following types (or items) of property.
(WARNING: If collateral is crops, fixtures, timber or minerals, read instructions on back.)

Check only if applicable
☐ This Financing Statement is to be filed for record in the real estate records.

Number of additional sheets presented _____
☐ Products of collateral are also covered.

6. This Statement is signed by the Secured Party instead of the Debtor to perfect a security interest in collateral
(Please check
appropriate box)
☐ already subject to a security interest in another jurisdiction when it was brought into this state, or when the debtor's location was changed to this state, or
☐ already subject to a financing statement filed in another county.
☐ which is proceeds of the original collateral described above in which a security interest was perfected, or
☐ as to which the filing has lapsed, or
☐ acquired after a change of name, identity or corporate structure of the debtor.

Use whichever signature line is applicable.

By _____

Signature(s) of Debtor(s)

By _____

Signature(s) of Secured Party(ies)

(1) Filing Officer Copy—Numerical
STANDARD FORM—FORM UCC-1 (Rev. 9/85) APPROVED BY THE SECRETARY OF THE STATE OF TEXAS — FORM 11-1548 — HART GRAPHICS, P.O. BOX 968, AUSTIN, TEXAS 78767

Before mailing — detach last 2 parts with this stub

prior recorded interests in the real estate. A fixture filing has priority against subsequent interests only when filed. If the Bank of Durango had advanced funds after the manufacturer had installed the oven, Only Oven would not enjoy a priority unless its security interest were already perfected by a fixture filing.

There are a few exceptions to this general rule regarding priority. The first exception concerns priority between a fixture lien and a construction mortgage. A construction mortgage is a mortgage given to secure funds advanced for the construction of improvements to real property.

CASE EXAMPLE

Claude Real Estate is building an office on land that it owns. The construction is being financed by Central Bank, which has agreed to advance funds as the work progresses. The bank has recorded a construction mortgage. Claude purchases plumbing fixtures from Little John, which perfects a security interest by properly recording a fixture filing statement. Soon after the building is completed, Claude fails and Little John attempts to remove the fixtures. Central Bank objects, claiming a prior interest on the basis of its construction mortgage.

In this situation, Little John would not be able to remove the plumbing fixtures. The law expressly gives priority to a construction mortgage recorded before the filing of a fixture security interest. In addition, the law provides that no security interest exists in ordinary building materials, such as bricks and lumber, once they are incorporated into a structure.

MOBILE HOMES

The Texas Business and Commerce Code offers a common solution to problems caused when lenders use as security personal property that can readily become a fixture. In other legal areas, major differences in the law's treatment of property whose character is uncertain continue to exist. One of these is the taxation and regulation of mobile homes. For example, a nonowner sale of a mobile home that is part of the sale of land can be done only through a licensed real estate broker because mobile homes in this situation are defined as real estate. However, the sale of a mobile home that is not attached to land can be performed by anyone because it is considered personal property.

A **mobile home** is a transportable structure built on a chassis and designed for year-round living. It is usually set up on a permanent foundation and connected to utilities. Mobile homes that are located on land owned by the owner of the mobile home are included in the definition of improvement for tax purposes. Therefore, these mobile homes are included as real property for ad valorem tax purposes. Mobile homes that are not located on property owned by the owner of the mobile home are personal property and subject to taxation as nonexempt personal property. Mobile homes can qualify as a homestead for gaining the partial tax exemption. Movement of mobile homes within the state must be reported to the Appraisal Districts that are affected by the removal.

SUMMARY

The term *property* generally refers to various rights a person has in a tangible item—a building, car or other possession—but it can also refer to something intangible, such as a lease or even the right to use a trademark. Possession of this "bundle of rights" depends on the laws a government creates and maintains for the benefit of citizens. A major development changing the laws regarding the use and sale of property is found in civil rights legislation.

Historically, personal property in general is differentiated from real property—land and buildings a person owns—because of the economic significance attached to land. Personal property is characterized as being movable, although in today's usage some personal property, such as a franchise, is intangible. Real estate professionals need to be aware of the distinction between the two kinds of property so that contracts and other legal documents will be written properly.

The legal distinction becomes important when courts determine whether an item attached to land or buildings becomes real property. If so, the item (such as built-in shelving or certain kitchen appliances) is characterized as a fixture and must not be removed upon sale of the realty. To determine whether or not an item is a fixture the courts look at the intent of the parties. However, if intent cannot be ascertained, then the courts will consider the relationship of the parties, the manner in which the item is annexed and the character and use of the item. There are two exceptions to the general principles of law relating to fixtures. These are trade fixtures and annual crops. Trade fixtures are removable within a reasonable time after the termination of a commercial lease. Annual crops are considered to be personal property.

Often a purchaser of fixtures uses the fixtures themselves as collateral to secure a loan for their payment. Section 9 of the Texas Business and Commerce Code provides protection for both buyer and seller in this type of secured transaction, when the two legal requirements of attachment and perfection are met. In the attachment process, three events occur: both parties consent in writing to the arrangement, value must be given by the secured party and the debtor must have rights in the collateral. In perfection, the secured party establishes priority in the collateral over other creditors through an official recording of the transaction. The law requires that all documents be both written and filed, as mortgage agreements would be.

In some areas the distinction between realty and personal property is not so clear. One example is mobile homes, which, although similar in many ways to realty, are still considered movable. Legal conflicts occur in many municipalities over the status of mobile homes. Controversy usually centers around issues of ownership and title, taxation and degree of mobility.

QUESTIONS AND CASE PROBLEMS

1. In 1968 Jacobs leased a building from Porter for use as a transmission shop. In 1980 Porter sold the building to Neely. At that time Jacobs was in arrears in his rent payments and Neely ordered Jacobs to vacate the premises. A dispute arose between Jacobs and Neely regarding ownership of six hydraulic lifts installed by Jacobs. Neely claimed ownership based on his warranty deed from Porter. Can Jacobs remove the six hydraulic lifts? Why?

2. Harris purchased a ten-acre tract of land at a foreclosure sale. The land was being developed as a mobile home park. The prior owner, Cantu, attempted to remove a metal building he had placed there. Harris claims that he is the owner of the building because under the terms of the trust deed he was to have and hold the premises and property "together with the rights, privileges and appurtenances thereto." The metal building was 14 feet by 30 feet and set on a three- to four-inch concrete slab. Harris argues that although the metal building was portable, when Cantu set it on the concrete slab the building became permanently attached to the land. The building had been placed on the property by Cantu as a temporary structure for use during development of the property. Is the metal building a fixture?

3. Stephens purchased a steel grain-drying bin from B. C. Manufacturing and executed a conditional sales contract and a financing statement. The financing statement was filed in the county clerk's office but not in the office of the registrar for deeds. The bin was placed on a concrete base on property owned by Newman Grove Grain Company. This property was later mortgaged to Battle Creek Bank. The mortgage was foreclosed, and Tillotson purchased at the foreclosure sale. B. C. Manufacturing sued for the value of the bin. Would B. C. Manufacturing be successful? Discuss.

5
Estates in Land

HISTORICAL CONSIDERATIONS

Interests in land existing in the United States today are the result of two different systems of ownership. For several centuries, both systems existed side by side in Europe. One of these systems was feudalism, in which everyone holding land except the sovereign owed rents or services to a superior. In the *allodial* system, on the other hand, all land was owned absolutely. The holder had no obligation to pay rents or services to another.

Allodium or absolute ownership was the basis of Roman real property law. After the collapse of the Roman Empire, feudalism gradually became dominant in most of Europe except in some sections where the Roman influence persisted. In many of these areas the Roman idea of absolute ownership continued as the basis for holding land. Land was held without obligation to superiors. The owner had an absolute title with few limitations or restrictions on rights to use or dispose of it.

Today, the allodial concept of ownership is the distinguishing feature of real property ownership in the United States. Private ownership of land is free and absolute, subject only to governmental and voluntary private restrictions.

The fall of the Roman Empire brought to western Europe a long period of intense disruption. Law and order, established and maintained by the military might and organizational genius of Rome, collapsed. The chaos that resulted for about 500 years led to extensive disintegration of organized society. In order to survive, the people of western Europe turned to local leaders for protection of family and wealth. It was during this period that feudalism developed. *Feudalism* is an economic and social system that is based primarily upon obligations owed to a superior in return for the right to occupy land.

Because most wealth consisted of land, which was also necessary for survival, people in a particular locality would join together and turn their land over to a local leader who, in exchange, would guarantee them protection and grant them rights in the land for a period of time. This practice, which proved relatively effective, spread throughout most of Europe over a period of several generations.

Local leaders who protected small groups often allied themselves to a stronger protector by a similar process. As a result, the interests of many people were sometimes united through a single piece of land. Frequently, several intermediaries existed between the person at the top and the actual occupant of the land.

In this system land was not owned in the sense that we think of ownership today. A person holding land was spoken of as being "seised" of the land. As a tenant, the occupant owed certain services that arose because he had possession, but the overlord also enjoyed rights arising out of the same parcel. In many instances this immediate overlord owed duties and services to another based upon his rights in the land.

The conquest of the Angles and Saxons by the Normans in 1066 brought a relatively advanced and sophisticated form of feudalism to England. The Norman dukes who became kings in England faced serious problems in a hostile environment. Their supply lines were long, they were opposed by most of the population and many of their followers were more interested in returning to Normandy than remaining in England. To consolidate his power and to induce his followers to remain in England, William the Conqueror, the first of the Norman dukes to serve as an English king, imported a modified form of the continental system of feudalism to England.

William declared all English lands forfeited to him because of the failure of the Angle and Saxon lords to recognize him as the rightful king. As supreme lord of all English land, he parceled it out as fiefs to his Norman followers and those Angles and Saxons who would swear allegiance to him. Those who acquired fiefs from the king, however, were not given absolute ownership. They held the land as tenants but were required, in return, to perform services for the king or their respective overlords. This practice is called *tenure*. **Tenure** is the principle that the occupier's use of the land is conditioned on his performance of certain duties and services for a superior.

Tenants who held land in military tenure, or knight service, agreed to furnish military service. Those who held in socage tenure were required to furnish supplies. Still others furnished personal service to the king in a type of tenure known as serjeanty. Finally, certain religious orders were given land as tenants for which religious support was required. Although all land was held eventually by the king, vassals to whom extensive grants of land were given allocated portions of their lands in a similar manner. The result was a system of landholding based upon tenancy very similar in many aspects to the system that existed on the Continent. In England, however, all land rights were derived from the Crown, then in the person of William the Conqueror.

In addition to the specific duties owed by the tenant, the relationship created other valuable rights for the lord. For example, if a tenant died with his heirs underage, the lord had the right to guardianship, which entitled him to all profits from the estate until the heir became of age. The lord also had the right to arrange a marriage for the heir. If the heir rejected his choice, the estate was subject to a substantial penalty. If a tenant died without heirs, his land *escheated*—that is, was returned to the lord's possession. The lord also had the right to collect contributions from tenants to defray the costs of knighting his oldest son, to provide a dowry for his oldest daughter and to ransom himself if he were taken prisoner.

Tenure in the United States

In the eastern part of the United States, some of the early colonial grants were based upon tenure. The proprietor held his land directly from the king. The small monetary payment required as a token of this relationship was called a quitrent. When the proprietor of a colony granted smaller tracts to individual settlers, each owed a quitrent by an extension of the feudal theory. These quitrents were very often ignored because of the ready availability of land on the frontier. In Massachusetts, Rhode Island and Connecticut, the tenurial system never existed; land there was held allodially. After the Revolution quitrents were abolished, and the notion prevailed that a person who owned land had an absolute title limited only by the state.

Vestiges of feudalism and tenure are retained in American real property law. One example is the law of escheat, in which the state is paramount, with land reverting to it if a person dies without heirs. Probably more important is the English concept of estates in land, for our legal system continues to recognize the idea that separate divisible interests can exist simultaneously in the same piece of land.

ESTATE

The feudal notion of tenure is the foundation of the doctrine of estates in land. This doctrine has substantially influenced the rights that individuals may have in real property. In the previous chapter property was defined as a collection of rights. Estates are based upon this concept of rights in land. Different rights are associated with different estates. The term *estate* as used in this context has a restrictive and technical meaning. It should not be confused with more common usage—that is, as a synonym for all of a person's assets.

In the system of tenure as it developed in England, land was separated from interests that might exist in it. Because land was one thing and interests in it another, several people could possess interests or estates in the same piece of land. This idea continues to be a feature of the law of English-speaking countries. Although a complete estate in land may exist at the present moment, it can be divided into various slices in such a way that each slice is regarded as existing now.

Although the nature, quality and extent of their interests often differ, each holder of an estate invariably has a present or future right of possession. Sometimes this right may be deferred until a future time, or it might even be conditional, but it is currently recognized by the courts.

As there are many possible interests in land, estates have numerous dimensions. These dimensions include the following:

1. the duration of the estate
2. the right to possession of the land
3. the right to transfer the land during the holder's lifetime
4. the right of the holder to transfer the land at his or her death
5. the right of the state to transfer the land at the death of the holder when he or she fails to make a will

Estates are divided into two categories depending upon the duration of the estate. Estates of an uncertain duration are **freehold estates.** The length of existence is not determined at the time the estate in land is created. It is unknown whether it will last for one day or 100 years. Estates that are created for a fixed period of time are called **nonfreehold estates.** The duration of such an estate is determined at its inception. A common nonfreehold estate is the lease for a stated period. Freehold estates are discussed in this chapter. Discussion of the nonfreehold estate is reserved for the chapters on landlord and tenant relationships (Chapters 24 and 25).

Freehold estates are further divided into present estates and future estates. A **present estate** is an estate in which the owner has the right to the present possession of the land. He or she has the right to use, possess and enjoy the land now. A **future estate** is an estate in which the owner may have the right to possession of the land at some time in the future. He or she cannot at the present time use, possess or enjoy the land. However, at some point in the future he or she may have the right to possession.

Finally, freehold estates are often classified by the freedom to convey the estate. If the owner of the land has the right to transfer all or any portion of his rights during his lifetime, then the estate is **alienable.** The transfer during his lifetime can be by gift or by sale. He can transfer all of his rights or only a portion of his rights. If the owner of the land has the right to bequeath the estate upon his death by will, then the estate is **devisable.** Assuming that the deceased leaves a validly executed and drawn last will and testament, the law will follow his directions regarding passage of the estate. But when a person dies without a valid will, the state by law names the heirs, referred to as the decedent's *heirs-at-law.* If the estate owned by the deceased will pass to his heirs-at-law when he dies intestate, the freehold estate is **descendible.**

TYPES OF FREEHOLD ESTATES

Keeping in mind these characteristics of freehold estates, we will begin to look at the various types of freehold estates. The freehold estates include these:

- fee simple absolute
- fee simple determinable and the possibility of reverter
- fee simple on a condition subsequent and the right of reentry
- fee simple subject to an executory limitation and the executory interest
- life estate and either remainder or reversion

Fee Simple Absolute

The fee simple absolute is the most extensive interest in land that a holder might possess. This estate contains the most complete collection of rights with respect to the land. Although the rights of use and possession are limited even in the fee simple absolute, it remains the greatest estate of all. Most land in the United States is held in fee simple absolute. The fee simple absolute is a present, alienable, devisable and descendible interest in land. The holder of this estate may voluntarily limit uses to which it may be put or carve out lesser estates from it.

No special language is required to create a fee simple absolute. However, it is common to find the following words in the conveyance that create the estate:

- To Jane; or
- To Jane, her heirs and assigns; or
- To Jane and her heirs.

Creation of the fee simple absolute is preferred over the lesser estates in Texas. The rule of law is that any inconsistencies in the language creating an estate will be resolved in favor of the fee simple absolute. (Tex. Prop. Code §5.001) Consequently, if the grantor intends to create a lesser estate, such as the life estate or a fee simple on a condition subsequent, he must by express and clear language make that intention known. In the absence of limiting language or in the presence of conflicting language, the court will hold that the estate created is a fee simple absolute.

Defeasible Estates

The defeasible estates are frequently referred to as *lesser freehold estates.* The rights associated with the defeasible estates are fewer than those associated with the fee simple absolute. The defeasible estates are the fee simple determinable, the fee simple on a condition subsequent and the fee simple subject to an executory interest. Common to these three defeasible estates is the imposition of a condition or event that can cause the holder to lose his or her estate in land.

CASE EXAMPLE

Mrs. Zahn, an environmentalist, wants to establish a wildlife sanctuary on 200 acres of land that she owns in Texas. Even after her death she wants the land to continue to be used as a wildlife sanctuary. She can control the future use of the land by creating a defeasible fee that will terminate if the land ceases to be used as a wildlife sanctuary.

Defeasible fees are present, alienable, devisable and descendible estates in land. They differ from the fee simple absolute in that there is a limitation, condition or event that may occur that will terminate the estate. Since there is a possibility that this *present* estate may terminate, the question arises concerning to whom the land will then be transferred. Who owns the *future* interest? For each type of defeasible fee there is a specific future estate.

The future estate can be one that is itself defeasible, or it can be absolute.

CASE EXAMPLE

Mrs. Zahn may transfer the 200 acres to the Texas Wildlife Society, provided that it is used as a bird sanctuary, and if it ceases to be so used, then she can provide that it will go to the American Audubon Society, provided that it is used as a bird sanctuary. Both of these estates are defeasible although one is a future interest. On the other hand, Mrs. Zahn could provide for the transfer to the Texas Wildlife Society, provided that it is used as a bird sanctuary, and if not then to her son, Jerome. Jerome's future interest in this case is not defeasible but absolute.

Fee Simple Determinable/Possibility of Reverter

The *fee simple determinable* is a defeasible estate that automatically terminates when a stated condition is fulfilled. The key distinguishing factor is the *automatic* termination of the estate. To create a fee simple determinable, the following language is commonly used:

- To the National Wildlife Society and its successors and assigns *so long as* the property is used as a wildlife preserve; or
- To the Roman Catholic Church *until* it is no longer used for charitable or religious purposes.

Since it is unknown when, if ever, these conditions may occur, the fee simple determinable has an indefinite duration. However, if the condition does occur, the grantee's interest terminates automatically and the land reverts back to the grantor. The grantor's future interest is called a *possibility of reverter*. Whenever a fee simple determinable is created, a possibility of reverter is also created. The possibility of reverter originally belongs to the grantor. However, this future interest is alienable, devisable and descendible and actually may be owned by someone else at the time the event or condition is met. Because the termination of the fee simple determinable is automatic, the holder of the possibility of reverter is not required to take any steps to assert his or her rights of ownership

Fee Simple on a Condition Subsequent/Right of Reentry

The second defeasible estate is called the *fee simple on a condition subsequent*. This defeasible estate *may* be terminated by the grantor or the grantor's successor when a stated condition is fulfilled. The key characteristic of this defeasible estate is the fact that the defeasible estate is *not* terminated automatically. Some action on the part of the holder of the future interest is required to terminate the estate.

To create a fee simple on a condition subsequent, the following language is commonly used:

- To the National Wildlife Society and its successors and assigns forever *on condition that* the land is used as a wildlife preserve, *but if* the land is used for any other purposes, Mrs. Zahn and her heirs shall have a right of entry and repossession; or
- To the Roman Catholic Church *provided that* the land be used as an orphanage, *but if* the land is ever used for another purpose, then Grantor, his heirs, or assigns shall have the right to retake possession of the property.

The future interest that the grantor has reserved for himself in these conveyances is called a *right of reentry.* Rights of reentry are alienable, devisable and descendible. The holder of the right of reentry must take steps to assert his right to possession. If he fails to make such an assertion, the right of reentry is lost. The holder of the right of reentry can assert his right to the land by taking possession within a reasonable time after the condition has been fulfilled, or, if that is not possible, the right can be asserted by filing a lawsuit to remove the prior interest holder from the land. If a lawsuit is required, it must be filed within a reasonable time. What constitutes action within a reasonable time is based on the notion of fairness or equity.

Fee Simple Subject to an Executory Limitation/Executory Interest

This is the last of the defeasible fees. The fee simple subject to an executory limitation is an estate that *may* be terminated by the holder of the *executory interest* when a stated condition is fulfilled. This defeasible estate is similar to the fee simple on a condition subsequent. However, it can be distinguished from the previous estate by the future interest associated with it. In the previous estate the grantor reserved the future interest. In the fee simple subject to an executory interest the grantor has conveyed the future interest to a third party at the same time as he created the defeasible fee.

The same type of language commonly used to create the fee simple on a

condition subsequent is used to create the fee simple subject to an executory limitation:

- To the Greater Southwest Archaeological Society *on the condition*
  that it be used as their headquarters, *but if* the land ceases to be used
  for this purpose; then to my son, Kevin; or
- To the State of Texas *provided that* it is used as a state park and, if it is
  not used as a state park, then to my daughter, Sandra.

Executory interests are alienable, devisable and descendible. An executory interest is lost if the holder fails to take possession of the property
upon the happening of the stated event or condition within a reasonable
time. As with the right of reentry, the holder of an executory interest can
assert his or her right to possession by filing a lawsuit against the other
party.

Problems with the Defeasible Fees and the Future Interests

The acceptance of the concept of possessory estates in land followed by a
future interest lends flexibility to the disposition of real property; in many
instances, however, future interests exist because a grantor wishes to limit
the free transferability of land. Often the creator of the estate wishes to control the use of the land not only during his or her lifetime, but after death as
well. Conditional and defeasible fees have been used in the past for this purpose and continue to be used today.

The defeasible fees and their future interests cause especially serious
problems. The fees are created to last forever and often do last for many
years. As a result, the future interests are merely expectant interests with
almost no present economic value. Often the current possessors of these interests are remote descendants of the original creator. Frequently they are
unaware that an interest exists. When a title search reveals the existence of
these interests, a person attempting to clear the title is presented with a difficult, if not insoluble, problem arising from the fact that often it is impossible to contact many of the parties who might retain an interest in the land
because of the future interest. Disputes can also arise as to whether the
condition or limitation has occurred.

A resolution of these title problems often requires court action. One of
the parties asserting a claim to the land will file a lawsuit called *trespass to
try title*, asking the court to determine who presently owns the land. Some
of these problems can also be cured through adverse possession. The doctrine of adverse possession is discussed later in this book. However, even
with a claim of adverse possession to bolster a party's assertion of ownership, the trespass to try title suit is frequently necessary.

Life Estate

A *life estate* is an estate of limited duration measured by a life or lives.
Granting an estate to an individual for life has been a common practice in

the United States. A life estate typically is measured by the life of the owner, but it may be measured by the life of some other person. If the holder of a fee simple absolute makes a grant "to *A* for life," *A* has an estate that terminates with his or her death. If the grant were "to *A* for the life of *B*," *A*'s estate would terminate upon the death of *B*. This type of life estate is called an estate pur autre vie. In modern practice, estates pur autre vie are seldom created.

No particular words are required to create a life estate; however, the grantor must clearly express that the estate is based upon someone's life. Any doubt regarding the intent of the grantor in creating the estate is resolved against the existence of a life estate. Life estates are alienable in Texas. The sale of a life estate conveys only the rights of the grantor.

CASE EXAMPLE

Sally owns a life estate in Blackacre based upon her life. Sally sells Blackacre to Tim. Tim receives a life estate in Blackacre based upon Sally's life. When Sally dies, Tim's interest in Blackacre terminates.

The future interest following the life estate is called either a *reversion* or a *remainder*. If the land reverts back to the grantor or his heirs upon termination of the life estate, the future interest is called a *reversion*. For example, if Blackacre is conveyed to Sue for life, Sue has a life estate and the grantor has a reversion. If the land passes to someone other than the grantor, then the future interest is called a *remainder*. For example, if Blackacre is conveyed to Mike for life, then to Dick, Mike has a life estate and Dick has a remainder.

Rights and Duties of Life Tenants

The holder of a life estate, usually called the *life tenant*, has an ownership interest in the land. This interest can be sold, mortgaged or leased, but its value can be difficult to ascertain. Any interest a buyer, mortgagee or lessee acquires ends with the death of the life tenant. Life tenants are entitled to rents and profits from the property while their tenancy lasts, but they may not use the property in a manner that will permanently reduce its market value. If they do so, the owner of the estate that follows may bring an action against them for waste.

Life tenants must make ordinary repairs to the property. They are responsible for annual property taxes but for only a proportionate share of special assessments for sewers, sidewalks and other permanent improvements. As a general rule, the life tenant is required to pay the interest on a mortgage but not the principal.

Occasionally disputes arise regarding maintenance of fire and casualty insurance on the property during the term of the life estate. Both the holder of the life estate and the holder of the future interest have an insurable interest in the property; however, neither is required by law to carry any type of insurance on the improvements. Although there is no obligation to insure, if insurance exists, then proceeds from the policy will be divided between the life tenant and the holder of the future estate. The division is determined by the economic value of each interest at the time of the loss. If the proceeds are inadequate to compensate fully both parties for their loss, the party who paid the premiums on the policy will be paid in full first.

One of the issues that frequently arises in the operation of a life estate concerns the relative rights of the owner of the life estate and those that take upon termination of the life estate. As previously mentioned, the life tenant cannot commit any waste of the property. This doctrine prohibits the permanent removal of minerals, timber or any natural resource from the land during the life estate by the life tenant. This rule is modified in Texas by what is called the "Open Mine" Doctrine. A life tenant cannot commit waste, nor is he entitled to royalties upon the sale of the minerals unless at the time the life estate comes into existence (1) the minerals are being removed by prior agreement with the grantor or (2) a valid agreement exists for removal of the minerals. If no minerals are presently being removed and no lease exists for their removal, then the life tenant cannot without the agreement of the remaindermen sell such rights to removal, nor is he entitled to receive the royalties from such a sale. However, in Texas the life tenant is entitled to receive interest on the royalties during the existence of the life estate.

Alternatives to the Creation of Defeasible Estates and Life Estates

The defeasible estates and the life estate were useful mechanisms for controlling the future ownership of land prior to the development of trusts. These interests are less common today because the trust allows for greater control and flexibility in accomplishing the purposes of the grantor. A *trust* is a legal relationship in which one person holds and manages property for the benefit of another. The creation and operation of a trust is controlled by the Texas Trust Code. (Tex. Prop. Code §111.001 et seq.) A trust involving real estate must be in writing. Trusts are discussed in Chapter 6.

Homestead

The interest in land called a *homestead* is a development of American law. Forty-three states have some type of homestead provision either by statute or by constitution. In Texas the first homestead exemption statute was passed in 1839, while Texas was still a republic. The primary purpose of the homestead law was to protect the family. In a lengthy treatise entitled *Homestead and Exemption* by Rufus Waples written in 1893, the policy in support of homestead laws was described as follows:

The policy of the state is to foster families as the factors of society, and thus promote the general welfare. To their permanency, the legislators seek to protect their homes from forced sales so far as it can be done without injustice to others.

The reasons which support this broad policy are cogent and readily apparent. Families are the units of society, indispensable factors of civilization, the bases of the commonwealth. Upon their permanency, in any community, depends the success of schools, churches, public libraries, and good institutions of every kind. The sentiments of patriotism and independence, the spirit of free citizenship, the feeling of interest in public affairs, are cultivated and fostered more readily when the citizen lives permanently in his own castle with a sense of protection and durability.

The first constitution for the state of Texas provided for protection of the family homestead. Subsequent constitutions provided similar protection. In 1973 the Texas Constitution was amended to extend the homestead protection to single adult persons. This change indicates that the homestead exemption now serves purposes other than protection of the family unit. It reflects a state policy that perceives an equally important social benefit in shielding some portion of a debtor's assets in order that he may rebuild his wealth and pay his debts. This is, of course, one of the purposes of the federal bankruptcy law.

Both the definition of a homestead and the rights of this estate are set out in the Texas Constitution. Neither the existence of the homestead nor the rights associated with it can be eliminated by the state legislature or waived by individual owners. The Texas homestead law is one of the most liberal among states that have enacted homestead exemption statutes. It has two characteristics that earn it this designation. First, it permits single people (without dependents) the same rights as a married person with dependents. Second, it protects the homestead without regard to its value. Many states have given limited homestead rights to those persons who are married or have dependents and have placed a dollar value limitation on the land that can be claimed as homestead. As a matter of fact, both of these limitations once existed in Texas as well.

The characterization of land as homestead confers three important rights. First, the land is exempted from forced sale by creditors of the owner, with some limited exceptions. Second, the homestead cannot be sold, mortgaged or encumbered without the joinder of the spouse. Third, the land is subject to a life estate in favor of the surviving spouse even if the homestead is not community property.

It should at least be mentioned that there are groups of businesses and individuals who would like to change the present homestead law to allow owners to mortgage the homestead for debts other than those presently allowed. Any change would require an amendment to the Texas Constitution and therefore must be submitted to Texas voters.

Designation of the Homestead

Homestead is the dwelling constituting the family residence, together with the land on which it is located. A family can have only one homestead. The Texas Constitution allows for 200 acres of land outside a city to be designated a homestead (rural homestead) or one acre of land inside the city to be designated a homestead (urban homestead). (Tex. Const. art. 16, §51, and for comparison see Tex. Prop. Code §41.002). Both include without regard to value all improvements made on the property for the purpose of a home or a place to exercise the family business. The constitutional provision further states that the temporary renting of the home will not terminate the homestead. No action on the part of the owner of the property is necessary in order for the property to be considered a homestead under the law. The key issue is whether the property is being used, is being developed for use or has been used as the home of the owner or his or her family. By statute a person can designate his or her homestead in writing and file the written declaration with the clerk of the court to prevent an attempted sale of the property. (Tex. Prop. Code §41.021 et seq.) However, this written designation is not necessary in order to be protected under the Texas Constitution. Many taxing authorities request the owner to disclose whether the property being taxed is a homestead for the purpose of properly assessing the taxes due. Failure to classify the property as a homestead for tax purposes will not affect the constitutional right of the owner to classify it as a homestead for other purposes.

If the property qualifies as a homestead, the Texas Constitution provides in Article 16, §50, that it shall be afforded the following protection:

> The homestead of a family, or of a single adult person, shall be, and is hereby protected from forced sale, for the payment of all debts except for the purchase money thereof, or a part of such purchase money, the taxes due thereon, or for work and material used in constructing improvements thereon, and in this last case only when the work and material are contracted for in writing, with the consent of both spouses, in the case of a family homestead, given in the same manner as is required in making a sale and conveyance of the homestead; nor may the owner or claimant of the property claimed as homestead, if married, sell or abandon the homestead without the consent of the other spouse, given in such manner as may be prescribed by law. No mortgage, trust deed, or other lien on the homestead shall ever be valid, except for the purchase money therefor, or improve-

ments made thereon, as herein before provided, whether such mortgage, or trust deed, or other lien shall have been created by the owner alone, or together with his or her spouse, in case the owner is married. All pretended sales of the homestead involving any condition of defeasance shall be void.

Protection from Forced Sale

As indicated in the constitutional provision quoted above, the homestead is protected from forced sale by a creditor unless the debt is incurred for the purpose of purchasing the land, for taxes due on the property or for improvements to the property if both spouses consented in writing to the improvements.

CASE EXAMPLES

Dick owes Big Bank $50,000 on a loan he made in order to purchase some equipment and inventory for his business, Dick's Stationery Store. Dick is in grave financial trouble and cannot pay Big Bank. Big Bank repossesses the business equipment and inventory. After these things are sold and the proceeds applied to the indebtedness, Dick still owes Big Bank $30,000. Can Big Bank force Dick to sell his home in order to recover the money due on the business loan? The answer is no. Dick's homestead is exempt from forced sale by a general creditor such as Big Bank.

Dick borrows $25,000 from Big Bank to remodel his home. After the remodeling is complete, Dick loses his job and cannot meet his monthly payments to Big Bank. Can Big Bank force Dick to sell his home in order to recover the debt for the remodeling? The answer is yes, if the agreement for home improvements was in writing.

The Texas Constitution also states that no lien can be created against the homestead except for the purchase money or improvements. Even if the homeowner attempts to create a lien, it is considered void. This additional provision clarifies the extent to which the homestead is exempt from forced sale by a general creditor. To understand the importance of this part of the law, consider the following illustration.

CASE EXAMPLE

Dick's wife has cancer. The medical bills for the treatment already total $40,000. Dick learns that a doctor in France has been successfully experimenting with a new treatment for cancer that has not yet been approved for use in the United States. Dick would like to take his wife to France for treatment but does not have the money and cannot borrow it unless he has some collateral for the loan. Dick has $78,000 in equity in his home. He signs an agreement with Big Bank, giving it a lien against the home and the right to foreclose if he defaults in the repayment of the debt. He also signs an agreement stating that he is not claiming the home as his homestead. Is the lien valid? Could Big Bank foreclose? The answer is no.

The Constitution does provide for three exceptions to the forced sale exemption. First, a lender who lent money to make the purchase of the homestead possible has the right to sell the property if the owner defaults. This is often referred to as a *purchase money mortgage*.

CASE EXAMPLE

Kevin borrows $56,000 from First Lender of Texas to apply toward the purchase of a $75,000 home. If Kevin defaults in his payments to First Lender, First Lender can foreclose even if Kevin lives in the home with his wife and five children and has officially designated it as his family homestead.

The second exception involves the collection of taxes by the state of Texas and any of its political subdivisions (such as cities, school districts, counties, etc.). These governmental units have the right to sell the homestead if the homeowner fails to pay the taxes assessed against the property. These are called *ad valorem* or *property taxes*. In addition, the federal government can force the sale of the homestead in order to collect delinquent federal income taxes.

Although the Texas Constitution does not specifically address the enforceability of the federal tax lien against a homestead, the issue is resolved by a provision in the Internal Revenue Code. The federal law specifically provides that any and all property of a taxpayer can be attached and sold by the federal government for the purpose of collecting delinquent taxes. In 1983 the U.S. Supreme Court was asked to rule on the forced sale of a homestead in Texas where the person claiming the homestead was *not* the delinquent taxpayer. To understand this case it is helpful to keep in mnd that a person can have a homestead right in property even if he or she does not own the property in fee simple.

CASE EXAMPLE

Ted buys a house in 1963 while he is single. This house is Ted's separate property under Texas law even if he subsequently marries. Ted marries Norma in 1969, and they live together in this house. Norma has a homestead estate in the house even though it is Ted's separate property. Ted owes the federal government $25,000 in delinquent income taxes for the years 1967–1969. The delinquent taxes are Ted's separate debt incurred before marriage. Can the Internal Revenue Service force the sale of Ted's house in order to recover the $25,000 in delinquent taxes? The answer is yes, even though Norma has a homestead estate in the house and is *not* personally liable for the taxes.

The third and final exception to the prohibition against forced sale involves loans made to improve the homestead. The Texas Constitution requires that the agreement to borrow be in writing and that both spouses consent to it. Generally, the courts have been careful to determine whether the proceeds of the loan were actually used for home improvement. If the loan proceeds were not applied toward the improvements, the lien against the homestead will not be enforced, and the creditor will not be able to force a sale of the house to pay the debt.

The protection against forced sale by a general creditor is very strong. Creditors who are contemplating accepting real estate as collateral for a loan must be very careful to ascertain whether that property is a homestead. If there is any doubt, the creditor is better advised not to accept the offered collateral. It is the creditor who will lose the most in the event of default by the debtor. It may appear somewhat harsh to prevent a creditor recovery against the homestead where the debtor has misled or deceived the creditor; however, there are two reasons for this outcome. First, the public policy in favor of the homestead is intended to protect the family unit. This includes protection of the children in the family from the acts of their parents or the protection of one spouse from acts of the other. Second, the Texas Constitution states that any purported lien is *void*. In law there is a clear distinction between an act that is void and one that is voidable. A void act is treated as if it never occurred. Consequently, in the case of a void lien against a homestead, the courts will not recognize that a lien ever existed. Compare this with a voidable act. In law a voidable act is one that exists, but for reasons of fairness and equity the courts refuse to give it legal significance. Therefore, if the Texas Constitution had stated that the lien was voidable instead of void, the courts could consider such things as the fraud or deceit of the debtor in deciding whether or not the lien should be enforced under the law. Obviously, the constitutional provision is written in the manner in which it is to provide the utmost protection to the family unit and, in the case of a single adult, to protect him from himself.

Marriage and Homestead

The second right provided by the Texas Constitution is the protection of the homestead against an attempted sale or encumbrance by one spouse. Any transfer of any kind must be joined in by both spouses if the property being transferred is their homestead. Transfers include sales, gifts, mortgages, liens and partial sales (such as the sale of mineral rights). This requirement extends to the transfer of separate property that qualifies as the homestead of the married couple. As illustrated above, Norma had a homestead right in Ted's separate property simply because she lived on the property. As a result, if Ted desires to sell the home or place a lien against the home, Norma must join in the transfer in order for it to be valid.

Life Estate in Surviving Spouse

The third right conferred by homestead is the life estate in the surviving spouse. The Texas Constitution states that homesteads will pass upon death as any other property, with the limitation that it cannot be partitioned during the lifetime of the surviving spouse so long as the survivor elects to use or occupy it as a homestead. This is true even though the homestead may have been the separate property of the deceased spouse. The survivor has the right to use and occupy it as her home until her death or until she elects to abandon it. Although the homestead right is in the nature of a life estate, it differs in one significant aspect. The homestead can be terminated either by the death of the surviving spouse or by abandonment of it by the surviving spouse, whichever occurs first. Whether the homestead has been abandoned is a factual issue and usually difficult to prove. The case that follows involves the issue of abandonment and the court's handling of it.

• CASE BRIEF •

McFarland acquired his interest in the property when his father died without a will in 1958. The property in question was purchased by McFarland's parents in 1948 and had been their home. McFarland occupied the premises after his father's death, sometimes with his mother. His mother would also spend time with the other children and at the time of the lawsuit had been residing with a son in Germany. McFarland had also raised two sons on the property. Rousseau obtained a judgment against McFarland and attempted to execute on that judgment by sale of the property claimed by McFarland as his homestead. Rousseau claimed that the homestead had been abandoned by McFarland and his mother. The court held that there was insufficient evidence of abandonment. When the homestead is created, it is presumed to continue until there is affirmative proof of abandonment. Proof of abandonment requires evidence that the owner has totally abandoned the property without an intention to return. A temporary absence is not adequate to prove abandonment by the mother or her son. *McFarland vs. Rousseau*, 667 S.W.2d 929 (Tex. Civ. App. 1984).

Dower and Curtesy

Dower is a life estate of a widow in one-third of any real property to which her husband had legal title during their marriage. *Curtesy* is a life estate of a widower in the real property to which his wife had legal title during their marriage. Neither of these two life estates is recognized in Texas. Passage of title to real property upon death is controlled either by a valid will or by the state intestacy law. These are discussed in Chapter 11.

Rule Against Perpetuities

The mere mention of this doctrine to many attorneys will strike fear in their hearts. This ancient English doctrine is so complex that there are few people who truly understand the mechanics of the rule. In simple terms, the rule states that all interests in land must vest, if at all, within a life or lives in being plus 21 years from the date it was created. The purpose of the rule is to prevent a decedent from continuing to control ownership of a tract of land centuries after his or her death. It requires that a future estate must vest within a certain time frame. That time frame is a life or lives in being plus 21 years. If the future interest cannot vest within that time period, then the future estate ceases to exist. The complexity of the rule is in calculating that time period. Fortunately, since most of us will never be forced to attempt the calculation, it is sufficient that we know that there is a limitation on the creation of future estates.

Figure 5.1: **CHARACTERISTICS OF THE MAJOR ESTATES IN LAND**

Estate Name	Chief Characteristics
Present Estates:	
Fee simple absolute	Complete set of property rights; alienable, devisable and descendible
Fee simple determinable	Incomplete set of property rights; limited by conditions or events set out in the conveyance; alienable, devisable and descendible; terminates automatically
Fee simple on condition subsequent and Fee simple subject to an executory limitation	Both of these estates contain an incomplete set of property rights; alienable, devisable and descendible; terminate only if the holder of the future interest asserts right to possession
Life estate	Alienable; terminates upon death of measuring life; cannot waste property
Homestead	Protected from forced sale by general creditor; cannot be sold or mortgaged without joinder of spouse; surviving spouse has a life estate; terminated by abandonment
Future Estates:	
Possibility of reverter	Follows termination of the fee simple determinable; alienable, devisable and descendible
Right of reentry	Follows termination of the fee simple on condition subsequent; alienable, devisable and descendible
Executory interest	Follows termination of fee simple subject to an executory interest; alienable, devisable and descendible
Remainder and reversion	Follows termination of a life estate; alienable, devisable and descendible

SUMMARY

Two systems have shaped real property ownership in the United States: the allodial system and the feudal system. The primary feature of modern real estate practice, however, is the allodial concept that private ownership of realty is free and absolute, subject only to governmental and voluntary restrictions. The feudal system, on the other hand, granted only the right to occupy land owned by a superior.

The continental version of feudalism was brought to England in the 11th century by William the Conqueror, a powerful king who parceled out land and granted tenure to those local lords who would swear allegiance to him. Tenants were required to provide soldiers and arms, supplies or other service to the king and the lords. Social and political pressures over the centuries brought an end to feudalism.

Nevertheless, some modern land policies have been carried over from that time. For example, the concept of estates in land has its roots in the feudal notion of tenure. Several types of ownership or estates in land exist: fee simple absolute, defeasible fees, future estates and life estates. All these forms have different legal rights.

The fee simple absolute is the greatest of the estates in land. The defeasible fees are lesser estates whose duration is terminated by the happening of some event or the fulfillment of some condition. Because these estates can terminate, there is a question regarding the future ownership of the land. Specific future estates are associated with each of the defeasible fees.

The life estate is granted for the life of the owner or some other person. After death of the life tenant, the person(s) named as remainderman takes possession. Legal problems frequently result from this relationship.

A very important estate in Texas is the homestead. The homestead estate is created and protected by the Texas Constitution. It confers three important benefits. First, it protects the land from forced sale by most creditors. Second, the homestead cannot be sold, mortgaged or encumbered without the joinder of the spouse. Third, it gives the surviving spouse a life estate in the homestead.

Finally, the law favors the creation of fee simple absolutes over all other estates in land. Consequently, if there is any doubt or any inconsistency in the language used to create the estate, the court will hold that a fee simple absolute was created.

QUESTIONS AND CASE PROBLEMS

1. (a) What is the chief characteristic of an estate? (b) Explain how the concept of estates has influenced the development of real estate law.
2. Define the following terms: freehold, future interest, alienable, devisable, descendible, dower, homestead, rule against perpetuities and allodium.
3. Sebastian Independent School District sued Ethel Ballenger for taxes on certain real estate. In 1941 Ethel had acquired by assignment whatever interest C. P. Barreda had in this real estate. However, there was some question regarding what interest, if any, C. P.

Barreda had in the land because of a prior conveyance to the county of Cameron in 1927. In the 1927 deed the following language appeared:

> ...to be used by the said County of Cameron solely for the control and carriage of excess flow from the Rio Grande in major floods...whenever the County of Cameron shall cease to maintain its said North Floodway or to use the premises hereby conveyed as a portion of said North Floodway, this grant shall cease in its entirety...and grantor...shall have the full right of re-entry.

The school district claimed that the conveyance to the county created an easement and, therefore, Ethel was the owner of the land under the assignment in 1941. What type of estate in land was created by the 1927 deed?

4. Troy and Ruby Vines were married in 1931. In 1951 they executed an oil and gas lease for a term of ten years. Ruby died in 1959 and by will left all her real property to Troy for his lifetime and the remainder to Harold Moore. The oil and gas lease expired in March 1961. On April 3, 1961, Troy executed a new oil and gas lease to Pan American Corporation. Who is entitled to the royalties paid under the 1961 lease?

5. During their marriage, Hiram and Lorene Fannin acquired a 7.9-acre tract of land in Upshur County, Texas. They resided on this property during their lifetime. In 1968 Hiram orally gave his granddaughter, Darla Overstreet, a house located on a portion of the 7.9-acre tract. Lorene Fannin did not join in the gift to Overstreet. Thereafter, there were two houses located on this tract, one occupied by the Fannins and other occupied by the Overstreets. In 1974 Lorene died. A few months later Hiram died. Ester Tolman was found to be the sole heir of both Lorene and Hiram. Tolman claims to be the owner of the entire 7.9-acre tract. Overstreet claims that she is the owner of the portion of the 7.9 acres on which her house sits. She alleges that she acquired it by gift from Hiram in 1968. Who owns the land and house that has been occupied by the Overstreets?

6. In 1904 John F. McElveen conveyed to the trustees of Independent School District a tract of one acre. The deed contained the following provision:

> Provided, always nevertheless notwithstanding, that in case it should so happen at any time that a free com-

mon school shall not be maintained on the described premises for a period of three consecutive years, then the said premises shall be considered abandoned and revert back to John F. McElveen.

Describe the interest of John F. McElveen in the one-acre tract. Does he have a right to sell his interest? Discuss.

6
Co-Ownership

CO-OWNERSHIP

Rights and interests in real estate may be divided in various ways, and a number of different interests often exist simultaneously in the same parcel. A common division of interests is horizontal in relationship to space. Chapter 2 indicated that one person might own the surface while others owned the minerals below or the airspace above the surface. Rights and interests are sometimes divided over time. For example, a life estate might be followed by a remainder in fee. Both estates are valuable, but the owner of the life estate has a present possessory interest. Simultaneously, the owner of the fee has a present interest, but the right to possession will not materialize until the life estate terminates in the future. A third division of rights, called *co-ownership,* exists when two or more persons own undivided interests in the same land at the same time. Generally in this type of ownership each person is entitled to a specific fraction of the parcel but also shares with the others a single right to possession and profits from the land. This is also referred to as *concurrent ownership.*

Co-ownership was important to the common law, and the various concurrent estates that developed at common law remain important today. A number of legal problems are associated with these common law concurrent estates. Many of these problems are reduced or eliminated if multiple owners use a partnership, corporation or trust to hold title to the property. As a result these devices are becoming increasingly important in real estate holdings and to a degree are replacing the common law forms of multiple ownership. This chapter discusses the traditional concurrent estates: tenancy in common, joint tenancy, tenancy by the entireties and tenancy in partnership.

In addition, the statutory form of co-ownership for married persons in Texas is discussed in some detail. This concurrent estate is called *commu-*

nity property. Finally, in this chapter some of the modern alternatives for multiple owners when investing in real estate are also presented. These alternatives include trusts and different types of real estate syndicates.

TENANCY IN COMMON

In Texas co-ownership of real property by persons not married to each other is usually held as tenants in common. A **tenancy in common** is a form of concurrent ownership in which each owner possesses an undivided right to the entire parcel of land, with each owner's rights similar to those possessed by a sole owner. To qualify as a tenancy in common, the parties must have the same type of interest in the land and the same right to possession. For example, the parties would each own an undivided fee simple absolute interest in the land. Parties can be tenants in common with respect to the lesser estates in land as well. For example, the parties can each have an undivided remainder interest in the land. The key characteristic among cotenants is the fact that each holds an undivided interest in the same estate in the land. If one person holds a life estate and another person holds a remainder, they would *not* be tenants in common because their interest in land is divided and is different.

Tenants in common may or may not hold the same proportional interest in the land. Among three co-owners each could own an undivided one-third interest, or one could have an undivided 50 percent interest and the other two each own an undivided 25 percent interest. If the conveyance creating the tenancy in common does not specify the proportional interest of each cotenant, then it is presumed to be equal shares. The tenancy in common terminates when it is divided or partitioned.

Rights and Responsibilities of Tenants in Common

Each tenant in common has an undivided right to possession of the entire parcel. At the same time, no tenant in common is entitled to the exclusive use of any part of the land. Cotenants are presumed to act on behalf of each other. This effectively prevents one cotenant from acquiring the land by adverse possession. It also means that, if one cotenant purchases the property at a foreclosure sale, he or she is purchasing it on behalf of all the cotenants, and title to the land continues to be held as a tenancy in common. Any profits or income generated by the property is shared proportionately among the cotenants, after payment of the maintenance expenses. Expenses that are absolutely necessary to preserve ownership of the property are shared proportionately by the cotenants. For example, if one cotenant pays the ad valorem taxes assessed against the property by the city, then he or she has a right to reimbursement from the other cotenants.

With the exception of property expenses that occur necessarily, such as ad valorem taxes, tenants in common are not required to consent to expenditures for development or improvement of property. Consequently, if all but one of the cotenants want to improve the property, and they cannot secure the consent of the remaining cotenant, they will bear the cost of the improvement and have no right to reimbursement from the dissenting cotenant. However, the courts will allow reimbursement from the proceeds from the sale of the property prior to division among the cotenants, provided the improvement sufficiently increased the value of the property to cover the cost of the improvement.

CASE EXAMPLE

Jason, Paula and Margaret have a fee simple absolute estate in Blackacre as tenants in common. Jason and Paula want to drill for oil on Blackacre. Margaret is opposed to the drilling operation. Can Jason and Paula proceed? The answer is yes. Can Jason and Paula demand that Margaret share the cost of the drilling operation? The answer is no. However, if the drilling is successful, Jason and Paula are entitled to recoup their drilling expenses prior to dividing the profits with Margaret.

Most third parties are reluctant to enter into transactions involving the land unless all the cotenants consent. For example, it would be difficult for Jason and Paula to find an oil exploration company that would be willing to drill on Blackacre. It is also difficult to sell an undivided interest in a tract of land or borrow against the land. These problems can create disputes among cotenants.

Many problems can arise with co-ownership. As illustrated above, one cotenant may desire to improve or develop the property while the others oppose the plan. The property may not be susceptible to possession and use by all the cotenants. It may be a single house on a city lot that, as a practical matter, can be occupied only by one of the cotenants. These types of problems can best be solved by agreement among the parties. However, when no agreement can be reached, partition of the property may be the only solution.

Partition

Partition, the act of dividing the realty and thereby terminating the joint ownership, is the historic method by which unwilling concurrent owners of real property may terminate the interests of fellow co-owners. Although courts traditionally ordered partition even when no statute authorized them to do so, today partition exists in some form by statute in every state. Many states make the remedy available to some holders of future interests. Under the law of almost all states, co-owners of personal property enjoy the right to partition to the same degree as co-owners of realty.

Partition may be voluntary or compulsory. Voluntary partitions are the result of agreement among the co-owners to end the relationship. They are usually carried out by deeds in which each co-owner is allocated a described portion of the realty by all the other part owners. It is also possible for all the co-owners to convey to a third party, the third party in turn conveying to each former co-owner his or her agreed-upon parcel. Voluntary partition agreements must be in writing and frequently will be accomplished by the use of a document called a *partition deed*. Voluntary partition requires not only the consent of all the parties to the act, but also agreement as to the division of the estate. Compulsory partition by judicial action is necessary when one or more of the multiple owners desire to terminate the relationship and agreement cannot be reached for dividing the property.

This right to partition is absolute, provided it does not interfere with homestead rights and has not been waived by agreement of the cotenants. If one of the cotenants has a right of homestead to the property, the court cannot partition it so long as it is subject to the homestead claim. The most common example of this situation occurring is upon the death of a spouse intestate. In that circumstance the deceased spouse's one-half interest passes to his or her children. The children would then own the property as tenants in common with the surviving parent. If the property was the homestead of the couple, the children cannot partition the property so long as the surviving spouse chooses to continue to use the property as the homestead.

However, in the absence of one of the exceptions mentioned above, the right to demand a partition exists without regard to the size of the cotenant's share. A tenant in common with an undivided one percent interest in the property can demand a partitioning. The fact that the interest of a co-owner is subject to a mortgage or other lien, though a complicating factor, will not defeat the right. So extensive is the right to partition that the state condominium statute must specifically prohibit the right of condominium owners to seek partition of the condominium elements that are owned in common.

Partition is based upon the land's value. In dividing the property, the court divides by value, not size. For example, a tenant in common with an undivided one-third interest would receive one-third of the land value, which may or may not be equal to one-third of the land mass. Partition is accomplished in one of three ways. The preferred method is by a physical division of the property. The court orders the property divided, allocating to each co-owner a share that is equivalent to his or her interest. Often, however, physical division is not practicable or desirable, and in these cases the property will be sold and the proceeds divided among the co-owners in relation to their interests. The third method involves physical division of the property into shares that are as nearly as possible equivalent in value to the interests of the individual owners. The court then orders monetary payment to those co-owners whose physical shares were not equivalent to their interest.

JOINT TENANCY

Joint tenancy is a form of co-ownership significant in that the entire estate passes to the survivor upon the death of the other joint tenant or tenants. The joint tenancy has been abolished in Texas. However, students should be familiar with this common law form of co-ownership since it does exist in other states. The principal feature of the joint tenancy is the right of survivorship. Upon the death of one of the co-owners, that person's interest passes automatically to surviving joint owners.

Traditionally, for a joint tenancy to be created or to continue, three "unities" are required. First, the unity of possession requires that each have an undivided right to possession. Second, the unity of interest requires that each receive a similar estate. For example, one joint tenant cannot hold as a life tenant while the other holds in fee simple. Finally, they have to take at the same time (unity of time) and from the same instrument (unity of title). If any of these unities terminates, the joint tenancy also ends. The new form of ownership is tenancy in common, a form in which the right of survivorship does not exist.

Although joint tenancies have been abolished in Texas, the parties can agree in writing at any time during the existence of the tenancy in common that there will be a right of survivorship. The common illustration of the contractual right of survivorship is the joint bank account. By agreement the two parties to the bank account have agreed that upon the death of one the bank account automatically vests in the survivor. Cotenants are permitted by state law to create the same contractual right with respect to real property. It should be remembered that the right of survivorship is looked upon with disfavor in Texas. Consequently, the creation of the right of survivorship must be specific and certain. A right of survivorship will not be inferred from ambiguous language.

COMMUNITY PROPERTY AND SEPARATE PROPERTY

Community property is a concurrent marital estate in real or personal property. An unmarried person cannot own community property. An unmarried person can hold property as a tenant in common with others but could never own community property. However, a married person can own both community property and separate property. A married person could also hold property as a tenant in common either with his or her spouse or with another person.

Before discussing community property rights, a clarification of the term married is appropriate. A heterosexual couple is married when they have obtained the appropriate license from the state and have exchanged vows before a person authorized in Texas to perform marriages. Persons authorized to perform marriages are generally religious ministers, rabbis, priests, justices of the peace and judges. In addition to this type of formal marriage, Texas also recognizes informal marriages. An informal marriage, frequently called a *common law marriage*, is recognized in Texas if three conditions exist. The couple must have agreed to be married. They must have lived in Texas as husband and wife, and they must have represented to others that they were married. Perhaps the most important of the three elements is the representation of marriage. A representation is made if the couple uses the name Mr. and Mrs. X or introduces each other as husband and wife. Texas also recognizes marriages performed under the laws of a foreign state or country or by the captain of a ship at sea.

One of the most litigated aspects of community property is the determination of whether the property is community or separate. This determination is important upon the death of a spouse because it affects to whom the property passes and how much of it passes. The determination is also important in the event of divorce and division of property. Finally, it is important to creditors of the parties who may consider accepting the property as collateral for an extension of credit.

The definition of community and separate property is found in both the Texas Constitution and the Texas Family Code. Article 16, §15, of the Texas Constitution reads as follows:

> All property, both real and personal, of a spouse owned or claimed before marriage, and that acquired afterward by gift, devise or descent, shall be the separate property of that spouse; and laws shall be passed more clearly defining the rights of the spouses, in relation to separate and community property; provided that persons about to marry and spouses, without the intention to defraud pre-existing creditors, may by written instrument from time to time partition between themselves all or part of their property, then existing or to be acquired, or exchange between themselves the community interest of one spouse or future spouse in any property for the community property then existing or to be acquired, whereupon the portion or interest set aside to each spouse shall be and constitute a part of the separate property and estate of such spouse or future spouse; and the spouses may from time to time, by written instrument, agree between themselves that the income or property from all or part of the separate property then owned by one of them, or which thereafter might be acquired, shall be the separate property of that spouse; and if one spouse makes a gift of property to the other that it is presumed to include all the income or property which might arise from the gift of property.

This constitutional provision defines separate property. All other property acquired by either spouse during marriage is community property. Further, there is a presumption that property possessed by either spouse during marriage is community property. The party claiming that the property is separate property must prove that it is separate property by evidence that places it in one of the categories listed in the constitutional provision. There is one other category of property that by statute is separate property. That category is property recovered for personal injuries sustained by the spouse during marriage. However, any recovery for loss of earning capacity is community property.

Inception of Title Rule

Characterization of property as community or separate property is determined on the date of acquisition. Therefore, property purchased one day before marriage is separate property. For example, assume that an engaged couple purchases real property five days before their marriage. Title to the property is in both their names. The down payment for the property comes from equal contributions from each person. The balance of the purchase price is paid from community funds after marriage. Is this property community or separate property? The answer is that it is separate property held by the married couple as tenants in common.

Similarly, under this inception of title rule, property purchased any time after marriage is community property. This is true even when the title to the property is held in only one of the spouse's names. There is one exception to this; it is called *tracing* and will be discussed later in this chapter. Once property is classified as separate or community property it remains so unless there is a written agreement between the parties to the contrary. Consequently, separate property remains separate even if community funds are used to maintain and pay for the separate property of one of the spouses.

Income generated by separate property during marriage is community property in Texas. This includes income generated by interest payments or rent. For example, the rental income from separate property pays the indebtedness, taxes and maintenance of the separate property. Even if the funds were generated from the property and used for the property, the funds are still community funds. Upon divorce the spouse who did not own the separate property could be entitled to equitable reimbursement.

Proceeds from the sale or exchange of separate property remain the separate property of the spouse. However, if the proceeds are commingled with community funds, the spouse could lose his or her separate funds to the community estate.

Management, Control and Disposition

Separate property is under the sole management, control and disposition of the spouse who owns it. Community property is subject to joint management, control and disposition. No spouse can dispose of community property against the will of the other spouse. Nor can one spouse impose any debt after purchase against community property without the written consent of the other. This is one of the reasons a determination of separate or community is important to creditors.

CASE EXAMPLE

Jane requests that a bank lend her $15,000 for her business. She offers as collateral a lot adjoining the business, which is owned in community with her husband. No lien can be created against this lot without the additional consent of Jane's husband. This is true even if Jane intends to repay the loan from proceeds from her business operations.

There is an exception to protect third parties who dealt with a married person and did not know that the property was community property. If the title to the property is in the sole name of one of the spouses, then the third party can assume that the spouse has the authority to deal with the property. The privilege is lost if the third party knew that the spouse was acting without authority or the third person was a party to a fraud being perpetrated against the absent spouse.

Division of Community Property

Community property can be divided and converted into separate property voluntarily or involuntarily. Voluntary agreements to divide or partition community property must be in writing and signed by both spouses. In 1980 the present constitutional provision was passed to allow married couples and to-be-married couples greater freedom in making prenuptial and postnuptial agreements. Persons intending to be married can now agree that property that would otherwise be community property or would be presumed to be community property will be separate property. This can be done in advance without knowing exactly what will be purchased during the marriage. If there is an agreement to partition future acquisitions, then the parties own the property as separate property as tenants in common. In addition, the spouses-to-be can agree that income from separate property will be the separate property of the owner of the property producing the income. The division consented to in a prenuptial agreement does not have to be exactly equal; however, each spouse must be receiving some part of the community estate. The same agreements discussed for couples to be married can also be entered into by married couples at any time during their marriage.

Whether or not there is an agreement concerning a particular piece of property can be difficult for an outsider to ascertain. A married couple can enter into any number of agreements concerning their property. How does an outsider know if the agreement is as represented? To alleviate some of the uncertainty, the Texas Family Code provides that an outsider can rely upon any document recorded in the county clerk's office. There is also a problem concerning marital agreements affecting the homestead. At this time it is uncertain whether a married person can waive his or her homestead interest in a particular tract of land by agreement. As explained in the previous chapter, the Texas Constitution does not allow for waiver of the homestead right. However, the right of a married couple or to-be-married couple to partition and divide their property is also part of the Texas Constitution. Consequently, there is a question regarding the effect of these two constitutional provisions on each other.

Community property can also be divided involuntarily upon divorce of the couple. Community property can be divided by the court in any manner that is equitable. Separate real property of a spouse, though, cannot be awarded to the other spouse upon divorce. Therefore, the characterization of property as separate or community can become very important. One method by which a person can protect the characterization of an asset as separate property is by tracing. Tracing requires proof that the source of the present property was the separate property of the party. A simple example of tracing is as follows:

CASE EXAMPLE

Mildred, a married woman, inherited Whiteacre from her mother. Whiteacre is Mildred's separate property. Since Whiteacre is located in a county far away from Mildred's home, she decides to sell it. She uses the proceeds from the sale of Whiteacre to buy another tract of land, Blackacre. Since Blackacre was purchased while Mildred was married, it is presumed to be community property. Mildred can prove that Blackacre is her separate property by tracing the source of the money she used for the purchase to the sale of Whiteacre.

Tracing can be more difficult when separate property and community property have been commingled.

CASE EXAMPLE

Mark, a married person, inherited Blueacre from his father. He sells Blueacre and deposits the proceeds from the sale, which is $250,000, in a certificate of deposit in his name. The interest on that certificate of deposit is rolled over into the certificate. A few years later the value of the certificate is $289,000. Mark withdraws the entire amount and purchases Redacre. The title to Redacre is in Mark's name only. Who owns Redacre? The principal amount in the certificate of deposit, $250,000, was the separate property of Mark; however, the interest earned on the certificate was community property. Separate and community property have been commingled. This case would probably be resolved by holding that Redacre is in part the separate property of Mark and in part the community property of Mark and his wife. To the extent Mark can trace the source of the present property to his separate property, Redacre is separate. For that portion that cannot be traced back to separate funds, Redacre is community property.

Improvement of Separate Property with Community Funds

Finally, with respect to the relationship of community and separate property, how do you account for community funds when they were used to improve and preserve the separate real property of one spouse? This issue usually arises upon divorce but can also arise upon the death of one of the spouses or upon the sale of the property. The real property remains separate property. Furthermore, the law in Texas does not give the community estate any legal interest in the separate property improved. However, the courts have resolved this inequity by giving the community estate a claim for reimbursement. The case that follows illustrates how the court should handle this situation.

CASE EXCERPT *Girard v. Girard,* 521 S.W.2d 714 (Tex. Civ. App.—Houston 1975). COLEMAN, Chief Justice.   This is an appeal from the judgment in a divorce case. The appellant, Dr. Louis J. Girard, makes no complaint of that portion of the decree awarding a divorce and the support and custody of the child of the marriage. His complaints are directed to that portion of the judgment relating to a house constructed upon a lot in River Oaks owned by Dr. Girard, the cost of which was paid with community funds.

. . . It is undisputed that the parties borrowed the sum of $135,000.00, and that both executed a note in that sum payable to the Benjamin Franklin Savings Association and secured by a lien on the River Oaks property. These funds, together with the additional sum of $12,000.00 of community funds, were used to pay the cost of construction of a house erected on the River Oaks lot. The evidence, therefore, shows that $147,000.00 of community funds were used to erect improvements on the separate property of the appellant. . . .

The River Oaks lot in question was improved with a residence at the time of the marriage of Dr. Girard and Mrs. Loraine Girard. This house was torn down in late 1968 so that the new house might be erected on the lot. Dr. Girard testified that the idea of tearing down his residence and building a new house was formulated by him in the middle or early Sixties prior to the time that he had met Mrs. Girard. Prior to their marriage they discussed the matter in detail and finally decided to tear the house down and build a new one. Construction was begun on the house in January of 1969 and was completed in May of 1970.

The parties stipulated that appraisals made by Robin Elverson were true and correct. These appraisals were admitted into evidence. It was Mr. Elverson's opinion that the lot was worth $115,000.00 to $125,000.00 in early 1970 and that the lot as improved was worth $340,000.00 to $380,000.00. . . .

Relying on the stipulated appraisals the trial court found a gross enhancement in value of the lot by reason of the improvements to be $225,000.00. His findings of fact reflect that from this enhancement figure the court deducted the costs of construction of $147,000.00 The result was a net enhancement in value of $78,000.00, and he allowed Mrs. Girard one-half of this figure as her share of the reimbursement due to the community. By deducting the cost of construction from the gross enhancement figure, the trial court required the community estate to reimburse itself for the expenditures made in improving Dr. Girard's separate estate. This was error. The estate benefited must reimburse the estate which made the contribution. . . . The error, however, is immaterial to the disposition of the case since neither party has made complaint of this action. Since the enhancement was greater than the cost of construction, the community estate's claim for reimbursement was limited to the sum of $147,000.00, the cost of construction. . . . The amount the court awarded Mrs. Girard as reimbursement for her share of community funds expended upon Dr. Girard's separate property was substantially less than one-half of the amount expended on said property and substantially less than one-half of the enhancement in value by reason of such expenditure. No harm has resulted to the appellant by reason of that provision in the judgment awarding Mrs. Girard a claim of $39,000.00 to be paid from the proceeds of the sale of the home by the respondent, or upon his death by his estate . . . .

The judgment is affirmed . . . .

TENANCY BY THE ENTIRETY

Tenancy by the entirety is a marital form of co-ownership recognized by nearly half of the states. It is *not* recognized in Texas. In Texas the marital form of co-ownership is community property. **Tenancy by the entirety** is co-ownership of property by husband and wife that is characterized by a right of survivorship in the surviving spouse.

A tenancy by the entirety is a more stable type of co-ownership than the joint tenancy. Because the marital partners are considered a single unit, neither husband nor wife can sever the tenancy without the other's consent. Unlike the joint tenancy, a sale by either the husband or wife does not terminate the tenancy or end the right of survivorship.

In many jurisdictions a tenancy by the entirety cannot be terminated by the forced sale of the husband's or wife's interest. This means that if either spouse individually incurs debts and then refuses to pay them, the creditor cannot attach—that is, judicially seize—his or her interest in the property. This rule has been criticized because it permits the debtor to escape responsibility while owning an interest in a valuable asset. In a few states, creditors of the husband, but not the wife, may reach the income, profits and title of the property. Whatever interest these creditors acquire is lost if the wife survives. Other states permit the separate creditors of either spouse to levy upon and sell the share of the debtor, whether husband or wife. If the opposite spouse survives, the creditor is deprived of his or her interest. If the creditor holds a joint judgment against both spouses, the creditor can attach the estate held by the entirety.

Tenancies by the entireties are terminated by divorce because the marital relationship is essential to this form of co-ownership. Upon divorce the parties become tenants in common.

TENANCY IN PARTNERSHIP

The common law did not recognize the partnership as a legal entity. As a result, property could not be held in the partnership name. This not only caused confusion but also frequently led to complex legal problems when a partner died or experienced financial difficulty. Creditors of an individual partner could then attach specific partnership property passed to that person's estate, and an individual partner could terminate the relationship by selling his or her interest in a particular property.

CASE EXAMPLE

Kane and Waldron entered into a partnership agreement to operate a creamery. Partnership funds were used to purchase real estate to operate the business. Title was taken in both Kane's and Waldron's names. A short time later, Kane died. At common law, his interest in the real estate would pass to his heirs, not to the surviving partner.

Texas and most other states have now adopted the Uniform Partnership Act, which creates the tenancy in partnership. (Tex. Rev. Civ. Stat. art. 6132b). One of the key characteristics of the tenancy in partnership is that a partner's interest in the partnership is treated as personal property even if the partnership owns real estate. Specifically, the Uniform Partnership Act permits the firm to buy, hold and sell real estate in the partnership name. Individual partners share ownership in particular property only as members of the firm. Spouses, heirs and creditors of individual partners have no rights in partnership property.

Individual partners may not assign partnership property unless the assignment involves the rights of all partners. Although an individual partner can transfer partnership real property, any such transfer is made only as an agent for other partners of the firm.

Upon the death of any partner, his or her share passes to the surviving partners. In the previous example, Waldron, as the surviving partner, acquires Kane's share. Waldron, however, possesses this property only for the purpose of liquidation inasmuch as Kane's death terminates the partnership. During liquidation, Waldron can operate the business without interference from Kane's legal representatives.

Kane and his heirs—in fact any partner—all have a valuable interest in the partnership. The interest stems from the individual's right to share in the profits and surplus of the firm. The interest is not in specific firm property. Under the Uniform Partnership Act, this interest is regarded as personalty, not real property. The partner's interest is unlike the interest of a joint tenant or a tenant in common. If the partner's interest is sold separately, the partnership is destroyed and the interest is not subject to partition.

INVESTMENT ALTERNATIVES FOR MULTIPLE OWNERS

Trust

The trust is a device that has been used in the United States and in England for several centuries. It has been an important instrument in law reform and the legal basis for some significant economic innovations. A ***trust*** is a legal relationship in which one party holds and manages property for the benefit of another.

CASE EXAMPLE

Elaine Morgan, a successful business executive, was married to Carl Morgan, a well-known musician. Carl had little interest in financial matters. In order to ensure that Carl had adequate income throughout his life, Elaine irrevocably transferred certain securities and real estate to Central Trust Company to be administered by the company with the income going to Carl for life. Upon Carl's death, the property was to go to the Juilliard School of Music.

Elaine has created a living or inter vivos trust. If she had made these provisions in a will, upon her death a testamentary trust would have been created. Today, trusts are used for many different purposes. They are used extensively in family estate planning of the type mentioned in the example, but they are also important in business. Trusts are frequently utilized to finance real estate ventures and to protect bondholder creditors of a corporation. Many large charities are organized as trusts; wealthy individuals convey assets to a trustee who administers them for some designated public benefit. Generally, trusts are governed by the Texas Trust Code. (Tex. Prop. Code §111.001 et seq.)

The premise upon which the trust is based is the division of property interests among owners. In a trust, one person or an institution is given title to specific property that is managed for the benefit of others. The property may be real or personal. In the example, Central Trust Company legally owns the securities and real estate, but it must administer them for Carl Morgan's benefit.

Trusts involving real property must be in writing, and it is generally recommended that all trusts be written. The Texas Trust Code does allow an inter vivos trust of personal property to be created by delivery of the property with oral instructions regarding the trust. All testamentary trusts—whether the property is real or personal—must be in writing and executed in the same manner as required for an effective will. Testamentary trusts that are frequently part of an estate plan often supplement a will.

The Fiduciary Relationship

Every trust must have a trustee to hold and manage the property. The trustee has a fiduciary duty, the responsibility for the utmost good faith and undivided loyalty to the beneficiary in administering the trust.

The doctrine of fiduciary responsibility applies to numerous legal relationships. Because some of these—such as the attorney-client and broker-seller relationships—are very important to real estate transactions, a brief outline of the duties common to all fiduciaries is in order. A fiduciary

(1) must act for the benefit of the other party in matters within the scope of the relationship, (2) must not profit at the other party's expense and (3) must make full disclosure of all information affecting transactions with the other party. In a case involving a trustee's fiduciary duties, Justice Cardozo once said:

> Many forms of conduct permissible in a workaday world for those acting at arm's length are forbidden to those bound by fiduciary ties. A trustee is held to something stricter than the morals of the marketplace. Not honesty alone but the punctilio of an honor the most sensitive is then the standard of behavior. As to this there has developed a tradition that is unbending and inveterate. Uncompromising rigidity has been the attitude of courts of equity when petitioned to undermine the rule of undivided loyalty by the "disintegrating erosion" of particular exceptions. Only thus has the level of conduct for fiduciaries been kept at a level higher than that trodden by the crowd. It will not consciously be lowered by any judgment of this court. *Meinhard v. Salmon*, 249 N.Y. 458, 464, 164 N.E. 545 (1928).

Under the terms of most trusts, trustees are usually granted extensive powers. Sometimes these powers are statutory, but they are also included in most well-drawn trust instruments. A trustee's powers will usually include, but not be limited to, making new investments, managing real estate, carrying on a business, selling property, borrowing money, reviewing mortgages, settling litigation, voting stock, collecting income and making distributions.

The fiduciary responsibility of the trustee protects the trust beneficiary. As a result trusts continue to be important in personal financial planning. Since World War II the trust has been one of several devices used by investors to organize real estate syndicates.

Real Estate Syndicate

A *real estate syndicate* generally can be defined as a group of investors who combine funds and managerial resources to develop, manage or purchase real estate for a profit or as a tax shelter. A real estate syndicate can take one of a number of legal forms. Probably the simplest is the tenancy in common. More important forms of ownership today are the S corporation, general and limited partnerships, joint ventures and real estate investment trusts (REITs). Each of these forms will be discussed in the following pages.

Tenancy in Common

The tenancy in common has been used by real estate investors for years. This form of ownership has the advantage of allowing the investors appreciable tax flexibility. Each co-owner is free to select the most beneficial tax treatment of his or her share. When the syndicate is organized as a partnership or corporation, the participants are bound by the tax characterization of the entity.

As a vehicle for syndication, the tenancy in common suffers from several legal and practical disadvantages. Individual owners are personally liable for all obligations arising out of property ownership. If someone is injured on the property or large debts are incurred, the individual assets of the co-owner can be reached. This compares unfavorably with the liability of the owners of a corporation, in which liability of each shareholder is limited to the amount that the shareholder has invested. The second legal drawback is the potential problem of marketability of property owned as a tenancy in common. If one of the owners dies or becomes insolvent and the remaining owners wish to sell their property, they usually must establish that the title is marketable. Death or insolvency of a co-owner clouds the title, causing delay and expense in clearing it to make it marketable.

Corporations

Corporations are legal entities that are chartered by the states. The law recognizes the corporation as a legal person and gives to it most of the powers, rights and duties that an individual may have. Among these rights is the power to acquire, manage, develop and own interests in land. Corporations are taxed separately from their shareholders, and, consequently, double taxation of the investor's interest can result. This problem can be alleviated by formation of an S corporation. This form allows investors to escape double taxation—that is, taxation of earnings of both the corporation and each shareholder. The S corporation allows the syndicate to pass income through without its being taxed at the corporate level. Thus the owners are not subject to the double burden associated with the ordinary corporation. Unfortunately, S corporations are limited to 35 shareholders, and severe limitations are placed upon the type of income allowed. Losses that a shareholder may take are also restricted. Because of these limitations and additional complex tax problems, S corporations are used only for relatively sophisticated syndications.

Partnership

Many syndicates are organized either as general or limited partnerships. A *partnership* is an association of two or more persons organized to carry on a business for profit. Both partnership forms also avoid double taxation—the nemesis of incorporation. A partnership is not taxed on its income; any income is taxed directly to the partners as individuals.

Investors who syndicate as a general partnership face three legal handicaps. Probably the most serious is the unlimited liability of the partners. Each partner is personally responsible for all partnership obligations, and his or her personal property can be reached if partnership assets are not sufficient to satisfy claims against the unit. A second handicap is the power of individual partners to make agreements binding the firm. Under Section 9 of the Uniform Partnership Act, "(e)very partner is the agent of the partnership for the purpose of its business . . . and the act of every partner binds the partnership. . . ."Finally, death, withdrawal or bankruptcy of one of the partners automatically terminates the partnership. The syndicate must be re-created by a new agreement. In order to facilitate securing capital for business ventures, many states have legislation that allows the creation of partnerships in which some of the members have limited liability. Partnerships of this kind are called *limited* or *special partnerships*. They are a popular form of organization for real estate syndicates.

Limited Partnership.   Texas and most other states provide for the creation of limited partnerships based upon the provisions of the Uniform Limited Partnership Act. (Tex. Rev. Civ. Stat. art. 6132a) This act defines a limited partnership as a partnership having as members one or more general partners and one or more limited partners. The limited partners are not liable to creditors of the partnership beyond the extent of their capital contribution.

CASE EXAMPLE

Anna, Ben and Carla Lane formed a limited partnership to invest in real estate. Anna, the general partner, invested $10,000 and agreed to manage the property. Ben and Carla, as limited partners, contributed $25,000 each. The project failed after accumulating debts of $65,000. Individual assets of Anna could be reached to cover any claims of creditors not satisfied upon liquidation. Ben's and Carla's individual assets could not be reached by the syndicate's creditors beyond the amounts of their initial investment.

In order to be considered a limited partner, the individual investor must be named as such in a certificate filed with the secretary of state. The individual must, in addition, avoid participation in management of the business. The limited partner who participates becomes a general partner and subject to all liability of the business. A limited partner's name may not appear in the partnership name. If it does, the limited partner becomes liable as a general partner. The purpose of this prohibition is to prevent the general public from extending credit to the partnership on the basis of the financial resources of a person who is a limited partner.

Although a limited partnership has some advantages over a general partnership as a vehicle for real estate syndication, both suffer because the partners' interests are not liquid; that is, they are difficult to transfer. Several reasons account for this lack of liquidity. First, a purchaser of a partner's interest cannot become a partner unless the remaining partners agree. In addition, a few states require that investors in limited partners have a minimum net worth as well as making a minimum investment. Some states even prohibit the transfer of limited partnership interests without the consent of a designated state official.

Joint Venture

A joint venture is a form of business organization very similar to the partnership. A joint venture is a business entity in which two or more persons have agreed to carry out a single undertaking for a profit. Most of the law that applies to partnerships also applies to the joint venture. Like a partnership, the joint venture is based upon agreement, and the members have a fiduciary relationship to each other. They share profits and losses; each enjoys the right to manage and direct the venture; and the venture is treated as a partnership for federal tax purposes.

The major difference between the partnership and the joint venture is that the latter is usually created to carry out a single transaction. Although some limited partnerships are created for a single purpose, most partnership operations are more extensive, carrying out a general business for a period of years. In a minority of jurisdictions, the authority of a member to bind the venture is more limited than that of a partner to bind the partnership. Finally, because a joint venture cannot be adjudicated a bankrupt, claims of creditors against the joint venture's real estate holdings are limited.

Real Estate Investment Trust (REIT)

During the late 19th century the American economy was expanding rapidly. Large sums of money were needed for investment in many segments of the economy. Real estate was no exception. Unfortunately, the corporate form of business organization that was used to attract capital into most business activity could not be used in real estate, because most of the states prohibited ownership of real property by corporations. The business trust, or Massachusetts trust, evolved to circumvent this prohibition. The trust had many advantages of the corporation, such as limited liability, ready transferability of shares and continuous existence. Because the trust was not a corporation, it was a permissible form of enterprise for real estate investment.

A *real estate investment trust* is an organization in which trustees own real estate or loans secured by real estate that they manage for beneficiaries who hold transferable shares representing their respective interests. The primary law regulating these trusts is the Texas Real Estate Investment Trust Act, passed in 1961. (Tex. Rev. Civ. Stat. art. 6138a) To create a trust, a declaration is filed with the county clerk in the county where the trust has its principal place of business. The operation of the business is run by one or more trust managers. Trust managers are elected by the shareholders of the trust. Real property acquired by the trust must be either improved or sold within 15 years of its acquisition.

Government Regulation of Syndicates

Both the federal and state governments exercise considerable control over the public sale of participation certificates in real estate syndicates. Although not all syndicates come within the purview of the federal or state securities law, many will be regulated in some way. As a general rule, if a syndicate is covered by the federal law it will also be covered under the Texas Securities Act. Therefore, the syndicate must comply with both state and federal requirements.

SUMMARY

Co-ownership of property is common in Texas and throughout the United States. Co-ownership can exist in a number of legal forms. The most common forms in Texas are tenancy in common and community property. In other states joint tenancies and tenancies by the entireties may be found.

A tenancy in common exists when two or more persons own an undivided interest in real estate. Each of the co-owners has an equal right to use and possess the property but cannot exclude the other cotenants. They are proportionately responsible for expenses of preserving the property. However, no cotenant is required to consent to improvement or development of the property. When cotenants cannot agree, they have the right to partition the property. This right is absolute, with two exceptions. First, if one of the cotenants has a right of homestead, then the property cannot be partitioned involuntarily. Second, if the parties have entered into an agreement waiving the right to partition, then the court will not interfere with the contractual agreement. Partitioning of property is based upon the land value and can be accomplished through a physical division of the land or a division of the proceeds from the sale of the land.

Although Texas has abolished the joint tenancy, cotenants are allowed to create a contractual right of survivorship. The right of survivorship means that upon the death of one of the co-owners that person's interest passes automatically to the remaining joint owner. This is a common provision found in joint bank accounts.

Community property is the marital form of co-ownership in Texas. The Texas Constitution defines separate property and states that all other property is community property. There is a presumption that all property acquired by a married couple during their marriage is community property. Property is characterized as community or separate on the date it is acquired by the party. This is called the *inception of title rule*. Once classified as separate or community, the property retains that characterization unless there is an agreement between the husband and wife to alter that classification. The Texas Constitution allows married couples a great deal of flexibility in making voluntary agreements regarding the classification of property. Community property can also be divided involuntarily by the court upon divorce. However, no court is permitted to take a spouse's separate property and transfer it to the other. If community funds have been used to maintain or improve another spouse's separate property, the contributing spouse has a right to be reimbursed upon divorce.

A tenancy in partnership is another form of co-ownership, and it is used primarily when co-owners have a business relationship. Tenants who own in partnership are regulated by the Texas Uniform Partnership Act, and the specific property is protected against the interest of spouses, heirs or creditors of individual co-owners. This form has become possible in recent times because of the recognition of the partnership as a legal entity.

Property may also be held and managed by another party in a trust—a legal device that has been the basis of significant economic innovations. Trusts are frequently used to finance real estate ventures and for estate planning. The person responsible for the property is known as the *trustee;* his or her relationship to the owner or beneficiary of the trust requires the utmost good faith and undivided loyalty. This is known as the *fiduciary duty.* The fiduciary relationship is pervasive in the real estate profession and its many transactions.

For business ventures in the real estate field, syndication is an important recent development. Through a syndicate, investors of many types can pool their resources to purchase, develop or manage real estate. Syndicates take many forms, including tenancy in common, S corporations, partnerships, joint ventures and real estate investment trusts (REITs). Knowledge of these developments and their legal requirements is essential to those engaged in commercial real estate sales, management or investment. Federal and state governments exercise considerable control over the public's participation in real estate syndicates.

QUESTIONS AND CASE PROBLEMS

1. During the past 15 years the S corporation and the limited partnership have been used extensively in real estate syndication. What factors account for this?

2. Outline some of the problems that real estate sales personnel face as a result of co-ownership of real property.

3. Davison and Cox are cotenants of certain real property that includes both surface and mineral rights. Davison wishes to develop the minerals on this property, but Cox refuses to consent to this development. Davison decides to proceed, and at his own expense he drills 16 wells. The drilling operations are successful. Is Cox entitled to share in the profits from these wells? Is Davison entitled to reimbursement from Cox for the $115,000 he expended in drilling? Finally, is Davison entitled to interest on the money he expended in drilling?

4. Melissa Rouse owned with her three sons a 50-acre tract of land as tenants-in-common. In 1931 Rouse, acting alone, conveyed to Dollery a "right-of-way over other lands of grantor between this tract and State Highway N. 58 at S.E. corner." The other lands referred to in the conveyance meant the 50-acre tract held in tenancy-in-

common. Subsequently, one of the sons, Henry Elliott, refused to allow Dollery to use the road. Dollery claimed an easement under the 1931 deed. Was Melissa's conveyance of a right-of-way to Dollery in 1931 binding on her cotenants?

5. Lawrence C. Evans sold an undivided one-half interest in 115 acres of land in Wharton County, Texas, to Mrs. Trumble and her husband, Lyle. The purchase price was $25,000. The Trumbles were residents of Boulder, Colorado (a non-community-property state). Each person contributed one-half of the purchase price from his or her separate property. The deed recited that the Trumbles were purchasing the land as joint tenants with right of survivorship. When Mr. Trumble died, he left all of his estate to his three sons. The sons claim an undivided one-fourth interest in the 115-acre tract. To support their claim, they allege that the Trumbles held the property as community property, not as joint tenants. Does the law of the state of Texas or the law of the state of Colorado govern this transaction? If you apply the law of Texas, what would be the likely result?

6. When the Cockerhams were married on May 16, 1949, the husband, E. A. Cockerham, owned an undivided one-half interest in a 320-acre tract, and his brother, Herman Cockerham, owned the other undivided half. The brothers conducted a farming and cattle operation on this property. In 1955 Herman wanted to sell his undivided half. The two brothers filed a suit to have the property partitioned. The court appointed a receiver, who sold the entire 320 acres to E. A. Cockerham and his wife. The purchase price was paid in part by the undivided interest owned by E. A. Cockerham and the balance from a loan he had obtained from John Hancock Mutual Life Insurance Company. The deed to the 320 acres was in the names E. A. Cockerham and wife, Dorothy Cockerham. Upon divorce would this 320 acres be the separate property of E. A. Cockerham or the community property of E. A. and Dorothy?

7
Condominiums, Cooperatives and Time-shares

In this chapter some of the special and unusual forms of property ownership—condominiums, cooperatives and time-shares are discussed. Each of these has special characteristics that distinguish it from ownership of land in fee simple. A purchase of one of these interests usually involves the imposition of duties or a limitation on use not found in fee simple absolute ownership.

CONDOMINIUM

Ownership of a *condominium* includes fee simple ownership of one unit in a multiple-unit structure combined with an ownership of an undivided interest in the land and those parts of the building denoted as part of the common elements. The concept of condominium ownership has blossomed in the United States since the mid-1960s. The notion of fee ownership, coupled with a release from the repair and maintenance chores of home ownership, made condominiums attractive to many people, especially to the elderly and to single-person households.

Condominiums did not present any fundamental legal problem. The common law had long recognized separate ownership of individual rooms or floors in a structure, which in essence is the nature of a condominium. Common or joint ownership of land and building was equally well established. Condominium ownership as a specific form, however, not only was new but also was a complex form of residential ownership. Describing the co-ownership, joint management, cross-easements and enforcement of individual responsibilities was part of the complexity. To provide some clarity and uniformity for this new area, states quickly began to adopt permissive condominium legislation. The Texas Condominium Act was initially passed in 1963. It can be found in its entirety in the Texas Property Code, beginning with §81.001.

This chapter discusses condominium ownership as it applies to residential units. The condominium form also is being used in commercial and some industrial property. The legal principles are the same, regardless of the use to which the condominium unit is put. Furthermore, many of the legal principles discussed may also be applicable to some townhome developments, patio home subdivisions and zero-lot line subdivisions. Although the law was not written specifically to include these types of property ownership, courts have borrowed these legal principles to resolve disputes concerning these other forms. In particular, the authority of some homeowners' associations in townhome communities can be very similar to the authority granted condominium associations.

Formation of a Condominium

The developer may purchase an existing multiple-family rental unit for conversion into a condominium. Alternatively, he or she may purchase land and obtain a construction mortgage for erecting the condominium structure. The completed condominium units are then sold to individuals. The individual purchasing the condominium unit attains a fee simple interest in the apartment unit. In addition, the individual becomes a tenant in common with the other unit owners of the land and all structures outside the walls of the individual apartments. These are known as the *common elements*.

The apartment owner, if necessary obtains a mortgage on his or her individual unit. Payment at the time of purchase is made to the condominium developer, who in turn pays off the construction mortgage as it pertains to that individual unit and its appropriate share of the common elements and has them released from the lien of the construction mortgage.

CASE EXAMPLE

Greg and Helene Burnside purchase a condominium unit from Condo Developers Inc. for $88,000. They obtain a mortgage on the unit for $81,000 from Security Bank, provide $7,000 of their own cash and deliver a check for $88,000 to Condo in exchange for a deed to the unit. Condo pays its mortgagee an amount sufficient to obtain a release for the Burnsides' unit and for one percent of the common elements. (There are 100 units of equal value in the development.)

Declaration

The **declaration** (also called the *master deed* or *master lease* as appropriate) is a special type of plat required under state law for each condominium development. The declaration is one of three documents mandated by state law. The other two documents are the bylaws and the deed to each individual unit.

The declaration is required for both new construction and conversion of an existing building. It is filed in the county where the property is located, and it is maintained by the county clerk in the condominium records for the county. The declaration must contain a legal description of the property; a general description of each unit, including square footage and identification by floor and unit number; a description of any area that is subject to limited control, such as carports and garages; a description of the common areas and each apartment's fractional interest in the entire condominium regime. Any changes or alterations to these declarations must be filed with the county clerk.

Declarations can also contain other matters, such as restrictive covenants. Restrictive covenants are discussed in Chapter 9, and the law discussed there is as applicable to condominiums as it is to other types of real property. Sometimes the condominium declaration will state that the association has a *right of first refusal* so that it can screen potential buyers of condominium units. When the existing owner of a unit has a willing buyer, the association is given a limited time in which to determine whether the prospective owner is satisfactory to them. If not, the association can purchase the unit under the same terms as offered by the buyer.

In addition, provisions are made for the contingency that the buildings might be destroyed substantially, by fire or some other disaster. The declaration can be amended at a meeting of the unit owners at which at least 67 percent of the ownership interests vote to amend.

Bylaws

The bylaws of a condominium development are not unlike the bylaws of any organization. Bylaws are rules that govern the internal operations of the condominium development. They provide for the selection of the board of directors of the association, meetings, regulations for the common elements, rights and responsibilities of unit owners, assessment and collection of monthly charges and other relevant matters.

The bylaws are very important to the property owners because they establish the rights and responsibilities of each with respect to the condominium regime. Prior to the purchase of a unit in a condominium project, the bylaws as well as the declaration should be read carefully. The courts strictly enforce the bylaws and will uphold action taken by the council of owners pursuant to the bylaws.

Individual Unit Deed

Just as other interests in land are conveyed by a deed, interests in a condominium can be created in a similar manner. The deed will describe the interior of the individual unit to be owned in fee simple along with that portion owned in common. The deed must be recorded to protect the unit owner from a fraudulent conveyance by the seller. In addition, it provides a chain of title that can be relied upon by a subsequent purchaser to ensure the marketability of the title.

Deeds to individual units are recorded in the real property records and should contain the legal description for the unit and the fractional interest in the common areas with reference to the recorded declaration or master deed. Ownership of the common area cannot be separated from ownership of the individual units.

Common Elements

Each condominium unit owner has a tenancy in common in the land and buildings and other structures not constituting the interior of his or her individual condominium unit. This ownership interest is undivided; that is, all unit owners have an equal right to all the common elements.

The common elements generally include hallways, elevators, recreational facilities, land, stairways, exterior of the buildings and so on. Sometimes the common area is divided into general common elements and limited common elements. The Texas Condominium Act defines the **general common elements** as that part of a condominium regime other than property that is part of or belongs to any unit. The percentage of the common elements ascribed to each apartment unit may be equal where the units are quite similar. Where significant differences exist among the units, however, the percentage may be based upon the differing values of the individual units. In any event, the amount attributable to each unit is designated in the declaration.

The **limited common elements** are that portion of the common elements allocated by unanimous agreement of the council of owners for the use by one or more but less than all of the apartments. This could include special corridors, the stairways and elevators in a particular building or sanitary services common to the units of a particular floor in a high-rise condominium.

The state statute provides that the expenses of administering, maintaining, repairing and replacing the common elements be paid for by an assessment of the unit owners made by the board of directors of the association. The board of directors is then responsible for repairing and operating the common elements. Unit owners are bound by the terms of the declaration to pay their shares of the assessment. Payment of the expenses cannot be avoided by waiving the right to use certain parts of the common elements. For example, a nonswimmer cannot reduce the monthly assessment by deducting an amount that would cover maintenance of the swimming pool.

Condominium Association

The **condominium association** is the organization that administers the operation of the common elements of the condominium project. The association, and its board of directors on a day-to-day operational level, carries out the business of caring for the condominium. Members of the board of directors are the representatives of the unit owners and bear a fiduciary relationship to those owners. Their responsibility to the unit owners is multifaceted. For instance, their fiduciary duty to the unit owners requires that the board deal fairly and carefully with the business interests of the unit owners. It must avoid participation in decisions that present conflicts of interest for individuals. In short, board members can be held legally liable for mismanagement or for secretly profiting from that management. Board members are not relieved of liability merely because they are "volunteer" or unpaid.

Assessments

The bylaws set out the rules for establishing regular and special assessments. An **assessment** is a periodic or one-time charge to cover the expenses of maintaining or improving the common elements. The association's board of directors, or a project manager appointed by it, normally collects the assessments and uses them in maintaining the condominium property. The original setting of the amount of the regular assessment, the changing of that amount and the imposition of a special assessment are determined by the terms of the bylaws. The bylaws are likely to place responsibility for establishing these assessments with the association or its board of directors.

The Texas courts have held that the association's decision regarding assessments shall not be set aside by the court unless the association failed to comply with the bylaws or its act was unreasonable and capricious. The following case illustrates the enforceability of assessments by the condominium association.

• CASE BRIEF •

Aquarius Condominium Owners Association, Inc., sued the Raymonds to collect assessments charged against them in connection with two condominium apartments they owned and for foreclosure against the apartments. The units were purchased by the Raymonds in 1973. The Raymonds had never paid any of the assessments made by the association and owed $39,965. The assessments accrued during the period 1973 to 1978. The Raymonds' justification for nonpayment was that the assessments were not made lawfully because of the existence of a rental pool. The association operated a rental pool in which the apartment owners could participate. The Raymonds contend that the expenses associated with the rental pool were not in any of the allowable categories of expenses under the bylaws. In finding for the association, the court stated that "condominium unit owners constitute a democratic subsociety, of necessity more restrictive in the use of condominium property than might be acceptable given traditional forms of ownership." The association was vested with broad discretion in exerting managerial and administrative responsibilities, including the privilege to determine the necessary expenses for the development and operation of the condominium project. The standard to be applied in reviewing action of the association is "reasonableness." The court concluded that the association could not enforce arbitrary and capricious rules, but if the items and services assessed can be reasonably identified as necessary to accomplish the purpose of creating a uniform plan for the development and operation of the condominium project, then it was permissible. *Raymond v. Aquarius Condominium Owners Association, Inc.,* 662 S.W.2d 82 (Tex. Civ. App.—Corpus Christi 1983).

When a unit owner refuses or is unable to pay an assessment, he or she is subject to enforcement procedures that are usually stated in the bylaws. The declaration or bylaws can establish that the council of owners will have a lien against the unit for any unpaid assessments. If this lien was a part of the declaration at the time the unit was purchased, it is a valid enforceable lien that can be foreclosed even when the unit is the homestead of the unit owner.

CASE EXCERPT *Johnson v. First Southern Properties, Inc.,* 687 S.W. 2d. 399 (Tex. Civ. App.—14th Dist. 1985)   ROBERTSON, Justice.   This is an appeal from a judgment approving a foreclosure sale. Johnson purchased a condominium apartment in November, 1978. After August, 1979, however, he failed to make any monthly maintenance fee payments. . . .

Among the papers on file at the time of purchase was the Condominium Declaration. This declaration states that the homeowner's council has a lien on each apartment for any unpaid assessments and obligates all co-owners of the project "to contribute, in proportion to their respective share in the Common Elements, to the payment of common expenses as a common charge covering the expenses of administration of the Project and the administration, maintenance, repair and replacement of the Common Elements, and other expenses authorized by the terms hereof." . . . Furthermore, the declaration authorized the council to enforce that lien through "nonjudicial foreclosure pursuant to Article 3810 of the Texas Revised Civil Statutes and [the] Co-owner[s] [hereby] expressly grant[ed] to the Board a power of sale in connection with said lien" through a trustee designated in writing by the Board. . . .

Johnson first argues that the forced sale for payment of debts violated his constitutional homestead protections. . . . The shelter of a homestead is not unassailable. Rather, a right, such as a lien, may prevail over a homestead claim if such right exists before the land becomes a homestead. . . .

It is firmly established in Texas law that to create a homestead the person claiming the homestead must prove concurrent usage and intent to claim the property as homestead. This determination becomes somewhat complicated when the "usage" follows the intent. During this interim period when the intention has not ripened into actual occupancy, the owner can, in effect, waive his homestead claim by making representations relinquishing that claim. Such representations can defeat a homestead without further reference to the homestead exemptions.

In the instant case, Johnson signed the papers relating to the purchase of the apartment on October 13, 1978, and moved in on November 1, 1978; consequently the interim rules come into play. The deed and the deed of trust represented that he took the apartment subject to the declaration, which declaration designated that the homeowner's council had an assessment lien. This, of course, amounted to a prior relinquishment of Johnson's homestead claim. We therefore hold that the assessment lien constituted a valid pre-existing debt which would overcome the homestead claim.

The case above has limited application to the enforceability of a lien against a homestead. For example, if the homeowners' association amended the declaration to create a lien against units for unpaid assessments, that lien would *not* be valid against those units that were homesteaded at the time of the amendment. Another limitation to note is the fact that the lien was recorded. If the creation of the lien appears in a bylaw that is *not* recorded, it would probably be unenforceable against a homestead. Problems regarding enforcement and collection of assessments are one of the reasons it is likely that the Texas Condominium Act will be amended.

In the absence of provisions in the declaration or bylaws regarding collection of assessments from delinquent apartment owners, two remedies are available to the homeowners' association. First, the association has the option of bringing a lawsuit against the delinquent party, obtaining a judgment and recording an abstract of that judgment. The judgment would be enforced in the same method described generally in Chapter 13. This process is also subject to the homestead rights of the individual. If the delinquent property owner cannot afford to pay the judgment and the apartment is his or her homestead, the homeowners' association may still be unable to collect the delinquency.

The second remedy that the homeowners' association has for collection of unpaid assessments is found in §81.208 of the Texas Property Code. It reads as follows:

> If an apartment owner conveys the apartment and assessments against the apartment are unpaid, the apartment owner shall pay the past due assessments out of the sale price of the apartment, or the purchaser shall pay the assessments, in preference to any other charges against the property except:
> (1) assessments, liens and charges in favor of this state or a political subdivision of this state for taxes on the apartment that are due and unpaid; or
> (2) an obligation due under a validly recorded mortgage.

This provision at least provides for priority over judgment liens and materialman's liens. Assuming the condominium is sold for an amount in excess of outstanding mortgages and tax debts, the homeowners' association will be next in line to collect for the delinquent assessments. However, even here there may be a question if the unit sold is a homestead. In §41.001 of the Texas Property Code, the proceeds from the sale of a homestead are declared to be exempt from seizure for a period of six months after the date of the sale. The relationship between §41.001 and §81.208 of the Texas Property Code remains unknown.

Tort Liability

Another issue of some importance to condominium ownership is liability for tort claims arising out of the ownership, use and maintenance of the common elements. The Texas statute on condominiums is silent on this point. However, in 1983 the Texas Supreme Court held that the individual property owners' liability is limited to their pro-rata interest in the regime as a whole. The primary reason for limiting the property owners' liability is their limited control over the common areas. Given the lack of control that an apartment owner has over the common areas, the court believed it would be unfair to hold each owner jointly and severally liable. For example, assume that Jane, a guest, is injured when she falls from a second-story balcony. The cause of the accident was defective construction of the rail surrounding the balcony. Since this railing was part of the common elements of the condominium regime, Jane is entitled to recover from each individual apartment owner an amount equal to his or her proportionate share in the common area. For simplicity, assume that there are ten units of equal size in the condominium regime. Each apartment is responsible for one-tenth of the cost of maintaining and repairing the common areas; therefore, Jane recovers one-tenth of her damages from each apartment owner. This also means that the liability of the individual apartment owners is limited to one-tenth of Jane's damages.

COOPERATIVE

Unlike the condominium unit owner, the cooperative owner or tenant does not have a fee simple interest in the apartment. Instead, the owner has shares of stock in the corporation that owns the land and building, along with a long-term proprietary lease. Occasionally the cooperative ownership is in a trust or partnership form rather than a corporate form.

The notion of a proprietary lease connotes that, unlike typical tenants, the cooperative tenants participate in the running of the cooperative through their stock interest in the corporation. The participation may be direct, when an individual is elected as a member of the board of directors, or indirect, when voting for directors or giving opinions to the elected directors. Despite the proprietary nature of the lease, however, it continues to be a lease and is governed by landlord-tenant law.

Financing a Cooperative

In a typical situation an investor purchases a multiple-unit dwelling to convert it into a cooperative. To finance the construction, the investor takes out a mortgage with a bank for 80 percent of the dwelling's value. The remaining 20 percent is paid by the investor initially but is recouped through the issuance of stock in the cooperative corporation to the future tenants. Future tenants pay their share of the 20 percent by purchasing stock when the enter the cooperative. In addition, each makes monthly payments that cover his or her share of the mortgage payment as well as operating expenses.

In addition to the mortgage share, each tenant as part of the monthly rent will pay a share of any other debt, taxes and operating expenses. As in a condominium, the share of these expenses may be on a per-unit basis or may vary with the relative value of the apartment. The amount of the annual or monthly assessment is determined by the board of directors of the corporation.

Differences Between Condominiums and Cooperatives

One difference between a cooperative and a condominium is the type of mortgage obtained. In the condominium each unit owner arranges for his or her own mortgage; in the cooperative there is a blanket mortgage for the entire unit. The blanket mortgage may be more difficult to obtain.

In the cooperative the ability of the tenants to sell their interest is restricted. Generally, the tenant needs the approval of the board of directors for the proposed new tenant. This procedure is a little more stringent than the right of first refusal used in the condominium area. These restrictions on the cooperative go beyond the outright sale and may prevent a tenant from assigning or subletting his or her share of the premises. The purpose behind these restrictions is to assure that a compatible group of tenants is assembled in the cooperative.

The cooperative form of ownership has advantages for the tenant compared to the usual landlord-tenant situation. The tenant is not subjected to annual rent increases and does not risk having the lease terminated arbitrarily. The cooperative tenant has a long-term lease and participates in any decision to raise the rent.

Like the condominium owner, the cooperative owner or tenant is subject to an extensive set of rules and regulations governing the cooperative. Failure to comply with the terms of the regulations may permit the board of directors to cancel the tenant's lease or to take some other action provided in the rules for redressing the violation.

Upon the death of the tenant any successor—an heir under the tenant's will or by law—must clear the screening of the board of directors. There is no automatic right on the part of successors to be able to continue the co-operative lease. This differs from a condominium, where the unit is owned in fee and can be freely passed on to successors.

There are some distinct advantages to fee simple ownership, of which the condominium owner is the beneficiary. The notion of fee ownership itself carries a certain feeling of security and psychological confidence that is not matched by the lease of the cooperative arrangement. Many of these advantages are tangible and specific.

The condominium owner is responsible for his or her own mortgage and is not as vulnerable to default as the cooperative owner, who shares a blanket mortgage with everyone else in the cooperative. The condominium owner can directly take advantage of certain tax benefits, such as property tax deduction, interest deductions, casualty loss deductions and depreciation allowance if the unit is rented, that are not available individually to the cooperative owners, although residential cooperatives may be able to take advantage of some federal tax benefits, such as property tax and interest deductions, if the cooperative is formed properly. Under §528 of the Internal Revenue Code, however, a condominium owner is permitted to make a tax-free contribution to the association for capital expenses, maintenance and operating expenses, provided the association meets the requirements of §528. Thus, a condominium owner can make a tax-free payment to the association for a new roof or for the pool lifeguard. A payment for similar expenses to a cooperative would not qualify.

Upon the sale of a condominium unit, the owner can sell at market value and pay the reduced capital gains rate on his or her gain. The cooperative owner generally must sell the stock back to the cooperative at a stipulated price. Often the stipulated price is the original price.

Cooperatives can be troublesome during difficult economic times. Initially, it may be more difficult to get a blanket mortgage loan than to get a mortgage loan on an individual condominium unit. Given the nature of the interdependence created by the blanket mortgage, the default of one or several cooperative owners can cause a default on the mortgage. Upon default all cooperative owners stand to lose their investments, even those who can afford to keep up their share of expenses. In a condominium, on the other hand, the default on an individual mortgage does not affect the other condominium owners. Nevertheless, the financial straits that caused the mortgage default are likely to prevent payment of condominium assessments; in this respect, delinquencies can place a financial strain on the other condominium owners.

One advantage the cooperative has over the condominium is that it is relatively easy to get rid of an incompatible tenant. A tenant who refuses to comply with the rules of the cooperative can be evicted in summary proceedings in most instances. Although a condominium owner who is in default on assessments can be ousted through a lien foreclosure, the procedure is likely to be more prolonged and expensive.

TIME-SHARES

Time-sharing has become a popular marketing device for resort developments in the United States. Time-sharing includes several very different types of ownership. Some of these forms include ownership of some type of interest in the real property, and other forms are mere rights of use with no interest in the property itself.

Time-sharing arrangements can be built upon several different legal principles. In some instances the arrangement is a variation of the tenancy in common. In others it is a variation of a cooperative. It could also be a lease. When it is built upon one of these types of legal ownership of property, it always includes a limitation as to the time of use. For example, a tenancy in common is an estate that includes more than one owner, with each co-owner owning an undivided interest. A time-sharing arrangement based upon the legal principles of the tenancy in common would introduce the characteristic of time with respect to possession of the property. An ordinary tenant in common has an equal right to possession with the other co-tenants. The time-share agreement limits the right to possession to a specific time period each year.

The time-sharing arrangement can also include principles of contract, partnership, license or corporate law. For example, a time-sharing arrangement based in contract would include the right to use a specific piece of property at a definite time each year for a certain number of years. At the expiration of that period the property would be owned by the developer, not the owner of the time-share.

Much of the criticism of time-sharing arrangements is a result of misleading marketing practices. The legal rights associated with time-sharing arrangements can vary significantly from development to development. The variety of legal rights that are being marketed as time-shares coupled with deceptive and misleading information by salespersons has prompted some states to enact legislation dealing specifically with time-shares.

In 1985, the Texas Legislature passed the Texas Timeshare Act. (Tex. Rev. Civ. Stat. art. 6573c) The law has four main effects. First, it requires developers to record a declaration regarding the time-share. The contents of the declaration are similar to that required of condominium development but in addition must include the amenities to be furnished. Second, this law requires that accurate and complete information regarding the legal aspects of time-share ownership be provided to prospective purchasers. The act details the information that must be included in advertisements and in the disclosure statement that must be given to prospective purchasers. Third, it provides for a period of rescission or cancellation if the purchaser did not visit the location of the time-share unit and have an opportunity to inspect a model unit. The purchaser has three days to rescind from the date on which he or she signed the agreement to purchase a time-share. If the purchaser rescinds within that time period, he or she is entitled to receive a full refund of the deposit. Fourth, the law declares that a time-share is an interest in land and, therefore, is subject to the Texas Real Estate License Act. The result of this provision is that, as of January 1, 1986, those who sell time-shares must be licensed salesmen or brokers unless specifically exempted under the provisions of the Texas Real Estate License Act. The licensing act is discussed in detail in Chapter 14.

Time-Share Ownership Forms

Some familiarity with the various types of ownership forms offered as time-shares is helpful. The information that follows is not exhaustive but does show the wide range of rights that can be associated with time-shares.

Vacation License

The purchaser pays the developer a sum of money for permission to use the property at a certain time each year for a stated number of years. This is a type of irrevocable license for the stated time period. The purchaser does not acquire any interest in the property.

Resort Club

The developer organizes a nonprofit corporation referred to as a "club." This club then obtains from the developer the right to use the property. The right of use granted to the club may be granted in the form of a purchase or a lease or a license. The club holds the units for use by its members. Purchasers acquire the right to use the resort property by joining the club. There is, of course, a membership fee. Club members have the right to use the resort property on a first come, first served basis. When purchasers use one of the units, they are required to pay a maintenance or usage fee to the club. In this type of arrangement, the purchaser of the time-share does not acquire any legal rights to the property.

Tenancy in Common

The purchaser of the time-share purchases an undivided interest in the property. In addition, the purchaser signs an agreement with all the other purchasers of time-shares in that property concerning the right to use the property. That agreement establishes the particulars of when, how and under what conditions each co-owner can use the property. The purchaser actually receives a deed to the property showing his or her undivided interest.

Interval Ownership

This is similar to the tenancy in common but includes in one conveyance the time element as well as the ownership element. The deed conveys to the purchaser a particular unit in the resort development at a certain time each year. Consequently, there is no need for the additional agreement described in the tenancy in common.

Stock Cooperative

A corporation is organized by the developer. The corporation owns the property. The purchaser of the time-shares owns stock in the corporation. The amount of stock owned by the purchaser determines which unit or which size unit is available for use and how many times a year it can be used.

SUMMARY

The condominium and the cooperative are devices by which owners acquire rights in individual units of a multiunit residential or office building. Many factors have combined to make the condominium popular, although until fairly recently condominium ownership was unusual in the United States. As a result of this new popularity, the various states, including Texas, have had to develop new laws and procedures for purchase of condos and for the protection of owners. A developer begins with the recording of a declaration. In addition, the condominium regime must establish a council of owners and adopt bylaws for management of the project. As individual apartments are sold, each owner receives a deed for his or her unit.

The declaration contains the legal description and lists restrictions on uses and legal requirements for each unit. The bylaws are the rules governing the internal operation of the condominium development. The deed to each unit is similar to the deed to any real property.

Each owner, in addition to fee simple ownership of a unit, has part ownership in the common elements of the structure. These include areas such as hallways, staircases, lobby and grounds. To administer these common elements, the condominium association is formed. Each owner is assessed a prorated amount of the total expense for operation of the common elements. Methods for measuring and collecting these assessments are established in the bylaws. State law provides two methods for collecting delinquent assessments: a lawsuit against the individual property owner and a preference lien against the apartment unit that is paid when the apartment unit is sold.

Another form of joint ownership is the cooperative. Individual owners in this form do not own their respective units; each owns a portion of stock in a corporation that owns the land and buildings. Instead of the fee simple interest enjoyed by condominium owners, the cooperative owner has a long-term proprietary lease, which is governed by landlord-tenant law.

A major difference between the condominium and cooperative is the type of mortgage obtained: each owner in a condominium obtains his or her own mortgage, while the cooperative usually carries a blanket mortgage on the entire complex. Taxation and liquidity benefits vary accordingly.

Another popular form of property ownership to develop in recent years is the time-share. The time-share can be built upon any number of legal principles discussed in this textbook; however, common to each is the element of sharing the unit with other people and a division of the time for use and possession of the unit. Because the legal rights associated with time-shares are so varied, ranging from a mere license to use the property to actual co-ownership of a particular unit, there were many complaints of deception and fraud in the marketing and selling of time-shares. As a result the Texas Timeshare Act was passed to regulate the advertising and selling of time-shares in Texas and allow the purchaser in certain instances the right to rescind the contract.

QUESTIONS AND CASE PROBLEMS

1. What are the common elements in a condominium arrangement? Distinguish between general common elements and limited common elements.
2. A condominium unit owner surrenders in writing her right to use the swimming pool, one of the common elements. Does that action relieve her of the responsibility of sharing the cost of maintaining the pool?
3. Compare and contrast condominiums with cooperatives.
4. Explain the ownership rights that can be acquired under the various types of time-shares.
5. Sondock purchased a condominium unit in the By the Sea Condominiums. At the time of his purchase, carports were assigned to each unit owner. Due to the cost of maintaining the carports, the council of co-owners voted to remove the covers. This removal was made in compliance with the bylaws. Sondock claims that the covered parking at the project was a property right and therefore cannot be eliminated or impaired by an amendment to the condominium declaration without 100 percent approval of the condominium owners. Will Sondock prevail?
6. Dutcher leased his condominium to Ted and Christine Owens. A fire that began in an external light fixture in a common area caused substantial property loss to Ted and Christine. Ted and Christine proved that the fire was caused by the negligence of the homeowners' association in failing to correct a known defect in the insulating box behind the light fixture. Ted and Christine sued Dutcher for their losses. Is Dutcher liable?

8

Easements and Other Nonpossessory Rights

EASEMENT

Most of the ownership interests considered in prior chapters provide the holder with a current or future right of possession. In these forms of ownership, the owner enjoys or will enjoy in the future the right to proceeds from the property and the right to occupy it to the exclusion of all others.

Some people have interests in real estate that are limited to use, not possession. These are referred to as *nonpossessory rights*. One important nonpossessory right is the easement. Easements are used extensively in real estate. For example, they are essential to the operation of utilities. They also provide a legal basis for condominium ownership, scenic and open-space protection and preservation of historic buildings. Indeed, few land developments would be successful without the extensive use of easements. Although easements are interests in real estate, the person who has an easement is never entitled to possession of the land itself, either currently or in the future.

An *easement* gives the holder the right to use another's land or buildings for a specified purpose. That purpose might be as simple as crossing the land to reach a beach or as complicated as using a portion of a neighbor's building to support one's own. The person who owns an easement has neither title nor estate in the land burdened by it. The easement holder's limited interest, however, is protected against interference by third parties, and it cannot be terminated at the will of the owner of the land that it burdens.

Frequently, easements authorize a person to perform a particular act. An example would be a right to use a neighbor's driveway to reach the back portion of a lot. These authorizing easements are called *affirmative easements*.

Others, called *negative easements,* prohibit the owner of the land from doing something that ordinarily an owner would be entitled to do. Easements of this nature are not as common. A negative easement might prohibit a landowner from constructing a building taller than a designated height in order to provide adjoining land with an unobstructed view; owners of lots in a development might be restricted from painting their houses a particular color. Easements are also classified as appurtenant or in gross.

Easement Appurtenant

An *easement appurtenant* is an easement that gives the owner of a *specific* piece of land the right to use another's land for a specified purpose.

CASE EXAMPLE

Stump and Levit own adjoining parcels of land at Lake Feather. Stump's property borders the lakefront; Levit's does not. Stump has, however, in a formally executed document, granted to Levit a right-of-way across the lakefront property to the beach. Stump has created an easement appurtenant.

An easement appurtenant involves two parcels of land, usually but not necessarily adjoining. The easement allows the possessor of one parcel to benefit by using the other parcel of land. The parcel that benefits is referred to as the dominant estate or *dominant tenement.* The owner of such easement is also called the *dominant tenant.* The property that is subject to the easement is known as the *servient estate.* Stump's property in the example above is the servient estate; Levit's, the dominant. An easement appurtenant cannot exist without a dominant estate.

If an easement is appurtenant, any conveyance of the dominant estate automatically includes the easement even if the easement is not mentioned in the deed. The easement is said to *run with the land.* When Levit sells his Lake Feather property to Bach, for example, Bach automatically acquires the right to cross Stump's property to get to the beach.

While the easement is automatically transferred with the dominant estate, it cannot be separated and conveyed independently. In the above examples, Levit cannot simply sell or convey to some neighboring landowner the right to cross Stump's property.

In addition to running with the land, an easement appurtenant is irrevocable. It cannot be canceled by the servient owner or terminated by a conveyance of the servient tenement. When the servient tenement is sold or otherwise conveyed, the property remains subject to the existing easement.

Easement in Gross

An *easement in gross* is an easement that confers to the holder of the easement the personal right to use another's land for a specified purpose. An easement in gross is not tied to another parcel of land as is the easement appurtenant. Thus an easement in gross exists without a dominant estate. Although a servient estate does exist, the privileges given by the easement belong to an individual. Stump, for example, might give the telephone company an easement to bury its line along the road bordering his Lake Feather property.

In the past, the easement in gross granted to an individual for a noncommercial purpose was considered a personal right or privilege. Only the person to whom the easement was given could use it. The easement could not be sold, assigned or otherwise transferred, and it terminated upon the death of its holder. For this reason, if the parties wished to have the easement continue or to have any value, they had to tie it to a dominant estate. If this were the case, it would be appurtenant and would run with the land. In Texas the creation of easements appurtenant are favored over the creation of easements in gross. Therefore, in the event the language creating the easement is ambiguous, the court will usually find that the parties intended to create an easement appurtenant.

Traditionally, the courts have treated easements in gross granted for commercial purposes differently. Commercial easements, because of their importance to the public, are considered freely transferable. As a result, a utility easement can be sold or assigned by one utility company to another.

Inasmuch as the easement in gross is not intended to benefit a parcel of land, it is considered a personal right in another's property. Because of this, it is frequently confused with a somewhat similar personal right—a license.

PROFIT

Most authorities consider the profit, correctly known as the *profit à prendre,* a type of easement. Others distinguish the profit from the easement as the profit allows the holder to take specified resources from the land. A person who has an easement does not have this right. Suppose, for example, that Stump grants the Cazenovia Lumber Company the right to take "any and all standing timber" from his property at Lake Feather. Although the lumber company does not have title to the timber, it has a right to remove it from the land. A **profit à prendre** is a nonpossessory interest in land that gives the holder of it the right to remove something from the land.

Few differences exist between easements and profits. Like other types of easements, a profit is an interest in land, but it is nonpossessory and limited to a particular purpose. The holder of the profit has a right of reasonable ingress and egress in order to use the right advantageously. In most states, unless specifically limited by the agreement, the owner of land does not lose the right to use the resource that is the subject of the profit. Like easements, profits may be appurtenant or in gross. The usual profit is in gross. This makes it a personal right not related to a dominant estate. Unlike the easement in gross, however, the profit in gross is freely transferable.

A common example of a profit à prendre in Texas is the hunting lease. Although the document is called a lease, it is in fact a profit à prendre because it creates a right to remove something from the land.

LICENSE

A *license* is a personal privilege to enter another's property for a specific purpose.

CASE EXAMPLE

Able and Baker are neighbors. Baker is having work done on his driveway, and Able gives him permission to park in Able's driveway for two weeks. Baker has a license.

Purchase of tickets to attend the theatre or a sporting event and obtaining a camping permit at a state park are other examples of licenses. Although both easements and licenses are intangible, an easement is an interest in land; a license is not. It is a right that is personal to the licensee, the party to whom it was given. Without a license, if Baker had parked in Able's driveway, Baker would be a trespasser.

Licenses may be created orally or may be in writing. Since they are personal, the licensor, the party giving the license, may revoke it at any time. If the license was created with a contract, the revocation is a breach of the contract. Nevertheless, although the licensee can collect damages, he or she cannot require the licensor to honor the agreement by specific performance. If Baker had rented space in Able's driveway, Able could revoke the license. Although Able would be responsible for money damages because of the revocation, Baker could not get a court order requiring Able to make space available.

Because licenses are personal, they are usually invalidated by the licensee's death and may not be transferred. An exception exists when the individual's license is coupled with an interest in the real estate. Under these circumstances the license is irrevocable. Instead of merely giving Baker permission to park in the driveway, Able sells Baker timber on Able's property. Baker, because of his interest in the timber, has, in addition, an irrevocable privilege to enter and remove it. Baker's license to enter the land is irrevocable because of the interest in the timber. The license is said to be coupled with an interest.

Licenses are sometimes the result of ineffective easements. Ordinarily an easement must be created by a written instrument. An oral easement may be construed as a license; if held to be a license, however, the grant would be revocable. Some states suspend the right to revoke a license if the licensee has made improvements on the land.

CREATION OF EASEMENTS

An easement is generally created in one of four ways: by written document, by implication, by prescription or by estoppel.

Creation of an Easement by a Written Document

The most effective method of creating an easement is by a written instrument describing the land and the location of the easement. Although most courts recognize that an easement can be created by implication or prescription, they have refused to accept the idea that an easement can be created orally. The reason is that an easement is an interest in real estate, and statutes in all states require that the creation of an interest in real estate be evidenced by a written document.

Usually the document creating an easement is very much like a deed, the written instrument used to convey title to land. Similar words are included, and the instrument is executed and recorded as a deed would be. However, there is no requirement of any specific language to create an easement. As a matter of fact, the courts will provide an interpretation of what was intended in the case of most ambiguities. For example, the exact location of the easement does not have to be included in the instrument. If the location is omitted in the instrument but the easement was in existence at the time of the conveyance, the court will find that it is that location that was intended by the parties. The one strict requirement concerning the location of the easement is an adequate description of the servient estate. A grant that does not sufficiently identify the estate to be burdened by the easement will fail. The case that follows illustrates the importance of the property description.

CASE EXCERPT *Pick v. Bartel;* 659 S.W.2d 636 (Supreme Court of Texas 1983) McGEE, Justice. We must determine the validity of a purported easement asserted by the Picks on a tract of land owned by the Bartels....

Andrew Truebenbach owned two adjacent tracts of land, one containing 165 acres and the other, 25 acres. Truebenbach sold the 165-acre tract to Pick. The deed, dated August 20, 1971, contained the following language:

> Grantors also guarantee grantees, their heirs and assigns, a right-of-way across the 25-acre tract sold to Walter Bartel.

The 25-acre tract was sold to Bartel by a deed dated August 25, 1971, and contained the following language:

> There is also a further stipulation this conveyance directs that the grantors are designating that a right-of-way for a road shall be allowed to be had through and over the said 25 acres at a location which will least interfere with the use of the 25 acres....

Both deeds were prepared by the same attorney, but were dated five days apart. Evidence concerning the location of a roadway on the Bartel tract was admitted at trial. There was conflicting testimony concerning the use of the roadway. According to the Picks, the primary use of the road was from November of 1979 when they moved onto the 165 acres until April of 1980 at which time, the Bartels placed locked gates at the entrances to the road preventing the ingress and egress of the Picks. . . .

An easement is an interest in land which is subject to the Statute of Frauds. . . . It is well settled that in order for a conveyance or contract of sale to meet the requirements of the Statute of Frauds, it must, insofar as the property description is concerned, furnish within itself or by reference to other identified writings then in existence, the means or data by which the particular land to be conveyed may be identified with specific certainty. . . .

The words in the Pick deed "sold to Walter Bartel" does not identify the alleged servient estate with sufficient certainty to satisfy the Statute of Frauds, nor does it refer to some other existing writing, by which the alleged servient estate may be identified with sufficient certainty. . . .

Moreover, since the Pick and Bartel deeds were dated five days apart, the 25-acre tract had not been sold to Bartel at the time the Pick deed was executed. No city, county or state is mentioned in connection with its location. No lot or block number is given nor is there an indication as to the amount of land. No description by any particular name appears. In fact, every essential element of the description is left to inference or to be supplied by parol. To permit the Picks to show by parol evidence what land was under consideration would be, in effect, to abrogate the rule requiring contracts or the conveyance of land to be in writing. . . . We hold that, as a matter of law, the description of the land subject to the alleged easement will not support a suit to establish a roadway easement.

The judgment of the court of appeals is affirmed.

The granting of an easement may be an independent transaction. Utility companies often seek easements when they need to run their lines over another's property. In many states the law gives these companies the right of eminent domain if the landowner refuses to grant the requested easement. Gas pipelines, sewers and roads are based upon easements from property owners.

Documents creating easement may do so by express grant or express reservation. An easement is created by *express grant* when the owner of a tract of land expressly grants a specific right to use the property to another.

CASE EXAMPLE
Morgan owns two adjoining lots at Lake Feather. She sells one to Betterman. Morgan's lot includes a private alley, and Morgan's deed to Betterman *expressly grants* Betterman the use of this alley.

An easement is created by *reservation* when the owner of a tract of land conveys title to another and specifically reserves an easement for himself or a third party.

CASE EXAMPLE

Morgan sells Betterman the lot with the alley and keeps the other for herself. Morgan's deed includes a clause that expressly reserves her right to use the alley.

Provisions expressly reserving an easement are usually found in a deed; some easements are created by will, but easements may also be included in a mortgage or lease.

An easement may also be created by a *contract* between the parties. This is not a preferred method, but if the courts will enforce by specific performance or injunction an agreement in which one party promises to allow another to use land for a limited purpose, an easement has been created.

If an easement is based upon a contract rather than a deed, difficulties can arise when the estate enjoying the benefit of the easement is transferred. The owner of the servient estate might claim that the easement was personal to the individual with whom the contract was made, and since that person no longer owns the property, the easement no longer exists. Most courts in this situation act as if the easement runs with the land. It may be enforced against the contracting party or a new owner of the servient estate if the latter had notice of the existence of the contract. Enforceable easements created by contract often involve reciprocal easements, such as those involved in a party wall agreement.

Party Wall

A *party wall* is a single wall located on the boundary of neighboring properties that simultaneously serves as a common support for buildings on each of the two parcels. In many metropolitan areas, adjacent buildings often share a single wall in order to save space and expense. Generally, a party wall is constructed on the boundary line between two parcels of real estate, with half of the wall on one side and half on the other. In the United States, the courts uniformly have held that each landowner owns that portion of the wall on his or her land and holds an *easement appurtenant* for support in the other half. If the party wall is entirely on the property of one landowner, the wall belongs to him or her; the other landowner normally has an easement in the wall.

Party walls are commonly constructed as the result of agreement, with each party contributing half of the cost. Because party walls have created many legal problems, these agreements must be drawn carefully. Related problems often involve use of the wall for advertising or purposes other than support.

Contributions for repairs to party walls generally can be compelled even if the agreement does not cover the question. The cost of improvements, however, must be borne by the owner who authorizes them. Neither owner can ordinarily remove the wall, but each may remove the remainder of the building without liability if reasonable care is taken.

Creation of an Easement by Implication

Courts sometimes presume that the parties intend to create an easement because certain facts exist when real estate is conveyed. The easement supposedly reflects the intention of the parties and is called an *easement by implication.* Courts have traditionally assumed easements by implication in two situations. In both, the easement results only if one or more parcels are severed from a larger tract under common ownership.

In the first situation, the effective use of one parcel (the dominant estate) depends upon continuation of a use already being made of the other. The other situation occurs if the severed portion is landlocked and cannot be used without passage across the other. This type is generally referred to as an *easement by necessity.* This second example of implied easement by necessity is much less common than the first example, which is based upon the effective use of a servient parcel that once was part of a single property.

Support for the creation of easements by implication is found in the idea that a sale of real estate includes that which is necessary to use the property beneficially. If a property owner visibly and continuously has used one part of the land for the benefit of the other, an easement is actually created when either part is sold separately. This is true even if neither party expressly makes any commitment creating the easement.

• **CASE BRIEF** •

In 1963 the parents of Arthur Beck and Doris Mills gave each of them a portion of their land. At the time of the conveyance there was a roadway across the land that was conveyed to Beck. This roadway had been used for some 40 years prior to the conveyances. Mills continued to use the roadway to go to and from her land until 1975, when Beck placed a lock on the gate crossing the roadway and ordered Mills to stop using it. Mills had access to her land by another route over a mountain range. Mills claimed that she had right-of-way over Beck's land. Beck claimed that, since there was no grant of an easement in the 1963 deeds, Mills had no easement. The court held for Mills. It concluded that she had an easement by implication. The use was apparent, permanent and reasonably necessary to the enjoyment of Mills's land. At the time of the 1963 partition the roadway was well defined and conspicuous. *Beck v. Mills*, 616 S.W.2d 353 (Tex. Civ. App.—14th District Houston 1981).

It is important to note in the above case that there was another access to Mills's land. However, the court still held that the easement was necessary. The distinction here is between absolute necessity and reasonable necessity. The alternative route to the Mills property was impractical. This is the difference between an easement by implication and an easement by necessity, which is discussed below. An easement by implication requires that the use be reasonably necessary. An easement by necessity requires that the use be absolutely necessary.

Easement by Necessity

An *easement by necessity* is an easement permitting the owner of a land-locked parcel to cross over a portion of land of which the easement formerly was a part. The courts will imply such an easement only for the limited purpose of ingress and egress and only if absolutely necessary.

Most courts consider the easement by necessity a form of implied easement. They reason that the parties intended that the grantee of a land-locked parcel have a means of access to the land. Without a right to cross the lands of the grantor, the grantee would derive no benefit from the conveyed property. A few courts have taken the position that presumed intent is not necessary. These courts feel that sound public policy dictates that no land should be inaccessible. Whatever theory prevails, two factors must be established for an easement to be created by necessity:

1. Both parcels must at one time have been part of a single unit.
2. There must be an absolute necessity for the easement.

CASE EXAMPLE

O'Mally purchased from Flynn a lot that was part of a larger parcel that abutted on Lake Feather. O'Mally did not think to get an easement to reach the lake across Flynn's remaining land. As a result, he had to drive more than five miles to use Lake Feather. If he sued to establish an easement by necessity, a court probably would reject his suit on the grounds that no real need existed.

Creation of an Easement by Prescription

Prescription is the term used to describe the acquisition of an intangible property right such as an easement through wrongful use of another's land for a period of time. In Texas the requisite time period is usually ten years.

Basic to the creation of the *easement by prescription* is the idea that an owner must take some legal action against wrongful use of his or her property within a certain period of time. An owner who does not do so is *estopped* or legally prohibited from asserting whatever rights he or she had.

At one time, the easement by prescription was justified on the presumption of a lost written document. Modern courts reject this presumption, but they continue to approve the prescriptive easement. Most courts apparently feel that land use will be stabilized and controversy reduced if the easement by prescription is recognized.

In addition to use for the designated period, two additional requirements must be met before a prescriptive easement is recognized. The use must be *continuous and uninterrupted* and *adverse* to the owner's interest. Over the years, both of these requirements have been the source of substantial litigation; the resulting interpretations have been both confusing and constantly changing.

A use that is adverse to the owner's interest must be open and notorious. It must be obvious enough that an owner reasonably concerned with protecting his or her property rights could readily discover it. A use is not adverse if the user has the owner's permission; no matter how long it continues, it will not ripen into an easement. If, however, the owner who has given permission revokes it, later use becomes adverse. Likewise, if the use made of the land differs from the permitted use, the use becomes adverse.

A difference of opinion exists as to the extent to which the use must be hostile to be considered adverse. *Hostile* means not ill will but that the wrongdoer actually claimed the right to use another's property. Many courts take the position that whenever an easement has been used for the prescribed period, the user did so under a claim of right. Under these circumstances, adverse use will be presumed unless the owner introduces sufficient evidence to overcome the presumption. Adverse use has thus been found in cases where the user actually believed that he or she owned the property. A use under these circumstances is clearly hostile to the owner's interest.

In a number of situations, however, use longer than the prescribed time is not presumed to be adverse. These include use by a relative, use of land that is open and unfenced, use by many people, none of whom claim an exclusive right and concurrent use by the owner.

Creation of an easement by prescription also requires that the use by the person claiming the easement be *continuous and uninterrupted. Continuous* use does not mean *constant use.* Use is continuous when a person uses the easement as the occasion may demand. It is also considered to be continuous so long as the easement is usable even if it is not presently being used. A critical factor is that the person claiming the right does not recognize a superior claim or abandon the use during the prescriptive period. In addition, the use does not have to be a continuous use by the same person. Most states allow *tacking*—the process of adding together periods of prescriptive use by a latter user who has succeeded to the interest of earlier users.

Uninterrupted and *continuous* are not synonymous. *Uninterrupted* refers to the failure of the owner of the land to act. For a use to be uninterrupted, the owner must not succeed in causing a discontinuance of the use. The running of the prescriptive period is stopped when a continuance is effected.

Easement by Estoppel

Estoppel is the legal term used to describe a situation in which a person is not permitted to deny the consequences of his or her actions. Occasionally courts have enforced oral contracts that create a limited interest in land. This is sometimes called an *easement by estoppel.* It is created by the court because it is equitable. The purpose of this doctrine is to protect a purchaser who, in reliance upon representations by the grantor that an easement exists or was granted, will suffer some detriment when it is discovered that in fact there is no easement. Frequently, this equitable doctrine is used when a purchaser of land is shown a plat or map indicating that certain areas are being reserved for streets, playgrounds or other open spaces.

Plats and Maps

Courts sometimes refer to an easement that arises when a document such as a deed refers to a plat or map with designated streets or areas as an easement by implication.

CASE EXAMPLE

Keene purchased several acres on the north side of Lake Feather. He subdivided the property and had prepared a map designating streets, parks and a beach area. Several of the lots were sold and described by reference to the map. Controversy arose between Keene and a number of the lot owners. Keene, as a result, attempted to restrict their use of the beach.

Courts in most states would rule that the lot owners had acquired easements, even if no easements were mentioned in their deeds. When a person buys property described by lot number on a particular map, that person acquires the right to use all common areas designated on the map. In Texas the easement attaches immediately upon the purchase of the property. Furthermore, the easement for a right-of-way exists even if the streets described in the plat are never opened by the city.

Dedication

Dedication is the granting by a private landowner of a portion of his or her property to the public or a governmental unit for public use. A typical dedication would be the setting aside by a developer of land to serve as streets into the development.

Litigation involving public easements in streets and other parcels of land is often complicated. Complications arise because almost all states have laws dealing with dedication of land designated for public use on plats and maps. When a plat is recorded, land indicated as set aside for public use becomes public property. In many states the local government automatically acquires an easement in the land. In other states the government acquires title to the designated areas.

A completed dedication solves numerous problems for landowners because the street or area becomes public and open to all users. Complications arise when the property is abandoned by the state. Does it revert back to the former owner, or do those whose interests may be injured now have private easements in the designated parcel? A majority of courts take the position that interests for which the easement was created continue to have a right to use the street.

A legal doctrine that can assist when an express dedication fails or is abandoned is the implied dedication. An implied dedication is established if there is evidence that the landowner intended to dedicate the land as a public road and the public used the road.

Frequently, when a person is asserting a claim to an easement he will support his claim with more than one theory. For example, he may claim that he has an easement by express grant or, alternatively, that he has an easement by necessity. The purpose for alleging that an easement was created in more than one way is to increase the chance of winning in court. The case that follows is a good illustration of this technique. In this case the plaintiff claimed that he had an easement by prescription or, alternatively, that an easement had been created by implied dedication. One theory failed; and the other succeeded.

CASE EXCERPT   *O'Connor v. Gragg,* 339 S.W.2d 878 (Supreme Court of Texas 1960)   SMITH, Justice.   On July 1, 1957, Gragg filed his first amended original petition alleging (1) that he had, by necessity, acquired an easement over and across O'Connor's land; (2) that he had acquired a private easement by prescription. . . .

On May 20, 1958, and during the progress of the trial, Gragg filed a trial amendment alleging that O'Connor's predecessors in title dedicated the roadway across the land "* * * to the public use as a public roadway, and that the public accepted such dedication and did in fact use such roadway as a public roadway. . . ." The theory that Gragg was entitled to a way of necessity was apparently abandoned. . . .

The permissive use of a roadway over the land of another contemporaneously with the owner's use of the same roadway is not adverse. The use of the roadway under the circumstances reflected by this record cannot ripen into a prescriptive right. In order for there to be an acquisition of a prescriptive right, an adverse use of the easement must be shown. . . .

However, the judgment of the trial court should not be reversed if there is evidence to support the finding of the jury on the issue of dedication. . . .

The evidence shows that the roadway in question has existed for more than 68 years; that it has been a well-defined and well-traveled road. . . . Walter Rickles testified that he was 75 years of age and born and reared on the Rickles Survey. He testified that he first remembers traveling the road in question in 1890; that he has recently traveled over the roadway and found that it still exists in substantially the same location as it was when he first knew it in 1890. . . .

Common law dedications, such as the one here involved, are subdivided into two classes, express and implied. This dedication falls in the latter class. The unequivocal acts and conduct of O'Connor and his predecessors in title show an implied intention to appropriate the roadway to public use. "* * * If the open and known acts are of such a character as to induce the belief that the owner intended to dedicate the way to public use, and the public and individuals act upon such conduct, proceed as if there had been in fact a dedication, and acquire rights which would be lost if the owner were allowed to reclaim the land, then the law will not permit him to assert that there was no intent to dedicate.". . .

The petitioners [O'Connor] are hereby restrained from obstructing the dedicated roadway or interfering with the use of said roadway by the public, including the respondent, W. A. Gragg, so long as said road remains devoted or appropriated to a public use. . . .

Easements for Light and Air

The energy crisis of the late 1970s spurred interest in prescriptive easements. Owners considering installation of solar heating units in buildings need assurance of enough sunlight to operate the units effectively. This need could be hindered if the owner of the adjoining parcel were to build a structure that would block much of the incoming light. Easements for light and air over a neighbor's land are a means of dealing with this problem, but the vast majority of American jurisdictions will not recognize this type of easement except where the parties have entered into an express agreement creating it. English courts have recognized a doctrine of "ancient lights." This doctrine allows an easement for light after a prescriptive period of 27 years, but the ancient lights concept has been rejected consistently by American courts. American courts have also refused to apply the concepts of implied easement or easement by necessity to create easements for light and air. The result is that the potential user of solar or wind-generated energy faces a substantial cost to ensure the required sunlight or air flow to operate his or her unit. The prospective user of these alternative energy sources must bargain with neighbors to prevent blocking of the necessary light or air flow. Few property owners are, however, willing to enter into agreements restricting the height of buildings on their land because this might markedly decrease the land's value.

Although Texas and most other states do not recognize an implied easement for light and do not recognize the doctrine of ancient lights, a homeowner may be afforded some protection through restrictive covenants. Therefore, restrictive covenants, discussed in detail in Chapter 9, should be consulted and considered in resolving the issue when it arises.

RIGHTS AND DUTIES

All easements, regardless of how they came into being, have certain rights and certain duties. The use of the servient estate is limited to the use stated in the easement. It cannot be altered unilaterally in any way. The owner of the easement may do all things that are reasonably necessary to the full use and enjoyment of the easement. However, he or she cannot do anything that would unreasonably increase the burden on the servient estate or interfere with the use of the servient estate not burdened by the easement. For example, the owner of the easement can choose the type of surface he wants on his or her right-of-way. But what if the owner of the easement erects a fence to prevent the cattle on the servient estate from coming onto the road? Has he unreasonably burdened the use of the servient estate? Clearly, if the fence prevents the cattle from grazing or watering on another section of the servient estate, there has been an unreasonable interference.

Sometimes the dominant tenement or estate is divided into two or more parcels. In such cases, provided that there is not an unreasonable number of new parcels, the courts have held that the existing easement runs with all of the newly created parcels. If, in an example given earlier in the chapter, instead of conveying his entire Lake Feather property, Levit had divided the parcel into two lots and sold one of them to Bach, both Bach's and Levit's land would have right-of-way across Stump's property.

The easement is shared with the owner of the servient estate to the extent that the owner of the servient estate can also use the easement. However, this use cannot destroy or interfere with the easement holder's use of the easement. Preservation of the easement is the duty of the owner of the easement. The owner of the servient estate has no responsibility for repair or maintenance. Easements appurtenant can be transferred, provided the dominant estate is also transferred. The two cannot be separated. Easements in gross are generally not transferable unless expressly agreed to by the parties.

TERMINATION OF EASEMENTS

Although an easement is actually a nonpossessory interest, in many respects it resembles a possessory interest. Like an estate, an easement may be created for a specific period, for life or for a designated purpose. Stump, who you recall granted an easement across his property to reach Lake Feather, might have limited the easement to a designated number of years or until a road was constructed to the lake. When an easement is created for a period of time or a designated purpose, it terminates either when the time expires or the purpose is accomplished. Easements for life terminate when the measuring life ends. An easement created by necessity does not last once the necessity disappears. Most easements, however, do not expire automatically. Like the fee simple, they have the potential to last forever.

A number of methods exist for terminating easements that do not expire automatically, including release, merger, abandonment, conveyance, eminent domain, estoppel and prescription. Each of these methods will be discussed in the balance of the chapter.

Once terminated, an easement will exist only if it is re-created. For example, assume an easement has been terminated by abandonment. Later the dominant estate is sold to another party who would like to begin using the old easement across the servient estate. Can he do so? The answer is no. In order for there to be an easement, it would have to be created again in one of the ways discussed previously.

Release

The holder of an easement appurtenant or in gross may extinguish it by means of a written agreement to give up the right. This document is referred to as a *release*. An oral release alone is ineffective. Except for automatic termination of easements, extinguishing by release is probably the most common method.

Merger

An easement terminates by merger when the holder of either the dominant or servient estate acquires the other. An easement establishes a right to use land owned by someone else. As a result, a person cannot have an easement in his or her own land. The principle applies whether the easement is appurtenant or in gross. Either expires if ownership changes in this way.

Abandonment

Although nonuse alone does not extinguish an easement, it may indicate an intention to abandon it. For an easement to terminate by abandonment, the holder's intention to give it up clearly must be established. This can be done if the holder discontinues use, states his or her intention to do so or acts in a manner consistent with discontinued use.

CASE EXAMPLE

Suppose Bach purchases additional land giving him frontage on Lake Feather. He builds a fence along his line abutting on Stump's land and clears a path across the newly acquired tract to Lake Feather. Bach has probably abandoned his easement across Stump's property.

Conveyance

An easement is terminated when the servient estate is sold to a person who has no knowledge of the easement's existence. When a written easement is not recorded, or when the easement is not visible from indications on the property, the servient estate may become free of the easement. Easements created by necessity and by prescription, however, are not subject to this doctrine.

Eminent Domain

The right of the state to take private property for public use applies to easements. If the state takes the servient estate for a purpose that is not consistent with the continued use of the easement, the dominant tenant loses his or her right to continue this use. This is true even if the dominant estate itself is not taken. The owner of the dominant estate is entitled to compensation for the loss in value of his or her easement right. Similarly, condemnation of the dominant estate may terminate the easement. This occurs if the condemnation and the new use destroy the usefulness of the easement.

Estoppel

Two factors must unite before the doctrine of estoppel is applied. First, a person must act in a manner that causes another to believe something. Second, the other person must rely upon the belief and stand to suffer some loss if reliance upon such belief should be barred or penalized.

An easement is extinguished by estoppel if the holder causes the servient estate owner to believe the easement will no longer be used and the servient owner relies upon this belief and suffers some damage as a result. The belief might be the result of a statement made by the easement holder or might be inferred from the person's conduct.

CASE EXAMPLE

Stump asked Bach to use another path across Stump's property to reach Lake Feather. Bach orally agreed to do so. Stump then built a tennis court that was partially on the original right-of-way. Bach found the new path inconvenient and demanded to be allowed to use the old recorded right-of-way. Bach's easement had been terminated by estoppel.

Prescription

An easement may be extinguished after the owner of the servient estate acts in a manner adverse to the easement for the prescriptive period. This use must be open, notorious and uninterrupted. That is, the servient owner must act in a manner similar to that which occurs when an easement is created by prescription.

CASE EXAMPLE

Stump builds a garage on his property, blocking Levit's right-of-way to Lake Feather. Levit does nothing about the garage because he has no interest in reaching Lake Feather. The prescriptive period in the state is ten years. Levit's easement will terminate by prescription unless he asserts his right before the end of the period.

SUMMARY

Ownership interests described in previous chapters are those that provide owners with the right of possession—either current or future. Not all interests provide possession, however. An important example of one type that does not is the easement, which provides only a right to use the property in a limited way, such as for operation of utilities or to gain access to a roadway or beach area. This type of easement is called an *affirmative easement*. Another type—negative easement—prohibits an owner of land from doing something an owner would normally have the right to do.

Two other distinctions are easements appurtenant and easements in gross. The former is the right of one owner—the dominant estate—to benefit from use of the land of another—the servient estate. Characteristics of this type of easement are that it runs with the land and it is irrevocable; that is, it cannot be canceled or terminated by sale of the realty. The easement in gross is not attached to the land but is personal to the owner of the land. It cannot be sold or otherwise transferred. However, commercial easements in gross, such as those utility companies enjoy, have been treated by the courts as transferable.

Another nonpossessory interest, generally considered a type of easement, the profit, entitles the holder to remove something of value, such as a crop or harvest, from the land. The profit, like other easements, may be either appurtenant or in gross. The profit is sometimes confused with a license, which grants permission only to enter another's land for a specific purpose. Licenses, which may be revoked by the grantor at any time, expire upon the grantor's death.

Easements may be created in four ways: by written document (express), by implication, by prescription or by estoppel. The written document has the legal validity of a deed and should be recorded with the deed. One type of easement best created by written agreement is the party wall—a wall shared by two neighboring buildings. Agreements relating to party walls ought to be drawn carefully by an attorney.

Easements by implication traditionally have been upheld by the courts in two kinds of situations. First, effective use of the dominant estate must depend on the continuation of the easement. In the second case, the land cannot be used at all without the easement, as, for example, in a landlocked parcel (easement by necessity). The existence of easements is a very important factor to check when selling or listing a property. Discovery of an easement would avoid complicated litigation resulting from the absence of written documents relating to the easement.

Easements may also be created by prescription over a period of time, usually specified by statute. This type of easement depends upon the continuous, open and adverse use of an easement, such as a roadway, without interruption by the owner of the servient estate.

Although easements have the potential to last forever, they may be terminated legally in a variety of ways.

QUESTIONS AND CASE PROBLEMS

1. Compare and contrast an *easement appurtenant* and an *easement in gross.*
2. Explain the factors that must exist for an easement to be created by prescription.
3. What is a license? How does it differ from an easement?

4. What is a profit? How does it differ from an easement? In what ways is it similar?

5. Hamilton and Tucker owned adjoining farms. For more than 40 years Mrs. Tucker, her predecessors in title, her agents and her employees had reached her farm by a roadway across the Hamilton farm.

   At one time the two farms had been a single unit, but it had been divided in 1884 by Mrs. Tucker's grandfather. He had given approximately 200 acres to each of his two sons. The Hamiltons had purchased their farm in 1972 from the widow of one of the sons.

   Upon purchasing the farm, the Hamiltons blocked the roadway to the Tucker place. Mrs. Tucker seeks an injunction to restrain this action. Will she succeed? Discuss.

6. In 1912 Clark subdivided a portion of his ranch adjoining and abutting on Lake Austin. He filed a plat of this subdivision with the county clerk of Travis County, Texas. In the plat he provided for two roads: an upper road that provided access to Lots 1–17 and a lower road that provided access to Lots 18–21. Between 1912 and 1950 the lower road was informally extended to cut across Lots 5–17 as a result of people simply driving across them at the same location. Since this "extension" was more convenient for access to the lake, the upper road was used infrequently and became overgrown with trees and underbrush. In 1950 Matthews sold a portion of Lot 6 to Duff, retaining the balance of Lot 6 and all of Lot 5 for himself. The deed did not expressly create an easement across Lot 6. Duff refused to allow Matthews to use that portion of the "extension" that crossed his land. Matthews claims that he has an easement by necessity over Duff's land because the upper road is no longer passable. Who is likely to prevail?

7. Southwestern Bell Telephone Company sued San Jacinto Sand Company seeking an injunction prohibiting the Sand Company from making excavations that would destroy cables, conduits and equipment of Southwestern Bell. Southwestern Bell had obtained a 30-foot utility easement across this property. Sand Company was dredging to a depth of 60 feet on either side of the 30-foot easement but was not dredging on the easement itself. Due in part to the nature of the sandy loam, the dredging caused the surface land along the 30-foot utility easement to deteriorate and disappear. Southwestern Bell claims that it has a right to lateral support of the land subject to the easement. Has Sand Company interfered with Southwestern Bell's use of its easement?

9

★

Control of Land Use

RESTRICTIONS ON LAND USE

The basic tenets of American property law are derived from feudal times in England. Between the king and the lowest serf was the great mass of landholders. The landholder was not an owner but had the right to use a parcel of land. In exchange for that right of use, certain duties were owed to the superior on the feudal scale. These duties might include military service or a portion of the crops grown on the land. Our system of private property has evolved from this scheme, in which each landholder owes certain obligations in exchange for the right of use, but the legal notion of private property in America had its own peculiar twist.

As in England, the landholders' *rights* gradually expanded into what we refer to as *ownership*. These rights eventually gave the owner almost absolute and unfettered control over his grant of land. William Blackstone, the great 18th-century authority on the common law, referred to a person's property right as "that sole and despotic dominion," thereby depicting the extensive freedom that accompanied land ownership. A person's ownership rights were never quite as absolute as Blackstone alleged, but the wide range of rights he connoted became indelibly etched in the minds of landowners in England and America.

The American difference applied not to the "rights" side of the equation but to the "duty" side. Almost from the inception of this country a landowner owed no duty to anyone except to refrain from acts on the property that would significantly interfere with another landowner's use of his or her property. Once the purchase price was paid, the buyer of land owed no additional duty to the seller. Our concept of property has always been long on the landowner's rights and short on any duties arising from that ownership.

Though most Americans still cling tenaciously to the idea of absolute ownership rights in land, those rights have sharply eroded in the 20th century. The subdivider of land usually places a significant number of restrictions on use in the deed to the new homeowner. Municipal codes contain an array of restraints on an owner's property rights. For instance, zoning laws limit an owner's use of the land. Other statutes or local ordinances require an owner to hook up to a sewer, to desist from playing loud music late at night, to refrain from keeping farm animals and to get a permit in order to build an addition to the house, to name only a few. This chapter will describe some of the private and public restrictions on an owner's use of his or her private property.

In addition to the traditional controls over land use, some of the recent developments in public land use controls will be discussed at the end of this chapter. These new developments include zoning for aesthetic and preservation purposes as well as governmental regulation of pollution and destruction of the environment.

RESTRICTIVE COVENANTS

One method of imposing restrictions on land use is through private agreements called *restrictive covenants*. A **restrictive covenant** is a contractual limitation placed on the use of land by individuals. The owner of land has the right to limit the land's use in any manner, provided it does not violate the law or public policy. Usually restrictive covenants are created by a developer at the time he or she subdivides and begins construction, typically as part of the developer's general development and building scheme. These restrictions are usually found with the plat of the subdivision or in a document called "Restrictive Covenants for XYZ Subdivision." These documents are filed in the real property records in the county where the land is located. The restrictions may also be listed in the deeds that convey title to the individual lots in the subdivision. Provided they are recorded, they are enforceable against all subsequent purchasers with actual or constructive notice of their existence. Covenants can also be created by all the landowners in a particular area, consenting to the placement of the restrictions on the land. This is less common due to the difficulty of reaching a consensus regarding what restrictions should be imposed.

Amending Restrictive Covenants

Restrictive covenants must be modified in the manner established by the agreements. If no such manner is established, it must be agreed to by all the landowners whose property is subject to the restriction as well as all lienholders whose rights may be affected. Modifications that require unanimous approval are difficult to obtain, as illustrated by the case that follows.

• CASE BRIEF •

Greenway Parks Home Owners Association brought this suit against William Crawford and others, seeking a declaratory judgment regarding restrictions on the use of land located within that subdivision that required a certain area to be used as a park. The land in question was located across the railroad tracks from the subdivision and had never been developed or used as a park. Other land in the subdivision also was restricted for park use and had been developed and used by the subdivision. Due to the location, Greenway Parks Home Owners Association desired to sell this tract of land and use the proceeds to maintain the other private parks in the subdivision. So long as the land was burdened by a restrictive covenant limiting its use to a park, it was not marketable. Therefore, Greenway Parks sought removal of the restriction. Crawford and others in the subdivision opposed the removal of the restriction. The court held that the restrictive covenant could not be removed without agreement of all the landowners. The fact that the land may be better used by the subdivision in some other way is irrelevant. *Peterson v. Greenway Parks Home Owners Association*, 408 S.W.2d 261 (Tex. Civ. App.—Dallas 1966).

A limited exception to the requirement of unanimity in creating, modifying and extending restrictive covenants was created by the Texas Legislature in 1985. The new law applies only to residential subdivisions that meet the following criteria (Tex. Prop. Code §201.001 et seq.):

1. The subdivision must be located within a city, town, village or the extraterritorial jurisdiction of a city, town or village.
2. The city, town or village must not have a comprehensive zoning ordinance.
3. The subdivision's restrictive covenants do not provide for automatic or indefinite extensions of the term of the restrictions or for additions or modification of restrictions by less than 75 percent of the owners of real property interests in the subdivisions.

If a subdivision meets the stringent criteria set out above, then it is possible for restrictive covenants to be modified, renewed, expanded or created upon approval by owners of at least 75 percent of the lots in the subdivision. However, the procedure established for modifying or renewing restrictive covenants by this method has very limited application and is lengthy and complex. It takes at least two years to create the changes and requires numerous filings and notices to property owners. Notices must also be sent to lienholders. Furthermore, even after the changes have been approved and the time period has elapsed, it is possible for a dissenting property owner to have his or her property exempted from the new or renewed restrictive covenants. In addition, the new restrictive covenants would not be binding on a lienholder who foreclosed unless the lienholder had approved the change. It remains to be seen whether this new law will have an impact on renewing, creating or modifying restrictive covenants. In subdivisions where restrictive covenants are due to expire and there is no procedure for renewing the restrictions, this law does, however, provide a mechanism for landowners to preserve the covenants.

Enforcement of Restrictive Covenants

Restrictive covenants are enforceable by any landowner or lienholder who was intended to benefit from the restriction. This usually means persons owning or making loans on land within the area covered by the restriction. Civic clubs and homeowners' associations that have been authorized by their members to act on behalf of the membership can also enforce the restrictions. In addition to these private parties, cities and towns in Texas that have no zoning ordinances have been given authority to enforce private restrictive covenants. A good example of a city in this category is Houston, which does not have a zoning plan. The city is allowed to sue to enjoin a violation of a private restrictive covenant and can withhold a building permit if the proposed construction would violate the covenants.

Restrictive covenants will be enforced according to their terms. If the covenant language is ambiguous, the court will interpret it in its narrowest meaning. The intent and the meaning of a covenant are determined at the date it was created, not at a later time. The covenant will not be changed or enlarged by time and circumstances. Interpretation of the meaning of a covenant is the area most frequently litigated. Texas courts have been consistently strict and literal in the enforcement of restrictive covenants. This has been and will continue to be a cause of frustration among those who would like the court to be liberal in its interpretation.

There are two reasons for the court's reluctance to extend or enlarge restrictive covenants. First, the law seeks to preserve a landowner's right to free use of his or her land. Second, a waiver of this right should be found only where the landowner had notice of the limitation and expressly or impliedly consented to the restriction. An ambiguous covenant does not give the notice necessary for the court to find that the landowner has given up a right. The case that follows illustrates the court's interpretation of restrictive covenants.

CASE EXCERPT *Davis v. Huey,* 620 S.W. 2d. 561 (Supreme Court of Texas 1981) WALLACE. Justice. Petitioners Tom H. Davis and Hattie Davis, husband and wife, appealed from a permanent injunction entered by the District Court ordering them to remove a portion of their residence built in a residential subdivision without approval of the developer pursuant to restrictive covenants of record....

Northwest Hills, Section 7, a residential subdivision in Austin, Texas, was developed by the Austin Corporation. In 1965, prior to the sale of any lots in the subdivision, the Austin Corporation filed in the Deed Records of Travis County certain restrictive covenants applicable to the subdivision. These covenants are contained in ten paragraphs, numbers 7 and 8 being the ones primarily at issue in this cause.

Paragraph 7 established the setback, front-line, side-line and rear-line limits of the lot in question. . . .

Paragraph 8 provides that prior to the commencement of construction on a lot, the lot owner is required to submit the construction plans to the developer or an architectural committee for approval.

. . . The Davises originally proposed to build a house on their lot to be situated twenty-five feet from the rear lot line. It is undisputed that the proposed placement of the house complied with the set-back restrictions in Paragraph 7. However, the developer, Austin Corporation, acting through David B. Barrow, Jr., refused to approve the Davises' plans on the basis that the proposed placement of the house on the lot was inconsistent with the general plan of the subdivision. In refusing approval, Barrow relied on the general authority of Paragraph 8 to refuse approval of a plan "on any ground, including purely aesthetic grounds, which in the sole and uncontrolled discretion" of the developer shall seem sufficient. After negotiations between the parties regarding placement of the house proved fruitless, the Davises began construction despite the lack of approval of their plans. Thereafter, the Hueys instituted proceedings, in which Barrow and Austin Corporation, intervened seeking to halt construction on the grounds that the disapproval of the plans was a reasonable good faith exercise of the authority granted by Paragraph 8; that the completion of the house would reduce the value of the surrounding property because of its size and placement; and the proposed construction would block the views of the Hueys and other neighbors. . . .

Although covenants restricting the free use of property are not favored, when restrictions are confined to a lawful purpose and are within reasonable bounds and the language employed is clear, such covenants will be enforced. . . . However, a purchaser is bound by only those restrictive covenants attaching to the property of which he has actual or constructive notice. One who purchases for value and without notice takes the land free from the restrictions. . . .

We find that the better reasoned view is that covenants requiring submission of plans and prior consent before construction are valid insofar as they furnish adequate notice to the property owner of the specific restriction sought to be enforced. Therefore, the question before this Court is whether the approval clause set out in Paragraph 8 of the restrictions placed the Davises on notice that their lot was subject to more stringent building site restrictions than those set out in the specific restriction governing set-back and side-lines, Paragraph 7. . . .

Moreover, the meaning of Paragraph 8 and accordingly the nature of the notice thereby furnished to the Davises, is determined at the date of the inception of the general plan or scheme, i.e. in 1965, the date of filing of the restrictions in the Deed Records of Travis County. . . .

. . . there is nothing in the record which will support a holding that a general plan or scheme had been adopted by the developer with respect to placement so as to place the Davises on notice of such restrictions. Barrow testified that at the time the restrictions were filed, the developers had no definite intentions concerning the regulation of placement under Paragraph 8. In addition, other than the specific restrictions on building site and size, there is no language in any of the covenants, particularly in Paragraph 8, which would place a purchaser on notice that his lot was subject to the placement limitation sought to be enforced. . . .

Based on the language of the restrictive covenants and Barrow's testimony, it is clear that a general scheme regarding the placement of houses on lots in Section 7 did not exist at the time the restrictions were filed but that the placement restrictions sought to be imposed were in response to developing conditions in the subdivision. Thus, the limitations on the Davises' free use of their property were not based on the restrictive covenants but rather on the voluntary decisions of neighboring lot owners who had the good fortune to construct their houses prior to the Davises. . . .

Accordingly, we hold that the refusal of the developer to approve the Davises' plans exceeded his authority under the restrictive covenants and was void.

Accordingly, we reverse the judgment of the courts below and render judgment that the Hueys take nothing.

Although the enforceability of restrictive covenants is generally governed by the rules previously discussed, there are two types of restrictions that by statute in Texas are unenforceable. They are covenants that require wood shingle roofs and covenants that prohibit the use of property by or the sale, lease or transfer of property to a person because of race, color, religion or national origin. (Tex. Prop. Code §5.025 and §5.026)

Termination of Restrictive Covenants

Restrictive covenants can be terminated by agreement of all the landowners, waiver, abandonment or changed circumstances. Termination by agreement can occur when the covenants are created for a certain time period or some contingency expressly set out in the covenants. Termination by agreement also occurs when all the property owners consent to a removal or termination of the restrictions or any one of the restrictions.

Termination by abandonment requires nonenforcement or noncompliance with the intent that the covenant be abandoned. Abandonment can be difficult to establish because intent can be difficult to prove. However, termination by waiver may occur even if there is no evidence of intent. Waiver occurs when the covenant has not been enforced for a sufficiently long period of time to justify the court's finding that the right to enforcement has been waived. Whether or not there has been a waiver depends on all the facts of the particular circumstance, and there is no established time period within which suit to enjoin the violation must be brought.

Related to the legal principles of abandonment and waiver is the doctrine of laches. The doctrine of laches is an equitable principle that allows a court to protect a property owner from enforcement of a restrictive covenant against him or her because it would be unfair. The court will find that enforcement is inequitable if there was a unreasonable delay in enforcing the restrictive covenant and the offending property owner reasonably believed that the restrictive covenants were no longer in effect. The doctrine of laches does not terminate the restrictive covenant. It simply makes it unenforceable against a particular property owner.

Termination by changed circumstances is very rare. Changed circumstances is an equitable doctrine that renders a restrictive covenant unenforceable if, due to changes within the neighborhood, the purpose of or the reasons for the restriction no longer exist. Most of the cases that have alleged that the area has changed in such a way that enforcement is no longer reasonable concern changes in the area surrounding the particular subdivision. The courts have consistently held that changes in the immediate area outside the subdivision will not justify termination of the covenant in the periphery of the subdivision. The courts have recognized that to hold otherwise would simply result in the changes moving into the subdivision. This would gradually erode the restriction in the entire subdivision.

RESTRICTIVE COVENANTS AND ZONING

Finally, the relationship between restrictive covenants and zoning ordinances should be mentioned. How are conflicts between deed restrictions and zoning ordinances resolved? In Texas the courts will enforce the more limiting of the two. For example, assume that the restrictive covenant limits construction to single-family residences, and the zoning ordinance limits the area to residential construction. A property owner desires to build a fourplex on a lot in the subdivision in compliance with the zoning ordinance. Can he do so? The answer is no. The court would enforce the more restrictive of the two, which in this case is the covenant. The landowner can build only a single-family residence on the lot.

OTHER PRIVATE RESTRICTIONS ON LAND USE

Although restrictive covenants are the most common and comprehensive method of private restrictions on land use, there are a few others that have been discussed in previous chapters. These other private restrictions include the defeasible fees discussed in Chapter 5, the easements discussed in Chapter 8 and the law of trespass discussed in Chapter 2. All of these legal principles can limit land use in some way, but these limitations are generally not as comprehensive as restrictive covenants.

Another legal doctrine that can be used to restrain use of land is the law of nuisance. A *nuisance* is an unreasonable interference by one party with another's use or enjoyment of his or her land. The notion of nuisance is an ancient creation to protect landowners from unfettered and wrongful use of land by a neighbor. It does not require a physical invasion of the complainant's land as does trespass. Such things as noise, dust, vibration and odors may constitute a nuisance. A party who is victimized by a nuisance will be able to get compensatory damages and may be able to enjoin the nuisance. However, a lawsuit involving a claim that a neighbor's use of his or her land is unreasonable can be difficult to win. The court will balance the equities between the parties and determine whether the benefit of the use outweighs the detriment being suffered. The legal principle that favors unrestricted use of land by its owner applies in nuisance suits as well as suits based upon restrictive covenants. An area where the law of nuisance has been used in recent times involves property located near a trash dump or hazardous waste disposal site. Private property owners using the law of nuisance will seek to enjoin a neighbor from using his or her property for the storage of such things as old tires, trash and hazardous chemicals because such use poses an unreasonable threat to their health and potential contamination of their property.

ZONING

Compared to the recognition by law of private restrictions on land use, public restraints are of recent vintage. Comprehensive control of land use is entirely a product of the 20th century. Shortly after the turn of the century, zoning codes began to appear. After a mixed judicial reception among the lower courts, the United States Supreme Court approved the notion of zoning in 1926. The approval was based legally upon the concept of nuisance. Zoning was merely a technique for ensuring that landowners did not unreasonably interfere with each other's use.

Gradually, the emphasis has shifted away from nuisance law and toward a basis in the states' police power. Under the police power the state can regulate land use for the purpose of protecting the public health, safety and welfare. Basing land use regulations on the broad back of the police power opened the door for creative regulation for a multitude of purposes and for the use of numerous control techniques. It ushered in the decade of the 1970s, which has been widely referred to as the era of the "quiet revolution of land use." This term is indicative of the proliferation of land use controls and of the changing character of those controls. Traditional zoning remains a major technique for controlling land use, but it is no longer the only approach. A sampling of the types of land use controls in addition to zoning will be discussed in this chapter.

Introduction to the "Taking" Issue

The state and federal governments, along with their designees, have the power of eminent domain. The federal and state constitutions state that governments may condemn land for a public use provided they give just compensation for it. In contrast, these governments have the power to *regulate* land for a public purpose under the police power, and when regulating they need not pay the restricted landowner. Traditional zoning is an example of a sanctioned form of police power regulation. However, there is a point at which a regulation may go too far and will be treated by a reviewing court as if it were an exercise of the power of eminent domain, or a *taking*. Since this taking was accomplished without the owner being paid just compensation, the regulation will be held to be unconstitutional. In other words, if the government wants to regulate in that fashion, it must use its powers of condemnation and pay the owner for the land.

An example of an ordinance that was held to be invalid was one passed by the city of Austin involving preservation of historic landmarks. In 1974 the city passed an ordinance that allowed the city council to designate buildings, sites and lands in the city as historic landmarks. It created a Historic Landmark Commission that recommended certain property for this designation. Once the property was either recommended for designation or actually designated a historic landmark no changes or repairs could be made to the exterior without approval. The ordinance further provided that upon notice from the city of a need for repairs to maintain the structural soundness of the building, the owner must make the repairs within 90 days. Lastly, the ordinance provided for a penalty in the amount of $200 or less if the owner made any changes or repairs or destroyed the property without compliance with the approval provision.

One of the most notable problems of the ordinance, discussed at length by the court of appeals, was the fact that the ordinance applied not only to designated historic landmarks but also to those recommended by the Historic Landmark Commission. No time limit was placed upon the date of recommendation and the date the city council must act on whether to follow that recommendation. Consequently, a building or area could be forced to comply with the ordinance for an indefinite time without the city council's having approved the designation. The result was very burdensome to property owners whose property was recommended for designation. The owners of the Driskill Hotel found themselves in this position and challenged the constitutionality of the ordinance. The court held that the ordinance created a servitude on the property without any provision for compensation as required by the Texas Constitution. Further, the court stated that the city council had delegated a legislative function to an advisory board without the authority to do so.

It is often said by courts that the rules for ascertaining when a taking occurs are few. Nevertheless one rule that seems pervasive is that the regulation cannot deny owners "all reasonable use" of their land. The certainty of the rule is shaken when one ponders the word *reasonable*. What is reasonable to one person is not to another, and what is reasonable today may not be ten years from now. Use of the word *reasonable* is indicative of the shifting sands of the entire area.

Zoning Codes

A *zoning code* is a comprehensive set of city ordinances that divides the city into zones and restricts land use within each zone to specified purposes. In its simplest form traditional zoning divides the municipality into districts for residential, commercial and industrial uses. Within each of these districts limitations are placed on the size and height of buildings, the siting of the building on the parcel, the density of development in the area, the minimum size of the parcel and perhaps the type of structure permitted on the site. The purchaser of a parcel of land must be aware not only of the restrictions revealed by a title search but also of the limitations placed upon the land by the zoning code.

The power to zone rests with the state as part of its general power to enact laws that promote the general welfare. The states have delegated this power to the cities and towns. In Texas this delegation was accomplished by the passage of article 1011a, Texas Revised Civil Statutes:

> For the purpose of promoting health, safety, morals, and for the protection and preservation of places and areas of historical, cultural or architectural importance and significance, or the general welfare of the community, the legislative bodies of cities, and incorporated villages is hereby empowered to regulate and restrict, the height, number of stories, and size of buildings, and other structures, the percentage of lot that may be occupied, the size of the yards, courts, and other open spaces, the density of population, and the location and use of buildings, structures, and land for trade, industry, residence or other purpose; and in the case of designated places and areas of historic, cultural or architectural importance and significance, to regulate and restrict the construction, alteration, reconstruction or razing of buildings and other structures.

Zoning in Texas is a municipal function. Cities and towns can enact zoning ordinances within their boundaries and can extend the zoning to include their extraterritorial jurisdiction. However, land lying outside this area is not subject to zoning. County governments have not been given the power to zone except in a very restricted situation. If approved by the voters in a county, the county can adopt zoning and building construction ordinances for areas of land surrounding some lakes.

In reviewing challenges made to zoning ordinances, the courts follow the rule that the ordinance is presumed to be valid, and the burden is on the party challenging it to prove its invalidity. The Texas courts have also stated that where reasonable minds could differ over whether a particular zoning or rezoning ordinance is in the interest of the health, safety and welfare of the community they will generally uphold the ordinance. Although the courts presume the validity of zoning ordinances, there are limits. As discussed previously, if a zoning ordinance so severely restricts the uses to which the land can be put and the result is a substantial destruction of its value, the ordinance will be struck down as an unconstitutional taking of property without just compensation.

Nonconforming Use

Most zoning codes are superimposed on partially developed localities. There is no guarantee that all development prior to zoning took place on optimal sites, as seen by the present drafters of the zoning code. These non-conforming uses present a problem. The owners cannot be ordered to discontinue their use immediately unless they are paid full value for the land. To do otherwise would be an unconstitutional taking of their land. The traditional solution was to permit the nonconforming use to continue and hope that it would eventually disappear.

The law regarding nonconforming uses has not left that disappearance purely to chance, however. The nonconforming user cannot enlarge that use. Whether the use has been enlarged will be a question for the fact finder (jury or judge). Similarly, a landowner who discontinues the nonconforming use will not be able to resume it later.

The nonconforming use is said to run with the land and not with the individual owner. The nonconforming user may convey his or her land to another, and the buyer can continue the nonconforming use. If the nonconforming building is substantially destroyed, it cannot be rebuilt in noncompliance.

Despite the precautions taken under the law to encourage the disappearance of nonconforming uses, they do not always fade away. Some localities have taken more direct steps to assure the discontinuance of these nonconforming uses. Ordinances have been passed placing a limit on the length of time the nonconformity will be permitted. So long as the time limitation is reasonable, such ordinances will be upheld by the courts. An important factor in determining reasonableness will be the life expectancy of the building in which the nonconformity is occurring. There are many examples of ordinances limiting the time allowed for nonconformity of advertising signs, but authorities have been reluctant to apply similar time limitations to other structures.

• CASE BRIEF •

Mrs. Gladys Jones owned a lot that was within an area annexed by the city of San Antonio in 1972. On annexation, this lot was zoned R-1, single-family residential. Mrs. Jones operated a sign manufacturing shop on the lot. The zoning ordinances for the city required that owners of land on which a nonconforming use is located must register the use with the city within one year after the territory was annexed. Mrs. Jones did not register her nonconforming use within the one-year period. Mrs. Jones challenged the constitutionality of the ordinance, claiming that it deprived her of property without due process of law. The court held that the registration ordinance was constitutional. The court stated that the purpose of the registration ordinance was to provide the city with knowledge of the nature and extent of nonconforming uses claimed within the city so it could plan for and monitor abandonment of the nonconforming use. *Board of Adjustment of the City of San Antonio v. Nelson*, 577 S.W. 2d. 783 (Tex. Civ. App.—San Antonio 1979).

Zone Change

The apparent inflexibility of the zoning code is mythical in most localities, although the uses permitted in a given zone may be inflexible. Zoning codes can be amended by the city or town, and these amendments are called *zone changes*. As previously mentioned, the zoning code is created to implement a plan—master plan, comprehensive plan or some less specific plan—but none of these plans is intended or can be expected entirely to reflect the future needs for the community. The plan may soon become dated. In addition, some areas of the locality may be zoned not so much for the anticipated use but as a holding zone until more definite decisions can be made. For instance, the northern one-half of a community could be zoned A-1 for agricultural use. The reason for this zoning would not be that this part of the town would be used for agriculture indefinitely, but that since development in the area was years away, the A-1 classification would create a holding zone. This approach would permit the town to postpone its ultimate zoning decision until the time for development was closer and it could better perceive the community needs. In addition, any attempt to use the land for other than agricultural purposes would require a zone change, which would allow the town to monitor closely development in the interim.

The zone change technique is a method for keeping the town's plan current and for reducing the inflexibility of the zoning code. Since the zoning code is legislation, it must be changed by the locality's lawmakers. Although a local government can move to change a zone designation, generally the moving party is a landowner or developer. He or she tries to convince the legislative body that the proposed use makes more sense than the use designated in the locality's plan. When granting a zone change, the city or town must be careful to establish the reasons for the change. The change must be presented as being justified by the current needs of the community. In this way the zone change is assured to be consistent with the notion that the locality is continuing to plan for its land use.

The ability to rezone is certainly necessary for a city to keep pace with a social and economic environment that is constantly changing. However, not all rezoning is constitutionally valid. If the rezoning is classified by the court as spot zoning, then the ordinance will be struck down by the court. *Spot zoning* is the singling out of a relatively small area for preferential treatment or relief from the previous zoning ordinance. In Texas two factors are critical to the determination of whether rezoning is valid. First, does the rezoning comply with the general plan for the community? Second, has there been a change in conditions or circumstances to justify the change? If either of these questions is answered in the negative, then the ordinance will in all probability be found to be spot zoning and invalid. Compare the facts in the two cases that follow. In the first case the court upheld the rezoning. In the second case the court struck it down because it was spot zoning.

• CASE BRIEFS •

The area that was rezoned is a 3.5-acre triangular-shape tract abutting a major east-west thoroughfare in the city of Bedford. In 1967, following the preparation of a land use plan, the city zoned this tract and that adjoining it residential. In 1970 this 3.5-acre tract was rezoned commercial. The land use plan prepared in 1967 recommended that more commercial districts were needed in the city. Between 1968 and 1970 substantially all of the property fronting Harwood Road in the area of the 3.5-acre tract had been rezoned from single-family residential to multiple-family residential or commercial. The court found that the rezoning of the 3.5-acre tract was in conformity with the plan. A plan is not necessarily fixed for all time. The 1967 plan recommended more commercial districts. The city was following that recommendation by gradually altering the uses for which the property fronting on Harwood Road could be used. *Bernard v. City of Bedford*, 593 S.W.2d 809 (Tex. Civ. App.—Forth Worth 1980).

The land rezoned in this case is a 4.1-acre tract at the corner of Crockett Road and Huffsmith Street in the city of Palestine. (Crockett Road is also U.S. Highway 287.) In 1960 the land was zoned residential. The area in which the tract is located contains some of the nicer homes in Palestine. The land is vacant. There are two nonconforming uses in the area. One is a church, and the other is a beauty shop operated from a residence. Both uses predated the 1960 zoning ordinances. The tract in question is surrounded by residences. Crockett Road was in 1960 and still is a heavily traveled highway. There have been three attempts to rezone this 4.1-acre tract to commercial. The court held that the rezoning singled out this particular tract for special treatment, which was not justified by changed circumstances. The rezoning was contrary to a long-established comprehensive plan. The changes in the area were minimal, involving widening of Crockett Road and the installation of commercial streetlights. These changes did not justify the rezoning of this tract of land. *Thompson v. City of Palestine*, 510 S.W.2d 579 (Tex. 1974).

Variance

In contrast to a zone change, a variance is not actually a change in the law. A **variance** is generally a modest deviation from the requirements of the zoning code granted by the city or a board of adjustment to an individual property owner. For instance, a landowner may gain a variance to allow him to set his proposed house back only 25 feet from the street rather than the 30 feet required under the zoning law. His parcel of land would continue to be zoned R-1 as it was before the variance.

Use variances can also be granted. Since they could permit a commercial use in a residential zone, however, they are more destructive to the local plan and are less likely to be granted. Typically, use variances can be granted only by the city council.

No one is entitled to a variance. Many cities have established boards of adjustments to hear petitions for variances and exceptions (to be discussed below). The board of adjustment must follow the guidelines established in the city zoning code regarding the granting of variances. It can authorize a variance only if literal enforcement of the ordinance would result in unnecessary hardship to a property owner. In addition, the granting of the variance cannot be contrary to the public interest and must be such that the purpose of the ordinance is still observed. The board's decision regarding the granting of the variance is usually upheld by the court. However, if the board's act is arbitrary or unjust to a particular property owner, its decision will be set aside by the court. The case that follows illustrates the appropriate use of a variance.

CASE EXCERPT   *Currey v. Kimple,* 577 S.W.2d 508 (Tex. Civ. App.—Texarkana 1978).   RAY, Justice.   This is a suit seeking relief from two variances granted by the Board of Adjustment of the City of Dallas. The variances were granted so that Mr. and Mrs. Louis T. Kimple... could build a tennis court on their residential lot... Mr. and Mrs. Frederick G. Currey, Dr. and Mrs. Heinz F. Eichenwald, and Mr. and Mrs. Edgar C. Hughes instituted suit against Mr. and Mrs. Louis T. Kimple, the City of Dallas, and the Board of Adjustment... seeking prohibitory and mandatory injunctive relief and the setting aside of the order of the Board granting the variances....

The Kimples purchased their lot in 1974 and employed an architect to plan alterations and additions on the land. The architect's plans showed how a tennis court would fit into the improvements, but the architect advised the Kimples that it would be necessary to get a variance from the Board of Adjustment before the tennis court could be constructed....

The evidence before the Board and before the trial court shows that the Kimples sought relief by the variance procedure from the literal application of the front yard and side yard set-back requirements of the city zoning ordinance due to the pie-shaped configuration of their lot. The Board found that the set-back requirements, when applied to the lot configuration, constituted an unnecessary hardship to the Kimple property and thus granted the small variances from the rigid enforcement of the front yard and side yard set-back requirements. The Board had made an on-site investigation and was well aware of the problem involved. Unnecessary hardship must be determined with regard to the facts and circumstances of the particular case. It is the duty of the Board to determine whether literal application of the zoning ordinance to the particular piece of property would be unreasonable in light of the general statutory purpose to secure reasonable zoning. The reasonableness test is viewed in light of the practical difficulty of applying the zoning ordinance to the property in question.... The trial court had before it evidence that the tennis court could not be constructed in 1977 in compliance with the front yard and side yard set-back requirements of the City without encroaching upon structures on the property which were present at the time Kimple acquired the property in 1974....

The Kimples are entitled to use their property to the fullest as it relates to a family dwelling and place for family recreation, limited only by the provisions of valid statutes and ordinances. In this case, Article 1011g(g) specifically authorized the variance procedure utilized by the Board and the City Council has authorized the Board under Division 29-700(j) to grant unnecessary hardship variances from setback requirements due to a parcel's irregular shape....

The judgment of the trial court is affirmed.

Exceptions

The zoning code can provide for special uses, called *exceptions*, that will be permitted even when inconsistent with the designated zone. Frequently, whether or not a particular use constitutes an exception under the zoning code is a question decided by the board of adjustment. Unlike variances or zone changes, exceptions are built right into the zoning ordinance. For instance, an R-1 (residential) zone may permit by exception the construction of a church, school or park within that district. The uses by exception are different from the permitted uses but are considered to be compatible with those uses. No special administrative clearance is necessary. So long as the proposed use coincides with the exception detailed in the zoning code, the landowner will be allowed to construct the excepted use.

Special-Use Permit

A special-use permit is similar to an exception. The zoning code establishes that certain uses of land can be made only under a permit from the city.

It has become common in zoning codes to omit certain uses from any of the zoning classifications. These uses are allowed only by getting a permit, which entails obtaining the approval of local zoning officials. Hospitals, churches, schools, recreational uses such as golf courses and cemeteries are handled in this fashion. Some of these uses may not be offensive in any specific zone, but the permit process retains control for community officials over their location in those situations where they may be objectionable. The special-use permit provides for flexibility in locating these uses for the applicant and maintains public control at the same time.

The special-use permit can be attacked on the basis that it is spot zoning, or unplanned zoning. However, this approach can be distinguished in several ways. Generally, special uses are enumerated as such in the zoning ordinance, giving rise to the notion that they may be appropriate uses in an array of zones, depending on surrounding conditions. Many of the uses are not intrinsically offensive; they are singled out for the special-use permit process so that they can be blended into the community in a planned way. This is the antithesis of spot zoning.

Even where the "permitted use" has greater potential for offending the area residents, such as a cemetery, jail or gas station, the purpose for segregating these uses in the zoning code is to ensure that they are placed on sites consistent with community needs.

Zoning Commissions and Boards of Adjustments

In Texas a city or town can establish two local bodies to assist it in zoning matters. They are zoning commissions and boards of adjustment. These two bodies serve different functions in the zoning area, and some familiarity with each is necessary to an understanding of zoning in Texas.

The *zoning commission* is an investigative body that makes recommendations to the city or town concerning the need for zoning or rezoning of the municipality. (Tex. Rev. Civ. Stat. art. 1011f) It gathers information, holds public hearings and makes written reports to the city council concerning its recommendations. If a zoning commission has been established by the city, all requests for zone changes must be submitted to it prior to consideration by the city council. The city appoints the members of the zoning commission. If a person is dissatisfied with the actions of the zoning commission, he can present his arguments for change to the city council.

Boards of adjustment are quasijudicial bodies that hear and decide petitions for variances, permits and exceptions to the local zoning ordinances. (Tex. Rev. Civ. Stat. art. 1011g) A person seeking an exception, variance or recognition as a nonconforming use applies to the board for a hearing on his or her case. The board hears testimony and decides whether the application should be granted. The decision of the board can be appealed to a district court.

Figure 9.1: SUMMARY OF LEGAL JUSTIFICATIONS FOR ZONING CODE VIOLATIONS

Unconstitutional Zoning Ordinance: A zoning ordinance that so restricts the landowner's right to use the land that it constitutes a "taking" of private property without compensation, which is prohibited by the state and federal constitutions.

Nonconforming Use: Land use that was in existence at the time the zoning code was passed and is inconsistent with the uses permitted in the zoning code.

Variance: A slight deviation from the zoning code granted by the local city or its board of adjustment to the landowner in order to prevent unnecessary hardship to a particular landowner.

Exception: A land use that is generally prohibited in the area but is allowed under the zoning code as a limited exception.

Special-Use Permit: A land use that is prohibited in the city unless a permit from the city or its board of adjustment has been issued.

SPECIAL ZONING ISSUES

Many communities have experienced special problems related to the use of land in their area. Zoning as described so far does not always deal adequately with these problems. This section provides a sampling of some of the special problems communities have encountered in the past and the methods that have been used to solve or alleviate those problems: growth management plans, contract zoning, planned unit developments, flood plain controls and conservation easements.

Growth Management Plans

Growth management plans are strategies devised by a community to control both when and where growth will occur. To date, growth management schemes have been adopted by communities on the fringe of urban and suburban growth. These communities have felt the financial pressures of a rapidly increasing population and have seen their exurban style of life disappearing. They have reacted by trying to monitor future growth closely.

Growth management plans are legal if the scheme meets the criteria of comprehensive preplanning, a rational connection between the reasonable restrictions in the plan and the public welfare–based goal of the scheme and a provision for low-income residential units where they are needed. The ultimate goal can be to maintain the existing character of the community or even to limit ultimate community growth, although the exact interpretation of these principles will have to evolve over time. It should be noted that only a small number of states have made any pronouncement on growth management schemes; therefore, we do not have assurance of their national acceptance at this time.

Contract Zoning

Contract zoning is a highly controversial concept. Under this approach the legislative body reviewing the zone change request may seek to obtain a contractual agreement from the developer that it will build in accordance with specifications more stringent than those required in the zoning code; for example, it may mandate a comprehensive landscaping plan for building and parking areas and less surface coverage by construction than allowed by the ordinance. The zoning contract provides the decision maker with needed flexibility; if not abused, it can serve the community welfare. Contract zoning is an unconstitutional delegation of a legislative function. Consequently, it is prohibited in Texas.

Planned Unit Development (PUD)

The *planned unit development* can be loosely defined as a development that is larger than the traditional subdivision, permits mixed uses within the development and attempts to provide a maximum amount of land for open space. This definition of a PUD is necessarily vague. As it has evolved, the PUD has become many things. It is a term used to describe a development that clusters houses on undersized lots in order to provide more open space to the residents. The term is used to depict a development that permits various types of housing within the same tract, such as townhouses, apartments and single-family housing. In another community it may be flexible enough to allow mixed uses, such as residential, commercial and even light industry (such as warehouses). Some zoning maps designate areas of the community as PUD zones, while other communities adopt a *floating-zone* concept in which the PUD becomes affixed to a particular land area when an appropriate proposal for mixed use is made to the community officials. Whichever cloak PUD wears, it provides the land use decision maker with additional flexibility in planning for growth within the community.

The original PUD concept was intended to provide for large-scale, relatively self-sufficient development on the order of a new town. A large PUD has the potential for creating an integrated community. It provides for generous quantities of open space in exchange for an increase in density in the living areas, with total density remaining the same. Since the size of the project necessitates development over several years, it permits medium-range community planning, with continuous updating through the section-by-section approvals. Where integrated multiple uses are permitted, it can provide for more proximity between residents and services and for a reduction in car miles and energy consumed. Since areas outside the extra-territorial jurisdiction of a city or town are usually not amenable to zoning by the county government, PUDs can be a useful tool for developing a community in an orderly fashion.

Floodplains

Floodplains simply refers to areas near waterways that are prone to flooding. Human beings have always tended to settle near streams, lakes and other bodies of water. The body of water provided a drinking supply, fishing and a convenient means of transportation. The first permanent settlements were made with a wary eye towards the ravages that a flood-swollen stream could cause. High, sheltered places near the water were favored over lower-lying areas that were more susceptible to flooding.

People slowly seemed to lose this sensitivity to the forces of nature. Settlements became more numerous in low-lying, flood-prone river valleys. Floods were either tolerated or, in more recent history, controlled by capital construction projects for dams, levees and dikes that alleviated the problem. In recent years it has become clear that, although dams and dikes may postpone or prevent some floods, sooner or later the dike weakens or the dam is not massive enough to handle a severe storm, and a flood ensues.

The cost of removing people from the floodplains throughout the world is prohibitive. Many people would not be willing to leave even if economic constraints did not prevail. In recent years, governments have undertaken measures to protect those living on the floodplain and to discourage others from building new structures or from repairing flood-damaged structures within the floodplain.

Some communities have used zoning as a method of controlling growth on the floodplain. A "floodplain district" would prohibit the building of new structures or filling or damming within the floodplain. It would prohibit any residential use. The purposes of this type of zoning would be to protect people who might choose to live on the floodplain unaware of the hazards in doing so; to protect those near the floodplain who would be injured by obstructions in the flow of floodwater; and to protect the public at large, who must bear the cost of disaster relief when persons on the floodplains lose their property because of flooding.

Although this zoning trend is aimed at keeping people out of the floodplain, the federal government is involved in protecting its residents. The national flood insurance program makes flood insurance available to landowners in flood-prone communities, where such insurance was previously exorbitantly expensive or simply unavailable. In essence, unless an individual in a flood-prone area has flood insurance, he or she will not be able to get a mortgage from the bank. If a community does not participate in the flood insurance program, federal aid or loans for use within the federally described flood hazard area will not be made available. An additional regulatory hook in the system is that a community must agree to establish land use controls for the flood-prone area before it is able to participate in the insurance program. In short, insurance will replace disaster relief in some measure, and new construction on the floodplain will be discouraged.

Conservation Easements

In 1983 the Texas Legislature enacted a law that allows for the creation of conservation easements. (Tex. Nat. Res. Code §183.001) It allows governmental bodies, charitable associations and individuals to create easements for the purpose of protecting or retaining natural, scenic or open-space values of real property. These easements are created in the same manner as any other easement would be created (discussed in Chapter 8). The act also allows for the creation of conservation easements in order to assure the availability of agricultural, forest and recreational land.

BUILDING CODES AND SUBDIVISION REGULATION

Two other areas of public regulation that impact land use within cities and towns in Texas should be mentioned. These are approval of plats by the city planning commission and compliance with the city building code. Plats and replats must conform to the general plan of the city. In addition, the city can promulgate standards based upon capacities of sewer and water mains, public utilities and general health, safety and welfare considerations. A plat or replat must be in compliance with these standards. Consequently, even a city that has not enacted a comprehensive zoning scheme can exercise some control over development and land use by its power to approve or disapprove plats and replats. As explained earlier, plats must be recorded for any subdivision within five miles of a city or town. No plat can be recorded unless it has been approved by the city planning commission. Furthermore, no building permits can be issued without approval of the plat.

Building codes were enacted by cities as part of their police power. A building code must have a reasonable basis and be uniform in its application. Although building codes are limited in nature; they can provide some control over land development and use. Through its building code the city can establish setback lines, side-lot lines, electrical and plumbing regulations and fire safety regulations. The city has the right to inspect and enforce its building code. It can require that a permit be obtained prior to construction and can halt construction if there is a violation of the code.

FEDERAL REGULATION OF LAND USE

Since the 1970s the federal government has become actively involved in land use regulation. Many of these laws are environmental protection laws. Others were passed to protect the consumer in the interstate sale of resort property. A few of these laws are discussed below. These laws have had and will continue to have a significant impact on land use and land value.

National Environmental Policy Act

The *National Environmental Policy Act* (NEPA) was enacted in 1969 and mandates that all federal agencies prepare environmental impact statements (EIS) for all actions that could have a significant effect on the quality of human environment. The EIS must include a discussion of the total environmental impact, the unavoidable adverse impacts, alternatives to the proposal, long-term as well as short-term effects of the action and any irretrievable commitment of resources. The EIS is a document that is supposed to gather the relevant environmental data and analyze it so that the administrator or the decision-making agency has a reasonably full understanding of the environmental consequences of the proposed action.

Clean Air Act

The purpose of the *Clean Air Act* is to cleanse, maintain and enhance the quality of the nation's air resource. The Clear Air Act of 1970, as amended, mandates that the Environmental Protection Agency (EPA) control pollutants that are harmful to public health and welfare. The EPA gathers together the full body of relevant information on a known harmful substance and issues what is known as a *criteria document.* Based on this document, the EPA then promulgates National Ambient Air Quality Standards for each "criteria pollutant." There are at present six criteria pollutants. Responsibility then shifts to the individual states to prepare state implementation plans (SIPs) for meeting the national standards within each designated air shed in the state. The state has three years after the approval of its SIP to meet health-related standards (primary) and a reasonable time to meet the welfare-related standards (secondary). It should be noted that the 1977 amendments to the act altered this time frame for the criteria pollutants that were originally listed by the federal government.

If the air quality in a specific region exceeds or is near the national standard, the state in its SIP will have to take affirmative measures to ensure that the standard is met and maintained. In order to accomplish this goal, an array of measures is available to the state and individual source of pollution. Emission-control devices have primacy under the statute, but taller stacks or heating-stack gases are permitted to be used in a limited way under the law. The statute provides as well for the use of transportation controls in order to meet national standards.

Clean Water Act

The purpose of the **Clean Water Act** (formerly the Federal Water Pollution Control Act) is to cleanse, maintain and enhance the quality of the nation's water resources. The water pollution statute of 1972, as amended provided that water bodies are no longer considered appropriate vehicles for getting rid of wastes.

The law uses effluent standards, or technology-based standards, along with water quality standards as the mechanisms for cleansing the nation's waterways from point sources of pollution. Point sources are those using a discrete conduit (a pipe) for their wastes. Industries were to adopt "best practicable technology" by 1977 and "best available technology" by 1983 as effluent standards. Some alteration of these dates can result from the 1977 amendments. The state will determine what use it wants to make of the stream or section of the stream (for example, trout fishing) and promulgate water quality standards for propagating that use. A point source of water pollution will have to adopt the stricter of the two standards.

The effluent standards will not have a direct effect on land use, as they only designate the technology that must be adopted by a new industrial pollution source. However, the water quality standard, which concerns itself with the quality of the ambient water, may be a deterrent to the location of water pollution sources. Industrial sources will have to be relatively clean in order to locate on a stream whose use is designated for drinking water or swimming. Others will be forced to locate on streams with lower water quality requirements.

Federal Interstate Land Sales Full Disclosure Act

The **Federal Interstate Land Sales Full Disclosure Act** is intended to protect residential land purchasers from unscrupulous sellers. This statute was an attempt to protect the increasing number of people, many at retirement age, who decided to seek homes in warmer climates. The industry that grew up to provide lots or homes, or both, for these people, who were often

Figure 9.2: **LAND USE CONTROLS**

Private:

Restrictive Covenants: Grantor creates limitations on the use of the land for the benefit of a group of landowners in a particular area, the violation of which is a breach of contract and can be enjoined.

Defeasible Fees: Grantor can create as a condition of ownership a limitation on use, the violation of which can result in a forfeiture of the estate.

Easements: Owner of the easement has a limited right of use in the servient estate, and owner of the servient estate cannot use it in a way that will interfere with the easement.

Trespass: Landowner cannot use his or her land in a way that would physically encroach on neighboring land without permission.

Nuisance: Landowner cannot use his or her land in a way that would unreasonably interfere with a neighbor's use and enjoyment of his or her land.

Public:

Zoning: A comprehensive set of laws enacted by a city or town that limits land use by sectors of the city.

Planned Unit Developments: A large development that mixes land use but segregates uses within the confines of the development.

Building Codes: A set of laws passed by local governments that regulate construction.

Plats: Drawings of land developments that show location and use and must be approved by the local government.

Environmental Legislation: Laws are passed by various levels of government for the purpose of preserving and protecting land as a resource.

---

thousands of miles away from their proposed homesites, was not entirely scrupulous. Beautiful brochures showed tree-lined streets, utilities in place and neatly subdivided lots, but the land often turned out to be untouched desert or wetland.

This 1969 law made it illegal for a developer to make use of any means of interstate commerce or the mails to sell or lease subdivision lots unless:

1. a *statement of record* was filed with HUD, fully disclosing information about the subdivision, and

2. a *property report* was provided to the buyer three days prior to signing the contract, which more briefly described the information in the statement of record. It is intended that the property report be read by the buyer prior to entering a contract.

The statute made it unlawful to use any scheme to defraud, to materially misrepresent pertinent information or to engage in any way in a fraudulent and deceitful transaction pertaining to this type of sale or lease.

There are numerous exemptions under the law. It excludes small subdivisions under 25 lots and subdivisions with uniformly large lots of more than 20 acres. The focus of the statute is to protect residential lot buyers who would usually purchase sight unseen, although visiting the site would not negate a buyer's rights. The buyer has several remedies, including voiding the sale and/or getting an administrative suspension of the developer's statement of record where the developer has violated the law. The administrator may seek an injunction whenever it appears that the developer is about to violate or has already violated the law. This statute has provided many potential homebuyers with protection against investing their life savings with dishonest developers.

SUMMARY

An owner has a wide range of rights connected with property. Currently, however, an increasing number of restrictions are placed on land use by both individuals and public agencies. Private restrictions on land use include many types of restrictive covenants and other legal limitations.

Restrictive covenants are usually created by a developer at the time he or she subdivides and begins construction of a subdivision. It can be difficult to amend restrictive covenants because in many cases all the landowners must consent to the amendment. Restrictive covenants are enforceable by any landowner or lienholder who was intended to benefit from the restriction. The courts are very strict in their interpretation of a restrictive covenant. Restrictive covenants can be terminated in a number of ways.

Public restrictions on land use have developed in this century, beginning with the appearance of zoning codes. Zoning is by far the most widespread method for controlling land use. The basic zones are residential, commercial, industrial and agricultural, but often communities have as many as 15 to 20 designated zones. Several bases exist for modifying the zoning regulation even in strictly zoned communities.

There are several exceptions to zoning ordinances. One of the more common is a nonconforming use. A nonconforming use is a use that was in existence at the time the zoning ordinance was enacted that is not in compliance with it. Most communities strive for the elimination of nonconforming uses within a zone. Other exemptions can be issued by boards of adjustment. Boards of adjustment are quasijudicial bodies that determine whether a landowner should receive a variance, a special-use permit or an exception to the zoning code.

Not all land use problems have been solved by traditional zoning. One special problem that has arisen for many communities is rapid growth that exceeds the city's ability to provide services. These cities have devised growth management plans that provide for orderly growth at a rate at which public services can be provided.

A trend that effectively mixes uses in one specific land area is the PUD, or planned unit development. Larger than a typical subdivision, the PUD provided a long-term plan for economic growth in an underused or vacant space. The plan might include various types of residences, stores and banks and perhaps even light industry or warehouses. The developer needs community approval for the plan at the outset and then must seek approval as each successive section is developed. This flexibility enables the builder to react and adapt to a changing marketplace. Unfortunately, it also provides opportunity for an unscrupulous builder to sabotage the plan by changing it frequently.

Subdivision is another popular method of controlling residential growth. Subdivision plans are designed by a builder, architect or developer and must be approved by the local planning authority. A subdivision plan should specify a percentage of land to be dedicated to parks and recreation and should allow for provision of necessary public services.

Cities also can control land use through enforcement of their building codes.

Finally, several federal statutes have been enacted that protect the physical environment. The passage of these laws, such as the Clean Air Act, the National Environmental Policy Act and the Clean Water Act, have substantially increased the role of the federal government in land use control. The federal government also found it necessary to intervene in interstate land sales to protect those purchasing land in another state. This was accomplished by the passage of the Interstate Land Sales Full Disclosure Act.

QUESTIONS AND CASE PROBLEMS

1. Why are courts unfavorably inclined toward restrictive covenants?
2. Describe the methods intrinsic in all zoning codes for retaining flexibilty in land use decision making.
3. Contrast a zone change request with a variance request.
4. Pete Robertson Enterprises, Inc. (PRE) purchased 20 acres of land in Phillietown. Advise them as to the proper action. (a) PRE plans to construct a warehouse on a portion of the parcel. It is zoned A-1 for agricultural use. (b) PRE plans to continue using an office building on the site for that purpose. The office building was constructed prior to adoption of the zoning code. The area is now zoned A-1 for agricultural use. (c) PRE plans to subdivide the parcel for single-family homes. The land is zoned R-1 for single-family homes, with a minimum lot size of one-half acre. According to PRE's sketch plan, three of the 32 lots will be slightly under one-half acre.
5. The town of Preston passed a sign control ordinance. Section 8 of the ordinance stipulated that all existing signs within the town must conform to the sign ordinance within five years from the date of its enactment. Marvin Miller has a large, flashing, nonconforming sign that he does not wish to remove. What arguments should Marvin assert? Would he be successful?
6. Southampton Civic Club sued to enjoin James and Erna Foxworth

from renting a garage apartment to a Rice University student. The civic club alleged that the renting of the apartment was a violation of a restrictive covenant. The restrictive covenant read as follows: "That no part of said property shall ever be used for the purpose of wholesale or retail business. . . .No apartment house or duplex will be permitted in the Addition, the object of this provision being to prohibit multiple housing throughout the entire addition." Will the Foxworth's be enjoined?

7. The Closes and Schoenhals reside in a residential subdivision in Perryton, Texas. Each of their deeds contains a restriction limiting use to residential. In 1959 the Schoenhals converted their garage into a beauty shop. From 1959 to 1964, the Schoenhals granddaughter operated a beauty shop from that converted garage. In 1960 the Closes purchased the house next to the Schoenhals. No lawsuit was filed to enjoin the Schoenhals from operating the beauty shop between 1959 and 1964. In 1964 the Schoenhals ceased the beauty shop operation. Between 1964 and 1969 the beauty shop was not in operation. During this period the Closes made more than $30,000 in improvements to their property. In 1969 the Schoenhals' granddaughter resumed the operation of the beauty shop. The Closes filed suit to enjoin the reopening of the shop. The Schoenhals defend on the grounds that the Closes have waited too long to bring suit. Who will prevail?

8. Mrs. Hunt, a homeowner, sued the city of San Antonio, contesting the validity of an ordinance rezoning two lots. The lots in question were reclassified from "A" to "D" designation. In an "A" district the uses were limited to family dwellings and accessory buildings. In a "D" district the uses included hospitals, clinics, schools, private clubs and apartment houses. Two doctors had requested the reclassification so that they could build a clinic on these two lots. Mrs. Hunt alleged that this was spot zoning. The city claimed that it had validly rezoned the lots pursuant to their police power. The city cited the following changes in the area to support the rezoning ordinance: (1) a parking lot had been built in the northeast corner of San Pedro and Summit catercorner to the lots; (2) a theatre parking lot had been built one block south of the lots; (3) enrollment had increased at the junior high school across San Pedro and to the south of the lots; (4) San Pedro Avenue had been widened to accommodate four lanes of traffic; and (5) traffic had increased on San Pedro Avenue in the vicinity of the lots. Is this spot zoning?

10

Title and Transfer of Title by Deed

TITLE

Title, as used in this chapter, is the totality of rights and obligations possessed by an owner. It is also used to refer to evidence of ownership. Title is one of the elusive concepts in real property law. Thorough understanding of the concept is complicated by at least two factors. First, the term is in general use in a number of different ways, and other terms have similar meanings. Second, concepts such as *estates* and *property* are associated with title, and their meanings sometimes seem to overlap.

Title is a word that has numerous meanings. People often use it in the same sense as ownership. If a real estate salesperson says that "Jane Brown has title to Lone Tree Ranch," that person usually means that Jane Brown is the owner of the ranch.

Sometimes *title* is used to refer not to ownership but to the acts and instruments by which a person becomes an owner. For example, title is transferred or *conveyed* primarily by the *deed,* an instrument that conveys title. The deed is not ownership but the means by which the owner of the land acquires ownership of the property.

People in real estate also use *title* to refer to the documents, records and acts that prove ownership. Two examples are the abstract of title and the title search. An *abstract of title* is a historical summary of the publicly recorded documents that affect title. A *title search* is an examination of these public records.

CASE EXAMPLE

Martin Ziebarth agreed to purchase a home from Keith Olvic. After signing

> the contract, Ziebarth asked his attorney for a title opinion. The attorney reviewed the appropriate records establishing the validity of Olvic's ownership and reported his findings to Ziebarth.
>   Olvic asked his attorney to prepare a deed to the property. The deed, when property executed and delivered, conveyed Olvic's title to Ziebarth.

Most titles are acquired through the voluntary acts of the parties. This fact applies whether the title is acquired by deed or by will. Title also can be acquired by operation of law. When the owner of real property dies without leaving a will, for example, statutes in each state indicate to which heirs the property shall pass. This is referred to as *intestate succession*. Titles acquired by operation of law also include those based upon adverse possession, judicial sale, accretion, escheat and eminent domain. Involuntary transfer is discussed in Chapter 11.

Historical Background

At one time in England real property was conveyed by a symbolic ceremony in which the owner delivered a twig, a stick or a handful of earth from the land to the new owner. The ceremony was known as *livery of seisin*. Ordinarily the ceremony took place before witnesses. If the conveyance was questioned, it was their testimony that established its validity. Although no written document was required, customarily one was prepared to provide additional evidence of what had occurred. The document was known as a *deed of feoffment* and is the forerunner of the modern deed.

In 1677 the English Parliament enacted the Statute of Frauds. This statute required a person wishing to enforce certain types of agreements to produce written evidence of the agreement, signed by the person against whom enforcement was sought. If no written evidence of the agreement existed, the plaintiff could not sue successfully. One transaction that the statute required to be in writing involved the transfer of an interest in real estate. As a result of this and similar legislation, the rule requiring a written document to transfer title to real estate became embedded in English law. When the American colonies became independent, each rapidly adopted this element of English law. As the United States expanded, the new states passed similar legislation. Today in the United States there is no such thing as an oral conveyance of title to real estate. In every state a written document is necessary.

The use of written documents to convey title to real estate led to an increased number of fraudulent transfers. Because of the importance of land, the ancient livery of seisin ceremony with the oral conveyance received a great deal of local publicity. People living in the vicinity of a transfer knew of the change. As written documents replaced livery of seisin, secret transfer could be made more readily. To prevent fraud that might stem from a secret transfer, Parliament passed the Statute of Enrollments. This law made deeds of freehold estates void unless recorded within six months of the transfer. The Statute of Enrollments is the predecessor of the recording acts, which are so important to conveyancing in the United States today.

Each state has legislation establishing a system for recording real property conveyances and encumbrances affecting real property. Proof of title in the United States is almost always based upon these records.

The recording statutes generally provide that conveyances not recorded are void against subsequent purchasers in good faith. Thus the original purchaser's failure to record can result in superior rights to the property going to one who subsequently purchases the same property from the original seller.

CASE EXAMPLE

Frank Kramer, the owner of a parcel of land, conveys it to Ginger Shields. Shields fails to record her deed. Kramer thereafter fraudulently conveys the same parcel to Elaine Simlo, who has no knowledge of the transfer to Shields. Simlo immediately records her deed. As a result her title is superior to that of Shields. The recording laws protect Simlo, the innocent purchaser.

Although recording is important in any real estate transaction, recording is not necessary to pass title. In the previous example, Ginger Shields has title to the parcel as a result of the conveyance from Frank Kramer. As far as Frank and the rest of the world are concerned, she is the owner. If, however, Ginger does not record the deed, and Frank fraudulently conveys to another. Ginger could lose all rights in the property. The recording process is discussed in Chapter 12.

DEED

A *deed* is the legal document that conveys title to real property. It is the primary method of transferring title. Therefore, it is one of the critical documents in the real estate transaction. Although problems involving deeds are ordinarily the concern of the attorney, the real estate professional needs to know the different types of deeds and to be familiar with the formal elements of a deed and the steps required for a deed to be executed properly.

The deed is a two-party instrument. One party, called the *grantor*, conveys real estate to the other party, the *grantee*. A deed does not have to follow any particular form to be valid. Any written document containing the few essential elements will be effective. Most states have adopted statutory forms for the different types of deeds. The statutory forms are almost always short, often a single page, and all the essentials are included. Although the statutory form is acceptable for all transactions, lawyers generally prepare a longer, more formal document.

In Texas the statutory form is found in §5.022 of the Texas Property Code, which reads as follows:

(a) The following form or a form that is the same in substance conveys a fee simple estate in real property with a covenant of general warranty:

The State of Texas,

County of _____.

Know all men by these presents, That I, _____

_____, of the

_____ [give name of city, town, or county], in the state aforesaid, for and in consideration of _____ dollars, to me in hand paid by _____, have granted, sold, and conveyed, and by these presents do grant, sell, and convey unto the said _____, of the

_____ [give name of city, town or county], in the state of _____, all that certain _____ [describe premises]. To have and to hold the above described premises together with all and singular the rights and appurtenances thereto in any wise belonging, unto the said _____, his heirs, or assigns forever. And I do hereby bind myself, my heirs, executors, and administrators to warrant and forever defend all and singular the said premises unto the said _____, his heirs, and assigns, against every person whomsoever, lawfully claiming to or claim the same, or any part thereof.

Witness my hand, this _____ day of _____, A.D. 19_____.

Signed and delivered in the presence of _____.

(b) A covenant of warranty is not required in a conveyance.

(c) The parties to a conveyance may insert any clause or use any form not in contravention of law.

Notice that the statutory form is written to convey a fee simple interest with the covenant of warranty. Consequently, this form would not be suitable for a conveyance of a lesser estate or a transfer without warranty.

Essential Elements of Deeds

A deed is a complicated instrument that should be drafted by an attorney. A properly drafted and executed deed is critical to any real estate sale. Errors in a deed can cause problems not only for the current owner but also for future generations of owners. Sale of the property, financing and even occupancy can be affected by errors that seem inconsequential. In order to help prevent these errors, the real estate salesperson needs some knowledge of the basic requirements of a valid deed. Since the deed should be drafted by an attorney, the salesperson's knowledge need not be extensive, but it should be sufficient to recognize potential problems. With this background the salesperson should be able to alert the drafter on issues that might lead to errors in the deed.

The minimum general requirements for an instrument to qualify as a deed are that it must (1) be in writing, (2) name the grantor and grantee, (3) contain a description of the property sufficient to identify it, (4) contain words of conveyance, (5) be signed by the grantor or his or her properly authorized agent and (6) be delivered to the grantee or his or her agent.

An instrument that fails to meet these minimum requirements will not convey title. In Texas, if an instrument was intended to convey title but does not, the document will be treated as a contract. The parties to the contract can seek its enforcement, and the court can require the grantor to execute a deed that will convey title to the grantee. (Tex. Prop. Code §5.002) A deed is presumed to convey the greatest estate in land that the grantor has. If the grantor is conveying a lesser estate, the deed must be precise and clear on that point. Any conflict in language will be resolved in favor of the greater estate. (Tex. Prop. Code §5.003) If the grantor purports to convey a greater estate in land than he or she actually owns, the deed will be interpreted as conveying whatever interest the grantor may have.

Words of Conveyance

The heart of a deed is the granting clause. A deed must contain words of conveyance sufficient to transfer an estate from one party to another. No particular words are necessary, provided that those used express an intention to convey title. Words customarily used are *grant, convey* and *bargain*. The word *grant* is used widely. A typical granting clause might read as follows: "Grantors...do by these presents grant, bargain, sell, and convey unto the said grantees forever...." "The words *quitclaim* or *release* is commonly found in quitclaim deeds.

A deed without words of conveyance does not transfer title: the courts, however, have been indulgent in interpreting words in order to give a deed effect.

Competent Grantor

To be valid; a deed must have a competent grantor. Any natural person except a minor or a person who lacks mental capacity may convey real estate by deed. Deeds made by minors or incompetents are not void, but they are voidable. *Voidable* means that the minor or incompetent retains the option of either ratifying or disaffirming the deed.

The minor wishing to disaffirm his or her transfer cannot do so until reaching the age of majority. The age of majority in Texas is 18. This should not be confused with the "legal drinking age." In a minority of states the age of majority is 21. Once having reached majority, the minor must institute proceedings to disaffirm within a reasonable time. If this is not done, the right is lost.

CASE EXAMPLE

In November 1948, John Spencer and his sister inherited land from their father. At the time John was a minor. He attained his majority on April 5, 1949. John's sister was of full age at her father's death. In December 1948, John and his sister sold the property to Alpheas MacLoon. Shortly thereafter, MacLoon conveyed part of the property to the Lymon Falls Power Company and the residue to William Hutchins. Three years later the power company commenced substantial improvements on the land. John Spencer attempted to disaffirm. The company's attorney pleaded that Spencer had a right to disaffirm when he reached majority, but the right had been lost because he failed to assert it within a reasonable time.

To cancel a deed for lack of mental capacity, evidence of grantor's incompetency must be clear and convincing. The test of mental capacity to make a deed is the grantor's ability to understand the nature and effect of the act at the time the conveyance is made.

• CASE BRIEF •

On January 11, 1969, Lillie Smith executed a deed conveying ranch land to her daughter-in-law, Faye Smith. At the time the deed was signed Lillie was in the Highland Nursing Home. She was 88 years old and had recently broken her hip. She was forgetful, had a catheter and could not control her bowel movements and sometimes required spoon feeding. She was very upset about her son's death on January 1. On January 21, 1969, she was declared incompetent by the county court. However, there was evidence that she could carry on a conversation and would answer when spoken to. There was evidence that she knew that she had signed the deed to her daughter-in-law. The trial court found that Lillie was competent at the time she executed the deed. The court of appeals upheld this finding. It stated that old age, sickness, distress in mind and body may or may not constitute unsoundness of mind; and unsoundness of mind at another time, prior to or after the making of a deed, may or may not indicate lack of mental capacity at the time of making the deed. The controlling question is the condition of the grantor's mind at the time the deed was executed. *Smith v. Smith*, 607 S.W.2d 617 (Tex. Civ. App.—Waco 1980).

A number of special rules apply to transfers of real property by corporations. The corporate officer who executes a deed must be authorized to do so. This authorization is obtained from the board of directors, which adopts a written resolution permitting the officer to act. In most states, if the corporation sells real estate that is a substantial portion of the corporation's assets, statutes require that the sale be approved by a designated portion of the shareholders, usually two-thirds or more. Nonprofit corporations are often required by statute to obtain approval by a majority of members before selling real estate.

A deed executed by a natural person should indicate the person's marital status, even though failure to include the grantor's marital status does not invalidate the deed. The reason for including reference to marital status is to assist in resolving disputes that may arise at a later time regarding an interest of an unknown spouse. As pointed out earlier, a spouse could have a community property interest or a homestead interest in the land being conveyed. If this interest is not conveyed, then title problems exist for the grantee. For example, in Texas both husband and wife must execute the deed if the property being conveyed is their homestead. This is true even if the property is the separate property of one of the parties. In other states the spouse may have a dower or curtesy interest, which can cause title problems if not addressed at the time the land is conveyed.

Grantee

A deed does not convey title unless it names an existing, identifiable grantee. Of course, few transactions exist in which the grantee does not have legal existence. One example might be a deed that designated an unincorporated association as the grantee. A deed naming this group would be invalid.

Some litigation has involved transactions in which a deed has been executed with the grantee's name left blank. Although this instrument does not pass title, most courts have reasoned that the intended grantee has authority to fill in his or her name. A subsequent conveyance by this person to a bona fide purchaser creates marketable title.

Ordinarily the determination of the proper designation of the grantee is a responsibility of the attorney or other person who drafts the deed. The real estate professional can aid this drafter by informing him or her of unusual circumstances regarding the name or marital status of the grantee or grantor. For example, during negotiations the real estate salesperson may learn of the grantee's use of another name or a variation in spelling.

Legal Description

Problems involving descriptions in deeds are, like those involving designation of the grantee, not primarily the concern of real estate personnel, but of legal personnel. Sales personnel, however, are apt to be aware of boundary controversies, which may result from or indicate description problems. Legal description and controversies involving boundaries are discussed in Chapter 3.

The salesperson who is aware of a boundary or description issue should urge the seller to obtain a resolution before placing property on the market. This will save time and embarrassment as well as prevent hard feelings that arise when the issues come up after agreement is reached.

Descriptions probably cause more litigation than any of the other formal requirements of the deed. Property to be conveyed must be described well enough in the deed to identify it with reasonable certainty. An imperfect description does not render a deed invalid, but the description must accurately depict the land in question. Presumably the grantor intended to convey *something*; the deed will usually be upheld unless the description is so vague or contradictory that the particular land cannot be ascertained.

Signature

To be valid a deed must be signed by the grantor; however, the grantee's signature is unnecessary. Signature may be by the grantor's mark or by any writing the grantor intends as a signature. If a grantor signs by a mark, his or her name should appear near the mark, and the act should be witnessed. By statute the signature must appear at the end of the instrument.

Attestation is the act of witnessing the execution of an instrument and subscribing as a witness. In general, the law does not require witnesses to a grantor's signature to establish a deed's validity. In many states witnessing and attestation are prerequisites to recording. The attesting witness subscribes the document for the purpose of verifying and identifying it. Usually two witnesses are required.

Acknowledgement is the act by which a grantor declares before a duly authorized official that a deed is genuine and executed voluntarily. In Texas, a deed must be either acknowledged or witnessed before it will be accepted for recording. The purpose of acknowledgement is to prevent forgery and fraud. The official witnessing the grantor's signature is charged with determining the grantor's identity. State statutes prescribes the officials before whom an acknowledgment may be made and the general form of the acknowledgment. (Tex. Rev. Civ. Stat. art. 6602) These matters are discussed more fully in Chapter 12. Neither attestation nor acknowledgment is required in order for the deed to be valid and pass title to the real property.

The grantor can authorize an agent to sign a deed on his or her behalf. The agent's authority to perform this on behalf of a grantor must be in writing and is typically created by a document called a *power of attorney*. A **power of attorney** is the general term used to describe a written instrument that authorizes a person, called an *attorney-in-fact*, to act as agent on behalf of another for the purposes set out in the instrument. In a real estate transaction, the parties should use a special or limited power of attorney that specifically authorizes the attorney-in-fact to convey the particular tract of land. The land being conveyed should be described in the power of attorney. Figure 10.1 is an example of a special power of attorney.

Normally, a power of attorney may be revoked at any time. In most cases the death of either the principal or the attorney-in-fact also revokes the power of attorney. The result is that the purchaser taking a deed signed by

Figure 10.1: **POWER OF ATTORNEY**

STATE OF TEXAS   §
COUNTY OF _____   §
 Know all men by these presents, that I, _____ of the City of
_____, County of _____, State of Texas, hereby make, con-
stitute, and appoint _____, my true and lawful attorney in
fact for me and in my name, place and stead, and for my use and benefit:
 I direct and authorize _____ to exercise, do, or perform
any act, right, power, duty, or obligation whatsoever that I now have or may acquire the legal right, power, or capacity to exercise, do, or perform in connection with, arising out of,
or relating to the sale and conveyance of the following real property: _____

To ask, demand, sue for, recover, collect, receive, and hold and possess all such sums
of money, debts, notes, checks, drafts, as are now, or shall hereafter become owned by, or
due, owing, payable, or belonging to me as a result of the sale and conveyance of the
aforesaid real property.
 To lease and to bargain, contract, and agree for the lease or sale, and convey on such
terms and conditions and under such covenants, as said attorney in fact shall deem
proper the real property legally described as follows:

 To sign, endorse, execute, acknowledge, deliver, receive and possess such applications, contracts, agreements, options, leases, mortgages, deeds, assignments, checks,
drafts, notes, or writing of whatever kind and nature as may be necessary or proper in the
exercise of the rights and powers herein granted.
 I grant to my said attorney in fact full power and authority to do and perform all and
every act and thing whatsoever requisite, necessary, and proper to be done in the exercise
of any of the rights and powers herein granted, as fully to all present, with full power of
substitution or revocation, hereby ratifying and confirming all that my said attorney in fact,
or his substitute or substitutes, shall lawfully do or cause to be done by virtue of this power
of attorney and the rights and powers herein granted.
 The rights, powers, and authority of said attorney in fact to exercise any and all of the
rights and powers herein granted shall commence and be in full force and effect from this
day forward, and such rights, powers, and authority shall remain in full force and effect
thereafter until written notice of termination is received by _____
_____.

Dated _____, 19 _____.

The State of Texas   §
County of _____   §
 Before me, the undersigned authority, on this day personally appeared _____
_____, known to me to be the person whose name is subscribed to
the foregoing instrument, and acknowledged to me that he executed the same for the purposes and consideration therein expressed.
 Given under my hand and seal of office on this the _____ day of
_____, 19_____

Notary Public in and for the State of Texas

an attorney-in-fact should be extremely cautious. The power of attorney should not be old, and the purchaser should require evidence that the principal is living. The purchaser should also insist that the power of attorney be recorded. This provides some protection because an unrecorded revocation is ineffective against a recorded power of attorney.

A power of attorney can also be affected by the mental capacity of the grantor. A power of attorney can become ineffective if the grantor is declared incompetent. This problem can be avoided by making the special power of attorney durable. A durable power of attorney is simply one that survives the subsequent incompetency of the grantor. A statement in the power of attorney that states it will not terminate on the future disability or incompetency of the grantor is sufficient.

Consideration

A deed does not have to state a consideration to be valid. The owner of land has the right to convey it as a gift as well as to sell it. Frequently, when this is done, the deed will recite that the land is being conveyed out of love and affection for the grantee.

A deed will usually recite at least a nominal amount of consideration. For example, it will recite that the land is being conveyed for "Ten dollars and other good and valuable consideration." The purpose of the recitation is to provide protection against creditors who may attempt to set aside the conveyance. If creditors can prove that the grantee gave no consideration, they may successfully levy against the property even though ownership has been transferred. The recitation of consideration is also important because the recording process protects only grantees who gave value.

CASE EXAMPLE
Elvis Carter borrowed money from Marilyn Duffy, a close personal friend. As security he gave her a mortgage on a parcel of land that he owned. Duffy did not record the mortgage. Later Carter conveyed the property to Helen Lehmen. The conveyance was a gift, and the deed stated no consideration. When Carter did not repay Duffy, she commenced a foreclosure action. Although her mortgage was not recorded, a court would direct the property be sold since Lehman was not a purchaser for value.

Even the recitation of a nominal consideration is effective. One of the reasons the nominal consideration is so common is that many buyers would prefer the purchase price to remain secret. If a creditor or third party should challenge whether the grantee actually bought the property, the grantee can disclose the full consideration at that time.

Delivery and Acceptance

A deed does not transfer title until delivered by the grantor and accepted by the grantee. Although manual transfer of the instrument is the common method of delivering a deed, manual transfer alone is insufficient to pass title. The grantor must *intend to pass title* and *surrender control of the instrument*. Unless these two components exist, the fact that the grantor has given up physical possession of the deed is of no consequence.

Conversely, even though physical transfer is the generally accepted procedure, delivery can be effective without it. Lord Coke, a noted English jurist of the 17th century, stated that "a deed may be delivered without any act of delivery."

Constructive or implied delivery, which is delivery without change of possession, is valid although rare. As with actual delivery, the essence of constructive delivery is the intention of the parties, not the manual act of transfer. If the grantor by words or acts manifests an intention to divest himself or herself of title and vest it in another, the law determines that delivery is sufficient. This follows, even though the instrument itself (but not control) remains in the hands of the grantor. For example, if a parent conveys title to a minor child, the deed would be delivered to the parent as the natural guardian of the child. Needless to say, proving constructive delivery can be difficult. However, if the parent records the deed, the courts will usually find that it has been constructively delivered.

With the exception of the example given above, delivery is ineffective unless the grantor parts with legal control of the instrument during his or her lifetime. The grantor may not retain the power to recall the deed from either the grantee or from a third party. Once a valid delivery has occurred the deed may, however, remain in the grantor's custody or be returned to the grantor for safekeeping.

A grantor may deposit a deed with a third party to satisfy the legal requirement of delivery. This is an effective delivery if the grantor has surrendered all control over the instrument and is powerless to recall it. A deed delivered to a third party is effective from that time even if the grantor dies or becomes insane before the grantee obtains possession of the instrument.

It is common in closing many real estate sales in Texas to deliver the executed deed to an employee of a title company, called a *closer*. The closer will record the instrument on behalf of the purchaser after all conditions of the earnest money contract have been fulfilled. The recorded deed is then delivered to the purchaser for safekeeping.

TYPES OF DEEDS

Several types of deeds are common in the United States. Ordinarily, in a real estate transaction, the type of deed that the seller will use is agreed upon in the sales contract. This is one of several reasons why each party should consult an attorney before signing the agreement. A seller is bound to furnish the type of deed stipulated by the agreement. Conversely, this is what the buyer must accept, although another type of deed might provide more protection.

All deeds must contain the essential elements discussed previously. Deeds differ from one another by the warranties or covenants contained in the instrument. The most common types of deeds are the general warranty deed, the special warranty deed and the quitclaim deed. In addition, others used in special circumstances include the deed without warranty (in some states this is called a *bargain and sale deed*), the trustee's deed, the sheriff's deed and the mineral deed.

Although standard forms are available for use, the grantor is free to modify the standard forms to include some warranties and exclude others. The language used in the deed determines the warranties that are included. Therefore, the document must be read in its entirety, and headings at the top of a document cannot be relied upon. For example, a document could be entitled "Quitclaim Deed," but if it contains the word *grant* or *convey,* the covenant of seisin and the covenant against encumbrances will be implied.

General Warranty Deed

The **general warranty deed** conveys title and promises the grantee and all subsequent owners that title from the sovereignty to the grantor is good. Figure 10.2 is an example of a general warranty deed. This promise specifically includes four warranties or covenants;

1. the covenant of seisin
2. the covenant against encumbrances
3. the covenant of quiet enjoyment
4. the covenant of warranty.

The first two covenants (seisin and against encumbrances) are implied by the use of the word *grant* or *convey* in the deed. (Tex. Prop. Code §5.023) The last two warranties are derived from the language in the deed by which the grantor promises to "warrant and forever defend the grantee against every person lawfully claiming" an interest in any part of the land.

By *covenant of seisin* the seller guarantees his or her ownership of the property and the existence of a right to convey.

The *covenant against encumbrances* is the seller's assurance that, at the time of conveyance, the property is free of *liens and encumbrances* (to be discussed more fully in Chapter 13). The covenant does not apply to those liens and encumbrances specifically excepted in the deed, because the buyer has agreed to accept them.

The *covenant of quiet enjoyment* and the *covenant of warranty* are very much alike. In both, the seller guarantees that the buyer will not be evicted by someone with a superior title. These covenants are not breached unless the buyer is actually evicted by a third party who has a better title. If this occurs, the buyer can sue the seller for damages.

The acts and persons covered by the covenants are quite extensive. The grantor is promising to protect the grantee from problems that may have arisen even before the grantor owned the land and about which the grantor

Figure 10.2: **WARRANTY DEED**

2251
Prepared by the State Bar of Texas for use by lawyers only
Revised 10-85
© 1985 by the State Bar of Texas

WARRANTY DEED

Date:

Grantor:

Grantor's Mailing Address (including county):

Grantee:

Grantee's Mailing Address (including county):

Consideration:

Property (including any improvements):

Reservations from and Exceptions to Conveyance and Warranty:

Grantor, for the consideration and subject to the reservations from and exceptions to conveyance and warranty, grants, sells, and conveys to Grantee the property, together with all and singular the rights and appurtenances thereto in any wise belonging, to have and hold it to Grantee, Grantee's heirs, executors, administrators, successors, or assigns forever. Grantor binds Grantor and Grantor's heirs, executors, administrators, and successors to warrant and forever defend all and singular the property to Grantee and Grantee's heirs, executors, administrators, successors, and assigns against every person whomsoever lawfully claiming or to claim the same or any part thereof, except as to the reservations from and exceptions to conveyance and warranty.

When the context requires, singular nouns and pronouns include the plural.

This form is reproduced here with the permission of the State Bar of Texas for informational purposes only. Further reproduction is not authorized without permission from the State Bar of Texas.

Figure 10.2 (continued)

(Acknowledgment)

STATE OF TEXAS
COUNTY OF

This instrument was acknowledged before me on the   day of   , 19   .
by

_____
Notary Public, State of Texas
Notary's name (printed):

Notary's commission expires:

(Corporate Acknowledgment)

STATE OF TEXAS
COUNTY OF

This instrument was acknowledged before me on the   day of   , 19   .
by
of
a   corporation, on behalf of said corporation.

_____
Notary Public, State of Texas
Notary's name (printed):

Notary's commission expires:

AFTER RECORDING RETURN TO: PREPARED IN THE LAW OFFICE OF:

was unaware. In addition, the grantor is promising that, with respect to these acts that could have occurred at any time prior to the present conveyance, he or she stands ready to defend not only the present grantee but also the subsequent owners. The following three examples illustrate this coverage.

CASE EXAMPLES

In 1955 the heirs of John Adams sold Blackacre to Kevin Baker. Kevin Baker, unaware that there might be a problem with his title to Blackacre, conveyed it by a general warranty deed to Idie Cross in 1969. Later that year an heir of John Adams, who had not joined in the conveyance to Baker, filed suit against Idie Cross, claiming an interest in Blackacre. If the heir's claim is substantiated, Kevin Baker has breached the covenants set out in the general warranty deed and will be liable to Cross for damages.

Lydia Long conveyed Whiteacre to Heather Peters by a general warranty deed in 1978. At the time of the conveyance Lydia's husband was missing and presumed dead. In order to sell the property she represented that her husband was dead. In 1984 Heather sold Whiteacre to Daniel Johnson. She also conveyed the title by a general warranty deed. In 1985 Lydia's missing husband appeared and asserted his community property interest in Whiteacre. If he substantiates his claim to Whiteacre, Lydia will be liable to Daniel Johnson for damages because the warranties she made to Heather also extend to all subsequent owners of Whiteacre.

King conveys Redacre to York in 1976 by a general warranty deed. York dies in 1982, and his heirs convey Redacre to Milton. In 1984, an illegitimate child of York proves that he is the only heir to York's estate. He files a lawsuit against Milton to recover Redacre. If he wins, Milton will *not* be able to recover any damages from King because the title problem arose after King's conveyance to York and his warranties cover only title problems arising before his conveyance in 1976. Milton's only remedy would be against his grantors, and their liability will depend upon what type of deed was used to convey title.

Covenants in a warranty deed do not assure the buyer that the seller has title. All they do is give the buyer a right to sue if a covenant is broken. Although they provide the buyer with some protection, that protection is limited by many factors. The seller who has made the warranties might become insolvent or leave the jurisdiction. As a result any judgment against the seller might be difficult to obtain or of little value. Because of the limited nature of the protection offered, a buyer should never rely only upon a warranty deed. Additional assurances, such as an attorney's opinion of title or title insurance, should be obtained.

Special Warranty Deed

The ***special warranty deed*** conveys title and provides a limited warranty to the grantee. The warranties described above are restricted. They cover only

Figure 10.3: **SPECIAL WARRANTY DEED**

2251
Prepared by the State Bar of Texas for use by lawyers only
Revised 10-85
© 1985 by the State Bar of Texas

S P E C I A L
WARRANTY DEED

Date:

Grantor:

Grantor's Mailing Address (including county):

Grantee:

Grantee's Mailing Address (including county):

Consideration:

Property (including any improvements):

Reservations from and Exceptions to Conveyance and Warranty:

Grantor, for the consideration and subject to the reservations from and exceptions to conveyance and warranty, grants, sells, and conveys to Grantee the property, together with all and singular the rights and appurtenances thereto in any wise belonging, to have and hold it to Grantee, Grantee's heirs, executors, administrators, successors, or assigns forever. Grantor binds Grantor and Grantor's heirs, executors, administrators, and successors to warrant and forever defend all and singular the property to Grantee and Grantee's heirs, executors, administrators, successors, and assigns against every person whomsoever lawfully claiming or to claim the same or any part thereof, except as to the reservations from and exceptions to conveyance and warranty by, through, and under Grantor but not otherwise.

When the context requires, singular nouns and pronouns include the plural.

This form is reproduced here with the permission of the State Bar of Texas for informational purposes only. Further reproduction is not authorized without permission from the State Bar of Texas.

Figure 10.3 (continued)

(Acknowledgment)

STATE OF TEXAS
COUNTY OF

    This instrument was acknowledged before me on the   day of   , 19   .
by

Notary Public, State of Texas
Notary's name (printed):

Notary's commission expires:

(Corporate Acknowledgment)

STATE OF TEXAS
COUNTY OF

    This instrument was acknowledged before me on the   day of   , 19   .
by
of
a   corporation, on behalf of said corporation.

Notary Public, State of Texas
Notary's name (printed):

Notary's commission expires:

AFTER RECORDING RETURN TO: PREPARED IN THE LAW OFFICE OF:

acts or events that arose during the time that the grantor owned the property and for which the grantor is responsible. The limited warranty coverage does extend to subsequent owners of the property. The special warranty deed is frequently used when one co-owner is conveying his or her interest to another co-owner. For example, if a tenant in common decides to sell his interest to his cotenants, he promises that he has not done anything that would affect the title to the property. Another situation in which the special warranty deed is used is the division of community property upon divorce. In this situation the grantor-spouse is promising that he or she has done nothing during the time he or she had an interest in the property that would affect the title. Figure 10.3 is an example of a special warranty deed.

Quitclaim Deed

Unlike the general or special warranty deed, the **quitclaim deed** does not purport to convey title but instead merely releases whatever interest the grantor has. If the grantor has title, the quitclaim deed conveys that title as effectively as a warranty or bargain and sale deed. A grantee who takes title by a quitclaim deed does not acquire any of the covenants that are given to a grantee accepting a warranty deed. If the contract does not mention the type of deed to be used, many states permit the seller to give a quitclaim deed.

The quitclaim deed is commonly used to clear a *defective* title. The defect could range from an incorrect description in a prior deed to an outstanding lien, a recorded easement, a recorded sales contract that failed to close or the release of a homestead right. Figure 10.4 is an example of a quitclaim deed.

CASE EXAMPLE

Martin Russo bought a tract of land in 1981 while he was single. In 1983 Martin married Jane. Two months after their marriage they decided to sell the land and move to another city. Martin contracted to sell the land to George and Kate Wilson. Even though Jane lived on the land for only two months, she could have a homestead claim to it. At closing, the Wilsons should insist that Jane sign a quitclaim deed releasing whatever interest she might have in the property.

Deeds Used in Special Circumstances

Another type of deed that is occasionally used in Texas is the **deed without warranty.** In some states this is called a *bargain and sale deed.* This deed contains none of the covenants found in a general or special warranty deed but differs from the quitclaim deed because it does purport to convey title. The grantor represents that he or she has an interest in the land but does not warrant the quality of that title. Consequently, it provides a benefit to the grantee not found in the quitclaim deed. It also can be relied upon by subsequent grantees. This is discussed in more detail in Chapter 12.

Figure 10.4: QUITCLAIM DEED

2250
Prepared by the State Bar of Texas for use by lawyers only.
Revised 10-85.
© 1985 by the State Bar of Texas

QUITCLAIM DEED

Date:

Grantor:

Grantor's Mailing Address (including county):

Grantee:

Grantee's Mailing Address (including county):

Consideration:

Property (including any improvements):

For the consideration Grantor quitclaims to Grantee all of Grantor's right, title, and interest in and to the property, to have and to hold it to Grantee, Grantee's heirs, executors, administrators, successors, or assigns forever. Neither Grantor nor Grantor's heirs, executors, administrators, successors, or assigns shall have, claim, or demand any right or title to the property or any part of it.

When the context requires, singular nouns and pronouns include the plural.

Figure 10.4 (continued)

(Acknowledgment)

STATE OF TEXAS
COUNTY OF

    This instrument was acknowledged before me on the   day of   , 19   .
by

_____
Notary Public, State of Texas
Notary's name (printed):

Notary's commission expires:

(Corporate Acknowledgment)

STATE OF TEXAS
COUNTY OF

    This instrument was acknowledged before me on the   day of   , 19   .
by
of
a   corporation, on behalf of said corporation.

_____
Notary Public, State of Texas
Notary's name (printed):

Notary's commission expires:

AFTER RECORDING RETURN TO: PREPARED IN THE LAW OFFICE OF:

Important variations on the deed without warranty are deeds that are generally described as fiduciary deeds. More specifically these include conveyances by administrators of estates, sheriffs and trustees. A *fiduciary* is a person who has been placed by law in a position of trust regarding property that is not his or her own—for example, the administrator or executor of a decedent's estate. The fiduciary might need to convey title to the decedent's real property but would not want to make guarantees or warranties concerning the title. A special form of deed similar to the bargain and sale deed will be used. The fiduciary guarantees only that he or she has been properly appointed and authorized to sell and convey. The deed does not make any other warranties.

The ***trustees's deed*** is the deed used to convey property that has been sold under a power of sale. Power of sale is the right to foreclose a lien against real property without a court order when there has been a default in the mortgage. This right is created in a document called a *deed of trust*. Deeds of trust and foreclosure are discussed in Chapters 21 and 22. A trustee's deed conveys title to the purchaser at the foreclosure sale. The trustee's deed warrants that the proper procedure for foreclosure and sale has been followed but contains no other warranties as to title.

A ***sheriff's deed*** is the deed to convey title when real property has been ordered sold by a court through the sheriff's office. The court can order real property that is not the owner's homestead sold to satisfy judgment debts. The court can also order real property sold to satisfy the mortgage debt against the property or some other type of lien, such as a tax lien. The sheriff's deed will recite the reason for the sale and the court order authorizing the sale.

A ***mineral deed*** is a deed that conveys only the mineral estate to the grantee. This deed was discussed in Chapter 2.

LIMITATION OF LAND USE

In addition to passing title, a deed may be used to regulate land use. This is accomplished through a condition in the instrument or through a covenant. Conditions must be included in the deed; covenants usually are, but a valid covenant may be created by an ancillary document.

Chapter 5 discussed the use of conditions to limit the use of an estate by creating an estate in land called a *defeasible fee* (fee simple determinable, fee simple on a condition subsequent and fee simple subject to an executory interest). That chapter indicated that, when a condition in a deed is fulfilled, the owner's estate is subject to termination. In some instances, depending upon the wording of the condition, termination is automatic; in others termination depends upon some action being taken by the person holding the reversionary interest.

As discussed in the previous chapter, restrictive covenants can also be included in a deed. A restrictive covenant limits the uses that may be made of the property, such as the type or location of buildings that may be erected upon it. See the previous chapter for a complete explanation of the creation, enforcement and termination of restrictive covenants.

Although both a covenant and a condition limit land use, the legal effects of the two differ. When a condition is fulfilled, the owner's interest is subject to termination. When a covenant is broken, the owner may be sued for damages or enjoined from breaking the contract, but the owner does not lose title to the property.

SUMMARY

In modern usage, *title* has many meanings. In real estate, the term refers to the totality of rights and obligations an owner possesses in the real estate, as well as the written record that is evidence of ownership. This official recording is crucial to the transfer of real estate in the United States today.

The deed is the legal instrument that conveys title when real property is bought and sold. As each sale occurs, the transfer is officially recorded, adding to the chain of title. The real estate professional needs to be familiar with state statutes concerning recording and with the various types of deeds.

The deed is such an important legal instrument that it should be drafted by an attorney. Errors in the written document can cause problems in the title for future generations. It is beneficial for real estate salespeople to know the elements necessary to create a valid deed. These requirements include words of conveyance that express the intention to convey title from one party (the grantor) to another (the grantee), a competent grantor and an identifiable grantee. The deed must contain a legal description of the property. It must be signed by the grantor or an authorized representative. Most deeds also state a consideration, and a deed can be challenged in court if no consideration has been given. Finally, delivery and acceptance must be demonstrated for a deed to be valid. One means for delivery to take place is by escrow; that is, the money payment and/or the document may be held by a third party until all conditions are met.

Several different types of deeds are used in Texas. The most common are the general warranty deed, the special warranty deed and the quitclaim deed. The general warranty deed contains four warranties. These covenants in general guarantee that the owner has the right to sell, that the property is free of liens or the claims of creditors and that the buyer will not be ousted by someone with superior title (a prior claim). If any of these covenants is broken, the buyer can recover damages from the seller. In practice, however, it is often difficult to collect such a judgment, so the buyer should instigate his or her own title search.

In the special warranty deed the grantor limits the warranties to actions that occurred during the time he or she owned the property. Finally, the quitclaim deed is a relinquishment of whatever rights the grantor may have in the property without any warranties of title. Other deeds are used to convey title to real property. Since no particular form is required, it is important to read the entire document to determine whether or not title is conveyed and if any warranties are made. The use of the word *grant* or *convey* implies the covenant of seisin and the covenant against encumbrances.

On occasion a deed is also used to limit the use to which land will be put. These restrictions or covenants usually appear in writing in the deed. If worded properly, these provisions run with the land and are difficult or impossible to terminate.

QUESTIONS AND CASE PROBLEMS

1. In Texas what covenants are implied from the words *grant* or *convey* in a deed?
2. Explain the difference between (a) a *general warranty deed* and a *special warranty deed* and (b) *deed without warranty* and a *quitclaim deed*.
3. Explain the assurances provided by a grantee by (a) covenant of seisin and (b) covenant of quiet enjoyment.
4. On March 7, Marlin Martin, who was very ill, executed a deed to his son Bill. Martin gave the instrument to Dr. Blaine, stating, "Take this deed and keep it. If I get well, I will call for it. If I don't, give it to Billy." On March 12 Martin died. Dr. Blaine delivered the deed as instructed. The grantee had it recorded. The grantee's sister claims the deed is ineffective. Is she correct? Discuss.
5. Dunlap owned a large farm, which he worked for many years with his son Sam. Dunlap had a daughter, Celeste, who lived in the city. Dunlap had often told Sam, Celeste and various relatives that Sam was to inherit the farm; nevertheless, nothing was ever done to ensure that it would happen. As Dunlap aged, he became senile and difficult to live with, but in lucid moments he talked about Sam's inheriting the farm. Because Sam knew that his father had no will, Sam had a deed prepared conveying the property to himself. Dunlap signed the deed. The execution of the instrument was done properly, according to state law. Two years later Dunlap died and Sam had the deed recorded. Celeste has sued to have the deed declared invalid. Will she be successful? Discuss.
6. On October 20, 1941, Edward Strawbridge executed and recorded the following instrument:

> State of Texas, County of Matagorda, know all men by these presents that I, Edward Strawbridge, of Escambia County, Florida, for and in consideration of One ($1.00) and other good and valuable considerations to me in hand paid by Ethel Strawbridge of the

City of Pensacola, Escambia County, Florida, that certain property described as follows:
[Here follows a sufficient description of the land involved in this suit.]
To have and to hold the above described property, together with all and singular the rights and appurtenances thereunto in anywise belonging unto the said
Ethel Strawbridge, her heirs or assigns forever.

The heirs of Edward Strawbridge challenged the conveyances, claiming
that the instrument was void because it did not contain any language
"granting" the property to Ethel. Does the conveyance fail because the instrument fails to contain a "granting" clause?

11

Inheritance and Involuntary Transfers

The transfer of real estate by deed is only one method by which title to property changes. Another very common occurrence is the transfer of ownership upon death. Upon an individual's death all of his or her property, real and personal, will pass either to those persons named in a will or, if none, to those persons deemed to be his or her heirs-at-law by state statute. In addition, there are transfers that take place against the owner's wishes. These involuntary transfers can occur due to foreclosure or condemnation, to name two circumstances. Although less common, involuntary transfers must be considered in determining land ownership. This chapter discusses transfers upon death, adverse possession, eminent domain and escheat and some transfers that result from natural forces. Transfers by foreclosure or judicial sales will be discussed in later chapters.

TRANSFERS BY INTESTACY

Upon an owner's death, title to land is commonly transferred by will. If the owner dies intestate, or without providing a will, title is transferred through the operation of a *statute of descent.*

CASE EXAMPLE

Henri DiMond, a bachelor, owned land in Waco, Texas. Henri's parents were dead. He did, however, have a brother Gene, who lived in Atlanta. Henri had no other close relatives. When Henri died without leaving a will, title to the Waco land passed to Gene DiMond.

A person such as Henri, who dies without leaving a will, is said to die *in-testate*; his property passes to his heirs according to laws of intestate succession, often referred to as *laws of inheritance*. Title so acquired is called *title by descent*. Since title to land is governed by the laws of the state in which it lies, intestate succession is determined by that state's laws. The details of these laws differ from one state to another. Because of the influence of English law, however, a common pattern of descent exists in the United States. Gene DiMond became the owner of the Waco land according to the Texas statute indicating those persons who are a decedent's heirs.

Laws of Inheritance

The general philosophy underlying the laws of inheritance is that property should descend to those persons the intestate individual probably would want to own it. If the decedent expressed no preference by executing a will, society assumes that he or she would want the property to go to those closely related by blood or marriage. In effect the state has written a will for the decedent. Unfortunately, the state's "will" may or may not reflect the desires of the decedent. Nevertheless, laws of inheritance benefit society at large by keeping property within the family and thereby preserving and protecting that important institution.

Per Stirpes and Per Capita Distinguished

Per stirpes is the distribution of an intestate's property to persons who take the share allocated to a deceased ancestor. A difficult question of fundamental fairness arises when a child who has children of his or her own dies before a parent. When the grandparent dies, should the surviving grandchildren share equally with their aunts and uncles, or are they entitled only to the share of the deceased parent?

> #### CASE EXAMPLE
> Trent Hightower died intestate. His wife had predeceased him by many years. They had three children: Stephanie, Joseph and Douglas. Stephanie and Joseph survived their father, but Douglas died before him. Douglas, however, left three children of his own: Trent, Jr., Eliza and Anne. Trent Hightower's estate was divided in thirds, with one-third going to Stephanie, one-third to Joseph and one-third to the children of Douglas. This allocation is *per stirpes* distribution.

Per Capita is the distribution of an intestate's property to persons who take equal shares as members of a class. State statutes generally establish the categories of person who will inherit upon death. The first category is typically the children of the decedent. If there are no children, then it usually passes to grandchildren. Per capita distribution means that if a person is a member of the class, he or she will share equally in the decedent's property with all other members of the same class.

CASE EXAMPLE

Mildred dies intestate. Her husband has predeceased her several years prior. At her death all five of her children were still living. The state plan for intestacy provided that all of her property shall pass to her children. Each child as a member of the class of persons who take upon intestacy will take an equal share, a per capita distribution.

Many state laws allow only per stirpes distribution if the heirs belong to different classes. If all of the heirs are members of the same class, they will share per capita. This is the case in Texas. Under the Texas plan the property of a decedent who is not survived by a spouse passes to his or her children and their lineal descendants. If the decedent is survived by two children and the three grandchildren of a deceased child (similar to the first case example), then the distribution is per stirpes. However, if none of the decedent's children survive him, then all of his grandchildren share per capita since all the heirs are members of the same class. (Tex. Prob. Code §43)

The Texas Plan of Descent and Distribution

Laws of descent and distribution are always complex and frequently confusing. It is important to remember two factors in the overall scheme for intestate succession in Texas. First, Texas is a community property law state. Consequently, the descent and distribution statute contains two plans: one that deals with community property and one that deals with separate property. Second, the descent and distribution statute is designed to provide for the children or lineal descendants of a decedent. This bias is so great that, even if the decedent is survived by a spouse who is also the parent of his or her children, the law decrees that the bulk of the decedent's estate will pass to the children. This can produce a financial hardship on the surviving spouse, particularly when the children are minors. Although several attempts have been make to amend this statute, none have been successful.

Upon death, the estate of a decedent immediately vests in his or her heirs-at-law. This is the case even when the heirs are unknown or cannot be located. The inherited property is subject to the debts of the decedent. This means that creditors must be paid in full, even if accomplishing that requires the sale of all of the decedent's estate. Assuming there is property remaining after the debts have been settled, there will be a hearing to determine the heirs of the decedent. The court will follow the order for descent and distribution set out in the law. The order of distribution is laid out in the charts that follow. Figure 11.1 shows the distribution of the estate of a decedent who is survived by a spouse. It includes both separate and community property. Figure 11.2 shows the distribution of the estate of a decedent who was not survived by a spouse. In this case there is no need to distinguish between separate and community property. (Tex. Prob. Code §§38 and 45).

FIGURE 11.1: **INTESTATE SUCCESSION: DECEDENT SURVIVED BY SPOUSE**

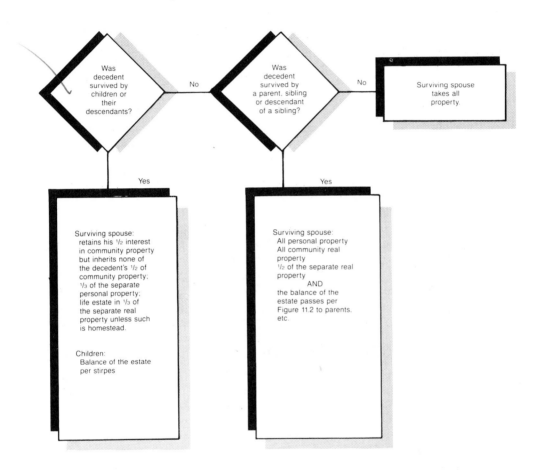

Was decedent survived by children or their descendants? — No → Was decedent survived by a parent, sibling or descendant of a sibling? — No → Surviving spouse takes all property.

Yes ↓

Surviving spouse:
retains his 1/2 interest in community property but inherits none of the decedent's 1/2 of community property; 1/3 of the separate personal property; life estate in 1/3 of the separate real property unless such is homestead.

Children:
Balance of the estate per stirpes

Yes ↓

Surviving spouse:
All personal property
All community real property
1/2 of the separate real property
AND
the balance of the estate passes per Figure 11.2 to parents. etc.

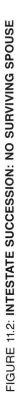
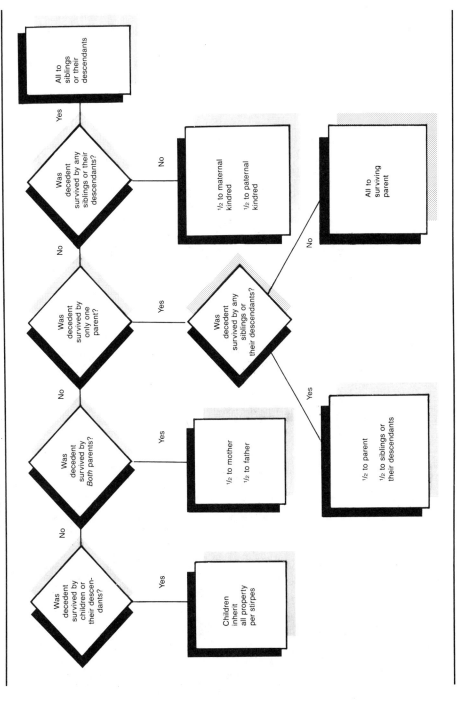

FIGURE 11.2: INTESTATE SUCCESSION: NO SURVIVING SPOUSE

A third situation that can arise creates some special problems. This is the problem of the simultaneous death of both spouses. By law in Texas a husband and wife are considered to have died simultaneously if their deaths occur within 120 hours of each other. There is no need to determine who died first. If the deaths fall within this time period, each is held to have survived the other, with the result that one-half of the community property passes through the husband's estate and the other half passes through the wife's estate. (Tex. Prob. Code §47)

CASE EXAMPLE

Sandra and her husband, Ernest Davis, were in a car accident. Sandra was killed instantly, and Ernest died the next day in the hospital. Neither Sandra or Ernest had a will. Sandra is survived by a brother. Ernest is survived by his parents. One-half of their community property passes to Sandra's brother, and the other half passes to Ernest's parents. If the simultaneous death statute did not exist, Sandra's share of the community property would have passed to Ernest since he survived her. Upon Ernest's death the next day, all of the estate would have passed to his parents.

TRANSFERS BY WILL

The conveyance of title to real property by will is called a **devise.** The conveyance is a form of gift that takes effect only upon the maker's death and is revocable during his or her lifetime. A person who makes a will is called a *testator* (or *testatrix*, if female). If the will is operative when the person dies, the person is said to have died *testate.* A person to whom real property is given by will is referred to as a *devisee.* Technically, a gift of personal property by will is a *bequest.* In reference to a bequest of money, the term *legacy* is often used; the receiver of the bequest is the *legatee.*

Proof of Death

It is axiomatic that neither a will nor an inheritance statute is operative until a property owner dies. Ordinarily, the occurrence and time of death are easy to determine, but problems arise in at least two instances. One instance is a disaster in which several closely related people die at approximately the same time; another is a situation in which a property owner has been missing for an extensive period.

Many wills solve the problem of determining who dies first in a common disaster by a provision in the instrument.

CASE EXAMPLE

Lance Beck and his wife Hilda were killed in a common disaster. Because of the nature of the accident, determining which one had died first was impossible. Lance's will left all his property to his wife if she survived him. If she did not, his estate was to go to his parents and to charity.

Lance's will contained the following provision. "In the event my wife and I shall die under such circumstances that there is insufficient evidence to determine the survivor, it shall be conclusively presumed that I survived her." As a result of this provision, the estate went to Lance's parents and the charities that he had named, not into his wife's estate.

As previously mentioned, Texas, like most other states, has enacted a law that deals with simultaneous deaths. If the decedent's will does not contain a provision regarding survival, then the simultaneous death law will apply.

States also solve by statute the problem caused by a missing owner. In most states and in Texas a person whose absence is unexplained for seven years is presumed dead. The presumption, however, may be rebutted.

Will

A *will* is a written instrument that provides for distribution of an owner's property after death. Our English legal heritage has had an extensive influence on requirements for making a valid will. As a result, similar requirements exist throughout the United States, although individual states deviate significantly from the common pattern. In most American jurisdictions, formality is a general characteristic of the procedure involved in executing a will. Formality is predicated upon a legislative desire to prevent fraud, undue influence, coercion or a testator's impetuousness. Legislatures apparently believe that ceremony helps to prevent rash actions. In addition, formality helps to memorialize the transactions. But even where there is formality, certain specific requirements must be met for a document to be a will.

In Texas two types of wills are valid. These are holographic wills and formal wills. In both of these wills, the testator must have had the legal competency to make the will on the date of execution. This legal competency is called *testamentary capacity.* Testamentary capacity exists when on the date the will was executed the testator had the capacity (1) to know the nature and general extent of his property, (2) to know those persons to whom he would probably devise his estate and (3) to make a plan for distributing his estate. Testamentary capacity is easier to prove than mental competency in other legal transactions. Its minimal requirements make it possible for an elderly person suffering from senility to execute a will during a period of lucidity.

For a will to be valid, it also must not have been revoked by the testator during his or her lifetime. Revocation occurs when the testator destroys the will or executes a subsequent will. There can also be a partial revocation of the will if the testator marks out a provision in the will. Finally, in Texas if a married person executes a will and then is divorced, any provision in the will devising property to the former spouse is revoked.

Before discussing the two types of wills, the relationship between intestacy and wills should be addressed. If a document that purports to be a will fails to qualify, either in whole or in part, the decedent's estate will pass pursuant to the intestacy laws. For example, if the testator executes a will and then destroys it, the will is revoked. If he or she dies prior to execution of a new will, he or she dies intestate. All of the decedent's estate then passes to his or her heirs-at-law as determined by the intestacy law.

It is also possible for a will to fail to dispose of all of the decedent's estate.

CASE EXAMPLE

On June 4, 1964, William Anderson executes a will. On that date he owned only one tract of land. He specifically described that land in his will and devised it to his sister, Maureen Mack. Anderson dies in 1984. On the date of death, he owned two parcels of land. However, he had never changed his will to include a provision disposing of this second parcel of land. In this case the first parcel passes pursuant to the terms of the will to Mack, and the second parcel of land passes to his heirs-in-law as determined by the intestacy laws. To avoid this problem, a will can be drawn to include a *residuary clause*, a provision that states that any property not specifically devised shall pass to a named devisee.

If the testator in the example above had had a residuary clause in his will providing that the remainder of his estate should pass to his nephew, then the second parcel would have passed pursuant to the terms of the will.

Holographic Wills

A *holographic will* is one entirely in the handwriting of the deceased person that disposes of his or her property upon death. The document must indicate that the decedent intended the writing to be his or her last will and testament. Witnesses to the execution of a holographic will are not required. However, the will must be completely in the decedent's handwriting. If any portion, including the date, is typed or written by someone else, the document will not qualify as a holographic will.

Formal Wills

A *formal will* is a written document that by its terms provides for distribution of the decedent's property at death and was properly witnessed as required by statute. The formal requirements are that (1) the decedent must have signed the will in the presence of two witnesses and (2) the witnesses must have signed their names in the presence of the decedent and at his or her request. Anyone 14 years of age or over can serve as a witness to a will. It is advisable for the witnesses not to be devisees under the will. In some cases the witness may forfeit his or her bequest. A will is not required to be in a particular form; however, it is a good practice to date the will.

Self-Proving Affidavits

A *self-proving affidavit* is an affidavit signed by the testator and the witnesses to the will in the presence of a notary public that states that (1) the instrument previously signed is the last will and testament of the testator, (2) the testator's execution was done freely, (3) the testator requested the witnesses to observe his or her signing and to sign as witnesses to the will, (4) the witnesses did sign as requested, (5) the testator was at least 18 years of age and of sound mind and (6) the witnesses were at least 14 years of age. The notary public takes the acknowledgement made by the testator and witnesses and signs and seals the affidavit.

This additional formality does not affect the validity of the will. The purpose of the self-proving affidavit is to facilitate the probating of the will after the testator's death. Without a self-proving affidavit the court must have proof that the signature on the document is genuine and that the decedent freely, knowingly and competently executed the will. This usually means that one of the witnesses to the will must be located and his or her testimony taken in court. Locating witnesses can be a very difficult task. If the witnesses cannot be located, then a handwriting expert may be required to offer testimony regarding the genuineness of the will. The self-proving affidavit makes such proof of execution and competency unnecessary unless a contest of the will is filed.

Doctrines Affecting Specific Bequests

Two legal doctrines related to distributions under the terms of the will should be mentioned. They are ademption and lapsed gifts.

CASE EXAMPLE

Bob devises Blackacre to his brother, Joe. However, before Bob dies he sells Blackacre and receives in exchange a ten-year note and some cash. Bob dies without changing the terms of the will. Is Joe entitled to receive the proceeds from the sale of Blackacre that remain at Bob's death? Under the doctrine of ademption the answer is no. The bequest had adeemed, or failed, and even though there may be identifiable proceeds, Joe receives nothing.

Another situation that can arise after a will is executed is the death of a devisee. Using the same example, assume Joe predeceased Bob, but Blackacre is still part of the estate upon Bob's death. No changes have been made in the will. Who inherits Blackacre? Under the law the bequest is held to have lapsed. If the will has a residuary clause, Blackacre would become part of the residue of the estate and pass to the persons named in the residuary clause. Most states have enacted "antilapse" statutes that are similar to the Texas statute. The Texas law states that, if the devisee was a lineal descendant of the testator, the gift does not lapse but instead passes to the children of the devisee (similar to a per stirpes distribution). In the example above, the Texas antilapse statute would not alter the outcome. Since Joe is Bob's brother, the antilapse law does not apply. However, if Joe had been Bob's son, under the Texas law Blackacre would go to Joe's children.

ADMINISTRATION OF ESTATES

Administration is the general term used to describe the management and settlement of a decedent's estate by a person appointed by the court. Many of the procedures for settling the estate of a person who dies intestate are similar to those for settling an estate where a will exists. A very important initial step is the appointment of a personal representative to act for the estate. The person charged with administration of the estate of an intestate decedent is called an *administrator*; the person who is appointed to administer the estate of a decedent who dies testate is an *executor*. (The terms *administratrix* and *executrix* are used to designate a woman who is serving as administrator or executor.) Sometimes the person nominated in a will as an executor is unable or unwilling to serve. Under these conditions, the court appoints an administrator with the will attached.

The administration of a decedent's estate is supervised by a special court called a *probate court* in the more populous counties and by the county courts in the less populous counties. The appointment of a personal representative is an important element in administering a decedent's estate. In the will, the testator almost always nominates an executor. The executor may be either a person or an institution, such as a trust company. The decedent's nominee is usually appointed by the court, unless that person is not qualified or refuses to serve.

Probate

The term *probate* literally means to prove; however, in law it has a narrower meaning. **Probate** is proving that a will is genuine and is the last will and testament of the maker. In the vast majority of cases, probate is a straightforward procedure. Ordinarily, the person nominated in the will as executor files a written application or petition for probate. In many jurisdictions, the probate court supplies the proper forms for this procedure. The petition alleges the testator's death and domicile at the time of death.

The will is usually filed with the petition unless it has been previously filed with the court. Notice of the filing of the application to probate or administer an estate is published in a newspaper of general circulation in the county or is posted at the courthouse.

After the notice period has expired, the applicant can request a hearing on his or her application. In the case of a will, the hearing includes testimony regarding the death of the testator, the residence of the testator at the time of death and the validity of the will being offered for probate. In the case of an intestate decedent, the court hears testimony regarding the death of the intestate, his or her residence at the time of death and the unsuccessful attempts to find a will.

In the case of a will, probate establishes that the will is valid and genuine. Probate does not establish the validity or meaning of particular provisions of the will. If the court is satisfied that the nominated executor is qualified to serve, this person will be furnished with *letters testamentary* as evidence of authority to settle the estate.

The procedures for the appointment of an administrator differ from those for the appointment of an executor, although both procedures are carried out by the same court. State statutes prescribe the persons eligible for appointment as administrator and the order in which they must be considered. The order, based upon relationship to the decedent, parallels the order of intestate inheritance. Preference is given to the surviving husband or wife. If there is no husband or wife, the relative next entitled to distribution is selected as administrator. The court selects form among those who stand in equal right the person best qualified to manage the estate. Usually, preference is given to residents of the jurisdiction. The court grants *letters of administration* to the person appointed to administer the intestate's estate. Administering an intestate's estate is usually more complex than the administration of an estate when there is a will to follow.

The personal representative, whether an executor or administrator, is authorized by the court to settle the decedent's estate. He or she is responsible for ensuring that assets are distributed in an orderly manner to those who are entitled to them. Although the personal representative has a wide variety of miscellaneous chores, four basic steps comprise the settlement of the estate:

- Collection of estate assets
- Processing and payment of claims against the estate
- Management of estate assets
- Accounting and distribution of estate assets

A will can be offered for probate at any time within four years of the testator's death. Will contests can also be filed at any time during that period. Applications for the administration of an intestate's estate must be filed within four years of the decedent's death. However, if no action is taken within this four-year time period, the county court can at any time thereafter hear testimony to determine the heirs of a decedent. This may be necessary in order to clear title to real property. It is important to remember that, regardless of when or if probate takes place, title to the property is actually transferred as of the date of death.

ADVERSE POSSESSION

Adverse possession refers to the acquisition of title to real property by wrongfully occupying it for a specified period of time. It is sometimes called *title by limitation* because it is based upon the running of a statute of limitation. A *statute of limitation* is a law that requires an injured party to bring a lawsuit within a certain time period or forfeit his or her right to request relief from the court. There are different statutes of limitations for different types of cases. For example, a suit for personal injuries arising from a car accident must be filed within two years of the accident. If the injured person fails to sue within that time frame, he loses his right to sue.

There are four different statutes of limitations that can affect the right of a landowner against a person who is adversely possessing his or her land. The landowner must file suit to remove the adverse possessor within the time period or lose his or her right to remove the adverse possessor.

CASE EXAMPLE

Tom Garret was the owner of a parcel of land. In 1945, Elswood Howard entered the premises and built a residence in which he lived until 1971, when he entered a nursing home. In 1973, Garret moved into the residence, which he later sold to Bonnie Cooke. Cooke checked the records before buying and found title in Garret. Cooke had no actual notice of Howard's possession for the 26 years.

When Howard recovered from his illness, he returned to the property and found Cooke in possession. In a suit brought by Howard against Cooke, the court probably would hold Howard entitled to possession, reasoning that because he had held the land adversely for longer than the statute required he had a good title against all the world.

Associated with each of the four statutes of limitations are special conditions of possession and claim that must be satisfied in order to acquire title by limitation. However, although each statute is unique, there are some requirements common to all four. These are discussed below.

The Elements of Adverse Possession

The common elements of adverse possession are that the possession by the adverse claimant must be actual, exclusive, hostile and continuous during the requisite time period. These requirements are expressive of judicial and legislative intention that possession must be sufficiently evident to give the owner notice of what is happening, that possession is without the owner's permission and that possession is exclusive and for the full term set by the statute.

Actual possession means use and possession by the claimant or his or her agent or tenant. Exclusive possession means that the claimant does not use or possess the land with the permission of someone else. His or her right to use the land does not depend on another person. Hostile possession includes acts that would give notice to the world that the claimant was asserting that he or she owned the property. A tenant, for example, cannot acquire rental property by adverse possession unless he or she clearly repudiates the permissive character of this possession, giving the owner clear notice of the invasion of property rights. The *intent* of the possessor can be crucial, especially in cases where possession is inadvertent.

Continuous possession means regular use of the land for the entire statutory period. If the land is abandoned, or if the true owner reenters either in the absence of the adverse possessor or simultaneously, the statutory term is interrupted and must start over again. A brief absence, such as a vacation, by the adverse possessor is probably not enough to defeat this requirement, however. With nonresidential property, what constitutes continuous and exclusive possession may be difficult to resolve.

A related issue arises when there is a succession of adverse possessors. Texas and most other states allow the "tacking" of one possessor's term to that of another if one acquired directly from the other, as with a sale or conveyance by will.

CASE EXAMPLE

Martin is the legal owner of a lot; however, Boyer has had adverse possession of it for five years (1940–1945). Boyer "sold" the lot to Lucas, who possessed it for eight years. Upon his death, Lucas devised the lot to Tenton in 1953. Tenton never lived on the land. When Tenton died in 1956, his heirs took possession of the lot again. In 1969 a lawsuit was filed by Tenton's heirs, claiming that they had acquired title by adverse possession. The statute of limitation in this case required ten years of adverse possession. Although neither Boyer or Lucas had adversely possessed the lot for ten years, Tenton's heirs would still win. The court would allow the heirs to add (tack) the possession by Boyer and Lucas and thereby meet the ten-year requirement.

Most of the litigation involving adverse possessors centers around the characteristics of the possession. Was the possession actual, exclusive, hostile and continuous? The following case illustrates the characteristics of possession that must be present in order for the possession to be adverse.

CASE EXCERPT   *McDonnold, Jr. v. Weinacht*, 465 S.W. 2d. 136 (Supreme Court of Texas 1971)
[Author's Summary of Facts:

McDonnold, the record owner, sued Weinacht to recover title to and possession of the NW/4 of Section 39, Block 13, H. & G.N.Ry.Co. Survey in Reeves County. Weinacht claimed that he had acquired title to this land by adverse possession under the ten-year statute. Weinacht had purchased three adjoining tracts in 1940 from Gould. He had also leased from Gould the SW/4 of Section 39. After the purchase, Weinacht repaired the fences surrounding his deeded property, which also happened to include the repair of a fence that in part enclosed the disputed land. In addition, Weinacht repaired a fence that bounded a portion of the leased land and the disputed land. During the period 1941 to 1954 Weinacht allowed his cattle to move freely from his deeded land to the leased land to the disputed land. The cattle and horses grazed on the disputed land as well as the other land. In addition, from time to time Weinacht would segregate cattle he had sold by enclosing them in the area of the disputed land. Weinacht also chopped the cockleburs and inkweed growing on the disputed land. Weinacht never paid taxes on the disputed land, nor did he render the property for tax purposes. On a few occasions when he may have had an opportunity to make a verbal claim of ownership on the disputed land he was silent.]

WALKER, Justice. . . . Defendants here rely, as they must, upon the grazing of livestock, chopping weeds and repair of existing fences. The tract in controversy was never separately enclosed, and no one has ever resided upon or cultivated the land in the trap. During the 1940–1954 period, there was no improvement of any kind on the 400 acres, not even a watering trough or salt box or improved road . . .

Unenclosed land has always been regarded as commons for grazing livestock in Texas, and it is well settled that the use of unenclosed land for grazing livestock does not, of itself, constitute adverse possession. . . .

It is accordingly well settled that the mere grazing of land incidentally enclosed as a result of the construction of fences built for another purpose does not constitute possession that will ripen into title by limitation. The adverse claimant who relies upon grazing only as evidence of his adverse use and enjoyment must show as part of his case that the land in dispute was designedly enclosed. . . .

Here there is no proof that the fences were originally built for the purpose of enclosing the NW/4 of Section 39, and neither the enclosure itself nor the work done by Weinacht on the fences warrants the conclusion that plaintiff's land was designedly enclosed. His repair or rebuilding of the fences along the east line of his deeded Section 36 and along the south line of his deeded Section 40 is clearly referable to his deed. They were designed to and did form part of the enclosure of his deeded land, and the fact that they also bounded the trap on the north and west was purely incidental. In these circumstances and in view of Weinacht's lease of the SW/4 from the Goulds, his repair of the fences bounding the trap on the south and east does not evidence an intention to enclose the disputed tract. It was simply the easiest and most economical way of maintaining an enclosure that would permit grazing on the SW/4. . . .

Defendants argue that the cutting of burs and poisonous weeds in the 400-acre trap adds something to their case. There is testimony that the weeds were cut "every year," but no one undertook to say whether this was done more than once a year or how long each operation lasted. Weinacht evidently had the right to cut weeds on the SW/4 he held under the Goulds, and his keeping the trap free of weeds could hardly be considered an appropriation of the remainder of the land in the enclosure. . . . This is in accordance with the general majority rule that cutting and gathering a natural crop does not constitute adverse possession. . . .

Defendants' repair of the fences, cutting weeds and permitting their livestock to graze on the disputed tract under the circumstances disclosed by this record did not constitute an actual and visible appropriation of the land. . . .

The Statutes of Limitations

Acquisition of title by limitation or adverse possession in Texas must meet the additional requirements imposed by one of the four statutes of limitations. The time periods provided in these statutes are three, five, ten and 25 years. (Tex. Civ. Prac. & Rem. Code §§16.024 – 16.028)

The three-year statute requires that the adverse possessor have title or color of title. *Title* is defined as a regular chain of transfers from the sovereignty. Sovereignty refers to the supreme governmental body that originally granted the land. This could be Spain, Mexico, the Republic of Texas or the state of Texas. *Color of title* means a consecutive chain of transfers down to the adverse possessor that is not regular. An irregular chain would be one in which an instrument was not recorded or some other defect that was not the result of some dishonesty or unfairness. The adverse possessor must be capable of producing a chain of documents that prove, in all fairness, that title should be in him or her.

The five-year statute of limitations requires that the claimant pay the taxes on the property and be claiming under a recorded deed. The major difference between the three-year and five-year statutes is the requirement of a chain of title from the sovereignty. Under the five-year statute the adverse possessor is not required to produce a chain of title to him or her. He or she must produce a recorded deed and proof of payment of taxes to support his or her other elements of adverse possession.

The ten-year statute is the general provision that requires adverse possession for a ten-year period. It is limited to the acquisition of 160 acres unless the adverse claimant has some type of written memoranda that increase the number of acres. There is no need to produce a deed or chain of title in support of the claim. The claimant must use the property in a manner sufficient to qualify as adverse possession.

Finally, Texas has a statute that provides for a 25-year period. The statute requires that the adverse possessor have adverse possession of the property for 25 years, be in good faith and have a recorded deed that purports to convey title to him or her. The only benefit gained from the 25-year statute concerns record owners that may be suffering from some type of legal disability at the time of the transfer to the adverse possessor. Legal disabilities include insanity and minority. Usually the presence of a legal disability tolls or extends the statute of limitations during the period of disability. The 25-year statute allows the running of the time period even though the record owner from whom the adverse possessor received the property may have been under a legal disability at the time. However, the adverse possessor must prove that he or she acted in good faith at all times. It can be difficult for an adverse possessor to prove good faith, and consequently this particular provision is used infrequently.

When Adverse Possession Does Not Apply

Although all the elements for adverse possession may exist, there are a few circumstances in which the adverse possessor will not acquire title to the land. For example, adverse possession cannot be applied against the state or against those whose interest is not yet a possessory right, such as a holder of a future interest. It cannot be applied against those who have certain disabilities, such as infants, the mentally incompetent and the insane. For a disability to prevent the running of the statute, however, it must exist at the time a right to sue accrues, usually when the adverse possessor enters the land. An intervening disability does not bar the running of the statute. In addition, the disability is personal to the owner at the accrual of the cause of action and cannot pass to his or her successors. The only exception for legal disabilities is the 25-year statute previously mentioned.

Finally, adverse possession cannot usually be asserted against a cotenant. If two or more persons own land as tenants in common, the possession by one is considered to be for the benefit of all. Consequently, it is not hostile. A rare exception may be possible if the cotenant in possession has notified the others that he or she is claiming exclusive possession and ownership of the property.

The Purpose of Adverse Possession

To many, adverse possession seems like a legal way of acquiring land without compensating the owner. There is also some question as to whether, with modern legislation like the Torrens systems, model title acts, recording acts and the like, society needs this ancient doctrine. Nevertheless, public policy has historically supported the doctrine. Those who defend the statute argue that the state has certain duties to citizens:

- It should eliminate stale claims since evidence and witnesses may be unavailable.
- It should discourage *laches*—that is, dilatory enforcement of one's rights.
- It should encourage full and efficient use of land.
- It should facilitate land transfer by providing a means to remove old title problems and thus "quiet men's estates."

It seems likely that adverse possession will continue to be an aspect of property law for the foreseeable future. The prudent owner of vacant land held for development or investment will make periodic inspections of the property to check against adverse possessors. The mere posting of "no trespassing" signs is probably not sufficient to protect the owner's interest.

EMINENT DOMAIN

Eminent domain is the power of government to take private property for public use. The power of eminent domain is one of the major attributes of sovereignty. In the United States, both federal and state governments are sovereign and may exercise this power. No specific constitutional grant is necessary for government to have the right to take private property for public use, although several state constitutions do contain provisions allocating the power of eminent domain to the state.

Eminent domain is a power that government may delegate. The result is that eminent domain is often exercised by villages, cities and counties as well as public bodies such as school boards and sanitation districts. The power can also be delegated to private corporations such as railroads, power companies and other public utilities. Upon a proper delegation, eminent domain may be exercised by individuals and partnerships. In any case, the status of the party exercising the power is not the critical factor. For a delegation to be proper, the property must be devoted to a public use.

Both the Texas Constitution (Art. 1 §7) and the U.S. Constitution (Fifth Amendment) require that the landowner be justly compensated when property is taken. Four substantive issues arise in all eminent domain cases: (1) what is a taking, (2) what is property, (3) what is the public benefit and (4) what is just compensation. All four of these issues have been construed broadly by the courts.

Taking, Property and Public Use

One issue that arises with respect to eminent domain is whether or not there has been a *taking* of a landowner's property. This most frequently is presented by the landowner who alleges that the government's action has deprived him or her of the beneficial use of his or her property. For example, a zoning ordinance that is so restrictive that the land cannot be used in any way by the owner is considered a taking. A taking also occurs when the government temporarily interferes with the beneficial use of land by its owner. For example, during the construction of a road access to the property may be blocked. This would constitute a temporary taking of property for which the property owner should be compensated. A taking is an act that deprives the landowner of the use, enjoyment or possession of property.

Another issue that is sometimes litigated is whether what the government has taken is *property*. Property includes any type of interest in land, either possessory or nonpossessory. Therefore, any of the interests in land that have been explained so far are property, including fee simples, easements, licenses, life estates and any other right in the property. The case that follows illustrates the broad definition of property.

• CASE BRIEF •

The San Antonio River Authority was engaged in a project of straightening, widening and deepening the channel of the San Antonio River. One of the results of this project was the diversion of waters of the river from their accustomed channel to a new channel some 200 feet to the west. Lewis had acquired the right to use water from an irrigation ditch that was fed with water from the San Antonio River. The project would destroy this source of water for the irrigation ditch. Lewis's property did not touch the San Antonio River at any point, and therefore he had no riparian rights. Nevertheless, he claimed that he owned certain water rights that were being taken by the project and for which he should be compensated. The Texas Supreme

Court agreed. It held that Lewis's water rights, although not riparian, were vested interests in property for which he must be compensated. *San Antonio River Authority v. Lewis*, 363 S.W.2d 444 (Tex. 1962).

The third issue that is raised in eminent domain cases is whether or not the property has been taken for the *public benefit. Public use* is broadly defined as a use that benefits the community. The U.S. and Texas Constitutions require that property acquired through eminent domain be used to benefit the public. Historically, in the United States, eminent domain has been used mostly to acquire land for public transportation systems and to satisfy government's need for space to conduct its business. As government has become increasingly involved in many aspects of life, the use of eminent domain has likewise increased. Today, government may use the power to acquire interest in land for diverse purposes such as parking lots to relieve congestion and traffic hazards, scenic beauty along highways and public recreation.

Although land taken by eminent domain must be used for a public purpose, different interpretations of this exist. A number of jurisdictions require that the property actually be used by the public. Even in these jurisdictions, the facility does not have to be open to the public, as long as some arm of government actually supervises the operation. Thus, public use is satisfied if a utility acquires property by eminent domain even if the general public cannot use the facility. A public utility commission supervises the overall business of the company and ensures that the property is used in the public interest.

In most jurisdictions, the public use requirement is met if some benefit to the public results from the acquisition of the property. This could be increasing employment in the community by acquiring land for a new industry or to eliminate a slum. The benefit does not have to be direct, nor does all of the public have to receive some advantage.

Neither actual use nor the public benefit approach is absolute in any jurisdiction. Courts have consistently looked at additional factors, such as the extensiveness of any benefits, the number of potential users, the extent to which the acquisition benefits private parties and the exclusiveness of the use.

• CASE BRIEF •

The vast bulk of the land in the state of Hawaii that was not owned by the state or federal government, was owned in fee simple by 72 private landowners. These landowners, who had acquired their titles through the descendants of Polynesian chiefs, refused to sell the land. Instead they would lease it on a long-term ground lease and allow the lessee to build a residence on it. At the termination of the lease the land and improvements reverted to the landowners.

In 1967 the Hawaiian legislature, exercising its power of eminent domain, passed a Land Reform Act designed to break up the concentration of land ownership and redistribute it to long-term lessees who had improved the leasehold. The act created a procedure for condemning a residential lot upon request of the lessee and transferring ownership to him or her upon payment of the price established by condemnation hearing.

The owners of the fee simples challenged the constitutionality of this land redistribution scheme, arguing that their property was not being taken for a public benefit. They complained that the state did not use nor did it intend to use any of the condemned lots but was merely forcing a landowner to sell to a particular lessee. This case was appealed to the U.S. Supreme Court, which found that the Land Reform Act was constitutional. The court found the public policy served and the public benefit derived was the destruction of oligopoly and the correction of the resulting inequities in the housing market. The fact that the land was transferred from one private landowner to another did not mean that the taking was for a private benefit rather than a public benefit. *Hawaii Housing Authority v. Midkeff*, 467 U.S. 229 (1984).

Just Compensation

Although the three issues discussed above can be raised in an eminent domain proceeding, the major issue is usually the amount owed to the property owner for the taking.

The principal measure of the owner's loss is the *fair market value* of the property at the time. The U.S. Supreme Court has held that *market value* and *just compensation* are synonymous. Market value is normally determined by what a willing buyer would pay in cash to a willing seller in an arm's-length negotiation. The seller is entitled to have the property valued at its highest and most profitable use, even if the property is not currently being used in that manner.

Market value is an elusive concept and courts have experienced difficulty in attempting to make fair and just awards. The emphasis in Texas appears to be to allow any testimony that may help in guiding the court to a fair compensation. This includes present use value and potential use value.

The most common method of determining value is to compare the property being taken with similar land recently sold. This information is generally presented to the courts through the testimony of expert witnesses. Real estate sales personnel are often expert witnesses in condemnation cases because they are familiar with the selling price of land. A good expert witness must be well prepared. He or she must be very familiar with the parcel of land involved as well as the selling price of comparable property.

Compensation for the value of the land does not always reflect the actual loss to the property owner. The taking of property can also affect other economic interests of the property owner. These interests include the cost of relocating a business or replacing a home or the diminished value of a portion of the original tract that was not taken.

CASE EXCERPT *State v. Schaefer;* 503 S.W.2d 813 (Supreme Court of Texas 1976) SAM D. JOHNSON, Justice This is a condemnation case wherein the State of Texas and McLennan County condemned .326 of an acre out of a .559-acre tract located on, and for the reconstruction of State and Federal Highway 31 and 84 in McLennan County, Texas. The property was owned by Richard L. Schaefer and his brother, Charles Schaefer, and had been used by them for the operation of a farm implement dealership. Trial to a jury resulted in a verdict of $25,000 for the property taken and $4,500 damage to the remainder. . . . .

The Schaefers' .559-acre tract had been the location of their farm implement business for approximately fifteen years. Several buildings were located on the property and were used in the operation of the business. After the condemnation only one building was left on the remainder. Charles Schaefer testified that the property remaining after the condemnation was not suitable for the operation of the business in that it was not large enough. He further testified, over objection, that the business was relocated on the other side of the highway and a short distance west from the subject property. . . .

Charles Schaefer testified that the property was worth $57,000. His testimony reflects that this figure was computed by combining $30,000 "replacement cost" for the main building, $12,000 "replacement cost" for the other buildings, $8,000 "replacement cost" for paving and ramps, and $7,000 for the entire tract of land. [Author's note: These figures were identical to the cost of the new buildings in the new location.] He also testified that the land with the buildings taken by the condemnors had a value of $49,000 and the remainder suffered $6,000 in damages. . . .

The condemnors called two witnesses at the trial, both of whom qualified as expert appraisers. One of the witnesses testified that the value of the land and improvements was $12,195 and the damage to the remainder was $5,165 for a total loss of $17,360. The other witness estimated the value of the land and improvements at $12,045 and the damage to the remainder at $3,030, for a total loss of $15,075. Using the income approach, one of the witnesses further testified that the value of the property was $15,325, based on annual gross rental income of $4,147 and a net rental income of $2,670. . . .

In the *City of Austin v. Cannizzo,* this court stated, "in the willing seller–willing buyer test of market value it is frequently said that all factors should be considered which would reasonably be given weight in negotiations between a seller and a buyer. . . ." And depending on the particular circumstances, removal, reconstruction or replacement costs of improvements located on the property taken or the property remaining may or may not be a proper subject of inquiry. . . . There is nothing in the foregoing cases, however, which authorizes the evidence complained of here. The entire focus in determining market value is directed on the property taken and the property remaining. The construction cost of a building other than the one condemned bears doubtful relevance to the market value of the condemned structure, particularly if the structures are dissimilar in size, material or construction. This is especially true when the new structure is on property wholly removed from the property in issue. When it is also considered that the condemned structures in the instant case were standing for several years, the relevance of evidence pertaining to the cost of new structures cannot be supported. . . .

We reverse the judgments of the trial court and the court of civil appeals and remand the case for a new trial.

To assist displaced landowners, both the state and federal governments have enacted laws that make it possible for a landowner to receive an amount in excess of the fair market value of the property taken. The federal law is called the Federal Uniform Relocation Assistance and Real Property Acquisition Policies Act of 1970. The federal law is substantively similar to the state law, which requires that the governmental agency pay some of the expenses associated with relocating. The state law is as follows:

> This state or a political subdivision of this state, may as a cost of acquiring real property, pay moving expenses and rental supplements, make relocation payments, provide financial assistance to acquire replacement housing, and compensate for expenses incidental to the transfer of the property if an individual, a family, the personal property of a business, a farming or ranching operation, or a nonprofit organization is displaced in connection with the acquisition." (Tex. Prop. Code §21.046 [b])

Both the federal statute and the state statute provide limits on the amount that will be paid for these expenses.

Condemnation Procedure

Some familiarity with the procedure followed by the governmental body in condemning can be helpful. If a voluntary agreement cannot be reached between the property owner and the agency, the agency must file a petition with the court, requesting condemnation of the property. This is usually filed in a county court at law in the county where in the land is located but also can be heard by a district court. The judge appoints a special commission consisting of three landholders in the county to hear testimony regarding compensation. This special commission holds a hearing in which both parties can present testimony regarding value. The special commission will offer an award to the property owner. Either party can appeal this award to the court and is entitled to a trial on any of the four issues, i.e., taking, property, public benefit or compensation. The governmental agency can request that the court grant it possession of the land pending the outcome of the condemnation proceeding. A bond in the amount of the expected award is required is most cases. However, if the agency is a city, county or the state, no bond is required.

ESCHEAT

Escheat is the reversion of property to the state when a person dies intestate with no heirs or when property is abandoned. As we have seen, the state law indicates the categories of relationship of those who are a decedent's heirs. The line for descent and distribution in Texas extends to very remote relatives. Therefore, it is rare for a person to die without any heirs. However, if the decedent dies without heirs, his or her property escheats to the state.

In Texas a person is presumed to have died intestate if no will is offered for probate within seven years of the individual's death. The person is presumed to have died without heirs if during that same seven-year period no claim has been made against the decedent's property and no acts of ownership have been exercised over the decedent's property. An act of ownership under escheat laws is the paying of taxes on the property to the state. A petition requesting the escheat of the property is filed by the state, and notice is given to anyone who may have a claim or interest in the property. If a claimant appears and denies the right of the state to escheat, there will be a trial to determine whether the claimant is an heir of the decedent. If no claim is made or the court finds that the only claimant is not an heir of the decedent, the court will enter an order granting the state's request. A suit to recover real property that has escheated to the state must be brought within two years of the judgment of the court allowing the escheat. Real property that escheats to the state becomes part of the permanent school fund. (Tex. Prop. Code §71.001 et seq.)

ACCRETION

Land that borders on a moving body of water is subject to significant changes over time. Several legal principles have been created to deal with the changes in size and shape that can occur due to water action. *Accretion* specifically refers to a gradual increase in riparian or littoral property as a result of deposits of sediment made by a body of water so as to create dry land where once there was only water. *Alluvion* is the term used for the land so created. *Reliction* is the word applied when water recedes and creates dry land without depositing more material. *Erosion* is simply the decrease is size of a piece of property as the result of water washing away material from the shore. Finally, *avulsion* is an abrupt and perceptible change in the size and shape of a tract as a result of unexpected events, such as a change in the course of a stream.

The general rule is that when accretion or reliction occurs the riparian or littoral land owner's boundary line and land area are extended to take in the alluvion, but when avulsion occurs it effects no change in boundary or title. One reason often given for the doctrine of accretion is that the landowner, who is subject to a diminution in the size of his or her tract through erosion, should have the corresponding benefit when the land is enlarged by natural processes. Another rationale for the rule is that the riparian or littoral owner is usually the only one in a position to use the land efficiently. A third explanation is the desirability of preserving the riparian owner's access to the water. The exclusion of avulsion from the general title-by-accretion rule is intended to mitigate the hardship that would result to abutting landowners when a river or stream abruptly changes course.

Because of these underlying policies, one necessary element of accretion, reliction or erosion is that it be a gradual and imperceptible change.

Another frequently stated requirement is that of *contiguity*; that is, that there be no separation between the riparian owner's original tract and the alluvion. It is not generally required that the alluvion be the result of natural causes alone. For example, if an upstream owner builds a levee or breakwater that affects water flow so as to increase accretion, the downstream riparian owner can still acquire title. An owner cannot, however, use the doctrine to enlarge property boundaries through his or her own acts.

Much of the case law in this area has to do with how to draw the boundaries once accretion, reliction or erosion has altered the shape of the land. Arising most often in suits for damages, declaratory judgment actions, quiet title cases or actions for ejectment, this issue is usually resolved by reliance on two general principles: that the share of each party should be proportionate in size and quality to the prior holding and that each party should have a fair share of the access to the water. The actual method of line drawing necessarily varies greatly, depending on the topography in each case. The courts will strive for an equitable solution and favor compromise settlements by the parties. The law varies somewhat from state to state, and the applicable rule is that of the jurisdiction in which the accretion occurred.

Texas Open Beach Law

There is one significant modification to the common law principles of accretion, alluvion, reliction, avulsion and erosion. This is the Texas statute concerning the beaches along the Gulf Coast. (Tex. Nat. Res. Code §61.011 et seq.) The law establishes an easement for the benefit of the public from the mean low tide to the line of vegetation. Property owners are forbidden to interfere with the public's right of use or easement to this area of the beach. If the shoreline remained constant, there would be no problem. However, the line of vegetation and the mean low tide can be altered gradually or suddenly by tidal action. The law does not specifically discuss the effect of changes in the mean low tide or line of vegetation from these natural causes. However, the public policy statement in the law favors the public's right to use the beaches over private property owners' rights to land they purchased.

Following hurricane Alicia in 1983, the line of vegetation moved inward along several miles of the Gulf Coast. Property owners along the coast who had been in compliance with the law prior to the hurricane were enjoined from rebuilding on the former site. To complicate matters further, the beach is gradually rebuilding itself by natural tidal action. Property owners have challenged the constitutionality of this law on the grounds that it allows the state to take private property without just compensation. The Texas Supreme Court has upheld the constitutionality of the law. Therefore, persons owning beachfront property along the Gulf of Mexico may find that their property boundaries are subject to continuing and radical changes.

The Texas Open Beach Law also requires owners of land located seaward of the Gulf Intracoastal Waterway to notify purchasers regarding the state's easement. This statutory notice and the penalties for failure to give the notice are discussed in Chapter 19.

SUMMARY

Real property is normally conveyed voluntarily be deed. Transfers also occur upon the death of the owner and can occur involuntarily by adverse possession, escheat or eminent domain.

Descent is the term given to the inheritance of real property when a person dies without a will. In this case the owner is said to have died intestate. Each state has enacted a statute of descent and distribution that establishes the heirs-at-law of an intestate decedent. In Texas distribution of property in part depends upon whether it was the separate or community property of the decedent.

When the deceased has made provision by will, the conveyance is by devise. Two types of wills are recognized as valid by Texas courts: holographic and formal wills. A holographic will is wholly in the handwriting of the decedent. A formal will must be signed, witnessed and attested to. In addition, for a will to be eligible for probate the testator must have possessed testamentary capacity on the date the will was executed and must not have revoked the will prior to death.

Wills and the administration of estates of persons who died intestate are monitored by a probate court. A personal representative is appointed to collect the estate assets, settle claims against the estate, manage the estate and distribute the estate to the heirs or beneficiaries. A will must be admitted to probate within four years after the death of the testator. Although the probating of any estate may take several years to complete, the title to the real property is transferred immediately upon the death of the decedent.

One way by which title passes involuntarily is adverse possession. To be adverse the possession must be actual, exclusive, hostile and continuous for a stated time period. There are four time periods in Texas that may affect the claim of adverse possession: three, five, ten and 25 years. Under each statute different conditions must be met.

Land also may be taken from a rightful owner by certain governmental bodies exercising the power of eminent domain. The right of eminent domain is exercised through the legal process of condemnation. Methods and procedures for exercising this power vary markedly from one area to another. Nevertheless, the U.S. and Texas Constitutions prohibit the taking of private property without just compensation, as do most state constitutions. When an owner does not wish to give up the land for the terms offered, some type of legal proceeding is required. Just compensation is based upon the fair market value of the property. The establishment of market value for a property may require testimony of an expert witness chosen from the real estate field.

The government may also acquire title by the process of escheat. This reversion of property occurs when a person who dies intestate has no heirs or when property is abandoned.

Boundaries of privately owned land will sometimes change by the action of water or other natural causes. These doctrines are called *accretion, alluvion, reliction, erosion* and *avulsion*. The Texas Open Beach Law governs disputes when the shore along the Gulf Coast changes.

QUESTIONS AND CASE PROBLEMS

1. Explain the difference between *accretion* and *avulsion*.
2. Discuss the major duties of a person appointed to settle a decedent's estate.
3. Eloise Williams executed a will in which she specifically devised her 103-acre home to her nieces and nephews. In 1976 Eloise sold the home and received a note in the amount of $80,000. In 1977 Eloise died. A residuary clause in the will left all property not specifically devised to the Masonic Homes for Crippled Children in Texas. The nieces and nephews claim that they are the owners of the $80,000 note. Who receives the $80,000 note?
4. In 1941 Ted married Sue. During their 27-year marriage, Ted and Sue had three children and acquired a house and lot in San Antonio, where they lived, and 300 acres in central Texas near Austin. In 1954 Sue's mother died and Sue inherited 20 acres in north Texas. Sue died intestate in 1967. Who are Sue's heirs at law and what does each inherit?
5. Fite filed suit against Pendley for court determination of the ownership of an L-shaped 40-foot strip of land in Potter County. Fite claimed title under a warranty deed dated 3/22/55 and by adverse possession. Pendley claims title by a warranty deed dated 8/19/79. The description of the property in both deeds included the L-shaped strip.

   In 1951 Fite's predecessor in title, Plunk, built a fence that enclosed the L-shaped strip that is in dispute. Between 1955 and 1977 Fite's tenant grazed cattle on Fite's land and the disputed strip. Fite maintained the fence and paid the taxes on it between 1972 and 1977.

   The Pendley's predecessor in title was Green. Green had acquired title to the disputed tract in 1947. Green resided on the property and was aware of the placement of the fence. The Pendley's allege that Fite had not acquired title by adverse possession because Plunk's placement of the fence was done with Green's permission. Who owns the disputed L-shaped 40-food strip of land?

6. York owned 28.083 acres of land near the San Jacinto Monument along the Houston Ship Channel. Over several years, 3.353 acres of this land became submerged by a shallow level of water. This submergence was caused by the removal of underground water. There was no erosion of the submerged land. Coastal Water Industrial Authority sought to condemn the land owned by York but refused to pay York for the 3.353 acres of submerged land. York claimed that he was due compensation for the entire 28.083 acres, not just the 26 acres above water level. Is York entitled to compensation for the 3.353 acres of submerged land?

12

Recording and Title Assurance

RECORDING

An important aspect of purchasing real property is determining whether the grantor has the right to convey the interest in the land that he or she claims to own. The purchaser would like to be assured that the title to the land is "good." A "good" or "indefeasible" title in Texas is one that is free from material defects of record and, therefore, not subject to being defeated or set aside. A good title is not a perfect title. In conveying real property, the grantor is required to convey a good title, not a perfect title.

Title is transferred if the instrument meets the requirements of a deed and is delivered during the lifetime of the grantor. A conveyance of real property is valid if it is in writing and signed by the grantor or his or her agent. The document must provide a description of the real property that reasonably identifies it. However, the fact that all conveyances of real property must be in writing does not assure a prospective purchaser that the title is good. Nor does it give the purchaser the means by which to determine whether the title is good.

Under common law, deeds and other instruments affecting the title to real property were not *recorded*, or officially entered into the public records. Problems arose for the owners when they lost or misplaced these deeds and other documents. Even more important, third parties had no way of knowing that a prior transaction had taken place. The person making a conveyance to an innocent third party may have previously conveyed to another and therefore had nothing to give to this subsequent party. These difficulties gave rise to the need for recording statutes. The primary intent of these statutes is to protect third persons by giving them notice that a prior transaction has occurred.

Recording statutes have been adopted by all states and provide a means for notifying third parties as to the ownership or other interests existing in a given parcel of land. The recording takes place when a deed, mortgage, easement or other legal instrument affecting the title to land is copied into the public record so that interested persons can discover the status of the title to the land. All entries regarding that title comprise the title history, also known as the *chain of title*.

Many centuries ago land could be transferred by a symbolic gesture, such as the giving of a handful of soil or a wild rose branch. Since England enacted the Statute of Frauds in 1677, however, a transfer of an interest in land must be in writing to attain legal recognition. The written document serves as proof of the transfer between the parties to the transaction—the buyer and the seller—and to anyone else who is aware of the writing. However, a prospective buyer unfamiliar with this transfer would have only the word of the seller as assurance that it did not take place. The buyer or the buyer's attorney can gain certainty about this transfer by referring to the public records to find the recording of the transaction. If the transaction is duly recorded, one can rely on it with relative safety. (Limitations on reliance upon the recording will be discussed later.) If the public records do not reveal the transaction, the prospective buyer would normally choose not to buy the parcel. The risk is that the seller is not telling the truth or that some other interest is outstanding in the land. To take a conveyance under these circumstances is to invite a lawsuit; under normal conditions it is too great a risk to the buyer. Thus the purpose of the recording act is to give to the prospective buyer and to the public *legal notice* of the status of a particular property.

Legal Notice

The public recording gives legal notice to third persons as to the existence of a transaction. Under the principle of *caveat emptor*, a prospective buyer or lender is charged with the responsibility of determining whether or not the seller holds title to the property and whether or not there are any encumbrances that would adversely affect the title. If an individual has legal notice of a defect or an encumbrance before acquiring an interest, that individual *holds this title subject to these prior rights*. Legal notice may take the form of actual notice, implied notice or constructive notice.

Actual Notice

Actual notice is information that is acquired by and known by the interest holder. A prospective purchaser may gain information from the seller or from other parties and from firsthand observation of the property.

CASE EXAMPLE

McCredy is negotiating an agreement to purchase Nagy's summer home. When McCredy inspects the premises, he finds several neighbors have been using a well on the property. If the neighbors have acquired and recorded an easement, that fact will appear on the record. If no easement is on the record, the users may have a prescriptive easement. If so, McCredy has actual notice of their easement.

An agreement between two parties gives *actual notice* to these two parties even if it is not recorded. However, unless a third party has actual notice of the parties' interests, an unrecorded deed gives no legal notice to the third party. Likewise, when a prospective purchaser is shown a house that is being occupied by someone other than the seller, he or she is put on notice that the occupant may have some kind of interest. The purchaser is thus obligated, under the theory of actual notice, to ascertain the status of this third party.

Implied Notice

Implied notice is information that would-lead a reasonable person to inquire further into the condition of the title. If a prospective interest holder has implied notice of a possible claim, he or she is said to have legal notice of any interest that would be discovered during the course of a reasonable inquiry into the condition of the title. *Failure to pursue such an investigation does not exempt the prospective interest holder from notice.*

For example, a purchaser should be careful about relying on a quitclaim deed in a chain of title. A quitclaim deed is a release of interest and will convey whatever interest the grantor had at the time of the conveyance. However, if the grantor had no interest at the time, the grantor conveys nothing to the grantee. The recording statute does not protect subsequent purchasers after a quitclaim deed from persons claiming an interest by an unrecorded document executed prior to the quitclaim.

CASE EXAMPLE

In 1967 Johnson conveys Blackacre to Gonzalez by a general warranty deed. Gonzalez does *not* record this deed. In 1969, Johnson conveys Blackacre to O'Connor by a quitclaim deed. O'Connor records this quitclaim deed. In 1970, O'Connor conveys Blackacre to Simmons. Gonzalez has title superior to Simmons even though he did not record his warranty deed. Simmons cannot rely on the quitclaim deed between Johnson and O'Connor. A quitclaim deed is implied notice of possible title problems that must be investigated by Simmons.

By contrast, the other deeds, including the deed without warranty, can be relied upon by a purchaser as proof of good title.

Constructive Notice

Constructive notice is information that can be discovered upon a careful inspection of the public records. Under the concept of constructive notice, a prospective interest holder is considered to have legal notice of any information recorded within the history of the title, *whether or not that individual has actual notice of the existence of the document.*

Constructive notice also charges the prospective interest holder with any information contained within recorded documents. A prospective interest holder can rely on the accuracy of the information contained in the recorded documents. The case that follows involves a document that was intended by the parties to be a mortgage, but its language indicated that it was a deed. The court held that a third party can rely upon the written content of the document.

• CASE BRIEF •

Mrs. Avila had acquired ownership of a home by deed in 1963. Mrs. Avila became delinquent in her notes to the mortgagee and borrowed $185 from her brother, Mr. Garcia. Mrs. Avila deeded the home to her brother at the same time the loan was made. Mrs. Avila continued to live in the house, and the deed was considered by Mrs. Avila and her brother as security for the $185. Mr. Garcia borrowed $5,067 from First Savings & Loan Association of El Paso and gave the savings and loan a lien against Mrs. Avila's home to secure repayment. Thereafter, Mr. Garcia transferred the home back to his sister, Mrs. Avila. When Mr. Garcia defaulted in the payment of his note to First Savings & Loan Association, First Savings & Loan Association foreclosed. Mrs. Avila claimed that the lien was invalid because Mr. Garcia never owned the home. The court held that the recorded documents appeared to be a deed from Mrs. Avila to Mr. Garcia. It reasoned that First Savings & Loan Association could rely on that document and thereby create a valid lien. Subsequent purchasers or lenders are not on notice of secret agreements between Mrs. Avila and Mr. Garcia. *First Savings & Loan Association of El Paso v. Avila,* 538 S.W.2d 846 (Tex. Civ. App.—El Paso 1976).

In addition to notice of all items contained in the public records, prospective interest holders are also considered to have constructive notice of all taxes that attach to the property.

TYPES OF RECORDING STATUTES

The recording statutes vary markedly from state to state, although their purpose is similar. They are designed to give notice to parties who are considering acquiring an interest in the land. The three general types of recording statutes are pure race, race-notice and notice.

A *pure race statute* provides that the first person who records an instrument prevails over all other takers from the same source. The recorder need not be acting in good faith and without notice of the prior instrument; all that matters is that he or she recorded first. In other words, the party who wins the race to the courthouse has superior title. Very few states have enacted pure race statutes.

A *race-notice statute* provides that a subsequent buyer will prevail only if he or she has no notice of the prior transaction and records first. The differences between these statutes and the pure race statutes are the additional requirements that the subsequent buyer be acting in good faith and without notice of the prior instrument.

A *notice statute* provides that the subsequent buyer will prevail over all interested parties who have not recorded their interest, provided he or she is acting in good faith and without notice of the prior instruments. Under this type of statute the subsequent buyer is not required to record his or her instrument in order to have superior title. The important factor is that the subsequent buyer did not know and could not determine from the public records that there were other interests in the property. The states are about evenly divided between race-notice and notice statutes.

The Texas Recording Statute

The recording statute adopted in Texas is a notice statute. It provides as follows:

> A conveyance of real property or an interest in real property or a mortgage or deed of trust is void as to a creditor or to a subsequent purchaser for a valuable consideration without notice unless the instrument has been acknowledged or proved and filed for record as required by law." (Tex. Prop. Code §13.001[a])

The following case illustrates the importance of recording.

• CASE BRIEF •

On May 9, 1860, Dignowitz executed a deed to McMillan for land in San Antonio. The deed was signed by his wife, who testified that she did not know whether it was delivered to McMillan, but she assumed that it was. This deed was not recorded until 1889.

In 1875, several years after the death of her husband, Mrs. Dignowitz conveyed the land to the city of San Antonio. Shortly thereafter the city conveyed the parcel to the United States, to be a part of a military reservation. At the time, the mayor of San Antonio orally mentioned a possible outstanding claim; but after an exhaustive search of the record, the attorney for the United States approved the title.

In a claim against the United States for trespass brought in 1889, the U.S. Supreme Court stated, "The inevitable conclusion as a matter of law is that the United States acquired a good and valid title, as innocent purchasers for valuable consideration, and without notice of a previous conveyance to McMillan." *Stanley v. Schwalby*, 162 U.S. 255 (1896).

It may seem unfair for the law to permit Dignowitz to make multiple conveyances of the same property. Theoretically, she no longer owns the property after the initial conveyance to McMillan and should be powerless to convey anything to San Antonio. This would be the case under the common law. Nevertheless, the impact of the recording statutes is to pry that title loose from McMillan and other nonrecording takers and to vest it in subsequent takers like the city of San Antonio.

The recording statute protects only good-faith purchasers for value or creditors. Consequently, persons who acquire the land through gift or inheritance are not protected even if they were unaware of the prior conveyance. To attain the protection of the statutes the purchaser must give consideration, that is some sort of value. The value need not be equal to the fair market value of the premises, but neither can it be nominal or merely recited in the deed without actual payment. It must be real value.

Furthermore, the subsequent purchaser must be without notice of the prior conveyance. If the purchaser has actual, implied or constructive notice of the prior conveyance, the recording statute does not apply.

CASE EXAMPLE
Albert conveys Blackacre to Ted by a general warranty deed in 1973. Ted does not record his deed. In 1974 Albert offers to sell Blackacre to Margie. While Margie is inspecting Blackacre she talks with Ted, who tells her that he owns Blackacre and shows her the 1973 deed from Albert. Albert tells Margie that Ted is incompetent and that the deed is not genuine. Margie can find no evidence of the transaction in the real property records. Margie purchases Blackacre and records her deed from Albert. Margie has legal notice of Ted's claim and therefore is not protected by the recording statute. Ted owns Blackacre.

Although recording is important, recording alone will not assure a purchaser of good title. Recording will not correct the following title problems:
* the rights of parties in possession
* forgeries
* defects in the instrument itself
* lack of capacity of the grantor to execute the instrument

In other words, recording will not make an invalid instrument valid, nor will it affect the rights of a person who has acquired title through adverse possession. Therefore, a prospective purchaser must not only look for a recorded instrument that conveys title to his or her seller but must also review all the instruments to determine their validity. Unfortunately, a review of the records will not disclose to a prospective purchaser whether or not all signatures are genuine. Further, the requirement of recording does not relieve the purchaser of the obligation to physically view the property and determine the names of the persons who are in possession of the land and the nature of their right to possession.

The Texas recording statute has one more requirement in order for the subsequent buyer to have superior title over an unrecorded interest. This is the requirement that the subsequent buyer's instrument be acknowledged or proved as required by law.

ACKNOWLEDGMENTS

An *acknowledgment* is an oath made to an authorized officer by the person who signed the document that he or she executed the instrument for the consideration and purposes stated in the document. The officer to whom this acknowledgment is made must certify in writing that the acknowledgment was made, and this certification must accompany the document. This practice is commonly referred to as *notarizing* a document.

Officers who are authorized to take acknowledgments in Texas include notaries public, court clerks and judges of the county courts. After taking the acknowledgment and making the certificate, the officer must sign and seal the document. (Tex. Rev. Civ. Stat. art. 6602) Acknowledgments are very important in the recording process. The absence of an acknowledgment or proper proof as required by law on a document is not notice of the interest conveyed in the document even if it is recorded. Similarly, a defective acknowledgment in a recorded document will not serve as constructive notice of the interest conveyed. A recorded deed containing a defective acknowledgment cannot be relied upon by a subsequent purchaser to show good title. Acknowledgments are also important because they make it possible to record the instrument.

The acknowledgment does not have to be taken on the date that the instrument was executed. It can be made at the time of or after the execution of the document.

An acknowledgment can also be corrected by the taking of another acknowledgment. Further, if an authorized officer is not available to take the acknowledgment, the acknowledgment can be made before two or more credible witnesses. Although there are other ways to prove the validity of a document, the acknowledgment is the most common practice in Texas.

The form of the acknowledgment is established by statute. There are long- and short-form acknowledgments. The short form acknowledgments are valid only on documents executed after August 31, 1981. The statutory acknowledgment forms are set out in Figure 12.1

THE RECORDING PROCESS

Instruments pertaining to real property are recorded with the county clerk in each county in which a portion of the land is located. The county

Figure 12.1: **STATUTORY SHORT AND LONG ACKNOWLEDGMENT FORMS**

Short Forms 1, 2, 3, 4

(1) Natural Person

STATE OF TEXAS
COUNTY OF _____

This instrument was acknowledged before me on ___(date)___ by _(name or names of_
person or persons acknowledging)

> _____
> Notary Public, State of Texas
> Notary's name printed:
>
> _____
> My commission expires: _____

(2) Attorney-in-fact

STATE OF TEXAS
COUNTY OF _____

This instrument was acknowledged before me on ___(date)___ by _(name of attorney-_
in-fact) _____ as attorney-in-fact on behalf of ___(name of principal)___ .

> _____
> Notary Public, State of Texas
> Notary's name printed:
>
> _____
> My commission expires: _____

(3) Partnership (By One or More Partners)

STATE OF TEXAS
COUNTY OF _____

This instrument was acknowledged before me on (date)by _(name of acknowledging_
partner or partners)_ , partner(s) on behalf of _(name of partnership)_ , a partnership.

> _____
> Notary Public, State of Texas
> Notary's name printed:
>
> _____
> My commission expires: _____

Figure 12.1 (continued)

(4) Corporation

STATE OF TEXAS
COUNTY OF _____

This instrument was acknowledged before me on ___(date)___ by (name of officer)
(title of officer)   of (name of corporation acknowledging), a _____ (state of
incorporation)_____ corporation, on behalf of said corporation.

_____
Notary Public, State of Texas
Notary's name printed:

_____
My commission expires: _____

Long Forms 1, 2, 3, 4

(1) Single Acknowledgment

STATE OF TEXAS
COUNTY OF _____

Before me, the undersigned authority, on this day personally appeared _____
_____, known to me to be the person whose name is subscribed
to the foregoing instrument and acknowledged to me that he executed the same for the
purposes and consideration therein expressed.

Given under my hand and seal of office on this _____ day
of _____, 19_____.

_____
Notary Public, State of Texas
Notary's name printed:

_____
My commission expires: _____

Figure 12.1 (continued)

(2) Corporate Acknowledgment

STATE OF TEXAS
COUNTY OF _____

Before me, the undersigned authority, on this day personally appeared _____ _____, _____ of _____, a corporation, known to me to be the person whose name is subscribed to the foregoing instrument, and acknowledged to me that he executed the same for the purposes and consideration therein expressed, in the capacity therein stated and as the act and deed of said corporation.

Given under my hand and seal of office on this _____ day of _____, 19_____.

_____
Notary Public, State of Texas
Notary's name printed:

_____
My commission expires: _____

(3) Attorney-in-Fact

STATE OF TEXAS
COUNTY OF _____

Before me, the undersigned authority, on this day personally appeared _____ _____, known to me to be the person whose name is subscribed to the foregoing instrument, as the attorney in fact of _____, and acknowledged to me that he subscribed the name of _____ thereto as principal and his own name as attorney in fact, and executed the same for the purposes and consideration therein expressed, in the capacity therein set forth.

Given under my hand and seal of office on this _____ day of _____, 19_____.

_____
Notary Public, State of Texas
Notary's name printed:

_____
My commission expires: _____

Figure 12.1 (continued)

---

(4) Partnership (By Member of)

STATE OF TEXAS
COUNTY OF _____

Before me, the undersigned authority, on this day personally appeared _____
_____, a member of the partnership firm of _____,
known to me to be the person whose name is subscribed to the foregoing instrument, and
acknowledged to me that he executed the same as the act of _____,
a partnership, for the purposes and consideration therein expressed, in the capacity
therein stated.

Given under my hand and seal of office on this _____ day
of _____, 19_____.

Notary Public, State of Texas
Notary's name printed:
_____

My commission expires: _____

---

clerk inspects all documents offered for recording to determine whether or
not they comply with the statutory requirements for recording. If they do
not, then the county clerk can refuse to record the documents. The requirements for recording in Texas are as follows:
1. The document must be in English.
2. It must be signed by the grantor.
3. It must contain the mailing address of each grantee.
4. It must be either acknowledged or proved in accordance with the
   applicable law.
5. The filing fee must be paid.
When the document is accepted for recording, the county clerk copies
and indexes the document. The documents are indexed in alphabetical order, chronologically, by the names of the grantors and grantees. The county
clerk maintains two indexes: a grantor's index (also called a *direct index*)
and a grantee's index (also called a *reverse* or *indirect index*). The indexes
refer the reader to a copy of the document itself by reciting the volume and
page number of the book where the document is kept or the film code number for the film on which the document was copied.

ABSTRACTS OF TITLES

The process of searching the records and creating an abstract of title is a
critical part of ascertaining whether title is good. Records that affect title to

real estate can be found in several different places: the real property records maintained by the county clerks, the court records and the tax records for the county, city and school district. The title searcher or abstractor compiles a summary of all the recorded transactions in a collection called an *abstract of title.* In Texas, abstracts of title are frequently prepared by title insurance companies.

The abstract covers the period from the date a sovereign government first conveyed the land to the date of the certification of the abstract. The length of an abstract depends on the number of transactions pertaining to that property. An abstract may be a few pages or thousands of pages.

The abstractor does not usually render an opinion regarding the title. It is the role of the abstractor to gather the information necessary so that an attorney can review the documents and render an opinion. However, it is important that an abstractor be familiar with the various types of legal documents and the types of interests and encumbrances. The more knowledgeable the abstractor is, the less likely it is that he or she will omit a document.

TITLE ASSURANCE

Purchasers can protect themselves against losses caused by defects in the title to the land that they are purchasing in various ways. The warranties of title found in general warranty deeds allow purchasers to recover damages from their grantors if one of the warranties is breached. The recording statute in Texas also provides purchasers protection. The recording statute will give them superior title over persons claiming under certain unrecorded documents. Purchasers can request that an abstract of title be prepared and review the documents that are included in the abstract. However, for most purchasers this will not be very beneficial. The legal effect of the documents would be unknown. All of these methods of assuring good title have their limitations; therefore, purchasers have sought other ways to protect their title to land. In Texas, this is most frequently accomplished by purchasing a policy of title insurance. Another less common method is to hire an attorney to review the records and issue a title opinion.

Title Insurance

In Texas the most common method of assuring title is to purchase a title insurance policy. There are two types of title insurance policies: an owner's policy and a mortgagee's policy. An owner's policy insures the owner of the property. The mortgagee's policy insures the mortgage company or lender. In exchange for a single premium the title company issues a policy that states that the title company will assume some of the risk of title defects.

An owner's policy benefits the owner and his or her heirs and devisees by insuring that they will have good title subject only to those limitations specifically listed in the policy. Coverage continues until the property is sold or transferred by the owner or his or her heirs or devisees. The policy cannot be assigned or transferred to the grantee. When the property is transferred, the owner's title insurance policy automatically becomes a warrantor's policy at no cost. This gives the grantor protection in the event that any of the warranties contained in the deed are breached. This warranty coverage lasts for 20 years. The amount of coverage remains the same throughout the life of the policy.

A mortgagee's policy protects the lender's lien interest in the property by insuring the mortgagee (lender) that the borrower's title is good and that the lien is valid. Coverage continues for the duration of the lien's existence. A mortgagee's policy is assignable to subsequent purchasers of the note. This is a separate policy and therefore requires the payment of a separate premium. This premium is nominal if both an owner's policy and a mortgagee's policy are issued simultaneously. Lenders usually require the borrower to provide them with a mortgagee's policy. The amount of coverage under a mortgagee's policy decreases as the principal balance due on the note is reduced.

The issuance of title insurance, the premiums and the terms of the policies are regulated by the Texas State Board of Insurance. A title insurance company's decision to issue a policy of insurance is based upon a review of the abstract of title to the property. Prior to issuing a policy to the buyer or the lender, the title company will prepare, upon request, a document called a *title commitment*. The title commitment will list in detail any problems with the title that have been discovered and any conditions that must be met before a title policy will be issued. In addition, it will list the exceptions to coverage. If the conditions set out in the commitment are satisfied, the title company will insure the title.

The title insurance company promises to defend the insured against claims made by persons claiming title based on recorded documents. The title policy usually covers forged instruments, undisclosed heirs, misfiled documents, incorrect marital status, confusion over similarity of names and mistaken legal interpretation of wills. Any of these defects will be defended by the title company.

If there is a loss, the title company will pay its insured for his or her loss to the extent of the policy limits. The maximum amount that can be collected for a total loss of the land is set out in the policy. Title insurance does not guarantee good title, nor does it guarantee that the insured will not lose the property to someone with superior title. Title insurance operates as do other types of insurance policies: it pays the insured for the value of the property lost.

Though title insurance does alleviate some of the shortcomings of the other methods of assuring good title, it is not a panacea. Title insurance does not protect the insured against all types of losses, and the amount it will pay for a loss is limited. The standard exceptions include the following:

1. restrictive covenants
2. boundary line disputes or encroachments
3. rights of parties in possession
4. taxes for the year of purchase and subsequent years
5. eminent domain
6. zoning
7. rights asserted to tidelands, shores of navigable water beds or streams or lakes
8. riparian rights
9. defects known to the purchaser and not disclosed to the title company

The title insurance company also can include special exceptions. These usually include certain listed liens, easements and mineral reservations. Further, the title insurance policy will state the interest in the land that is being insured and the value that is being insured. This insurance is, of course, limited to coverage under the policy and to acts occurring prior to the date the insured purchased the property. Figures 12.2 and 12.3 are examples of title insurance policies.

Many misunderstandings arise about coverage under a title insurance policy. The case that follows, although long and difficult to read, explains the responsibilities of the title company to the insured. To summarize, these are the main points regarding coverage made by the Texas Supreme Court in this case:

1. A title insurance company must defend the insured's title if a defect is evident even if no legal action has been taken against the insured and no attempt to dispossess the insured has been made.
2. A title insurance company does have the option to attempt to cure or remedy the title defect through appropriate legal action or the execution of appropriate legal documents.
3. A title insurance company is *not* liable to the insured for damages caused by the loss of a sale due to a title defect.
4. If the title defect cannot be cured, the title insurance company must pay the insured for the value of his or her loss.
5. The value of the insured's loss is determined by the following formula: difference between the land value without defect and the land value with defect on the policy date divided by land value without defect multiplied by policy limits.

Figure 12.2: **SAMPLE TITLE INSURANCE POLICY**

T-2 Mortgagee Policy—Form Prescribed by State Board of Insurance of Texas—Revised 3-1-1985

STEWART TITLE
GUARANTY COMPANY

a Texas corporation, hereafter called the Company, for value received, will pay to the Insured named in Schedule A hereof, as interest may appear, all loss or damage not exceeding the amount stated in Schedule A which the Insured, or the heirs, devisees, executors, administrators, successors or assigns of the Insured may sustain or suffer by reason of the failure of, defects in, encumbrances upon, or liens or charges against the title of the mortgagors or grantors to the estate or interest in the land described in the mortgage or trust deed identified in Schedule A, existing at or prior to the date of this policy, including mechanics' and materialmen's liens now having priority, or now existing but incomplete, which may hereafter be completed so as to gain priority over the lien of the Insured, and not excepted to in Schedule B hereof, subject to the Conditions and Stipulations hereof.

Subject to the provisions of Schedule B and the Conditions and Stipulations, the Company insures that at the date of filing said mortgage or trust deed for record, the title to the estate or interest in the land described therein was as shown in Schedule A, and said mortgage or trust deed was a valid first lien thereon, unless superior liens are set out in Schedule B. The Company insures that any assignments noted in Schedule A, whether recorded or not at the date hereof, are good and valid and vest title to said mortgage or trust deed in the Insured free and clear of liens, except as specified in Schedule B.

This policy inures to the use and benefit of the lawful owner or owners of the evidence of debt identified herein and to any subsequent owner or owners thereof, under and in accordance with the terms and conditions hereof (all of said present and subsequent owner or owners of said debt identified herein being included within the term "Insured" as used herein), provided always that it shall not be the duty of the Company to trace the ownership of such evidence of debt or of this policy; and, in the absence of satisfactory proof of such ownership at the time liability hereunder accrues, any payment made to the named Insured, or a legally appointed successor, upon surrender of this policy for endorsement, shall be deemed to be in satisfaction of all demands hereunder pro tanto.

IN WITNESS HEREOF, the STEWART TITLE GUARANTY COMPANY has caused this policy to be executed by its Chairman and President under the seal of the Company, but this policy is to be valid only when it bears an authorized countersignature, as of the date set forth in Schedule A.

STEWART TITLE
GUARANTY COMPANY

Carlos Morris
Chairman of the Board

Countersigned:

Stewart Morris
President

STEWART TITLE GUARANTY CO.
INCORPORATED
★
1908
TEXAS

582 (Rev. 3-1-85)

Figure 12.2 (continued)

CONDITIONS AND STIPULATIONS

1. The following terms when used in this policy mean:

   (a) "land": The land described, specifically or by reference, in Schedule A, and improvements affixed thereto which by law constitute real property.

   (b) "date": The effective date, including hour if specified.

   (c) "mortgage": Mortgage, deed of trust, trust deed, or other security instrument.

2. (a) The Insured, should his rights remain as a lienholder only, shall be protected under this policy for the period of limitation applicable to the indebtedness secured by the lien herein described calculated from the original maturity date of such indebtedness or from a subsequently renewed and extended maturity date whichever is later, provided that the Company shall have no liability by reason of any invalid renewal and extension agreement of either the indebtedness or the lien or by reason of the failure to record any such renewal and extension agreement.

   (b) If the Insured acquires the land under foreclosure, or other legal manner, in extinguishment of a debt, or in a legal manner under the Federal Housing Administration Mortgage Insurance Contract, or in any legal manner as a direct or indirect consequence of the guaranty of insurance of the Veterans' Administrator, this policy shall continue in force as of the date of the policy; provided that the amount of the insurance hereunder after such acquisition, exclusive of costs, attorney fees and expenses which the Company may become obligated to pay, shall not exceed the least of:

      (i) The amount of insurance stated in Schedule A;

      (ii) The market value of the land or equity insured as of the date of the policy;

      (iii) The amount of the unpaid principal of the indebtedness, not including additional principal indebtedness prior to foreclosure or acquisition, created subsequent to the date of the policy, plus interest thereon and expenses of foreclosure; or

      (iv) The amount paid by any governmental agency or instrumentality, if such agency or instrumentality is the Insured claimant, in the acquisition of such estate or interest in satisfaction of its Insurance Contract or Guaranty.

   (c) The coverage of this policy shall continue in force as of the Date of Policy in favor of an Insured so long as such Insured retains an estate or interest in the land, or holds an indebtedness secured by a purchase money mortgage given by a purchaser from such Insured, or so long as such Insured shall have liability by reason of covenants of warranty made by such Insured in any transfer or conveyance of such estate or interest; provided, however, this policy shall not continue in force in favor of any purchaser from such Insured of either said estate or interest or the indebtedness secured by a purchase money mortgage given to such Insured.

3. Whenever any action or proceeding shall have been commenced against the Insured, asserting any claim of title, lien, charge, defect or encumbrance hereby insured against, or if a defense is interposed against a foreclosure by the Insured or by the privies of the Insured legally entitled to protection under the terms hereof by reason of any claim as to the validity, or priority of the lien insured herein, or if a restraining order or other injunctive remedy is applied for to prevent the sale of the estate or interest in the land in satisfaction of the debt by reason of any claim as to the validity or priority of the lien insured herein, and process shall have been served upon the Insured, it shall within a reasonable time, and in ample time for defense therein, notify the Company in writing of the particulars of such action or proceeding, giving the number of this policy

and agreeing to render all reasonable assistance therein; whereupon the company is bound to proceed at once to the defense of the title. At its option, it may (a) re-establish the status quo of the Insured by effecting settlement and dismissal of such action or proceeding; (b) at its own cost and charges pursue such action or proceeding to final determination in the court of last resort and comply with the judgment of the court in behalf of the Insured up to the amount of this policy: (c) at any time pay the Insured the amount of this policy in discharge of all obligation hereunder. In the absence of notice as aforesaid, the Company is relieved from all liability with respect to such claim or demand; provided, however, that failure to notify shall not prejudice the claim of the Insured, if such Insured shall not be a party to such action or proceeding; nor be served with process therein nor have any knowledge thereof, nor in any case unless the Company shall be actually prejudiced by such failure.

4. When the Company shall have settled a claim under this policy, all right of subrogation shall vest in the Company unaffected by any act of the Insured, but such subrogation and transfer shall be in subordination to the lien of the Insured under its said mortgage or trust deed, and to the claim of the insured to receive and be fully paid the amount of principal and interest and other monies, if any there be, secured by said mortgage or trust deed.

5. Nothing contained in this policy shall be construed as a guarantee against the consequences of the exercise and enforcement or attempted enforcement of governmental police powers over the land described herein.

6. A statement in writing of any loss or damage, for which it is claimed the Company is liable, shall be furnished to the Company within ninety-one days after such loss or damage shall have been determined, and no right of action shall accrue under this policy until thirty days after such statement shall have been furnished, and no recovery shall be had under this policy unless action shall be commenced thereon within two years after the expiration of said last mentioned period of thirty days; and a failure to furnish such statement of loss or damage, and to commence such action within the time hereinbefore specified, shall be a conclusive bar against the maintenance of any action under this policy.

7. So long as any one or more persons are personally liable for the indebtedness described in this policy, the Insured may release any one or more persons from personal liability for the payment of said indebtedness; provided, however, that in no event shall any release be made of any warranties of title; and further provided that no release shall be executed except in consideration of the assumption of such indebtedness by a bona-fide purchaser of the land.

8. All payments under this policy shall reduce the amount insured pro tanto.

9. This policy does not insure against loss or damage by reason of defects, liens, encumbrances, adverse claims, or other matters (a) created, suffered, assumed or agreed to by the insured claimant; (b) not known to the Company and not shown by the public records but known to the Insured claimant either at Date of Policy or at the date such claimant acquired the insured mortgage and not disclosed in writing by the insured claimant to the Company prior to the Date such insured claimant became an Insured hereunder; (c) resulting in no loss or damage to the insured claimant; or (d) attaching or created subsequent to Date of Policy (except to the extent insurance is expressly afforded herein as to any statutory or constitutional lien for labor or material).

10. All notices required to be given the Company and any statement in writing to be furnished the Company shall be addressed to it at P.O. Box 2029, Houston, Texas 77252.

11. COMPLAINT NOTICE: Should any dispute arise about your premium or about a claim that you have filed, contact the agent or write to the company that issued the policy. If the problem is not resolved, you may also write the State Board of Insurance, Department C, 1110 San Jacinto Blvd., Austin, Tx, 78786. This notice of complaint procedure is for information only and does not become a part or condition of this policy.

STEWART TITLE
GUARANTY COMPANY

Figure 12.2 (continued)

T-1 Owner Policy Schedules – Form Prescribed by State Board of Insurance of Texas – Revised 3-1-1983

SCHEDULE A

GF No.

Owner Policy No. 0-5801-   Date of Policy:

NAME OF INSURED:

Amount

1. The estate or interest in the land insured by this policy is (Fee Simple, Leasehold, Easement, etc. – Identify or Describe)

2. The land referred to in this policy is described as follows:

SCHEDULE B

This policy is subject to the Conditions and Stipulations hereof, the terms and conditions of the leases or easements, insured, if any, shown in Schedule A, and to the following matters which are additional exceptions from the coverage of this Policy.

1. The following restrictive covenants of record itemized below (insert specific recording data or state "None of Record").

2. Any discrepancies, conflicts, or shortages in area or boundary lines, or any encroachments, or any overlapping of improvements.

3. Taxes for the year 19   and subsequent years, and subsequent assessments for prior years due to change in land usage or ownership.

4. The following lien(s) and all terms, provisions and conditions of the instrument(s) creating or evidencing said lien(s).

Fold   Fold

Countersigned   **STEWART TITLE**
                                                                  GUARANTY COMPANY

BY _____
            Authorized Countersignature

Figure 12.3: OWNER'S TITLE INSURANCE POLICY

T-1 Owner Policy—Form Prescribed by State Board of Insurance of Texas—Revised 3-1-1985

STEWART TITLE
GUARANTY COMPANY

STEWART TITLE GUARANTY COMPANY, a Texas corporation, hereinafter called the Company, for value does hereby guarantee to the Insured (as herein defined) that as of the date hereof, the Insured has good and indefeasible title to the estate or interest in the land described or referred to in this policy.

The Company shall not be liable in a greater amount than the actual monetary loss of the Insured, and in no event shall the Company be liable for more than the amount shown in Schedule A hereof, and shall, except as hereinafter stated, at its own cost defend the Insured in every action or proceeding on any claim against, or right to the estate or interest in the land, or any part thereof, adverse to the title to the estate or interest in the land as hereby guaranteed, but the Company shall not be required to defend against any claims based upon matters in any manner excepted under this policy by the exceptions in Schedule B hereof or excluded by Paragraph 2, "Exclusions from Coverage of this Policy", of the Conditions and Stipulations hereof. The party or parties entitled to such defense shall within a reasonable time after the commencement of such action or proceeding, and in ample time for defense therein, give the Company written notice of the pendency of the action or proceeding, and authority to defend. The Company shall not be liable until such adverse interest, claim, or right shall have been held valid by a court of last resort to which either litigant may apply, and if such adverse interest, claim, or right so established shall be for less than the whole of the estate or interest in the land, then the liability of the Company shall be only such part of the whole liability limited above as shall bear the same ratio to the whole liability that the adverse interest, claim or right established may bear to the whole estate or interest in the land, such ratio to be based on respective values determinable as of the date of this policy. In the absence of notice as aforesaid, the Company is relieved from all liability with respect to any such interest, claim or right; provided, however, that failure to notify shall not prejudice the rights of the Insured if such Insured shall not be a party to such action or proceeding, nor be served with process therein, nor have any knowledge thereof, not in any case, unless the Company shall be actually prejudiced by such failure.

Upon sale of the estate or interest in the land, this policy automatically thereupon shall become a warrantor's policy and the Insured shall for a period of twenty-five years from the date hereof remain fully protected according to the terms hereof, by reason of the payment of any loss, he, they or it may sustain on account of any warranty of title contained in the transfer or conveyance executed by the Insured conveying the estate or interest in the land. The Company shall be liable under said warranty only by reason of defects, liens or encumbrances existing prior to or at the date hereof and not excluded either by the exceptions or by the Conditions and Stipulations hereof, such liability not to exceed the amount of this policy.

IN WITNESS HEREOF, the STEWART TITLE GUARANTY COMPANY has caused this policy to be executed by its Chairman and President under the seal of the Company, but this policy is to be valid only when it bears an authorized countersignature, as of the date set forth in Schedule A.

STEWART TITLE
GUARANTY COMPANY

Carlos Morris
Chairman of the Board

Countersigned

Stewart Morris
President

581 (Rev. 3-1-85)

Figure 12.3 (continued)

T-1 Owner Policy Schedules—Form Prescribed by State Board of Insurance of Texas—Revised 3-1-1983

SCHEDULE A

GF No.

Owner Policy No. 0-5801-   Date of Policy:

NAME OF INSURED:

Amount

1.   The estate or interest in the land insured by this policy is (Fee Simple, Leasehold, Easement, etc.—
Identify or Describe)

2.   The land referred to in this policy is described as follows:

SCHEDULE B

This policy is subject to the Conditions and Stipulations hereof, the terms and conditions of the leases or easements, insured, if any, shown in Schedule A, and to the following matters which are additional exceptions from the coverage of this Policy:

1.   The following restrictive covenants of record itemized below (insert specific recording data or state "None of Record").

2.   Any discrepancies, conflicts, or shortages in area or boundary lines, or any encroachments, or any overlapping of improvements.

3.   Taxes for the year 19   and subsequent years, and subsequent assessments for prior years due to change in land usage or ownership.

Fold   Fold

4.   The following lien(s) and all terms, provisions and conditions of the instrument(s) creating or evidencing said lien(s):

Countersigned:

STEWART TITLE
GUARANTY COMPANY

BY _____
       Authorized Countersignature

5812-3 (25M 10-85)

Figure 12.3 (continued)

GENERAL CONDITIONS AND STIPULATIONS

1. Definitions

The following terms when used in this policy mean:

(a) "land": The land described, specifically or by reference, in Schedule A, and improvements affixed thereto which by law constitute real property.

(b) "public records": Those records which impart constructive notice of matters relating to the land.

(c) "knowledge": Actual knowledge, not constructive knowledge or notice which may be imputed to the Insured by reason of any public records.

(d) "date": The effective date, including hour if specified.

(e) "insured": The Insured named in Schedule A and, subject to any rights or defenses the Company may have had against the named Insured or any person or entity who succeeds to the interest of such named Insured by operation of law as distinguished from purchase, any person or entity who succeeds to the interest of such named Insured by operation of law as distinguished from purchase including but not limited to the following:

(i) heirs, devisees, distributees, executors and administrators;

(ii) the successors in interest to a corporation resulting from merger or consolidation or the distribution of the assets of such corporation upon partial or complete liquidation;

(iii) the partnership successors in interest to a general or limited partnership which dissolves but does not terminate;

(iv) the successors in interest to a general or limited partnership resulting from the distribution of the assets of such general or limited partnership upon partial or complete liquidation;

(v) the successors in interest to a joint venture resulting from the distribution of the assets of such joint venture upon partial or complete liquidation;

(vi) the successor or substitute trustee of a trustee named in a written trust instrument; or

(vii) the successors in interest to a trustee or trust resulting from the distribution of all or part of the assets of such trust to the beneficiaries thereof.

2. Exclusions from the Coverage of this Policy

THE POLICY DOES NOT INSURE AGAINST LOSS OR DAMAGE BY REASON OF THE FOLLOWING:

(a) LACK OF ADEQUATE TITLE IN THE INSURED PROPERTY TO ALLOW IT TO BE USED, SOLD, TRANSFERRED, LEASED OR MORTGAGED FOR ANY PURPOSE INTENDED BY THE INSURED NOR LOSS OF OPPORTUNITY OR ECONOMIC EXPECTATION.

(b) Governmental rights of police power or eminent domain unless notice of the exercise of such rights appears in the public records at the date hereof; and the consequences of any law, ordinance or governmental regulation including, but not limited to, building and zoning ordinances.

(c) Any titles or rights asserted by anyone including, but not limited to, persons, corporations, governments or other entities to tidelands, or lands comprising the shores or beds of navigable or perennial rivers and streams, lakes, bays, gulfs or oceans, or to any land extending from the line of mean low tide to the line of vegetation, or to lands beyond the line of the harbor or bulkhead lines as established or changed by any government, or to filled-in lands, or artificial islands, or to riparian rights, or the rights or interests of the State of Texas or the public generally in the area extending from the line of mean low tide to the line of vegation or their right of access thereto, or right of easement along and across the same.

(d) Defects, liens, encumbrances, adverse claims, or other matters (1) created, suffered, assumed or agreed to by the Insured; (2) not known to the Company and not shown by the public records but known to the Insured either at the date of this policy or at the date the Insured acquired an estate or interest insured by this policy and not disclosed in writing by the Insured to the Company prior to the date such Insured became an Insured hereunder; (3) resulting in no loss or damage to the Insured; (4) attaching or created subsequent to the date of this policy; (5) resulting in loss or damage which would not have been sustained if the Insured had paid value for the estate or interest insured by this policy; or (6) the homestead or community property or survivorship rights, if any, of any spouse of any Insured.

3. Defense and Prosecution of Actions

(a) In all cases where this policy provides for the defense of any action or proceeding, the Insured shall secure to the Company the right to so provide defense in such action or proceeding, and all appeals therein, and permit it to use, at its option, the name of the Insured for such purpose.

(b) The Company shall have the right to select counsel of its own choice whenever it is required to defend any action or proceeding, and such counsel shall have complete control of said defense.

(c) The Company shall have the right at its own cost to institute and without undue delay prosecute any action or proceeding or to do any other act which in its opinion may be necessary or desirable to establish the title to the estate or interest as insured, and the Company may take any appropriate action under the terms of the policy, whether or not it shall be liable thereunder, and shall not thereby concede liability or waive any provision of this policy. When, after the date of the policy, the Insured notifies the Company as required herein of a lien, encumbrance, adverse claim or other defect in title to the estate or interest in the land insured by this policy which is not excluded or excepted from the coverage of this policy, the Company shall promptly investigate such charge to determine whether the lien, encumbrance, adverse claim or defect is valid and not barred by law or statute. The Company shall notify the Insured in writing, within a reasonable time, of its determination as to the validity or invalidity of the Insured's claim or charge under the policy. If the Company concludes that the lien, encumbrance, adverse claim or defect is not covered by this policy, or was otherwise addressed in the closing of the transaction in connection with which this policy was issued, the Company shall specifically advise the Insured of the reasons for its determination. If the Company concludes that the lien, encumbrance, adverse claim or defect is valid, the Company shall take one of the following actions: (1) institute the necessary proceedings to clear the lien, encumbrance, adverse claim or defect from the title to the estate as insured; (2) indemnify the Insured as provided in this policy; (3) upon payment of appropriate premium and charges therefor, issue to the current Insured or to a subsequent owner, mortgagee or holder of the estate or interest in the land insured by this policy, a policy of title insurance without exception for the lien, encumbrance, adverse claim or defect, said policy to be in an amount equal to the current value of the property or, if a mortgagee policy, the amount of the loan; (4) indemnify another title insurance company in connection with its issuance of a policy(ies) of title insurance without exception for the lien, encumbrance, adverse claim or defect; (5) secure a release or other document discharging the lien, encumbrance, adverse claim or defect; or (6) undertake a combination of 1. through 5. herein.

(d) Whenever the Company shall have brought an action or interposed a defense as required or permitted by the provisions of this policy, the Company may pursue any such litigation to final determination by a court of competent jurisdiction and expressly reserves the right, in its sole discretion, to appeal from any adverse judgment or order.

(e) Whenever requested by the Company, such insured shall give the Company all reasonable aid in any such action or proceeding, in effecting settlement, securing evidence, obtaining witnesses, or prosecuting or defending such action or proceeding, and the Company shall reimburse such insured for any expense so incurred.

(f) Any action taken by the Company for the defense of the Insured or to establish the title as insured, or both, shall not be construed as an admission of liability, and the Company shall not thereby be held to concede liability or waive any provision of this policy.

4. Payment of Loss

(a) No claim shall arise or be maintainable under this policy for liability voluntarily assumed by the Insured in settling any claim or suit without written consent of the Company.

(b) All payments under this policy, except payments made for costs, attorney fees and expenses, shall reduce the amount of the insurance pro tanto; and the amount of this policy shall be reduced by any amount the Company may pay under any policy insuring the validity or priority of any lien excepted to herein or any instrument hereafter executed by the Insured which is a charge or lien on the

Figure 12.3 (continued)

GENERAL CONDITIONS AND STIPULATIONS Continued
(continued and concluded from reverse side of Policy Face)

land, and the amount so paid shall be deemed a payment to the Insured under this policy.

(c) The Company shall have the option to pay or settle or compromise for or in the name of the Insured any claim insured against by this policy, and such payment or tender of payment, together with all costs, attorney fees and expenses which the Company is obligated hereunder to pay, shall terminate all liability of the Company hereunder as to such claim. Further, the payment or tender of payment of the full amount of this policy by the Company shall terminate all liability of the Company under this policy.

(d) Whenever the Company shall have settled a claim under this policy, all right of subrogation shall vest in the Company unaffected by any act of the Insured, and it shall be subrogated to and be entitled to all rights and remedies of the Insured against any person or property in respect to such claim. The Insured, if requested by the Company, shall transfer to the Company all rights and remedies against any person or property necessary in order to perfect such right of subrogation, and shall permit the Company to use the name of the Insured in any transaction or litigation involving such rights or remedies.

5. Policy Entire Contract

Any action, actions or rights of action that the Insured may have, or may bring, against the Company, arising out of the status of the title insured hereunder, must be based on the provisions of this policy, and all notices required to be given the Company, and any statement in writing required to be furnished the Company, shall be addressed to it at P. O. Box 2029, Houston, Texas 77252.

6. This policy is not transferable.

7. COMPLAINT NOTICE

Should any dispute arise about your premium or about a claim that you have filed, contact the agent or write to the company that issued the policy. If the problem is not resolved, you may also write the State Board of Insurance, Department C, 1110 San Jacinto Blvd., Austin, Tx, 78786. This notice of complaint procedure is for information only and does not become a part or condition of this policy.

STEWART TITLE
GUARANTY COMPANY

CASE EXCERPT *Southern Title Guaranty Company, Inc. v. Prendergast*, 494 S.W.2d 154 (Supreme Court of Texas 1973) REAVLEY, Justice. This is a suit on a title insurance policy by the insured, Vincent Prendergast and wife, against the insurer, Southern Title Guaranty Company. Prendergast bought 22 acres of Harris County land for $10,233 in 1964. His owner's policy in that amount was issued by Southern Title Guaranty Company on February 17, 1964. In July, 1965, Prendergast entered into a contract to sell the 22 acres for $25,000. The prospective purchaser objected to the title on the ground that an undivided one-tenth outstanding interest was owned by Theresa Krug Matlage. Prendergast called upon Southern Title Guaranty Company to purchase the Matlage interest for him, but this was not done and the sale of 22 acres for $25,000 was lost. Prendergast then sued to recover the damages to which he was entitled under his title policy. . . .

There is the question of whether the insured may sue on the policy merely because of the failure of this title. The insurance company insists that eviction should be a prerequisite to this suit, as it is to a suit for breach of a covenant of warranty. . . . By the terms of the policy the company does more than agree to warrant and defend the insured against anyone claiming adverse title. The policy contract begins by saying in emphatic type: "The Southern Title Guaranty Co., Inc. . . . Does hereby guarantee to Vincent Prendergast and his wife, Leola Prendergast . . . that they have good and indefeasible title to the following described real property. . . ." This is the basic assurance of the contract, and a failure of that guarantee gives rise to a cause of action for damages. . . .

In the second trial a jury verdict was obtained, the findings being that—in July of 1965 when the resale was lost—the value of full fee title to the 22 acres was $25,000 while the value of the land with an outstanding one-tenth interest was only $10,200. The difference between these two figures being thought to be Prendergast's damages, the trial court rendered judgment for the amount of the policy limit, $10,233. This judgment has been reversed by the Court of Civil Appeals because its effect would be to give to the insured the benefit of his 1965 bargain rather than to indemnify him for the failure of the title guaranteed on the date of the policy. We agree that the trial court judgment was erroneous, but we disagree with the opinion of the Court of Civil Appeals in two respects which will become significant when the trial court reaches the case once more.

Our first disagreement is with respect to the effect of the proportionate payment provision of the policy. It provides that if there is established an outstanding interest in "less than the whole of the property, then the liability of the Company shall be only such part of the whole liability limited above as shall bear the same ratio to the whole liability that the adverse interest, claim, or right established may bear to the whole property, such ratio to be based on respective values determinable as of the date of the policy." This application of this provision is not limited to the situation where outstanding title to a physically identifiable segment of the acreage is established. It applies in all cases where there is a loss of title "for less than the whole of the property"—meaning anything less than the title and acreage insured. It simply means that the parties deal with the insured property on the assumption that its value is equal to the amount of the policy and this assumption is to be applied whether the insured loses part or all of what the policy insures. . . .

If the amount of the policy is the same as the value of what is insured, the assumption of the policy is correct and the recoverable loss is the value of the outstanding interest. This value may or may not bear the same fractional relationship to the total value as the undivided interest or portion of the land area (lost to the insured) bears to the whole title and property. A one-tenth interest in land might carry an added bargaining weight and be worth more than one-tenth of what the market would allow to the whole.

If the market value of the whole property and the policy amount differ, the ratio of the quoted provision must be applied. This avoids an advantage to insurer or to insured. To illustrate, suppose the jury were to find the values for the 22 acres as of the date of the policy to have been as follows: $25,000 for the whole, $4,800 for the one-tenth, and $20,200 for the land with an outstanding one-tenth. . . . If the policy provision is applied and the ratio of $4,800 to $25,000 is used, the recovery would be 19.2% of $10,233 or $1,964.74. . . .

A final question, perhaps a determinative one, is presented by the attempt of the insurance company to introduce into evidence a quitclaim deed from the executor of the estate of Theresa Krug Matlage, which deed is said to cure any defect in Prendergast's title. The trial court refused to admit the deed, and this ruling was upheld by the Court of Appeals. . . .

Southern Title Guaranty Company filed no suit to cure this defect because Prendergast did not request that action, and during the first trial and appeal the company expressed its willingness to prosecute such a suit. After that appeal and after the death of the adverse claimant, the company was finally successful in purchasing the quitclaim deed which it contends resolves the matter. We hold that it should not be precluded from making that proof and mitigating the damages owed to Prendergast. If upon a new trial it appears that the defect in Prendergast's title is cured, his damages will be no more than nominal.

The judgment of the Court of Civil Appeals is affirmed. The case is remanded to the trial court for further proceedings consistent with this opinion.

Attorney's Title Opinion

An *attorney's title opinion* is the professional judgment of a lawyer as to the condition of the title based on the facts revealed in the abstract. This method of assuring good title is much less common than the title insurance policy except when dealing with minerals in which the mineral lessee generally requires an opinion by its attorney.

There are no requirements concerning the form of, content of or exceptions to an opinion in Texas. The title opinion is based on an abstract of title and consequently does not protect the purchaser from problems or defects that do not appear in the records. The title opinion will list the exceptions to and limitations on the attorney's liability. Therefore, the opinion should be read with care. The standard exceptions found in title insurance policies are usually the standard exceptions included in a title opinion.

If an attorney is negligent in the preparation and issuance of the title opinion, the buyer could have the right to sue the attorney for damages. A judgment for damages, however, is only as good as the ability of the judgment debtor to pay. If the attorney (judgment debtor) is financially sound, the buyer may recover the financial loss resulting from the attorney's professional error. If the attorney is not solvent, the money judgment may be uncollectible, and the buyer will not obtain financial satisfaction.

Torrens Certificate

The *Torrens certificate* is a type of land title registration available in a few states. It is not available in Texas. Furthermore, even in states where the Torrens system exists, it is not compulsory and exists along with the recording system previously described. The advantage of the system is that it eliminates the need for a title search, and the Torrens certificate shows the status of the title at any time.

The Torrens system can be used when a landowner applies in writing to the county court to have a title registered. A current title search is made and provided to the court, which holds a type of *quiet title action*. In this action all parties who may have an interest in the parcel are notified and given a chance to be heard by the court. The purpose of the notice and hearing is to obtain assurance that all encumbrances to the title are known prior to issuance of a Torrens certificate. When the court is satisfied that the landowner is the titleholder and that all liens and encumbrances to that title have been revealed, it orders the certificate of title to the parcel to be registered.

Henceforth, the certificate of title will depict the exact state of the title. The original is filed with the recorder, and a copy goes to the owner. A party alleging to have an interest arising prior to the registration of the Torrens certificate will be precluded from attacking the present owner's or any subsequent owner's title, unless his or her interest was recorded on the original certificate. To assure that the Torrens certificate is always up to date, any conveyance, mortgage, lien or other encumbrance upon the parcel will not be valid until it is entered on the original certificate. Further, title does not pass until the registration takes place. If there is a defect of title, suit is usually against the state for the loss. A state fund is provided for such lawsuits.

As with the normal recording system, under the Torrens system it is usually necessary to go beyond the recorder's office (or the certificate) to determine whether there are unpaid taxes or special assessments, zoning and buildings restrictions or federal court judgments that may affect the parcel.

For reasons not completely clear, the Torrens system has not been used widely. Perhaps the title searching apparatus already in place has successfully resisted the abolition of the title search. There is also the initial expense of having the title registered and the fact that the system is voluntary, both of which militate against its wide adoption. The Torrens system has been adopted to some degree by 15 states, but it does not seem to be spreading rapidly and is not likely to replace the present recording system in the foreseeable future.

SUMMARY

Statutes that govern the recording of transfers of real estate have been adopted by all the states. Their primary intent is to protect buyers of real estate by informing them of the status of a title to the land in question. Each successive act of recording serves as legal notice to the public of a transaction that changes the status of ownership.

Legal notice falls into three categories. When information is acquired personally by the interested party, it is called *actual notice.* Implied notice, a second type, is imposed by the law when conditions exist that would cause a reasonable person to inquire further. Finally, constructive notice occurs when information on record could have been uncovered in a reasonable search.

Statutes governing recording are established and enforced by the states. They can be classed in three types that relate to the priority of ownership of any claimant to the property. In the first type, pure race, the statutes provide that the first person to record has priority. The second type, race-notice statutes, provide that a subsequent buyer can claim ownership by recording first, but only if he or she had no notice of the prior conveyance. Notice statutes, the third type, provide that a subsequent buyer takes precedence over an earlier one if the prior transaction was not on record at the time of sale.

The Texas recording statute requires that documents affecting title to land be acknowledged and recorded. The Texas statute is a notice-type statute. A subsequent purchaser without notice will have superior title over a titleholder under a prior unrecorded deed. Although there is no requirement that a deed be recorded in order for it to convey title, the grantee can protect his or her title from subsequent purchasers only by recording.

Acknowledgments are oaths made to a proper authority by the person signing the document. In the oath the signor swears that he or she has executed the document for the reasons set forth in the document. There are several ways to make an acknowledgment. However, the most common is to execute it in the presence of a notary public on the date the document is signed.

Deeds and other instruments pertaining to land are recorded in the county where the land is located. The county clerk reviews each document offered to it for filing to determine whether or not it meets the statutory requirements. After accepting the document, the county clerk indexes the instrument and copies it into the official records for the county. An abstractor reviewing the title to a tract of land will begin his or her search with these records maintained by the county clerks. In addition, the abstractor will review the court records of the county in which the land is located and the tax records for the taxing units. The abstractor will create a chain or history of the title to the property from these records. This is called *abstract of title.*

It is from an abstract of title that an attorney will render a title opinion.

The title opinion is one method of title assurance. The title opinion is the attorney's professional opinion regarding the condition of the title based upon the abstract. The title opinion will usually list some exceptions to coverage and therefore should be read with care.

The most common method of obtaining assurance that title to the property is good is to purchase a title insurance policy. There are two types of title insurance policies: an owner's policy and a mortgagee's policy. Title insurance policies offer the purchaser, the seller and the lender protection from certain title defects. The title company promises to defend the insured against persons claiming title based upon recorded documents. There are several standard exceptions to title insurance policies. In addition, coverage under a policy is limited to an amount specified in the policy. Consequently, even with title insurance a purchaser retains some risk of loss as a result of a defective title.

QUESTIONS AND CASE PROBLEMS

1. (a) Explain the purpose of recording statutes. (b) What must a plaintiff establish to be protected by this type of legislation?
2. Define *constructive notice* and explain how it might affect a person who purchases real estate.
3. Describe the title searching process.
4. What are the prerequisites that must be met for an instrument to be recorded?
5. Explain why title insurance is often advisable even when the grantee receives a warranty deed.
6. Dowse sold land to Pender by warranty deed dated April 1, 1979. The deed was recorded on June 3, 1979. On May 29, 1979, Dowse fraudulently sold the same land to Petez. Petez recorded his deed on June 4, 1979. Petez had no actual knowledge of the deed to Pender. As between Pender and Petez, who has the superior claim in (a) a race-notice jurisdiction. (b) a race jurisdiction. (c) Texas? Explain.
7. In August 1967, Woods purchased 130.437 acres of land in Panola County from Massey. About two weeks after Woods acquired title, he found Gross and Janes Company cutting timber on the land. Gross & Janes had a timber deed from Darnell Lumber Company. This deed was recorded on February 8, 1967. This deed recited that conveyance of timber was "the same as conveyed to Grantor by Timber Deed dated Jan. 3, 1967, from G. W. Massey to Darnell Lumber Company." The earlier timber deed from Massey to Darnell was never recorded. Is the timber deed held by Gross & Janes valid against Woods?

13
Involuntary Liens against Title

LIEN

A **lien** is a claim against another's property securing either payment of a debt or fulfillment of some other charge or obligation. Liens are important in all spheres of commercial law. They take many forms and are subject to extensive variations from state to state. Despite these differences, the underlying concept of all liens is much the same. The purpose is to provide security for a debt or completion of some action or obligation. A lien cannot exist in the absence of a claim against another person.

Although courts sometimes refer to liens as property, a lien is not a property right in the thing itself. The lienholder has neither title nor the rights of a titleholder. His or her only right is to have an obligation satisfied out of proceeds from the sale of the property. A lien thus differs from an estate, which is the right to possess and enjoy property.

Because the fundamental nature of a lien is security, interests in real estate are frequently the subject of liens. Land and buildings provide excellent security. They are valuable, their value is relatively stable and they are difficult, if not impossible, to move or conceal. Further, in the United States, land is subject to a system of recording that gives constructive notice to anyone who might deal with land titles without being aware of charges upon them.

Liens are either voluntary or involuntary. *Voluntary liens* are those a property owner tends to apply to his or her property. The usual function of a voluntary lien is to secure long-term credit. Funds are advanced to the property owner, who agrees to repay the debt and provide a lien on the property as security. One example is a real estate mortgage, which in many states is regarded as a lien. Real estate mortgages are discussed extensively in Chapters 21 and 22. A number of involuntary liens are also important to real estate practitioners. *Involuntary liens* are created by law to protect interests of persons who have valid claims against the owner of real property. The claim might arise out of a judgment, sale or furnishing of a service of some kind. Involuntary liens are also created to aid government in the collection of taxes and special assessments.

This chapter discusses some general aspects of liens, with particular emphasis on involuntary liens involving real estate. Specific liens that apply to real property discussed in detail are the mechanic's lien, the judgment lien and the tax lien.

The voluntary liens are discussed in detail in Chapters 21 and 22. These are mortgage liens that take two forms: deed of trust liens and vendor's liens. Since those liens are usually created when property is sold, discussion of them is reserved for the section concerning the sale of real property.

Historical Background

Both personal and real property are subject to lien. The emphasis of early English law was on the personal property lien. As far back as the 12th century, English courts recognized the right of a landowner to retain possession of cattle that strayed upon his land until the owner paid for damages. This right was later applied to other situations, and possession became the basis for the common law lien. Under the common law, when a lien existed, the lienor had the right to retain possession of property until the debtor met the obligation. The debtor's title was in no way affected. If the lienor surrendered possession, the lien was lost. The original common law lien did not permit the lienor to sell the property.

Because the common law lien was based upon possession, it was never particularly important to real estate. The *equitable lien* was more significant in the development and use of real estate as security. English law recognized two avenues for the administration of justice—law and equity. The equitable lien was originally recognized in equity, though not in law, to apply property to satisfy a specific debt or obligation. The holder of an equitable lien did not have the right to obtain or retain possession of the property. Unlike the common law, equity provided for enforcement of the lien by ordering the property sold and the proceeds applied to the debt. The equitable lien is the basis for much of mortgage law as it has developed in the United States.

MECHANIC'S AND MATERIALMAN'S LIENS

By statute in most states, contractors and suppliers who work on real estate or furnish materials for such work are entitled to a lien if they are not paid. The lien provides them with a means of compelling payment since the property can be sold to satisfy the claims. Generally, the lien attaches to both buildings and the land, and the work must have been done at the owner's request. The mechanic's lien is not the only action unpaid suppliers or contractors may take. By filing for the lien, they do not lose the right to recover on the contract. Mechanic's liens may also be known as *material-man's liens* or *contractor's liens.*

CASE EXAMPLE

Eldon Horn and his wife purchased a lot. Shortly thereafter they contracted with Jamco Builders for the construction of a home on the lot. Jamco subcontracted some of the work to Mid-American Homes. Mid-American, as required by law, notified the Horns of its right to place a lien against the real estate. Jamco did not pay for the subcontracted work, and Mid-American filed a mechanic's lien against the property. This established its right to petition a court to have the property sold and the proceeds applied against the debt.

Valid reasons exist for granting contractors and suppliers a special lien against real property. In trying to collect for services and materials, they are at a disadvantage when compared with credit sellers of personal property. When not paid, the seller of personal property can usually take the item back. This remedy does not exist for the contractor and supplier, whose work and material have been incorporated into an immovable structure. Except for the mechanic's lien, these claimants would be limited to suing for the contract price, but winning damages for the contract price does not necessarily give the plaintiff a claim to the improved property. The mechanic's lien does because a court can order the property sold and the proceeds applied against the debt. The lien also has nuisance value in that, until the debt is paid, a purchaser takes title subject to the lien. The mechanic's lien laws thus aid many small entrepreneurs who might be reluctant or financially unable to take judicial action to collect an unpaid claim.

Mechanic's lien laws also encourage economic activity. Because a substantial amount of construction is done on credit, these laws increase security for the contractors, subcontractors and suppliers who have invested their capital. The additional security induces financial institutions to provide more credit for additional projects in the construction industry.

Mechanic's lien laws did not exist at common law. They developed in the United States during the 19th-century in response to the needs of those involved in the expanding building activity in American cities. Every state in the United States now has some type of mechanic's lien legislation. Since this legislation is often merely the ad hoc response to problems of a particular area and time, it is extremely varied and often complicated. In those jurisdictions that have a basic mechanic's lien statute, political pressures may lead to substantial amendments, which increase variability and add further complications. Any person in real estate working with transactions involving mechanic's lien laws must be particularly concerned with local statutes on the subject.

The importance of the materialman's and mechanic's lien in Texas is evidenced by the fact that the lien is a creature of both statutory and constitutional law. These are two separate and distinct liens. A person may have a right to a statutory mechanic's lien but not to a constitutional lien. Similarly, a person may not meet the technical requirements for creating a statutory lien but may meet the requirements for a constitutional lien. Both liens should be considered when improvements have been made to real estate.

The Constitutional Lien

The Texas Constitution provides as follows:

> Mechanics, artisans, and material men, of every class, shall have a lien upon the buildings and articles made or repaired by them for the value of their labor done thereon, or material furnished therefor; and the Legislature shall provide by law for the speedy and efficient enforcement of said liens. (Tex. Const. art. 16, §37)

Although the Texas Legislature has passed laws creating a statutory materialman's lien, a contractor can still assert protection under this constitutional provision. The constitutional lien is usually resorted to if the materialman has failed to meet the procedural requirements of the statutory lien.

The constitutional lien protects only contractors who have a direct contractual relationship with the owner of the real property. The materialman must have dealt directly with the owner pursuant to an oral or written agreement. Subcontractors are not covered. The right to the constitutional lien exists only if the work was performed on an article or building on the land. The lien arises automatically. There is no requirement that an affidavit be filed or any type of notice be given. However, the lien can be lost if the property is sold to someone who had no knowledge of the lien. The constitutional lien is enforced by suit against the owner to foreclose the lien. The lien has limitations but can be useful if the statutory lien has failed for technical reasons.

The Statutory Lien

The statutory lien laws have been codified in the Texas Property Code, beginning with §53.001. The persons who can file a statutory lien are so numerous and broad that they include every type of workman or materialman who furnishes labor or materials in the construction of buildings or improvements: contractors, subcontractors, laborers, suppliers and manufacturers of specially fabricated items.

The lien claimant must have provided labor or materials for improvement of property. *Labor* is defined as that performed in direct prosecution of the work, whether it is original construction or repairs. The term *materials* includes materials used in construction or repair, the reasonable rental of the equipment used or ordered for use in the construction and specially fabricated items, whether or not they were ever used. A specially fabricated article is an item that was ordered and made for use at that particular job and is unsuitable for use elsewhere.

Improvements are also defined broadly in the Texas statute. They include all types of construction on the land, ranging from buildings to the creation of artificial lakes or ponds. The term *improvement* also includes such things as sidewalks, irrigation systems, the planting of orchard trees and preparatory work such as the clearing of land.

The improvements must be made to private land and at the request, directly or indirectly, of some interest holder. The lien can attach to the fee simple absolute interest or any lesser interest. The interest to which the lien attaches depends upon who requested the work. If the work was requested by the owner of the fee simple absolute, then the lien attaches to that interest. However, if the work was performed under contract with the lessee, then the lien is against the leasehold estate. Liens cannot be placed against property owned by a governmental entity. Materialmen who perform labor or furnish materials on public jobs are protected by a bonding system that will be discussed later.

Perfecting the Statutory Lien

Most of the issues on materialman's liens in Texas concern securing or perfecting the lien. **Perfection** is the term used to indicate the legal steps necessary to establish an enforceable lien. A person may have a statutory right to a lien, but if he fails to timely perfect that right, he loses the lien. Consequently, the procedure for securing the lien is critical if the lien is going to benefit the materialman. As is true in most states, the procedure for perfecting a lien involves giving notice to the owner and filing a lien affidavit in the public records. Both the giving of notice and the filing must occur within a certain time period. Figures 13.1 and 13.2 are examples of a lien affidavit and of a notice to the owner. Lien affidavits are filed with the county clerk of the county in which the land improved is located.

The methods for perfecting the lien differ for the various types of laborers or materialmen. Those persons in a direct contractual relationship with the owner have a longer period of time to perfect their lien and are required to give fewer notices. Persons not in a direct contractual relationship with the owner, such as subcontractors and laborers, are required to give more notices within a shorter time frame.

Regardless of when it was perfected, a lien is treated as if it had been perfected on the first day that work was begun on the improvement. This is called the *relation back doctrine.* This is an important principle of law because it affects the priority for payment when more than one person has a lien against property. Priority is discussed later in this chapter.

Figure 13.1: **MATERIALMAN'S LIEN AFFIDAVIT**

The State of Texas §
County of Hudspeth §

I, Willie C. Cramer, Affiant, as President of Willie's Roofing Service, Inc., Claimant doing business in the City of Sierra Blanca, Hudspeth, Texas, Claimant having furnished materials and/or labor to improve the property and improvements to secure the amount of the claim therefor, makes this affidavit and states:

1. That Henry Lee King is the owner or reputed owner of said land and Henry Lee King is the owner or reputed owner of the improvements located thereon.

2. That Wallace T. Harrison is the original contractor on the job or that portion thereof for which the hereinafter described material and/or labor were furnished.

3. That said materials and labor were furnished to Wallace T. Harrison, original contractor, pursuant to a contract with such party, it having been furnished for the improvements or property located in Hudspeth, Texas, and described as follows:

Blackacre

Said house, building, or improvements located thereon are described as follows:

horse stable

The amount of the claim is $1,690.00, and said amount is just, reasonable, and unpaid, and a general statement of the kind of work done and materials furnished by claimant is as follows:

roof installed

This lien for the amount shown above is upon the land and the improvements described above.

_____
Willie C. Cramer. Affiant
as President
for Willie's Roofing Service, Inc.

SWORN AND SUBSCRIBED TO before me, under my official hand and seal of office, on the _____day of _____, 198___.

_____
Notary Public in and for
Hudspeth County, Texas

Figure 13.2: **NOTICE TO THE OWNER**

April 12, 1983

Henry Lee King
P.O. Box 2345
Sierra Blanca, Texas

Wallace T. Harrison
300 Main Street
Sierra Blanca, Texas

Dear Interested Parties:

Willie's Roofing Service, Inc., furnished the materials and labor for the new roof that was installed on the horse stable at Blackacre. An invoice for this work is enclosed. This work was performed at the request of Wallace T. Harrison. Mr. Harrison has been billed for this work but has not paid the bill. There remains due and owing at this time $1,690.00.

A materialman's lien affidavit has been filed today in the amount of $1,690.00. Two copies of the lien are enclosed. This lien is to attach to the land, improvements and the retainage fund which the owner is required to establish. Pursuant to state law the owner can retain funds for the payment of this claim. If this claim remains unpaid, the owner may be personally liable unless the owner withholds payments from the contractor to pay this claim.

Upon receipt of payment, Willie's Roofing Service, Inc., will release this lien.

Sincerely yours,

Willie C. Cramer

CASE EXAMPLE

MJ Contractors, Inc., began clearing the land for construction on June 1, 1982. The owner made prompt payment to MJ Contractors until December 10, 1982. On January 30, 1983, MJ Contractors filed a lien affidavit and sent two copies of it to the owner, thereby timely and properly perfecting its statutory lien. The lien is treated as if it had been filed on June 1, 1982, the date the work was begun.

The treatment of subcontractors and others not in a direct contractual relationship with the owner is very different from the treatment of contractors. The Texas law has attempted to balance the interest of the property owner and these subcontractors. The property owner who has paid the original contractor expects him to pay his subcontractors and suppliers and views the imposition of any additional liability as unjust. On the other hand, the subcontractor, supplier and laborer have provided a valuable service to the landowner and should receive some protection from him. Consequently, the Texas law imposes limited liability upon the owner. Liability is imposed on the property owner in two ways. First, the subcontractor can trap the funds by notifying the owner prior to the time that the owner pays the original contractor for the work. Second, the owner is required to retain ten percent of the contract price for 30 days following completion of the work for the benefit of subcontractors. This is called a *retainage fund*.

Trapping Funds in the Hands of the Owner

Trapping of funds occurs when the owner receives written notice of a sub-contractor's claim prior to payment to the contractor. Assuming the notice contains the information required by law, the owner must protect the sub-contractor. If the owner elects to pay the contractor despite the notice, then the owner will be liable to the subcontractor if the subcontractor is not paid. If the owner had not received notice of the claim prior to payment, the owner would not be liable.

CASE EXAMPLE

King, the owner of Blackacre, has contracted with Harrison for the con-struction of a horse stable. In performing this contract, Harrison subcon-tracted the roofing of the stable with Willie. Willie performed his work and is now owed $2,300 by Harrison. Harrison requests payment from King in the amount of $4,500, which includes the roof and other work performed by Harrison in the last two weeks. King pays Harrison as requested, but Harri-son does not pay Willie. Since Willie did not notify King that he was owed $2,300 before the payment to Harrison, Willie cannot perfect his material-man's lien. He failed to trap funds as required by Texas law. Willie must rely on his contract with Harrison and Harrison's solvency for payment. If Willie had notified King in advance of King's payment to Harrison, then Willie could hold King liable for the $2,300 and foreclose a properly perfected lien against the real property.

In addition to the preliminary notice described in the example, the sub-contractor must also file with the county clerk a lien affidavit within the statutory time period and mail a copy of the lien affidavit to the original contractor and the owner. If the subcontractor fails to take both steps within the time required, the lien will not be considered perfected.

Retainage Fund

The owner is also required to retain ten percent of the contract price for 30 days after the project is completed for the benefit of subcontractors, suppli-ers and laborers. This is called a *retainage fund*. The retainage fund is man-datory. If the owner does not set it aside, he or she will be liable for payment of all properly perfected liens whether or not the funds had been trapped previously. The liability of the owner is limited to the amount he or she should have retained. If ten percent of the contract price is not sufficient to pay all the lien claimants, then the lien claimants will share ratably.

CASE EXAMPLE

Using the previous case example, Willie has another remedy. If Willie perfects his lien by filing the lien affidavit within 30 days after the work is completed, then even though he failed to trap the payment Willie will have a lien against the retainage fund. If King failed to withhold the retainage, Willie's lien is against the property, and he can file suit to foreclose. However, if King withholds ten percent of the contract price for 30 days after the work is completed, his liability is limited to the amount in the fund. Willie would be paid out of this fund.

The case that follows discusses the subcontractor's lien rights under each of the two methods for perfecting the lien. The statutory procedure for creating the lien must be followed precisely if the lien is going to be enforceable. The case also discusses the relation back doctrine and the issue of priority.

CASE EXCERPT *First National Bank in Graham v. Sledge,* 653 S.W.2d 283 (Supreme Court of Texas 1983) CAMPBELL, Justice. This is a mechanic's and materialman's statutory lien case. The First National Bank in Graham sued the owner, Guy Meacham, and five subcontractors to remove a cloud from title to land caused by lien affidavits filed by the subcontractors. . . .

Meacham, the owner of two lots in Graham, Texas, contracted with Harris, a general contractor, to build a house on each lot. The contract price was $23,383 per house. Meacham and Harris executed a mechanic's lien contract for each lot and Meacham gave Harris a mechanic's lien note for each contract. Harris assigned the mechanic's lien contracts and notes to the First National Bank as collateral for interim construction money advanced to Harris. Harris completed one house, but took bankruptcy before completing the other. The subcontractors, unpaid, filed lien affidavits in the Young County lien records. The subcontractors then mailed a copy of each lien affidavit to Meacham. . . .

Because a subcontractor is a derivative claimant and unlike a general contractor, has no constitutional, common law, or contractual lien on the property of the owner, a subcontractor's lien rights are totally dependent on compliance with the statutes authorizing the lien. . . .

The Act provides two methods by which a subcontractor can perfect a lien on the owner's property. Article 5463 [now Tex. Prop. Code §§53.081–53.084] is a "trapping" statute. It provides the subcontractors can trap, in the owner's hands, funds payable to the general contractor if the owner receives notice from the subcontractors that they were not being paid. . . . Article 5469 [now Tex. Prop. Code §§53.101–53.105] often referred to as the "retainage" statute, is a duty statute. It provides that it shall be the duty of the owner to retain 10% of the contract price owing to the general contractor, and that the fund be retained in the owner's hands for 30 days after the work is completed. . . .

To determine whether the subcontractors have valid liens, we must compare the steps the subcontractors took to perfect their liens with the statutory requirements. . . .

The only notices sent to Meacham within the statutory time limit consisted of one copy of each subcontractor's lien affidavit without the invoice copies attached. These notices did not contain the statutory warning that unless Meacham paid the claim or it was otherwise settled he might be held personally liable and his property subjected to a lien.

We hold the subcontractors have not perfected a lien under Article 5463. . . . The statutory warning is a condition precedent; without it no lien can be imposed under article 5463. . . .

We must next determine if the subcontractors have perfected a lien under article 5469. Again the question hinges on the notice requirements to perfect the lien. The notice requirements of article 5469 are not the same as the requirements of article 5463. Because 5469 fixes a duty on the owner to retain 10% of the contract price regardless of notice of the claim, there is no requirement that the statutory warning be given to perfect a lien under article 5469. . . . We hold the copy of the lien affidavit timely received by the owner satisfied this requirement. . . .

We must now determine the inception and priority of the liens on Meacham's property. The bank and the subcontractors each seek a declaratory judgment that their liens are superior. The bank acquired its lien when the general contractor assigned the construction contracts and promissory notes to the bank in return for interim financing. Therefore, the bank holds the same position of priority as the general contractor. The date of the inception of the bank's lien is the date the general contractor's mechanic's and materialman's lien contracts were recorded in the lien records of the county. The subcontractors' liens are also effective as of that date because they furnished material or labor to the general contractor in connection with the construction contracts.

Although the bank's lien and the subcontractor's liens have the same time of inception, we hold article 5469 gives the subcontractor's liens preference over the bank's lien to the extent of the $3,638.30 which should have been retained. Article 5469 was enacted to protect mechanics, artisans and materialmen by providing a single protective fund to satisfy their unpaid claims. . . .

Foreclosure and Termination

The foreclosure of a materialman's lien is accomplished by the filing of a lawsuit against the property owners in which the claimant requests foreclosure. There will be a trial to determine whether the claimant has a right to foreclose the materialman's lien. If the court is satisfied that the right exists, it will order the lien foreclosed and the property sold at public auction by the sheriff.

Foreclosure and public sale is one method of terminating the lien and collecting payment. Another more common method is payment of the amount by the owner and obtaining from the materialman a release of the lien. Frequently, the owner of the property intends to develop and then sell the improved property. At the same time the property is transferred, the materialman's lien must be satisfied in order to convey a clear title to the land. If the lien is not released, the new owner takes the land subject to the lien. This means that the materialman can still pursue foreclosure of the perfected lien; consequently, settlement of the lien is required as a condition of purchase.

Liens may also be terminated by a *waiver*. The contractor or subcontractor waives in writing his or her right to assert a lien against the property. Because this is an important right, the waiver is enforced only against a materialman who signed it.

Finally, mechanic's liens are also extinguished by the lienor's failure to foreclose within the statutory time period. In Texas that is four years from the date the owner defaulted in his or her obligation to the materialman. The purpose of this statute of limitation is to eliminate the cloud on the title resulting from a properly filed mechanic's lien claim.

Homesteads

Materialman's liens can be created and attached to real property that is a homestead. They are created in the same manner as was generally described above, with one additional requirement. That requirement is the execution of a written contract and the recording of that contract prior to the date the work is begun. If the owner is married, both the husband and wife must sign the contract. Contracts executed after September 1, 1987 contain a warning next to the signature line that alerts the homeowner to the fact that ownership of his home could be lost if he breaches the contract for home improvement. A contractor is liable under the Deceptive Trade Practices Act (see Chapter 16) if the warning is not given. Loans made for home improvements are discussed in more detail in Chapters 21 and 22.

Public Projects

As mentioned earlier, mechanic's liens cannot be filed against publicly owned property. There is no right, either statutory or constitutional, in Texas to charge government-owned land with the debt even if improvements were made to land. However, to protect subcontractors in Texas who perform labor or supply material to a public project, the original contractor is usually required to post a payment bond. If a subcontractor is not paid, then the subcontractor can file a claim against the payment bond. The existence of a bond does not encumber the land.

JUDGMENT LIENS

A *judgment lien* is a lien that automatically arises against all property of a defendant when a plaintiff wins a judgment against him or her. (Tex. Prop. Code §52.001) The judgment lien in Texas is perfected against real property by recording an abstract of judgment with the county clerk in each county where the judgment debtor owns property. The judgment does not have to specify any particular piece of property to be enforceable against that property. The abstract of judgment includes the names of the plaintiff and defendant in the lawsuit, the date of the judgment, the amount of the judgment and, of course, the party against whom the judgment was taken.

CASE EXAMPLE

Justin Lane purchased a lot. Lane was the defendant in a tort case, and a judgment was entered against him for $8,500. Lane refused to pay the judgment as he felt that it was unfair. When Lane attempted to sell the lot, the purchaser's attorney refused to certify that the title was marketable because of a judgment lien resulting from the tort case.
the lot, the purchaser's attorney refused to certify that the title was marketable because of a judgment lien resulting from the tort case.

The judgment lien continues for ten years from the date of recording and can be renewed. It is an involuntary lien attaching to all of the debtor's property. The lien establishes the claim of the *judgment creditor* against the defendant's real estate and helps to ensure that the plaintiff will eventually collect the judgment. While the lien exists, a sale or mortgage of the property is subject to the judgment creditor's interest. As a result, the defendant often pays the judgment to free the property from the judgment creditor's lien. Ultimately, however, the real estate can be levied against and sold if the judgment is not paid. The only real property exempt from forced sale is a homestead. Proceeds from the sale of a homestead are also exempt for six months after the date of the sale. (Tex. Prop. Code §41.001)

The judgment lien is foreclosed by a procedure called *execution*. The judgment creditor requests the sheriff to sell at public auction real property owned by the judgment debtor. The judgment creditor must provide the sheriff with the legal description of the real property owned by the judgment debtor. The sheriff sends notice of the execution to the judgment debtor, who has an opportunity to pay the judgment prior to the date of sale. Judgment liens can be executed only against real property that is not the homestead of the debtor.

Legal Effect

Real estate personnel, especially those involved in sales, should be especially concerned with judgment liens that attach to fee simple ownership. A properly perfected judgment lien creates a cloud on the title to the real estate that must be removed prior to the closing of the sale of the real property. Failure to secure a release of the judgment lien can result in the purchaser's losing the property to a judgment creditor of the seller. Problems can arise when the seller has the same name as a judgment debtor. It can be difficult to determine whether the seller and the judgment debtor are the same person. Frequently, a title company will issue a title insurance policy, provided the seller will execute an affidavit that he or she is not the same person as the person named in an abstract of judgment.

TAX LIEN

The power of the government to levy taxes is commonly coupled with the right to place liens on real and personal property to facilitate tax collection.

Liens are encountered as part of the tax structure at all levels of government. In addition to federal and state governments, counties, cities, towns and villages as well as nonpolitical units such as school and water utility districts are authorized to use liens as security when taxes are unpaid.

Although tax liens may be placed against both real and personal property, liens on real property are generally more effective than those on personal property. Several reasons exist for this. Personal property is easier to conceal than real property. Personal property can be moved from the taxing district or disguised with little difficulty. Real property's value is relatively stable, whereas many types of personal property deteriorate when used. As a result, personal property is often not of sufficient value to cover the defaulted tax.

In Texas the taxation of real estate is the most common type of taxation used by governmental entities to collect revenue. Governmental units can also assess sales taxes, special-use taxes and taxes against personal property. However, it is the taxation of real property that receives the most attention. By statute in Texas the tax lien attaches automatically on January 1 of each year against the property on which the tax will be imposed or assessed for that year. The lien is only for taxes due as a result of the ownership of that particular piece of property. After the tax has become delinquent, the taxing authority can file suit to foreclose the tax lien. These suits for foreclosure of tax liens will be tried, and, if the taxes are found due, the court will order the property sold.

If the property is sold, the former owner has the right to redeem the property. It can be redeemed anytime during the two years immediately following the recording of the tax deed by paying the purchaser the amount he or she paid for the property plus a penalty provision of 25 percent of the amount if redeemed during the first year and 50 percent of the amount if redeemed during the second year. This right of redemption applies only to tax foreclosure sales.

Federal Tax Lien

The federal taxing authority uses liens against real property to aid in the collection of federal income, estate and gift taxes. Federal tax liens for income taxes are not valid against a mortgagee, pledgee, mechanic's lienor, purchaser or judgment creditor until a notice of lien is filed. Liens for federal estate taxes do not require recording or filing. They come into existence against all of a decedent's taxable assets automatically upon that person's death. Relatively simple procedures have been developed to release a decedent's real property from the tax lien. These are designed to facilitate sale of the property. They ordinarily require a bond by the estate or partial payment of the tax. Federal gift taxes also attach automatically upon all gifts made. If the tax is not paid, the donee can be personally liable up to the value of the gift.

LIENS AGAINST MINERAL PROPERTY

The development of minerals has long been an important part of the Texas economy. There are many laws concerning mineral rights and the development of minerals. One of these laws provides that a mineral contractor or subcontractor has a lien to secure payment for labor or services related to mineral activities. (Tex. Prop. Code §56.001) Although mineral contractors and subcontractors may be covered under the statutory mechanic's lien previously discussed, there is some doubt. The question arises because mineral development may not constitute an "improvement" to the land. This special law leaves no doubt that mineral contractors and subcontractors do have the right to a lien against the mineral estate and in some cases the land itself.

The law covers most activities related to mineral development, such as drilling, mining or repairing of wells, pipelines, mines and quarries. The lien can attach to the land, the leasehold, the well or any personal property used in the operation of the development. However, the lien will not attach to the fee simple absolute unless the work is being performed at the request of the landowner. If the leaseholder requests the work, the lien attaches to the leasehold estate.

The lien against mineral property is perfected by filing an affidavit no later than six months after the day the indebtedness accrued with the county clerk in the county where the mineral property is located. In addition to this affidavit, the subcontractor must notify the property owner that the lien has been filed. The owner's liability to subcontractors is limited to the amount that the owner owes the original contractor when the notice is received. Foreclosure of the lien against mineral property is the same as foreclosure of a mechanic's lien.

CONSTRUCTION LOANS

Loans made for construction of improvements or repairs on land are usually secured by a lien against the land. This lien is created by a deed of trust. The creation and enforcement of deed of trust liens are discussed in Chapters 21 and 22.

PRIORITY

The numerous liens that have been described in this chapter can encumber a single piece of real property. If the property owner fails to pay the debts secured by the liens, the property will be sold and the proceeds paid to the lienholders. If the proceeds are insufficient to pay all lienholders in full, which of these lienholders will lose? The issue of priority is very important to a lienholder. The following rules regarding priority in Texas apply to all types of liens, including deed of trust liens and vendor's liens discussed later in this textbook.

    1. Federal tax liens have priority over all other liens.

Figure 13.3: **SUMMARY OF MAJOR CHARACTERISTICS OF INVOLUNTARY LIENS**

Type of Lien	Method of Perfection	Foreclosure	Redemption
Materialman's and Mechanic's Lien:			
Original Contractor—Constitutional Lien	self-executing but should record to protect against subsequent purchasers and creditors—if homestead, see additional requirements below	by court order	none
Original Contractor—Statutory Lien	file lien affidavit and send copies of it to landowner within 120 days after debt accrues	by court order	none
Subcontractors—Statutory Lien	trap funds by giving notice to landowner prior to payment to general contractor and file lien affidavit within time period or file lien against retainage fund within time period	by court order	none
All Contractors—Homesteads	follow procedure set out above and have written contract signed by husband and wife recorded prior to beginning work	by court order	none
Judgment Liens	file abstract of judgment in each county where debtor owns property	by writ of execution	none
Tax Liens:			
Federal tax liens	file affidavit except for estate and gift taxes	by non-judicial fore-closure	none
County, city or school district	self-executing	by court order	two years
Liens Against Mineral Property	file affidavit and notify property owner	by court order	none

2. State and local tax liens have priority over mortgage liens.
3. Liens are given priority in the order that each was recorded except:
   - liens that have been expressly subordinated by agreement of all the parties;
   - mechanic's liens whose priority date is determined by the date the work was begun or the contract recorded; and
   - fixture liens created under article 9 of the Texas Business and Commerce Code (see Chapter 4) to the extent that particular law gives the fixture lien priority.
4. A materialman will be allowed to remove any materials from the land, provided he or she can remove them without damage to the land.

SUMMARY

A lien is a claim against property that either secures payment of a debt or binds a party to fulfill some other obligation. Although a lien does not transfer title to the lienholder, it establishes the right to have an obligation met out of proceeds from sale of the property.

Because land and buildings provide excellent security for a debt, liens occur frequently in real estate practice. Liens are classed as voluntary—those the property owner enters willingly—and involuntary—those attached by legal process to satisfy creditors. The home mortgage is an example of a voluntary lien. Involuntary liens important to the real estate professional are the mechanic's (or materialman's) lien, the judgment lien and the tax lien.

The mechanic's lien provides contractors or suppliers who furnish labor or materials to improve buildings or land the right to seek a sale of the property to satisfy unpaid claims. The value of the improved property acts as security for the labor and supplies furnished. Usually, building supplies are sold on credit, and the additional security induces financial institutions as well as suppliers of materials to provide more credit for the construction industry.

There are two types of materialman's liens in Texas: the constitutional lien and the statutory lien. The constitutional lien is a self-executing lien that protects materialmen who deal directly with the owner of the land improved. The statutory lien must be perfected but covers subcontractors, laborers and suppliers as well as original contractors. To perfect the statutory lien, the materialman must file a properly executed lien affidavit and notify the owner of the land that a materialman's lien is claimed against the property. Notice and filing must be accomplished within a certain time period. The time for filing the lien and the type of notice required differ for subcontractors and contractors. The procedure that a subcontractor must follow is more complex. There are two ways a subcontractor can be secured: trapping funds in the hands of the owner and attaching a lien against the retainage fund. This scheme reflects the legislature's attempt to balance the interest of subcontractors with the interest of the owner and create an equitable system for protecting both against a contractor who is not paying his or her bills.

Materialman's liens can be terminated in several ways. The most common is by a release that is executed when the debt is paid. However, if the owner does not voluntarily settle the debt, the lien claimant can sue to foreclose the lien. After a trial the court can sue to foreclose the lien. After a trial the court can order the sheriff to sell the property and apply the proceeds to the amount owed to the materialman.

Another common type of involuntary lien is the judgment lien. The judgment lien arises automatically when a plaintiff obtains a judgment against a defendant in a lawsuit. The judgment lien is perfected by recording an abstract of judgment. The lien is foreclosed by the sheriff's selling the property pursuant to a writ of execution.

The tax lien is created by an owner's failure to pay taxes. It may be filed against real property by governments at all levels. There are federal tax liens as well as state tax liens. The state tax lien is foreclosed by judicial action after a trial. If the property is sold to satisfy the tax debt, the owner has two years in which to redeem the property.

Mineral contractors and subcontractors are provided special protection under the law. Since there is some question as to whether these materialmen would be covered under the general statutory lien, they can be assured of protection by following the requirements set out in the special statute.

Frequently, a property owner who defaults in the payment of one debt is also delinquent in others. Consequently, persons with liens against land of the debtor are concerned with priority among competing creditors. Tax liens are always paid first from the proceeds from the sale of the land. Other lienholders are then paid in the order in which the lien was filed. There are some exceptions to this general rule.

QUESTIONS AND CASE PROBLEMS

1. When a contractor improves real property, the work is done on the basis of a contract with the owner. A contractor who is not paid can sue for breach of that agreement. Explain why a contractor should also be entitled to file a mechanic's lien against the property.

2. Kile borrowed $15,000 from Chatfield, giving her a promissory note to cover the debt. The note was unsecured, but Chatfield knew that Kile owned substantial unmortgaged real property. A short time later Hude won a judgment against Kile for $150,000. When Kile filed as a bankrupt, both Chatfield and Hude claimed priority in the real estate. Which of the two has the superior claim? Explain.

3. Kniveton, Inc., performed well services under an oral contract with Levens Corporation. Levens Corporation had an oil and gas leasehold on the properties where Kniveton, Inc., performed its services. Levens did not pay Kniveton the $3,106.45 due for the well services. On May 14, 1980, Kniveton filed its materialman's lien. On May 16, 1980, Levens sold its leasehold to Efficient Energy Systems, Inc. Thereafter, Levens filed bankruptcy. Kniveton sued Efficient Energy to foreclose its lien. Efficient Energy defended on the ground that it had not assumed the obligation of Levens to pay Kniveton. Is there any merit to this defense? If Kniveton is allowed to foreclose, against what interest can it foreclose?

4. Rhoades purchased from Miller 25½ cubic yards of ready-mix concrete to be used in the construction of a building on Rhoades's property. Miller performed, but Rhoades did not pay Miller for his work. On March 8, 1966, Miller filed a materialman's lien that did not comply with the statutory requirements. When Miller sued to foreclose the lien, Rhoades defended alleging that the lien was invalid. Miller claims that even though he did not have a valid statutory lien, he did have a constitutional lien. Is Miller right?

14

Texas Real Estate License Act

Many phases of a real estate transaction are performed by representatives who act on behalf of another. Real estate transactions frequently involve complex legal and financial issues that are better performed by trained persons. For many years the state of Texas has regulated those persons who represent others in any type of real estate transaction. The Texas law that licenses and regulates persons in the real estate field is called the Texas Real Estate License Act. In addition to the Texas Real Estate License Act, real estate agents are subject to other laws that will be discussed in Chapters 15 and 16.

The Texas Real Estate License Act (Tex. Rev. Civ. Stat. art. 6573a, hereafter referred to as *the act*) is the principal law affecting the real estate profession. Therefore, it is important that persons anticipating a career in this field be thoroughly familiar with this statute. In this chapter provisions of this law will be explained in detail. The complete text of the law can be found in the appendix to this book. In addition to the statute itself, the Texas Real Estate Commission has issued several regulations that interpret the provisions of the act. Some of these regulations will also be covered in this chapter.

The act contains 20 sections that regulate several aspects of the real estate business. A general overview of the act is beneficial to an understanding of the various sections. The act can be divided into ten areas as follows:

1. It establishes the Texas Real Estate Commission and defines its authority and responsibility.
2. It defines the activities that are regulated under the act, the per-

sons who must be licensed and the persons who are exempt from coverage.

3. It establishes the qualifications that must be met in order to receive a license from the commission.

4. It defines the obligations of a licensee to the commission and prohibits licensees from engaging in certain conduct or activities.

5. It creates the procedural and substantive framework for suspension or revocation of a license.

6. It creates a Texas Real Estate Broker-Lawyer Committee that among other duties, drafts the standard contract forms.

7. It establishes the qualifications for licensing real estate inspectors and regulates the activities of real estate inspectors.

8. It creates two funds to aid in compensating persons injured by a licensee: the real estate recovery fund and the real estate inspection recovery fund.

9. It defines the civil and criminal penalties for violations of the statute.

10. It limits the circumstances under which a licensee may sue to recover a commission.

THE TEXAS REAL ESTATE COMMISSION

The Texas Real Estate Commission (TREC) is a state agency consisting of nine members. The commissioners are appointed by the governor with the approval of the senate. Each member must be a citizen of Texas and a qualified voter. Six of the members must be real estate brokers with at least five years of experience. Three of the members must be persons who are neither licensees nor persons with a financial interest in the practice of a real estate broker.

The commissioners hold office for staggered terms of six years. Every two years three of the members of TREC are replaced. TREC hires officers and employees to assist in administering the provisions of the act. The Texas Real Estate Commission has its principal office in Austin, Texas. In 1987, TREC had approximately 95 employees.

TREC has the authority to establish regulations governing the conduct and ethics of licensees. Periodically it reviews the promulgated regulations and makes revisions. Proposed regulations and revisions are published in the *Texas Register*, and public reaction and suggestions are considered before the regulation becomes final. The Texas Legislature, acting through its appropriate committee, can veto any proposed rule and demand the repeal of any effective rule. In addition to this rule-making power, TREC has the important function of administering the provisions of the act and monitoring the activities of its licensees. In carrying out the act, TREC oversees the licensing of brokers and salesmen, accredits the proprietary schools that offer real estate courses, investigates verified complaints against licensees, conducts hearings involving revocation or suspension of a license, and, effective January 1, 1986, licenses and regulates real estate inspectors. TREC is the primary state agency with responsibility for licensing and regulating real estate brokers, salesmen and inspectors.

PERSONS REGULATED UNDER THE ACT

Section 1 of the act states:

> It is unlawful for a person to act in the capacity of, engage in the business of, or advertise or hold himself out as engaging in or conducting the business of a real estate broker or a real estate salesman within this state without first obtaining a real estate license from the Texas Real Estate Commission. It is unlawful for a person licensed as a real estate salesman to act or attempt to act as a real estate agent unless he is, at such time, associated with a licensed Texas real estate broker and acting for the licensed real estate broker.

The purpose of the act is to regulate all persons who engage in activities traditionally performed by real estate brokers. This is true whether those people call themselves brokers, advisors, consultants, finders or apartment locators. The act, to avoid any confusion regarding activities that are conducted by real estate brokers, defines the term *real estate broker*. In §2 of the act *real estate broker* is defined to include:

> a person who, for another person and for a fee, commission, or other valuable consideration, or with the intention or in the expectation or on the promise of receiving or collecting a fee, commission, or other valuable consideration from another person:
> (A) sells, exchanges, purchases, rents, or leases real estate;
> (B) offers to sell, exchange, purchase, rent, or lease real estate;
> (C) negotiates or attempts to negotiate the listing, sale, exchange, purchase, rental or leasing of real estate;
> (D) lists or offers or attempts or agrees to list real estate for sale, rental, lease, exchange, or trade;
> (E) appraises or offers or attempts to or agrees to appraise real estate;
> (F) auctions, or offers or attempts or agrees to auction real estate;
> (G) buys or sells or offers to buy or sell, or otherwise deals in options in real estate;
> (H) aids, attempts, or offers to aid in locating or obtaining for purchase, rent, or lease any real estate;
> (I) procures or assists in the procuring of prospects for the

purpose of effecting the sale, exchange, lease, or rental of real estate; or

(J) procures or assists in the procuring of properties for the purpose of effecting the sale, exchange, lease, or rental of real estate.

The activities of a real estate broker under the act include almost every aspect of the real estate business. If the activity is conducted in the state of Texas, then the person must be licensed by TREC. This is true even if the property being offered for sale or lease is located in another state.

Some of the less obvious business activities covered by the act include property management companies and apartment locator services. TREC has promulgated regulations stating that persons who represent to the general public that they are in the property management business must be licensed. TREC has also clarified any confusion regarding licensure of persons who operate apartment locator or home-finding services. The regulation states that the compilation of rental vacancies available in an area is an activity requiring a real estate license, even if the property is not shown, sold, leased or managed by the apartment locator service.

Persons in the real estate business can choose any type of business organization form in which to operate. A person may conduct the activities as an individual or sole proprietorship. The person may choose to join with others and form a partnership or a corporation to engage in the same activities. Obviously a person who operates his or her real estate business as a sole proprietorship must be licensed individually. If the business is conducted as a partnership, each individual partner who engages in real estate brokerage activities must be licensed. It is also possible, though not required, that the partnership be licensed by the commission. If the business is organized as a corporation, any officer or employee of the corporation who is engaging in the activities set out above must be individually licensed. In addition, the corporation itself must be licensed. If the corporation has not been licensed, then neither it nor its employees or independent contractors can force the payment of a commission even if the employee or independent contractor is licensed. The case that follows illustrates the importance of licensing the corporation.

• CASE BRIEF •

Henry S. Miller Company is a Texas corporation engaged in the real estate brokerage business. In 1975 the Miller Company entered into a listing agreement with Jones Lake Company, Inc., to sell a warehouse located in Dallas. Miller Company, acting through an employee, Jerry McCutchin, found a buyer for the property. As part of the sale, the buyer, Treo Enterprises, agreed to pay Miller Company the $15,000 commission due by Jones Lake Company, Inc. Treo Enterprises executed a promissory note in the amount of $15,000, payable to Miller Company. Treo defaulted in its payments to Miller Company under the note, and Miller Company sued to collect the balance due. At the time of the transaction Miller Company was not licensed by the Texas Real Estate Commission; however, McCutchin was a licensed broker. One of the justifications for nonpayment used by Treo was that a person may not bring a suit for collection of a commission unless he or she was a licensed broker or salesperson at the time the services were begun. Treo argued that Miller Company could not sue because the corporation was not licensed. Miller argued that there was no need to license the corporation, provided the employee who performed the services was licensed. The court agreed with Treo. It reasoned that, since it was clear that Miller Company, not McCutchin, contracted to perform the brokerage services, and corporations are legally recognized as persons, then §20 of the act required that the corporation be licensed at the time the services were begun in order to collect the commission due by Treo. *Henry S. Miller Company vs. Treo Enterprises*, 585 S.W.2d 674 (Tex. Civ. App.— Texarkana 1978).

Exemptions

Although coverage under the act is quite broad, ten categories of persons are specifically exempted from regulation under the act. The exemptions are found in §3, which reads:

The provisions of this Act shall not apply to any of the following persons and transactions, and each and all of the following persons and transactions are hereby exempted from the provisions of the Act, to wit:

(a) an attorney at law licensed in this state or in any other state;

(b) an attorney in fact under a duly executed power of attorney authorizing the consummation of a real estate transaction;

(c) a public official in the conduct of his official duties;

(d) a person acting officially as a receiver, trustee, administrator, executor, or guardian;

(e) a person acting under a court order or under the authority of a will or a written trust instrument;

(f) a salesperson employed by an owner in the sale of structures and land on which said structures are situated, provided such structures are erected by the owner in the due course of his business;

(g) an on-site manager of an apartment complex;

(h) transactions involving the sale, lease, or transfer of any mineral or mining interest in real property;

(i) an owner or his employees in renting or leasing his own real estate whether improved or unimproved;

(j) transactions involving the sale, lease, or transfer of cemetery lots.

An attorney-in-fact is a person acting under a power of attorney to execute documents such as those instruments necessary to close the sale or purchase of a specific piece of real property. Powers of attorney were discussed in Chapter 10. This is a very restricted exemption. The regulation interpreting this provision states that "An unlicensed person cannot use the power of attorney method to engage in the real estate agency business." (22 T.A.C. §535.32) Therefore, it would be reasonable to conclude that a person who regularly and for a fee acts as an attorney-in-fact for another for buying or selling real estate must be licensed. However, a husband who was given a power of attorney by his wife to execute documents and consummate the sale of real property is clearly exempted from the licensing requirement.

Persons serving as trustees, administrators, executors or guardians are also exempted from this act. This is true no matter how frequently or how many tracts of land are bought, sold, rented or leased. The activities of guardians and administrators are to a large extent supervised by the court. Typically, the sale, purchase, or rental of property that is part of an estate must be approved by the court.

Owners of property base their choice of executors and trustees on confidence in the ability and integrity of the people they have chosen. Requiring the person chosen to be licensed would unnecessarily limit an owner's freedom in choosing an executor or a trustee. Furthermore, the law regarding the responsibilities of trustees and executors provides adequate protection.

Another important exemption is for persons who are employed as landmen. A *landman* is a person who negotiates options and contracts for the purchase of mineral leases and mineral deeds. Landmen can operate independently of any one company but frequently are employed by a company in the oil and gas business. Companies such as Exxon, U.S.A., Pennzoil, and Coastal States have large departments of employees who are landmen.

Finally, an exemption that is frequently encountered and is the most controversial of the exemptions is for salespersons who are employed by the builder-owner of new structures. One of the reasons this is a controversial exemption is that it is difficult to determine the public policy served by excepting from the act's coverage this group of persons. The result, though, is obvious. The state has no direct control over the qualifications, competency or conduct of persons who sell new housing on behalf of a developer-owner. For example, John Smith, Inc., a developer and builder of residential subdivisions, may hire salespersons who are not only unlicensed by the state of Texas but who may also lack any training in real estate transactions. Thus these persons are not subject to the same stringent code of conduct imposed by TREC on its licensees. In other words, exemption from the licensing requirement means exemption from *all* aspects of the act. The following case brief illustrates this point.

• CASE BRIEF •

Young was hired by Del Mar Homes, Inc., to sell homes that Del Mar had built upon real estate it owned. Young was not licensed as either a sales-person or a broker. A dispute regarding duties and compensation arose be-tween Young and Del Mar, resulting in termination of Young's employment. At the time of his termination, Young had earned $19,551 in commissions, which were not due and payable until the sales were closed. These clos-ings took place after the date of termination. Young sued Del Mar for the commissions after Del Mar refused to pay. Del Mar defended on the grounds that the Texas Real Estate License Act prohibited suits for com-missions if (1) the agent was not licensed at the time the contract was made or (2) there was no writing evidencing the right to a commission. The court held that, although Del Mar correctly stated the law in Texas, Young as an employee of an owner-builder was exempt from any and all requirements of the Texas Real Estate License Act. *Young v. Del Mar Homes, Inc.*, 608 S.W.2d 804 (Tex. Civ. App.—Houston 14th 1980).

Penalties

Engaging in the activities of a real estate broker without a license from the commission and for which there is no exemption is both a civil violation and a criminal violation of the law. The commission has the authority to request that the court stop or enjoin the person from engaging in the activ-ity. An injunction also can be instituted by the county attorney, the district attorney or the attorney general. A person who is found guilty of acting as a real estate broker or real estate salesman without first obtaining a license can be fined between $100 and $500, imprisoned in the county jail for a term of less than one year or both. This is a misdemeanor offense. A corpo-ration that is found guilty of engaging in brokerage activities without a li-cense can be fined not less that $1,000 or more that $2,000 for its first infraction. An individual's second conviction for the same offense can be punished by a fine between $500 and $1,000, imprisonment for a term of less than two years or both. The corporation's fine for a second offense is not less than $2,000 or greater than $5,000.

The guilty party is also required to return any compensation he or she earned to the persons who paid the fee. At the court's discretion, the guilty party can be required to pay the injured party an amount in excess of the fee as a penalty. The penalty cannot exceed three times the amount of the fee actually paid by the injured party.

QUALIFICATIONS FOR OBTAINING A LICENSE

TREC issues two types of licenses: the salesman's license and the broker's license. If licensed, the salesman and broker can perform the same range of real estate activities. However, a salesman can perform those activities only if associated with a broker. The broker is responsible for the conduct of his or her salesmen even if the salesmen are not supervised directly by the broker. By contrast, brokers act independently. They can establish their own real estate business and contract directly with persons for the sale of their services.

To qualify for a license either as a salesman or as a broker, the applicant must be a citizen or the United States or a legal alien, must be at least 18 years of age, must be a resident of the state of Texas for at least 60 days prior to the date of the application and must be of good moral character. Good moral character refers to the qualities of honesty, trustworthiness and integrity. The mere fact that an applicant has a civil judgment against him or her, or a criminal conviction, or has been adjudged bankrupt does not necessarily preclude the applicant from meeting the requirement of good moral character. However, if the judgment or conviction or bankruptcy was in part based upon the dishonesty, misrepresentation or fraud of the applicant, then securing a license may be difficult.

In addition to these general requirements, the applicant is required to demonstrate that he or she is competent. The competency of an individual is determined by an examination that is given several times a year by the Texas Real Estate Commission. Different examinations are administered to prospective salesmen and brokers. The examinations test the applicant's knowledge of real estate principles, finance, law, appraisal, math and investments.

Applicants must also provide TREC with satisfactory evidence of completion of educational courses beyond high school The applicant for a salesman's license must complete at least 12 semester hours or 180 classroom hours of postsecondary education. Of these at least six semester hours or 90 classroom hours must be core real estate courses, including a course in principles of real estate of at least two semester hours and one or more of the eight other core real estate courses enumerated in §7(a) of the act or approved by TREC. The remaining hours must be completed in related courses as defined by TREC. "Related courses" are considered on a course-by-course basis, but, in general, college-level business courses and basic courses in English, mathematics, psychology and speech will meet this requirement.

The core real estate courses specifically set out in §7(a) of the act are principles of real estate, real estate appraisal, real estate law, real estate finance, real estate marketing, real estate mathematics, real estate brokerage, property management and real estate investments. One of the courses that has been approved by TREC is real estate law: contracts. Additional approved courses are added by TREC periodically. The courses must be completed at an accredited college, university or proprietary school specifically authorized and approved by TREC.

During the first three years that a salesman is licensed, he or she must continue to complete postsecondary courses consisting of real estate core courses. The salesperson will not be recertified after the first year unless he or she has completed at least another two semester hours or 30 classroom hours each year for the next three consecutive years. Consequently, by the third recertification, the salesman will have completed a total of 18 semester hours of postsecondary education of which at least 12 semester hours were in the core real estate courses. Following the third recertification there is no requirement that the salesman continue to complete courses.

Applicants for a broker's license must meet all of the conditions required for a salesman's license. In addition, the broker must have completed a total of 60 semester hours or 900 classroom hours of postsecondary education. Of these hours, the applicant must have completed at least 12 semester hours in the core real estate courses. The applicant for a broker's license must have had at least two years of experience as a licensed salesman in the state of Texas during the three years preceding the application. The competency of an applicant for a broker's license is tested by an examination administered by the commission. The examination for the broker's license is more stringent than the test for the salesman's license.

Finally, both salespersons and brokers are required to complete three classroom hours of coursework on federal, state and local laws governing housing discrimination or community reinvestment or three semester hours in constitutional law.

When the act was originally enacted, it provided that anyone licensed under the prior law was exempt from the examination requirement of the act. This type of provision in the law is called a *grandfather clause* and is sometimes included when licensing requirements are changed by the legislature. Another special group of potential licensees are nonresidents who are licensed under the laws of another state. Texas does not have reciprocity. This means that those who are licensed as brokers or salesmen in another state cannot engage in brokerage activities in Texas unless they also are licensed here. To obtain a Texas license, the person licensed by another state must meet the same educational and competency requirements discussed above. An applicant's transcript of courses taken will be evaluated for similarity with the core real estate courses required here. The applicant will be tested using the same test given for salesmen or brokers as appropriate. The experience requirement for the broker's license can be met by real estate activities engage in outside the state, provided that they are substantially similar to the type of experience a salesman in Texas would gain during the two years.

REGULATION OF ACTIVITIES

TREC is involved not only in determining the qualifications of persons interested in engaging in real estate brokerage activities but also in regulating the activities of its licensees. All brokers are required to maintain a fixed office within the state of Texas and to notify TREC of any changes in that office. The act further requires that the broker prominently display his or her license and that of any salesmen for whom he or she is responsible. These licenses are displayed in the office of the broker. If a broker withdraws his or her sponsorship of a salesman, then the salesman's license must be returned to TREC until another licensed broker assumes sponsorship of the salesman.

In addition to keeping track of its licensees, the commission has the authority to investigate the actions of licensees and to review records maintained by the licensees. These investigations may be begun by the commission after receipt of a written complaint or upon TREC's own motion. A licensee's failure to produce documents or provide requested information is a sufficient ground for suspension or revocation of his or her license.

In §15 of the act, several of the grounds for suspension or revocation of a license are enumerated. Since this is a lengthy provision of the act, it is not reproduced verbatim here. However, the complete text is printed in the appendix. Some of the acts for which a license could be revoked or suspended include:

1. failing to disclose on whose behalf the agent is acting;
2. commingling money to be escrowed with his or her own funds;
3. splitting a commission with someone who is not licensed;
4. failing to include a definite termination date in a listing agreement;
5. pursuing a flagrant course of misrepresentation;
6. failing to advise a purchaser in writing that he or she should have a title examination performed by an attorney or obtain a policy of title insurance;
7. procuring a real estate license by fraud or misrepresentation; and
8. entering a plea of guilty or nolo contendre or being found guilty of a felony involving fraud.

There are many other reasons for suspension or revocation of a license, including conduct described in §15 as well as conduct prohibited elsewhere in the act. This listing merely shows the range of activities that can be unlawful. A salesperson or broker may also be liable for monetary damages or criminal sanctions if his or her misconduct warrants it.

It is important to note that in the litany of reasons for suspension or revocation of a license there are several grounds that do not require that the licensee acted intentionally. A broker or salesman may find himself in violation of the act without intending to have violated it. A licensee is expected to know and understand the provisions of the act and all the regulations promulgated by TREC. Ignorance or misunderstanding is not an excuse or justification for noncompliance.

For example, §15(6)(E) states that it is a ground for license suspension or revocation if a licensee fails "within a reasonable time properly to account for or remit money coming into his possession which belongs to others, or commingling money belonging to others with his own funds." Licensees are not required to act as escrow agents, but frequently they do. If a licensee agrees to hold the earnest money pending the closing of the sale, then he or she holds the money in a fiduciary capacity. What does the licensee do if a dispute arises between the seller and the buyer regarding the earnest money? The section quoted above requires the agent to account for the money within a reasonable time. First, what does it mean to account for the money, and second, what is a reasonable time?

• CASE BRIEF •

In March 1976, Kilgore, a broker, received $500 earnest money from Mr. and Mrs. Brown as deposit toward the purchase of land from Mr. and Mrs. Hearn. The deal fell through in April 1976. Both parties claimed the $500. The commission informed Kilgore on August 31, 1976, that he should remit the money to one of the parties. On November 17, 1976, Kilgore deposited the money with the court. On December 7, 1976, after a hearing before the commission, Kilgore's license was suspended for 90 days. Kilgore appealed the decision of the commission to the district court. The commission held that Kilgore had failed to account for the money within a reasonable time. Kilgore claimed that he had accounted for the money even though he did not remit it to either party. The court disagreed with Kilgore's interpretation of the phrase *account for.* It agreed with the commission and stated that *to account for* means to pay to the one entitled to receive it the money held in escrow. *Kilgore v. Texas Real Estate Commission,* 565 S.W.2d 114 (Tex. Civ. App.—Fort Worth 1978).

TREC in its regulations has provided licensees with guidance in interpreting this provision. It defines a *reasonable time* as 30 days after demand is made for an accounting or remittance. It has also defined *properly account for or remit* as meaning to pay the money to the party or parties entitled to the money if it can be reasonably determined to which party or parties the money should be paid. A provision regarding payment of the earnest money is usually included in the earnest money contract, and the licensee is bound to abide by the terms of that agreement. However, if the licensee cannot reasonably determine to whom the money should be paid, then he or she can deposit it with the court. One way to avoid some of the pitfalls of serving as an escrow agent is to include in the earnest money contract a provision that gives the licensee the right to demand a written authorization or release from the parties prior to disbursing the earnest money. Then, if the licensee fails to receive the written release, he or she can deposit the money with the court without encountering the problems confronting Kilgore in the case described above.

Revocation and Suspension

A licensee whose license is the subject of a possible suspension or revocation is entitled to a public hearing. Written notice of the allegations and the time and place of hearing must be given to the licensee. The hearing takes place before a representative of the commission who renders a decision based upon the evidence presented at the hearing. A licensee can be represented by an attorney at the hearing. The manner and procedure for conducting the hearing is established in regulations promulgated by the commission. If the licensee disagrees with the report of the hearing officer, he or she can request a hearing by the entire commission. Following a decision by the entire commission, the licensee can appeal to a district court.

The district court's review of the commission's decision is limited. The district court acts as an appeals court in these cases; therefore, representation at the commission's hearing and full presentation of evidence at the hearing are very important. The district court will review the transcript of the hearing and decide whether the decision reached by the commission is supported by substantial evidence and otherwise complies with the law and the regulations. An appeal must be filed in the district court within 30 days from the date the licensee is notified of the commission's decision.

A willful violation of any provision of the Texas Real Estate License Act is a misdemeanor. Although an unintentional act may be grounds for license suspension or revocation, a licensee cannot be found guilty of a crime unless his or her misconduct was willful. If a licensee is found guilty of a willful violation of the act, he or she can be fined up to $500, imprisoned for a term not to exceed one year or both.

UNAUTHORIZED PRACTICE OF LAW

A problem frequently encountered by licensees is a request from a client for legal advice. Licensees must understand the fundamentals of real estate law in order to perform competently many of the brokerage activities; however, they are not lawyers. The giving of legal advice and the preparation of legal documents constitutes practicing law. Practicing law without being licensed as an attorney at law is both a civil and criminal offense in this state.

Section 16 of the act addresses the problem of the unauthorized practice of law by a broker or salesman. It reads as follows.

> A license granted under the provisions of this Act shall be suspended or revoked by the commission on proof that the licensee, not being licensed and authorized to practice law in this state, for a consideration, reward, pecuniary benefit, present or anticipated, direct or indirect, or in connection with or as a part of his employment, agency, or fiduciary relationship as a licensee, drew a deed, note, deed of trust, will, or other written instrument that may transfer or anywise affect the title to or an interest in land, except as provided in the subsections below, or advised or counseled a person as to the validity or legal sufficiency of an instrument or as to the validity of title to real estate.

Brokers and salesmen are allowed to complete contract forms that have been promulgated by TREC or prepared by a lawyer or the property owner. The promulgated forms are discussed in detail in Chapter 19. Use and completion of these forms do not constitute the unauthorized practice of law. However, significant deviation or redrafting of these forms by a broker or salesman would constitute the unauthorized practice of law. Regulations promulgated by the Texas Real Estate Commission direct licensees to limit their additions and deletions to the forms to (1) filling in blanks, (2) adding factual statements and business details requested by the principal and (3) striking out only those parts desired by the principal and necessary to conform the contract to the intent of the principal. In reviewing the contract form with a principal, the licensee can explain the meaning of the factual statements and business details but cannot give legal advice.

Understanding the fine line between brokerage activities and practicing law often can be difficult. In an attempt to provide some guidance on this difficult question, the Texas Real Estate Commission has passed several rules on the issue of the unauthorized practice of law. These are found in §537.11 of the Rules of the Texas Real Estate Commission. The complete text of this section is included in the appendix.

The regulations require licensees to use the promulgated earnest money contract forms, lease forms and contract addenda forms whenever possible. Licensees are forbidden to give their opinion as to the legal effect of any contract or other document affecting title to real estate. Licensees are forbidden to give their opinion regarding the status or validity of title to a parcel of real estate. Licensees are also cautioned to advise their clients to seek the advice of an attorney whenever a transaction involves unusual matters. These restrictions are not meant to inhibit a licensee from discussing and disclosing with his or her principal all the facts that might affect the transaction or the title to the real estate. Certainly, if the licensee is aware of facts that might create a cloud or encumbrance against the title, the broker or salesman has a duty to explain these facts to his or her principal. A broker or licensee should never hesitate to discuss facts with clients. As a matter of fact, a licensee who fails to disclose or explain facts pertinent to a real estate transaction to clients would be in violation of his or her fiduciary obligation to the clients. Practicing law does not include a discussion of facts, but it does include giving advice as to the legal implications of the facts. A licensee must avoid giving his or her opinion regarding the legal effect of the facts.

CASE EXAMPLE

Assume that Higdon, a licensed broker, has a listing agreement for the sale of a home with Nancy and Marvin Spencer, the heirs of Samuel Spencer, the deceased landowner. Robert Spencer, a disinherited child of Samuel, calls Higdon and tells him that he plans to contest the will of the deceased and claims an ownership interest in the home. Higdon has a duty to notify his clients, Nancy and Marvin, that Robert has contacted him and the content of the communication. By doing this, Higdon is disclosing facts to his client. However, if Higdon also tells his clients that Robert has no grounds for challenging Samuel's will or that Robert cannot sue Nancy and Marvin, then he is giving legal advice. This constitutes the unauthorized practice of law.

Broker-Lawyer Committee

The act establishes the Texas Real Estate Broker-Lawyer Committee, an independent committee consisting of 12 members, six appointed by the Texas Real Estate Commission and six appointed by the president of the State Bar of Texas. The purpose of this special committee is the drafting and revising of standard contract forms that can be used by real estate licensees. The act directs that the forms prepared by this committee should be those that will expedite real estate transactions, reduce controversies and protect the interests of the parties to the transaction. TREC has the option of taking the forms developed by this committee and establishing regulations that require licensees to use these forms. The act does specifically provide, though, that a licensee can use other forms, provided they were prepared by an attorney at the request of the property owner or were prepared by the property owner. As a result of the activities of the Broker-Lawyer Committee, most of the real estate transactions in the state involve the use of one of the promulgated forms.

REAL ESTATE RECOVERY FUND

The act prohibits licensees from acting dishonestly or fraudulently in brokerage activities they perform for others. The prohibited activities described earlier are grounds for suspension or revocation of the license. In addition, the person with whom the licensee dealt has a civil lawsuit against the dishonest licensee. If the injured party obtains a judgment against the licensee and is unable to collect, he or she may be able to recover from the real estate recovery fund.

The fund is established in §8 of the act from $10 contributions assessed against each new licensee. The purpose of the fund is to compensate persons who have suffered actual damages due to the fraud or dishonesty of a licensee. There is at the present time some question as to the extent of coverage under this section. The section states that any person injured due to a violation of §15(3) or §15(4) of the act could be eligible to recover from the fund, provided he or she meets the other criteria. Section 15(4) in the original law was the list of infractions that is now found in §15(6). When §15 was revised by the state legislature in 1983, the sections were renumbered, resulting in the present confusion. TREC has continued to allow recovery from the fund if a proper party was injured by one of the acts described in §15(6), even though literally the law does not specifically provide for the coverage. It is expected that when the state legislature meets in 1989 this technical problem will be corrected.

In order to recover from the fund, the injured party must show that the fund covers the type of conduct engaged in by the licensee and that he or she has been unable to collect from the licensee. The request for payment from the fund is made to the court that heard the civil lawsuit. If the court finds that the injured party should be paid from the fund, the court will order TREC to pay the injured party from the recovery fund. Collection from the fund is limited to actual damages sustained by the injured party and does not include punitive or exemplary damages. The licensee's license is automatically revoked and cannot be reinstated until he or she has repaid the recovery fund the amounts paid out on his or her account plus interest. The bankruptcy of the licensee does not relieve the licensee of this duty to repay the fund.

REAL ESTATE INSPECTORS

In 1985 the act was amended to strengthen TREC's regulation of real estate inspectors. Real estate inspectors are persons who represent themselves to the public as being trained and qualified to inspect improvements to real property and who accept employment for the purpose of performing such an inspection for a buyer or seller of real property. A person cannot act as an inspector unless he or she has been licensed by TREC. The procedure for obtaining a real estate inspector's license is similar to the procedure followed by salespeople and brokers. The applicant must be at least 18 years of age, a citizen of the United States or a legal alien and a resident of Texas for at least 60 days prior to the filing of the application. The applicant must provide proof that he or she has successfully completed 90 classroom hours of core real estate inspection courses. Real estate inspection courses are courses approved by TREC in the following areas: electrical, mechanical, plumbing, roofing and structural performance. Finally, the competency of the applicant is tested by an examination given periodically by TREC in Austin. This provision does not apply to persons in the business of structural pest control, such as termite inspectors. It also does not apply to persons who are in the business of making repairs and do not represent themselves as being inspectors of improvements.

Section 18(C)(i) of the act sets out certain conduct that is specifically prohibited. A representative sample of some of the prohibited activities is:

1. accepting a job if it or the fee is contingent upon a certain outcome or report;
2. performing an inspection in a negligent manner;

    3. acting as both a real estate inspector and a real estate broker or salesman; and

    4. acting in any manner that is fraudulent, dishonest or deceitful.

In addition, a real estate inspector is required to include in each contract of employment a conspicuous notice to the purchaser that reminds the buyer that he or she has certain rights under the Texas Deceptive Trade Practices Act that are in addition to his or her contractual rights. If the buyer has entered into an earnest money contract that contains a property condition addendum, the real estate inspector is required to obtain a copy of the completed form. The inspector must check and issue a written report to the buyer on the items designated for inspection in the addendum. The property condition addendum is discussed in Chapter 19.

SUMMARY

The Texas Real Estate License Act is an important law regulating the activities of persons who are in the real estate business. The act creates the Texas Real Estate Commission to oversee the enforcement of the law. Everyone in the real estate business in Texas should be thoroughly familiar with this law and the regulations promulgated by the commission.

The act requires that anyone who represents another in exchange for a fee in a real estate transaction must be licensed by TREC. The real estate activities requiring licensing include buying, selling, leasing, renting, appraising and auctioning of real estate. Ten categories of persons are specifically exempted from the coverage by the act, including attorneys at law, on-site apartment managers, administrators and executors. Unlicensed persons who engage in real estate activities that are not exempted from coverage under the act are guilty of a misdemeanor. They will also be responsible for returning any compensation received for their services.

Two types of licenses are issued by TREC: the salesman's license and the broker's license. Applicants must prove to TREC that they are qualified to represent others in real estate transactions. This is accomplished by meeting certain educational criteria, passing a competency examination, and showing evidence of good moral character. An applicant for a broker's license must also have experience as a salesperson.

TREC is very actively involved in regulating its licensees. Licensees must maintain an office and notify the commission of any changes in location. TREC also has the right to investigate complaints against a licensee and to review records maintained by a licensee. It can suspend or revoke a licensee's license if he or she has violated a provision of the act or a regulation of the commission. The act establishes many rules that must be adhered to by licensees. If a complaint is made against a licensee, he or she has the right to a hearing before the commission and the right to appeal that decision to a district court.

Licensees, in performing services for their clients, frequently are concerned with legal aspects of the transaction. It is both a civil and a criminal offense for a person to practice law without being licensed as an attorney. Practicing law includes preparing legal documents and giving legal advice. TREC has promulgated regulations that can guide licensees in avoiding the unauthorized practice of law.

The act also regulates the activities of real estate inspectors. A real estate inspector is a person who is employed to inspect improvements to real estate. An inspector must be licensed by TREC and must follow the rules regarding business practices set out in the act and in regulations promulgated by the commission.

QUESTIONS AND CASE PROBLEMS

1. List the real estate activities that are included in the definition of a *real estate broker* under the Texas Real Estate License Act.

2. The Texas Real Estate Commission sued Nancy Long for violation of the Texas Real Estate License Act. Nancy is a real estate appraiser who appraises residential buildings for Hamilton Mortgage Corporation. The Texas Real Estate Commission requested the court to order Nancy to stop appraising real property because Nancy had not been licensed by the commission. Nancy defended on the grounds that she was not buying or selling real estate and was exempt from the provisions of the act. Who prevails? Why?

3. List some of the acts for which a licensee can have his or her real estate license suspended.

4. Harold and Hattie Bench sued Jonathan Realty, Inc., for fraud. Jonathan Realty, Inc., misrepresented the zoning classification of the property and the income-producing capability of the property. Jonathan had also failed to disclose that it was the true owner of the property. On October 29, 1980, Mr. and Mrs. Bench obtained a judgment against Jonathan for $30,000. Of that amount, $10,000 represents actual damages and $20,000 represents punitive damages. Jonathan Realty, Inc., is bankrupt. Will Mr. and Mrs. Bench be able to collect any part of the $30,000? Why? Is there an action that the Texas Real Estate Commission can take against Jonathan Realty, Inc.?

5. Four property owners in a Montgomery County subdivision filed complaints with the Texas Real Estate Commission, alleging that Kelley, a broker, misrepresented the date on which roads in the subdivision would be completed and the date by which utilities would be installed. The contract signed by each purchaser stated that the completion date for roads and services would be December 31, 1983. The purchasers alleged that Kelley had convinced

them that the roads and services would be completed by August of 1981. Neither the roads nor the utilities were completed by August 1981, although they were complete by December 1983. Kelley had sold 250 out of the 268 unimproved lots in the subdivision, and these were the only purchasers who filed complaints with TREC. After a hearing, TREC revoked Kelley's license. Kelley appealed the revocation to a district court in Harris County. Should the district court affirm TREC's order revoking the license? Why?

15
Agency

As discussed in the previous chapter, persons who represent others for a fee in a real estate transaction must be licensed and are regulated by the Texas Real Estate License Act. However, this is not the only law that governs persons who perform services in the real estate field. Another law, equally important, is the law of agency. *Agency* is the legal relationship in which one party acts for another in dealing with third parties. The person who acts for the other is the *agent,* and the person for whom the agent acts is the ***principal.*** In a typical real estate sale, the broker is the agent for the seller, who is the principal. The rules of agency thus apply to many real estate transactions.

The agency relationship between a seller/principal and a broker/agent is only one of the many agency relationships that can arise in a real estate transaction. There can also be an agency relationship between a broker and his or her salesmen. Furthermore, an agency relationship can arise between a buyer and a broker. The key to determining whether there is an agency relationship between two people is whether one of the two is representing and acting on behalf of and at the request of another person.

The agency relationship is very common in all business activities. Corporations always act through agents. Employees are agents of their employers. Lawyers and stockbrokers are agents for their clients. One of the reasons agency relationships are so common is that it is impossible for each of us to act and do everything for ourselves. Therefore, we seek the assistance of persons who are competent and whom we trust to act on our behalf. In this chapter the creation, responsibilities and termination of the agency relationship will be explained.

AGENCY

The relationship between agents and principals is a very special relationship. It is based upon the trust and confidence of the parties and is a fiduciary relationship. The agent is a **fiduciary.** The fiduciary holds a position of confidence and trust; the principal, in selecting the broker as fiduciary, has relied upon his or her integrity, fidelity and ability. This relationship of confidence and trust requires high standards of conduct, and the broker must exercise good faith and loyalty in all matters relating to the agency.

Good faith and loyalty require the broker to advance the principal's interest even at the expense of his or her own. A broker may not purchase the principal's property unless the principal has complete knowledge of all the facts and freely consents to the sale. This prohibition applies even if the broker can show that the transaction was beneficial to the principal and that the principal was not injured in any way.

CASE EXCERPT *Wilson v. Donze,* 692 S.W.2d 735 (Tex. Ct. App.—Fort Worth 1985) HOPKINS, Justice.   Ken Wilson appeals from a judgment rendered on a jury verdict awarding Anthony and Lena Donze $24,900 actual damages and $35,000 exemplary damages for breach of Wilson's fiduciary duty as a real estate broker for the Donzes. . . .

A review of the record reveals evidence that in May, 1982, Wilson telephoned and asked the Donzes if their property was for sale. He was informed that it was and that the sale price was $85,000. . . . he was advised by the Donzes that they did not do business with brokers, they sold their own land and did not pay commissions. Wilson said if he could just sell their property, he would obtain his fee from the buyer. The Donzes agreed that Wilson could view the property and later told him he could show it to the couple. (Wilson had located the Bullards who expressed an interest in this type of property.) . . . About ten days later, Wilson again called and told the Donzes the couple wanted the property and he would have the papers prepared immediately. . . . The sales contract Wilson presented for the Donzes' signature on June 2, 1982, named Ken/Car Investments, Inc., trustee or assigns, as purchaser of the Donzes' property for $85,000 and provided for an earnest money escrow deposit of $1,000. Ken/Car Investments, Inc. was a business owned by Wilson and his wife. . . .

One June 1, 1982, Powers (another real estate agent acting with Wilson) secured from the Bullards (the couple referred to by Wilson as being interested in the Donze property) an offer to purchase the property for $100,000. At the time, Powers told them he did not believe their offer would be accepted and that he thought it would take $115,000 to close the deal.

The Bullards indicated that if it took $115,000, they would pay it. Pursuant to Powers' suggestion, the Bullards gave him their check for $10,000 as an earnest money deposit. On June 2nd, the same day Wilson entered into a contract as Ken/Car Investments, Inc., trustee or assigns to purchase the Donze's property for $85,000, Powers called the Bullards and told them their $100,000 had been rejected and that it would take $115,000 to buy the property. The Bullards agreed and a completed contract naming Ken Wilson, trustee, as seller was delivered to the Bullards later the same day. . . .

After the two sales contracts had been executed, the Donzes and the Bullards met one time and discussed the fact that the Bullards were buying the property but did not discuss the price being paid. Apparently, each couple thought the sale and purchase was between them and without the intervention of a middle man. . . .

Wilson contends that since the Donzes received the price they asked for the property and are happy with the Bullards as eventual owners of the property, they have no right to complain. We disagree. As real estate broker for the Donzes, Wilson had the obligation to obtain for them the best price possible, even if the Donzes had set a lesser price. . . .

The duty of good faith and loyalty controls situations in which the broker can represent both parties. If a broker has the authority to enter into a contract for either buyer or seller, the broker violates the fiduciary duty if he or she accepts compensation from both. Courts reason that it is impossible for a broker under these circumstances to satisfy the diametrically opposed interests of both parties.

Abstract terms such as *trust, good faith* and *loyalty* indicate the general scope of the broker's responsibility to his or her employer. In Texas, the fiduciary duties of an agent to a principal are:

1. the duty to act in good faith;
2. the duty to be loyal;
3. the duty to disclose all matters relating to the agency relationship;
4. the duty to account for money coming into the agent's possession;
5. the duty to follow the instructions of the principal; and
6. the duty to exercise reasonable care and skill in performance of the agent's duties.

Just as there are obligations imposed on the agent in the relationship, the principal also assumes certain responsibilities to his or her agent. These duties are:

1. the duty to inform of known dangers or hazards the agent will encounter;
2. the duty to compensate;
3. the duty to reimburse for expenditures reasonable and necessary to performance; and
4. the duty to indemnify.

Establishing an Agency Relationship

An agency relationship can be created in writing, orally or by the conduct of the parties. The key elements to establish an agency relationship are: (1) an express or implied request on the part of the principal to the agent;(2) to perform some task or series of tasks for the principal and (3) expressed or implied acceptance by the agent.

The agency relationship is a voluntary relationship. Agency cannot be forced on either the principal or the agent. The principal must ask the agent to act, and the agent must consent. Although written agreements are preferred, a principal can make his or her request verbally, and the agent can consent by simply acting on the principal's behalf.

Once an agreement is reached between an agent and the principal regarding the terms of the agency relationship, it is a legally enforceable contract. Thereafter, if either party wrongfully terminates the relationship or fails to perform his or her obligations, a suit for damages can be filed against the breaching party. In the case that follows, the court found that an agency relationship had been created even though there was no written agreement.

CASE EXCERPT *West v. Touchstone*, 620 S.W.2d 687 (Tex. Ct. App.—Dallas 1981) AKIN, Justice. This is an appeal from a summary judgment rendered in favor of defendant Gifford Touchstone against plaintiffs Robert H. West, Lorraine West. . . .

The Wests are the owners of certain real property. In May 1975, they entered into an exclusive listing agreement with Touchstone to sell the property. In August 1976, West informed Touchstone by letter that the exclusive listing agreement had terminated. In 1977, Touchstone was contacted by a party (Millican) who expressed an interest in purchasing West's property. Touchstone had previously shown the property in question to this prospective purchaser in 1975 when he was acting as West's exclusive agent. Touchstone advised West of the prospective purchaser's interest in the property and agreed to assist in bringing the parties together. During this period, West was attempting to negotiate a sale of the property with the Dallas Housing Authority (DHA). Touchstone wrote a letter to the Dallas City Manager, which was subsequently forwarded to the DHA, stating that the tentative purchase price which West and the DHA were discussing was excessive and that the market value for comparable land in the area was far less than the discussed purchase price. West alleges that Touchstone's letter and subsequent contacts with officials at the DHA resulted in the DHA's failure to purchase the property.

West's second amended petition alleged causes of action against Touchstone for breach of fiduciary duties. . . . The gravamen of West's complaints is that Touchstone was acting as their agent at the time he wrote the letter in question and that his communications with Dallas officials constituted violation of his duty of loyalty as their agent. . . .

Touchstone contends that, as a matter of law, he has established that he was a mere middleman between West and Millican and as such, owed West no fiduciary duties. We disagree. An agent is one who consents to act on behalf of and subject to the control of another, the principal, who has manifested consent that the agent shall so act. The relationship between agent and principal is a fiduciary relationship. . . . Applying this definition of an agent to the facts of this case, we hold that a fact issue exists as to whether Touchstone was the agent of West and, therefore, owed him fiduciary duties. The fact issue is presented by the affidavit of Robert H. West which states that Touchstone agreed to negotiate with Millican in order to get Millican to increase the amount of his offer. Additionally, the information obtained by Touchstone with respect to the proposed sale to DHA was obtained during his discussions with West as to the proposed Millican negotiations. Taken as true, this testimony indicates that Touchstone was acting on behalf of, and with the consent of, West and that Touchstone was thus West's agent. . . .

An interesting aspect of this case is the fact that Touchstone could not have sued West for compensation for services rendered. The Texas Real Estate License Act forbids licensees to sue for a commission unless there is a written agreement. Consequently Touchstone has not only assumed all the fiduciary duties that an agent owes to a principal but also was acting gratuitously.

Authority of Agents

The second element in the agency relationship is that there be a request to the agent to perform some task. The task may be to find prospective purchasers for a piece of property, to negotiate leases for an office building, to maintain and manage an apartment complex or to appraise or auction a piece of property. This is called the *express authority* of the agent. It reflects both the duty and the power of the agent to act on behalf of the principal and thereby bind the principal. **Express authority** is the authority the principal confers upon an agent explicitly and distinctly. The express authority may be stated orally to the agent or may be written. For example, a principal may authorize a broker to lease office space in an office building. This is the express authority of the agent. In carrying out his or her express authority, the broker will engage in activities such as advertising, showing the property and executing leases. This is called the *implied authority* of the agent. **Implied authority** is the agent's authority to do those things necessary and proper to accomplish the express terms of the agency. Advertising, showing the office space and executing leases is reasonably necessary in order to accomplish the task assigned to the agent by the principal.

An agent's power to bind a principal is limited to those acts that were either expressly or impliedly authorized. Therefore, defining the task or the authority of the agent is important. Care should be taken by the broker to determine from the principal precisely what is expected from him and the limits on his authority.

CASE EXAMPLE

Karen, a real estate broker, is retained to sell the Walker's home. Karen's express authority is to find prospective purchasers who will make offers for the purchase of the house to the Walkers. In carrying out this function, Karen has the implied authority to advertise, show the property and assist in negotiations. However, Karen has no authority to sign an earnest money contract even if the purchaser is willing to pay the Walkers' asking price. Similarly, Karen has no authority to lease the house. Neither express nor implied authority was conferred on Karen to do these acts.

Terminating the Agency Relationship

Since the agency relationship is a fiduciary relationship, it can be revoked or terminated at any time by either the principal or the agent. The revocation of the agency relationship can be either rightful or wrongful. The agency is properly terminated by written agreement of both parties, by completion of the task that was the subject matter of the agency or by a substantial breach of the agency relationship by the other party. Principal and agent may agree at the time the agency relationship is created that it will exist for a definite time, such as 30 days, six months or one year. The agency terminates automatically at the time specified by the agreement. The principal and agent could also agree to an agency at will. An agency at will gives either party the right to revoke or terminate the agency at any time, provided the party is acting in good faith. An example of bad faith would be termination of an agency in order to avoid payment of a commission.

An agency is also automatically terminated when the task is completed. For example, assume that the agent is hired to lease the vacant office space in Twin Towers. When all the office space in Twin Towers is leased, the agency terminates. Finally, the agency relationship can be terminated by the nonbreaching party if the other has violated the agreement.

CASE EXAMPLE

King hires Hugh Ribbons Management Company to manage the apartment complex called Graceful Pines for one year. After six months, King discovers that Ribbons has been depositing into King's bank account only a portion of the rent it collects from the tenant's. The balance of the rent is being embezzled by Ribbons. King can terminate the agency relationship because Ribbons has breached its fiduciary duties to King.

An agency relationship is wrongfully terminated when either the principal or the agent revokes the agency without just cause and in violation of the agreement.

CASE EXAMPLE

Curtis signs a listing agreement with Jay Lang's Real Estate Company to sell his house. The term of the agreement is six months. After three months, Curtis decides that he does not want to sell his house and sends Lang's a letter terminating the agency relationship. Curtis has the power to revoke the agency with Lang's but his revocation was not justified and is in violation of the written listing agreement. Lang's can sue Curtis for the damages caused by Curtis's wrongful revocation of the agency.

These are some of the general principles of agency law that are applicable to any type of agency relationship. As previously mentioned, several different agency relationships are common in real estate transactions. Each of these will be discussed below.

RELATIONSHIP BETWEEN BROKERS AND SALESMEN

The legal responsibility of a person who hires someone else to act for him or her depends upon the relationship between them. As a general rule, the more extensively the person for whom the job is being done controls the manner in which it is accomplished, the greater that person's responsibility. For example, an employer has appreciable control over how an employee works. Thus, if the employee is acting within the scope of his or her employment, the employer is responsible for any harm the employee causes. In real estate brokerage, the client who "hires" a broker has little control over the manner in which the broker performs the task. The broker is said to be an independent contractor. This is also frequently the case between a sponsoring broker and his or her salesmen. If the broker does not directly supervise and control his or her salespeople, the salesmen are independent contractors.

Liability

The agent's classification as an independent contractor or as an employee is important for several reasons. First, the principal's liability for the acts of an employee are greater than his or her liability for the acts of an independent contractor.

CASE EXAMPLE

King, a licensed broker, agrees to sponsor Grant, a salesman. King directs which houses Grant will show and to whom. Each morning King meets with Grant to tell him his activities for the day. Grant runs a red light on his way to meet a prospective client, and the injured driver sues King. King is liable to the injured driver for Grant's negligence. Grant is an employee of King because King's supervision of Grant was so extensive.

However, if King has not directly supervised or controlled the day-to-day activities of Grant, the result would be different.

CASE EXAMPLE

King, a licensed broker, has agreed to sponsor Harry, a salesman. King has established some general policies that he expects Harry and the other salespeople to follow. King meets with Harry regularly to discuss Harry's activities and provide some professional guidance; however, Harry chooses his clients, negotiates the listing agreements and for the most part acts independently of King. Harry runs a red light on the way to meet a prospective client, and the injured driver sues King. King is not liable for Harry's negligence because Harry is an independent contractor.

Needless to say, most principals would prefer to hire independent contractors and thereby limit their liability for the negligent and malicious acts of an agent. Between a sponsoring broker and his or salesmen, the Texas Real Estate License Act, as discussed in the previous chapter, does not permit a broker to relieve himself or herself of all liability arising from negligent or wrongful conduct of a salesman. A sponsoring broker is liable if any of his or her salesmen violate the Texas Real Estate License Act. This is the case whether the salesman is an employee or an independent contractor. The broker is responsible to both the Texas Real Estate Commission and any person injured as a result of the salesman's acts.

A salesman's conduct in performing any of the real estate activities described in Chapter 14 is attributable to the broker through whom he or she works. For example, if a real estate salesman fails to notify the seller of a prospective purchaser, he or she has breached one of his or her fiduciary duties to the seller. The broker would also be liable to the seller for this breach even if the broker did not personally know that there was a prospective purchaser.

Salesmen must also be aware of the broker's activities with respect to a real estate transaction. If the broker's conduct causes a forfeiture of a commission, the salesman is not entitled to be compensated. This is true even when the salesman acted in good faith and procured a buyer who actually purchased the property.

• CASE BRIEF •

Martin and Morgan are licensed real estate salesmen who are employed by Forestier, a licensed real estate broker. Martin and Morgan, on behalf of Forestier, induced Southern Cross Industries, Inc., to sign an exclusive listing agreement with Forestier. A prospective purchaser, Dunlap Sales and Service Corporation, was located by Martin, who prepared an earnest money contract. Forestier did not notify Southern Cross of the prospective purchaser and instead offered to buy the property at a price below the offer made by Dunlap. There was no evidence that either Morgan or Martin participated in this deception. Ultimately the sale to Forestier failed, and the property was sold to Dunlap. The court found that Forestier had a duty to disclose to Southern Cross Dunlap's interest in purchasing the property. Forestier has breached that duty and was not entitled to a commission. The court then stated, "Since Martin and Morgan are entitled to compensation only if their former employer, Forestier, is, our holding that Forestier breached a fiduciary duty owed to appellants precludes Martin and Morgan from recovering any compensation from Southern Cross." *Southern Cross Industries, Inc. v. Martin, et al.,* 604 S.W.2d 290 (Tex. Civ. App.—San Antonio 1980).

Payment of Taxes

The second benefit for the principal in hiring independent contractors instead of employees is the nonpayment of the various types of employer taxes. An employer is required by law to contribute to the employee's social security account, to withhold federal income taxes and to contribute to the state's unemployment compensation fund. In addition, an employer is required to maintain worker's compensation insurance. Consequently, it is less expensive for a principal to hire an independent contractor. A sponsoring broker who treats his or her salesmen as independent contractors is relieved from making these tax and insurance payments on behalf of the agent. The salesman's tax payments will then be higher than they would be if he were an employee. This salesman is considered to be self-employed. Under the federal tax laws self-employed persons are responsible for making all of their social security contributions.

From a broker's perspective, the limited liability and relief from the tax and insurance payments are incentives to claim that all of his or her salesmen are independent contractors. However, the courts are not bound to accept a broker's classification of the salesman as an independent contractor, even if the salesman agrees in writing to the classification. The court will look at the actual manner in which the broker and salesman acted to determine whether or not the salesman is an employee or an independent contractor. The more control the broker has over the physical activities of a salesman, the greater the probability that the court will hold that the salesman is an employee. Furthermore, the same salesman could be an employee for tax purposes but not an employee for liability purposes. The reason this can occur is that the tax law definition of *employee* is different from the definition used generally.

BROKER-BROKER RELATIONSHIPS

It has become a common practice for real estate brokers to form contractual relationships whereby the brokers agree to share the commission. The most common contract is that created by membership in a multiple-listing service and the existence of a multiple-listing agreement. However, this is not the only type of agreement that can exist between or among brokers. A broker may solicit the aid of another broker in finding a purchaser or locating property for sale. The courts have considered this relationship a joint venture or subagency that can be either written or verbal. If such a relationship exists, the brokers owe each other the same fiduciary duties that are present in an agency relationship. These fiduciary duties include among others the duty to be loyal and to disclose information.

RELATIONSHIP BETWEEN BROKERS AND SELLERS

Many owners of real property find it beneficial to hire a broker to assist them in selling property. The primary reason for hiring brokers is their expertise. Brokers are experienced in marketing property. They have been trained in salesmanship techniques and can present the property to prospective purchasers in a manner that is likely to result in its sale. Brokers are also experienced in financing and can advise the seller and prospective purchasers of the options for financing the property. Brokers are also familiar with the legal aspects of a real estate transaction and can advise the seller if the services of an attorney are required. Finally, brokers are experienced in negotiating the sale of property and in an objective manner can protect the interest of the seller in contract negotiations and at the closing of the transaction.

The first step in hiring a broker is discussion regarding the authority, responsibilities and compensation of the broker. The most common method of establishing an agency relationship between a seller and a broker is through a written agency contract called a *listing agreement.*

Listing Agreements

The terms of the listing agreement are established by the parties to the contract. The Texas Real Estate License Act has three requirements for all listing agreements. First, the listing agreement must be in writing and signed by the person to be charged. Second, the listing agreement must specify a definite termination date. Third, if the property is located along the Gulf Coast, the contract should contain a section explaining the availability of Texas coastal natural hazards information.

No particular form is required. However, the listing agreement should be specific and clear concerning the parties' agreement. For example, the property to be sold should be identified adequately so that the court will know when the commission is due. The listing agreement can be in the form of a letter, memorandum or contract.

There are five common types of listing agreements: open listing, exclusive agency, exclusive right to sell, multiple listing and net listing. Illustrations of some of these listing agreements are included in this chapter.

Open Listing

An *open listing* is an agreement that entitles the broker to compensation only if his or her activities bring about the sale of the property. Unless the agreement clearly indicates otherwise, courts presume that a listing is open. An owner who enters into an open listing agreement may list the property with any number of brokers. The broker who brings about the sale is entitled to the commission. Authority of the broker is automatically revoked without notice when the owner enters into a contract to sell the property.

In an open listing the owner retains the right to negotiate a sale on his or her own. If the sale is effected by the owner without the aid of a broker, no commissions are due and all listings are automatically terminated. The owner has no commitment until the broker has procured a buyer who is ready, willing and able to buy. In order to escape paying a commission, a

Figure 15.1: **SAMPLE OPEN LISTING**

TAR **TEXAS ASSOCIATION OF REALTORS®**

REAL ESTATE LISTING AGREEMENT (NON-MLS)
RESIDENTIAL PROPERTY
(OPEN LISTING)

TO: _____, REALTOR*, _____, Texas

I. For and in consideration of the mutual agreement herein, by and between _____, hereinafter called Owner, and _____, hereinafter called REALTOR*, Owner does hereby appoint REALTOR* as a non-exclusive Agent to sell the following real estate situated in _____ County, Texas, known as _____ (address), and further described as Lot _____, Block _____, Addition, City of _____, or as described on attached exhibit with the following fixtures, if any: curtains and rods, draperies and rods, valances, blinds, window shades, screens, shutters, awnings, wall-to-wall carpeting, mirrors fixed in place, ceiling fans, attic fans, mail boxes, television antennas, permanently installed heating and air conditioning units and equipment, built-in security and fire detection equipment, lighting and plumbing fixtures, water softener, trash compactor, garage door opener with controls, shrubbery and all other property owned by the seller and attached to the above described property. The real estate and fixtures named herein are hereinafter referred to as the "Property".

II. The selling price of the Property shall be $_____ or any other price that Owner may accept, to be payable on the following terms _____

or any other terms that Owner may accept. Owner authorizes REALTOR® to receive a deposit in an amount acceptable to Owner and within a reasonable time to deposit same in trust with a title company authorized to do business in this state, or in a custodial, trust or escrow account maintained for that purpose in a banking institution authorized to do business in this state.

III. Owner does hereby certify and represent that Owner has fee simple title to and peaceable possession of the Property with all improvements and fixtures thereon, and the legal authority and capacity to convey such Property by a good and sufficient General Warranty Deed. Owner further certifies and represents that the property has no known latent structural defects or any other defects, except the following: _____

Owner agrees to convey said Property by General Warranty Deed, and provide a ( ) Title Policy or ( ) Abstract at _____ (Owner's or Purchaser's) expense, and pay other customary closing costs. Owner shall not rent or lease the herein described property during the term of this agreement without the prior written approval of REALTOR®.

IV. Owner agrees to pay REALTOR®, in cash, at the time of closing or upon the happening of any of the following events, whichever first occurs, a commission of _____ of the gross sales price of said Property: (1) a) if REALTOR® shall during the term of this agreement produce a purchaser ready, willing and able to buy said Property at the price and terms above listed, or at any other price and terms Owner has agreed to accept; b) if REALTOR® shall procure a purchaser who enters into a contract to purchase the property during the term of this agreement and who closes the sale during the term of this agreement or after the expiration of this agreement, or (2) if during the term of this agreement Owner prevents the sale of said Property by attempting to cancel this agreement and Owner receives the earnest money, or any portion thereof, as liquidated damages, one half of which (but not exceeding the herein recited commission) shall be paid by Owner to REALTOR® as additional compensation, or if Owner sues purchaser for specific performance and damages, commission is payable when Owner recovers damages for such default by suit, compromise settlement or otherwise, and then only in an amount equal to one-half of portion collected not exceeding the commission. No commission will be payable if sale does not close, without fault on the part of REALTOR®. If the property is destroyed by fire or other casualty loss, and if Owner, without fault, is unable to restore same before the closing date and the earnest money contract. The commission provided herein shall be negotiated by the agreement had been sold, conveyed, or otherwise transferred within _____ days after the termination of this authority or any extension thereof to anyone with whom REALTOR® has had negotiations prior to final termination provided Owner has received notice in writing which includes the names of said prospective purchasers on or before _____ days after expiration of this agreement or any extension thereof. However, Owner shall not be obligated to pay such compensation if a valid exclusive listing agreement is entered into during the term of said protection period with another licensed real estate broker and the sale, lease, or exchange of the Property is made during the term of said protection period.

REALTOR® may divide any commission paid hereunder with any other licensed Broker or Brokers. The person who closes any sale covered by this Agreement is hereby directed to and authorized to collect and disburse all commissions due hereunder. In the event it becomes necessary for REALTOR® to retain any attorney or initiate legal proceedings of any nature in order to secure payment of the real estate commission provided for herein, in addition to all other sums to which REALTOR® may be entitled, REALTOR® shall be entitled to recover costs of suit and reasonable attorney's fees from Owner.

V. Owner hereby authorizes REALTOR® to cooperate and act in association with other brokers in procuring or attempting to procure a purchaser for the Property and Owner agrees that said cooperating brokers may act as subagents for REALTOR®. REALTOR® hereby promises and agrees to attempt to dispose of the Property in accordance with the terms and conditions of this Agreement. In pursuit of such efforts, REALTOR® is authorized to advertise at his discretion the Property by all such means and methods REALTOR® deems best and place a "FOR SALE" sign on the premises.

VI. Owner hereby authorizes REALTOR® and any subagents of REALTOR® to require that any or all contracts of sale submitted by REALTOR® to Owner to bind the sale of the Property include a written disclosure advising the prospective purchaser that certain information relating to the Property has been received by REALTOR®, and any subagents of REALTOR®, in writing from Owner and/or other sources and that REALTOR® and subagents of REALTOR® do not warrant or guarantee such information.

VII. OWNER HEREBY REPRESENTS AND WARRANTS TO REALTOR® AND ANY SUBAGENTS OF REALTOR® THAT ALL WRITTEN INFORMATION RELATING TO THE PROPERTY PROVIDED TO REALTOR® BY OWNER IS TRUE AND ACCURATE. OWNER IS HEREBY ADVISED THAT REALTOR® AND ANY SUBAGENTS OF REALTOR® SHALL RELY UPON SAID WRITTEN REPRESENTATIONS AS TO THE TRUTH AND ACCURACY THEREOF FOR THE PURPOSE OF PROVIDING SAID INFORMATION TO PROSPECTIVE PURCHASERS AND FOR THE PURPOSE OF GIVING WRITTEN NOTICE OF SAID RELIANCE TO PROSPECTIVE PURCHASERS. OWNER IS HEREBY ADVISED THAT, IF SAID INFORMATION IS FALSE OR INACCURATE, OWNER MAY BE HELD LIABLE FOR DAMAGES CAUSED BY SAID FALSITY OR INACCURACY.

VIII. Owner hereby agrees to notify REALTOR® of any prospective purchasers with which Owner is negotiating for the sale of the Property to avoid duplication of effort or the unnecessary expenditure of REALTOR's® time. Owner reserves the right to sell the Property to any purchaser not procured or produced by REALTOR® provided Owner enters into a contract to sell the Property to said purchaser prior to the time REALTOR® produces or procures a purchaser ready, willing, and able to buy the Property at the price and terms above listed or at any other price and terms Owner has agreed to accept.

IX. Owner herein authorizes the lending institution having any loan outstanding in any way secured by the Property to furnish promptly to REALTOR® all the current information that REALTOR® may request.

X. REALTOR® and cooperating real estate brokers shall not be responsible in any manner for loss of personal or real property due to vandalism, theft, freezing water pipes or any other damage or loss whatsoever. Owner is advised to notify his insurance company and request a "Vacancy Clause" to cover the Property in the event the same is vacant or to be vacated. This Property will be offered, shown and made available for sale to all persons without regard to race, color, religion, national origin or sex. Owner acknowledges that he has read this Agreement, understands its contents, received a copy thereof and that there are no existing agreements or conditions, other than as set forth herein. This Agreement is binding upon the parties hereto, their heirs, administrators, executors, successors and

(TAR-040) 10/85   Page 1 of 2 Pages

Figure 15.1 (continued)

assigns. If this agreement is signed by more than one person, it shall constitute the joint and several obligation of each. This contract contains the entire agreement of the parties and cannot be changed except by their written consent.
    XI. SPECIAL PROVISIONS:

    The REALTOR'S® compensation for services rendered in respect to this listing is solely a matter of negotiation between the REALTOR® and Owner, and is not fixed, controlled, recommended, suggested or maintained by any persons not a party to this listing agreement. The division of a commission or fees between the REALTOR® and a cooperating broker, if any, is not fixed, controlled, recommended, suggested or maintained by any persons other than REALTOR® and subagent.

    This Agreement shall begin on the _____ day of _____, 19 _____ and shall continue in full force and effect until midnight on the _____ day of _____, 19_____.
    Dated at _____, Texas, this _____ day of _____,
19_____.

_____   _____
REALTOR®   OWNER

BY: _____ **TEXAS ASSOCIATION OF REALTORS®** _____
                                              OWNER

_____   _____
ADDRESS   ADDRESS

SAMPLE

dishonest owner, suspecting that a broker is about to submit an offer, might revoke the broker's authority and attempt to deal directly with the potential buyer. An owner who revokes in bad faith under these circumstances is subject to liability if the property is sold to a buyer located by the broker. Some open listings contain provisions entitling the broker to a commission after the expiration of the listing if the property is purchased by one to whom it had been shown by the broker.

Exclusive-Agency Listing

An *exclusive-agency listing* agreement is an agreement with a broker that makes the broker the owner's exclusive agent but reserves to the owner the right to sell the property on his or her own without incurring the obligation to pay a commission. An exclusive agency protects the broker against appointment by the owner of other brokers. The broker does not have to fear the loss of a commission if another broker arranges a sale of the property. However, if the owner of the property finds a buyer without the assistance of the broker, no commission is due the broker. An owner must act in good faith and provide the broker with a reasonable opportunity to secure a sale of the property.

Exclusive-Right-To-Sell Listing

An *exclusive-right-to-sell listing* agreement is an agreement in which the owner agrees that the broker will be his or her exclusive agent and the owner further agrees to pay the broker a commission regardless of how the property is sold. Under this type of listing the broker is entitled to a commission even if the property is sold by the owner without any assistance from the broker. This is the most common type of listing agreement used in residential sales. It eliminates any disputes regarding who procured the buyer. If the property is sold at any time during the term of the listing agreement, then a commission is due.

Multiple Listing

A *multiple listing* is an agreement in which the seller agrees to make the property available to any broker who is a member of the multiple-listing exchange. A multiple-listing exchange is a group of brokers who have agreed to share listings and to divide the commission received for negotiating the sale. Notice that a multiple-listing agreement is not actually a type of listing but rather a service. For example, either an exclusive-right-to-sell or an exclusive-agency listing could be placed in a multiple-listing service. Submission of a listing to such an exchange creates a unilateral offer of subagency to the other exchange members unless limited by the regulations of the exchange. The listing broker and the selling broker each receive a percentage of the commission as agreed upon between the brokers. Property can be listed in a multiple-listing exchange only with the written consent of the property owner.

Figure 15.2: **SAMPLE EXCLUSIVE-AGENCY LISTING**

 TEXAS ASSOCIATION OF REALTORS®

REAL ESTATE LISTING AGREEMENT
MULTIPLE LISTING SERVICE
RESIDENTIAL PROPERTY
(EXCLUSIVE AGENCY)

TO: _____ REALTOR®, _____, Texas

I. For and in consideration of the mutual agreement herein, by and between _____, hereinafter called Owner, and _____, hereinafter called REALTOR®, Owner does hereby appoint REALTOR® as the sole and exclusive Agent to sell the following real estate situated in _____ County, Texas, known as _____ (address), and further described as Lot _____, Block _____, Addition, City of _____, or as described on attached exhibit with the following fixtures, if any: curtains and rods, draperies and rods, valances, blinds, window shades, screens, shutters, awnings, wall-to-wall carpeting, mirrors fixed in place, ceiling fans, attic fans, mail boxes, television antennas, permanently installed heating and air conditioning units and equipment, built-in security and fire detection equipment, lighting and plumbing fixtures, water softener, trash compactor, garage door opener with controls, shrubbery and all other property owned by the seller and attached to the above described property. The real estate and fixtures named herein are hereinafter referred to as the "Property".

II. The selling price of the Property shall be $_____ or any other price that Owner may accept, to be payable on the following terms _____

_____ or any other terms that Owner may accept. Owner authorizes REALTOR® to receive a deposit in an amount acceptable to Owner and within a reasonable time to deposit same either in trust with a title company authorized to do business in this state, or in a custodial, trust or escrow account maintained for that purpose in a banking institution authorized to do business in this state.

III. Owner does hereby certify and represent that Owner has fee simple title to and peaceable possession of the Property with all improvements and fixtures thereof, and the legal authority and capacity to convey such Property by a good and sufficient General Warranty Deed. Owner further certifies and represents that the property has no known latent structural defects or any other defects, except the following: _____

_____

Owner agrees to convey said Property by General Warranty Deed, and provide a (   ) Title Policy or (   ) Abstract at _____ (Owner's or Purchaser's) expense, and pay other customary closing costs. Owner shall not rent or lease the herein described property during the term of this Agreement without the written approval of REALTOR®.

IV. Owner agrees to pay REALTOR® _____ commission of _____ the following events, whichever first occurs, a commission of _____ of the gross sales price of said Property if a) REALTOR® shall during the term of this agreement produce a purchaser ready, willing, and able to buy said Property at the price and terms listed, or at any other price and terms Owner has agreed to accept, or b) if REALTOR® shall procure a purchaser who enters into a contract to purchase the property during the term of this agreement and who closes the sale during the term of this agreement or after the expiration of this agreement, or (2) if during the term of this agreement Owner prevents the sale of said Property by attempting to cancel this agreement, by adversely renting the Property during the period of this agreement, or otherwise; or (3) if during the term of this price Owner has agreed to accept; provided, however, that if a purchaser procured by REALTOR® defaults in the performance of an earnest money contract promulgated under this agreement and Owner receives the earnest money, or any portion thereof, as liquidated damages, one half of which (but not exceeding the herein recited commission) shall be paid by Owner to REALTOR® as additional compensation, or if Owner sues purchaser for specific performance and/or damages, the commission is payable only if and when Owner collects damages for such default by _____ after first deducting the expenses of collection an only _____ amount to _____ of said portion _____ collected, but not exceeding the amount of REALTOR®'s fee stated herein. No commission will be due _____ the _____ close _____ (1) Owner, without fault, is unable to deliver an Abstract or Title _____ required _____ earnest _____ with _____, or (2) any _____ property is damaged or destroyed by fire or other casualty _____ res _____ same to its _____ ous condition by the closing date under the _____ hest m _____ c _____ comm _____ vic _____ has been n _____ iated by a _____ etween the parties hereto and shall be paid if P _____ sold _____ nveyed _____ or trans _____ hin _____ nation of this authority or any extension thereof to anyone with whom REALTOR® has had negotiations prior to final termination provided Owner has received notice in writing which includes the names of said prospective purchasers on or before _____ days after expiration of this agreement or any extension thereof. However, Owner shall not be obligated to pay such compensation if a valid exclusive listing agreement is entered into during the term of said protection period with another licensed real estate broker and the sale, lease, or exchange of the Property is made during the term of said protection period.

REALTOR® may divide any commission paid hereunder with any other licensed Broker or Brokers. The person who closes any sale covered by this Agreement is hereby directed to and authorized to collect and disburse all commissions due hereunder. In the event it becomes necessary for REALTOR® to retain any attorney or initiate legal proceedings of any nature in order to secure payment of the real estate commission provided for herein, in addition to all other sums to which REALTOR® may be entitled, REALTOR® shall be entitled to recover costs of suit and reasonable attorney's fees from Owner.

V. REALTOR® represents that he is a member of the _____ Multiple Listing Service, and REALTOR® binds himself that he will properly file this listing with said service. Owner hereby acknowledges that such filing constitutes a blanket unilateral offer of subagency to all members of said Service and Owner hereby agrees that said members may act in association with REALTOR® in procuring or attempting to procure a purchaser for the Property. REALTOR® hereby promises and agrees to use his best efforts in attempting to dispose of the Property in accordance with the terms and conditions of this agreement. In pursuit of such efforts, REALTOR® is authorized to advertise at his discretion the property by all such means and methods REALTOR® deems best and place a "FOR SALE" sign on the premises and to remove any and all other signs offering the Property for sale. If REALTOR® ceases to be a member of the _____ Multiple Listing Service, this listing shall be deleted from said Service. REALTOR® shall so notify Owner immediately, and upon written notice to REALTOR®, Owner may declare this agreement null and void.

VI. Owner hereby authorizes REALTOR® and any subagents of REALTOR® to require that any or all contracts of sale submitted by REALTOR® to Owner to bind the sale of the Property include a written disclosure advising the prospective purchaser that certain information relating to the Property has been received by REALTOR®, and any information in writing from Owner and/or other sources and that REALTOR® and subagents of REALTOR® do not warrant or guarantee such information.

VII. OWNER HEREBY REPRESENTS AND WARRANTS TO REALTOR®, ANY SUBAGENTS OF REALTOR®, THE _____ BOARD OF REALTORS®, AND THE _____ MULTIPLE LISTING SERVICE THAT ALL WRITTEN INFORMATION RELATING TO THE PROPERTY PROVIDED TO REALTOR® BY OWNER IS TRUE AND ACCURATE. OWNER IS HEREBY ADVISED THAT REALTOR®, ANY SUBAGENTS OF REALTOR®, THE _____ BOARD OF REALTORS®, AND THE _____ MULTIPLE LISTING SERVICE SHALL RELY UPON SAID WRITTEN REPRESENTATIONS AS TO THE TRUTH AND ACCURACY THEREOF FOR THE PURPOSE OF PROVIDING SAID INFORMATION TO PROSPECTIVE PURCHASERS AND FOR THE PURPOSE OF GIVING WRITTEN NOTICE OF SAID RELIANCE TO PROSPECTIVE PURCHASERS. OWNER IS HEREBY ADVISED THAT, IF SAID INFORMATION IS FALSE OR INACCURATE, OWNER MAY BE HELD LIABLE FOR DAMAGES CAUSED BY SAID FALSITY OR INACCURACY.

VIII. Owner hereby agrees to notify REALTOR® of any prospective purchasers with which Owner is negotiating for the sale of the Property to avoid duplication of effort or the unnecessary expenditure of REALTOR®'s time.

(TAR-035) 1/85   Page 1 of 2

Figure 15.2 (continued)

IX.   Owner herein authorizes the lending institution having any loan outstanding in any way secured by the Property to furnish promptly to REALTOR® all the current information that REALTOR® may request.

X.   _____ OWNER AUTHORIZES _____ OWNER DOES NOT AUTHORIZE the _____ Multiple Listing Service to furnish sales price and terms to any bona fide taxing authority which shall in writing request such information (Owner initials in appropriate blank).

XI.   A lock box device enables cooperating REALTORS® to gain access to the Property. It is a container placed on the Property by REALTOR® in which the key to the Property is placed. The lock box device itself is locked and opened by a special key. Whoever possesses a key to the lock box device has access to the Property at any time, even in Owner's absence. Owner recognizes the risk involved in such an arrangement, but in order to facilitate the showing of the Property. _____

_____ OWNER AUTHORIZES REALTOR® to place a lock box device on the Property. (Owner initials blank).

XII.   REALTOR® and cooperating real estate brokers shall not be responsible in any manner for loss of personal or real property due to vandalism, theft, freezing water pipes or any other damage or loss whatsoever. Owner is advised to notify his insurance company and request a "Vacancy Clause" to cover the Property in the event the same is vacant or to be vacated. This Property will be offered, shown and made available for sale to all persons without regard to race, color, religion, national origin or sex. Owner acknowledges that he has read this agreement, understands its contents, received a copy thereof and that there are no other existing agreements or conditions, other than as set forth herein. This agreement is binding upon the parties hereto, their heirs, administrators, executors, successors and assigns. If this Agreement is signed by more than one person, it shall constitute the joint and several obligation of each. This contract contains the entire agreement of the parties and cannot be changed except by their written consent.

XIII.   SPECIAL PROVISIONS:

The REALTOR'S® compensation or fees for services rendered to the Owner is solely a matter of negotiation between REALTOR® and Owner, and is not fixed, controlled, recommended, suggested or maintained by any persons not a party to this listing agreement. The division of a commission or fees between the REALTOR® and a cooperating broker, if any, is not fixed, controlled, recommended, suggested or maintained by any persons other than REALTOR® and subagent.

This agreement shall begin on the _____ day of _____ 19_____, and shall terminate at 5:00 p.m. on the _____ day of _____ 19_____ ("termination date"). However, if on such termination date there is a pending earnest money contract ("contract") in effect between Owner and a purchaser which has not closed and funded, this agreement shall continue in effect beyond such termination date and then terminate on: (1) the _____ day of _____ 19_____ (the estimated closing date of such contract), or (2) the closing and funding of such contract, or (3) the termination of such contract as therein provided, whichever occurs earlier.

Dated _____, Texas _____ of _____, 19_____.

SAMPLE

REA_____   OWN_____

BY: _____   _____
                                       OWNER

ADDRESS _____   ADDRESS _____

(TAR-035) 1/85   Page 2 of 2 Pages

Figure 15.3: **SAMPLE EXCLUSIVE-RIGHT-TO-SELL LISTING**

 TEXAS ASSOCIATION OF REALTORS®

REAL ESTATE LISTING AGREEMENT
MULTIPLE LISTING SERVICE
RESIDENTIAL PROPERTY
(EXCLUSIVE RIGHT TO SELL)

TO: _____ REALTOR®, _____, Texas

I. For and in consideration of the mutual agreement herein, by and between _____

hereinafter called Owner, and _____, hereinafter called REALTOR®. Owner does

hereby appoint REALTOR® exclusive agent and grant REALTOR® the exclusive right to sell the following real estate situated in

_____ County, Texas, known as _____, and

(Address)

further described as Lot _____ Block _____

_____

_____ Addition, City of _____

or as described on attached exhibit with the following fixtures, if any: curtains and rods, draperies and rods, valances, blinds, window shades, screens, shutters, awnings, wall-to-wall carpeting, mirrors fixed in place, ceiling fans, attic fans, mail boxes, television antennas, permanently installed heating and air conditioning units and equipment, built-in security and fire detection equipment, lighting and plumbing fixtures, water softener, trash compactor, garage door opener with controls, shrubbery and all other property owned by the seller and attached to the above described property. The real estate and fixtures named herein are hereinafter referred to as the "Property".

II.   The selling price of the Property shall be $_____ or any other price that Owner may accept, to be payable on the following terms _____

_____

or any other terms that Owner may accept. Owner authorizes REALTOR® to receive a deposit in an amount acceptable to Owner and within a reasonable time to deposit same either in trust with a title company authorized to do business in this state, or in a custodial, trust or escrow account maintained for that purpose in a banking institution authorized to do business in this state.

III.   Owner does hereby certify and represent that Owner has fee simple title to and peaceable possession of the Property with all improvements and fixtures thereof, and the legal authority and capacity to convey such Property by a good and sufficient General Warranty Deed. Owner further certifies and represents that the property has no known latent structural defects or any other defects, except the following: _____

Owner agrees **TEXAS ASSOCIATION OF REALTORS®**) Abstract at

_____ (Owner's or Purchaser's) expense, and pay other customary closing costs. Owner shall not rent or lease the herein described property during the term of this Agreement without the written approval of REALTOR®.

IV.   Owner agrees to pay REALTOR®, in cash, at the time of closing or upon the happening of any of the following events, whichever first occurs, a commission of _____ of the gross sales price of said Property: (1) a) if REALTOR® shall during the term of this agreement produce a purchaser ready, willing, and able to buy said Property at the price and terms above listed, or at any other price and terms Owner has agreed to accept, or b) if REALTOR® shall procure a purchaser who enters into a contract to purchase the property during the term of this agreement and who closes the sale during the term of this agreement or after the expiration of this agreement, or (2) if during the term of this agreement Owner prevents the sale of said Property by attempting to cancel this agreement, by adversely renting the Property during the period of this agreement, or otherwise; or (3) if during the term of th~~~~~~~~reed to sell, said P~~~~~~ is sol~~~~~xchan~~~~~~Ow~, or any ot~~~~~~, the price listed, or any other price

SAMPLE

if Property is sold, conveyed, or otherwise transferred within _____ days after the termination of this authority or any extension thereof to anyone with whom REALTOR® has had negotiations prior to final termination provided Owner has received notice in writing which includes the names of said prospective purchasers on or before _____ days after expiration of this agreement or any extension thereof. However, Owner shall not be obligated to pay such compensation if a valid exclusive listing agreement is entered into during the term of said protection period with another licensed real estate broker and the sale, lease, or exchange of the Property is made during the term of said protection period.

REALTOR® may divide any commission paid hereunder with any other licensed Broker or Brokers. The person who closes any sale covered by this Agreement is hereby directed to and authorized to collect and disburse all commissions due hereunder. In the event it becomes necessary for REALTOR® to retain any attorney or initiate legal proceedings of any nature in order to secure payment of the real estate commission provided for herein, in addition to all other sums to which REALTOR® may be entitled, REALTOR® shall be entitled to recover costs of suit and reasonable attorney's fees from Owner.

V.   REALTOR® represents that he is a member of the _____ Multiple Listing Service, and REALTOR® binds himself that he will properly file this listing with said service. Owner hereby acknowledges that said filing constitutes a blanket unilateral offer of subagency to all members of said Service and Owner hereby agrees that said members may act in association with REALTOR® in procuring or attempting to procure a purchaser for the Property. REALTOR® hereby promises and agrees to use his best efforts in attempting to dispose of the Property in accordance with the terms and conditions of this agreement. In pursuit of such efforts. REALTOR® is authorized to advertise at his discretion the property by all such means and methods REALTOR® deems best and place a "FOR SALE" sign on the premises and to remove any and all other signs offering the Property for sale. If REALTOR® ceases to be a member of the _____ Multiple Listing Service, this listing shall be deleted from said Service. REALTOR® shall so notify Owner immediately, and upon written notice to REALTOR®, Owner may declare this agreement null and void.

VI.   Owner hereby authorizes REALTOR® and any subagents of REALTOR® to require that any or all contracts of sale submitted by REALTOR® to Owner to bind the sale of the Property include a written disclosure advising the prospective purchaser that certain information relating to the Property has been received by REALTOR® and any subagents of REALTOR®, in writing from Owner and/or other sources and that REALTOR® and subagents of REALTOR® do not warrant or guarantee such information.

VII.   OWNER HEREBY REPRESENTS AND WARRANTS TO REALTOR®, ANY SUBAGENTS OF REALTOR®, THE _____ _____ BOARD OF REALTORS®. AND THE _____MULTIPLE LISTING SERVICE THAT ALL WRITTEN INFORMATION RELATING TO THE PROPERTY PROVIDED TO REALTOR® BY OWNER IS TRUE AND ACCURATE. OWNER IS HEREBY ADVISED THAT REALTOR®, ANY SUBAGENTS OF REALTOR®, THE _____ BOARD OF REALTORS®. AND THE _____ MULTIPLE LISTING SERVICE SHALL RELY UPON SAID WRITTEN REPRESENTATIONS AS TO THE TRUTH AND ACCURACY THEREOF FOR THE PURPOSE OF PROVIDING SAID INFORMATION TO PROSPECTIVE PURCHASERS AND FOR THE

(TAR-033) 1/85   Page 1 of 2 Pages

Figure 15.3 (continued)

PURPOSE OF GIVING WRITTEN NOTICE OF SAID RELIANCE TO PROSPECTIVE PURCHASERS. OWNER IS HEREBY ADVISED THAT, IF SAID INFORMATION IS FALSE OR INACCURATE, OWNER MAY BE HELD LIABLE FOR DAMAGES CAUSED BY SAID FALSITY OR INACCURACY.

VIII. Owner covenants to refrain from negotiation with any prospective purchasers or their agents or representatives who may contact Owner directly, and shall direct all such prospects and their agents or representatives to REALTOR®.

IX. Owner herein authorizes the lending institution having any loan outstanding in any way secured by the Property to furnish promptly to REALTOR® all the current information that REALTOR® may request.

X. _____ OWNER AUTHORIZES _____ OWNER DOES NOT AUTHORIZE the _____ Multiple Listing Service to furnish sales price and terms to any bona fide taxing authority which shall in writing request such information (Owner initials in appropriate blank).

XI. A lock box device enables cooperating REALTORS® to gain access to the Property. It is a container placed on the Property by REALTOR® in which the key to the Property is placed. The lock box device itself is locked and opened by a special key. Whoever possesses a key to the lock box device has access to the Property at any time, even in Owner's absence. Owner recognizes the risk involved in such an arrangement, but in order to facilitate the showing of the Property, _____ OWNER AUTHORIZES REALTOR® to place a lock box device on the Property. (Owner initials blank).

XII. REALTOR® and cooperating real estate brokers shall not be responsible in any manner for loss of personal or real property due to vandalism, theft, freezing water pipes or any other damage or loss whatsoever. Owner is advised to notify his insurance company and request a "Vacancy Clause" to cover the Property in the event the same is vacant or to be vacated. This Property will be offered, shown and made available for sale to all persons without regard to race, color, religion, national origin or sex. Owner acknowledges that he has read this agreement, understands its contents, received a copy thereof and that there are no other existing agreements or conditions, other than as set forth herein. This agreement is binding upon the parties hereto, their heirs, administrators, executors, successors and assigns. If this agreement is signed by more than one person, it shall constitute the joint and several obligation of each. This contract contains the entire agreement of the parties and cannot be changed except by their written consent.

XIII. SPECIAL PROVISIONS:

TEXAS ASSOCIATION OF REALTORS®

The REALTOR'S® compensation for services rendered in respect to this listing is solely a matter of negotiation between the REALTOR® and Owner, and is not fixed, controlled, recommended, suggested or maintained by any persons not a party to this listing agreement. The division of a commission or fees between the REALTOR® and a cooperating broker, if any, is not fixed, controlled, recommended, suggested or maintained by any persons other than REALTOR® and subagent.

This agreement shall begin on the _____ day of _____ 19 ____, and shall terminate at 5:00 p.m. on the _____ day _____ ("Expiration date"). However _____ termination date there is a pending _____ contract ("contract") in _____ between _____ er _____ ch has not _____ ded, this agreement shall continue in eff _____ beyond such term _____ date _____ n te _____ c _____ 1) the _____ er _____ of _____ 19 ____ (the esti _____ sing date _____ contra _____ 2) the _____ fundi _____ f _____ contract, _____ mination of such contract as therein provid _____ wer _____ s ea _____

D _____ at _____ as _____ day of _____ , 19 ____ .

REALTOR® _____   OWNER _____

BY: _____   OWNER _____

ADDRESS _____   ADDRESS _____

Net Listing

A *net listing* agreement is an agency agreement between a broker and the owner in which the owner establishes a selling price and agrees to compensate the broker by allowing him or her to retain the amount between the selling price and the amount for which the property is actually sold. Net listing agreements are discouraged in residential sales. Sellers frequently rely upon the broker's experience in establishing a selling price. There is great potential in this type of listing agreement for abuse or at least a dispute between a seller and a broker. A seller often believes that the broker should have advised him or her to establish a higher selling price. For this reason the Texas Real Estate Commission has promulgated the following rule:

> A broker should take net listings only when the principal insists upon a net listing and when the principal appears to be familiar with current market values of real property. When a broker accepts a listing, he enters into a fiduciary relationship with his principal, whereby, the broker is obligated to make diligent efforts to obtain the best price possible for the principal. The use of a net listing places an upper limit on the principal's expectancy and places the broker's interest above his principal's interest with reference to obtaining the best possible price. Net listings should be qualified so as to assure the principal of not less than his desired price and to limit the broker to a specified maximum commission.

The net listing agreement can also be open, exclusive agency or exclusive right to sell. The term merely refers to the calculation of the commission due.

Fiduciary Duties—Agent to Seller

The listing agreement establishes an agency relationship between the broker and the seller. As explained earlier, once an agency relationship is created, certain fiduciary duties arise. A broker as an agent of the seller owes those fiduciary duties to the seller. The Texas Real Estate Commission has promulgated three canons of professional ethics that further support the importance of the fiduciary duties in the agent-seller relationship. These canons address three areas of the broker's conduct: fidelity, integrity and competency. They are as follows:

> §531.1. A real estate broker or salesman, while acting as an agent for another, is a fiduciary. Special obligations are imposed when such fiduciary relationships are created. They demand:
> (a) that the primary duty of the real estate agent is to repre-

sent the interests of his client, and his position, in this respect, should be clear to all parties concerned in a real estate transaction; that, however, the agent, in performing his duties to his client, shall treat other parties to a transaction fairly;

(b) that the real estate agent be faithful and observant to trust placed in him, and be scrupulous and meticulous in performing his functions; and

(c) that the real estate agent place no personal interest above that of his client.

§531.2. A real estate broker or salesman has a special obligation to exercise integrity in the discharge of his responsibilities including employment of prudence and caution so as to avoid misrepresentation, in any wise, by acts of commission or omission.

§531.3. It is the obligation of a real estate agent to be knowledgeable as a real estate brokerage practitioner. He should:

(a) be informed on market conditions affecting the real estate business and pledged to continuing education in the intricacies involved in marketing real estate for others;

(b) be informed on national, state, and local issues and developments in the real estate industry; and

(c) exercise judgment and skill in the performance of his work.

Understanding fiduciary duties and ethical responsibilities can be difficult because the obligation is phrased in general terms. The law is intentionally vague on these standards. In determining whether or not a broker has violated a fiduciary duty, the courts consider all the facts and circumstances of each individual case. A slight variation in the facts might cause a court or a jury to consider an act a violation in one case and not in another. As a result it is difficult to say that a broker will be liable for certain conduct. Fortunately, the Texas Legislature and the Texas Real Estate Commission have established that certain conduct will definitely be grounds for license suspension. Conduct that is grounds for suspension is also likely to be satisfactory evidence of a breach of fiduciary duty to the seller. The list that follows contains excerpts from the Texas Real Estate License Act and regulations enacted by the Texas Real Estate Commission. A broker should remember that adherence to these standards alone may not be sufficient in any given circumstance. The broker's conduct must also conform to the general fiduciary duties and canons of ethics previously enumerated.

1. A broker must make clear to all parties to a transaction whom he or she is representing and by whom he or she is being compensated. A broker cannot be compensated by more than one party to a transaction without the full knowledge and consent of all parties.

2. A broker must properly account for or remit money coming into his or her possession that belongs to others within a reasonable time. Reasonable time is deemed to be 30 working days after demand for an accounting or remittance is made. *Properly account for* means to pay the money to the party or parties entitled to receive it. If that cannot be reasonably determined, then the broker can pay the money into the registry of a court.

3. A broker cannot commingle money belonging to others with his or her own funds.

4. A broker cannot accept or charge an undisclosed commission or profit on expenditures made for a principal.

5. A broker must disclose when he or she is engaging in a real estate transaction on his or her own behalf.

6. A broker must avoid conduct that constitutes dishonest dealings, bad faith or untrustworthiness.

7. The broker must act competently in performing any act for which a person is required to be licensed. He or she should not undertake a service or handle a transaction for which he or she lacks the necessary expertise.

8. A broker is required to disclose to his or her principal all known information that would affect the principal's decision on whether or not to accept or reject offers; however, the agent is not required to inform the principal of offers received after a contract has been entered into between the buyer and seller.

9. A broker must within a reasonable time deposit money he or she receives as escrow agent in a real estate transaction either in trust with a title company or in an escrow account maintained for that purpose.

10. A broker cannot disburse money held in escrow before the transaction has been closed or the transaction otherwise terminated.

11. A broker cannot place a sign on real estate offering it for sale or lease without the written consent of the owner.

Dual Agency

Fiduciary duties are owed by an agent to his or her principal. At times confusion or misunderstanding can arise concerning for whom a broker is acting. As stated in the list above, the broker and his or her salesman should make clear to all parties for whom they are acting. Although it may be unusual for a broker to represent a buyer in a real estate transaction, such an agency relationship can be established. *Dual agency* is the representation of both buyer and seller by the same agent. The courts in Texas are suspicious of a broker who is a dual agent, but they permit dual agency if both buyer and seller are fully informed and consent to this relationship. If the agent will receive a commission from both buyer and seller, then this fact must be disclosed and consent from both buyer and seller obtained. This is the case even if the agent is not a dual agent. There are two common situations in which there can be confusion regarding for whom the salesman or broker is acting.

The first situation arises from the use of multiple-listing services. A buyer may contact a real estate broker or salesman regarding a particular piece of property. In the course of discussing the property with the broker, the broker checks the multiple-listing service to determine if there is comparable property that the buyer may be interested in viewing. Whom does that broker represent? The general rule is that the broker represents the seller in this situation. The broker is considered a subagent for the listing broker. There are two reasons for this general rule. First, the seller in fact hired all members of the multiple-listing service when he or she signed the multiple-listing agreement. Second, the broker will share in the commission to be paid by the seller if the broker locates a buyer for the property. This general rule can be altered if the buyer specifically engages the broker to represent him or her. Therefore, it is important that the broker ascertain from the buyer what the buyer's expectations are regarding the broker's services and make clear to the buyer whether the broker will be representing the buyer or the seller.

An issue of dual agency also can arise if different salesmen working for the same broker represent the buyer and the seller. Since the broker is responsible for and directs the acts of both of his salesmen, indirectly he is an agent for both buyer and seller. For example, salesman A sponsored by the broker has obtained a listing agreement with seller A. Salesman B, also sponsored by the broker, has obtained a listing agreement with seller B. Seller A and seller B, with the help of their salesmen, negotiate an exchange of their properties. The broker is a dual agent. Unless both seller A and seller B have been informed of the dual agency and expressly consented to it, the broker will forfeit any commission earned. The licenses of the broker and the salesmen are also subject to suspension or revocation.

Perhaps the greatest hazard to a broker with respect to dual agency is that it can be created so easily and unintentionally. A selling broker can innocently mislead a prospective buyer into believing that he or she in fact represents the buyer. If the buyer perceives such representation of his best interest by the broker, there is a serious question of dual agency. If the seller discovers this real or imagined relationship, he or she might be able to avoid the payment of any commission. It is incumbent upon the broker to make clear to the buyer that the broker represents the seller and only the seller.

Fiduciary Duties—Seller to Agent

Just as an agent has obligations to the seller, the seller in turn has fiduciary duties to the agent. The principal obligation is the duty to compensate the broker for his or her services. The broker or salesman expects that upon faithful performance of his or her obligations to the principal he or she will receive compensation. Only persons licensed by the Texas Real Estate Commission are entitled to receive a commission. Disputes sometimes arise between broker and owner over whether or not the broker has earned a commission. One reason may be that terms of the parties' agreement are vague, without clear provisions as to matters that later become subjects of disputes.

• CASE BRIEF •

Webb, the owner, executed a listing agreement granting Eledge an exclusive agency with sole right to sell or exchange property described as 918-20 Slide Road in the City of Lubbock, Texas. Eledge produced a lessee who executed a ten-year lease for a total rental of $270,000, payable in monthly installments. Webb refused to pay Eledge a commission for securing this lease. Eledge sued. The court held that the street address was not sufficient to identify the property with reasonable certainty without resort to extrinsic evidence. The extrinsic evidence presented indicated some confusion regarding the accurate street address for this property. *Webb v. Eledge,* 678 S.W.2d 259 (Tex. Civ. App.—7 Dist. 1984).

In addition, legal misunderstandings may arise. The seller makes the agreement believing that no commission is due until the property has been paid for and plans to pay the commission out of the purchase price. On the other hand, the broker expects compensation for finding a purchaser whose offer is accepted even if title never passes. Potential problems involving payment also occur because payment is not a primary concern of the parties when the broker is hired.

When there is a problem concerning the commission, some brokers as a matter of policy refuse to litigate. They believe that a lawsuit can damage their reputation. They reason that adverse community reaction to litigation outweighs monetary gain even if they win. It is true that litigation is unpleasant and should be avoided, but civil suits are not extensively publicized. In fact, the word-of-mouth injury to the broker's reputation caused by a quarrel over commissions with a dissatisfied owner probably occurs even if the broker does not sue. A broker should not avoid litigation to collect a commission that has been earned, although all other solutions to the problem should be exhausted first.

Commission disputes generally involve two questions. Although frequently interrelated, either question may be the subject of the dispute. One common question is "Has the broker done the job he or she was hired to do?" The other is "When has the broker's job been accomplished so as to entitle him or her to a commission?"

In one typical scenario, the broker locates a buyer who is willing to purchase the property on terms agreeable to the seller. When presented with an offer, the seller refuses to accept for one reason or another, although he or she previously indicated that the terms were acceptable. In another common situation, the broker negotiates a contract between buyer and seller, but the seller cannot perform because the title is defective. Or, perhaps the owner just decides not to sell and refuses to honor the agreement. The broker cannot compel performance of the contract, and the buyer, reluctant to sue, looks for property elsewhere. The broker, feeling that he or she has performed, now seeks to recover a commission.

For the broker to be entitled to a commission, a number of threads must come together. Initially, the court needs to determine what the broker was hired to do. The broker may have been hired to sell or lease property on specific and detailed terms. If so, the broker's sole responsibility is to find a buyer on these terms. Once this has been accomplished, the broker is entitled to the fee even if the parties never enter into a contract. When there is a variance between the terms authorized by the owner in the listing agreement and those tendered by the prospective buyer, the broker is not entitled to a commission if the owner refuses to contract.

Generally, both the amount of compensation and the right to compensation are determined by the listing agreement. The right to a commission must be stated in the listing agreement. The two most common clauses controlling the right to a commission are referred to as *procuring cause* and *exclusive right to sell*. Texas courts will enforce both clauses. Both clauses require that the buyer be ready, willing and able to purchase the property.

Ready, willing and able means that the buyer is capable of present performance. The test of whether the buyer is ready and willing is his or her intention at the time the contract is made. Intent at the time the contract is to be consummated (closed) is not material. Most courts infer readiness and willingness if the buyer submits an offer on terms stipulated by the owner. A buyer is said to be able if he or she has the financial ability to complete the transaction.

A buyer is considered financially ready and able to buy under any of three conditions:

- The buyer has cash on hand to complete the sale.
- The buyer has sufficient personal assets and a strong credit rating that ensures with reasonable certainty that he or she can complete the sale.
- The buyer has a binding commitment for a loan with which to finance the sale.

One common provision in the listing agreement is the requirement that the broker be the procuring cause in bringing about a "meeting of the minds" between buyer and owner. A broker is the procuring cause of a sale if he or she initiates a series of continuous events that result in a sale upon the owner's terms. Merely introducing buyer and seller would be enough if the seller takes over the negotiations and completes the transaction. If the broker is unable to obtain an offer and abandons his or her efforts, the owner is not liable for a commission if the sale is completed without the broker's aid.

• **CASE BRIEF** •

Ramesh, a buyer of real estate, hired Johnson to find an apartment complex in Houston with which Ramesh could effectuate a tax-deferred exchange of real estate. Johnson located the Alta Vista apartments and negotiated a contract between Ramesh and Municipal Engineering Company for $532,000. The contract provided that Johnson was due $28,000 in commissions at closing. The contract gave Ramesh the right to rescind the transaction if, on inspection of the apartments, he found them unsatisfactory. After conducting an inspection, Ramesh refused to close the sale because the building's roof needed substantial repairs. The contract was rescinded. Within a week after the rescission, Ramesh, acting through another broker, Rushton, and without the knowledge of Johnson, entered into a new contract to buy the Alta Vista Apartments for the same price but with different financing arrangements. Ramesh agreed to pay Rushton $10,000 for his services. Johnson sued Ramesh for the $28,000 in commissions due under the prior contract, alleging that he was the procuring cause of the sale. Ramesh argued that the prior contract had terminated and that Johnson had not assisted in securing the second contract. The court disagreed and held in favor of Johnson. The court stated that the broker's right to a commission continues for a reasonable time after termination of the earnest money contract by mutual rescission of the buyer and seller unless there is some new independent intervening cause for the ultimate sale. A new independent and intervening cause is an event that destroys the causal connection between the first event and the result such that the result was actually caused by the occurrence of a second event. In this case there was none. *Ramesh v. Johnson*, 681 S.W.2d 256 (Tex. Civ. App.— 14th Dist. 1984).

The other common provision in the listing agreement is an exclusive-right-to-sell provision. Under this clause the agent is entitled to receive a commission if the property is sold during the listing term even if he or she did not find the buyer or negotiate the sale. Property is considered sold when a binding contract is entered into by the buyer and seller. The closing date does not affect the right to receive the commission. In an exclusive-right-to-sell contract the broker does not have to prove that he or she procured the buyer. However, there still must be proof that the buyer was ready, willing and able to purchase the land.

Special Problems in Collecting Commissions

Most of the litigation pertaining to commissions in Texas concerns the seller's termination of the listing agreement before its stated termination date or a seller's postponement of a sale until after the termination date in an attempt to avoid payment of a commission. In both instances the agent is entitled to damages and in some cases his or her full commission.

In Texas, as elsewhere, a broker or salesman can negotiate contracts for the seller or buyer but cannot bind him or her to the terms. The final approval of the contract must be in writing by the seller and buyer. Also, a seller or buyer can revoke the brokerage contract at any time for any reason. Despite the fact that the principal has the power to revoke, he or she will be liable to the agent for damages if he or she breaches the brokerage contract. The amount of damages the broker is entitled to receive may or may not equal the amount of the commission. If the broker can show that he or she had procured a ready, willing, and able buyer at the time the seller revoked the listing agreement, the broker will receive his or her commission. If the broker has not procured a buyer, then the measure of his or her damages shall be the reasonable profit the broker anticipated, and it is presumed to equal the amount of the commission.

The other frequently litigated situation concerns sales made after the termination of the contract to persons who were first introduced to the seller during the listing agreement by the agent. In Texas, as elsewhere, the courts will look at all the facts to determine whether the seller and buyer acted in good faith. Texas courts have repeatedly held that, if the purpose of the delay in consummating the sale is to avoid payment of the commission, the broker will be entitled to receive it. In further protection of the broker, the courts in Texas have held that, even if the agent could not have sued the seller to collect his or her commission, the agent can sue the buyer if the buyer encouraged, induced or conspired with the seller to prevent the agent from receiving the commission. This type of lawsuit is called *tortious interference with a business contract*.

A somewhat different problem arises when, through no fault of the seller, the buyer refuses to close after a binding contract has been executed. Is the agent entitled to receive a commission even though the sale is never consummated? The general rule in Texas is that the agent whose listing agreement contained a procuring cause clause is entitled to receive a commission. Upon signing of the earnest money contract the risk that the buyer will default is assumed by the seller. However, a modification to this rule does exist. If the earnest money contract contained a provision that in the event of default by the buyer the seller has the option to sue for specific performance or forfeiture of the earnest money, then the agent's compensation may be limited to the amount of the earnest money he or she is due to receive in the event of forfeiture. The election is in the hands of the seller. If the seller chooses to retain the earnest money rather than sue for specific performance, then the agent must accept the seller's decision. In that event the agent is not entitled to receive a commission but is limited to a share of the forfeited earnest money.

Forfeiture of Commission

A broker's conduct in the real estate transaction may cause a forfeiture of the commission. First, the broker must be licensed at the time the listing agreement was executed. Subsequent licensing does not cure this problem.

CASE EXAMPLE

Udoph, a broker, has had his license suspended for 30 days. During this period, one of Udoph's salesmen secures a listing agreement with the Fowlers. Three months later Udoph is successful in locating a buyer for the Fowlers' property. This buyer is ready, willing and able to purchase the property under the terms of sale set out in the listing agreement. By this time Udoph's license has been reinstated. Can Udoph force the payment of the commission? No; since Udoph was not licensed at the time the listing agreement was signed, he cannot support a claim for commission. Similarly, there also would be a forfeiture if the salesman working for King was not licensed at the time the Fowlers signed the listing agreement.

Commissions are also forfeited if there is a breach of a fiduciary duty by the broker or the salesman in the conduct of the transaction. Failure to account for money held in trust, undisclosed dual agency, failure to disclose information to the seller and other breaches of a fiduciary nature are grounds for forfeiture of a commission.

Finally, the Texas Real Estate License Act requires that the listing agreement be in writing and signed by the seller in order for the broker to be entitled to a commission.

The written agreement can take any form, such as a letter or memorandum. The broker can also forfeit his or her commission by violating certain duties owed to the buyer. These are discussed in the next section.

DUTIES OF AGENT TO BUYER

In the traditional real estate transaction, the broker is hired by the seller. In the past, American courts have generally held that the broker's sole responsibility is to the seller. Courts have regarded the relationship between broker and buyer as one of *caveat emptor*, reflecting the relationship between seller and buyer. This is not the case if the broker has been hired by the buyer. Then the broker is the buyer's representative.

The traditional legal view of the relationship between buyer and broker in the standard transaction is not in accord with the realities of the marketplace. Certainly the accepted legal relationship between buyer and broker does not meet the expectations of most buyers of residential property. Because of the broker's superior knowledge and skill, buyers frequently rely heavily upon a broker. Many buyers are not even aware that the broker is the seller's agent and not their own. Few brokers, apparently, make this clear to them. All of this places the broker in the dubious position of being able to influence the buyer with little fear of legal responsibility.

In recent years, however, courts in a few states have suggested that brokers do have limited duties to the buyer. A primary duty is to communicate the seller's price accurately to the buyer and to make known to the seller any offer made by the buyer. These courts have also held that a broker has a duty to act honestly in relationships with the buyer. Although the relationship between buyer and broker is generally not fiduciary, practices in which the broker takes some advantage of the buyer are considered to be against the public interest.

The Texas Real Estate License Act establishes that the broker or salesman owes the buyer certain duties even though the broker is representing the seller. These duties include the duty:

1. to refrain from making material misrepresentations;
2. to disclose unknown latent structural defects or other defects known to the broker or salesperson;
3. to disclose whether the broker or salesman is the owner of the property;
4. to advise a purchaser in writing prior to closing that the purchaser should either have an abstract covering the property examined by an attorney or obtain a title insurance policy;
5. to treat the buyer fairly; and
6. to refrain from discriminating on the basis of race, color, sex, religion or creed.

A buyer can sue the agent for damages incurred as a result of a breach of any one of these duties. Depending on the type of breach, the buyer may be able to rescind the contract and receive his or her money back. This also can lead to a suit by the seller against the brokers for breach of his duty to exercise care in representing the seller. The problems of misrepresentation and fraud are discussed in detail in the following chapter.

Although it is logical that the buyer could sue the agent for breach of one of these duties, the issue has arisen as to whether the agent would forfeit the commission owed to the agent by the seller even though the agent produced a ready, willing and able buyer. The Texas Supreme Court held that the commission would be forfeited in the following case.

CASE EXCERPT   *Jones v. Del Andersen and Associates,* 539 S.W. 2d 348 (Supreme Court of Texas 1976)   GREENHILL. Chief Justice.   This suit was brought by Del Andersen, doing business as Del Andersen & Associates, to recover a real estate commission. Suit was brought against Mrs. Joy Jones, the owner of the property for which a purchaser was procured. . . .

Joy Jones owned the Deluxe Motel in Comanche, Texas. In December of 1973, she and Del Andersen & Associates entered into a real estate listing agreement which gave Andersen the exclusive right to list the motel for a period of 360 days. Under the agreement, Mrs. Jones agreed to pay Andersen a commission of 6% of the selling price "in the event that within the listing period: 1) DEL ANDERSEN & ASSOCIATES procures a purchaser for said price. . . ." Andersen subsequently located a prospective purchaser, Mr. and Mrs. Joseph Gallant, who executed a purchase contract for the motel during the listing period. The contract of sale, however, was never consummated. Andersen brought suit contending that the Gallants were ready, willing and able purchasers, and that he was therefore entitled to his commission. . . .

Mrs. Jones contended that the suit was barred by the following provisions of Section 28, Article 6573a:

> At the time of the execution of any contract of sale of any real estate in the State, the Real Estate Salesman, Real Estate Broker, Real Estate Agent or Realtor shall advise the purchaser or purchasers, in writing, that such purchaser or purchasers should have the abstract covering the real estate which is the subject of the contract examined by an attorney of the purchaser's own selection, or that such purchaser or purchasers should be furnished with or obtain a policy of title insurance; and provided further, that failure to so advise as hereinabove set out shall preclude the payment of or recovery of any commission agreed to be paid on such sale. . . .

Andersen contends that Section 28 is not applicable. He argues, and the court of appeals agreed, that it does not apply where the suit for commission is based upon a listing agreement rather than a contract of sale. Andersen also contends that the purpose of the statute is to protect purchasers of real property; therefore it must be construed to apply only in cases where the purchaser is to pay the commission; and since this suit is against the seller, Section 28 should be no bar.

In determining the meaning of a statute, the dominant consideration is to ascertain the intention of the Legislature. This intention is to be found in the language of the statute itself. With these rules of construction in mind, we cannot give Section 28 the limited construction advocated by Andersen. To do so would require that we read into the statute words which are not there. It contains no language indicating that it applies only to commissions which are "payable by purchasers" or which are "based upon a contract of sale." Instead, the statute precludes "the payment of or recovery of any commission agreed to be paid."

. . . The Legislature could reasonably conclude that the most effective means of protecting prospective purchasers is to deny the realtor his commission any time he fails to supply the required information. . . .

We recognize that such a statute, construed as it is intended, can lead to harsh results in individual cases. For example, it appears that in the present case the purchasers did in fact seek legal advice concerning the seller's title, even though Andersen had failed to so advise them. However, when we have determined the legislative intent expressed in unambiguous language, our function is not to question the wisdom of the statute. In the absence of constitutional infirmities, we must apply it as written.

We therefore hold that Andersen's suit for his commission is barred by Section 28, Article 6573a. (Author's Note: The substance of Section 28 is now found in Section 20 of Article 6573a.)

SUMMARY

Real estate transactions are frequently facilitated by the use of persons who are trained and experienced in the field. A trained professional is hired to act on behalf of a landowner. This is called an *agency relationship*. Agency relationships are common to many different business activities. In the area of real estate, agency relationships are established between brokers and sellers, brokers and buyers, and brokers and salesmen.

Agency is a voluntary relationship. It can be created in writing, verbally or by the actions of the parties. The key elements to the formation of any agency relationship are an agreement between two parties that one, called the *agent*, will perform some task on behalf of another, called the *principal*. An agent is a fiduciary. The principal can expect and demand that his or her agent act loyally, competently and with integrity in advancing the principal's interest. Agents must avoid all potential conflicts of interest. Principals are also obligated to protect their agents from liability incurred on the principal's behalf. The chief duty of the principal is to compensate the agent.

The authority of an agent to act on behalf of the principal is limited to those acts expressly granted to the agent and those acts that are reasonably necessary to carry out the express grant. These are called the *express* and *implied authority* of an agent. In any agency relationship it is important for the agent and principal to define clearly the scope of authority.

An agency relationship can be revoked at any time by either party. However, if the termination violates a contract between the agent and principal, the breaching party will be liable for monetary damages caused by the breach. An agency relationship also can be properly terminated for cause, by agreement of the parties, by completion of the task or by expiration of the term of the agency.

One of the many agency relationships is the one that can be created between a broker and a salesman. In this relationship there are two primary considerations. First is the liability of the broker to third parties for the conduct of his or her salesmen. A broker can limit his or her liability for the salesman's conduct by treating the salesman as an independent contractor. An independent contractor is an agent who is not supervised directly by the principal. Although a broker can limit his or her liability in this way, the broker cannot avoid all responsibility. The Texas Real Estate License Act holds the sponsoring broker liable for any violation of the act committed by his or her salesmen. The second consideration for a broker in deciding how to treat his or her salesmen is tax liability. If the broker is an employer, then the broker must withhold federal income tax, contribute to the employee's social security and pay the state and federal unemployment tax. These tax payments are not required of the broker if his or her salesmen are independent contractors.

The most common agency relationship in real estate transactions is the relationship between a broker and a seller. This relationship is usually created by a written contract called a *listing agreement*. A listing agreement must be in writing and signed by the seller. There are different types of listing agreements. They are classified by the method by which the commission is calculated and by the provision regarding when a commission is due. In Texas a broker is not entitled to a commission unless he or she has a written agreement.

The Texas Real Estate License Act and the regulations promulgated by the Texas Real Estate Commission provide the broker and salesman with some guidelines concerning their fiduciary duties to the seller. These legislated duties include such specific obligations as disclosing to the seller when the broker or agent is acting on his or her own behalf in a transaction and properly accounting for money the agent is holding in escrow.

Brokers and salesmen should be particularly careful to explain to sellers and buyers for whom they are acting. Buyers are frequently confused about the loyalty of a salesman and expect or assume that if they initiate the contact the salesman or broker will be representing them. This is an area of increasing litigation that can sometimes be avoided through a clear explanation by the broker of his or her obligations to the buyer.

The most frequently litigated dispute by brokers against sellers concerns payment of the commission. The terms of the listing agreement establish when a commission is due. A general requirement is that there be a buyer ready, willing and able to purchase the property. The two principal clauses affecting the accrual of a commission are procuring cause provisions and exclusive-right-to-sell provisions. In either of these clauses a commission may be due even if the sale did not close. Occasionally the agent's conduct causes a forfeiture of the commission. Breach of a fiduciary duty such as undisclosed dual agency can cause a forfeiture. Lack of a license at the time the listing agreement is signed is another ground for forfeiture.

Finally, of increasing importance is the obligation of a broker or salesman to a buyer who is not the agent's principal. The Texas Real Estate License Act clearly establishes that brokers owe potential buyers some minimum standards of care. These include disclosure of latent structural defects known to the broker and a general duty to treat buyers fairly.

QUESTIONS AND CASE PROBLEMS

1. Explain why classifying a real estate salesman as an independent contractor does not relieve the broker of responsibility for the salesman's actions.
2. Compare and contrast *express authority* and *implied authority*. Provide some examples of implied authority.

3. In the traditional real estate transaction, what are the broker's duties to the buyer?

4. Ed Kelly listed property with Dave Gould Realty. Gould showed the property to Nadine McNicols, a real estate developer. McNicols had numerous questions relating to zoning, and Gould referred her to Kelly's attorney, who answered her questions and supplied her with additional information.

When McNicols learned that Gould was showing the property to other prospective buyers, she made an offer directly to Kelly. Kelly accepted the offer but refused to pay Gould a commission. What argument could be made for Kelly? For Gould? Who would win if Gould sued? Why?

5. Sam Guidi, a real estate broker, learned from a friend that Arro, Inc., was interested in buying vacant land for a warehouse. Knowing that Byron Lane owned land that he was trying to sell, Guidi phoned Lane, who quoted him a price of $35,000 for the parcel. Lane knew that Guidi was a broker, but no commission or other arrangements were discussed. Guidi obtained an offer of $28,000 from Arro, which Lane rejected. Shortly thereafter Lane contacted Arro directly and entered into a contract at $33,000. In a suit by Guidi against Lane for a commission, what resulted? Why?

6. John T. Withers, a licensed broker, was hired by Hall to find a purchaser for some land owned by Hall. The purchaser, William Clements, discussed the property with Withers and demanded that Withers surrender his commission and told him that he would get the property directly from Hall. Hall did sell the property to Clements, and Clements agreed with Hall to "take care of Withers." Withers was not paid his commission. The contract between Withers and Hall was unenforceable because it did not identify the land to be sold. Withers sued Clements. Clements defended on the ground that the listing agreement between Withers and Hall was unenforceable and therefore he was not liable. Withers claimed that Clements tortiously interfered with the agreement between Withers and Hall and that for that reason Clements was liable. Between Clements and Withers, who will prevail? Why?

7. V/W Realty Sales Agency, a licensed real estate broker, sued Long Meadows Country Club, Inc., for $90,000, which represented the commission due. Long Meadows had executed an earnest money contract with John Jamail for $1.5 million. At the time of the contract, Jamail deposited $10,000 as earnest money. Jamail defaulted. Long Meadows elected to keep the earnest money and waived its right to sue for specific performance. V/W Realty alleged that it was entitled to receive the $90,000 commission even though the sale was never consummated. V/W Realty alleged that the com-

mission was earned when the earnest money contract was signed by Long Meadows and Jamail. V/W Realty also argued that the decision by Long Meadows not to sue Jamail for specific performance and instead to retain the earnest money did not relieve Long Meadows of its contractual agreement with V/W Realty. Who prevails and why?

8. Riley, a real estate broker, was retained by Powell to sell an apartment complex. Riley notified several other brokers that the complex was for sale for around $600,000. Riley received one offer on the complex in the amount of $700,000 but did not tell Powell about it. In August 1979, Riley agreed to purchase the apartments for $420,000. A dispute arose between Riley and Powell regarding the terms of a second lien note that Powell had agreed to carry. Powell refused to close the sale. Riley sued Powell for specific performance of the contract. Who is likely to win? Why?

16
Fraud and Misrepresentation

No evidence exists that misrepresentation and fraud are more prevalent in real estate than they are in other sectors of the economy. If, however, deceptive acts occur in a real estate transaction, they probably have a greater impact than they do in other areas. Several reasons account for this. First, most real estate transactions involve large sums of money; as a result, people who feel deceived are more apt to complain or take legal action to assert their rights. A second reason is that licensing laws in every state have placed substantial supervisory responsibility upon brokers for the conduct of salesmen, as was seen in Chapter 15. Unauthorized and even unintentional deception by the salesman can subject the broker to liability, including the loss of license. Finally, in many transactions little direct contact takes place between buyer and seller. Inasmuch as information is often transmitted through a third party, misunderstanding and error can result in the buyer or seller, or perhaps both, feeling that they have been deceived.

Fraud is a deceptive act or statement deliberately practiced by one person in an attempt to gain an unfair financial advantage over another. If the false representation was not made intentionally, it is often called *misrepresentation*. **Misrepresentation** is a false statement negligently or innocently made that was a material factor in the victim's decision to contract. Both fraud and misrepresentation can serve as the basis for rescinding a contract or recovering damages caused by the reliance on the false statement. The remedy available often depends upon the extent to which the person making the false statement intended to deceive. Fraud and misrepresentation are also grounds for suspension or revocation of the real estate license under the Texas Real Estate License Act. Furthermore, a victim who is unable to recover damages awarded by the court from the licensee may be able to recover some or all of the damages from the recovery fund. This was discussed in Chapter 14.

In Texas there are three ways an injured party can recover for fraud or misrepresentation. First, there is a lawsuit based upon common law fraud. This is an action in tort that was created by the courts to assist victims of fraud to recover damages from the offending party. Second, there is a lawsuit based on a statute found in §27.01 et seq. of the Texas Business and Commerce Code. This statute specifically prohibits fraud in real estate transactions. Third, there is a lawsuit based upon a statute called the Deceptive Trade Practices–Consumer Protection Act. This statute is found in §17.45 et seq. of the Texas Business and Commerce Code.

It is important to remember throughout this chapter that fraud or misrepresentation can be committed by any party or agent in the real estate transaction, including sellers, buyers, brokers and salesmen.

COMMON LAW FRAUD

Actions for common law fraud usually require proof that (1) an intentional (2) misstatement of a material fact was (3) justifiably relied on and (4) resulted in damages. Although it is relatively simple to list these elements, their application in practice is much more difficult.

Intentional

An intentional, conscious misrepresentation is an essential element of actionable frauds. Courts usually refer to this as an intention to deceive. The technical term *scienter* is also used. Scienter exists if a person knowingly makes a false statement or asserts that something is true or false without actual knowledge of whether or not this is the case. An evil intention is not necessary, nor is it required that the speaker intend to injure the other party.

Early cases found the requisite intent only in those situations in which the speaker had actual knowledge of the falsity of the representation; the courts equated intent to deceive with knowledge of falsity. This restrictive interpretation did not long survive. Today all American jurisdictions find scienter not only when the speaker knew the representation to be false but also when the representation was made either without belief in the statement's truth or with reckless disregard of its truth or falsity. Included are statements made by a person who realizes that he or she does not have sufficient basis or information to justify them.

Negligent misrepresentation is an area of increasing concern for brokers and salesmen. As discussed in the previous chapters, brokers and salesmen have both a legal and an ethical duty to be knowledgeable and exercise reasonable care in performing real estate activities. Courts have held that, if brokers should have known that their statements regarding real estate were false, they will be liable for any harm caused to the person to whom the misrepresentation was made. In determining what a broker or salesman should know, the courts inquire as to whether a reasonable broker or salesman would generally have knowledge or experience that would have alerted him or her to the possible falsity of the statement. Furthermore, courts have held that brokers should not make statements regarding the property without checking the accuracy of their statements. The case that follows illustrates this principle.

• CASE BRIEF •

Stone, a licensed real estate agent, bought 18.639 acres of a 70-acre tract owned by Goodstein. Of paramount concern to Stone in carving out the 18.639 acres was that any land containing an oil and gas pipeline easement be excluded. The agent for Goodstein, aware of Stone's requirement and that Stone intended to construct a mobile home park on the purchased land, represented that all the pipeline easements were outside the 18.639 acres. Mobile home sites cannot be constructed over such easements. Stone sued Goodstein and his agent when it was discovered that a high-pressure gas pipeline ran under a portion of the 18.639 acres. The court held that the agent would be liable even though he was unaware of the pipeline easement. The court stated that he was reckless about making statements without knowing if they were true or false. Further, the court held that Stone was under no obligation to make an independent investigation and acted reasonably in relying upon the agent's statement. *Stone vs. Lawyers Title Insurance Corp.*, 537 S.W.2d 55 (Tex. Civ. App.—Corpus Christi 1976).

Misstatement of a Material Fact

An important premise of American contract law is that adults are competent and have the ability to make rational decisions. As a result, courts do not aid those who rely upon representations not worthy of belief. Judges reason that the rational person discounts statements that are not factual.

Although the rule that only factual representation can be the basis for fraud is clear, often it is difficult to determine what statements are factual. A fact is something that is knowable, a physical object that actually exists or existed or an event that is under way or has taken place. Understanding what the law means by a representation of fact is often clarified by considering statements generally considered by courts as not factual. These include opinions and estimates, predictions, guesses and promises.

Promises require a special word of caution. As will be seen in the chapter on contracts (see Chapter 18), a person who makes a promise that later is broken is subject to a suit for breach of contract. Fraud is usually not the basis for the injured party's action. However, the Texas statutory remedy for real estate fraud found in the Texas Business and Commerce Code does apply to promises as well as statements of fact.

Puffing is a statement of opinion made by a seller to induce the purchaser to buy. Sellers have a natural tendency to commend the item they are selling. Such expressions as "I built it with the best," "It's the best building in town" and "You have nothing to worry about; it's a good well" are examples. This type of statement is often referred to as "puffing" or "dealer's talk." Statements of this nature are not actionable as fraud, even though false, since courts treat them as expressions of opinion. A leading American jurist, Judge Learned Hand, explained why in the following language.

> There are some kinds of talk no sensible man takes seriously, and if he does he suffers from his credulity. If we were all scrupulously honest, it would not be so; but as it is, neither party usually believes what the seller says about his opinions, and each knows it. Such statements, like the claims of campaign managers before election, are rather designed to allay the suspicion which would attend their absence than to be understood as having any relation to objective truth. *Vulcan Metals Co. v. Simmons Mfg. Co.*, 248 F. 853 (2nd Cir. 1918).

Although generally the law does not protect the credulous buyer who relies upon the seller's opinion, a number of situations exist in which courts allow recovery for fraud based upon nonfactual statements. Opinions expressed (1) by a person who enjoys a relationship of trust and confidence or has superior knowledge, (2) by an expert hired to give advice or (3) by a person who actually does not have this opinion are all actionable.

Compare the case example below with the case brief that follows it. In the first instance the statement of opinion was a basis for fraud. In the second case the court held that the statement of opinion was not the basis for fraud.

CASE EXAMPLE

Mel Erickson, a licensed real estate broker, specialized in investment properties. Tillitz, a wealthy rancher, wished to invest in a multifamily dwelling. Erickson showed Tillitz several properties. After inspecting one large unit, Erickson stated, "That's a fine building, and the return on your investment would be substantial." At the time, Erickson had never inspected the records and was unaware of some major problems with the heating units.

Tillitz purchased the building, lost money and sued Erickson for fraud. Because of Erickson's superior knowledge, many courts would consider the statement as the basis for fraud.

• CASE BRIEF •

McMinn, Welling and Luciano were partners doing business under the name Mangum Road Center. Mangum Road Center was constructing a shopping center on Mangum Road in the city of Houston, Texas. In August

1961, DiSclafani entered into negotiations to lease space in the Mangum Road Center shopping center. During the negotiations Luciano told DiSclafani "that a substantial part of the yet uncompleted section would be occupied by a large drugstore," and that the building "would be completed within a short time." DiSclafani executed a lease with the partnership for space in the shopping center. Six months later DiSclafani vacated the premises in violation of the lease. The partnership sued DiSclafani for breach of the lease. DiSclafani defended, claiming that he was fraudulently induced into executing the lease by the statements of Luciano regarding the drugstore and the completion date. In fact no drugstore had occupied the shopping center, and the shopping center had not yet been completed. The partnership claims that the statements were opinions and not facts. The partnership anticipated or intended that there would be a drugstore and that the center would be completed soon but did not promise or commit itself to those statements. The court found for the partnership on the ground that the statements were simply opinions and not facts. *Mangum Road Center v. DiSclafani,* 450 S.W.2d 130 (Tex. Civ. App.—Houston 1969).

The most difficult legal questions arise in cases in which a buyer has suffered a loss because of the seller's failure to speak. In some instances the seller simply fails to disclose an element important in the transaction. In others the seller employs some trick or scheme to conceal a condition or fact that is material to the transaction.

The cases that involve concealment are much easier to decide than those that merely involve silence. Active efforts to hide something usually overcomes any reluctance courts have to refuse relief on the grounds of caveat emptor.

As a general rule, a party's silence—even silence concerning a critical factor—is not actionable as a misrepresentation. American contract law does not ordinarily require an individual to disclose facts detrimental to the agreement. In a few instances, however, there is a positive obligation to disclose known facts. Courts call this a *duty to speak.* In the following situations, courts in most states have ruled with consistency that a person must speak out about relevant circumstances and facts known to him or her.

- A hidden defect exists that is likely to result in personal harm to persons using the property.
- A hidden defect exists that is likely to limit a use the seller knows the buyer intends to make of the property.
- The seller enjoys a confidential relationship with the buyer.
- The buyer has asked a question that the seller has truthfully answered, but the situation changes and the answer is now false.

Another troublesome problem exists where the seller has made an oral or written representation that is only partially true. Like silence and concealment, the "half-truth" is a misrepresentation actionable as fraud. In many cases a half-truth is more misleading than a statement that is completely false. The half-truth can more easily lull the listener into accepting other representations that are made.

Reliance

To be successful in an action for fraud, the injured party must prove that (1) he or she acted in reliance upon the false information and (2) the reliance was justified. A person cannot have relied upon false information if the information was acquired after the person acted, nor may a person rely upon statements that investigation indicates are false.

CASE EXAMPLE

Grace Kiner was interested in purchasing a music store from Helen Little. Kiner's marketing strategy required large volumes of potential customers. Little informed Kiner that on the average 250 people came in daily. Little knew that this was false.

Upon several occasions, Kiner visited the store, remaining for appreciable periods of time. After Kiner purchased the store, it became apparent that Little's statement was false. As a result, Kiner sued to rescind. Rescission would be denied if the jury determined that Kiner had relied upon her own inspection, not Little's statement.

In spite of the previous example, the fact that a purchaser makes an independent investigation does not in itself show reliance only upon his or her own judgment. In these situations, the courts must weigh the circumstances of the particular case to determine whether continued reliance upon the misrepresentation after investigation is justifiable. Critical factors are such elements as (1) the background of the person investigating, (2) the amount of time available to investigate, (3) the sources of information available and (4) the techniques needed to secure correct information.

Courts use different criteria to determine whether reliance is justifiable. Some states measure the plaintiff's conduct against that of a reasonably prudent person. If a jury decides that a reasonably prudent person, one who uses ordinary care under the circumstances, would not have relied upon the statement, the plaintiff's reliance was not justified. Most states have rejected this standard. The test that is applied is tailored to the particular individual to whom the misrepresentation has been made. Courts in these states take the position that the law should not protect positive, intentional fraud practiced upon the simpleminded or unwary. At the same time, a person who has special knowledge and competence is not justified in relying upon statements that an ordinary man might believe. Similarly, a person whose background and information are those that a normal person might have is not barred from recovery because he or she carelessly accepts a misrepresentation; but if the alleged fact is preposterous, reliance is not justified, and recovery for fraud will be denied.

Material

Not only must the misrepresentation be a misstatement; it must also be material. A person is not justified in acting upon a false statement that is trivial in relation to the entire transaction. Inconsequential information of this nature is not material and thus not grounds for suit. On the other hand, some false statements that in themselves seem to be of no significance are important in particular situations. Consider the following examples, in both of which representations are false.

CASE EXAMPLES

Rex Todor is purchasing a house in Memphis, Tennessee. The salesman states, "Elvis Presley's uncle once lived here."

Rex Todor is purchasing an inn in Memphis, Tennessee. The salesman states, "Elvis Presley often stayed here."

In the first example, the misrepresentation would not be material. A reasonable person would not consider this a significant factor. If, however, the speaker knew that this was important to the buyer, the result would be different. Courts ordinarily will not allow a person knowingly to practice a deception, even though the supposed fact might be unimportant to most people. In the second example, the misrepresentation is material. The fact that Elvis Presley had often stayed at a particular inn would increase the property's value as an attraction for tourists.

Materiality also has a second dimension, which causes some legal problems. Frequently, a false statement is only one of several reasons that causes the person to act. A difficult factual question exists when the plaintiff has numerous bits of valid information upon which a decision could logically be reached, but, in addition, has been given some information that is false. It is the view of most courts that for the false information to be material, it must have substantially contributed to the plaintiff's decision to act. If without this information the injured party would not have contracted, the false information may be the basis of an action for deceit. Whether the information is material is a question for the jury.

STATUTORY FRAUD IN REAL ESTATE TRANSACTIONS

In §27.01 of the Texas Business and Commerce Code, fraud is defined as either

1. a false representation of a material fact made to a person to induce him to enter into a contract and relied upon by him in entering into the contract; or
2. a false promise to do an act that is material and made with the in-

tent of not fulfilling it and to induce the person to enter into the contract and that is relied upon by that person.

The first part of this definition is similar to a common law action for fraud. The second part expands the common law to include promises to perform future acts. As previously pointed out, the failure to perform a promised act at common law is a breach of contract rather than fraud.

Under the statute, fraud can be committed by any party in the real estate transaction, including sellers, brokers, salesmen and buyers. Although there are few cases involving a fraud perpetrated by a buyer on a seller, the statute does protect both parties. Furthermore, the statute pertains to any phase of the real estate transaction, including negotiating the sale, financing the purchase and closing. The only limitation is that the transaction must involve real estate. The case that follows discusses several of the elements necessary to prove fraud under the statute and the awarding of exemplary damages.

CASE EXCERPT   *Trenholm v. Ratcliff*, 646 S.W.2d 927 (Supreme Court of Texas 1983)   SPEARS, Justice.   Trenholm, a homebuilder, sued Ratcliff, a developer, under . . . the fraud in real estate transaction provisions of the Business and Commerce Code. . . .

In November 1975, Ratcliff held a "draw meeting" to solicit local builders. The meeting was attended by several builders, including George Trenholm. At the meeting Ratcliff discussed the Greenhollow development, and invited builders to purchase lots in the subdivision. During the presentation, Ratcliff stated a mobile home park located near Greenhollow would be a future shopping center. At the conclusion of his presentation, Ratcliff invited questions. George Trenholm asked:

> Ray, you talked in, around and about this mobile home park through your presentation, and you definitely left me with the impression that it's going to be moved, but before I buy any lots I specifically want to know what disposition is going to be made on that property.
> Ratcliff answered:
> Don't worry about it, that's zoned commercial, and that property has already been sold. Those people have been notified that their leases will not be renewed, so the park should close up sometime in April and after that, why, after they get everything moved out over there, they will come in and bulldoze it down so by June or July it will be like there's never been a park there, and that will coincide actually just fine with the grand opening out there.

Trenholm built eighteen houses in the Greenhollow development. Six houses were built for his account, and twelve were built pursuant to a joint venture with Richardson Savings & Loan. Richardson Savings & Loan would furnish the money, and Trenholm would build and sell the houses. The profits or losses of the joint venture would be split 50/50 between them.

. . . The Greenhollow subdivision did poorly and on June 23, 1976, a meeting was held by Ratcliff to discuss the slow sales. Trenholm asked about the continued presence of the mobile home park, and he was told that the park would not be moved. The closings on seven of the twelve joint venture lots were held after June 23. The houses were ultimately sold at a net loss. . . .

Ratcliff contends the necessary elements of a common law fraud action have not been established. . . . The elements of actionable fraud in Texas were stated in *Wilson vs. Jones* as follows:

> (1) that a material representation was made; (2) that it was false; (3) that, when the speaker made it, he knew it was false or made it recklessly without any knowledge of its truth and as a positive assertion; (4) that he made it with the intention that it should be acted upon by the party; (5) that the party acted in reliance upon it; and (6) that he thereby suffered injury.

Ratcliff argues that the "trailer park representations" are matters of opinion or predictions of future events, and therefore, Trenholm must prove that Ratcliff knew they were false at the time they were made. . . .

Ratcliff's representation was not merely an expression of an opinion that the trailer park would be moved in the future. He falsely represented that the trailer park had been sold, and that notices had been given to the tenants. These are direct representations of present facts which are so intertwined with his future prediction that the whole statement amounts to a representation of facts. . . .

The court of appeals affirmed the take nothing judgment, holding. . . that Trenholm did not rely on Ratcliff's representations as to seven of the houses [reference here is made to the lots that did not close until after Trenholm knew that the mobile home park would not be moved]. . . .

The court of appeals reasoned that Trenholm did not rely on Ratcliff's false representations because he discovered Ratcliff's fraud prior to the purchase of seven of the twelve joint venture lots. The Trenholms' reliance did not occur when they purchased the joint venture lots, but rather, when the Trenholms entered into the agreement obligating themselves to build the houses. The reliance occurred in April 1976, prior to the June 23, 1976 discovery of Ratcliff's fraud. . . .

Furthermore, Trenholm could not have backed out of the joint venture agreement without suffering injury. The joint venture agreement provided that the Trenholms could not recover their share of the profits under the agreement until ALL of the houses had been built and sold. If Trenholm had abandoned the agreement after discovering the fraud, he would have given up his right to whatever profits were still possible. Additionally, Trenholm testified his other loan agreements with Richardson would not have been renewed if he had abandoned the joint venture agreement. . . .

Ratcliff argues Trenholm is not entitled to exemplary damages. . . .Conscious indifference to the rights of others is also sufficient for an award of exemplary damages. Ratcliff was aware prior to the draw meeting that the trailer park would be a drawback and concern the builders. So to induce them to buy lots, he falsely represented that the mobile home park had been sold and the land had been zoned commercial. This is some evidence to support a jury inference that Ratcliff made the misrepresentation with a conscious disregard for the rights of Trenholm. . . .

We reverse the judgment of the court of appeals, and render judgment for

Trenholm on the jury verdict for actual damages of $190,500.00 and exemplary damages of $250,000.00, with lawful interest from the date of the trial court judgment.

This statutory protection for false statements is very similar to common law fraud actions. If the elements for common law fraud are present, then there is also a violation of the statute. In addition, this statute clearly covers false statements made innocently by the speaker.

CASE EXAMPLE
Jordan, the seller, states to Hinds, a prospective buyer, that the roof is in good condition. Jordan based his statement concerning the roof on two facts known to him at that time: first, that the roof does not leak; and second, that he had been told recently by a roof specialist that the roof was good for another three to five years. Shortly after Hinds buys the property and moves in, the roof begins to leak. Although Jordan's statement was made innocently and based upon the information he had, it was nevertheless false. Hinds will be able to recover his actual damages from Jordan.

REMEDIES FOR COMMON LAW FRAUD AND STATUTORY FRAUD

The remedies available to the injured party depend in part upon whether the false statement was made intentionally, negligently or innocently. Assuming the elements for either common law fraud or statutory fraud are proven, the injured party has the following remedies from which to choose:
1. Refuse to perform, using the deceit as a defense if sued for breach of contract.
2. Affirm the contract and sue for damages.
3. Rescind the contract.
4. Rescind the contract and sue for damages.

Rescission is the disaffirmation or cancellation of a transaction. If the injured party elects to rescind the contract on the basis of fraud or misrepresentation, he or she is entitled to recover whatever consideration was given. The injured party must also return the consideration or property he or she had received. The purpose of rescission is to place both parties to a transaction in the position that they would have been in had the contract or transaction not taken place. Frequently, rescission alone does not fully compensate the injured party for his or her economic loss. Therefore, the victim may also elect to sue for damages.

Damages

In an action for fraud and deceit, a plaintiff is not entitled to recover damages unless actual monetary loss can be proved. Ordinarily, this requirement is met easily because usually the relationship between the misrepresentation and monetary injury is clear. Few people would sue for misrepresentation unless they believed the deception caused them to lose money. The costs and trauma of litigation make it an expensive way to prove a person a liar if the plaintiff lost nothing.

Generally, the more acute legal problem involves the amount of the damages, not their existence.

CASE EXAMPLE

Sam Tremain purchased a building site in a development for $28,000. In making this purchase, Tremain relied on the developer's false representation that plans called for a community swimming pool within walking distance of the site. The sites adjacent to Tremain's sold for $27,000 and $28,500. They were comparable in size to his.

Although the seller did build a pool, it was more than three miles away. Sites near the pool sold for $40,000. In a suit against the seller for damages based on misrepresentation, Tremain argued that he was entitled to $12,000. The developer argued that Tremain could not recover because he suffered no damage. He contended the site Tremain purchased was worth what he paid for it.

Courts in the United States use two different rules to measure damages in this type of situation.

Benefit-of-the-Bargain Rule

Damages calculated under the **benefit-of-the-bargain rule,** are measured by the difference between the value of what the deceived party actually received and what would have been received had the misrepresentation been true. This is sometimes called the *loss-of-bargain.* Under this rule, Tremain would be entitled to $12,000. Benefit-of-the-bargain damages are sometimes difficult to establish because they often depend upon subjective testimony of what something would be worth under conditions that do not actually exist. In some situations, courts can simplify this problem by measuring damages as the cost of putting the property in the condition that would bring it into conformity with the value as represented.

Out-of-Pocket Rule

Using the **out-of-pocket rule,** damages are measured by the difference in value between what the injured party actually gave up and what the party received. If a court were to follow the out-of-pocket rule, Tremain would be entitled to very little. The lot that he purchased was worth approximately what he paid for it.

In some states there is only one method by which damages can be calculated. In Texas, the court will apply the rule that most adequately compensates the injured party for every loss that is the natural and direct result of the fraud.

Exemplary Damages

Exemplary damages are damages awarded as a punishment to the wrong-doer in addition to those actually incurred by the injured party. These damages also are called *punitive damages.* To recover exemplary damages for fraud and deceit, the plaintiff must have suffered actual damages. In most states, exemplary damages will not be awarded unless the action is gross, oppressive and committed with ill will. Thus a person whose misrepresentation was the result of negligence or was made innocently would not be responsible for exemplary damages.

The purpose of exemplary damages is to deter others from committing similar acts. The award of exemplary damages is discretionary with the jury. Exemplary damages usually include an amount sufficient to cover the injured party's attorney fees and an amount the jury considers appropriate to dissuade others. Exemplary damages must have some fair relationship to the compensatory damages that have been proved. Exemplary damages awards that shock the conscience of the court will not be permitted.

Also important to a victim of misrepresentation is the cost of bringing suit against the perpetrators of the fraud. Although the common law action for fraud did not allow for the recovery of such expenses, the Texas statute specifically directs that the victim, if successful in court, will recover the expenses of the litigation such as attorney fees, expert witness fees and costs of court.

Vicarious Liability

Although it is clear that the person who makes the false statement is liable and should be responsible, a second concern is to what extent the seller will be liable for a broker's misrepresentation or a broker will be responsible for a seller's misrepresentation. The law imposes on the person who will benefit from the transaction and who knows of the misrepresentation the duty to disclose the falsity of the statement. If a broker knows a seller has made a false statement and fails to tell the purchaser that the statement made by the seller is false, then the broker will be liable for punitive damages. Similarly, if the seller is aware that a broker is representing that the house slab is in perfect condition, and he or she knows that this is not true, then the seller will be liable to the purchaser for actual and punitive damages unless the seller discloses to the purchaser that the slab was not in perfect condition.

Waiver

Waiver is the intentional surrender of a known right or privilege. Under certain circumstances one who has been induced to enter a contract because of fraud or deceit waives the available remedies. Generally, waiver occurs when a person discovers the fraud and then does nothing about it. American courts have generally taken the position that, once a person learns that he or she has been deceived, ordinarily that person must take some action, or the contract based upon the deception will be confirmed.

Most courts are reluctant to find that a victim has waived the right to complain of the fraud or deception. Probably the most common bar to suing a party for fraud or misrepresentation is the failure to file the lawsuit within the statutory period. The statutory period is either two or four years, depending upon the theory of recovery used.

An injured party also waives any right to sue for deceit if, upon discovery of the fraud, he or she enters into a new arrangement concerning the subject matter of the contract. Tremain surrenders his right both to sue for damages and to rescind if, with knowledge of the developer's misrepresentation, he enters into a new contract for the same site at a reduced price. Tremain would also waive his right to sue for damages if he entered into a new contract that extended the period of time allowed to pay the purchase price or substituted another site for that agreed upon in the original agreement.

Real estate contracts sometimes contain provisions stating that the purchaser has not relied upon any representations made by the owner or broker or that the property is being purchased "as is." A modification of this is a statement that the purchaser has personally examined the property and enters the contract relying solely upon his or her own inspection. A typical example is a clause such as "buyers agree that they have entered into this contract relying upon their own knowledge and not upon any representations made by the seller or any other person." Clauses of this type do not waive the injured party's rights to sue for fraudulent representations made by an owner or a broker. The courts reason that to accept such clauses as defenses would provide the seller and the seller's agent with a license to commit fraud. Most buyers would neither recognize the significance of the language nor consider that it applied to outright deception. To allow its enforcement would violate the clear public policy of protecting people who act on the basis of deceptive statements.

DECEPTIVE TRADE PRACTICES–CONSUMER PROTECTION ACT

The Deceptive Trade Practices–Consumer Protection Act was passed by the Texas Legislature in 1973. As the act was originally drafted, real estate transactions were excluded from coverage. In 1975 the act was amended to include transactions involving real property purchased or leased for use. This law has had a significant impact on the manner in which business transactions are conducted in Texas. The purpose of the law is to protect consumers against false, misleading and deceptive business practices, unconscionable actions and breaches of warranty.

This law creates a powerful weapon for consumers. There are two reasons for its effectiveness. First, proving that a deceptive act has occurred is easier under this law than under the previous statute regarding fraud in real estate transactions and is certainly simpler than the common law cause of action for fraud. Consequently, it provides an efficient method for protecting consumers from unscrupulous or unethical trade practices. Second, the law provides that consumers can recover more than their actual losses if they are successful. Although an injured party can recover punitive damages for fraud, the Deceptive Trade Practices Act does not require proof that the defendant intended to deceive or mislead. The mere occurrence of a deceptive act can result in damages in excess of the actual economic losses.

The first use of the Deceptive Trade Practices Act in the real estate area involved cases concerning breach of warranty in the sale of new homes. The initial draft of the law allowed a consumer to recover three times the amount of actual damages suffered as a result of defective or unworkmanlike construction in a new home purchase. This generous remedy prompted consumers to bring all breach of warranty cases under the Deceptive Trade Practices Act. In recent years the law has been used by consumers against sellers of used homes, brokers and lenders. The law no longer provides for the automatic trebling of damages; however, it still allows for a recovery of damages in excess of the actual economic loss. This chapter will focus on those provisions of the act prohibiting deceptive or misleading conduct.

The act protects only consumers; therefore, it is important to understand the definition of *consumer. Consumer* means "an individual, partnership, corporation, this state, or a subdivision or agency of this state who seeks or acquires by purchase or lease, any goods or services. (T.B.C.A. §17.45[4]) Specifically excluded are business consumers with assets of $25 million or more. Goods include both real and personal property. Services include any type of labor or work performed for another and for which compensation is received.

Deceptive Acts

The act prohibits all false, misleading or deceptive acts in the conduct of business. The law specifically enumerates 23 activities that are violations of the act. Although an awareness of the enumerated prohibited acts is important, a violation of the act is not limited to those listed. The enumerated acts include the following.

1. misrepresenting or causing confusion and misunderstanding regarding the source, approval, certification or affiliation of goods or services;

2. misrepresenting the characteristics, benefits, qualities or uses of goods or services;

3. misrepresenting that goods are new;

4. disparaging the goods, services or business of another by misleading or false representations;

5. misleading advertising, such as advertising goods or services for sale

with intent not to sell them as advertised or a fraudulent representation that one is going out of business;

6. making false or misleading statements concerning the reasons for a price reduction;

7. misrepresenting the authority of an agent to negotiate the final terms of a consumer transaction;

8. representing that a contract, agreement, warranty or guaranty confers rights or benefits that it does not;

9. representing that work or services have been performed when in fact they were not; and

10. failing to disclose information concerning goods or services that were known at the time of the transaction if the purpose of the lack of disclosure was to induce the consumer into a transaction into which the consumer would not have entered had the information been disclosed.

There are two aspects of the enumerated acts that are important to remember. First, there is no requirement that the consumer prove that the offending party *intended* to deceive or misrepresent the facts. In most cases an innocent misrepresentation is as much a violation of the act as a fraudulent misrepresentation. In other words, it is not a defense to a lawsuit brought under this act that the actor did not *know* that his or her statements were false. Second, the act prohibits not only misrepresentations but also misleading statements. A misleading statement is one that leads the consumer in the wrong direction or creates a misconception of the facts.

• CASE BRIEF •

Mrs. LeSassier contracted with Orkin Extermination Co., Inc., for termite extermination services. On the date the serviceman came to Mrs. LeSassier's home, she let him in and then returned to her employment. Almost a year later she noticed evidence of termite activity. Orkin returned and treated her home. When she continued to have problems, she hired another firm to exterminate her home. She had the damage repaired and sued Orkin, alleging violation of the Deceptive Trade Practices Act in that Orkin had "represented that work or services had been performed when such work or services had not been performed." Orkin defended that the Deceptive Trade Practices Act did not apply because there was no verbal assertion made by it that the termite treatment had been performed. The court held that the serviceman's coming to Mrs. LeSassier's home, beginning treatments and then leaving, never to return, was a representation that all the treatments called for in the contract had been performed. *Orkin Exterminating Co., Inc. v. LeSassier*, 688 S.W.2d 651 (Tex. Civ. App.—9 Dist. 1985).

Unconscionable Conduct

The Deceptive Trade Practices Act also provides that a consumer can sue if he or she has suffered actual damages produced by unconscionable action by another. Unconscionable action is a form of deception and therefore should be explored. The act defines it as follows:

(5) "Unconscionable action or course of action" means an act or practice which, to a person's detriment:
(a) takes advantage of the lack of knowledge, ability, experience, or capacity of a person to a grossly unfair degree; or
(b) results in a gross disparity between the value received and consideration paid, in a transaction involving transfer of consideration.

Unconscionable action is a type of equitable relief afforded to a person who has been tricked or swindled to such an extent that it would be unfair to allow the transaction to stand. Unconscionability is a difficult legal concept to grasp because it is intentionally vague. In the case that follows, the Texas Supreme Court provides some guidance in understanding the type of conduct prohibited.

CASE EXCERPT *Chastain v. Koonce,* 700 S.W.2d 579 (Supreme Court of Texas 1985) KILGARLIN, Justice. This deceptive trade practices case requires us to first determine if petitioners are consumers under the Deceptive Trade Practices–Consumer Protection Act. If so, we must examine whether the evidence supports a finding that respondents committed an unconscionable action or course of action....

In 1979, Charles Koonce and J. P. Stroud began to sell five-acre tracts on the northern boundary of their 320 acre farm. At trial, there was ample testimony that Koonce and Stroud told the purchasers that lot 1 at the northeastern corner would be commercial but that lots 2 through 15 would be restricted for residential use only. Claiming they relied on these representations, the Chastains and the other three couples independently purchased lots 4, 5, 6, and 9 by warranty deed....

In January 1981, Koonce and Stroud sold lot 2 to David Metts. About seven months later, after the Chastains and other residential purchasers had constructed houses on their lots, Metts built an oilfield pipe storage yard on his property....

The statute itself defines a consumer to be an "individual...who seeks or acquires by purchase or lease, any goods or services."...In addition...this court also determined that the goods or services sought or acquired by lease or purchase must form the basis of the complaint. Koonce and Stroud contend that the purchasers do not meet this second part of the test because they are complaining about lot number 2, a piece of property which none of the couples sought or acquired...The DTPA is to be construed liberally to promote its underlying purposes "which are to protect consumers against false, misleading, and deceptive business practices, unconscionable actions, and breaches of warranty."...

The purchasers here are complaining of conduct occurring during the transaction which resulted in the purchase of these lots. Koonce and Stroud made representations calculated to induce these purchasers to buy the lots and which enhanced the desirability of the property. Thus, the purchasers are complaining about an aspect of the lots purchased and the transaction involved....

Having decided that the purchasers are covered by the DTPA, we now may consider the second point of error, which complains that there was evidence to support the jury finding of unconscionability. . . .

Under the facts of our case, the purchasers failed to show any disparity between the value received and the consideration paid in the transaction. . . .

The only other way in which the purchasers can recover is to show that Koonce and Stroud took advantage of the purchasers' lack of knowledge, ability or capacity to a GROSSLY unfair degree. We must assume that every word of a statute was used for a purpose and every word in that statute must be given effect if possible . . .

Thus we must find evidence not simply that Koonce and Stroud took unfair advantage of the purchasers but that the advantage was grossly unfair. . . .

The term "gross" should be given its ordinary meaning of glaringly by noticeable, flagrant, complete and unmitigated. . . . The courts have had no problem determining what constitutes a gross disparity under subdivision B of section 17.45(5). A slight disparity between the consideration paid and the value received is not unconscionable; a glaring and flagrant disparity is. Unfairness is perhaps a more nebulous term than disparity, but this is not a reason to create a new definition for "gross."

Taking advantage of a consumer's lack of knowledge to a grossly unfair degree thus requires a showing that the resulting unfairness was glaringly noticeable, flagrant, complete and unmitigated. Based on the record as a whole, we find no evidence that the Chastains and the other three couples were taken advantage of to a grossly unfair degree. . . .

Although we find that the purchasers have standing to sue under the DTPA, we affirm the court of appeals' judgment that there is no evidence of unconscionability. . . .

Producing Cause

The consumer must prove that the misleading, deceptive or fraudulent act was a producing cause of his loss. A ***producing cause*** is a contributing factor that in the ordinary sequence produces injury or damage. In common law and statutory fraud causes of action, the injured party is required to prove that the misrepresentation was of a material fact and that the misrepresentation directly caused his or her economic loss. Under the Deceptive Trade Practices Act the consumer is not required to prove that the deceptive act related to a material fact or that the consumer relied upon that misrepresentation. Furthermore, the consumer is not required to prove that the misleading or deceptive act directly caused his or her injury.

The two cases that follow illustrate the breadth and depth of the Deceptive Trade Practices Act. In the first case a broker was held liable for a misrepresentation concerning the square footage of a house found in the multiple-listing service. Another real estate agent showed this information to prospective purchasers. The broker who was sued and held liable had been hired by the seller, had relied on information the seller had given him, and had had no contact with the prospective buyers. In the second case, the sellers were held liable for oral statements made to the purchasers both before and after the execution of the earnest money contract. The contract itself stated that the used home was being sold "as is" and that the buyer had the right to inspect the house and reject the contract if repairs in excess of $1,000 were necessary.

• CASE BRIEFS •

Jerry and JoAnn Cameron purchased a house. The house had been listed for sale by the sellers with their real estate agent, Terrell and Garrett, Inc. Terrell and Garrett had listed the house in the multiple-listing service and in doing so included a statement that the house contained 2,400 square feet. The Camerons were shown this information about this house by their real estate agent. Subsequently, the Camerons closed the sale and moved in. The Camerons then had the house measured and discovered that it contained 2,245 square feet of heated and air-conditioned space. However, if the garage, porch and wall space was included, there was a total of 2,400 square feet. The Camerons sued Terrell and Garrett, Inc., under the Texas Deceptive Trade Practices Act, alleging misrepresentation. They claimed that Terrell and Garrett, Inc., had falsely represented in the MLS Guide the number of square feet in the house. They sought actual damages of $3,419.30 ($22.06 × 155 sq. ft.).

The jury found for the Camerons, but the trial judge set aside the verdict and entered the judgment in favor of Terrell and Garrett, Inc. On appeal the court reversed the lower court decision and rendered judgment for the Camerons. The court stated that Terrell and Garrett had misrepresented the number of square feet through the MLS Guide and that the Camerons were consumers under the law even though there was no contact with Terrell and Garrett. Terrell and Garrett represented the seller. Cameron was required to prove that they had been adversely affected by the misrepresentation. *Cameron v. Terrell and Garrett, Inc.,* 618 S.W.2d 535 (Tex. 1981).

On February 8, 1983, Barnes/Segraves Development Company, seller, and the Weitzels, buyers, signed a contract to purchase a remodeled home. The written contract gave the Weitzels the right to inspect, among other things, the plumbing and air-conditioning systems in the house. The contract provided that, if the Weitzels were dissatisfied with the systems, they could reject the contract. A contract addendum further provided that failure of the buyer to inspect and give written notice of repairs to the seller constituted a waiver of buyer's inspection rights and amounted to buyer's consent to purchase the property as is. The Weitzels did not inspect the house. Prior to and after the signing of the contract the seller had told the Weitzels that the plumbing and air-conditioning systems complied with the Fort Worth building code specifications. After moving into the house the Weitzels found that the equipment did not function properly and was not in compliance with the city code. The Weitzels claimed that the oral representations were deceptive acts under the Deceptive Trade Practices Act. Barnes/Segraves asserted as their defense the written contract provision regarding inspections, repairs and waiver. The seller also argued that the buyer did not rely upon the representations and in fact had notice prior to consummation of the sale that the city had posted a "condemned" notice sign on the house. The court held for the Weitzels. The court reasoned that the buyers were not seeking to contradict the terms of the written agreement, nor were they claiming a breach of contract. Therefore, the verbal misrepresentations were admissible to prove a violation of the Deceptive Trade Practices Act. Next the court stated that the act does not require proof that the Weitzels relied upon the oral misrepresentation. Reliance is not an element of "producing cause." The court did point out that, had the seller remained silent and not spoken to the quality or characteristics of the plumbing and air-conditioning system, the seller would not have been liable. The contract provision regarding inspection, repairs and waiver would have been controlling. *Weitzel v. Barnes*, 691 S.W.2d 598 (Tex. 1985).

Damages Under the Act

The Deceptive Trade Practices Act provides that the prevailing consumer can recover his or her actual damages, attorney fees and court costs. In addition, the judge or jury can award the consumer a sum of money in excess of his or her actual out-of-pocket losses. This aspect of the law makes it enticing to consumers and elicited an outcry from many businesses. The consumer may receive two times that portion of the actual damages not exceeding $1,000. For example, if a purchaser was actually damaged in the sum of $2,300, he could receive the $2,300 plus an additional $2,000 ($2 \times \$1,000$). Further, if the court finds that the defendant committed the prohibited act knowingly, the plaintiff could receive three times the amount of damages in excess of $1,000. Using the previous example, the calculation would be as follows: three times the first $1,000 of actual damages, or $3,000, and not more than three times the amount of actual damages in excess of $1,000 ($1,300 \times 3$), or $3,900. This brings the total judgment to $6,900.

Defenses to a DTPA Case

The Texas Deceptive Trade Practices Act is a powerful weapon because it simplifies the issues that must be proved by the plaintiff, allows recovery of damages in excess of actual loss and mandates that the winning party recover attorney fees and court costs incurred in bringing the suit. How can a person limit his or her liability for a deceptive or misleading act or practice? The act specifically makes unenforceable any waiver (written or oral) by the consumer to sue under the Deceptive Trade Practices Act. However, the act does establish a procedure for limiting liability and for recovery of damages from a consumer if the suit is filed in bad faith.

The consumer must give 30 days' written notice to the defendant of his or her specific complaint and the amount of actual damages and expenses, including attorney fees. The defendant then has 30 days to respond to the complaint and tender to the consumer a written offer of settlement. If the consumer ignores or rejects this offer and the court later determines that the offer is the same or substantially the same as the actual damages found by the court to have existed, then the defendant's liability can be limited to the amount of the offer if it is less than that awarded by the court. The law also states that the tender of an offer of settlement is *not* an admission of guilt.

A second defense and one particularly important to brokers and salespeople is the giving of timely written notice to the consumer of the broker's reliance on some other written information. This can greatly assist brokers and salespeople because they frequently rely upon information provided by others, such as the seller, an appraiser, an engineer or perhaps even a governmental agent. The key to the success of this defense is that (1) the broker or agent must have received the information in writing; (2) the broker must give written notice to the consumer prior to consummation of the sale that the broker is relying upon this written information and (3) the broker must establish that he or she did not know and could not have known that the information was false or inaccurate. It is important for a broker or an agent to remember that reliance upon the written information must be reasonable considering his or her expertise in the area. However, a broker or an agent who can prove that he or she has met this defense will not be liable for the consumer's damages.

SUMMARY

Fraud is a deceptive act practiced deliberately by one person in an attempt to gain an unfair advantage over another. Misrepresentation is a false statement made negligently or innocently that was a material factor in the victim's decision to contract. In Texas there are three methods for holding a person liable for fraud or misrepresentation in a real estate transaction: common law fraud, statutory real estate fraud and the Deceptive Trade Practices Act.

To establish common law fraud, the plaintiff must prove an intentional misrepresentation of a material fact. In addition, he or she must establish that the misrepresentation was justifiably relied upon and that it resulted in damages. Fraud may also exist if a person conceals a material fact, such as a hidden defect, or deliberately makes a statement that is only partially true.

Statutory fraud under §27.01 of the Texas Business and Commerce Code is similar to common law fraud. However, in addition to protecting parties from false representations of material facts, it also defines fraud as a false promise to do an act when the promisor has no intention of performing at the time the promise was made. Statutory fraud clearly covers innocent misrepresentations as well as negligent and intentional misrepresentations.

The remedies for common law fraud and statutory fraud are the same. The victim can rescind the contract, sue for damages or refuse to perform his or her obligations under the contract. In Texas the calculation of dam-

Figure 16.1: **COMPARISON OF ACTIONS FOR FRAUD AND MISREPRESENTATION**

Cause of Action	Factors to Be Proven	Remedies
Common Law Fraud	1. Was a false statement made? 2. Was it made intentionally or negligently? 3. Was the misstatement a material fact? 4. Was the misstatement relied upon? 5. Was anyone injured?	1. rescission; 2. actual damages and rescission; 3. actual damages; 4. exemplary damages
Statutory Fraud	1. same factors as for common law fraud 2. Was a false promise made with intent not to perform? 3. Did the person who benefited from the misrepresentation know that it had been made and fail to disclose truth?	1. same remedies as for common law fraud; 2. attorney fees, court costs and expert witness fees
Deceptive Trade Practices–Consumer Protection Act	1. Were any acts specifically listed committed? 2. Were any deceptive acts committed? 3. Were any misleading statements made? 4. Were any false statements made, including innocent misstatements? 5. Was an unconscionable act or course of action practiced against the victim? 6. Were any of the acts listed above the producing cause of harm to the victim?	1. actual damages; 2. $2 \times$ actual damages not exceeding $1,000; 3. $3 \times$ actual damages exceeding $1,000; 4. attorney fees and court costs

ages can be made using either the benefit-of-the-bargain rule or the out-of-pocket rule. Under the benefit-of-the-bargain rule, damages are measured by the difference between what the injured party actually received and what he or she would have received if the deceitful statement had been true. Under the out-of-pocket rule, damages are measured by the amount the injured party actually gave up in relation to value received.

The right to prosecute for fraud may be lost, or waived, by the victim under certain circumstances. For example, an injured party waives his or her right if, upon discovery of the fraud, he or she enters into a new contract concerning the subject matter of the contract. Attempts to avoid liability for misrepresentations by inserting a waiver provision in the contract are generally unenforceable.

Finally, the third remedy available to victims of fraud or misrepresentation is the Deceptive Trade Practices Act. This act is a powerful weapon for consumers who have been deceived in a real estate purchase or lease. The act prohibits not only false statements but also misleading statements or acts. A consumer who can prove that a misleading act was the producing cause of the injury can recover his or her actual damages, attorney fees, court costs and additional compensation up to twice the amount of the actual losses. One defense that can be particularly useful to brokers is giving written notice to a buyer or seller that they are relying upon written information supplied by someone else. If this notice is given in a timely and proper manner, the broker is relieved from liability for false or misleading statements contained in such written reports.

QUESTIONS AND CASE PROBLEMS

1. (a) How does the benefit-of-the-bargain rule for measuring damages differ from the out-of-pocket rule? (b) Which is more beneficial to the injured party?
2. Under what circumstances might a court award punitive damages in a case involving fraud?
3. In May 1963, Mr. Reed, a salesman for S. J. Guthrie Company, sold Mr. and Mrs. Mitchell a house constructed by Frank Short. Mr. Reed made the following statements to the Mitchells during the course of the negotiations:
   • The house was of sound nature and good workmanship.
   • Short was "a good builder."
   • The Mitchells were buying a good sound house that they could live in for 15 or 20 years and still have no bad maintenance problems other than just normal.

   In June 1967, the house and foundation began to crack and buckle, the walls began to separate from the floors and large cracks developed on the walls and ceilings of the house. The Mitchells sued Frank Short for fraud. Short defends on the grounds that Reed was not authorized to make the statements and that the statements were nothing more than opinion or puffing. Decide.

4. Holleman sued National Resort Communities for fraud and rescission of a contract. Holleman had purchased a lot in a resort development from National. At the time of the purchase, Holleman was told by a salesman for National that the road to the purchased lot would be paved immediately. One week after the purchase, a heavy rain washed out the existing road. Holleman requested that National pave the road as promised by the salesman. National refused, stating that it was not developing that area. Has National violated the Texas statute on fraud in real estate transactions? Explain.

5. Chapa entered into a contract with Jim Walter Homes, Inc., for the construction of a house on a lot owned by Chapa. The cost of the home was $12,385. At the time of the purchase several oral and written representations were made, including that the construction would be performed in a "good, substantial and workmanlike manner." Shortly after Chapa moved into the house, he noticed sagging Sheetrock, leaky plumbing, and numerous other problems, including electrical. Chapa sued Jim Walter Homes, Inc., for violation of the Texas Deceptive Trade Practices Act, alleging false, misleading and deceptive acts, specifically violation by misrepresenting the quality of the house. Decide.

6. Kaye was interested in buying a large piece of land from Katzenberry, who lived nearby. Katzenberry did not want to sell the land to a buyer who would use it for commercial purposes; he asked Kaye what he planned to do with the property. Kaye told Katzenberry that he was going to build a house on part of it and probably would use the rest for a garden. This was true, but before the closing Kaye changed his mind and made plans to build a hamburger stand next to his house. Katzenberry learned of this and refused to convey the property. Kaye sued for breach of contract, defense— fraud. Would Kaye be successful? Discuss.

17

Fair Housing Laws

Fair housing laws have been passed at all levels of government: federal, state and local. The most important of these laws were those passed by the United States Congress. These are discussed in detail in this chapter. Legislation passed by the Texas Legislature is also discussed, but its application is not as comprehensive as the federal laws. In addition, some cities have enacted local ordinances that prohibit certain types of discrimination in housing. Although these are not discussed in this chapter, these local ordinances are generally similar to the federal statutes. However, in some instances local laws have been passed to deal with a special local need or problem.

INTRODUCTION TO FAIR HOUSING

The term *fair housing* is used to express a national policy against many types of discrimination in housing. The second half of the 20th century has seen increasing involvement of government in housing in the United States. Types of housing regulations discussed elsewhere in the text include zoning and subdivision regulations, rent controls and mortgage regulations. During the same period government has exhibited an interest in assuring, through legislation, that no member of our society is refused an opportunity to obtain decent housing.

The voluntary or enforced separation of one group from another in residential location based on religious association, ethnic background, race or a combination of these factors is referred to as *segregation in housing.* Until quite recently, segregation was the American way of life. People were routinely segregated from one another on the basis of race, ethnic background and religious preference. Ethnic identity has traditionally been a source of pride among most people. This pride led to the Irish immigrants living in the Irish section of a city, the Germans in the German section and the Poles in the Polish section. Second- and third-generation descendants of these immigrants, however, began to drift away from their ethnic neighborhoods and become assimilated into the general population. The security provided by the support structure of the extended family in the ethnic community was no longer a necessity for the children and grandchildren of these immigrants. "Americanization" of language and customs along with ethnic intermarriages lessened their emotional and psychological bonds to their ethnic beginnings. Also, in most cities a parallel slow progression toward ethnic integration began in housing. Although this ethnic integration continues, it has by no means been uniformly successful for all ethnic groups.

Further, this assimilation and integration process did not occur in the area of racial segregation. Racial integration may have failed to parallel ethnic integration because of the highly visible differences among the races. Probably it also involves a host of.social and cultural attitudes. Lack of integration among the races was seen in the housing market as well.

Racial segregation was institutionalized by the real estate industry. Developers, banks and real estate agents adopted practices that facilitated the continued separation of the races. For instance, it would not have been considered a good business practice for a real estate agent to negotiate the sale of a house to a black in a white neighborhood. Embittered whites would be likely to employ an embargo against the real estate agent because it was contended, sometimes accurately, that property values would become relatively depressed in such an integrated area. Lost business and depressed property values were negative inducements to real estate agents who relied on a percentage of the selling price for their commission.

"Separate but Equal" Facilities

In the late-19th-century case of *Plessy v. Ferguson*, 163 U.S. 537 (1896), the U.S. Supreme Court affirmed the doctrine that "separate but equal" was the law of the land. The *separate but equal* doctrine was a legal principle that permitted the states to enforce separation of the races so long as each race was provided with "equal" services or facilities. This concept was used to separate the races in many sectors of American life, including public transportation, education and accommodations. In housing, some state and local governments passed laws confining blacks and whites to separate sections of cities for residential living. This practice was considered constitutional as long as both black and white sections were provided. Economic and social pressures also were factors separating races in residential areas.

The separate-but-equal interpretation of the Constitution prevailed until the mid–20th century. Prior to that some erosion of the doctrine began to appear, especially in cases involving housing. In *Buchanan v. Warley*, 245 U.S. 38 (1917), the Supreme Court struck down a city ordinance that prohibited blacks from moving to predominantly white streets and whites from migrating to predominantly black streets. The basis for the decision had nothing to do with the doctrine of separate but equal facilities. The legislation was held to be an undue restraint on a person's constitutionally protected right to *sell* property, since it excluded an entire race from the available market.

The separate-but-equal doctrine played a more prominent role in a case decided 30 years later in 1947.

• CASE BRIEF •

Shelley, a black man, pursuant to a contract, received a warranty deed to a parcel of land in the city of St. Louis. Unknown to Shelley, a former owner of the property had entered into an agreement with other property owners in the area restricting the sale of the property to members of the Caucasian race.

Kraemer and other property owners brought suit in the Missouri courts to prevent Shelley from occupying the premises. The lower courts in Missouri refused to enforce the agreement, but the Supreme Court of Missouri held the restrictive covenant enforceable. Shelley appealed to the United States Supreme Court.

The Supreme Court reversed the Missouri court, holding that "in granting judicial enforcement of the restrictive agreements . . . the States have denied petitioners the equal protection of the laws and that, therefore, the action of the state courts cannot stand." *Shelly v. Kraemer,* 334 U.S. 1 (1947).

In *Shelley v. Kraemer,* the court did not rule that the racially based restrictive covenants were unconstitutional, but only that the states, including their courts, must refrain from enforcing racial discrimination. Obviously, the effectiveness of a restrictive covenant is markedly reduced where enforcement in the courts is not available. Unless the party restricted by the covenant voluntarily complies with the limitation based on race, it is legally unenforceable.

The *Shelley* decision was quickly followed by several other cases that made it clear that courts could no longer be used as vehicles for enforcing racially discriminatory practices in housing. For example, in 1950 the Chicago Real Estate Board amended a relevant section of its Code of Ethics. The board rewrote a section that advised real estate agents never to introduce members of a race or nationality into a neighborhood where the act would be detrimental to local property values. All reference to race or nationality was deleted from the Code of Ethics.

Equal Protection

The separate-but-equal doctrine provided equality in theory, but it has been well documented that it had little relation to equality in fact. Black and white schools were equal neither in physical plant nor in the quality of education children obtained in them. In housing as well, the quality of housing for blacks and whites and the locations of that housing were not equal.

In 1954, beginning with the school desegregation cases, the separate-but-equal doctrine was laid aside, and equal protection became the constitutional mandate. The **equal protection** doctrine is a constitutional mandate that all people be treated equally under the law. In the school desegregation cases the plaintiffs were black children who, pursuant to statutes in Kansas, South Carolina, Virginia and Delaware, attended schools segregated on the basis of race. In each of these states with the exception of Delaware, federal district courts had denied relief to the plaintiffs, citing the separate-but-equal doctrine of *Plessy v. Ferguson.* In the Delaware case, the state supreme court adhered to the doctrine but ordered plaintiffs admitted to the white schools because of their superiority to the black schools. Plaintiffs appealed to the U.S. Supreme Court, which rejected the language of *Plessy v. Ferguson.* In an important decision the court stated:

> We conclude that in the field of public education the doctrine of "separate but equal" has no place. Separate educational facilities are inherently unequal. Therefore, we hold that the plaintiffs and others similarly situated for whom the actions have been brought are, by reason of the segregation complained of, deprived of the equal protection of the laws guaranteed by the Fourteenth Amendment. *Brown v. Board of Education*, 347 U.S. 483 (1954).

After the decision in *Brown v. Board of Education*, the country began the slow process of racially integrating society. In the late 1950s and early 1960s several states and cities enacted fair housing laws with varying degrees of coverage. These statutes were a prelude to the entry of the federal government into the fair housing arena. Since the federal government is now the focus for regulation of discrimination in housing, the remainder of this section will concentrate on several federal legislative enactments.

FEDERAL FAIR HOUSING LEGISLATION

Ten years after *Brown v. Board of Education*, Congress enacted the Civil Rights Act of 1964. This act included some prohibitions regarding discrimination in housing; however, it was not until this law was amended four years later that significant progress was made toward ensuring equal opportunity in housing. During this time, a law passed in 1866 was resurrected. This law, which had been dormant for almost a century, became another weapon for ensuring that discrimination in housing was eliminated.

Civil Rights Act of 1866

In 1866, following the end of the Civil War, Congress enacted one of the first laws protecting the civil rights of all citizens. The concern at that time was to ensure that black citizens enjoyed the same legal rights as white citizens. The act provided that "[A]ll citizens of the United States shall have the same right, in every state and territory as is enjoyed by white citizens thereof to inherit, purchase, lease, sell, hold, and convey real and personal property." The obvious intent of the statute is to prohibit discrimination based on race or color in real estate transactions.

Despite the significant implications that this law may have had on housing discrimination during that 100-year period, it seemed to have been forgotten. However, in 1965 this old law was discovered and used to combat discrimination in housing. In that year Mr. and Mrs. Jones filed suit against the Alfred H. Mayer Company, complaining that Mayer had refused to sell them a home in the Paddock Woods community of St. Louis County in Missouri because they were black. They alleged that this refusal to sell was a violation of their civil rights as protected under the 1866 law. At issue in *Jones v. Mayer* was the interpretation and application of the 100-year-old law. In 1968 the case reached the Supreme Court of the United States, which ruled in favor of the Joneses. The Supreme Court stated that the 1866 law prohibited *all* discrimination against blacks in the sale or rental of housing. Furthermore, the court pointed out that the language of the act included both discrimination by a governmental body and discrimination by a private landowner. Mayer Company's discriminatory act was prohibited by law, and Jones could recover damages from Mayer. This case and the 1866 act remain an important part of the fair housing laws in the United States. The case that follows illustrates the breadth of coverage under this law.

• CASE BRIEF •

Cheryl Walker and her brother, James E. Walker, filed suit alleging that G.M. Pointer had violated their civil rights as protected by the Civil Rights Act of 1866. The Walkers are white but associated with blacks. Pointer evicted the Walkers from their apartment on December 16, 1968, claiming that they had failed to pay their rent on time and disturbed other tenants in the complex by playing loud music. The Walkers claim that they were evicted because of their association with blacks. The evidence at trial proved that the Walkers had in fact paid their rent in a manner and within a time period not unlike other tenants in the complex. There was also testimony that the policy of the apartment management was one of discrimination against blacks. Assistant managers were warned against renting to blacks and were told to report to the manager if any black guests were seen in the apartment complex. Pointer argued that the Walkers had no claim because they were white and that the Civil Rights Act of 1866 was enacted to protect blacks. The court rejected this argument, stating, "In this case, according to plaintiff's allegations, they are direct victims of black racial discrimination, discrimination directed at them because of their black associations. Since this discrimination has disturbed their leasehold, they should be entitled to relief under §1982 as if their skin was black." *Walker v. Pointer,* 304 F. Supp. (56 N.D. Tex. 1969).

Civil Rights Act (1964)

For almost 100 years Congress ignored the reality of housing discrimination in the United States. But during the political turmoil of the 1960s, Congress took another step toward assuring fair housing opportunities for all citizens when it enacted the Civil Rights Act of 1964. Among other civil rights guarantees, this law prohibited discrimination based on race, color or national origin in most housing programs and activities in which the federal government rendered financial assistance. The agency granting the financial aid could reject an application for money or terminate assistance already granted, as a sanction for housing discrimination.

The 1964 law did not cover conventional mortgages because they did not involve federal aid. Most FHA and VA loans that required federal insurance or guarantees were excluded from coverage as well. One authority estimates that the statute applied to only about half of one percent of the houses purchased. Consequently, the impact of the 1964 Civil Rights Act upon racial discrimination in housing was far from dramatic.

The Fair Housing Act (1968)

Although a major effort was mounted in Congress in 1966 to get approval of more comprehensive fair housing legislation, the majority of the Congress was unwilling to go along. In 1968, however, Congress made its first comprehensive venture into fair housing by passing Title VIII of the Civil Rights Act of 1968, which is also called the Fair Housing Act. (42 U.S.C.A. §3601 et seq.)

The 1968 act prohibited discrimination based on race, color, religion, sex (in a later amendment) or national origin by someone either selling or leasing residential property. Residential property included any building occupied or designed for occupation, as well as any vacant land sold for the construction of a dwelling.

The act was amended in 1972 by a requirement that equal opportunity posters be displayed at brokerage houses, model home sites, mortgage lender offices and other similar locations. The poster must contain the slogan "Equal Housing Opportunity" and must carry a brief equal housing opportunity statement. Failure to display such a poster will be treated as prima facie evidence of discrimination; that is, in the absence of evidence to the contrary it will be presumed that the broker discriminates in violation of the law.

Although the Fair Housing Act of 1968 significantly increased the number of transactions and activities covered, there remain several exceptions worth noting. First, the act does not apply to the sale or rental of commercial or industrial properties. Second, certain persons are exempted even when the sale or rental involves residential property. Persons exempted are those who meet all of the following criteria:

    1. The person does not own more than three houses at any one time.

2. The person is living in the house or was the last person to live there. If this residency requirement is not met, then the exception applies to only one sale every 24 months.

3. In addition, the exempt person may not use a broker, agent or salesperson to facilitate the sale.

4. The person also must refrain from any form of discriminatory advertising.

CASE EXAMPLES

Williams owns a house in town, one at the beach and another in the mountains. She lives in each during various parts of the year. She can discriminate in the sale of the beach house (or either of the others) so long as she sells it herself (without a broker) and does not advertise that there is a discriminatory preference or limitation.

Johnson also owns the same assortment of houses. He lives in the town house only and rents the other two. In addition to the restrictions mentioned above, Johnson is permitted to sell no more than one of the rental houses every two years if he wants to discriminate against buyers.

A third exception occurs when the owner of a multiple-family dwelling with no more than four units resides in one of the units and rents out the other units. Finally, occupancy of dwellings owned by religious organizations may be confined to the members of that organization, provided that membership in that organization is not based upon the categories protected by the Fair Housing Act.

Despite these exceptions, coverage of the act is comprehensive. Since most single-family homes are sold through the use of a broker, and most multiple-family dwellings have more than four units, the bulk of sales and rentals would be covered by the statute.

The 1866 Civil Rights Act and the Fair Housing Act of 1968 Compared

The 1866 act prohibits only discrimination based upon race or color (in the sale or rental of property). By comparison, the Fair Housing Act prohibits discrimination based on race or color but also includes discrimination based on religion, sex or national origin. The Fair Housing Act prohibits more types of discrimination.

However, where the 1866 act does apply there are no exceptions to coverage. Consequently, a person exempt under the 1968 Fair Housing Act is still bound to comply with the 1866 Civil Rights Act. Referring back to the case examples in the previous section in which Williams and Johnson were allowed to discriminate under the Fair Housing Act, their conduct would be prohibited under the 1866 Act if the discrimination was based on race or color.

Finally, the 1866 act is limited to discrimination in the sale or rental of property. By contrast, the Fair Housing Act in addition prohibits discriminatory advertising and discrimination in the exaction of terms and brokerage activities.

Conduct Specifically Prohibited by Law

The Fair Housing Act of 1968 prohibits certain actions when based on discrimination as defined in the law. For example, *refusal* to sell or lease, or to otherwise refuse to negotiate or to make a dwelling available, is illegal. Moreover, *variation* in the terms of the sale or lease, as in provision of services or facilities in the sale or rental of a dwelling, is also prohibited.

• CASE BRIEF •

Filippo, a broker, refused to accept from a black person a purchase offer of $22,500, the price quoted to the buyer by Filippo's sales associate. Filippo instead told the black offeree that the selling price was $26,950. Later Filippo accepted a purchase order from a white buyer at $22,500 for the same property. As a result, Filippo's license was suspended for 45 days. Filippo appealed the suspension, but his appeal was rejected. *Filippo v. Real Estate Commission of District of Columbia*, 223 A.2d 268 (D.C. 1966).

Any *statement or advertisement* in the sale or lease of a dwelling, if it indicates a discriminatory preference or limitation based upon classifications defined in the law, is illegal.

CASE EXAMPLE

Cartwright and Lindsay visited a real estate firm where they indicated to a salesperson an interest in purchasing property in a certain section of Detroit. The salesperson stated that the section was fine "if you like a busted community." When asked what was meant by "busted community," the salesperson indicated that it was one that blacks had moved into. The salesperson also stated that housing values in that community are down and will continue to go down and that, while the schools are OK, "You know what will happen eventually." The salesperson then suggested another community.

Representation that a dwelling is not available for inspection, sale or rental, when in fact it is available, is also illegal. Other illegal acts include *denying membership* or *limiting participation* in real estate brokerage firms or their multiple-listing pools, *blockbusting* and *redlining*.

Blockbusting

Blockbusting is the practice of inducing the sale or rental of any dwelling by indicating that a particular class of persons has entered or will enter the neighborhood. The purpose of the tactic is to scare homeowners into selling or renting at an amount lower than they would have otherwise.

• CASE BRIEF •

Bowers and a number of other real estate firms in Northwest Detroit conducted solicitation campaigns in Northwest Detroit involving fliers, telephone calls and door-to-door canvassing. As part of their campaign, fliers were allegedly delivered to "Resident." One flier contained the legend "We think you may want a friend for a neighbor . . . know your neighbors." Another mailing also addressed to "Resident" purported to carry "neighborhood news." It announced that a real estate agency had just bought a house at a specific address in the recipient's neighborhood, that the named sellers had received cash and that the recipient might receive the same service. The recipients lived in changing neighborhoods. This conduct was judged to be illegal. See *Zuch v. Hussey*, 394 F. Supp. 1028 (E.D. Mich. 1975).

Redlining

Redlining is the practice by a lender of requiring more stringent loan requirements in certain parts of a city or denying a loan because of its location in the city. The term is derived from the actual business practice of dividing the city into sectors marked off with red lines on a map to indicate undesirable locations. Although redlining is often a strictly economic decision by a lending institution, it has been found to be illegal in some cases because it results in discrimination.

• CASE BRIEF •

The Laufmans, a white couple, purchased a home in a predominately black neighborhood. When financing was denied by the Oakley Building and Loan Company, the Laufmans sued. They argued that the defendant had redlined areas in the community in which minority group families were concentrated.

The defendant moved for summary judgment. The court denied the motion. In denying the motion, the court stated that "although not altogether unambiguous, we read this [§§3604 and 3605 of the Civil Rights Act of 1968] as an explicit prohibition of 'redlining' " *Laufman v. Oakley Building and Loan Co.*, 408 F. Supp. 489 (D. Ohio 1976.)

Permitted Discrimination

All discrimination in housing is not illegal. As mentioned within the discussion of the Fair Housing Act (1968), private individuals can continue to discriminate based upon religion, sex or national origin so long as they can comply with the terms of the statutory exemption.

All discrimination is not based upon prohibited categories. It is not uncommon to find discrimination based on age, financial reputation, marital status, number of children, position in life or the like.

CASE EXAMPLES

Polcyk has a policy of refusing to rent his apartments located in the area of a university to undergraduate students because some are notorious for loud parties and damaging the interiors of apartments. Nothing is illegal about Polcyk's discrimination.

Barton leases her garden-style apartments only to persons 55 years of age or older without children. This clearly discriminates against those under 55, against persons with children and against the children themselves. There is, however, nothing illegal about Barton's leasing practice.

There may be some sound social reasons for discriminating. Many elderly people find the continuous presence of small children in their living environment an annoyance or even an unreasonable interference with their enjoyment of their land or leased premises. This is not to say that all elderly react the same way. Although many would thrive on the presence of children, those who are annoyed should have housing available to them that provides the quiet they seek.

The Federal Fair Housing Act of 1968 states that an aggrieved party has two types of remedies: administrative and judicial. These remedies are not mutually exclusive, and the party need not exhaust the administrative remedies before turning to judicial remedies. Nor need the party choose one remedy over the other prior to satisfaction.

Statutory Remedies

Under the Civil Rights Act of 1866 a person may file a suit under §1982 of the Federal Procedural Code in a federal district court seeking redress for harm done by discrimination based on race or color in the transfer of property. No specific remedies are provided by the law, but it was indicated in *Jones v. Mayer* that courts should frame effective equitable remedies. In practice, what the courts seem to be doing is permitting the same remedies in §1982 suits as are authorized in the Fair Housing Act of 1968.

The discussion of statutory remedies will focus on the administrative and judicial remedies provided under the Fair Housing Act of 1968.

Administrative Remedies

Administrative remedies are remedies that can be granted by a federal or state agency, such as the Department of Housing and Urban Development (HUD). If a person believes that he or she has been the victim of a discriminatory practice, then the complaining party must file a complaint within 180 days of the occurrence of the discriminatory action with the Department of Housing and Urban Development. HUD then has 30 days to investigate the complaint.

If the complaint is filed in a state that has a law "substantially equivalent" in provision to the 1968 federal Fair Housing Act, HUD must notify the appropriate state authorities and turn the case over to them. Should the state undertake to act on the complaint within 30 days of its notification, HUD loses jurisdiction of the matter unless, as the statute expresses it, "justice demands" its continued interest. The "justice demands" language permits HUD to retain jurisdiction if, for instance, the state has consistently failed satisfactorily to resolve a given type of complaint. In short, it permits HUD to oversee the appropriate handling of the matter. Texas does not have a state law comparable to the 1968 federal Fair Housing Act. Consequently, HUD has jurisdiction to investigate complaints.

When HUD retains jurisdiction over the matter, it must investigate the complaint within 30 days. If HUD finds that discrimination has occurred, it can use the tools of conference, conciliation and persuasion in order to obtain satisfaction for the complainant. When HUD is pursuing the matter, it is seeking to obtain the following relief for the complaining party (1) access to the same or similar housing (2) compensation for out-of-pocket expenses and (3) money for the hurt or embarrassment that may have occurred. In addition, when it is appropriate, HUD will attempt to get institutional change as well by getting the real estate firm to agree actively to seek minority clients for its products. It should be noted that there is nothing that compels the party accused of discrimination to confer, conciliate or be persuaded. If HUD's efforts fail, the complainant has 30 days to file suit in federal district court or the appropriate state court where the state has a substantially equivalent statute.

Judicial Remedies

Judicial Remedies are those remedies that can be granted by a court. Since a large number of the people who are the victims of discrimination are poor, most people are likely to pursue their administrative remedies within HUD. HUD does the investigating and negotiating, so there is no need for the complainant to hire a lawyer, and thus the procedure is cheaper. Also, the HUD approach involves a less formal procedure. It should be noted, however, that the Fair Housing Act does provide for the appointment of an attorney where the court deems it to be "just," enabling the victim to commence litigation without paying any fees, costs or security.

Within 30 days of HUD's failure to attain satisfaction for the complainant, or within 90 days after the discriminatory action occurred, the complainant can file a lawsuit in federal district court. The complaining party may choose to pursue both remedies simultaneously. One benefit of this dual course of action is that the court may enjoin the landlord or seller from renting or selling the premises while HUD is attempting to negotiate a settlement. Needless to say, this action by the court will place pressure upon the landlord or seller to settle on HUD's terms.

The complainant, whether before HUD or in court, will have to prove that he or she met the objective (nondiscriminatory) requirements set out by the landlord or seller in the transaction, that the rental or sale would probably have taken place had the complainant been of a different race or religion and so on, and that the offer was made in good faith and refused.

Several methods can be used to establish the complainant's prima facie case.

The complainant may also use a statistical approach to satisfy the burden of proof. If he or she can show that no members or an unexplainably small number of minority people live in the landlord's housing, a prima facie case of discrimination usually exists.

The complainant who successfully proves his or her case in court has available a full array of legal and equitable remedies. The court may grant compensatory damages and punitive damages. It may grant injunctions or issue other appropriate judicial orders.

One of the lingering issues under the Fair Housing Act of 1968 is whether the complainant must prove that the defendant's conduct had discriminatory intent or merely that it had a discriminatory effect. About half the federal appeals courts have approved the more lenient discriminatory effect test, but the more stringent discriminatory intent test is favored by the Reagan administration.

TEXAS FAIR HOUSING LAWS

Article I, §3a of the Texas Constitution states that "Equality under the law shall not be denied or abridged because of sex, race, color, creed or national origin." This is referred to as the Texas Equal Rights Amendment and it was passed in 1972. Although it prohibits discrimination on the basis of race, color, creed and national origin, it has been most frequently used in support of complaints of sex discrimination. One reason this state constitutional guarantee has not been used to support other types of discrimination complaints is the existence of the equal protection clause of the United States Constitution and the federal fair housing laws previously discussed. Another limitation on the usefulness of the Texas amendment is that it provides for equality only under the law. The phrase *under the law* has been interpreted as meaning some type of state action or private conduct that is encouraged by or closely related to state action. The Fair Housing Laws passed by the U.S. Congress cover a greater range of activities than is encompassed by the Texas Equal Rights Amendment.

Restrictive covenants are common in many residential developments. In cities that do not have zoning ordinances, the presence of restrictive covenants is the main limitation on land use. As previously discussed, restrictive covenants exist that prohibit the mixing of races in a subdivision. Texas enacted a law in 1969 that voids any restrictive covenant that prohibits the use by or the sale, lease or transfer to a person because of race, color, religion or national origin. (Tex. Prop. Code §5.026) In addition to making such restrictions null and void, the statute requires that a court dismiss any action seeking to enforce such a covenant.

A third Texas law that prohibits discriminatory practices is the Texas Real Estate License Act. As discussed in Chapter 14, this law establishes the licensing requirements for real estate brokers and salespersons, prohibits certain conduct and activities of its licensees and establishes a Texas Real Estate Commission to enforce and monitor those requirements. The licensing law specifically prohibits discriminatory practices by its licensees. The law provides that the Texas Real Estate Commission can suspend or revoke a license if the licensee is found to have discriminated against an owner, potential purchaser, lessor or potential lessee on the basis of race, color, religion, sex, national origin or ancestry. (Tex. Rev. Civ. Stat. art. 6573a, §15[AA])

The type of discrimination specifically mentioned as being prohibited includes steering prospective homebuyers or lessees interested in equivalent properties to different areas according to their race, color, religion, sex, national origin or ancestry. These practices are also prohibited by federal law. Although steering is specifically mentioned, the licensing act prohibits any type of discriminatory practices engaged in by a licensee. In addition to license suspension or revocation, a licensee can be sued by the injured party under one of the federal laws.

CASE EXCERPT   *United States v. Mitchell* 580 F.2d. 789 United States Court of Appeals—5th Cir. 1978 GODBOLD, Circuit Judge. In this case under the Fair Housing Act, 42 U.S.C. §3601 et seq., the Attorney General sued John T. Mitchell, his real estate company, and his agents, seeking damages and an injunction to end racially discriminatory housing practices. The district court granted the injunction after finding that the defendants had "steered" blacks into a separate section of a large apartment complex. . . .

The complex, located on eight acres, is comprised of 18 buildings with 12 apartments in each building. Between 1973 and 1975, ninety-five percent of all blacks renting in the complex were rented apartments in the same section comprised of four buildings at a remote end of the complex. Fifty-three percent of all black tenants were located in the same building within this section. Black tenants testified that they were shown apartments only in this section. Vacant apartments in the "white" section were not shown, offered, or made available to blacks. . . .

Under 42 U.S.C. §3604(a) an agent or owner may not refuse to sell or rent after a bona fide offer, refuse to negotiate for the sale or rent of a dwelling, or "otherwise make unavailable or deny, a dwelling to any person because of race, color, religion, sex, or national origin." Steering blacks to a particular group of apartments in a complex effectively denies access to equal housing opportunities. The Fair Housing Act prohibits not only direct discrimination but practices with racially discouraging effects; steering evidences an intent to influence the choice of the renter on an impermissible racial basis. . . .

The fact that a large majority of Mitchell's black tenants were clustered in a defined area is highly probative of a §3604(a) violation. Statistics, although not dispositive, "have critical, if not decisive significance." Therefore, a significant discriminatory effect flowing from rental decisions is sufficient to demonstrate a violation of the Fair Housing Act.. . . .

Affirmed.

LENDING PRACTICES AND FAIR HOUSING

In addition to the federal laws previously discussed, there are two other statutes concerning lending practices that affect the opportunity to buy housing. These two statutes are the Community Reinvestment Act and the Equal Credit Opportunity Act. The purpose of these statutes is to make financing available without regard to race, religion, sex or national origin. The laws also encourage financial institutions to make funds available to all areas of the community they serve.

Community Reinvestment Act

The Community Reinvestment Act was passed in 1977. (12 U.S.C.A. §2901 et seq.) It gives the Comptroller of the Currency, the Federal Reserve System, the Federal Deposit Insurance Corporation and the Federal Home Loan Bank Board the specific authority to create regulations to require financial institutions to meet the needs of all segments of the local community they serve by providing credit services as well as deposit services. Each of the federal agencies has enacted regulations that require that financial institutions (1) establish boundaries for the community they are attempting to serve; (2) list the types of credit (such as residential loans, housing rehabilitation loans, home improvement loans, farm loans, small business loans) they are prepared to offer to the local community and (3) report how its current business practices are meeting the special credit-related needs of the community. A financial institution's performance in the area of community reinvestment can affect its ability to obtain permission to expand, relocate, merge or consolidate.

Equal Credit Opportunity Act

The Equal Credit Opportunity Act (ECOA) makes it unlawful for any creditor to discriminate against an applicant regarding any aspect of a credit transaction on the basis of race, color, religion, national origin, sex, marital status, age or receipt of public assistance. The act also limits the type of information that can be asked on credit applications and requires the creditor to notify the applicant within 30 days of action that has been taken. If credit is refused, the creditor must furnish the reason if requested to do so by the applicant.

The purpose of ECOA is to ensure that a person who applies for credit will be considered on the basis of ability to pay. Although the act applies primarily to consumer credit, business credit when not excluded by action of the Federal Reserve Board is also covered.

Under ECOA, creditors may ask questions about a person's spouse, marital status or age, but use of this information is permitted only for the purpose of determining creditworthiness. For example, a borrower applying for a joint account might be asked about his or her marital status if the spouse is to be permitted to use the account or the borrower is relying upon alimony, child support or separate maintenance payments to repay the credit.

Figure 17.1: **SUMMARY OF FAIR HOUSING LAWS**

Title of Law	Classes Protected	Transactions Covered	Exceptions	Remedies
1866 Civil Rights Act	race and color	sale, rental, and inheritance	none	judicial: damages and injunctions
Fair Housing Act of 1968	race, color, religion, sex and national origin	sale, rental, advertising, terms and brokerage	commercial and industrial property; persons owning fewer than three houses; persons residing in one of four units; and certain religious groups	file complaint with HUD and/or file a lawsuit: damages and injunctions
Texas Real Estate License Act	race, color, religion, sex, national origin and ancestry	sale or rental	applies *only* to real estate licensees	suspension or revocation of license
Community Reinvestment Act	all segments of local community	extension of credit	applies *only* to financial institutions	can affect expansion or relocation
Equal Credit Opportunity Act	race, color, religion, national origin, sex, marital status, age and receipt of public assistance	extension of credit	applies *only* to businesses that extend credit	damages

Information about age may be used to evaluate a borrower's length of employment or length of residence.

Creditors may not ask questions about a person's sex, race, color, religion or national origin, except in the case of a home mortgage; creditors are allowed to collect this information to show that they are complying with the law. The borrower does not have to supply answers, and failure to do so will not affect the credit application. Although a borrower can be asked to select a title such as Ms., Miss, Mr., or Mrs., the application must first indicate that this is optional.

An individual who is denied credit and can establish that the creditor has violated the Equal Credit Opportunity Act may recover his or her actual damages and punitive damages up to $10,000. The plaintiff who brings a successful action under ECOA is also entitled to reimbursement for court costs and reasonable attorney fees.

SUMMARY

Fair Housing is the term given to the national policy of abolishing discrimination in housing on the basis of race or ethnic origin. Segregation of one group from another has long been a characteristic of residential patterns. The civil rights movement, begun in the latter half of this century, however, has as its goal equal opportunity for members of all races to achieve adequate housing as well as employment.

Earlier in this century restrictive covenants in housing were upheld by the courts in most cases. More recently, however, those clauses forbidding sale of property to blacks have been held unenforceable.

The doctrine of equal protection under the law provided by the Constitution started with the landmark school desegregation case of *Brown v. Board of Education* in 1954.

Ten years later Congress enacted the Civil Rights Act (1964), which refused federal assistance in the form of loans or mortgage guarantees to those who practice racial discrimination. This move had a limited impact on private housing, however. A more comprehensive venture into fair housing is found in the Fair Housing Act of 1968. This act prohibits discrimination based on race, color, religion, sex or national origin in the sale or rental of a dwelling. An earlier Civil Rights Act, passed in 1866, had been largely ignored by the courts. In 1968 the United States Supreme Court gave new life to this old statute in the case of *Jones v. Mayer.*

Certain acts, when based on discrimination, are currently prohibited by law. These acts include refusal to sell or lease a dwelling, variation in terms of a sale or lease from one party to another, advertising that excludes certain groups and false representation that an available dwelling is no longer available. Also prohibited are the real estate practices of blockbusting, redlining and steering. Further, refusing membership in a multiple-listing pool on the basis of race is illegal.

Under the Fair Housing Act the party who suffers discrimination is entitled to bring a complaint to the Department of Housing and Urban Development (HUD). The party may also file in a federal court. Judicial remedies are often more effective than the administrative remedies of HUD because that agency lacks both the enforcement mechanisms and the budget to conduct the necessary investigations.

Legal remedies available to wronged parties may include collection of damages, both compensatory and punitive, and injunctions or other judicial orders. Nevertheless, the number of cases handled by both HUD and the courts continues to be small.

Texas does not have a comprehensive statute prohibiting discrimination in housing. However, the federal legislation has been effective in eliminating housing discrimination within the state. In addition, the Texas Real Estate License Act prohibits licensees from discrimination based upon race, color, religion, sex, national origin or ancestry. A licensee who is found guilty of discriminatory practices can have his or her license either suspended or revoked.

A second important aspect in housing is the availability of financing to purchase or improve real estate. There are two federal laws that require lenders to make financing available in a nondiscriminatory manner. These are the Community Reinvestment Act and the Equal Credit Opportunity Act.

QUESTIONS AND CASE PROBLEMS

1. Compare the coverage of the Fair Housing Act (1968) with that of the Civil Rights Act (1866).

2. Defendants operated 119 buildings within the city of New York, containing 15,484 apartments, with rentals ranging from $140 to $400 per month. To be eligible to rent an apartment a family had to have a weekly net income equal to 90 percent of the monthly rental or, alternatively, the family had to obtain a cosigner of the lease who had a weekly net income equal to 110 percent of a month's rent. These financial requirements excluded a large percentage of black and Puerto Rican applicants. Suit was brought against the defendants seeking injunctive relief on grounds that the requirements violated federal civil rights statutes. What do you think was the result? Why?

3. Greenwood was a salesperson in an office visited by Bago, a prospective buyer. Bago expressed an interest in a property in a specific area of Detroit. Greenwood told Bago that she had some nice property listed outside of the city. She stated, "The school system is poor in Detroit." Later she asked, "Do you read the newspapers? Even the police are afraid to live in the area, and they are supposed to protect us." Greenwood gave Bago several listings in Detroit and

a suburb and suggested that he compare prices, indicating that prices were lower in Detroit because blacks lived there. Greenwood further indicated that she would sell him any property he was interested in, wherever it was located. What, if any, violation of fair housing legislation has Greenwood committed? Support your answer.

4. Marshall and Barnett, two black men, wished to buy homes in a development called Johnson Estates. Twelve homes remained to be sold in the development. The agent for Johnson Estates told them that the company would have difficulty selling the other homes if sales were made to Barnett and Marshall. He offered to build them identical homes elsewhere. He also told them that closing costs would not be charged if they could find purchasers for some of the remaining homes but that he would sell them the homes as the law required. Commonly, white purchasers were not required to pay closing costs. What violations of fair housing legislation is the agent guilty of?

18

Basic Contract Law

Citizens are obliged to obey laws the government imposes upon them. No one likes to pay taxes, but failure to do so results in penalties. The obligation to pay taxes arises from a legislative act. Obligations may also arise by individual agreement. Two or more persons may come together in agreement to be bound by their own "private legislation." The law will enforce that agreement through the courts if certain ingredients are present. A promise or an agreement between two or more parties that is enforceable by law is called a *contract*.

Contracts are the essential fabric of commercial transactions. Most people enter into contracts on a daily basis, by asking for fuel at a gas station, ordering a sandwich to carry out or purchasing a paper from a newsstand. Real estate listing and purchase agreements, leasehold agreements, options and mortgages are more complex forms of contracts. Each of these agreements is governed by contract law. Every state has its own body of contract law—derived from the common law and from statutes. The general body of contract law applies to all commercial agreements, including real estate agreements.

A contract entitles each party to certain rights, as well as imposing certain duties upon both. When a legally binding contract exists, each party is assured that, should the other party not perform in accordance with the terms, the court will offer a remedy to the aggrieved party. The remedy may be in the form of money damages or a requirement for *specific performance*—that is, that the party perform in accordance with the terms of the contract. A contract thus provides an incentive for each party to perform.

This chapter covers basic principles of law relating to contract formation, contract interpretation and contract enforcement. The following two chapters discuss specific types of real estate contracts, such as the earnest money contract and options. However, before one can understand the specific contract terms a basic understanding of contract law is necessary. Of particular interest to brokers is the process of negotiating or forming a binding agreement between a buyer and a seller.

ELEMENTS OF CONTRACTS

Real estate and other contracts are governed by the general body of contract law. Certain essential ingredients must be present in an agreement in order for an enforceable contract to exist. Basic to the agreement are the *offer* and *acceptance* that are genuinely made. Moreover, the parties must possess the requisite *capacity*, or state of mind, to contract. *Consideration* must be present, and the subject matter of the contract must be *legal*. These and other elements of contracts will be covered in the following sections.

Offer

An **offer** is a proposal made with the intent that upon acceptance by the person to whom it is made a contract will be formed. The person making the offer is called an *offeror*, and the person to whom the offer is made is called the *offeree*. If Mary offers to sell her house to Martin for $70,000, Mary is the offeror and Martin is the offeree. If Martin offers to buy Mary's house for $70,000, Martin is the offeror and Mary is the offeree.

The offer must state with *specificity* what the offeror is willing to do and what is expected in return. Terms of an offer must be certain enough to be interpreted by a court. A clear identification of the property to be conveyed and the names of the parties are essential inclusions within the offer. Indefinite or vague terms such as "a price to be determined by the parties at a later date" are not sufficiently definite to constitute a valid offer. The fact that there is a written document evidencing the offer will not cure a vague term. The case that follows illustrates a document that failed in part because it lacked specificity.

• CASE BRIEF •

Sisk and Parker entered into a written agreement concerning two tracts of land owned by Parker. Sisk agreed to purchase Tract 1 for $9,000. This part of the agreement was performed fully. The second part of the agreement stated that Fisk and Parker would form a corporation for the purpose of owning and operating an apartment complex to be built on Tract 2. The written agreement further stated that Parker would furnish the land and that Sisk would construct the apartments. The plans and specifications for the apartment complex were to be agreed upon by the parties, and a loan for the cost of construction was to be secured by the corporation. The corporation was never formed, the loan commitment was never secured and the parties never agreed upon the plans and specifications for the apartment project. Parker sued Sisk for breach of contract. The court of appeals found that the agreement between Sisk and Parker as to Tract 2 was unenforceable. It held that the provisions regarding Tract 2 were no more than an agreement to agree in the future. "Since either party by the very terms of the agreement could refuse to agree to anything to which the other party might agree on essential matters, and there was no subsequent agreement, no enforceable agreement resulted with legal consequences flowing therefrom. In such an event it is impossible for the law to affix any obligation to such agreement." *Sisk v. Parker,* 469 S.W.2d 727 (Tex. Civ. App.—Amarillo 1971).

An offer must be *communicated* in order to be effective. Communication may be actual or constructive. *Actual* communication occurs when an offeree receives and reads or hears the offer. *Constructive* communication occurs when a reasonably prudent offeree, under the circumstances, should have read the contents of the offer, regardless of whether an actual reading occurred.

An offeror has the power to control the terms of a contract. The offeror may make a reasonable offer or an unreasonable offer. If it is to ripen into a contract, the offeree must accept the terms of the offer. Before acceptance certain events may occur that will cause the offer to terminate.

Termination of an Offer

If unaccepted, an offer may terminate in several ways, including revocation, rejection, lapse of a reasonable time, destruction of the subject matter, death of the offeror, insanity of the offeror or illegality of the subject matter of the offer.

Revocation. An offeror may withdraw an offer any time before the offeree's acceptance. The revocation becomes effective upon actual communication to the offeree. If the offeree receives a revocation prior to acceptance, the offer is terminated. Any purported acceptance after receipt of a revocation merely operates as a new offer, which the original offeror may accept or reject. The revocation need not in every instance be communicated by the offeror to the offeree in order to be effective. Sometimes a revocation is implied. An implied revocation occurs when the offeree hears from a reliable source that the offeror has acted in a manner incompatible with the outstanding offer.

Rejection. An offeree may simply reject an offer by communicating to the offeror a refusal to accept the offer. If the offeree makes a counteroffer, an implied rejection of the offer results. An offeree who communicates a rejection of an offer and then decides to accept the offer has actually rejected the offer. The purported acceptance merely results in a counteroffer, which the original offeror is free to accept or reject.

Lapse of Reasonable Time. An offeror may specify an expiration date for an offer. A purported acceptance after the specified date is ineffective. If no date is specified, then the offer lapses after a reasonable period of time.

What is considered reasonable varies from case to case, depending upon the circumstances. In general, however, an offer to purchase realty will not expire as rapidly as, for example, an offer to purchase shares of stock because the price of stock normally fluctuates more rapidly than that of realty.

Destruction of the Subject Matter.   Destruction of the subject matter of the offer, before acceptance, results in a termination of the offer. If a seller offers to sell Redacre and the house on it to a prospective purchaser, the offer will automatically terminate, before acceptance, upon the destruction of the house. This would be true even if the prospective purchaser was unaware of the destruction. Nevertheless, a *contract* does not necessarily terminate because of the destruction of the subject matter.

Death of the Offeror.   Death of the offeror prior to the offeree's acceptance results in a termination of the offer whether the offeree knows of the death or not. If the offeree accepts the offer and then the offeror dies, a contract exists. However, death will normally not excuse performance of one's contractual obligation, unless the performance involves personal services.

Insanity of the Offeror.   An offer terminates before acceptance in the event the offeror becomes insane. Otherwise, the offeror would be at a disadvantage because an insane person does not normally possess the faculties necessary to decide to revoke an offer. A *contract* for the sale of realty, however, is not affected should a party become insane after entering the contract; the guardian or other representative of the insane person is required to perform.

Illegality of the Subject Matter.   A change in the law may cause an offer that was legal when made to become illegal. Such a change causes an offer to terminate. Similarly, a valid contract that later becomes illegal due to a change in law is generally unenforceable.

Acceptance

Acceptance is the offeree's assent to the terms of the offer. The offeree has the power to create a contract merely by communicating an acceptance. The offeree does not have the authority to modify the terms of a proposal. In fact, should the offeree change the terms of the offer, the variation results in a *counteroffer*. A counteroffer actually results in a rejection of the original offer. The original offeror may then reject or accept the counteroffer.

CASE EXAMPLE

Allen offers to sell Solid Rock to Baldoro for $70,000. Baldoro responds, saying, "I accept your offer, $20,000 down and $10,000 a year for five years." Baldoro's response is a counteroffer because it differs from Allen's offer. Allen's offer was for $70,000 in cash. Baldoro's response included only $20,000 in cash and the balance to be financed by Allen. Allen can either reject or accept the counteroffer.

At times an offeree appears to add terms to an offer when in fact the new terms were implied within the original offer. In such a case the purported terms will not defeat the acceptance.

CASE EXAMPLE

Allen offers to sell Solid Rock to Baldoro for $70,000. Baldoro responds by saying, "I accept, provided the title is good." Since the law implies in Allen's offer that Allen will tender good title, Baldoro has added no new terms and acceptance is valid.

The offer and the acceptance constitute the agreement. It may not always be feasible or possible to determine which party made the offer and which party accepted. In many instances, after final negotiations, the entire agreement is reduced to writing. Both parties then sign the agreement. It is only academic in such a case to break the agreement down to the offer and acceptance components. However, the party who signed first could be considered the offeror and the second signer the offeree. In reality this is not always true, because a contract may have resulted prior to the signing of the agreement. In such a case the signing is merely the evidence of the oral agreement.

Manifest Intent

Courts often articulate that there must be a "meeting of the minds" before an agreement can exist. This subjective test requires an examination of the psyche of each of the parties, which is, of course, impractical and usually impossible. The more acceptable approach is the *objective test*, one that is designed to determine whether the parties manifested an *intent* to be bound. Regardless of the mind of the offeror, if a reasonable offeree believes an offer to have been communicated seriously, then an acceptance of the offer ripens into a contract. This is true even when the offer was made in excitement or jest.

Transmittal of Acceptances and Revocations

An acceptance is effective upon actual communication to the offeror or the offeror's agent. The offeror may expressly name an agent, or one may be implied. The law deems that an offeror impliedly invites acceptance from the offeree by the same mode of communication the offeror used to communicate the offer. This is known as the *implied agency rule*. If an offeror communicates an offer by mail, then the mailboxes would be the offeror's implied agents. Under that circumstance the deposit of an acceptance in the mail results in a valid acceptance at the time of deposit. The offeror assumes the risk of nondelivery of the acceptance in such a case, so that even if the offeror never receives the acceptance, it is nonetheless effective at the moment of delivery to the mailbox. Of course, the offeror may eliminate this risk by expressly stating as a term of the offer that acceptance is effective only upon actual receipt by the offeror.

An offer may be revoked anytime before it is deemed accepted. Revocation is effective upon actual receipt by the offeree. The implied agency rule does not operate in the area of revocation.

CASE EXAMPLE

Jan. 3. *A* offers by mail to sell Landacre to *B* for $2,000 an acre.
Jan. 4. *B* deposits an acceptance in the mail.
Jan. 5. *A* mails a letter to *B* revoking her previous offer.
Jan. 6. *B* receives the letter of revocation.
Jan. 7. *A* receives the letter of acceptance.
A contract exists on January 4 since an effective acceptance was delivered to *A*'s implied agent prior to actual receipt by *B* of *A*'s letter of revocation.

The law of transmittal of acceptances and revocations is based upon fairness and establishes firm rules that a businessperson may rely upon in decision making.

Reality of Assent

There must be reality of assent to an agreement between the parties; the *appearance* of assent is not sufficient. Any nonassenting party may avoid the contract. Causes that may intervene to negate a party's assent include fraud, innocent misrepresentation, mistake, undue influence and duress.

Fraud is an intentional misrepresentation of a material fact that induces justifiable reliance to the detriment of a party. The area of fraud is examined in detail in Chapter 16. The defrauded party not only may seek rescission of the contract but also may have an action in tort to recover damages against the defrauder. *Innocent misrepresentation* is an unintentional misrepresentation of a material fact that induces justifiable reliance to the detriment of a party. In contrast to fraud, the misrepresenter does not do so intentionally. Consequently, most courts permit the party relying on the material fact to rescind the contract but deny recovery for damages.

Mistake is an unintentional error. When both parties enter into a contract under a mistaken belief as to a material matter related to the contract, either party may rescind the contract. If, for example, a seller and buyer of Redacre enter into a real estate sales contract under the misimpression that the property is an historical landmark when in fact it is not, rescission is available to either party. If only one party is mistaken concerning a material fact, rescission is not generally an available remedy unless the mistake should have been obvious to the other party.

Undue influence is the exertion of dominion over another person that destroys that person's ability to exercise independent judgment. Undue influence cases giving rise to a right of rescission involve situations where one party has developed a total dependency upon another. An elderly aunt be so mentally overpowered by a suave nephew that she conveys her land to him at his insistence. Or a sick patient may develop such a trust in a nurse that he loses his power to resist the nurse's plea to convey his property to her. *Duress* is coercion that overcomes a party's will. Duress results when one is coerced to enter into an agreement by force or threat of force. The threat must be of such a nature as to place a reasonable person in fear, such as the threat of bodily harm.

Capacity

For a legally binding agreement to exist, both parties must have the *capacity*, or legal ability, to enter into the contract. Some persons have no capacity to contract. Their contracts are designated as void. Other persons possess limited capacity to enter into contracts. Their contracts are classified as voidable. Examples of both categories are discussed below.

Insane Persons

An insane person, under the law, is one who lacks the requisite reason to comprehend the nature and consequences of transactions. Any contract entered into by a person who has been determined to be insane by a court—that is, one who has been *adjudicated insane*—is automatically void. Since such information is a matter of public record, all are deemed to be on notice that the person cannot enter into a valid contract and may not be held liable because the court has determined him or her to be insane. A person who is *actually insane*, but has not been adjudicated insane by a court, is deemed to possess limited capacity to enter into contracts. His or her contracts are classified as voidable. A *voidable contract* is one that may be voided or validated at the option of the party who possesses limited capacity. During the course of the insanity, up to a reasonable time after being restored to sanity, a person who is actually insane may elect to *disavow* the contract and treat it as void. In such a case the insane person must tender back the property received and is then entitled to return of the property he or she previously conveyed. Or, after being restored to sanity, that person may *ratify* the contract and treat it as valid.

Insane persons are obligated to pay for the necessities of life for which they contract and receive. Although the contract itself is void, the court will require the insane person to pay the reasonable value of the property or services received. Necessities are those things reasonably necessary for the care and comfort of the insane person. For example, an insane person can contract for and is obligated to pay for medical services.

Minors

The law seeks to protect the immature as well as the insane. For that reason the law discourages adults from contracting with them. In some states those under the age of 21 are considered minors, but in most, including Texas, minors are those under 18. (This should not be confused with the legal drinking age.) Generally, a contract entered into with a minor is voidable by the minor. That means that the minor may choose to disaffirm the contract anytime during minority and up to a reasonable time after attaining majority. If the contract is executory (unperformed), then that disaffirmance releases the minor from the obligation to perform the contract. If the contract is executed (performed), then the disaffirming minor need only give back to the adult that which remains of what he or she received from the adult. Then the minor would be entitled to a full return of the money or property originally conveyed to the adult. In most states, however, when the transaction involves a completed sale of the minor's realty, the minor is obliged to await the age of majority before disaffirming the transaction.

Just as insane persons are required to pay for any necessities for which they contract, so are minors. Although minors may still disaffirm contracts for necessities, they will nonetheless be required to pay the reasonable value of the property or services received. Normally, real estate that provides housing is not deemed to be a necessity for a minor since the minor can live with his or her parents. Generally, a minor's parents are not liable for their child's contractual obligations or debts. However, a parent may become liable by agreement. Such an agreement may involve the parents' co-signing a contract or a promissory note guaranteeing payment.

Intoxicated or Drugged Persons

Contracts entered into by a person who is intoxicated or under the influence of drugs are voidable if the drug renders such a person unable to appreciate the nature and consequences of his or her acts. Most courts are less sympathetic to this classification of persons than minors and will permit disaffirmance of a completed contract only if the sound person can be restored to the original position, suffering no loss.

Consideration

The third element necessary for contract formation is consideration. *Consideration* is a promise, act or forbearance bargained for and given in exchange for a promise, act or forbearance. Generally, if a defendant's promise is not supported by consideration, then it is unenforceable. In order for a promise to be supported by consideration, it must result in a benefit to the promisor (the one who makes a promise) *or* a detriment to the promisee (the one to whom a promise is made). The benefit or detriment may be in the form of a return promise, an act or a forbearance.

A *return promise* to do something that one was not otherwise obligated to do is sufficient consideration. Most real estate contracts take the form of a promise for a promise. This type of contract is designated *bilateral*.

CASE EXAMPLE

Burnside promises to pay Yerkes $25,000 for Needleacre, and Yerkes promises to sell Needleacre to Burnside for $25,000. All the details of the contract are reduced to writing. Since there is a promise for a promise, a bilateral contract exists. Each promise is supported by consideration supplied by the other's promise.

An *act* may constitute good consideration for a promise. If the promisor is bargaining for the act, the performance of the act usually constitutes a legal benefit to the promisor as well as a legal detriment to the promisee. Such a contract is termed *unilateral* because there is only one promise.

CASE EXAMPLE

Burnside promises to convey Needleacre to Johannes if Johannes cares for Burnside's mother for her life. Johannes cares for Burnside's mother for her life. Since there is a promise for an act, the contract is unilateral. The act is sufficient consideration to support Burnside's promise since it was bargained for and results in a detriment to Johannes.

Consideration may take the form of a *forbearance.* Such a contract is also unilateral, since there is only one promise.

CASE EXAMPLE

Burnside promises to convey Needleacre to Lasser if Lasser will not sue him for fraud. Lasser gives up his right to sue Burnside. Since there is a promise for a forbearance, the contract is unilateral. The forbearance is sufficient consideration to support the promise because it was bargained for and results in a detriment.

In a unilateral contract, the act or forbearance constitutes both the consideration and the acceptance. If the promisor is looking for a promise and receives an act, then the act does not constitute sufficient consideration because it was not "bargained for and given in exchange." Similarly, in the event the promisor is looking for an act, a return promise is insufficient consideration.

CASE EXAMPLE

Irma Keeton promises to tender a deed to her property to Vera Stanley if Stanley produces and tenders $60,000 cash to her by July 1. Stanley promises to produce and tender the cash on July 1. There is no contract, since Keeton is bargaining for the act of payment of $60,000 and Stanley has made only a promise. If Stanley tenders $60,000 by July 1, a contract results, obligating Keeton to tender the deed to the property.

Promissory Estoppel

Promissory estoppel is a doctrine that prevents a party from denying that a promise is supported by consideration. The doctrine of promissory estoppel is applicable in certain cases when no consideration exists, but it is necessary to enforce a promise in order to avoid an injustice. The following ele-

Figure 18:1: **CONTRACT FORMATION ILLUSTRATED**

Jack and Jill view house with agent.

Jack and Jill discuss terms of offer with agent, who writes out offer.

Agent presents offer to seller.

Seller increases selling price (counteroffer), and agent writes down terms of new offer.

Agent presents counteroffer to Jack and Jill.

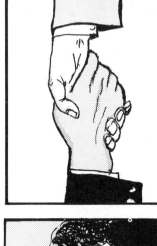

Jack and Jill accept counteroffer— contract is formed.

ments must also be present: (1) a promise (2) calculated to induce reliance, (3) actual justified reliance by the promisee and (4) injury.

CASE EXAMPLE

Montrasor is in arrears on her mortgage payments and requests additional time from the mortgagee to permit her to pay the arrearage. The mortgagee extends the time by 90 days. There is no consideration to support the promise to extend. Thirty days thereafter Montrasor makes substantial improvements to the property in reliance on the mortgagee's promise. The mortgagee files an action in foreclosure prior to the expiration of the 90 days. Since the ingredients of promissory estoppel are present, the mortgagee's promise not to foreclose for 90 days is enforceable.

Lawful Purpose

A contract must possess a legal purpose. Any contract that runs afoul of the Constitution, a statute or public policy is illegal and hence void. A party to an illegal bargain normally will not be assisted by the courts. Simply, the courts will leave the parties to an illegal bargain in the same position as they are found. There are some exceptions to this rule.

Sometimes the parties to the contract are not deemed to be *in pari delicto*— that is, not at equal fault. A landlord who lets property to a tenant who uses the property to traffic drugs may be innocent of the illegal purpose for which the property was intended. In that instance, the courts aid the innocent party in the collection of the rents. An elderly man who is tricked out of his real estate or other property will be protected in many jurisdictions regardless of the fact that he was a willing participant in an unscrupulous scheme.

When a contract involves an illegal provision, the courts may excise that portion and enforce the remainder of the contract. However, if the legal provision is so interconnected with the whole so as to render it nonseverable, the entire contract would be rendered void.

STATUTE OF FRAUDS

As explained in the first section of this chapter, an agreement is a contract only if four elements are present: an offer and acceptance, consideration given and received, capacity to contract and a legal subject matter. Contracts can be either oral or written. In most cases an oral agreement is as enforceable as a written contract. Nevertheless, there are problems associated with verbal contracts. One of those problems is proving the existence and the terms of that contract. In a suit for breach of contract, the plaintiff must prove that a contract was formed. The plaintiff must convince the judge or jury that an offer was accepted and must also convince the judge or jury of what consideration was promised or given by the parties. The existence of a written document signed by both parties makes proving the existence and terms of a contract easier.

Another problem associated with proving the existence of an oral contract is the possibility that one person may perpetrate a fraud on another by lying about the formation of the contract or its terms. Centuries ago, courts, in handling contract disputes, found that it was not uncommon for a party to pay witnesses to fabricate testimony to support a nonexistent oral contract. Lawyers and judges began to believe that one way to prevent fraud and perjury in contract cases was to require that the plaintiff have written evidence of the contract. In 1677 the British Parliament enacted a law that required that contracts for the sale of real estate be in writing to be enforceable. Following that British precedent, all of the states have enacted statutes that require that contracts for the sale of real estate be written and signed to be enforceable by a court. Laws that require that certain contracts be in writing to be enforceable by the courts are called **statutes of fraud**, the name originating from the British statute whose purpose was to prevent fraud and perjury.

Two statutes in Texas require that contracts for the sale of real estate be in writing to be enforceable by a court. The pertinent provisions of these statutes are as follows:

(a) A promise or agreement described in Subsection (b) of this section is not enforceable unless the promise or agreement, or a memorandum of it, is
(1) in writing; and
(2) signed by the person to be charged with the promise or agreement or by someone lawfully authorized to sign for him.
(b) Subsection (a) of this section applies to...
(4) a contract for the sale of real estate;
(5) a lease of real estate for a term longer than one year;
(6) an agreement which is not to be performed within one year from the date of making the agreement;
(7) a promise or agreement to pay a commission for the sale or purchase of
(A) an oil or gas mining lease;
(B) an oil or gas royalty;
(C) minerals; or
(D) a mineral interest. (Tex. Bus. & Com. Code §26.01)

A conveyance of an estate of inheritance, a freehold or an estate for more than one year, in land and tenements, must be in writing and must be subscribed and delivered by the conveyor or by the conveyor's agent authorized in writing. (Tex. Prop. Code §5.021)

It is important to remember that the written memorandum is proof of an oral contract. In other words, a written document is useless if one of the four elements necessary for formation of a contract is missing. The case that follows illustrates the relationship between the Statute of Frauds and contract formation.

• CASE BRIEF •

Misener-Collins Company, Ltd., and L. P. Botello entered into a written "sale contract." The written document identified the parties to the agreement, described the real estate being sold and was signed by both parties. The part of the agreement in dispute concerned the terms for payment of the purchase price. The written document contained the following:

2. The purchase price is $200,000.00 payable as follows: $5,000.00 cash, of which Buyer has deposited with the undersigned agent $5,000.00 as part payment, receipt of which is hereby acknowledged by agent, Emillo Chito Davila.

The court held that the written document met the requirements of the Statute of Frauds even though it did not specifically set out the terms for paying the balance due of $195,000. However, the agreement was unenforceable because the parties never reached a verbal agreement concerning how or when the $195,000 was to be paid. If the parties had orally agreed on this essential term, then the agreement would have been an enforceable contract. *Botello v. Misener-Collins Company*, 469 S.W.2d 793 (Tex. 1971).

Memorandum

The Statute of Frauds requires that there be a writing signed by the person against whom enforcement is sought. The statute does not describe the contents or the form of the writing. The form can be a letter, a memorandum, a note, a formal document or a series or collection of any of these written instruments. The agreement can be handwritten, typed or printed. The writing is not required to include all of the terms of the contract. For example, although the purchase price must be in writing, the method for paying it does not need to be in writing. The courts have held that the following must be in writing: (1) the identity of the parties, (2) the description of the real estate and (3) essential terms and conditions (such as consideration).

The memorandum may be prepared anytime before suit on the contract is commenced. Loss or destruction of the memorandum does not render the contract unenforceable. In such a case, the existence of the memorandum may be proved by witnesses or other documents. In most jurisdictions, the Statute of Frauds is deemed waived unless it is pleaded as a defense in court.

A written memorandum for the sale of real estate will be enforced only against the party who signed the memorandum. Consequently, it is possible that a purchaser of a parcel of real estate may not be legally able to enforce the contract against the seller, while the seller may be legally able to enforce the contract against the purchaser. The reverse is also true.

CASE EXAMPLE

Bill Barley, seller, contracts with John Harley, buyer, for the sale of Lodgeacre, with complete details of the sale contained in a writing. Barley signs the writing, but Harley neglects to sign. The contract is enforceable against Barley but not against Harley, because Harley did not sign.

The best way to ensure compliance with the Statute of Frauds is to require that all parties sign the real estate purchase contract. Although the entire agreement of the parties need not be reduced to writing, as a practical matter it is best to do so. This prevents uncertainty and provides a controlling document to resolve disputes.

Part Performance—An Exception

There are certain exceptions to compliance with the Statute of Frauds. The most notable exception is the doctrine of *part performance*. There are various views as to what constitutes an act of part performance sufficient to remove a contract from the Statute of Frauds so that a writing will not be required.

In Texas a buyer can enforce an oral contract for the sale of land if the buyer can prove that (1) there was an oral contract, (2) he or she paid consideration for the property, (3) he or she took possession of the land and (4) he or she made valuable improvements on the land. There must be satisfactory proof of all four elements before a court will enforce an oral agreement. The case that follows illustrates the difficulty of proving the exception of part performance to the Statute of Frauds.

• CASE BRIEF •

Potts and Elizey each agreed to convey to Harris an 11.1-percent interest in certain land located near Lake Livingston. Harris introduced his canceled checks showing payment of the consideration. The land in question had been subdivided and platted as "Lake Livingston Subdivision." It contained 250 lots. The land was vacant, unimproved land prior to the agreement. After the agreement was made, streets were graded and culverts were placed at the subdivision entrance and low places for drainage. The property owners, including Harris, borrowed the money to pay for these improvements. There was a promissory note showing Harris as a codebtor, and Harris had canceled checks showing his payments on the note. Harris cleared three of the lots by cutting the trees and bushes. He set up a table on the cleared area for the purpose of writing contracts for the sale of lots. Harris and another owner, Holleman, procured and erected permanent street signs on the property. Harris went out to the property on several occasions to show lots to prospective buyers. The court held that these activities on the part of Harris did not satisfy the requirements of part performance because there was no evidence that Harris took possession or occupied the property. Although Harris constructed valuable improvements, the requirement of possession is distinct and different from the requirement that the buyer make valuable improvements. Having failed to offer proof of one of the essential elements, Harris has failed to meet his burden of proof. *Harris v. Potts,* 545 S.W.2d 126 (Tex. 1976).

CONTRACT INTERPRETATION

All the essential terms of an agreement must be definite and certain in order for an enforceable contract to exist. Courts will not normally construct terms or fill in gaps where the instrument is deficient. It is the duty of the courts to interpret language within a contract and to give effect to the intent of the parties. If the language is ambiguous and the court cannot arrive at the intent of the parties, then it will not enforce the instrument. In a real estate purchase contract, the parties and property must be identified. Essential terms left open for future negotiation may invalidate the contract.

Courts use various rules for interpreting contractual provisions, each designed to ascertain the intent of the parties. Words are assigned their plain meaning and are read in the context of the entire contract. Technical terms are given their common meaning within the industry. For example, terms such as *escrow, balloon payment, wraparound mortgage, contract for deed* and others are common in real estate contracts. Courts will look to the real estate industry to determine the meaning of these technical terms.

If there is a conflict within two or more provisions in the contract, the court will resolve the conflict by using the following rules:

1. Specific provisions have precedence over general provisions.
2. Handwritten provisions have precedence over those that are typewritten.
3. Typewritten provisions will prevail over those that are printed (typeset).

The key purpose of all rules of construction is to give meaning to the intent of the parties.

Parol Evidence

Parol evidence is oral testimony or other evidence extraneous to the written instrument. Parol evidence is not admissible for the purpose of varying, adding to or contradicting the terms of a contract. The rule, however, does not exclude parol evidence consistent with the writings of the parties. Nor does the rule exclude parol evidence for the purpose of clarifying ambiguous terms in the contract or to prove that the writing was induced by fraud, illegality, duress, undue influence or mistake.

CASE EXCERPT   *Weinacht v. Phillips Coal Co.*, 673 S.W.2d 677 (Tex. Civ. App.— 5th Dist. 1984) ALLEN, Justice. Don Weinacht appeals a summary judgment granted in favor of the appellees, Phillips Coal Company and Murff F. Bledsoe.

It is undisputed that the parties entered into a written coal lease for a primary term of 25 years. The written lease recited that Weinacht, as lessor, was to receive a royalty equal to 5% of the actual sales price of the coal at the mine. Three years after the execution of the lease, Weinacht brought suit against Phillips and Bledsoe alleging breach of contract and fraud. Weinacht contended that the parties orally agreed that if Phillips gave a higher royalty in a coal lease to any other landowner in the county, then Phillips would increase Weinacht's royalty to match the higher royalty. Weinacht alleged that Phillips had given an 8% royalty in the county, that Phillips had failed to raise Weinacht's 5% royalty to 8%, and that such failure had deprived Weinacht of nine million dollars in royalties. Phillips and Bledsoe moved for summary judgment on the basis that enforcement of the alleged oral agreement was barred by the statute of frauds and by the parol evidence rule. Summary judgment was granted in favor of Phillips and Bledsoe, and Weinacht brings this appeal. . . .

It is settled that when contracting parties have concluded a valid integrated agreement, whether written or oral, dealing with the particular subject matter they have between them, the parol evidence rule will prevent enforcement of prior or contemporaneous agreements which are inconsistent with the integrated agreement. . . .

Initially, Weinacht claims that the parol evidence rule does not bar enforcement of the oral agreement because the written agreement is not a final integrated agreement between the parties. Absent pleading and proof of ambiguity, fraud, accident or mistake, a written instrument presumes that all prior agreements of the parties relating to the transaction have been merged into the written instrument. Its provisions will be enforced as written and cannot be added to, varied, or contradicted by parol testimony. . . .

Next, Weinacht claims that the parol evidence rule does not apply because the oral agreement is collateral to, and not inconsistent with, the written agreement. We disagree. The parol evidence rule does not preclude enforcement of prior contemporaneous agreements which are collateral to, not inconsistent with, and do not vary or contradict the express or implied terms or obligations thereof. To be collateral, the agreement may and must be such as the parties might naturally make separately and would not ordinarily be expected to embody in the writing; and it must not be so clearly connected with the principal transaction as to be part and parcel thereof. We hold that the alleged oral agreement in the instant case is not collateral to, and is inconsistent with, the written agreement between the parties, and that the parol evidence rule prevents the enforcement of the alleged contemporaneous oral agreement.

We hold that the trial court correctly entered summary judgment in favor of Phillips Coal Co. and Murff F. Bledsoe. The judgment is affirmed.

The parol evidence rule does not prevent the parties from amending their original written contract. Evidence of a subsequent agreement altering the original contract is admissible. The subsequent agreement must itself conform to all the requirements for a contract to be enforceable. If it fails this test, then it does not alter the original obligations of the parties. A subsequent agreement should also clearly reference the written contract being amended. Otherwise, the parol evidence rule might prevent the intended amendment from being effective.

ASSIGNMENT

Contract benefits and obligations can be transferred from one person to another. The present transfer of a contract right from one person (the assignor) to another (the assignee) is called an *assignment.* For example, the purchaser, as a party to an executory (unperformed) contract, is the equitable owner of the property; the purchaser has a right to receive title to the property from the seller in accordance with the terms of the contract. This right may be transferred to a third party. An assignee succeeds to the rights that were previously invested in the assignor. The assignee of a right to receive a deed may enforce that right against the seller.

An assignee is bound to perform the obligations the assignor promised the seller, including payment of the purchase price. Failure to perform on the part of the assignee constitutes a breach of the agreement and results in liability for damages. An assignment does not relieve the assignor from obligations under the contract. In the event that the assignee does not perform, the seller may hold the original purchaser (assignor) responsible for performing in accordance with the agreement.

The seller, as a party to an executory contract, has an equitable interest in the purchase price; the seller has a right to receive the purchase price in accordance with the terms of the contract. The seller may assign the right to receive this purchase price. The same rules that apply to the assignment of a purchaser's rights also apply to the assignment of a seller's rights.

There are a few limitations on the right to assign contracts. Of course, the parties can agree and include in their contract a prohibition against assignment. However, the most notable limitation with respect to earnest money contracts are those in which the seller is extending credit to the buyer as part of the consideration. An earnest money contract is not assignable if the seller is financing the purchase of the property for the buyer. This limitation on assignability protects a seller who agreed to finance the purchase (or a part of the purchase) based on a particular buyer's situation.

BREACH OF CONTRACT

The failure of a purchaser to tender the purchase price for the property at the appointed time is one example of a breach of contract. Another example is the seller's failure to tender title to the purchaser at the appointed time. Any nonperformance of a term within the contract may give rise to a breach of that contract. The law provides remedies in the event of breach. These serve as incentives to both parties to live up to the terms of the agreement.

Anticipatory Breach

It is not always necessary to await the day designated for performance to determine that a party is in breach. Sometimes an anticipatory breach occurs. An anticipatory breach is a breach of contract that occurs as a result of repudiating a contract before the date due for performance. In order to constitute an anticipatory breach, the nonperforming party must communicate to the other party an intention not to perform. Or, an intention not to perform may be determined from a party's behavior.

CASE EXAMPLE

R. Brower, a contractor, agreed to paint John Dooley's home for $2,500. Pursuant to the contract the work was to begin August 1. Thereafter, Brower informed Dooley that he was going out of business and asked him to find someone else to do the work. On July 15 Dooley learned from a reliable source that Brower had gone out of business, had sold all of his equipment and had dishonored all of his existing contracts. Under such a circumstance, Dooley may treat Brower as in anticipatory breach of contract and immediately sue for damages.

Substantial Performance

The law recognizes that humans, frail as they are, cannot always perform their contracts according to the exact specifications. Consequently, if the closing date is set for April 5 and the purchaser desires it to be moved to April 7, the two-day delay does not amount to a material breach, barring a provision in the contract to the contrary or exceptional circumstances. In the area of building contracts, a contractor who builds a home and incurs minor deviations from the specifications may nonetheless have substantially complied with the contractual provisions. In such a case, the contractor will be entitled to the contract price less the cost to remedy the deviations to the property. If, for example, a contractor complies with all the specifications under a $60,000 building contract but fails to paint three out of 14 window panels, the contractor is entitled to $60,000 less the cost of having the window panels painted. This legal doctrine is called **substantial performance** and has the effect of relieving one of the parties of his or her obligations under the contract even though that party has failed to perform totally and completely.

• CASE BRIEF •

John H. Vance, d/b/a Vance Construction Company, entered into a construction contract with My Apartment Steak House of San Antonio in March 1978. The restaurant was to be completed by August 10, 1978. Various delays occurred for which each party blames the other. On September 25, 1978, Steak House notified Vance that the contract was terminated and thereafter denied him access to the property for further work. At that time the restaurant was substantially completed. Steak House withheld $20,000 from the original contract. Vance sued for $8,298, which he claims represents the difference between the $116,000 contract price and the cost to complete the construction. Steak House cross-claimed against Vance for $43,488.75 for defective construction and failure to complete the contract. The court held that, since Vance had substantially performed the building contract, he was entitled to recover the full contract price less the cost of remedying the defects. The burden of proving the reasonable cost of repairing and completing the building was on the contractor. *Vance v. My Apartment Steak House of San Antonio, Inc.*, 677 S.W.2d 480 (Tex. 1984).

There is no substantial performance if the utility of the property or its purpose is significantly affected by the contractor's deviation. If the specifications in the contract called for gas heating and the contractor installed oil heating instead, the deviation would amount to a breach, and the contractor would not be entitled to any compensation. Some courts do, however, permit the contractor to recover the reasonable value of the services rendered and goods supplied where a substantial deviation is not willful.

Remedies for Breach of Contract

A general overview of the remedies a court can grant was given in Chapter 1. In this chapter the three remedies most frequently sought when a contract has been breached are discussed. Those three remedies are damages, specific performance and rescission. However, before a court will grant relief to the complaining party, the court must be convinced that the plaintiff was ready, willing and able to perform his or her obligations under the contract. For example, if a seller complains of the buyer's breach, the seller must show that he or she was ready and willing to tender a deed conveying marketable title to the land. Similarly, the buyer who sues the seller for failing to perform must show that he or she has obtained or was able to obtain the funds with which to purchase the property.

Many real estate contracts contain a clause that describes the options available to the nonbreaching party when the other party defaults. All of the earnest money contracts promulgated by the Texas Real Estate Commission contain such provisions. Generally these contracts provide that the seller or buyer can elect to sue for damages, rescind the contract and retain the earnest money or sue for specific performance. These are in most cases mutually exclusive options. For example, a seller cannot be granted both specific performance and rescission. The court will usually award only one remedy unless the remedy is inadequate to compensate the injured party fully. If the remedies are insufficient, the court can combine the remedies in any manner that will avoid inequity.

Specific Performance

Specific performance is a court decree mandating a party to perform according to the contract. The buyer is entitled to the deed after completion of the requirements under the contract. Should the seller refuse performance, a court may award specific performance requiring the seller to execute a deed in favor of the buyer. Refusal by the seller to comply with the decree may result in contempt of court and punishment. The court may also execute a deed in the buyer's favor, or—in the event of the seller's refusal to perform in accordance with the decree—the very court decree may be deemed to pass title to the buyer. In many jurisdictions, specific performance is also available to a seller against a defaulting buyer. A decree of specific performance in such a case compels the purchaser to pay the purchase price and accept title to the property.

A court will grant specific performance only if the party seeking it has "clean hands." If one of the parties has taken advantage of the other's disabled condition, for example, or has been guilty of fraud, the court would deny this equitable relief.

Rescission

Rescission is the cancellation of a contract that results in the parties being restored to the position they were in before the contract was made. If the seller defaults, the buyer may elect to rescind the contract and recover his or her earnest money. This is a good choice if the market value of the property has declined. However, a buyer cannot unilaterally and without cause rescind a contract. The seller must have breached the contract.

If the buyer breaches the contract, the seller may choose to cancel the contract and retain the earnest money as liquidated damages. *Liquidated damages* are damages that the parties to the contract have stipulated as being reasonable compensation in the event of a breach. Many real estate contracts contain a provision that states that the earnest money deposit can be treated as liquidated damages by the seller in the event of the buyer's default. Liquidated damage clauses are enforceable provided the sum stipulated is reasonable considering all the circumstances.

Rescission is also available as a remedy by a party who executed the contract as a result of fraud, innocent misrepresentation, mistake, duress or undue influence. Additionally, a contract may be rescinded by mutual consent of the parties.

Damages

Money recoverable by one suffering a loss or injury due to breach of the contract is called *damages.* A buyer may incur actual damages when the seller breaches the obligation to tender the deed. The damages may be in the nature of the loss of the bargain. Translated into monetary terms, loss of the bargain is the difference in the market value of the property at the date set for closing and the contract price. That difference represents the value of damages to which the purchaser is entitled, assuming that the market value of the property at the time of breach is greater than the contract price. Additionally, damages may include the deposit made by the purchaser and actual costs incurred incident to the contract. Incidental expenses include attorney fees for handling the purchase transaction as well as the expense related to a title search.

CASE EXAMPLE

Joe Deal, seller, refused to tender his deed to John Tiehl, purchaser, on March 13, the date set for closing. Tiehl had previously paid Deal $5,000 to be applied to the purchase price of $85,000. Tiehl additionally expended $500 for a title search of the property. The market value of the property was $90,000 on March 13. In an action by Tiehl against Deal for damages Tiehl will be entitled to $5,500, computed as follows: $90,000 (market value)–$85,000 (contract price) = $5,000 + $500 (title search). Tiehl will also be entitled to a return of the $5,000 deposit.

As stated previously, when the buyer breaches the contract, the seller can elect to retain the earnest money as liquidated damages. Whether or not the seller would elect to do so depends upon the market value of the property at the time of default. If the land has retained its value or increased in value, then the seller may be in a better position if he or she rescinds the contract and retains the earnest money. If the land has decreased in value, the seller may sue for damages. Damages in such a case are computed by deducting the market price from the purchase price minus any earnest money payment forfeited to the seller.

CASE EXAMPLE

Robert Peterson breaches his agreement to tender the purchase price of $75,000 to Susan Ely on August 17. The market price of the property fell to $70,000 on that date. Peterson had previously paid $5,000 as earnest money to Ely. Ely retained the $5,000. She is entitled to damages as computed: $75,000 (purchase price)–$70,000 (market value) = $5,000–$5,000 (earnest money forfeited) = $0.

DISCHARGE

Discharge is the release of a party's obligation to perform under the contract. Generally, discharge occurs when a party has totally or substantially performed. However, there are other events that can result in a discharge.

Conditions

Frequently, real estate contracts will contain conditions that will affect the obligation of one of the parties to perform. A condition is a contingency that the parties agree will alter or affect the obligation to perform. Conditions are classified as either conditions precedent or conditions subsequent. A **condition precedent** is a contingency or condition that must exist before a party becomes liable for performing. An example of a condition precedent is the "back-up" contract. A back-up contract is an agreement between a buyer and seller in which the buyer and seller become obligated to each other only if a prior earnest money contract is discharged.

CASE EXAMPLE

James Holt, seller, and Martha Campeau, buyer, have entered into an earnest money contract. Timothy Sands views the property and offers to buy it from Holt if Campeau changes her mind or defaults. Sands and Holt enter into a contract that is contingent upon the sale to Campeau. Hold is obligated to sell and Sands is obligated to buy *only if* Campeau fails to purchase the property. Campeau's default is a condition precedent.

A **condition subsequent** is a contingency that terminates one of the party's obligation to perform. Conditions subsequent are very common in real estate contracts. One example is a condition regarding the buyer's ability to obtain a loan. The buyer agrees to purchase the property provided he or she can obtain suitable financing. If the buyer cannot obtain the financing he or she can cancel the contract and recover the earnest money. The option to cancel or proceed rests with the buyer. The existence of the condition subsequent (inability to obtain the loan) discharges the buyer's obligations under the contract.

Act of the Parties

The parties to a contract can mutually agree to cancel. If such an agreement is reached, the parties are discharged. The parties may also agree to a novation. A **novation** is the substitution of a new party and the release of the original party. A novation is valid only if all three parties agree to the substitution.

CASE EXAMPLE

Cary is indebted to Ponce in the amount of $5,000. Ponce is indebted to Darin in the amount of $5,000. Cary, Ponce and Darin agree that Ponce will release Cary of the debt, Darin will release Ponce and Cary will pay $5,000 directly to Darin.

The parties can also agree to change or substitute the kind of performance originally required under the contract. This agreement is called an **accord** and the performance of the agreement is referred to as a **satisfaction**. An accord and satisfaction discharges a party from his or her original obligation.

CARY

$5,000

$5,000

Ponce $5,000   Darin

CASE EXAMPLE

Castor Andora was indebted to Andrea Hammer, a former employer, in the amount of $2,000. Hammer made a demand for the amount. Andora was out of work and did not have the money. He offered, however, to paint Hammer's house in lieu of the $2,000. Hammer agreed, and Andora, pursuant to the agreement, painted Hammer's house. This constitutes an accord and satisfaction. Andora is discharged of any further obligation to pay Hammer $2,000.

Operation of Law

Finally, the law in some cases will discharge a party from his or her contractual obligation. If the contract involves the personal services of one of the parties, then the death or insanity of that party releases him from his obligations. For example, if the buyer contracts with the builder-seller to construct a house, then the death of the builder would discharge his or her obligation to perform the contract. This was a contract for the personal services of the builder. By contrast a contract that does *not* involve personal services is not discharged by the death or insanity of one of the parties.

A contract also is discharged if the subject matter of the contract becomes illegal. Suppose that a contractor enters into a contract with a shipper to transport specified building materials from a foreign country. Should the U.S. government issue an embargo forbidding the transport of goods from that foreign country, the parties would be discharged from their contractual obligations.

Finally, discharge can occur by operation of law if the circumstances make it impossible or impractical for a party to fulfill his or her obligation under a contract. The event making performance impossible cannot be caused by a party's intentional or negligent act. For example, if the buildings that are being sold are destroyed by fire through no fault of the seller, then the parties are discharged from their obligations under the contract. This can be changed by agreement of the parties by including a stipulation in the earnest money contract.

Figure 18.2: **IS THE AGREEMENT ENFORCEABLE?**

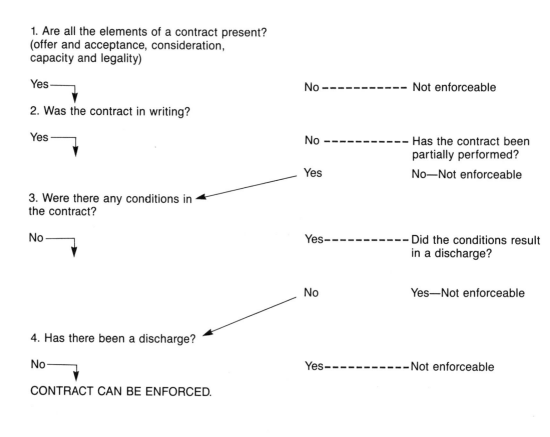

1. Are all the elements of a contract present?
(offer and acceptance, consideration,
capacity and legality)

Yes ⟶   No ---------- Not enforceable

2. Was the contract in writing?

Yes ⟶   No ---------- Has the contract been
                                             partially performed?
                             Yes   No—Not enforceable

3. Were there any conditions in ⟵
the contract?

No ⟶   Yes ---------- Did the conditions result
                                             in a discharge?

                             No   Yes—Not enforceable

4. Has there been a discharge? ⟵

No ⟶   Yes ---------- Not enforceable

CONTRACT CAN BE ENFORCED.

SUMMARY

A contract is a promise or an agreement that is enforceable by law. Contracts entitle the parties to certain rights but also entail obligations. Basic to any contract is an offer, an acceptance and consideration. In addition, both parties must possess the capacity to contract, and the subject matter of the contract must be legal.

In a real estate transaction, an offer is a proposal to sell or purchase property. The offer may be terminated at any time before acceptance, and in such a case no contract exists. An acceptance involves an assent to the terms of an offer. In real estate transactions the offer and acceptance are often communicated by an agent, usually the salesperson or broker. Even after acceptance, however, the contract may be voided because of fraud, misrepresentation or other conditions such as duress. Consideration is another necessary element and involves a benefit to the promisor or a detriment to the promisee that was bargained for and given up in exchange for a promise or an act. Capacity requires that both parties be sane and of legal age to contract. Finally, persons may not contract for an unlawful purpose.

Contracts pertaining to real estate must be supported by a written memorandum signed by the party against whom it is sought to be enforced. The law requires such written evidence in order to deter fraud and perjury in real estate transactions. The law requiring a writing is called the *Statute of Frauds*. There is one notable exception to the Statute of Frauds, called *part performance*.

Although the parties to a real estate contract are required to write and sign their oral agreement, frequently the written document does not include all the terms of the contract or contains ambiguous terms. When this occurs, the courts must interpret the meaning of the contract by trying to determine the intent of the parties. The courts follow several rules of construction in interpreting contract terms. One of the more important and more difficult rules to understand is the parol evidence rule. Under this rule the courts will not hear oral testimony of contemporaneous agreements inconsistent with the written document.

Each party to a contract is expected to perform his or her obligations as promised. However, the courts realize that complete performance is not always possible and therefore recognize the doctrine of substantial performance. Under the doctrine of substantial performance a party is allowed to recover for the work he or she has actually done even though that party did not fully complete all of his or her obligations under the contract as promised. Nevertheless, the party who fails to fully perform his or her obligations under a contract is guilty of a breach of contract. Breach of contract gives the nonbreaching party several remedies. These remedies include specific performance, rescission and damages.

Occasionally the law will excuse a party from performance of his or her obligations under a contract. This is referred to as a *discharge*. Discharges occur when the parties agree to cancel a contract or when performance has become impossible through no fault of the parties.

QUESTIONS AND CASE PROBLEMS

1. Name the elements of a contract and define each.
2. What are the elements necessary to satisfy the Statute of Frauds? Give an example of a case involving a real estate transfer that is excepted from the Statute of Frauds.
3. Explain the remedies available to a buyer when the seller breaches the contract for the sale of real property. Explain the remedies available to the seller in the event of the buyer's breach.

4. On February 13, 1968, KVET Broadcasting Company signed a contract to purchase a tract of land owned by Tiemann. The signed contract was delivered to Herzog, a licensed real estate broker, for presentation to Tiemann. The purchase price in the contract was $2,650 per acre. Tiemann, who had been wanting $3,000 per acre, was disappointed in the price and requested Herzog to ask if KVET would "split the difference." As an alternative Tiemann asked Herzog to see if KVET would consider a seven-percent interest rate on the note provided for in the contract. When Herzog called KVET on February 14 and informed it of Tiemann's proposal, KVET told Herzog that the offer was withdrawn. On February 15 Tiemann signed the original contract. Was KVET's offer terminated by Tiemann's inquiries regarding "splitting the difference" and raising the interest rate on the note? If the offer had not been terminated by Tiemann's inquiries, was notice to Herzog of withdrawal on February 14 an effective termination of the offer?

5. A written earnest money contract contained the following provision regarding the purchase price:

> $2,000.00 to be paid by Purchaser upon the signing of this Earnest Money contract. $23,000.00 to be paid by Purchaser upon the closing of said purchase, and the balance to be represented by a promissory note to be signed by the Purchaser, together with interest at the rate of six per cent (6%) per annum, payable, both principal and accrued interest in equal annual installments until fully paid. Said note to contain the usual default and attorney's fee clauses and to be secured by vendor's lien, superior title and usual Deed of Trust lien on said property.

The seller refuses to complete the sale and claims the contract is void because the term "usual Deed of Trust lien" is too ambiguous to be ascertainable. How would a court determine the intent of the parties, and could it determine the meaning of this phrase?

6. Mrs. Cowart, a recently divorced woman, was employed by Dr. Sessions. As part of the divorce settlement she acquired the home, which was subject to a purchase money lien. Mrs. Cowart was four months delinquent in the mortgage and in somewhat of a financial bind. She was also contemplating a move to Louisiana and a new marriage. Dr. Sessions agreed to buy the house from Mrs. Cowart and in his own handwriting wrote the following "contract":

1-5 1978

RECEIVED FROM John L. Sessions (400.00) four hundred & no/100 DOLLARS Agreed that this 400.00 is a down payment on a Brick Home owned by Effie Cowart—Location 2½ miles on left on Airport Road (Lost Scott Rd.) west of U.S. 96. Total price is 400.00 plus 150.00 a month until 20,000.00 is paid. Dr. Sessions is to assume present payment on the Brick Home on Lost Scott Road.

This "contract" was signed by Mrs. Cowart. When Mrs. Cowart refuses to close the sale, Dr. Sessions sues for specific performance. Will Dr. Sessions prevail?

19

★

Earnest Money Contracts

The previous chapter explained the legal principles relating to contract formation, interpretation and remedies. In this chapter specific terms and conditions commonly included in the real estate purchase contract will be discussed.

In Texas the most frequently used contract by which land is purchased is called an ***earnest money contract.*** The earnest money contract is a bilateral contract in which the buyer promises to purchase the property and the seller promises to convey good title to the property upon payment of the purchase price. The parties are free to establish their own terms and conditions of sale, including an agreement by the seller to finance a portion of the purchase price.

Because the earnest money contract is a contract for the sale of land, it must be in writing under the Texas Statute of Frauds. Some of the provisions typically found in the earnest money contract are included to satisfy the Statute of Frauds. However, most of the provisions are included by the parties to clarify the details of the agreement. The first section of this chapter discusses some of the topics that should be included in an earnest money contract. The next section covers the role of the broker in completing the earnest money contract and the use of the forms promulgated by the Texas Real Estate Commission. The third section of the chapter explains in detail the different forms promulgated by the Texas Real Estate Commission.

PROVISIONS OF EARNEST MONEY CONTRACTS

As explained in the previous chapter, the Texas Statute of Frauds requires that the following provisions for the sale of land be in writing: (1) the identity of the parties, (2) the description of the land, and (3) essential terms and conditions such as the consideration. Some of the provisions that follow satisfy these requirements; however, many go beyond these minimal considerations to address and define more completely the agreement of the parties.

Date

The contract should be dated. Although the date is not required to satisfy the Statute of Frauds, it is frequently important to know when the contract was made. It is not uncommon for other provisions in the earnest money contract to set time limits that reference the date of the contract as the beginning date for the running of the time period. For example, a clause within the contract might read, "Buyer shall obtain financing within 90 days of the signing of this contract."

Parties

The identity of the parties to the contracts is required under the Statute of Frauds. In naming the parties it is important to insert accurately the proper names of the seller and the buyer. It is advisable to use the name of the seller as shown on the deed by which he or she acquired the property. In inserting the buyer's name it is important to use the name that the buyer would like to appear in the deed.

The marital status of the buyer and seller also should be determined and included in the contract. This is commonly accomplished by inserting a phrase such as *a single man* or *a single woman* following the party's name. If the buyer or seller is married, the contract should use a designation such as "Ann Smith and husband, Joe Smith." If either of the parties is married, it is advisable to ascertain the interest of the spouse in the property. If the seller's spouse has any interest in the property either by community property law or by homestead right, the spouse must be included as a seller and must consent to the sale. Because Texas recognizes common law marriages, the potential claim of a common law spouse must also be considered and provided for in the contract.

If the seller or buyer is a corporation or a partnership, the earnest money contract should designate the business entity by its proper name.

Earnest Money

Contrary to popular belief, the deposit of earnest money is not necessary to validate a contract unless the seller specifically makes it a condition of the sale. The consideration given by the buyer is his or her promise to buy the property. Therefore, a deposit of earnest money is not necessary to have an enforceable contract. If earnest money is deposited, it may be a nominal sum, such as $100, or it may be as substantial as ten percent of the purchase price. The earnest money is deposited with an escrow agent. At closing the earnest money is applied toward the purchase price.

Method of Payment

The Statute of Frauds requires that the sales price be set out in writing but does not require that the method for paying the consideration be reduced to writing. Nevertheless, it is good practice to write down not only the total price but also the method by which it will be paid, including any contingencies related to financing arrangements.

Form of Deed

Several types of deeds can be used to convey good title to the buyer. Because the type of deed used can make a difference to both buyer and seller, this issue should be discussed, and specific reference to the type of deed should be included in the earnest money contract.

Property Description

The description of the property is required to be in writing by the Statute of Frauds. Although the preferred method of describing property is by a complete legal description, any narrative that is sufficient to identify with certainty the land that is being sold is adequate. What constitutes an adequate description is discussed in Chapter 3.

In describing the property to be sold it is also advisable to list any fixtures or items of personal property that are to be included in the sale. A detailed list in the earnest money contract can prevent disputes at a later date.

Possession

The date on which the seller is required to surrender possession to the buyer is subject to negotiation and should be addressed specifically in the contract. This date can be before or after the closing. If possession is not to take place on the same date that legal title is transferred, a landlord-tenant relationship is created and should be addressed in the earnest money contract or a separate lease agreement.

Closing

The contract normally states the date and place of closing. Closing procedures are discussed in detail in Chapter 23. At closing the buyer pays the seller the agreed-upon consideration, and the seller passes title by signing and delivering the deed to the buyer. Normally, time is not of the essence in real estate closings. This means that failure to close on the date specified in the contract is not fatal and does not result in a discharge of the party's contractual obligations. If the buyer is acting in good faith and is able to close within a reasonable time after the date specified, the seller must complete the sale. The parties can, of course, agree within the earnest money contract that time is of the essence. If there is such an agreement, then failure to close on the date specified is a breach of contract and can result in the contract's termination.

Signing

The Statute of Frauds requires that the contract be signed by the party against whom enforcement is sought. However, it is advisable to have both parties sign the earnest money contract. There is no requirement that the contract be witnessed, acknowledged or recorded to be enforceable. However, to protect the purchaser's interest against subsequent bona fide purchasers for value, the purchaser may want to record the contract or a memorandum of the contract. If the document is to be recorded, it must be acknowledged or witnessed. It is unusual to record earnest money contracts in Texas, but if the contract is to be recorded, the broker must advise the parties to consult with an attorney before signing. (22 T.A.C. §537.11)

THE BROKER'S ROLE

Real estate sales are frequently facilitated by a licensed real estate broker or salesperson. The buyer and seller rely upon the broker's advice in completing the earnest money contract as well as in negotiating the terms of the sale. As explained in Chapter 14, the drafting of legal documents, such as contracts, is practicing law. Only licensed attorneys in Texas are allowed to practice law. Consequently, brokers must be careful in handling real estate transactions that necessitate the preparation of legal documents.

As explained in Chapter 14 a broker is allowed to use contract forms prepared by the seller or his or her Texas-licensed attorney. In addition, brokers are allowed to fill in the blanks on forms required and prepared by a governmental agency or forms prepared by attorneys and authorized for use in the particular transaction. However, most often a broker will use one of the contracts promulgated or approved by the Texas Real Estate Commission.

In order to assist brokers, the Texas Real Estate Commission has promulgated earnest money contract forms and contract addenda forms that meet the needs of most residential real estate sales. Brokers and salesmen are required to use the promulgated forms whenever possible. Furthermore, they are limited to filling in the blanks on the standard forms, deleting inappropriate provisions and including factual statements when necessary to augment the standard provisions. If the standard forms are not appropriate, the broker or salesman must use a contract drafted by an attorney licensed in Texas.

There are six different earnest money contracts promulgated by TREC for use by brokers and salesmen. They are:

1. One to Four Family Residential Earnest Money Contract (Resale) All Cash, Assumption, Third Party Conventional or Owner Financed
2. Residential Earnest Money Contract (Resale)—FHA Insured or VA Guaranteed Financing
3. Unimproved Property Earnest Money Contract
4. Farm and Ranch Earnest Money Contract

5. New Home Residential Earnest Money Contract (Incomplete Construction) and

6. New Home Residential Earnest Money Contract (Completed Construction)

Brokers and salesmen should choose the form that most closely describes the verbal agreement of the buyer and seller. Each of these forms is reproduced in this book and should be studied with care.

The first form, Figure 19.1, entitled "One to Four Family Residential Earnest Money Contract (Resale) All Cash, Assumption, Third Party Conventional or Owner Financed," is designed for use when all the following general conditions exist:

1. The sale is of residential as opposed to commercial real estate.
2. The structures are used as opposed to new.
3. The buyer will be paying for the property by one of the following means:
   a. all cash;
   b. assumption of an existing mortgage against the property;
   c. the seller is financing a portion of the sales price; or
   d. the buyer will be borrowing funds from someone other than the seller, and the loan is not to be insured by the Federal Housing Administration (FHA) or guaranteed by the Veterans Administration (VA).

The individual clauses included in this earnest money contract will be discussed in detail later in this chapter.

The second form, entitled "Residential Earnest Money Contract (Resale) FHA Insured or VA Guaranteed Financing" (and reproduced in Appendix C), is designed for use when all the following conditions exist:

1. The sale is of residential as opposed to commercial real estate.
2. The structures are used as opposed to new.
3. The buyer will be paying for the property by one of the following means:
   a. a loan insured by the Federal Housing Administration or
   b. a loan guaranteed by the Veterans Administration.

Many of the individual provisions of the earnest money contract are the same clauses included in the prior contract form. The most significant difference in the two forms is in Paragraph 4, on financing arrangements. Paragraph 4 of this form includes matters that are unique to FHA or VA financing. For example, if the sales price of the property exceeds the FHA appraised value, then either the seller can reduce the price or the buyer can terminate the contract and recover his or her earnest money.

The third form, entitled, "Unimproved Property Earnest Money Contract" (reproduced in Appendix C), is designed to be used in a sales transaction in which the land contains no permanent improvements but the buyer intends to build a one- to four-family residence on the land. It contains many of the same provisions found in the first form. The most notable dif-

Figure 19.1 ONE TO FOUR FAMILY RESIDENTIAL EARNEST MONEY CONTRACT (RESALE) ALL CASH, ASSUMPTION, THIRD PARTY CONVENTIONAL OR OWNER FINANCED

02-08-85

ONE TO FOUR FAMILY RESIDENTIAL EARNEST MONEY CONTRACT (RESALE) ALL CASH, ASSUMPTION, THIRD PARTY CONVENTIONAL OR OWNER FINANCED

PROMULGATED BY TEXAS REAL ESTATE COMMISSION

NOTICE: Not For Use For Condominium Transactions

1. PARTIES: _____(Seller) agrees to sell and convey to _____(Buyer) and Buyer agrees to buy from Seller the property described below.

2. PROPERTY: Lot _____, Block _____, _____
Addition, City of _____, _____, County, Texas, known as
_____(Address); or as described on attached exhibit, together with the following items, if any: curtains and rods, draperies and rods, valances, blinds, window shades, screens, shutters, awnings, wall-to-wall carpeting, mirrors fixed in place, ceiling fans, attic fans, mail boxes, television antennas, permanently installed heating and air conditioning units and equipment, built-in security and fire detection equipment, lighting and plumbing fixtures, water softener, trash compactor, garage door openers with controls, shrubbery and all other property owned by Seller and attached to the above described real property. All property sold by this contract is called the "Property".

3. CONTRACT SALES PRICE:
    A. Cash payable at closing .... $_____
    B. Sum of all financing described in Paragraph 4 below .... $_____
    C. Sales Price (Sum of A and B) .... $_____

4. FINANCING: (Check applicable boxes below)
    ☐ A. ALL CASH: This is an all cash sale; no financing is involved.
    ☐ B. ASSUMPTION:
        (1) Buyer's assumption of the unpaid principal balance of a first lien promissory note payable to _____
        in present monthly installments of $_____, including principal, interest and any reserve deposits, with Buyer's first installment payment being payable on the first installment payment date after closing, the assumed principal balance of which at closing will be $_____.
        (2) Buyer's assumption of the unpaid principal balance of a second lien promissory note payable to _____
        in present monthly installments of $_____, including principal, interest and any reserve deposits, with Buyer's first installment payment being payable on the first installment payment date after closing, the assumed principal balance of which at closing will be $_____.
    Buyer's assumption of an existing note includes all obligations imposed by the deed of trust securing the note.

    If the total principal balance of all assumed loans varies in an amount greater than $350.00 at closing either party may terminate this contract and the Earnest Money shall be refunded to Buyer. If the noteholder on assumption (a) requires Buyer to pay an assumption fee in excess of $_____ in B(1) above or $_____ in B(2) above and Seller declines to pay such excess or (b) raises the existing interest rate above _____% in B(1) above or _____% in B(2) above, Buyer may terminate this contract and the Earnest Money shall be refunded to Buyer. The cash payable at closing shall be adjusted by the amount of any variance in the loan balance(s) shown above.
    NOTICE TO BUYER: Monthly payments, interest rates or other terms of some loans may be adjusted after closing. Before signing the contract, examine the notes and deeds of trust to determine the possibility of future adjustments.

    ☐ C. THIRD PARTY FINANCED:
        ☐ 1. A third party first lien note of $_____, due in full in _____year(s), payable in initial monthly payments of principal and interest not exceeding $_____ for the first _____year(s) of the loan.
        ☐ 2. A third party second lien note of $_____, due in full in _____year(s), payable in initial monthly payments of principal and interest not exceeding $_____ for the first _____year(s) of the loan.
    NOTICE TO PARTIES: Before signing this contract Buyer is advised to determine the financing options from lenders. Certain loans have variable rates of interest, some have monthly payments which may not be sufficient to pay the accruing interest, and some have interest rate "buydowns" which reduce the rate of interest for part or all of the loan term at the expense of one or more of the parties to the contract.

    ☐ D. TEXAS VETERANS' HOUSING ASSISTANCE PROGRAM LOAN:
        This contract is also subject to approval for Buyer of a Texas Veterans' Housing Assistance Program Loan (the Program Loan) in an amount of $_____ for a period of at least _____ years at the interest rate established by the Texas Veterans' Land Board at the time of closing.

    ☐ E. SELLER FINANCED: A promissory note from Buyer to Seller in the amount of $_____, bearing _____% interest per annum, and payable:
        ☐ 1. In one payment due _____after the date of the note with interest payable _____.
        ☐ 2. In installments of $_____ [ ] including interest [ ] plus interest beginning _____ after the date of the note and continuing at _____intervals thereafter for _____year(s) when the entire balance of the note shall be due and payable.
        ☐ 3. Interest only in _____installments for the first _____year(s) and thereafter in installments of $_____ [ ] including interest [ ] plus interest beginning _____after the date of the note and continuing at _____ intervals thereafter for _____year(s) when the entire balance of the note is due and payable.
        ☐ 4. This contract is subject to Buyer furnishing Seller evidence of good credit within _____days from the effective date of this contract. If notice of disapproval of Buyer's credit is not given within five (5) days thereafter, Seller shall be deemed to have approved Buyer's credit. Buyer hereby authorizes Buyer's credit report to be furnished to Seller.
        Any Seller financed note may be prepaid in whole or in part at any time without penalty. The lien securing payment of such note will be inferior to any lien securing any loan assumed or given in connection with third party financing. If an Owner's Policy of Title Insurance is furnished, Buyer shall furnish Seller with a Mortgagee's Title Policy.

    Buyer shall apply for all third party financing or noteholder's approval of Buyer for assumption and waiver of the right to accelerate the note within _____ days from the effective date of this contract and shall make every reasonable effort to obtain the same. Such financing or assumption shall have been approved when Buyer has satisfied all of lender's financial conditions, e.g., sale of other property, requirement of co-signer or financial verifications. If such financing or noteholder's approval and waiver is not obtained within _____days from the effective date hereof, this contract shall terminate and the Earnest Money shall be refunded to Buyer.

5. EARNEST MONEY: $_____ is herewith tendered by Buyer and is to be deposited as Earnest Money with _____, at _____(Address), as Escrow Agent, upon execution of the contract by both parties. ☐ Additional Earnest Money of $_____ shall be deposited by Buyer with

001

TREC NO. 20-0

Figure 19.1: (continued)

One To Four Family Residential Earnest Money Contract — Page Two

02-08-85

·the Escrow Agent on or before _____, 19____.

6. TITLE: Seller shall furnish to Buyer at Seller's expense either:

☐ A.   Owner's Policy of Title Insurance (the Title Policy) issued by _____
in the amount of the Sales Price and dated at or after closing: OR

☐ B.   Abstracts of Title certified by an abstract company (1) from the sovereignty to the effective date of this contract (Complete Abstract) and (2) supplemented to the Closing Date (Supplemental Abstract).

NOTICE TO SELLER AND BUYER: AS REQUIRED BY LAW, Broker advises Buyer that Buyer should have an Abstract covering the Property examined by an attorney of Buyer's selection, or Buyer should be furnished with or obtain a Title Policy. If a Title Policy is to be obtained, Buyer should obtain a Commitment for Title Insurance (the Commitment) which should be examined by an attorney of Buyer's choice at or prior to closing. If the Property is situated in a Utility District, Section 50.301 Texas Water Code requires the Buyer to sign and acknowledge the statutory notice from Seller relating to the tax rate and bonded indebtedness of the District.

7. PROPERTY CONDITION: (Check A or B)

☐ A.   Buyer accepts the Property in its present condition, subject only to any lender required repairs and_____

☐ B.   Buyer requires inspections and repairs required by any lender and the Property Condition Addendum attached hereto.

On Seller's receipt of all loan approvals and inspection reports, Seller shall commence repairs and termite treatment required of Seller by the contract, any lender and the Property Condition Addendum. if any, and complete such repairs prior to closing. Seller's responsibility for the repairs, termite treatment and repairs to termite damage shall not exceed $_____. If Seller fails to complete such repairs, Buyer may do so and Seller shall be liable up to the amount specified and the same paid from the proceeds of the sale. If the repair costs will exceed the stated amount and Seller refuses to pay such excess, Buyer may (1) pay the additional cost or (2) accept the Property with the limited repairs unless such repairs are required by lender or (3) Buyer may terminate this contract and the Earnest Money shall be refunded to Buyer. Buyer shall make his election within three (3) days after Seller notifies Buyer of Seller's refusal to pay such excess. Failure of Buyer to make such election within the time provided shall be deemed to be Buyer's election to accept the Property with the limited repairs, and the sale shall be closed as scheduled; however, if lender required repairs prohibit Buyer's acceptance with the limited repairs, this contract shall terminate and Earnest Money shall be refunded to Buyer.

If the repair costs will exceed five (5) percent of the Sales Price of the Property and Seller agrees to pay the cost of such repairs, Buyer shall have the option of closing the sale with the completed repairs, or terminating the sale and the Earnest Money shall be refunded to Buyer. Buyer shall make this election within three (3) days after Seller notifies Buyer of Seller's willingness to pay the cost of such repairs that exceed five (5) percent of the Sales Price. Failure of Buyer to make such election within the time provided shall be deemed to be Buyer's election to close the sale with the completed repairs.

Broker(s) and sales associates have no responsibility or liability for inspections or repairs made pursuant to this contract.

8. BROKER'S FEE: _____, Listing Broker, and any Co-Broker represent Seller unless otherwise specified herein. Seller agrees to pay Listing Broker the fee specified by separate agreement between Listing Broker and Seller. Escrow Agent is authorized and directed to pay Listing Broker said fee from the sale proceeds.

9. CLOSING: The closing of the sale shall be on or before _____, 19____, or within seven (7) days after objections to title have been cured, whichever date is later (the Closing Date); however, if financing or assumption approval has been obtained pursuant to Paragraph 4, the Closing Date shall be extended daily up to fifteen (15) days if necessary to complete loan requirements. If either party fails to close this sale by the Closing Date, the non-defaulting party shall be entitled to exercise the remedies contained in Paragraph 16 immediately and without notice.

10. POSSESSION: The possession of the Property shall be delivered to Buyer on _____in its present or required improved condition, ordinary wear and tear excepted. Any possession by Buyer prior to or Seller after closing that is not authorized by the Buyer's Temporary Residential Lease or Seller's Temporary Residential Lease Forms promulgated by the Texas Real Estate Commission shall establish a landlord-tenant at sufferance relationship between the parties.

11. SPECIAL PROVISIONS: (Insert factual statements and business details applicable to this sale.)

12. SALES EXPENSES TO BE PAID IN CASH AT OR PRIOR TO CLOSING:

A.   Loan appraisal fees shall be paid by _____

B.   The total of the loan discount and any buydown fees shall not exceed $ _____of which Buyer shall pay the first $ _____ and Seller shall pay the remainder.

C.   Seller's Expenses: Prepayment penalties on any existing loans paid at closing, plus cost of releasing such loans and recording releases; tax statements; ½ of any escrow fee; preparation of deed; preparation and recording of any deed of trust to secure assumption; any Texas Veterans' Housing Assistance Program Participation Fee; other expenses stipulated to be paid by Seller under other provisions of this contract.

D.   Buyer's Expenses: Application, origination and commitment fees; private mortgage insurance premiums and any loan assumption fee; expenses incident to new loan(s) (e.g., preparation of note, deed of trust and other loan documents, survey, recording fees, copies of restrictions and easements, Mortgagee's Title Policies, credit reports, photos); ½ of any escrow fee; any required premiums for flood and hazard insurance; any required reserve deposits for insurance premiums, ad valorem taxes and special governmental assessments; interest on all monthly installment payment notes from date of disbursements to one (1) month prior to dates of first monthly payments; expenses stipulated to be paid by Buyer under other provisions of this contract and any customary Texas Veterans' Housing Assistance Program Loan costs for Buyer.

E.   If any sales expenses exceed the maximum amount herein stipulated to be paid by either party, either party may terminate this contract unless the other party agrees to pay such excess.

13. PRORATIONS: Taxes, flood and hazard insurance (at Buyer's option), rents, maintenance fees, interest on any assumed loan and any prepaid unearned mortgage insurance premium which has not been financed as part of any assumed loan and which is refundable in whole or in part at a later date shall be prorated through the Closing Date. If Buyer elects to continue Seller's insurance policy, it shall be transferred at closing.

14. TITLE APPROVAL:

A.   If abstract is furnished, Seller shall deliver Complete Abstract to Buyer within twenty (20) days from the effective date hereof. Buyer shall have twenty (20) days from date of receipt of Complete Abstract to deliver a copy of the examining attorney's title opinion to Seller, stating any objections to title, and only objections so stated shall be considered.

B.   If Title Policy is furnished, the Title Policy shall guarantee Buyer's title to be good and indefeasible subject only to (1) restrictive covenants affecting the Property (2) any discrepancies, conflicts or shortages in area or boundary lines, or any encroachments, or any overlapping of improvements (3) taxes for the current and subsequent years and subsequent assessments for prior years due to a change in land usage or ownership (4) existing building and zoning ordinances (5) rights of parties in possession (6) liens created or assumed as security for the sale consideration (7) utility easements common to the platted subdivision of which this Property is a part and (8) reservations or other exceptions permitted by the terms of this contract. Exceptions permitted in the Deed and zoning ordinances shall not be valid objections to title. If the Title Policy will be subject to exceptions other than those recited above in sub-paragraphs (1) through (7) inclusive, Seller shall deliver to Buyer the Commitment and legible copies of any documents creating such exceptions that are not recited in sub-paragraphs (1) through (7) above at least five (5) days prior to closing. If Buyer has objection to any such previously undisclosed exceptions, Buyer shall have five (5) days after receipt of such Commitment and copies to make written objections to Seller. If no Title Commitment is provided to Buyer at or prior to closing, it will be conclusively presumed that Seller represented at closing that the Title Policy would not be subject to exceptions other than those recited above in sub-paragraphs (1) through (7).

C.   In either instance if title objections are raised, Seller shall have fifteen (15) days from the date such objections are disclosed to cure the same, and the Closing Date shall be extended accordingly. If the objections are not satisfied by the extended closing date, this contract shall terminate and the Earnest Money shall be refunded to Buyer, unless Buyer elects to waive the unsatisfied objections and complete the purchase.

D.   Seller shall furnish tax statements showing no delinquent taxes, a Supplemental Abstract when applicable, showing no additional title exceptions and a General

Figure 19.1: (continued)

One To Four Family Residential Earnest Money Contract concerning ———————————————— Page Three 02-08-85
(Address of Property)

Warranty Deed conveying title subject only to liens securing payment of debt created or assumed as part of the consideration, taxes for the current year, restrictive covenants and utility easements common to the platted subdivision of which the Property is a part and reservations and conditions permitted by this contract or otherwise acceptable to Buyer. Each note shall be secured by vendor's and deed of trust liens. A vendor's lien and deed of trust to secure any assumption shall be required, which shall automatically be released on execution and delivery of a release by noteholder. If Seller is released from liability on any assumed note, the vendor's lien and deed of trust to secure assumption shall not be required. In case of dispute as to the form of the Deed, note(s), deed of trust or deed of trust to secure assumption, forms prepared by the State Bar of Texas shall be used.

15. CASUALTY LOSS: If any part of Property is damaged or destroyed by fire or other casualty loss, Seller shall restore the same to its previous condition as soon as reasonably possible, but in any event by Closing Date. If Seller is unable to do so without fault, Buyer may terminate this contract and the Earnest Money shall be refunded to Buyer.

16. DEFAULT: If Buyer fails to comply herewith, Seller may either (a) enforce specific performance and seek such other relief as may be provided by law or (b) terminate this contract and receive the Earnest Money as liquidated damages. If Seller is unable without fault, within the time herein required, to (a) make any non-casualty repairs or (b) deliver the Commitment or (c) deliver the Complete Abstract, Buyer may either terminate this contract and receive the Earnest Money as the sole remedy or extend the time for performance up to fifteen (15) days and the Closing Date shall be extended pursuant to other provisions of this contract. If Seller fails to comply herewith for any other reason, Buyer may either (a) enforce specific performance hereof and seek such other relief as may be provided by law or (b) terminate this contract and receive the Earnest Money, thereby releasing Seller from this contract.

17. ATTORNEY'S FEES: Any signatory to this contract, Broker or Escrow Agent who is the prevailing party in any legal proceeding brought under or with relation to this contract or transaction shall be additionally entitled to recover court costs and reasonable attorney fees from the non-prevailing party.

18. ESCROW: The Earnest Money is deposited with Escrow Agent with the understanding that Escrow Agent (a) is not a party to this contract and does not assume or have any liability for performance or non-performance of any signatory (b) has the right to require from all signatories a written release of liability of the Escrow Agent which authorizes the disbursement of the Earnest Money (c) is not liable for interest or other charge on the funds held and (d) is not liable for any losses of escrow funds caused by the failure of any banking institution in which such funds have been deposited, unless such banking institution is acting as Escrow Agent. If any signatory unreasonably fails to deliver promptly the documents described in (b) above, then such signatory shall be liable to the other signatories as provided in Paragraph 17. At closing, the Earnest Money shall be applied first to any cash down payment required, then to Buyer's closing costs and any excess refunded to Buyer. Any refund or payment of the Earnest Money under this contract shall be reduced by the amount of any actual expenses incurred on behalf of the party receiving the Earnest Money, and Escrow Agent will pay the same to the creditors entitled thereto.

19. REPRESENTATIONS: Seller represents that as of the Closing Date (a) there will be no unrecorded liens, assessments or Uniform Commercial Code Security Interests against any of the Property which will not be satisfied out of the Sales Price, unless securing payment of any loans assumed by Buyer and (b) assumed loan(s) will be without default. If any representation in this contract is untrue on the Closing Date, this contract may be terminated by Buyer and the Earnest Money shall be refunded to Buyer. All representations contained in this contract shall survive closing.

20. AGREEMENT OF PARTIES: This contract contains the entire agreement of the parties and cannot be changed except by their written agreement. Texas Real Estate Commission promulgated addenda which are a part of this contract are (list): ————————————————————————————————

21. NOTICES: All notices shall be in writing and effective when delivered at the addresses shown below.

22. CONSULT YOUR ATTORNEY: The Broker cannot give you legal advice. This is intended to be a legally binding contract. READ IT CAREFULLY. Federal law may impose certain duties upon Brokers or Signatories to this contract when any of the signatories is a foreign party, or when any of the signatories receives certain amounts of U.S. currency in connection with a real estate closing. If you do not understand the effect of any part of this contract, consult your attorney BEFORE signing.

SELLER'S ATTORNEY: ———————————————   BUYER'S ATTORNEY: ———————————————

EXECUTED in multiple originals effective the ———— day of ————, 19—— (BROKER: **FILL IN THE DATE OF FINAL ACCEPTANCE.**)

Buyer ————————————————   Seller ————————————————

Buyer ————————————————   Seller ————————————————

Buyer's Address ———————— Phone No. ————   Seller's Address ———————— Phone No. ————

AGREEMENT BETWEEN BROKERS

Listing Broker agrees to pay ————————————————————————————————, Co-Broker, a fee of ———————— of the total sales price when the Broker's fee described in Paragraph 8 is received. Escrow Agent is authorized and directed to pay Co-Broker from Listing Broker's fee at closing.

Co-Broker ———————— License No. ————   Listing Broker ———————— License No. ————
By: ————————   By: ————————

Co-Broker's Address ———————— Phone No. ————   Listing Broker's Address ———————— Phone No. ————

EARNEST MONEY RECEIPT

Receipt of $———————— Earnest Money is acknowledged in the form of ————————————————

Escrow Agent ————————————————   By ————————

Date ———————— , 19 ————

The form of this contract has been approved by the Texas Real Estate Commission. Such approval relates to this contract form only. No representation is made as to the legal validity or adequacy of any provision in any specific transaction. It is not suitable for complex transactions. Extensive riders or additions are not to be used. (02-85) TREC NO. 20-0. This form replaces TREC NOS. 1-1, 4-0 and 6-0.

001

ference is the omission of the clause regarding the condition of the structures and repairs to them.

The fourth form entitled "Farm and Ranch Earnest Money Contract" (see Appendix C) was promulgated May 22, 1987, and its use is mandatory beginning December 1, 1987. It is suitable for use when the following conditions exist: (1) The land characteristics include the existence or creation of mineral, royalty or timber interests; or (2) the preponderance of the property's value is in the land rather than the improvements. Mineral and royalty interests were explained in Chapter 2. Easements and timber rights were discussed in Chapter 8.

The last two forms designed for use in the sale of new homes were also promulgated May 22, 1987, and their use is mandatory beginning December 1, 1987. These two forms will be discussed in more detail in Chapter 20.

In addition to the six promulgated earnest money contract forms there are two earnest money contract forms that have been developed and approved for use on a voluntary basis by the Texas Real Estate Commission:

1. Residential Condominium Earnest Money Contract (Resale) All Cash, Assumption, Third Party Conventional or Seller Financing. (This form is included in Appendix C.)
2. Residential Condominium Earnest Money Contract (Resale) FHA or VA Financing

In addition, the Texas Real Estate Commission has promulgated the following contract addenda forms that can be used in conjunction with the above earnest money contracts as appropriate. These forms are entitled:

1. Property Condition Addendum
2. Addendum for Sale of Other Property by Buyer
3. Addendum for Second or "Back-Up" Contract
4. Seller Financing Addendum
5. Financing Conditions Addendum
6. VA Release of Liability/Restoration of Entitlement
7. New Home Insulation Addendum

These seven forms are reproduced in this chapter and preceded by a brief discussion of their use.

In addition to the seven addenda forms promulgated by TREC there are two forms approved for use by TREC. They are:

1. Addendum for Property Located Seaward of the Gulf Intracoastal Waterway
2. Condominium Resale Certificate. (This form is reproduced in Appendix C.)

Finally, the Texas Real Estate Commission has promulgated two lease forms to be used when possession of the property will be transferred at any time other than the time of closing. As previously mentioned, the parties may agree to transfer possession of the property either before closing, in which case the buyer is "renting" the property, or after closing, in which case the seller is "renting" the property. These two lease forms are included in Appendix C.

STANDARD CONTRACT PROVISIONS

The earnest money contract forms promulgated by the Texas Real Estate Commission are so widely used that they are a good model for discussing specific contract provisions. In this section the earnest money contract entitled "One To Four Family Residential Earnest Money Contract (Resale) All Cash, Assumption, Third Party Conventional Or Owner Financed" will be reviewed paragraph by paragraph. Many of the clauses used in this contract are also used in the other contract forms, however, there are differences, as pointed out earlier. Therefore, those forms should be reviewed carefully by the broker prior to their use.

Paragraph 1: Parties

---

1. PARTIES: _____ (Seller) agrees to sell and convey to _____ (Buyer) and Buyer agrees to buy from Seller the property described below.

This paragraph fulfills the Statute of Frauds requirement that the seller and buyer be identified. As mentioned earlier in this chapter, it is advisable to use the correct names of the buyer and seller. In checking the seller's name, the broker should read the deed by which the seller acquired the property. This will help the broker determine if there are any outstanding interests in the property that should be resolved prior to closing, as well as provide the broker with the name to be inserted in the earnest money contract.

Paragraph 2: Property

---

2. PROPERTY: Lot _____, Block _____, _____ Addition, City of _____, _____, County, Texas, known as _____ (Address); or as described on attached exhibit, together with the following items, if any: curtains and rods, draperies and rods, valances, blinds, window shades, screens, shutters, awnings, wall-to-wall carpeting, mirrors fixed in place, ceiling fans, attic fans, mail boxes, television antennas, permanently installed heating and air conditioning units and equipment, built-in security and fire detection equipment, lighting and plumbing fixtures, water softener, trash compactor, garage door openers with controls, shrubbery and all other property owned by Seller and attached to the above described real property. All property sold by this contract is called the "Property."

As required by the Statute of Frauds, the standard form provides a place for insertion of the legal description of the property. It is important to remember that even in incorporated areas there may be a need for a metes-and-bounds description. For example, a tract of land containing a portion of an adjoining lot may be more accurately described by metes and bounds if such a description is available. Because it is not uncommon for land to be surveyed prior to closing, the metes-and-bounds description may be readily available. This description could be copied and attached as an exhibit to the contract.

This paragraph also enumerates several items of personal property and fixtures that are included in the sale. Such things as curtains, ceiling fans, garage door openers with controls, and water softeners are listed. If this form is being used, the seller should carefully review this list and determine if there are any items listed that he or she intended not to sell. If there are, then these items should be crossed out and the deletion initialed by both parties.

On the other hand, if the buyer wants to purchase items of personal property not included in the list in paragraph 2, these items will have to be enumerated separately in the space provided in paragraph 11 or attached as an exhibit to the contract. For example, if the property has a swimming pool, the buyer may want all of the pool equipment, such as the pool sweep, brooms and vacuums, included in the sale. Since these are not physically attached to the property and not specifically listed, the buyer will have to add these items to the contract by listing them.

Paragraph 3: Contract Sales Price

---

3. CONTRACT SALES PRICE:
   A. Cash payable at closing. . . . .$_____
   B. Sum of all financing described in Paragraph 4 below . . . .$_____
   C. Sales Price (Sum of A and B) . . . .$_____

This paragraph states the consideration being given in exchange for the real estate. As drafted, the provision lists the cash down payment separate from the financed portion of the sales price. The total sales price is stated on line C of this paragraph. The total sales price is fixed. The down payment and the financed portion are approximations in the case of an assumption.

For example, the buyer and seller have agreed to a total sales price of $68,000 with the buyer agreeing to assume the existing mortgage, which has an estimated principal balance due of $55,000. Line C would be completed by inserting the figure $68,000, and line B would contain the amount $55,000. Consequently, line A would be the difference between lines C and B, which is $13,000. At closing the actual balance due on the mortgage is $55,249. The cash down payment is reduced by $249 to $12,751 so that the total sales price remains fixed at $68,000. This is discussed in more detail under paragraph 4.

Paragraph 4: Financing

---

4. FINANCING: (Check applicable boxes below)
   ☐ A. ALL CASH: This is an all cash sale; no financing is involved.
   ☐ B. ASSUMPTION:
        (1) Buyer's assumption of the unpaid principal balance of a first lien prom-
        issory note payable to _____
        in present monthly installments of $_____, including principal,
        interest and any reserve deposits, with Buyer's first installment payment
        being payable on the first installment payment date after closing, the
        assumed principal balance of which at closing will be $_____.
        (2) Buyer's assumption of the unpaid principal balance of a second lien
        promissory note payable to _____
        in present monthly installments of $_____, including principal,
        interest and any reserve deposits, with Buyer's first installment payment
        being payable on the first installment payment date after closing, the
        assumed principal balance of which at closing will be $_____.
    Buyer's assumption of an existing note includes all obligations imposed by the deed of trust securing the note.

    If the total principal balance of all assumed loans varies in an amount greater than $350.00 at closing either party may terminate this contract and the Earnest Money shall be refunded to Buyer. If the noteholder on assumption (a) requires Buyer to pay an assumption fee in excess of $_____ in B(1) above or $_____ in B(2) above and Seller declines to pay such excess or (b) raises the existing interest rate above _____% in B(1) above or _____% in B(2) above, Buyer may terminate this contract and the Earnest Money shall be refunded to Buyer. The cash payable at closing shall be adjusted by the amount of any variance in the loan balance(s) shown above.
    NOTICE TO BUYER: Monthly payments, interest rates or other terms of some loans may be adjusted after closing. Before signing the contract, examine the notes and deeds of trust to determine the possibility of future adjustments.
   ☐ C. THIRD PARTY FINANCED:
       ☐ 1. A third party first lien note of $_____, due in full in _____ year(s),
          payable in initial monthly payments of principal and interest not exceed-
          ing $_____ for the first _____ year(s) of the loan.
       ☐ 2. A third party second lien note of $_____, due in full in _____ year(s),
          payable in initial monthly payments of principal and interest not exceed-
          ing $_____ for the first _____ year(s) of the loan.
    NOTICE TO PARTIES: Before signing this contract Buyer is advised to determine the financing options from lenders. Certain loans have variable rates of interest, some have monthly payments which may not be sufficient to pay the accruing interest, and some have interest rate "buydowns" which reduce the

rate of interest for part or all of the loan term at the expense of one or more of the parties to the contract.

☐ D. TEXAS VETERANS' HOUSING ASSISTANCE PROGRAM LOAN: This contract is also subject to approval for Buyer of a Texas Veterans' Housing Assistance Program Loan (the Program Loan) in an amount of $_____ for a period of at least _____ years at the interest rate established by the Texas Veterans' Land Board at the time of closing.

☐ E. SELLER FINANCED: A promissory note from Buyer to Seller in the amount of $_____, bearing _____% interest per annum, and payable:

   ☐ 1. In one payment due _____ after the date of the note with interest payable _____.

   ☐ 2. In installments of $_____ [   ] including interest [   ] plus interest beginning _____ after the date of the note and continuing at _____ intervals thereafter for _____ year(s) when the entire balance of the note shall be due and payable.

   ☐ 3. Interest only in _____ installments for the first _____ year(s) and thereafter in installments of $_____ [   ] including interest [   ] plus interest beginning _____ after the date of the note and continuing at _____ intervals thereafter for _____ year(s) when the entire balance of the note is due and payable.

   ☐ 4. This contract is subject to Buyer furnishing Seller evidence of good credit within _____ days from the effective date of this contract. If notice of disapproval of Buyer's credit is not given within five (5) days thereafter, Seller shall be deemed to have approved Buyer's credit. Buyer hereby authorizes Buyer's credit report to be furnished to Seller.

   Any Seller financed note may be prepaid in whole or in part at any time without penalty. The lien securing payment of such note will be inferior to any lien securing any loan assumed or given in connection with third party financing. If an Owner's Policy of Title Insurance is furnished, Buyer shall furnish Seller with a Mortgagee's Title Policy.

Buyer shall apply for all third party financing or noteholder's approval of Buyer for assumption and waiver of the right to accelerate the note within _____ days from the effective date of this contract and shall make every reasonable effort to obtain the same. Such financing or assumption shall have been approved when Buyer has satisfied all of lender's financial conditions, e.g., sale of other property, requirement of cosigner or financial verifications. If such financing or noteholder's approval and waiver is not obtained within _____ days from the effective date hereof, this contract shall terminate and the Earnest Money shall be refunded to Buyer.

This paragraph details the parties' agreement concerning the method of payment. There are five options provided in this paragraph: (1) all cash, (2) assumption, (3) third-party financing, (4) Texas Veterans Housing Assistance Program Loan and (5) seller financing. The buyer and seller should select the appropriate option or options. The boxes should be checked as needed and that portion of the paragraph completed in detail as suggested. It is possible for a buyer to combine options. For example, a buyer may be assuming an outstanding loan and financing a portion with another lending institution.

In that case the box adjacent to subparagraphs B and C would be checked. Subparagraph B is then completed by identifying the current lender, the current monthly payment and the principal balance at closing. Although it is sometimes difficult to determine accurately the principal balance at closing, the parties should be able to make a close approximation of that balance. Making a close estimate of this amount is important because this subparagraph allows for only a margin of error of plus or minus $350. This means that, if the principal balance exceeds the approximation by more than $350, the buyer or seller could elect to terminate the contract. This subparagraph also establishes an upper limit on the buyer's obligation concerning assumption fees and increases by the lender in the rate of interest on the note. Careful consideration should be given before inserting these figures.

The buyer in our example was also going to obtain a loan from another lender; therefore, subparagraph C is checked. This subparagraph establishes limits on the amount to be borrowed, the length of time that the buyer will have to repay the debt and the monthly payment. The interest rate is not mentioned specifically; however, it is implicit in the monthly payment, which includes both principal and interest.

If the seller is financing any portion of the purchase price, then subparagraph E should be checked. In seller financing it is important that the parties reach an understanding at this point regarding the terms of the loan. Although this subparagraph does not address all of the issues, it does require the parties to reach an agreement regarding the amount to be financed, the interest rate and the method by which the loan will be repaid. However, it does not discuss whether the loan can be assumed or whether the note can be called due if the property is transferred. For additional terms, the Seller Financing Addendum must be used whenever possible. If the addendum is still inadequate, then the parties should write the other provisions and attach them to the contract.

Finally, paragraph 4 requires the buyer to apply for the loan within a certain time period and to obtain approval of the loan within another established time frame. In setting these time periods the buyer and seller should be aware of what is reasonable in the mortgage market serving the area in which the real estate is located.

This paragraph does not address FHA or VA financing arrangements. If the buyer is choosing either of these financing options, then the standard form entitled "Residential Earnest Money Contract (Resale) FHA Insured or VA Guaranteed Financing" should be used.

Paragraph 5: Earnest Money

---

5. EARNEST MONEY: $_____ is herewith tendered by Buyer and is to be deposited as Earnest Money with _____, at _____(Address), as Escrow Agent, upon execution of the contract by both parties. ☐ Additional Earnest Money of

$\underline{\hspace{5cm}}$ shall be deposited by Buyer with the Escrow Agent on or before $\underline{\hspace{4cm}}$, 19$\underline{\hspace{1cm}}$.

This paragraph sets out the amount of earnest money to be deposited by the buyer and with whom that deposit shall be made. It is common practice in Texas for a title company to serve as escrow agent. If a title company is chosen, it is advisable to include the address of the title company because title companies frequently have several branch offices.

Paragraph 6: Title

6. TITLE: Seller shall furnish to Buyer at Seller's expense either:
   ☐ A.   Owner's Policy of Title Insurance (the Title Policy) issued by $\underline{\hspace{3cm}}$
          in the amount of the Sales Price and dated at or after closing; OR
   ☐ B.   Abstracts of Title certified by an abstract company (1) from the sovereignty to
          the effective date of this contract (Complete Abstract) and (2) supplemented
          to the Closing Date (Supplemental Abstract).
   NOTICE TO SELLER AND BUYER: AS REQUIRED BY LAW, Broker advises Buyer
   that Buyer should have an Abstract covering the Property examined by an attorney of
   Buyer's selection, or Buyer should be furnished with or obtain a Title Policy. If a Title
   Policy is to be obtained, Buyer should obtain a Commitment for Title Insurance (the
   Commitment) which should be examined by an attorney of Buyer's choice at or prior
   to closing. If the Property is situated in a Utility District, Section 50.301 Texas Water
   Code requires the Buyer to sign and acknowledge the statutory notice from Seller re-
   lating to the tax rate and bonded indebtedness of the District.

This paragraph requires the seller to purchase for the buyer either a policy of title insurance or an abstract of title. Title insurance and abstracts of title were discussed in Chapter 12. One of the boxes should be checked. In residential sales it is more common for the seller to purchase an owner's policy of title insurance than it is for the seller to provide an abstract.

This paragraph also includes the statutory notice concerning title insurance that brokers are required to give buyers and the notice that sellers are required to give to buyers concerning any water district.

Paragraph 7: Property Condition

7. PROPERTY CONDITION: (Check A or B)
   ☐ A.   Buyer accepts the Property in its present condition, subject only to any
          lender required repairs and $\underline{\hspace{3cm}}$
          $\underline{\hspace{8cm}}$
          $\underline{\hspace{8cm}}$

☐ B.   Buyer requires inspections and repairs required by any lender and the Property Condition Addendum attached hereto.

On Seller's receipt of all loan approvals and inspection reports, Seller shall commence repairs and termite treatment required of Seller by the contract, any lender and the Property Condition Addendum, if any, and complete such repairs prior to closing. Seller's responsibility for the repairs, termite treatment and repairs to termite damage shall not exceed $_____. If Seller fails to complete such repairs, Buyer may do so and Seller shall be liable up to the amount specified and the same paid from the proceeds of the sale. If the repair costs will exceed the stated amount and Seller refuses to pay such excess, Buyer may (1) pay the additional cost or (2) accept the Property with the limited repairs unless such repairs are required by lender or (3) Buyer may terminate this contract and the Earnest Money shall be refunded to Buyer. Buyer shall make his election within three (3) days after Seller notifies Buyer of Seller's refusal to pay such excess. Failure of Buyer to make such election within the time provided shall be deemed to be Buyer's election to accept the Property with the limited repairs, and the sale shall be closed as scheduled; however, if lender required repairs prohibit Buyer's acceptance with the limited repairs, this contract shall terminate and Earnest Money shall be refunded to Buyer.

If the repair costs exceed five (5) percent of the Sales Price of the Property and Seller agrees to pay the cost of such repairs, Buyer shall have the option of closing the sale with the completed repairs, or terminating the sale and the Earnest Money shall be refunded to Buyer. Buyer shall make this Selection within three (3) days after Seller notifies Buyer of Seller's willingness to pay the cost of such repairs that exceed five (5) percent of the Sales Price. Failure of Buyer to make such election within the time provided shall be deemed to be Buyer's election to close the sale with the completed repairs.

Broker(s) and sales associates have no responsibility or liability for inspections or repairs made pursuant to this contract.

The condition of the property is always an area that is ripe for dispute between buyer and seller. This paragraph attempts to address the issue of repairs before they become a problem. There are two options provided in this paragraph. Subparagraph A should be checked if the buyer is agreeing to purchase the property in its present condition without any inspections, with only those repairs listed specifically in this subparagraph or required by the lender. For example, the buyer may be willing to accept the property as is, provided a new roof is installed. This would be the appropriate place to insert a requirement that the seller must replace the roof. This subparagraph also ties back into paragraph 4 concerning financing. If the lender requires certain repairs as a condition for making the loan, then these repairs would have to be made. For example, the lender may require repair of the foundation as a condition of the loan. If this repair is not performed, then the buyer would be excused from performing. Other than repairs required by the lender and any repair listed specifically, the buyer agrees to accept the property in its present condition.

Subparagraph B should be checked if the buyer wants to have the property inspected prior to closing. The types of inspections should be enumerated in the Property Condition Addendum and the addendum attached to this contract. This form is discussed in more detail later in this chapter; however, the types of inspections the buyer may want include termite, structural, equipment and mechanical, plumbing and electrical. Given that this provision is fraught with potential problems for the seller as well as the buyer, the paragraph requires the parties to discuss who will be responsible for making those repairs and when the buyer can rightfully reject the property because the repairs are needed. The provision does this in two ways. First, it establishes a limit on how much the seller will be required to spend in remedying any defects. Second, it provides that, if repairs exceed five percent of the sales price, the buyer can elect to terminate the contract even if the seller is willing to make the needed repairs.

For example, assume the total sales price of the house is $100,000. After all inspections are made, the total cost of repairs is $3,400, but the seller had agreed to pay only $2,500 to make repairs. The seller is willing to pay $2,500 to make repairs but refuses to spend any more than that amount. The buyer has three options at this point: (1) accept the property with the limited repairs, (2) pay for the additional repairs or (3) terminate the contract and recover the earnest money. The paragraph does require the buyer to elect his or her option within three days after the seller notifies the buyer that the seller will pay only the $2,500. Failure of the buyer to make his or her choice within that time period is construed as the buyer's willingness to take the property with the limited repairs unless the repairs are required by the lender.

It should be noted that, if the seller is willing to make the $3,400 worth of repairs, the buyer must accept the property and close the transaction. However, a buyer may begin to question the wisdom of buying this house if extensive and unexpected repairs are needed. The buyer may not want to buy the house even if the seller is willing to pay for all the needed repairs. For that reason this paragraph establishes that, if the total cost of repairs is greater than five percent of the sales price, the buyer can terminate the contract. For example, if the total cost of repairs was $7,500, the buyer would not be required to accept the property even if the seller voluntarily made all the repairs, since the total repairs cost in excess of five percent of $100,000, or $5,000.

Paragraph 8: Broker's Fee

---

8. BROKER'S FEE: _____, Listing Broker, and any Co-Broker represent Seller unless otherwise specified herein. Seller agrees to pay Listing Broker the fee specified by separate agreement between Listing Broker and Seller. Escrow Agent is authorized and directed to pay Listing Broker said fee from the sale proceeds.

This provision identifies the listing broker by name and states that any co-broker also represents the seller. It also authorizes the escrow agent to pay the listing broker's fee from the sale proceeds. Notice that this paragraph does not state the amount of the fee but instead references the separate listing agreement that does stipulate the amount of the fee. The result is that the broker cannot rely upon the earnest money contract to support his or her claim for a commission. The right to a commission must have been established in a separate agreement.

Paragraph 9: Closing

9. CLOSING: The closing of the sale shall be on or before _____ _____, 19____, or within seven (7) days after objections to title have been cured, whichever date is later (the Closing Date); however, if financing or assumption approval has been obtained pursuant to Paragraph 4, the Closing Date shall be extended daily up to fifteen (15) days if necessary to complete loan requirements. If either party fails to close this sale by the Closing Date, the non-defaulting party shall be entitled to exercise the remedies contained in Paragraph 16 immediately and without notice.

This provision establishes the date by which the seller and the buyer should be ready to complete the transfer of title and payment of the consideration. The closing date should allow a reasonable amount of time for completion of all the tasks the buyer and the seller must perform prior to closing. Closing and settlement procedures are discussed in more detail in Chapter 23. The clause does allow for an automatic extension of seven days to cure title defects and 15 days to complete loan requirements, provided the loan has been approved. Failure to close by the stated date or within one of the automatic extension periods is considered a default.

Paragraph 10: Possession

10. POSSESSION: The possession of the Property shall be delivered to Buyer on _____ in its present or required improved condition, ordinary wear and tear excepted. Any possession by Buyer prior to or Seller after closing that is not authorized by the Buyer's Temporary Residential Lease or Seller's Temporary Residential Lease Forms promulgated by the Texas Real Estate Commission shall establish a landlord-tenant at sufferance relationship between the parties.

This paragraph is completed by filling in the date on which possession shall be transferred. The date can be the same as that set for closing or any other time agreed to by the parties. If possession is to be transferred either before or after closing, the parties should consider using one of the standard lease forms promulgated by the Texas Real Estate Commission. If no agreement is reached concerning lease terms, a tenancy at sufferance is created. Tenancies at sufferance are explained in Chapter 24.

Paragraph 11: Special Provisions

11. SPECIAL PROVISIONS : (Insert factual statements and business details applicable to this sale.)

If a standard contract addenda form is not suitable for addressing special considerations, and the special provision is short enough that it can be inserted in this space, then it should be written here. If the space allowed is inadequate, the parties should write their agreement on a separate sheet of paper and attach it to the contract. It is a good idea to reference those exhibits here.

Paragraph 12: Sales Expenses to Be Paid in Cash at or Prior to Closing

12. SALES EXPENSES TO BE PAID IN CASH AT OR PRIOR TO CLOSING:
    A. Loan appraisal fees shall be paid by _____.
    B. The total of the loan discount and any buydown fees shall not exceed $_____ of which Buyer shall pay the first $_____ and Seller shall pay the remainder.
    C. Seller's Expenses: Prepayment penalties on any existing loans paid at closing, plus cost of releasing such loans and recording releases; tax statements; ½ of any escrow fee; preparation of deed; preparation and recording of any deed of trust to secure assumption; any Texas Veterans' Housing Assistance Program Participation Fee; other expenses stipulated to be paid by Seller under other provisions of this contract.
    D. Buyer's Expenses: Application, origination and commitment fees; private mortgage insurance premiums and any loan assumption fee; expenses incident to new loan(s) (e.g., preparation of any note, deed of trust and other loan documents, survey, recording fees, copies of restrictions and easements, Mortgagee's Title Policies, credit reports, photos); ½ of any escrow fee; any required premiums for flood and hazard insurance; any required reserve deposits for insurance premiums, ad valorem taxes and special governmental assessments; interest on all monthly installment payment notes from date of disbursements to one (1) month prior to dates of first monthly payments; expenses stipulated to be paid by Buyer

under other provisions of this contract and any customary Texas Veterans' Housing Assistance Program Loan costs for Buyer.

E. If any sales expenses exceed the maximum amount herein stipulated to be paid by either party, either party may terminate this contract unless the other party agrees to pay such excess.

There are several expenses associated with the purchase of real estate in addition to the purchase price, and they can amount to several thousands of dollars. Two benefits are gained by including this clause in the earnest money contract. First, it calls the buyer's and seller's attention to the presence of these expenses and thereby eliminates some of the "surprise" later on. Second, it establishes who is responsible for the expenses. For example, the seller is required to pay for the tax statements and half of the escrow fee, among other fees. The buyer is required to pay for the loan application fee and half of the escrow fee, among others.

One of the bigger expenses in financing the purchase of real estate is the loan discount fees, often referred to as *points*. The lender usually quotes the loan discount or buydown fee in terms of points. One point is one percent of the amount borrowed. This provision establishes a dollar limit on the amount of discount and buydown fees and states that the buyer will pay a certain amount toward these fees. Any difference between the total and the buyer's share will be paid by the seller.

For example, assume the buyer is planning to borrow $70,000. At the time lenders are charging between two and four points for home mortgages. The buyer and seller agree that the maximum number of points they are willing to pay is three. To convert three points to a dollar amount, take three percent of $70,000, which is $2,100. This figure is inserted in the first blank in subparagraph B. The buyer and the seller also agree that the buyer will be responsible for $1,400 and the seller will pay anything over $1,400 and up to $2,100. The second blank should be completed by inserting $1,400. If the buyer is able to obtain a loan by paying only two points, or $1,400, then the seller will not incur any of the expense associated with the loan discount fee. In setting the dollar amount the parties must be familiar with local lending requirements at the time and set a reasonable amount given the market conditions.

Paragraph 13: Prorations

---

13. PRORATIONS: Taxes, flood and hazard insurance (at Buyer's option), rents, maintenance fees, interest on any assumed loan and any prepaid unearned mortgage insurance premium which has not been financed as part of any assumed loan and which is refundable in whole or in part at a later date shall be prorated through the

Closing Date. If Buyer elects to continue Seller's insurance policy, it shall be transferred at closing.

Owners of real property are frequently required to pay certain expenses in advance. For example, hazard insurance is usually paid on a yearly basis in advance. When property is sold during the year for which the premium was paid, it is reasonable that the seller receive credit for the part of the premium that covers the period after the sale. Similarly, the owner pays other expenses at the end of a year to cover expenses incurred during that year. Real property taxes are an example of this type of expense. This proration provision states that these expenses will be divided between buyer and seller in proportion to the amount of time each owns the real property with which the expenses are associated. For example, assume that the closing occurs on March 31, 1987. The buyer owns the property for nine months during the year 1987, and the seller owned the property for three months during 1987. Since the seller has paid the insurance premium for the entire year, the buyer owes the seller $9/12$, or three-fourths of the premium. Similarly, since the buyer will pay the property taxes on December 31 for the entire year, the seller owes the buyer $3/12$, or one-fourth, of the total tax due.

Paragraph 14: Title Approval

14. TITLE APPROVAL.
    A. If abstract is furnished, Seller shall deliver Complete Abstract to Buyer within twenty (20) days from the effective date hereof. Buyer shall have twenty (20) days from date of receipt of Complete Abstract to deliver a copy of the examining attorney's title opinion to Seller, stating any objections to title, and only objections so stated shall be considered.
    B. If Title Policy is furnished, the Title Policy shall guarantee Buyer's title to be good and indefeasible subject only to (1) restrictive covenants affecting the Property (2) any discrepancies, conflicts or shortages in area or boundary lines, or any encroachments, or any overlapping of improvements (3) taxes for the current and subsequent years and subsequent assessments for prior years due to a change in land usage or ownership (4) existing building and zoning ordinances (5) rights of parties in possession (6) liens created or assumed as security for the sale consideration (7) utility easements common to the platted subdivision of which this Property is a part and (8) reservations or other exceptions permitted by the terms of this contract. Exceptions permitted in the Deed and zoning ordinances shall not be valid objections to title. If the Title Policy will be subject to exceptions other than those recited above in sub-paragraphs (1) through (7) inclusive, Seller shall deliver to Buyer the Commitment and legible copies of any documents creating such exceptions that are not recited in sub-paragraphs (1) through (7) above at least five (5) days prior to closing. If Buyer has objection to any such previously undisclosed exceptions, Buyer shall have five (5) days after receipt of such Commitment and copies to make written objections to Seller. If no Title Commitment is

provided to Buyer at or prior to closing, it will be conclusively presumed that Seller represented at closing that the Title Policy would not be subject to exceptions other than those recited above in subparagraphs (1) through (7).

C. In either instance if title objections are raised, Seller shall have fifteen (15) days from the date such objections are disclosed to cure the same, and the Closing Date shall be extended accordingly. If the objections are not satisfied by the extended closing date, this contract shall terminate and the Earnest Money shall be refunded to Buyer, unless Buyer elects to waive the unsatisfied objections and complete the purchase.

D. Seller shall furnish tax statements showing no delinquent taxes, a Supplemental Abstract when applicable, showing no additional title exceptions and a General Warranty Deed conveying title subject only to liens securing payment of debt created or assumed as part of the consideration, taxes for the current year, restrictive covenants and utility easements common to the platted subdivision of which the Property is a part and reservations and conditions permitted by this contract or otherwise acceptable to Buyer. Each note shall be secured by vendor's and deed of trust liens. A vendor's lien and deed of trust to secure any assumption shall be required, which shall automatically be released on execution and delivery of a release by noteholder. If Seller is released from liability on any assumed note, the vendor's lien and deed of trust to secure assumption shall not be required. In case of dispute as to the form of the Deed, note(s), deed of trust or deed of trust to secure assumption, forms prepared by the State Bar of Texas shall be used.

This provision addresses the quality of the title that the buyer is to receive from the seller. It refers back to paragraph 6. Subparagraph A requires the seller to deliver the abstract to the buyer within 20 days of the contract date and gives the buyer 20 days from that time to have it examined. Subparagraph A is applicable only if the seller agreed to furnish an abstract instead of a title insurance policy in paragraph 6.

The seller's furnishing a policy of title insurance is the more common method of assuring good title. If title insurance is being provided, subparagraph B applies. Subparagraph B enumerates the standard exceptions in Texas listed in the title insurance policy. It is important that the buyer understand what the standard policy excepts and that the seller is contemplating providing the buyer with only a standard owner's policy of title insurance.

Subparagraph C gives the seller 15 days to cure any title defect raised by the buyer. If these objections cannot be cured, then the buyer can terminate the contract and recover his or her earnest money.

Subparagraph D states that the seller shall convey title by a general warranty deed and that there will be no encumbrances against the title except those disclosed specifically to the buyer. However, the buyer is warned here that he or she must take the property subject to any utility easements, restrictive covenants and taxes for the current year.

Paragraph 15: Casualty Loss

---

15. CASUALTY LOSS: If any part of Property is damaged or destroyed by fire or other casualty loss, Seller shall restore the same to its previous condition as soon as reasonably possible, but in any event by Closing Date. If Seller is unable to do so without fault, Buyer may terminate this contract and the Earnest Money shall be refunded to Buyer.

Although it is unusual for the property to be damaged as a result of fire, windstorm, hail or vandalism prior to closing, it can happen. In that event the seller can restore the property to the condition it was in on the date of the earnest money contract, provided this can be accomplished prior to the closing date. However, if the seller cannot do so, the buyer has the option to terminate the contract. The buyer and seller are free to reach any other agreement should a casualty loss occur. If an agreement is reached, it should be drawn up as a formal written amendment to the contract.

Paragraph 16: Default

---

16. DEFAULT: If Buyer fails to comply herewith, Seller may either (a) enforce specific performance and seek such other relief as may be provided by law or (b) terminate this contract and receive the Earnest Money as liquidated damages. If Seller is unable without fault, within the time herein required, to (a) make any non-casualty repairs or (b) deliver the Commitment or (c) deliver the Complete Abstract, Buyer may either terminate this contract and receive the Earnest Money as the sole remedy or extend the time for performance up to fifteen (15) days and the Closing Date shall be extended pursuant to other provisions of this contract. If Seller fails to comply herewith for any other reason, Buyer may either (a) enforce specific performance hereof and seek such other relief as may be provided by law or (b) terminate this contract and receive the Earnest Money, thereby releasing Seller from this contract.

As explained in the previous chapter, a default occurs when one of the parties fails to perform his or her obligations as promised in the contract. Thus far we have examined 15 contractual provisions that impose duties on the two parties to the contract. For example, in paragraph 4 (financing) the buyer is obligated to apply for a loan within a certain time period. Assume that the time period is ten days. If the buyer fails to make a loan application within ten days, he or she is in default. Another example, would be the obligation imposed on the seller in paragraph 7 to make repairs up to a certain amount. Assume that that provision was completed by inserting the figure $1,200 and that the seller refuses to pay for such repairs. The seller in this situation is in default. When one of the parties defaults, what options are available to the nonbreaching party? In some of the provisions discussed previously, the clause explained the rights of the party if there is a default. For example, the repair provision states that, if the seller fails to make the required repairs, the buyer can make the repairs and deduct the cost from the purchase price.

Paragraph 16 covers the potentiality of default by either the buyer or the seller. It states that, if the buyer defaults, the seller has two options: (1) the seller can sue for specific performance or (2) terminate the contract and retain the earnest money.

The provision regarding the seller's default is more complex. If the seller defaults because he or she is unable to make the repairs required in paragraph 7 or because he or she is unable to deliver a title commitment, then the buyer's only remedy is to terminate the contract and recover the earnest money. However, if the seller defaults for any other reason, then the buyer has the same options as the seller: (1) to sue for specific performance or (2) to terminate the contract and recover the earnest money.

Although both the buyer and the seller have the remedy of retention of the earnest money, this can be as difficult a remedy to effectuate as the remedy of specific performance. Paragraph 18 discussed below, concerning the escrow agent, can make it difficult for the nonbreaching party to obtain the earnest money.

Paragraph 17: Attorney's Fees

---

17. ATTORNEY'S FEES: Any signatory to this contract, Broker or Escrow Agent who is the prevailing party in any legal proceeding brought under or with relation to this contract or transaction shall be additionally entitled to recover court costs and reasonable attorney fees from the non-prevailing party.

This provision provides that, if one of the parties to the contract incurs attorney fees and courts costs in asserting his or her rights under the contract, he or she will be entitled to recover those expenses from the losing party.

Paragraph 18: Escrow

---

18. ESCROW: The Earnest Money is deposited with Escrow Agent with the understanding that Escrow Agent (a) is not a party to this contract and does not assume or have

any liability for performance or non-performance of any signatory (b) has the right to require from all signatories a written release of liability of the Escrow Agent which authorizes the disbursement of the Earnest Money (c) is not liable for interest or other charge on the funds held and (d) is not liable for any losses of escrow funds caused by the failure of any banking institution in which such funds have been deposited, unless such banking institution is acting as Escrow Agent. If any signatory unreasonably fails to deliver promptly the documents described in (b) above, then such signatory shall be liable to the other signatories as provided in Paragraph 17. At closing, the Earnest Money shall be applied first to any cash down payment required, then to Buyer's closing costs and any excess refunded to Buyer. Any refund or payment of the Earnest Money under this contract shall be reduced by the amount of any actual expenses incurred on behalf of the party receiving the Earnest Money, and Escrow Agent will pay the same to the creditors entitled thereto.

If earnest money is being held in escrow, this clause establishes how and when the earnest money will be disbursed by the escrow agent. If the sale closes as planned by the parties, then the escrow agent applies the earnest money toward the down payment and the buyer's closing costs and refunds any excess. If there is a default and the sale does not close, the the escrow agent will not disburse the deposit until he or she has received a written release from both buyer and seller. If the defaulting party wrongfully refuses to sign a release, the nonbreaching party is forced to sue in court to recover the funds. Furthermore, it should be pointed out that the escrow agent is not required to pay interest on the earnest money even though he or she may have possession of it for several years while the litigation is pending.

Paragraph 19: Representations

19. REPRESENTATIONS: Seller represents that as of the Closing Date (a) there will be no unrecorded liens, assessments or Uniform Commercial Code Security interests against any of the Property which will not be satisfied out of the Sales Price, unless securing payment of any loans assumed by Buyer and (b) assumed loan(s) will be without default. If any representation in this contract is untrue on the Closing Date, this contract may be terminated by Buyer and the Earnest Money shall be refunded to Buyer. All representations contained in this contract shall survive closing.

This paragraph assures the buyer that there are no unrecorded liens, assessments, encumbrances or claims against the property that will not be taken care of by the seller at or before closing. If there are liens or claims that are not being assumed expressly by the buyer and have not been satisfied by the seller, the buyer can terminate the contract and recover his or her earnest money.

Paragraph 20: Agreement of Parties

20. AGREEMENT OF PARTIES: This contract contains the entire agreement of the parties and cannot be changed except by their written agreement. Texas Real Estate Commission promulgated addenda which are a part of this contract are (list): _____

This provision should alert buyer and seller to the requirements of the parol evidence rule explained in the previous chapter. All agreements concerning the sale of the real estate must be in writing and included in this contract. The parties are prohibited from later claiming that the agreement regarding a contract term was different or inadvertently deleted from the contract. It also provides a space where the parties can list the addenda that are part of the contract. Contract addenda are discussed in the next section.

Paragraph 21: Notices

21. NOTICES: All notices shall be in writing and effective when delivered at the addresses shown below.

This provision is direct and avoids the problems of oral notices. If either party is required to notify the other of some condition or option, the notice must be in writing to be effective and delivered to the address listed for the party in the contract.

Paragraph 22: Consult Your Attorney

22. CONSULT YOUR ATTORNEY: The Broker cannot give you legal advice. This is intended to be a legally binding contract. READ IT CAREFULLY. Federal law may impose certain duties upon Brokers or Signatories to this contract when any of the signatories is a foreign party, or when any of the signatories receives certain amounts of U.S. currency in connection with a real estate closing. If you do not understand the effect of any part of this contract, consult your attorney BEFORE signing.

This clause draws attention to the fact that this document is a *contract* and that if any provision of the contract is not understood the party should consult with an attorney before signing the contract. It does no good to take the contract to an attorney after it has been signed by both parties. The provision also reminds the broker, the seller and the buyer that the broker is not an attorney and cannot give legal advice. Buyers and sellers should remember that the sale of real estate is an expensive and complex transaction. Parties should know and understand their rights *before* they sign a contract.

Finally, this paragraph gives broad notice to the seller, buyer and broker that federal law may impact upon this transaction. Specifically, this general notice refers to the following transactions:

1. A transaction in which the seller is a foreign national, the buyer will not occupy the property as his or her principal residence and the sales price is more than $300,000. In this case, the buyer is required by the Foreign Investment in Real Property Tax Act (FIRPTA) of 1984 to withhold ten percent of the sales price and pay it to the Internal Revenue Service.

2. A transaction in which either the seller or the buyer is a foreign national and the subject property is agricultural (ten acres or more in size or $1,000 or more in agricultural products raised and sold from it). In this case, the transaction must be reported to the Agricultural Stabilization and Conservation Service (ASCS) in the county where the property is located.

3. A transaction in which any of the signatories receive more than a certain amount (currently $10,000) in cash as a result of the transaction.

CONTRACT ADDENDA

As stated earlier, the Texas Real Estate Commission promulgated seven special conditions additions that can be used as appropriate with one of the standard earnest money contract forms. Each of these addenda addresses a contract condition that occurs frequently in the sale of residential property but is not always part of the basic agreement of the parties. These addenda, when attached to the earnest money contract, are part of the contract between the parties and can amend the standard contract. The Texas Real Estate Commission requires its licensees to use these special addenda whenever appropriate rather than drafting a special provision. Each of these forms is reproduced in this section and accompanied by a brief explanation.

Property Condition Addendum

If the buyer has checked subparagraph B of paragraph 7 of the promulgated earnest money contract, this addendum must be completed and attached to the contract. This addendum, shown as Figure 19.2, specifies the inspections the buyer requires prior to the purchase of the property. These inspections are made at the buyer's expense and are waived by the buyer if the buyer fails to have a licensed inspector make the specified inspections. The addendum allows the parties to limit the time period in which the inspections are to be made and written notice of the results are provided to the seller. The buyer is also required to provide a written list of repairs the buyer is expecting and demanding that the seller make. The cost of repairs and limitations is governed by paragraph 7 of the earnest money contract previously discussed. The only repairs required under this addendum are repairs to items checked for inspection, repairs caused by termite damage and treatment of the buildings for termites if infestation is found upon inspection. The form does set aside space for establishing an affirmative duty to make repairs in addition to those listed in paragraph 7 of the earnest money contract and in addition to those discovered upon inspection.

Sale of Other Property by Buyer

Frequently, a buyer is planning a move from a residence he or she presently owns to another. All of the buyer's savings are in his or her present home in the form of equity. The buyer's ability to buy the new home is contingent on his or her ability to sell the existing home. In that situation this contract addendum, shown as Figure 19.3, should be completed and attached to the earnest money contract. This additional provision allows the buyer to terminate the contract and obtain a refund of the earnest money if the buyer is unable to sell the home by the date specified in the addendum. As protection to the seller, the addendum allows the seller to continue to show and offer the property for sale, and, if another buyer is located, the seller can demand that the contingency be removed and the first buyer deposit additional earnest money. If the buyer refuses, then the seller can terminate the contract and refund the earnest money to the buyer. At that point the seller is free to sell the property to someone else.

This addenda form was modified by TREC in 1987 to include a provision stating that time is of the essence. This means that the dates in the addendum must be strictly adhered to by the parties. This is the only form promulgated by TREC that requires a strict adherence to the dates for performance.

Second or "Back-up" Contract Addendum

This additional provision allows for two earnest money contracts for the purchase of the same property to be pending at the same time (Figure 19.4). The second contract is contingent on the first contract's terminating by a certain date. This provision makes the first contract's termination a condition precedent to the obligations under the second contract.

Seller Financing Addendum

The standard earnest money contract discussed at length in this chapter covers many of the terms to be included when the seller is financing all or a portion of the purchase price. The Seller Financing Addendum draws the parties' attention to three other issues that relate to seller financing: the assumability of the note, the method for paying taxes and insurance, and remedies if the buyer defaults in payment of the first lien note. The form, shown as Figure 19.5, provides the parties with options in handling each of these situations. The parties should check the appropriate boxes in completing the form.

Financing Conditions Addendum

This form was used more frequently prior to the promulgation of the present earnest money contracts. It provides several options with respect to conventional financing, which are now covered in the standard earnest money contract form discussed in this chapter. However, it is still used for its clear handling of loan buydown arrangements. If the form is used and all of its sections completed by the broker, care should be taken to prevent a conflict with the terms included in the principal document. It is shown as Figure 19.6.

New Home Insulation Addendum

The "New Home Insulation Addendum," Figure 19.7, was designed to meet the disclosure requirements concerning insulation established by the Federal Trade Commission. Completion of the form requires identification of each segment of the house that has been insulated, with a description of the thickness of the insulation and its R-value. In completing the form, the seller and broker should *not* guess or estimate. The documentation accompanying the insulation should be consulted.

VA Release of Liability/Restoration of Entitlement Addendum

This form, Figure 19.8, should be used whenever the buyer is assuming a VA-guaranteed loan and the seller wants to be released from any further liability on the note. The seller-veteran has three options when a VA loan is assumed. He or she can remain liable on the note and simply allow the buyer to assume payments. The buyer in this situation does not have to be a veteran. The second option for the seller-veteran is to seek a release from the VA as to any further personal liability on the note. This release can be made a condition of sale. If the veteran does not obtain the required release, the seller can cancel the contract. The third option for the veteran-seller is to seek a release *and* restoration of his or her entitlement. If the veteran's entitlement is restored, he or she will be able to purchase another home with a VA-guaranteed loan. The earnest money contract can be conditioned upon the granting by the VA of a release and restoration of entitlement. The form should be completed to reflect the seller's choice with respect to these options.

Figure 19.2: **PROPERTY CONDITION ADDENDUM**

PROPERTY CONDITION ADDENDUM

02-08-85

PROMULGATED BY TEXAS REAL ESTATE COMMISSION

ADDENDUM TO EARNEST MONEY CONTRACT BETWEEN THE UNDERSIGNED PARTIES CONCERNING THE PROPERTY AT _____

(Street Address and City)

CHECK APPLICABLE BOXES:

☐ A.   TERMITES: Buyer, at Buyer's expense (except at Seller's expense in VA transactions), may have the Property inspected by a Structural Pest Control Business Licensee to determine whether or not there is visible evidence of active termite infestation or visible termite damage to the improvements. If termite treatment or repairs are required, Buyer will furnish a written report to Seller from such Licensee within _____days from the effective date of this Contract, but no treatment or repairs will be required for fences, trees or shrubs. Buyer's failure to furnish such report to Seller within the time specified shall constitute a waiver of Buyer's right to any treatment and repairs.

☐ B.   INSPECTIONS: Buyer, at Buyer's expense, may have any of the items designated below inspected by inspectors of Buyer's choice. Repairs will only be required of items designated by this Contract for inspection and reported to be in need of immediate repair or which are not performing the function for which intended. Failure of Buyer to furnish written inspection reports and to designate the repairs to which Buyer is entitled by this Contract within the times specified below shall be deemed a waiver of Buyer's repair rights.

STRUCTURAL: Buyer requires inspections of the following: (check applicable boxes)

☐ foundation, ☐ roof, ☐ load bearing walls, ☐ ceilings, ☐ basement, ☐ water penetration, ☐ fireplace and chimney, ☐ floors,
☐ and _____
_____
_____

Within _____days from the effective date of this Contract, Buyer will furnish Seller written inspection reports with a designation of repairs if repairs are required.

EQUIPMENT AND SYSTEMS: Buyer requires inspections of the following: (check applicable boxes)

☐ plumbing system (including any water heater, wells and septic system), ☐ electrical system, ☐ all heating and cooling units and systems,
☐ any built-in range, oven, dishwasher, disposer, exhaust fans, trash compactor, ☐ swimming pool and related mechanical equipment, ☐ sprinkler systems,
☐ gas lines (inspection by private inspector) ☐ gas lines (inspection by gas supplier) ☐ and _____
_____
_____

Within _____days from the effective date of this Contract, Buyer will furnish Seller written inspection reports with a designation of repairs if repairs are required.

☐ C.   OTHER REPAIRS: Seller shall make the following repairs in addition to those required above: _____
_____
_____

All inspections shall be by persons who regularly provide such service and who are either registered as inspectors with the Texas Real Estate Commission or otherwise permitted by law to perform inspections. Repairs shall be by trained and qualified persons who are, whenever possible, manufacturer-approved service persons and who are licensed or bonded whenever such license or bond is required by law. Seller shall permit access to the Property at any reasonable time for inspection or repairs and for reinspection after repairs have been completed. Seller shall only be responsible for termite treatment and repairs to termite damage, repairs to items specifically designated above for inspection, and repairs specifically described in Paragraph C, subject to the provisions of Paragraph 7 of this Contract. Broker and sales associates shall not be liable or responsible for any inspections or repairs pursuant to this Contract and Addendum.

SELLER _____   BUYER _____

SELLER _____   BUYER _____

The Form of this Addendum has been approved by the Texas Real Estate Commission for use only with similarly approved or promulgated forms of contracts. No representation is made as to the legal validity or adequacy of any provision in any specific transactions. (Rev. 02-85) TREC No. 2-2. This form replaces TREC No. 2-1.

001

Figure 19.3: SALE OF OTHER PROPERTY BY BUYER

05-22-87

PROMULGATED BY THE TEXAS REAL ESTATE COMMISSION

ADDENDUM FOR
SALE OF OTHER PROPERTY BY BUYER

ADDENDUM TO EARNEST MONEY CONTRACT BETWEEN THE UNDERSIGNED PARTIES
CONCERNING PROPERTY AT

_____

(Street Address and City)

A. The contract is contingent upon (1) sale of Buyer's property at _____
_____ , **AND** (2) Buyer's receipt of the sale proceeds by 5:00 p.m.
on _____ , 19 _____ (the Contingency). If the Contingency is not satisfied or waived by Buyer by the above
time and date, the contract shall terminate and the Earnest Money shall be refunded to Buyer.
NOTICE TO PARTIES: The date inserted in this Paragraph should not be later than the date inserted in Paragraph 9 of the contract.

B. Seller's Property may continue to be shown and offered for sale to other prospective buyers until such time as Buyer notifies Seller that the Contingency has been satisfied or waived, and Buyer has deposited the additional Earnest Money specified in Paragraph C below.

C. If Seller accepts a bona-fide written offer to purchase Seller's Property, Seller shall notify Buyer (1) of such acceptance **AND** (2) that Seller requires Buyer to waive the Contingency. Buyer shall, by 5:00 p.m. on the _____ day after Seller's notice to Buyer, (a) notify Seller of Buyer's waiver of the Contingency **AND** (b) deposit $_____ with Escrow Agent as additional Earnest Money; otherwise the contract shall terminate and the Earnest Money shall be refunded to Buyer.

D. Notwithstanding the provisions of Paragraph 4 of the contract, if Buyer waives the Contingency, but approval of any loan or loan assumption is conditioned upon sale of Buyer's property described in Paragraph A above, Buyer shall be in default if such condition is not satisfied by the date provided for in Paragraph 4 of the contract, and Seller shall be entitled to exercise the remedies specified in the default paragraph of the contract.

E. For purposes of this Addendum time is of the essence, and strict compliance with the times for performance stated herein is required.

F. All notices shall be in writing and effective when delivered in accordance with the contract.

_____   _____
Buyer   Seller

_____   _____
Buyer   Seller

The form of this Addendum has been approved by the Texas Real Estate Commission for use only with similarly approved or promulgated contract forms. Such approval relates to this form only. No representation is made as to the legal validity or adequacy of any provision in any specific transactions. It is not suitable for complex transactions. (Rev. 05-87) TREC NO. 10-1. This form replaces TREC No. 10-0.

005

Figure 19.4: **SECOND OR "BACK-UP" CONTRACT ADDENDUM**

05-22-87

PROMULGATED BY THE TEXAS REAL ESTATE COMMISSION

ADDENDUM FOR
SECOND OR "BACK-UP" CONTRACT

ADDENDUM TO EARNEST MONEY CONTRACT BETWEEN THE UNDERSIGNED PARTIES
CONCERNING PROPERTY AT

_____

(Street Address and City)

A. The Earnest Money Contract to which this Addendum is attached is contingent upon the termination of a previous contract between
    Seller and _____ ,
    dated _____ , 19 _____ , for the sale of Seller's Property (the "Contingency").

B. If the previous contract is terminated on or before 5:00 p.m. on _____ , 19 _____ , this
    contract shall no longer be subject to the Contingency and the effective date of this contract shall be amended to be the date of termination of
    the previous contract.

C. If the previous contract is not terminated within the time specified in Paragraph B, this contract shall terminate and the Earnest Money shall
    be refunded to Buyer.

_____   _____
                  Buyer   Seller

_____   _____
                  Buyer   Seller

The form of this Addendum has been approved by the Texas Real Estate Commission for use only with similarly approved or promulgated contract
forms. Such approval relates to this form only. No representation is made as to the legal validity or adequacy of any provision in any specific
transactions. It is not suitable for complex transactions. (Rev. 05-87) TREC NO. 11-1. This form replaces TREC No. 11-0.

005

Figure 19.5: **SELLER FINANCING ADDENDUM**

05-22-87

PROMULGATED BY THE TEXAS REAL ESTATE COMMISSION

SELLER FINANCING ADDENDUM

NOTICE: Not For Use In Farm And Ranch Or Commercial Transactions

ADDENDUM TO EARNEST MONEY CONTRACT BETWEEN THE UNDERSIGNED PARTIES CONCERNING PROPERTY AT

_____

(Street Address and City)

A. The promissory note (the Note) described in Paragraph 4 of the Earnest Money Contract payable by Buyer (Maker) to the order of Seller (Payee) shall be payable at the place designated by Payee.

B. The deed of trust securing the Note shall include the provisions checked below:

    1. ASSUMABILITY OF NOTE: (check only one)

        ☐ a. ASSUMPTION WITHOUT CONSENT: The Property may be sold without the consent of the Payee, provided any subsequent buyer assumes the Note.

        ☐ b. ASSUMPTION WITH CONSENT: The Property may be sold to a subsequent buyer who assumes the Note, with no change in interest rate or terms; provided the subsequent buyer obtains prior written consent from the Payee. Consent will be based on the subsequent buyer's credit history, and shall not be unreasonably withheld. If all or any part of the Property is sold, conveyed, leased for a period longer than three (3) years, leased with an option to purchase, or otherwise sold (including by contract for deed), without the prior written consent of the Payee, then the Payee may at his option declare the outstanding principal balance of the Note, plus accrued interest, to be immediately due and payable. The creation of a subordinate lien, any sale thereunder, any deed under threat or order of condemnation, any conveyance solely between makers, the passage of title by reason of the death of a maker or by operation of law shall not be construed as a sale or conveyance of the Property.

        ☐ c. DUE ON SALE: If all or any part of the Property is sold, conveyed, leased for a period longer than three (3) years, leased with an option to purchase, or otherwise sold (including any contract for deed), without the prior written consent of the Payee, then the Payee may at his option declare the outstanding principal balance of the Note, plus accrued interest, to be immediately due and payable. The creation of a subordinate lien, any sale thereunder, any deed under threat or order of condemnation, any conveyance solely between makers, the passage of title by reason of the death of a maker or by operation of law shall not be construed as a sale or conveyance of the Property.

    2. TAX AND INSURANCE PAYMENTS: (check only one)

        ☐ a. WITHOUT ESCROW: Maker shall furnish to Payee, before the taxes become delinquent, copies of tax receipts showing that all taxes on the Property have been paid. Maker shall furnish to Payee evidence of current paid-up insurance in accordance with the terms of the deed of trust securing the Note.

        ☐ b. WITH ESCROW: Maker shall, in addition to the principal and interest installments, deposit with the Payee a pro rata part of the estimated annual ad valorem taxes on the Property and a pro rata part of the estimated annual insurance premiums for the improvements on the Property. These tax and insurance deposits are only estimates and may be insufficient to pay total taxes and insurance premiums. Maker shall pay any deficiency within thirty (30) days after notice from Payee. Maker's failure to pay the deficiency shall constitute a default under the Deed of Trust. In the event any superior lienholder on the Property is collecting escrow payments for taxes and insurance, this Paragraph shall be inoperative.

C. CROSS-DEFAULT: The deed of trust securing the Note shall include a provision that any act or occurrence which would constitute default under the terms of any lien superior to the lien securing the Note shall constitute a default under the Deed of Trust securing the Note.

_____   _____
Buyer/Maker   Seller/Payee

_____   _____
Buyer/Maker   Seller/Payee

The form of this Addendum has been approved by the Texas Real Estate Commission for use only with similarly approved or promulgated contract forms. Such approval relates to this form only. No representation is made as to the legal validity or adequacy of any provision in any specific transactions. It is not suitable for complex transactions. (05-87) TREC NO. 26-0.

006

Figure 19.6: **FINANCING CONDITIONS ADDENDUM**

PROMULGATED BY THE TEXAS REAL ESTATE COMMISSION

FINANCING CONDITIONS ADDENDUM
(To be used only for Conventional Loans)

**ADDENDUM TO EARNEST MONEY CONTRACT BETWEEN THE UNDERSIGNED PARTIES
CONCERNING THE PROPERTY AT** _____
(Street Address and City)

Paragraph 4 of the contract is replaced and superseded by this Addendum.

4. FINANCING CONDITIONS: This contract is subject to approval for Buyer by a third party of a conventional loan (the Loan) of not less than the amount of the Note, ☐ with ☐ without private mortgage insurance, as described below:

☐ A. A flexible interest rate Loan for a minimum term of _____ years with monthly payments based upon a _____ year amortization, with the initial interest rate not to exceed _____ % per annum, with the following provisions:

☐ (i) None of the following.

☐ (ii) The initial interest rate may be adjusted at the end of _____ years; and may be adjusted thereafter every _____ years to the rate determined by the lender.

☐ (iii) The maximum interest rate adjustment at any adjustment period shall not exceed _____ % per annum.

☐ (iv) The maximum interest rate that may be paid by the Buyer at any time during the Loan term shall not exceed _____ % per annum.

☐ (v) The maximum payment adjustment for principal and interest at any adjustment period is _____ % of the previous payment for principal and interest.

☐ (vi) The monthly principal and interest payment shall not exceed $_____ during the loan term. If the monthly payments will not amortize the Loan over its remaining term, the Loan term may be extended by the lender. If the monthly interest accruing on the Loan exceeds the amount of the monthly payments, the excess will be added to the Loan principal.

☐ B. Buydown Loan for a minimum _____ year term with annual interest of _____ % for the first loan year, _____ % for the second loan year, _____ % for the third loan year, _____ % for the fourth loan year, _____ % for the fifth loan year and _____ % thereafter. In addition to the Sales Expenses in Paragraph 12, a buydown fee not to exceed $_____ shall be paid by
_____

This contract is also subject to the approval by the lender of any third party Second Note. Buyer shall apply for all financing within _____ days from the effective date of this contract and shall make every effort to obtain approval. If all financing cannot be approved within _____ days from the effective date of this contract, this contract shall terminate and the Earnest Money shall be refunded to Buyer without delay.

_____   _____
Seller   Buyer

_____   _____
Seller   Buyer

107

Figure 19.7: **NEW HOME INSULATION ADDENDUM**

PROMULGATED BY TEXAS REAL ESTATE COMMISSION

NEW HOME INSULATION ADDENDUM

ADDENDUM TO EARNEST MONEY CONTRACT BETWEEN THE UNDERSIGNED PARTIES CONCERNING PROPERTY AT _____

(Street Address and City)

As required by Federal Trade Commission Regulations, the information relating to the insulation installed or to be installed in the home being purchased under the contract is as follows:

A. Exterior walls of improved living areas insulated with _____ insulation to a thickness of _____ inches which yields an R-Value of _____ .

B. Walls in other areas of the home insulated with _____ insulation to a thickness of _____ inches which yields an R-Value of _____ .

C. Ceilings in improved living areas, insulated with _____ insulation to a thickness of _____ inches which yields an R-Value of _____ .

D. Floors of improved living areas not applied to a slab foundation insulated with _____ insulation to a thickness of _____ inches which yields an R-Value of _____ .

E. _____ insulated with _____ insulation to a thickness of _____ inches which yields an R-Value of _____ .

All stated R-Values are based on information provided by the manufacturer of the insulation.

_____   _____
              Seller   Buyer

_____   _____
              Seller   Buyer

The form of this contract has been approved by the Texas Real Estate Commission. Such approval relates to this contract form only. No representation is made as to the legal validity or adequacy of any provision in any specific transaction. It is not suitable for complex transactions. Extensive riders or additions are not to be used. (6-82) TREC No. 13-0   **107**

Figure 19.8: **VA RELEASE OF LIABILITY/RESTORATION OF ENTITLEMENT**

PROMULGATED BY TEXAS REAL ESTATE COMMISSION

VA RELEASE OF LIABILITY/RESTORATION OF ENTITLEMENT
(ASSUMPTION OF LOAN CONTRACT)

**ADDENDUM TO EARNEST MONEY CONTRACT BETWFEN THE UNDERSIGNED PARTIES
CONCERNING PROPERTY AT** _____
(Street Address and City)

Buyer shall accept from Seller a deed containing the VA-required assumption clause and shall furnish promptly such information and documents required by VA to release Seller from VA liability or to restore Seller's VA entitlement as indicated below.

(Check A or B)

☐ A. VA RELEASE OF SELLER'S PERSONAL LIABILITY TO THE GOVERNMENT ON LOAN TO BE ASSUMED

(Check only 1 or 2)

    ☐ 1. This contract is contingent upon the approval of a release of Seller's VA liability being received by Seller on or before the Closing Date. If such approval is not received by this date, the contract shall terminate and Earnest Money shall be refunded to Buyer without delay.

    ☐ 2. If approval of the release of Seller's VA liability has not been received by Seller on or before the Closing Date, Buyer shall continue to aid in the receipt of same after closing.

☐ B. RESTORATION OF SELLER'S VA ENTITLEMENT FOR A VA GUARANTEED LOAN*

Buyer is a veteran and will apply promptly to VA for substitution of Buyer's entitlement for that of the Seller on the loan being assumed; and

(Check only 1 or 2)

    ☐ 1. This contract is contingent upon the approval of the restoration of Seller's VA entitlement being received by Seller on or before the Closing Date. If such approval is not received by this date, the contract shall terminate and Earnest Money shall be refunded to Buyer without delay.

    ☐ 2. If approval of the restoration of Seller's VA entitlement has not been received by the Seller on or before the Closing Date, Buyer shall continue to aid in the receipt of same after closing.

The provisions of this addendum shall survive closing.

*NOTICE: VA will not restore Seller's entitlement unless Buyer is a Veteran, has sufficient unused VA entitlement, and is otherwise qualified. If restoration is important to Seller, Seller should require receipt thereof prior to closing.

_____   _____
Seller   Buyer

_____   _____
Seller   Buyer

The form of this contract has been approved by the Texas Real Estate Commission. Such approval relates to this contract form only. No representation is made as to the legal validity or adequacy of any provision in any specific transaction. It is not suitable for complex transactions. Extensive riders or additions are not to be used. (6-82) TREC No. 12-0   **107**

Special Provisions for Gulf Coast Property

The Texas Open Beach Law requires that the Gulf Coast beaches from the mean low tide to the vegetation line remain open to the public. This public easement was explained earlier. In 1986 the Texas Open Beach Law was amended. The amendment required that the seller of property in any county touching the Gulf of Mexico notify the purchaser that the State of Texas has an easement along the Gulf of Mexico. In 1987 the law was amended again to limit the number of property owners who are required to give the statutory notice. The law presently requires that the sale of any real property physically located seaward of the Gulf Intracoastal Waterway or seaward of the longitudinal line denoted as 97°12'19" must include the following warning:

> The real property described in this contract is located seaward of the Gulf Intracoastal Waterway to its southernmost point and then seaward of the longitudinal line also knows as 97 degrees 12', 19" which runs southerly to the international boundary from the intersection of the centerline of the Gulf Intracoastal Waterway and the Brownsville Ship Channel. If the property is in close proximity to a beach fronting the Gulf of Mexico, the purchaser is hereby advised that the public has acquired a right of use or easement to or over the area of any public beach by prescription, dedication, or presumption, or has retained a right by virtue of continuous right in the public since time immemorial, as recognized in law and custom.

The Texas Real Estate Commission has approved an addendum entitled "Addendum for Property Located Seaward of the Gulf Intracoastal Waterway" that contains this warning.

The penalties for failing to complete this addendum or give the required notice contained in this addendum are quite severe. The law provides that the failure to give the warning constitutes a deceptive act under the Texas Deceptive Trade Practices Act. Failure to give the warning is also grounds for termination of the earnest money contract by the buyer. If the buyer elects to terminate the contract, he or she is entitled to a full refund of the earnest money.

SUMMARY

Earnest money contracts are the most frequently used contract for the purchase and sale of land in Texas. Upon signing of the contract both the buyer and the seller become obligated to perform faithfully the obligations assumed in that agreement. Earnest money contracts must be in writing and should be signed by both parties. The buyer and the seller are free to negotiate and include any terms, conditions and contingencies mutually agreeable.

The written earnest money contract must contain the identity of the parties, a description of the real property and the purchase price. In addition, it is advisable for the parties to date the contract, describe the method of payment, specify the type of deed to be used to convey title and set a closing date and a date for transfer of possession.

Brokers and salesmen play a significant role in negotiating earnest money contracts. Sellers and buyers frequently rely upon the broker's expertise in completing the earnest money contract. However, the drafting of legal documents such as earnest money contracts can be done only by licensed attorneys or the parties themselves. Brokers and salesmen are prohibited by statute from engaging in the practice of law. To assist brokers and salesmen, the Texas Real Estate Commission has promulgated standard earnest money contracts, leases and contract addenda that can be completed by licensees. There are six basic earnest money contract forms and seven different addenda from which to choose. Brokers and salesmen should read each of these forms and understand their use in order to choose competently and complete the necessary documents. If none of the forms are adequate to describe the agreement of the parties, then an attorney should be hired by either the seller or the buyer to prepare the document.

QUESTIONS AND CASE PROBLEMS

1. On March 23, 1979, the seller and the buyer executed an earnest money contract for the sale of the following property:

> All of Lots 1 and 2, Horde Buchanan subdivision to the City of Lubbock, Lubbock County, Texas, bearing municipal street address of 2202 Memphis, Lubbock, Texas, and otherwise known as Southern Manor Apartments, together with all improvements thereon and all furniture and fixtures located therein, subject to all easements, restrictions, and zoning ordinances of record. . . .

The seller agreed to provide the buyer with a general warranty deed "conveying good and marketable title subject to any liens to be created or assumed under the contract." The contract provided that the buyer would assume a note executed by the seller payable to State Savings & Loan of Lubbock, Texas, with an unpaid principal balance of $208,705.83.

The contract further provided that "Seller warrants that there are no liens on the items of personal property in the premises." The closing date was set forth in the contract as May 1, 1979. The buyer refused to close the sale because the deed of trust securing the loan from State Savings & Loan included a lien against all furniture, fixtures, appliances and goods located on the premises. Seller claims that the contract specifically provided that buyer would assume that indebtedness and deed of trust and sues to force the buyer to purchase the property subject to the indebtedness. Is the seller entitled to specific performance of this contract?

2. The buyer and seller have reached the following verbal agreement concerning the sale of Lot 2, Block 16, of the Lincoln Subdivision in Dallas, Texas:

 1. Buyer's Name: Raul Lopez

 2. Seller's Name: Bradford T. Hopkins

 3. The purchase price is $78,000; with ten percent down, an assumption of a fixed rate loan with Guaranty Federal Savings & Loan in the original amount of $70,000 and an estimated balance due of $68,750. The difference between the down payment and the amount assumed to be carried by the seller at ten percent interest to be paid in full within two years, amortized over two years with equal monthly payments of principal and interest. The deed of trust to Guaranty requires their prior written approval before the loan can be assumed and an assumption fee of $45 paid. Mr. Lopez is not interested in buying the house if the interest rate rises above 13 percent. It is presently fixed at 12 percent.

 4. Structural, mechanical, electrical and plumbing inspections are required. Termite inspection is also to be made and any problems relating to the existence of termites or damage caused by termites to be repaired by seller. Seller is liable to make repairs up to $1,500.

 5. The sale is contingent on buyer selling his present home on or before June 15, 1987. There is presently a contract outstanding on buyer's home with a closing date of June 10, 1987.

 6. Closing of this sale should be on or before June 20, 1987. Possession to be transferred to buyer within seven days after closing.

 7. Seller to furnish a standard policy of title insurance from State Title Company. State Title Company will serve as the escrow agent, and buyer has agreed to deposit $1,000.

 8. Buyer and seller have agreed that the sale will include a ten- by 15-foot metal building presently situated on the lot, a redwood picnic table and a bug light.

Complete the appropriate TREC forms to show the agreement of the parties. Is there any information not provided that the parties to the contract should consider?

20

Other Real Estate Contracts

Contracts for the sale of land can be written in a number of different ways. The earnest money contract for the sale of a used home discussed in the previous chapter is only one type of contract. Although this book does not cover all the terms that could be included in a contract for the sale of land, it does provide a representative sample of provisions and contracts. In this chapter, three additional types of contracts will be explained. These contracts are earnest money contracts for the sale of new homes, contracts for deed and options. These contracts frequently contain provisions and characteristics found in the earnest money contracts previously discussed. The contracts must comply with the general requirements for enforceability discussed in Chapter 18. However, these contracts serve special purposes and contain differences that should be understood. This chapter focuses on the differences.

NEW HOME CONSTRUCTION AND SALES

Although the resale of houses is very common, there are many people who buy newly constructed homes or build their own dream home. The person or firm hired to construct the house is called the general contractor or builder.

The general contractor is obligated to provide the materials and labor necessary to construct the planned house. Much of the work is performed by subcontractors, whom the general contractor will hire and be solely responsible for. The general contractor is neither an employee nor an agent of the buyer but is classified legally as an independent contractor. The independent contractor agrees to provide a house to specifications, but the buyer has no direct control while the contractor is performing the services contracted for.

The general contractor may be constructing homes in a subdivision in compliance with the model home selected by the buyer or may be hired to construct an individually designed house on a lot owned by the buyer. Although these are the most common arrangements, others exist as well. The buyer may choose to act as his or her own general contractor, hiring and coordinating the subcontractors or unit contractors.

One of the chief responsibilities of the contractor is to coordinate the work of the subcontractors. If the general contractor fails to coordinate the work reasonably and that failure causes injury to the buyer or to a subcontractor, the general contractor will be liable in a suit for damages.

The contractor has a duty to inspect the materials brought onto the construction site. If such materials have defects that are reasonably discoverable upon an inspection, and the contractor fails to inspect them or inspects but does not reject the defective materials, the contractor will be liable for injury caused by those materials. Injury includes the final product being a less valuable house, and the contractor will be liable for money damages for the difference between the value of the house contracted for and the one actually built.

Contracts for the purchase of real property that include the construction of the buildings require a few additional contractual provisions. These provisions concern the manner and time of construction. The contract terms should address the building of the house in compliance with the plans and specifications, in a good and workmanlike manner and within the agreed-upon time period.

In May 1987, the Texas Real Estate Commission promulgated two earnest money contract forms for use in the sale of new homes. These contract forms must be used by brokers and salesmen after December 1, 1987, unless one of the exceptions discussed in Chapter 19 exist. These forms are:

1. New Home Residential Earnest Money Contract (Incomplete Construction)
2. New Home Residential Earnest Money Contract (Completed Construction)

These forms are designed to be used if the following conditions exist:

1. The house is *not* a condominium.
2. The house is either to be constructed, under construction or construction has been completed but the house never has been occupied.
3. The purchaser is buying the lot with the house. (The buyer did not own the lot previously.)

The "New Home Residential Earnest Money Contract (Incomplete Construction)" is reproduced in this chapter as Figure 20.1. The form for completed construction is very similar and is included in the Appendix C. Briefly, some of the features of the earnest money contracts are:

1. Options for choosing the method of financing the purchase include all cash, conventional loan, FHA-insured loan, VA-guaranteed loan, Texas Veterans Housing Assistance loan and seller financing.
2. It recommends that the escrow agent be a disinterested third party.
3. The seller represents that there are no unrecorded liens at the time of closing.
4. The TREC-promulgated addenda discussed in the prior chapter can be used as appropriate to modify the forms.

Plans and Specifications

The plans and specifications are an integral part of the contract between the builder and the buyer. The plans should contain sufficient detail concerning construction to prevent disputes regarding the size of rooms, the materials to be used and the amenities to be included. Buyers who are relying on a model they were shown by a builder should carefully inspect the model and note any differences between the model and their house that they would like to include in the contract. It is important for the parties to remember the parol evidence rule and the statute of frauds. If certain specifications are discussed and agreed to orally, these should be reduced to writing and included in the earnest money contract to avoid running afoul of either of these two rules.

Assuming the contract does contain sufficient detail of the plans for the house, the buyer and builder are required to follow those plans. If problems arise during construction that require a change in the plans, these changes should be written and signed by both builder and buyer. These written orders for change are amendments to the contract and are enforceable. Significant deviations from the plans should be evidenced by a written amendment to the earnest money contract; otherwise, the variance could be considered a default in the contract giving rise to one of the contractual remedies previously discussed.

Slight deviations or variances from the plans and specifications are allowed under the doctrine of substantial performance. The doctrine of substantial performance allows the builder minor infractions of the contract without substantial penalty. Nowhere is the doctrine of substantial performance more important than in construction contracts. For example, assume the builder has completed construction of the house with the following exceptions: a light fixture in the bathroom has not been installed, the baseboard in the three bedrooms has been primed but not painted and seven of the floor tiles in the kitchen have popped up and need to be relaid. Is the builder entitled to receive his last draw of $6,500 from the buyer? Can the buyer refuse to pay this amount until the builder has corrected the items listed? This type of dispute is very common in new home construction. In all probability a court would find that the builder has substantially performed the contract and is entitled to receive this last draw less the cost of remedying the enumerated defects.

Figure 20.1: NEW HOME RESIDENTIAL EARNEST MONEY CONTRACT

05 22 87

NEW HOME RESIDENTIAL EARNEST MONEY CONTRACT

(Incomplete Construction)

PROMULGATED BY TEXAS REAL ESTATE COMMISSION

Notice: Not For Use In Condominium Transactions

1. **PARTIES:** ______________________ (Seller) agrees to sell and convey to ______________________ (Buyer) and Buyer agrees to buy from Seller the property described below.

2. **PROPERTY:** Lot __________, Block __________, __________ Addition, City of __________, __________ County, Texas, known as __________ (Address); or as described on attached exhibit, together with the improvements, fixtures and all other property located thereon or placed thereon pursuant to Paragraph 7 below. All property sold by this contract is called the "Property".

3. **CONTRACT SALES PRICE:**

   A. Cash payable at closing .... $__________

   B. Sum of all financing described below excluding any FHA Mortgage Insurance Premium (MIP) or VA funding fee .... $__________

   C. Sales Price (sum of A and B) .... $__________

4. **FINANCING:** (Check applicable boxes below)

☐ A. ALL CASH: This is an all cash sale; no financing is involved.

☐ B. THIRD PARTY CONVENTIONAL FINANCING:

☐ 1. A third party first lien note of not less than $ __________, due in full in ______ years, payable in initial monthly payments of principal and interest not exceeding $ __________ for the first ______ year(s) of the loan.

☐ 2. A third party second lien note of not less than $ __________, due in full in ______ years, payable in initial monthly payments of principal and interest not exceeding $ __________ for the first ______ year(s) of the loan.

☐ C. FHA INSURED FINANCING:

A Section __________ FHA insured loan of not less than $ __________, due in full in ______ years, payable in initial monthly payments of principal and interest not exceeding $ __________ for the first ______ year(s) of the loan.

As required by HUD-FHA, if FHA valuation is unknown, "It is expressly agreed that, notwithstanding any other provisions of this contract, the Purchaser (Buyer) shall not be obligated to complete the purchase of the Property described herein or to incur any penalty by forfeiture of Earnest Money deposits or otherwise unless the Seller has delivered to the Purchaser (Buyer) a written statement issued by the Federal Housing Commissioner setting forth the appraised value of the Property (excluding closing costs and MIP) of not less than $ __________, which statement the Seller hereby agrees to deliver to the Purchaser (Buyer) promptly after such appraised value statement is made available to the Seller. The Purchaser (Buyer) shall, however, have the privilege and option of proceeding with the consummation of this contract without regard to the amount of the appraised valuation made by the Federal Housing Commissioner. The appraised valuation is arrived at to determine the maximum mortgage the Department of Housing and Urban Development will insure. HUD does not warrant the value or the condition of the Property. The Purchaser (Buyer) should satisfy himself/herself that the price and the condition of the Property are acceptable."

If the FHA appraised value of the Property (excluding closing costs and MIP) is less than the Sales price (3C above), Seller may reduce the Sales Price to an amount equal to the FHA appraised value (excluding closing costs and MIP) and the parties to the sale shall close the sale at such lower Sales Price with appropriate adjustments to 3A and 3B above.

☐ D. VA GUARANTEED FINANCING:

A VA guaranteed loan of not less than $ __________, due in full in ______ years,

☐ 1. with interest at maximum rate allowable at time of loan funding if the loan is a fixed rate loan or

☐ 2. with interest not to exceed ______ % per annum for the first ______ year(s) of the loan if such loan is not fixed rate.

VA NOTICE TO BUYER: "It is expressly agreed that, notwithstanding any other provisions of this contract, the Buyer shall not incur any penalty by forfeiture of earnest money or otherwise or be obligated to complete the purchase of the Property described herein, if the contract purchase price or cost exceeds the reasonable value of the Property established by the Veterans Administration. The Buyer shall, however, have the privilege and option of proceeding with the consummation of this contract without regard to the amount of the reasonable value established by the Veterans Administration."

If Buyer elects to complete the purchase at an amount in excess of the reasonable value established by VA, Buyer shall pay such excess amount in cash from a source which Buyer agrees to disclose to the VA and which Buyer represents will not be from borrowed funds except as approved by VA. If VA reasonable value of the Property is less than the Sales Price (3C above), Seller may reduce the Sales Price to an amount equal to the VA reasonable value and the parties to the sale shall close the sale at such lower Sales Price with appropriate adjustments to 3A and 3B above.

☐ E. TEXAS VETERANS' HOUSING ASSISTANCE PROGRAM LOAN:

A Texas Veterans' Housing Assistance Program loan of $ __________ due in full in ______ years at the interest rate established by the Texas Veterans' Land Board at the time of closing.

☐ F. SELLER FINANCING: A promissory note from Buyer to Seller of $ __________, bearing ______ % interest per annum, and payable:

☐ 1. In one payment due __________ __________ after the date of the note with interest payable __________.

☐ 2. In installments of $ __________ ☐ including interest ☐ plus interest beginning __________ after the date of the note and continuing at __________ intervals thereafter for ______ year(s) when the entire balance of the note shall be due and payable.

☐ 3. Interest only in __________ installments for the first ______ year(s) and thereafter in installments of $ __________ ☐ including interest ☐ plus interest beginning __________ after the date of the note and continuing at __________ intervals thereafter for ______ year(s) when the entire balance of the note shall be due and payable.

INITIALED FOR IDENTIFICATION BY BUYER __________ AND SELLER __________

TREC No. 23-0

005

Figure 20.1: (continued)

New Home (Incomplete Construction)—Page Two   05/22/87

☐ 4. This contract is subject to Buyer furnishing Seller evidence of good credit within _____ days from the effective date of this contract. If notice of disapproval of Buyer's credit is not given within five (5) days after receipt by Seller, Seller shall be deemed to have approved Buyer's credit. Buyer hereby authorizes Buyer's credit report to be furnished to Seller.

Any Seller financed note may be prepaid in whole or in part at any time without penalty. The lien securing payment of such note will be inferior to any lien securing any loan given in connection with third party financing described above. If an Owner's Policy of Title Insurance is furnished, Buyer shall furnish Seller with a Mortgagee's Title Policy.

Buyer shall apply for all third party financing within _____ days from the effective date of this contract and shall make every reasonable effort to obtain the same from _____ as lender, or any lender that will make the loan at no greater loan expense (including but not limited to discounts or other charges however designated) to Seller than charged by the designated lender. Such financing shall have been approved when Buyer has satisfied all of lender's financial conditions; e.g., requirements of sale of other property, co-signer, or financial verifications. If such financing is not approved within _____ days from the effective date hereof, this contract shall terminate and the Earnest Money shall be refunded to Buyer.

NOTICE TO PARTIES: Before signing this contract Buyer is advised to determine the financing options available from lenders. Certain loans have variable rates of interest, some have monthly payments which may not be sufficient to pay the accruing interest, and some have interest rate "buydowns" which reduce the rate of interest for part or all of the loan term at the expense of one or more of the parties to this contract.

5. **EARNEST MONEY:** Buyer shall deposit the sum of $ _____ as Earnest Money with
_____, at _____ Address,
as Escrow Agent, upon execution of the contract by both parties. ☐ Additional Earnest Money of $ _____ shall be deposited by Buyer with the Escrow Agent on or before _____, 19 _____. If Buyer fails to deposit the Earnest Money or any additional Earnest Money, Seller may terminate this contract.

NOTICE: Escrow Agent should be a disinterested third party. Review Paragraph 18 before selecting Escrow Agent.

6. **TITLE:** Seller shall furnish to Buyer at _____'s expense either:

☐ A. Owner's Policy of Title Insurance (the Title Policy) issued by _____
in the amount of the Sales Price and dated at or after closing; OR

☐ B. Abstracts of Title certified by an abstract company (1) from the sovereignty to the effective date of this contract (Complete Abstract) and (2) supplemented to the closing date (Supplemental Abstract).

NOTICE TO SELLER AND BUYER: AS REQUIRED BY LAW, Broker advises Buyer that Buyer should have the Abstract covering the Property examined by an attorney of Buyer's selection, or Buyer should be furnished with or obtain a Title Policy. If a Title Policy is to be obtained, Buyer should obtain a Commitment for Title Insurance (the Commitment) which should be examined by an attorney of Buyer's choice at or prior to closing. If the Property is situated in a Utility District, Section 50.301, Texas Water Code requires the Buyer to sign and acknowledge the statutory notice from Seller relating to the tax rate and bonded indebtedness of the District. If the Property is situated seaward of the Gulf Intracoastal Waterway, attach an addendum containing the statement required by Section 61.025, Texas Natural Resources Code.

7. **PROPERTY CONDITION:**

A. CONSTRUCTION DOCUMENTS: All improvements shall be completed with due diligence in accordance with the plans and other specifications, finish out schedules or allowances initialed by the parties hereto, incorporated herein and identified as _____ together with the following changes or
alternates: _____
_____ and any other change orders hereafter agreed to by the parties in writing (all called Construction Documents).

B. COST ADJUSTMENTS: Increase in costs resulting from change orders or items selected by Buyer which exceed the allowances specified in the Construction Documents shall be paid by Buyer as follows: _____

Decrease in costs resulting from change orders and unused allowances shall reduce Sales Price and loan amount accordingly.

C. BUYER'S SELECTIONS: If the Construction Documents permit selections by Buyer, Buyer's selections will conform to Seller's normal standards or will not, in Seller's judgment, adversely affect the marketability of the Property, Buyer will make required selections within _____ days after receipt of written notice from Seller.

D. COMPLETION: If construction has not already commenced, it shall commence on or before _____, 19 _____, or within _____ days after Loan approval, whichever is later. The improvements shall be substantially completed in accordance with the Construction Documents and ready for occupancy not later than _____, 19 _____. The improvements shall be deemed to be substantially completed in accordance with the Construction Documents upon the final inspection and approval by all applicable governmental authorities and any lender. If delay of construction is caused by reason of Buyer's acts or omissions, provided Seller has exercised reasonable and continued diligence, or by reason of acts of God, fire or other casualty loss, strikes, boycotts or non availability of materials for which no substitute of equal quality and price is available, the time of such delays shall be added to the time allowed for substantial completion of the construction, but in no event shall such time extensions exceed a total period of _____ days. Seller may substitute materials, equipment and appliances of equal quality for those specified in the Construction Documents.

E. WARRANTIES: In connection with all improvements, fixtures and all other property located on or made a part of the Property:
☐ Seller makes no express warranties, OR
☐ Seller makes the express warranties stated in Paragraph 11 or attached.
Seller agrees to assign to Buyer at closing all assignable manufacturer warranties.

F. INSULATION: Insulation information required under Federal Trade Commission Regulations is included in an attached addendum unless previously disclosed to Buyer in writing.

8. **BROKER'S FEE:** _____ (Broker) and any co-broker represent Seller unless otherwise specified herein. Seller agrees to pay Broker the fee specified by separate agreement between Broker and Seller. If there is no separate agreement, Seller agrees to pay Broker in _____ County, Texas, on closing of this sale, or on termination of this contract by agreement of the parties (except as permitted by the terms of this contract), on Seller's default a total cash fee of _____ of the total Sales Price (including any additional amounts pursuant to 7 B above) or upon Buyer's default, one half of any Earnest Money to which Seller is entitled under Paragraph 16 not to exceed the amount of the cash fee. Escrow Agent is authorized and directed to pay Broker said fee from the sale proceeds.

9. **CLOSING:** The closing of the sale shall be within _____ days after the improvements have been substantially completed in accordance with the Construction Documents and are ready for occupancy, or within seven (7) days after objections to title have been cured, whichever date is later (the Closing Date). If financing approval has been obtained pursuant to Paragraph 4, the Closing Date shall be extended daily up to fifteen (15) days if necessary to complete loan requirements. If either party fails to close this sale by the Closing Date, the non defaulting party shall be entitled to exercise the remedies contained in Paragraph 16 immediately and without notice. Seller's obligation to complete all improvements shall survive closing.

10. **POSSESSION:** The possession of the Property shall be delivered to Buyer on _____. The parties agree to use the Buyer's Temporary Residential Lease Form promulgated by the Texas Real Estate Commission (TREC), if Buyer takes possession prior to closing. In the absence of such written lease, any possession by Buyer prior to closing shall establish a landlord tenant at sufferance relationship between the parties.

INITIALED FOR IDENTIFICATION BY BUYER _____ AND SELLER _____

Figure 20.1: (continued)

11. **SPECIAL PROVISIONS:** Insert factual statements and business details applicable to this sale. A licensee shall not add to a promulgated earnest money contract form factual statements or business details for which a contract addendum, lease or other form has been promulgated by TREC for mandatory use. 22 TAC §537.11(d).

12. **SALES EXPENSES TO BE PAID IN CASH AT OR PRIOR TO CLOSING:**

   A. Loan appraisal fee shall be paid by _____

   B. (1) Conventional or FHA Sale: The total of the loan discount and any buydown fees (excluding any Texas Veterans' Housing Assistance Program Participation Fee) shall not exceed $ _____ of which Buyer shall pay the first $ _____ and Seller shall pay the remainder.

       (2) VA Sale: The total of the loan discount and buydown fees (excluding any Texas Veterans' Housing Assistance Program Participation Fee) shall not exceed $ _____ which shall be paid by Seller.

   C. Seller's Expenses: (1) Lender, FHA or VA completion requirements, and any other inspections, reports or repairs required of Seller; (2) releases of existing loans, including prepayment penalties and recordation; tax statements; preparation of deed; one-half of escrow fee; (3) for VA loans, expenses VA prohibits Buyer from paying (e.g., preparation of loan documents, copies of restrictions, photos, excess cost of survey, remaining one half of escrow fee); (4) any Texas Veterans' Housing Assistance Program Participation Fee not exceeding $ _____ ; (5) other expenses stipulated to be paid by Seller under other provisions of this contract.

   D. Buyer's Expenses: (1) Application and origination fees; (2) interest on the notes from dates of disbursements to one (1) month prior to date of first monthly payments; (3) all prepaid items (e.g. required premiums for flood and hazard insurance, reserve deposits for insurance, ad valorem taxes and special governmental assessments); (4) loan related inspection fees; (5) any customary Texas Veterans' Housing Assistance Program loan costs; (6) expenses stipulated to be paid by Buyer under other provisions of this contract and

       (a) FHA Buyer: (1) expenses incident to any loan (e.g., preparation of loan documents, survey, recording fees, copies of restrictions and easements, amortization schedule, Mortgagee's Title Policy, credit reports, photos); one half of escrow fee.

       (b) VA Buyer: (a) expenses incident to any loan (e.g., that portion of survey costs VA Buyer may pay by VA Regulation; recording fees, Mortgagee's Title Policies, credit reports).

       (c) Conventional Buyer: (1) private mortgage insurance premiums; (2) expenses incident to any new loan (e.g., preparation of loan documents, survey, recording fees, copies of restrictions and easements, Mortgagee's Title Policies, credit reports, photos); (3) one half of escrow fee.

       (d) Cash Buyer: (1) recording fees; (2) one half of escrow fee.

   E. The VA Loan funding fee or FHA MIP in the amount of $ _____ is to be paid by _____ . If paid by Buyer, it is to be ☐ paid in cash at closing ☐ added to the amount of the loan to the extent permitted by lender. If financed, the amount is to be added to the loan amount in Paragraph 3B by lender in the loan documents but is not part of the Contract Sales Price.

   F. If any expenses exceed the amount herein stipulated to be paid by either party, either party may terminate this contract unless the other party agrees to pay such excess. In no event shall Buyer pay charges and fees expressly prohibited by FHA, VA or Texas Veterans' Housing Assistance Program Regulations.

13. **PRORATIONS AND TAXES:** Current taxes, any rents and subdivision dues and assessments shall be prorated through the Closing Date. If Seller's change in use of the Property prior to closing or denial of a special use valuation claimed by Seller results in the assessment of additional taxes for periods prior to closing, such additional taxes shall be the obligation of Seller, and such obligation shall survive closing.

14. **TITLE APPROVAL:**

   A. If abstract is furnished, Seller shall deliver Complete Abstract to Buyer within twenty (20) days from the effective date hereof. Buyer shall have twenty (20) days from date of receipt of Complete Abstract to deliver a copy of the examining attorney's title opinion to Seller stating any objections and only objections so stated shall be considered. However, the following items shall not be recited as objections to title by Buyer: liens securing payment of debt created as part of the consideration, taxes for the current year, restrictive covenants and utility easements common to the platted subdivision of which the Property is a part, existing building and zoning ordinances, and any exceptions permitted by the terms of this contract.

   B. If Title Policy is furnished, the Title Policy shall guarantee Buyer's title to be good and indefeasible subject only to (1) restrictive covenants affecting the Property (2) any discrepancies, conflicts or shortages in area or boundary lines, or any encroachments, or any overlapping of improvements (3) taxes for the current and subsequent years and subsequent assessments for prior years due to a change in land usage or ownership (4) existing building and zoning ordinances (5) rights of parties in possession (6) liens created as security for the sale consideration (7) utility easements common to the platted subdivision of which this Property is a part and (8) reservations or other exceptions permitted by the terms of this contract. If the Title Policy will be subject to exceptions other than those recited above in items (1) through (7) inclusive, Seller shall deliver to Buyer the Commitment and legible copies of any documents creating exceptions that are not recited in items (1) through (7) above at least five (5) days prior to closing. If Buyer has objection to any such previously undisclosed exceptions, or to any unrecorded easement or adverse condition with respect to the boundaries which are revealed by any survey of the Property, Buyer shall have five (5) days after receipt of such Commitment, copies, and survey to make written objections to Seller. If no Commitment is provided to Buyer at or prior to closing, it will be conclusively presumed that Seller represented at closing that the Title Policy would not be subject to exceptions other than those recited above in items (1) through (7).

   C. In either instance if title objections are raised by Buyer or Title Company named in Paragraph 6A, Seller shall have fifteen (15) days from the date such objections are disclosed to cure the same, and the Closing Date shall be extended accordingly. If the objections are not timely cured, this contract shall terminate and the Earnest Money shall be refunded to Buyer, unless Buyer elects to waive the unsatisfied objections and complete the purchase.

   D. Seller shall furnish tax statements showing no delinquent taxes; a Supplemental Abstract, when applicable, showing no additional title objections; and a General Warranty Deed conveying title subject only to liens securing payment of debt created as part of the consideration, taxes for the current year, restrictive covenants and utility easements common to the platted subdivision of which the Property is a part, existing building and zoning ordinances, and any exceptions or reservations acceptable to Buyer. Each note shall be secured by vendor's and deed of trust liens. In case of dispute as to the form of the deed (and in Seller financed transactions, the note and deed of trust), forms prepared by the State Bar of Texas shall be used.

15. **CASUALTY LOSS:** If after the construction is substantially completed, any part of the Property is damaged or destroyed by fire or other casualty loss, Seller shall restore the same to its previous condition, and the Closing Date shall be extended for a maximum of fifteen (15) days if necessary for Seller to do so. If Seller is unable to do so without fault, this contract shall terminate and the Earnest Money shall be refunded to Buyer.

16. **DEFAULT:** If Buyer fails to comply herewith, Seller may either seek such relief as may be provided by law or terminate this contract and receive the Earnest Money as liquidated damages, thereby releasing Buyer from this contract. If Seller is unable without fault, within the time herein required to (a) make any noncasualty repairs or (b) deliver the Commitment or (c) deliver the Complete Abstract, Buyer may either terminate this contract and receive the Earnest Money as the sole remedy or extend the time for performance up to fifteen (15) days and the Closing Date shall be extended pursuant to other provisions of this contract. If Seller fails to comply herewith for any other reason, Buyer may either seek such relief as may be provided by law or terminate this contract and receive the Earnest Money, thereby releasing Seller from this contract.

17. **ATTORNEY'S FEES:** Any party to this contract, Broker, co broker or Escrow Agent who prevails in any legal proceeding brought under or with relation to this contract or transaction shall be additionally entitled to recover court costs and reasonable attorney's fees.

INITIALED FOR IDENTIFICATION BY BUYER _____ AND SELLER _____

005 TREC No. 25-0

Figure 20.1: (continued)

New Home (Incomplete Construction)—Page Four

18. **ESCROW**: The Earnest Money is deposited with Escrow Agent with the understanding that Escrow Agent (a) is not a party to this contract and does not assume or have any liability for performance or non-performance of any party to this contract (b) has the right to require from all parties and brokers a written release of liability of the Escrow Agent which authorizes the disbursement of the Earnest Money (c) is not liable for interest or other charge on the funds held and (d) is not liable for any losses of escrow funds caused by the failure of any banking institution in which such funds have been deposited, unless such banking institution is acting as Escrow Agent. If any party or broker unreasonably fails to deliver promptly the document described in (b) above, then such party or broker shall be liable as provided in Paragraph 17. At closing, the Earnest Money shall be applied first to any cash down payment required, then to Buyer's closing costs and any excess refunded to Buyer. Any refund or payment of the Earnest Money under this contract shall be reduced by the amount of any actual expenses incurred on behalf of the party receiving the Earnest Money, and Escrow Agent shall pay the same to the creditors entitled thereto. If the Earnest Money is deposited with the Seller, this paragraph is not applicable.

19. **REPRESENTATIONS**: Seller represents that as of the Closing Date there will no unrecorded liens, assessments or Uniform Commercial Code Security Interests against any of the Property which will not be satisfied out of the Sales Price. If any representation in this contract is untrue on the Closing Date, this contract may be terminated by Buyer and the Earnest Money shall be refunded to Buyer. All representations contained in this contract shall survive closing.

20. **AGREEMENT OF PARTIES**: This contract contains the entire agreement of the parties and cannot be changed except by their written agreement. Texas Real Estate Commission promulgated addenda which are part of this contract are: (list) _____

_____

21. **NOTICES**: All notices shall be in writing and effective when delivered at the addresses shown below.

22. **CONSULT YOUR ATTORNEY**: The Broker cannot give you legal advice. This is intended to be a legally binding contract. READ IT CAREFULLY. If you do not understand the effect of any part of this contract, consult your attorney BEFORE signing. Federal law may impose certain duties upon brokers or parties to this contract when any party is a foreign party or when any party receives certain amounts of U.S. currency in connection with a real estate closing.

BUYER'S   SELLER'S
ATTORNEY: _____   ATTORNEY: _____

EXECUTED in multiple originals effective the _____ day of _____, 19 _____ **(BROKER: FILL IN THE DATE OF FINAL ACCEPTANCE.)**

_____   _____
Buyer   Seller

_____   _____
Buyer   Seller

_____   Phone No.   _____   Phone No.
Buyer's Address   Seller's Address

AGREEMENT BETWEEN BROKERS

Broker agrees to pay _____ (Co-Broker) a fee
of _____ of the total sales price when the Broker's fee described in Paragraph 8 is received. Escrow Agent is authorized and directed to pay Co-Broker from Broker's fee at closing.

_____   _____
Co-Broker   License No.   Broker   License No.

By: _____   By: _____

_____   Phone No.   _____   Phone No.
Co-Broker's Address   Broker's Address

EARNEST MONEY RECEIPT

Receipt of $ _____ Earnest Money in the form of _____
is acknowledged and is accepted subject to the terms of the contract.

Escrow Agent _____   By: _____

Date _____, 19 _____

The form of this contract has been approved by the Texas Real Estate Commission. Such approval relates to this contract form only. No representation is made as to the legal validity or adequacy of any provision in any specific transaction. It is not suitable for complex transactions. Extensive riders or additions are not to be used. (05-87) TREC NO. 23-0.

005

Good and Workmanlike Construction

A second issue that arises in the sale of a new home concerns the quality of the workmanship and materials used in the building. Some of the issues of quality in materials can be addressed in a well-drafted section on specifications. For example, the parties can specify the grade carpet to be installed, the brick manufacturer to be used or the brand of appliances to be installed. These detailed specifications can serve as some control over quality of materials. However, drafting a provision concerning quality in workmanship can be difficult because it is by its nature somewhat ambiguous. The builder's notion of "good workmanship" may be significantly different from the buyer's perception. However, an even greater problem arises when the contract contains no provision regarding quality. In that case, is the buyer required to accept any level of workmanship? In 1968 the Texas Supreme Court held that a builder-vendor impliedly warranted to the buyer that the new home was built in a good and workmanlike manner. This is called the *implied warranty of habitability.* It is not necessary for the buyer and builder to agree expressly in the contract that the home will be habitable upon completion. Good workmanship is a reasonable expectation that does not have to be stated in the contract. This implied warranty covers only latent structural defects. For example, the warranty would protect the buyer against such major problems as improper electrical wiring, foundation defects, faulty plumbing and inadequate roof supports.

This implied warranty can be waived expressly by the buyer. The buyer can agree in writing that the builder has made no implied warranties of any kind in the sale of the house. The courts have long recognized the basic principle that two parties to a contract can set their own standards for performance. Consequently, the buyer should read carefully before signing any documents to determine whether or not any promises regarding the workmanship are being made and whether the buyer is waiving the implied warranty of habitability. A waiver can appear in any of the closing documents. The court has held that a waiver of the implied warranty found in the promissory note was valid.

Homeowners' Warranty Program

Frequently, the builder will make specific warranties regarding his or her work in the contract. These are called *express warranties.* For example, the builder may warrant that the house will be free from defects for one year. Another type of warranty program, which has been in existence since 1973, provides for a ten-year combined warranty and insurance package in the sale of new homes. The program is sponsored by the National Association of Home Builders, and participation in the program is voluntary. A builder who wishes to offer the warranty program to his or her customers must register with the plan, agree to observe construction standards set by the program and pay a one-time premium on each house when it is sold. During the first two years of ownership, the buyer notifies the builder of major construction defects or problems in the plumbing, heating, electrical and cooling systems, and the builder is required to make repairs to correct the defects. During the last eight years of the coverage, the buyer files claims for reimbursement with a private insurance company. Again only major structural defects are covered under the plan. The homeowners' warranty plan is widely available throughout Texas and is usually substituted for the implied warranty of habitability. Its major advantage over the implied warranty of habitability is the existence of an insurance company that will cover the cost of repairs in the event there is a major structural problem with the dwelling and the builder cannot or does not make the needed repairs.

Property Condition Provision—TREC Form (incomplete construction)

Paragraph 7 of the new home earnest money contract included in this chapter contains six subparagraphs related to the construction of the house. First, the paragraph allows for the incorporation of the plans and specifications as part of the contract. The plans and specifications should be reviewed carefully by the parties. If any changes were verbally agreed to during negotiations, these modifications should be written, initialled by the parties, referenced on the plans and included in the construction documents attached to the earnest money contract. The contract also attempts to eliminate the disagreements that can arise due to subsequent verbal change orders. This provision requires that all change orders be in writing and approved by both buyer and seller. The seller is allowed to substitute materials, equipment and appliances of equal quality to those listed in the construction documents. This right of substitution can be modified in writing by the parties at the time the contract is made.

Because changes in the plans can result in a change in the sales price, Subparagraph B of Paragraph 7 requires the parties to specify how increases in cost will be handled. The contract automatically provides that decreases in cost shall be subtracted from the sales price and loan amount.

The time period for completing the construction of the house is covered in Subparagraph D. This requires the insertion of a beginning date—if construction has not yet begun—and the completion date. The house is considered completed when it is ready for occupancy. The provision defines substantial completion as the point in time when the house has received the final approval of the governmental authority or the lender. Minor details that do not affect the habitability generally would not make the house incomplete. This subparagraph also addresses delays caused by acts of God, the buyer's acts or omissions, fire or casualty loss, strikes, boycotts and nonavailability of materials. It allows the parties to insert the number of days that can be added to the completion date for these delaying factors.

Workmanship is always an important factor for a buyer. The TREC contract allows the parties to select whether any express warranties concerning the construction of the house will be made by the seller. If the parties agree to include express warranties, the warranties either can be typed in the space provided in Paragraph 11 or written on a separate sheet of paper that is attached to the contract and referenced in Paragraph 11. The seller should furnish the description of the warranties. For example, if the seller has offered to provide the buyer with coverage under the Homeowners' Warranty Program, the seller must write a description of the coverage that can be included in the earnest money contract. This description should be referenced in Paragraph 11 and the appropriate box checked in Paragraph 7.

The implied warranty of habitability is not mentioned in the TREC form. The TREC form does not refer to any type of implied warranty. The subparagraph described above only covers express warranties. Therefore, unless a disclaimer of the implied warranty is inserted and agreed to by the parties, the seller-builder does warrant in an implied manner that the house was built in a good and workmanlike manner.

CONTRACT FOR DEED

A *contract for deed* is a legally enforceable agreement between a buyer and a seller whereby the buyer promises to make periodic installment payments to the seller toward the purchase price of real property and the seller promises to convey title to the property upon receipt of the last installment. It is also called a *land installment contract*. The rules that attach to ordinary contracts also apply to contracts for deed. The agreement must be supported by consideration and entered into by parties who have the capacity to contract.

The contract for deed is a method of financing a real estate transaction. Although this may sound like seller financing under an earnest money contract, there are significant differences. First, if the seller under an earnest money contract agrees to finance the purchase for the buyer, he or she actually transfers legal title to the buyer by deed prior to payment in full by the buyer. Under a contract for deed, legal title is not transferred until the final payment is made. During the contract term the buyer enjoys only an equitable title to the land. An *equitable title* is the right of the buyer to obtain ownership to the land when the buyer has fulfilled all the terms of the contract for deed, including payment of the full purchase price. Upon final payment, transfer of ownership by deed is required. In the event the seller refuses to execute the deed transferring title, a court can impose the remedy of specific performance.

The second difference between seller financing under an earnest money contract and the contract for deed is the execution of a debt instrument. In the earnest money contract, the loan or seller financing is evidenced by a promissory note in which the buyer promises to pay the seller the difference between the down payment and the purchase price. The loan is secured by a lien against the property sold, which is frequently referred to as a *purchase-money mortgage*. The lien is created by a document called a *deed of trust* and by a vendor's lien retained in the warranty deed. The mortgage documents are signed by the purchaser at closing when legal title is transferred. In this situation the seller has the rights of an ordinary lender. The rights of a lender are discussed in Chapters 21 and 22. By contrast, the financing terms are part of the contract for deed. The seller under a contract for deed remains the owner of the property. This gives the seller substantially greater rights than those held by the ordinary lender.

Contract Terms

As previously stated, all contracts for the sale of land must be in writing. This requirement extends to contracts for deed. The contract for deed should be supported by a written memorandum. The parties are free to agree on the terms of the contract, and the courts will enforce those terms to the extent that they do not offend public policy. Over the years certain typical terms have emerged. Generally, the specifics of the terms reflect the relative bargaining strength of the buyer and seller. It appears that the seller traditionally has possessed the upper hand.

Price

Normally the buyer pays a modest down payment and periodic installments. The installment payments include principal and interest. The installments may be payable monthly, quarterly, annually or at any other agreed-upon interval. Unless otherwise stated, taxes and insurance are the seller's responsibility because the seller is the legal owner of the property until the entire purchase price is paid. Neither statute nor custom prevents an allocation of taxes and insurance to the parties on the basis of their respective interests in the property. In most cases, however, the bargaining position of the seller is usually strong enough to require the buyer to assume the whole burden of these charges. This is not an unreasonable burden because the buyer receives the present beneficial use of the property and expects full ownership in the future.

Waste, Removal and Inspection

The buyer is normally in possession of the premises in an installment contract. Consequently, the installment buyer is in the best position to maintain the premises and keep them in good repair. Customarily, the parties include a clause in the contract that makes the buyer responsible for the maintenance. Similarly, the installment contract may include a clause against committing waste or removing fixtures or improvements without the consent of the seller. Failure of a buyer to comply with these clauses is a breach of the contract that gives rise to various remedies discussed in this chapter.

The seller needs the right to inspect the premises in order to police these provisions. For that reason a clause similar to the following is often included: "Seller shall have the right to enter on and inspect the property and the buildings and improvements thereon at least once each calendar month."

Assignment

In the absence of a provision in the contract prohibiting assignment, the buyer is free to transfer his or her interest in the land contract. Assignment does not, however, relieve the installment buyer of the obligation to continue making installment payments to the seller. The seller may desire to limit the buyer's right of assignment, being concerned that the assignee (one to whom the property is transferred) may be more likely to jeopardize the seller's interest in the property than the installment buyer. For this reason the installment contract normally includes a provision prohibiting assignment without the seller's written consent.

At any time before title passes, the seller is free to transfer the property to someone other than the installment buyer. Installment payments are then directed to the new owner. The sale is subject to the rights of the installment buyer, who remains entitled to the property upon fulfillment of the terms of the installment contract. The seller's power to assign may be limited by agreement but normally is not because of the purchaser's weaker bargaining position.

Conveyance

The buyer's ultimate objective is to receive good title to the property. Upon performance of the contractual obligations, including payment of the last installment, the seller is obligated to give a good title to the property by conveying the deed to the buyer. This requirement is normally reflected in a clause that reads as follows:

> When the buyer has paid the full purchase price with interest due and in the manner and at the time as required by the terms and conditions of this contract; and, if the buyer performs all other covenants and agreements required of the buyer by the terms and conditions of this contract, seller agrees to convey the above described property to the buyer by deed of general warranty.

Advantages to the Buyer

Most purchasers are not financially able to raise the entire purchase price in one lump sum; consequently, they must obtain financing in order to purchase the realty. A buyer, however, may not be able to secure financing from a lending institution because of an inability to meet down payment requirements or because of an unsatisfactory credit rating. Or the lender may refuse to extend credit because of the marginal value of the property. Of course, the seller may be able to extend this financing, but sellers normally do this only if adequately protected. The land contract gives a form of protection because the property remains in the name of the seller and in the event of default the seller may be able to cut off the buyer's interest quite simply, unless the contract for deed has been recorded.

The principal advantage that the installment contract offers to buyers is the ability to purchase the property. For little or no down payment, buyers are able to gain an interest in, and derive the benefit of, the property. The land installment contract increased in popularity as a financing tool in the early 1980s when high interest rates decreased the borrowing power of many people.

Advantages to the Seller

The land installment contract may also benefit the seller. Such benefits may include attracting buyers and continued incidents of legal ownership.

The main advantage to sellers is that the land installment contract provides a means for increasing the demand for property by attracting buyers who could otherwise not purchase the property because of an inability to secure outside financing. The ability to set the schedule of repayment so that it is affordable to the buyer often places the seller in a position to increase the purchase price above the market level and/or charge higher interest than the seller is paying on the mortgage. Normally, however, the property is priced in accordance with the market. The attractive terms often permit the sale of otherwise unattractive property.

The land installment contract secures the payment of the buyer's indebtedness and gives the seller certain incidents of legal ownership. As discussed earlier, the seller may assign the property subject to the contract or mortgage the property up to the indebtedness. This is attractive to a seller who may reap the benefits of incidents of ownership while involved in a sale of the property.

Disadvantages to the Buyer

The land installment contract may present certain disadvantages to the buyer. These disadvantages may arise should the seller die or fail to transfer good title or should the contract be unrecorded or should the buyer not be afforded the right to prepay the amount due under the installment contract.

Problems Created by the Death of the Seller

Although the land contract is enforceable against the seller's heirs upon death, as a practical matter enforcement may be very costly. The buyer may be forced to hire an attorney to accomplish the transfer. The beneficiaries may be difficult to locate, and the property may be tied up in probate for years. Should there be a large number of beneficiaries, the situation becomes more laden with concurrent ownership interests and difficulties. Since minor and incompetent beneficiaries may require the appointment of a guardian, resolution may be even further complicated and delayed. Similar problems are also present when the seller assigns the installment contract to another who dies.

Unwillingness or Inability to Transfer Good Title

The seller might refuse to transfer the title to the buyer after fulfillment of the contract. The buyer, who is legally entitled to the deed, may be forced to institute a costly suit seeking specific performance. Even worse, after the buyer pays the installments in conformity with the contract, the seller may not have good title. Normally, the seller has agreed to convey title to the buyer upon receiving the final payment. By prevailing authority the seller is not required to maintain marketable title during the pendency of the contract, although a few courts have taken a contrary view. The buyer could obtain protection by insisting upon a contract provision requiring the seller to maintain marketable title or by obtaining title insurance.

Title Problems

Upon completion of all terms of the contract, including payment of the last installment, legal title passes to the buyer. The deed can be recorded in the buyer's name. Until the last installment is paid, the seller holds the deed, and the property remains in the seller's name. During this interval the seller may encumber the property with mortgages or other liens. Unless the buyer is protected, he or she may pay the entire purchase price and find the property totally encumbered. By recording the land installment contract, however, the buyer can secure protection against most future encumbrances. Recording places all prospective mortgagees and lienors on notice of the buyer's interest in the property, and title problems are less likely to arise.

If the contract is unrecorded and the seller encumbers or sells the property, the installment contract buyer may be without remedy. A claim against the seller for damages will not necessarily help the buyer should the seller not be solvent. Sellers often discourage or impede the recording because it is easier to resell the property upon the buyer's default if the contract is not recorded.

Recording only protects the purchaser from subsequent transactions; therefore, the buyer should require proof of title in the seller as a condition of entering into the contract, should be sure the contract is immediately recorded and should require a clause within the contract clarifying that the seller agrees to tender a deed to the property free of all liens and other encumbrances, except as specified.

Disadvantages to the Seller

From the seller's viewpoint the land installment contract is often a compromise sometimes negotiated as a result of an inability to sell the property for cash. Two reasons may exist for this inability. High market interest rates may make it impractical for purchasers to obtain conventional financing, or the purchaser's financial status may prevent him or her from obtaining a loan from a lending institution. Because the land contract does often attract buyers who are otherwise not able to purchase the property because of their financial status, risk of default is high. Default may result in the buyer's forfeiture of all rights in the property. The buyer's interest may revert to the seller, in which case the seller is burdened with the property once again and must reenter the real estate market, necessitating additional brokerage costs and attorney fees. If the buyer has recorded the contract, the seller must have this cloud on the title removed before good title can be conveyed to a subsequent purchaser. This procedure can be costly.

Seller's Remedies

A seller possesses several remedies against a buyer who fails to pay or who otherwise defaults under the terms of the installment contract, including specific performance of the contract or damages, rescission, forfeiture and foreclosure. These remedies have been covered in general earlier. Forfeiture, however, deserves special attention as a seller's remedy under the land installment contract.

Often included within the terms of a land contract is a forfeiture clause, which provides that in the event the buyer fails to abide by the terms of the contract, the seller has the right to terminate the contract, retake possession of the property and retain all prior payments. Traditionally, these forfeiture clauses have been upheld by the courts. When enforced, the defaulting buyer loses all equity in the property, and the seller often receives a substantial windfall. The forfeiture penalty may be very severe to a defaulting buyer.

Although forfeiture is considered to be an appropriate remedy for the seller, Texas law does provide some protection to real estate that is or will be the residence of the purchaser. This protection is in the form of a notice requirement and opportunity to cure. The law is as follows:

> A seller may enforce a forfeiture of interest and the acceleration of the indebtedness of a purchaser in default under an executory contract for conveyance of real property used or to be used as the purchaser's residence only after notifying the purchaser of the seller's intent to enforce the forfeiture and acceleration and the expiration of the following periods:
>
> (1) if the purchaser has paid less than 10 percent of the purchase price, 15 days after the date notice is given;
>
> (2) if the purchaser has paid 10 percent or more but less than 20 percent of the purchase price, 30 days after the notice is given; and
>
> (3) if the purchaser has paid 20 percent or more of the purchase price, 60 days after the date notice is given. (Tex. Prop. Code §5.061)

The law specifically states that the right to redeem set out in the above statute cannot be waived by the purchaser. It is important to note that the statutory right to notice and cure is limited to real estate that is being used or will be used as the residence of the purchaser. Frequently, the installment land contract is used to buy unimproved land (which will not be the principal residence) or second homes in a resort area. In that instance the protection afforded by the statute would not be available to the purchaser. However, the courts are protective of purchasers buying property under a land installment contract and generally will interpret the statute to have the broadest coverage possible. For example, the real property can be the residence of the purchaser even when it is temporarily rented.

The statute also sets out the requirements concerning the form and content of the notice. Notice must be conspicuous and printed in ten-point boldfaced type or uppercase typewritten letters and sent to the purchaser's residence or place of business by registered or certified mail. The notice must contain the following statement:

NOTICE
YOU ARE LATE IN MAKING YOUR PAYMENT UNDER THE CONTRACT TO BUY YOUR HOME. UNLESS YOU MAKE THE PAYMENT BY _____ THE SELLER HAS THE RIGHT TO TAKE POSSESSION OF YOUR HOME AND TO KEEP ALL PAYMENTS YOU HAVE MADE TO DATE.

A seller who complies with the provisions of this statute is allowed to evict the purchaser from the real estate if the purchaser fails to cure his or her delinquency by the due date set out in the notice. If the seller has accelerated the balance due on the contract, the purchaser must pay the entire contract price by that date.

Buyer's Remedies

The buyer possesses several possible remedies against a seller who fails to convey title or otherwise defaults under the terms of the contract. The remedies of specific performance, rescission and damages discussed earlier are all available.

OPTION

An option is an agreement between an owner of property (optionor) and another (optionee) whereby the optionee has a right to purchase property within a specified time for a designated price. Under an option agreement the optionor agrees not to revoke an offer to sell for a period of time. Unlike a buyer, the optionee is not under an obligation to purchase the property but may elect to do so within the time specified in the option agreement.

The option confers upon the optionee the right to buy, whereas a buyer under a purchase contract or a land installment contract is under an obligation to buy.

Unless there is consideration to support the optionor's promise to keep the offer open, the optionor may revoke the offer at any time prior to acceptance. Consideration sufficient to support an optionor's promise to keep an offer open may be in the form of a payment of a sum of money.

• CASE BRIEF •

On July 1 Jack Kelvin made an offer to Harry Hilton to sell specified property for $25,000. Kelvin agreed to keep the offer open for 30 days. On July 15 Sally Hammond offered Kelvin $30,000 for the property. On July 21 Kelvin accepted Hammond's offer. On July 23 Kelvin revoked his offer to Hilton. On July 25 Hilton accepted Kelvin's original offer. Since there was no consideration to support Kelvin's offer to Hilton, Kelvin's revocation on July 23 was effective. *See Echols v. Bloom*, 485 S.W.2d 798 (Tex. Civ. App. 1972).

In addition to requiring consideration, an option must be in writing, signed by the optionor, describe the property and specify the price and any other conditions of sale. The absence of any of these elements makes the option unenforceable.

Other clauses contained within the option agreement pertaining to the sale of the property are those normally found within a purchase contract. The precise manner of exercising the option should be detailed, including the time and place of delivery of the notice to exercise the option. The following is an example of a notice specification:

> Notice of the exercise of this option to purchase Cornacre shall be delivered in writing to the optionor at (his) (her) place of business at (address) on or before midnight (date).

When the optionee elects to exercise the option, the optionee becomes a buyer and both parties are bound by the terms of the sale included within the option agreement. The terms should be specific so as to avoid unenforceability of the agreement. The purchase price should be designated with provision as to whether the price paid for the option is to be applied to reduce the purchase price. The price of the option may have been as nominal as $1 or may be very substantial in the case of highly speculative property. Options are desirable from the optionee's viewpoint under several circumstances.

CASE EXAMPLES

A land developer may desire ten parcels of land. The developer wants all or none. Instead of purchasing the parcels one by one, the developer may choose to attempt to purchase options on all the parcels from the various owners. If successful, the developer, upon exercise of each, acquires all the desired parcels. If the developer cannot secure options on all the parcels, then only the price paid for the options is lost.

A charitable organization desires to build a physical structure to house its operations. It locates the land but does not have the cash or the financing to purchase the land. By purchasing an option to buy the land it may be in a better position to solicit sufficient funds from contributors to permit the exercise of the option. If the organization's efforts fail to raise the funds, then only the option price is lost.

A parcel of land is located in an area that may be developed in the future and hence cause the value of the land to increase substantially. An investor may desire a long-term option to buy the land. If the area is developed and the value of the land rises, the investor may make a substantial profit by exercising or assigning the option. On the other hand, in the event the area is not developed and the value of the land is less than the price stated in the option, the investor will not exercise the option and has lost only the price paid for the option.

An option is assignable by the optionee unless assignment is prohibited expressly within the agreement. The optionee's assignee has the same rights under the option as the optionee. Upon exercise of the option by the prescribed manner, the assignee is entitled to the property subject to the terms of the option agreement.

The optionor has a right to sell the property that is under option in absence of a prohibition against sale within the option agreement. In such a case if the sale occurs, the optionor's buyer takes subject to the option, if on notice of the option. Notice need not be actual. If the option has been recorded, then any buyer would be deemed on constructive notice.

SUMMARY

This chapter completes the discussion of real estate contracts. In addition to the earnest money contract, there are three situations requiring a special contract. These are the sale of a house that is under construction or is to be constructed, a sale in which the buyer does not obtain legal title for a long period of time and an option to purchase real estate at some future time.

There are two standard contracts prepared by the Texas Real Estate Commission for use in the sale of new homes. Contracts for the sale of new homes should contain specific provisions regarding the construction of the home. Two of the more important aspects of these construction contracts are provisions establishing the specifications for the house and the quality of workmanship.

The specifications of construction must be included in the contract if they are to be enforced by the court. If the builder deviates substantially from the specifications, the court can award the homeowner one of the remedies discussed in Chapter 18. Of similar concern to the homebuyer is the quality of workmanship. In the absence of an agreement, there is an implied warranty in the sale of new homes by the builder that the house was built in a good and workmanlike manner. In some sales this implied warranty is replaced by a homeowners' warranty plan.

The second special contractual situation arises when the seller finances the purchase price of the land and retains legal title until the land is paid in full. The document used to evidence this type of sale is called a *contract for deed.* For the duration of the contract for deed the buyer has possession of the property and an equitable title to it. There are problems associated with the contract for deed not typically found when the earnest money contract is used. Therefore, buyers and sellers should be careful in using and drafting the contract for deed.

Finally, a buyer may be interested in buying a tract of land but not yet ready to commit to the purchase. In this situation an option contract could be entered into by the buyer and seller. The option enables a buyer to elect to purchase property at some future time for an agreed-upon price. Options should be drawn with the same care as any other real estate contract. It should contain specific and definite terms regarding price, legal description, method of payment and time and place of delivery of notice to exercise the option. To make the option contract valid, the buyer must pay consideration to the seller.

QUESTIONS AND CASE PROBLEMS

1. Describe the differences among a contract for deed, an earnest money contract and an option.
2. Compare and contrast the implied warranty of habitability and the homeowners' warranty program.
3. The Warrens contracted with Denison, a building contractor, for the construction of a house on the Warrens' property in Tahoka, Lynn County, Texas. After Denison constructed the house, the parties were unable to consummate the transaction. The Warrens refused to make any further payments to Denison. Denison sued for the unpaid balance of $48,400. The Warrens' defense is that Denison did not complete the contract in a good workmanlike manner. The cost to correct the defects in the dwelling was $1,961.50. Who is most likely to win and why?
4. On November 3, 1976, Ritter Homes, Inc., purchased a lot upon which it built a house. On July 27, 1977, the lot and finished house were sold to James E. Wobig. Mr. Wobig and his family occupied the house for three months and then sold it to Gupta. Sometime later the roof began to leak, and the patio pulled away from the rest of the house. Gupta discovered that this was caused by excessive

settlement in the slab foundation. Cracks also appeared in the garage slab and the driveway. None of these defects were apparent at the time of the sale and were not known to Wobig. Gupta sues Wobig and Ritter Homes, Inc., for breach of the implied warranty of habitability. Discuss the likelihood that Gupta will succeed against either party.

5. Maxwell and Dale were interested in buying a tract of land from Lake. Two earnest money contracts were drafted, and earnest money of $5,000 was deposited on each, but Maxwell and Dale were unable to obtain financing, and the deals collapsed. Subsequently, Maxwell and Dale leased the property from Lake for a three-year term commencing June 15, 1980. Under paragraph 35 of the lease agreement, Lake gave Maxwell and Dale a one-year option to purchase the property. In a letter to Maxwell and Dale dated May 11, 1981, Lake extended the option to purchase for an additional year, until June 15, 1982. On June 15, 1982, Maxwell and Dale hand-delivered a letter to Lake, purporting to exercise the option. Two days later, they delivered a cashier's check for $5,000 to Safeco Title and a letter to Lake in which they advised him that they were "ready, willing and able to pay the balance of the purchase price in full" and offered to do so. On the same day, June 17, 1982, Lake refused to close the sale, contending that the option was not exercised properly because the sale had to be closed before June 15, 1982. The lease was silent regarding the method of exercising the option. Did Maxwell and Dale properly exercise the option?

21

★

Financing and Mortgages

From the purchase of a family's modest first home to the million dollar commercial sale, financing is the key to almost every successful real estate transaction. People and institutions lend money because lending is profitable; much of the profitability stems from the risk entailed. A lender's risk is reduced when its loan is secured by property—an automobile, real estate, a firm's inventory or some other kind of valuable asset. When a loan is secured, the lender has a right to sell the security and apply the proceeds against the debt if the borrower fails to pay or violates some other term of the loan agreement.

A lien against real estate created to secure the repayment of a loan is called a *mortgage.* As security, real estate has several advantages over personal property. Mortgages, therefore, increase the attractiveness of lending to individuals and firms.

Not all loans are secured. Sometimes a lender will advance funds on the basis of the borrower's character and reputation. If the borrower *defaults*—that is, fails to pay according to the terms of the agreement—and the creditor wins a judgment, the creditor has a right to attach the borrower's nonexempt assets. Claims of a secured creditor take priority over this type of judgment, however.

The true nature of a mortgage, no matter what its form, is to establish a security right against a debtor's interest in real property. Most often the debtor's interest will be fee simple ownership, but legally mortgages may cover almost any interest in real estate that may be sold or assigned. Mortgages may be applied to rental income, life estates, estates for years, remainders and reversions, as well as other valuable property rights. Most of these interests in real estate are seldom the subject of mortgage loans, however, because they are often of limited duration or conditioned upon something that cannot be controlled.

Mortgages are frequently created in order to induce a lender to loan money to the borrower for the purpose of buying the land that will be subjected to the mortgage. Most lenders are reluctant to lend large sums of money without some type of security. Mortgages are also commonly created to secure repayment of a home improvement loan. Again, since these loans are usually for large sums of money, the lender wants more than the borrower's mere promise to repay the debt as a guarantee that the loan will be repaid. Mortgages can also be used to secure obligations that are quite unrelated to the property mortgaged.

CASE EXAMPLE

Ray Adams wished to go into business for himself as a plumbing and heating contractor. He planned to hire one or two employees and open up a small showroom from which to sell plumbing fixtures. Although Ray had saved enough money to get started, he was advised by some of the manufacturers whose lines he wished to carry that he should have a line of credit with a local bank. Ray's bank was willing to give him a $45,000 line of credit; as security the bank asked for a mortgage against rental property that he owned.

As you can see from this example, one of the fundamental principles relating to mortgages is the existence of a debt. A mortgage cannot exist without a debt. The financing of land purchases, development or improvement therefore involves two steps. First is the creation of a debt, which is usually evidenced by a document called a *promissory note*. Second is the creation of a mortgage by a document called a *deed of trust*. The **promissory note** is a written acknowledgment of the existence of the debt with a promise to repay the loan according to the terms set out in the note. The **deed of trust** is a conditional conveyance of a piece of real property to a trustee for the benefit of the lender to secure repayment of the indebtedness. Although there is no requirement that the note and deed of trust be separate documents, this is typically the case. The use and terms of promissory notes and deeds of trust will be explained in this chapter.

In addition to the note and deed of trust, another type of interest may exist in the financing of real estate purchases. This interest is called a *vendor's lien*. The vendor's lien is also a lien against real property to secure repayment of a debt. However, the similarity with the mortgage created by a deed of trust ends there. The vendor's lien is a creation of state law, and it arises automatically whenever the seller extends credit to the buyer for the purchase of the real property. It can also be created by express reservation in the deed even if a third party extends credit. In that instance, the seller assigns his or her vendor's lien to the lender. The vendor's lien will be explained in more detail in this chapter.

The need to borrow money is common in today's society. Individuals, partnerships, corporations and even state, local and federal governments borrow money. A borrower who fails to understand the terms of the note or the deed of trust stands to lose the mortgaged property to the lender. An understanding of financial arrangements is difficult but also very important. Many laws have been written to protect borrowers and assist them in understanding the terms of the loan. Some of these laws will be explained in this chapter.

Mortgage, Mortgagor and Mortgagee

Many common terms are not used with the precision they deserve, and the term *mortgage* is one of these. It is often confused with the underlying debt. Each month many people speak about paying "the mortgage," but what they pay is not the mortgage. They pay a debt so that a creditor will not have to turn to the mortgage, which secures the debt.

Many people, even some actually involved in real estate, are troubled by the terms *mortgagor* and *mortgagee*. This confusion arises because they ignore the true nature of the mortgage. They think of the funds the lender is advancing as the mortgage. Naturally then they have a tendency to refer to the lender as the mortgagor, but the funds are not the mortgage. The mortgage is the instrument the borrower gives to create a security right in the lender. The borrower thus is the mortgagor, just as the person who sells a home and gives a deed is the grantor. The mortgagee is the person or firm to whom the mortgage is given. Like the grantee of a deed, the mortgagee is the recipient of an interest in real estate.

LOAN APPLICATION AND COMMITMENT

Not too many years ago, a person who wanted to borrow on a mortgage from a bank, savings and loan or other financial institution was asked to appear before a loan committee for interrogation. Today most mortgage loans start with an application made on a printed form supplied by the lender. The information needed to complete the application is ordinarily given to a loan officer, and the form is signed by the party requesting the loan. The information provided in a loan application must be accurate and complete. An applicant who deceives or misleads a lender in a loan application can be both civilly and criminally liable.

The application serves two purposes: it supplies the lender with information necessary to decide whether the loan should be granted, and it serves as the borrower's *offer* to enter into a contract. If the lender approves the loan, it notifies the borrower and furnishes a formal commitment, often called a *loan approval*. The commitment, if it does not modify the terms in the application, is an *acceptance* of the offer. The parties have entered into a contract to make a loan with real property as security. Ordinarily the commitment contains a clause terminating the contract if the borrower does not take advantage of the loan within a specified time.

Sometimes the lender modifies the terms in the application, in effect making a *counteroffer*. The counteroffer becomes a contract only if the bor-

Figure 21.1: **REAL ESTATE LIEN NOTE**

2408
Prepared by the State Bar of Texas for use by lawyers only
Revised 11/82, 8/84, 10/85
1985 by the State Bar of Texas

REAL ESTATE LIEN NOTE

Date:

Maker:

Maker's Mailing Address (including county):

Payee:

Place for Payment (including county):

Principal Amount:

Annual Interest Rate on Unpaid Principal from Date:

Annual Interest Rate on Matured, Unpaid Amounts:

Terms of Payment (principal and interest):

Security for Payment:

Maker promises to pay to the order of Payee at the place for payment and according to the terms of payment the principal amount plus interest at the rates stated above. All unpaid amounts shall be due by the final scheduled payment date.

On default in the payment of this note or in the performance of any obligation in any instrument securing or collateral to it, the unpaid principal balance and earned interest on this note shall become immediately due at the election of Payee. Maker and each surety, endorser, and guarantor waive all demands for payment, presentations for payment, notices of intention to accelerate maturity, notices of acceleration of maturity, protests, and notices of protest.

If this note or any instrument securing or collateral to it is given to an attorney for collection or enforcement, or if suit is brought for collection or enforcement, or if it is collected or enforced through probate, bankruptcy, or other judicial proceeding, then Maker shall pay Payee all costs of collection and enforcement, including reasonable attorney's fees and court costs, in addition to other amounts due. Reasonable attorney's fees shall be 10% of all amounts due unless either party pleads otherwise.

Interest on the debt evidenced by this note shall not exceed the maximum amount of nonusurious interest that may be contracted for, taken, reserved, charged, or received under law; any interest in excess of that maximum amount shall be credited on the principal of the debt or, if that has been paid, refunded. On any acceleration or required or permitted prepayment, any such excess shall be canceled automatically as of the acceleration or prepayment or, if already paid, credited on the principal of the debt or, if the principal of the debt has been paid, refunded. This provision overrides other provisions in this and all other instruments concerning the debt.

Each Maker is responsible for all obligations represented by this note.

When the context requires, singular nouns and pronouns include the plural.

PREPARED IN THE LAW OFFICE OF

This form is reproduced here with the permission of the State Bar of Texas for informational purposes only. Further reproduction is not authorized without permission from the State Bar of Texas.

rower accepts these new terms. In practice, especially for construction lending and financing commercial real estate, the *commitment* is more important than the application. For these types of financing, the terms of the loan the lender is willing to make generally differ from the loan for which the borrower applied. The commitment becomes the basis for the contract; the parties are obligated by its terms if the counteroffer is accepted by the borrower.

Because it is the basis of a contract between borrower and seller, all of the major loan provisions should be indicated clearly and precisely. If the contract is breached, litigation may ensue. Since neither the lender nor the borrower is entitled to specific performance, each has only damages as a remedy.

When the lender refuses to honor the contract, the borrower's damages are relatively easy to calculate. They are the increased cost of obtaining the loan from some other source. Ordinarily the bulk of this cost would be the difference between the interest charged on the two loans. If the borrower does not use the funds, damages to the lender are very difficult to measure. In a number of cases the courts have held that the lender is entitled only to nominal damages. Because of problems associated with measuring the damages, many commitments for major loans contain provisions for a nonrefundable commitment fee paid by the borrower. When the fee involved is reasonable, the forfeiture of this amount has generally been accepted by courts as valid liquidated damages.

PROMISSORY NOTES

The promissory note is a contract between the borrower and the lender. The typical note includes the amount borrowed, the interest rate, the time and method for repayment as well as the borrower's obligation to pay. The note is signed by the debtor, and the original is held by the creditor until the loan has been repaid. It is uncommon for a note to be recorded or even witnessed in Texas. Promissory notes pertaining to the purchase of real estate are sometimes called *real estate lien notes*. An example of a note is shown in Figure 21.1

Debtors who sign promissory notes are obligating themselves to repay the debt. As a result, if the borrower defaults in any of the terms of the note, the lender can sue the debtor and obtain a personal judgment against him or her. This judgment can be collected by attaching the nonexempt assets of the debtor. The promissory note does *not* create a lien against any property, and therefore foreclosure is *not* a remedy available to the creditor if the only document the creditor has is a promissory note.

There are various types of notes, classified by the terms regarding the rate of interest, the time of repayment, the method of repayment and the purpose of the loan. All notes contain the promise to repay, the name of the creditor, an option to accelerate the note in the event of default and a provision to charge the debtor with the expense of collecting the debt.

The interest rate for a loan can be fixed for the duration of the note or can change over time. If the rate of interest is fixed, then the mortgage is called a *fixed-rate mortgage*. If the rate of interest can increase or decrease during the lifetime of the note, then the mortgage is called a *flexible-rate mortgage*. There are different types of flexible-rate mortgages. In some promissory notes there will be a limit on how much the interest rate can change. In others there are no caps or limits. The note should be read with care to determine if the interest rate can be changed and, if so, when and by how much.

Promissory notes are also classified by purpose. For example, a loan to purchase a residence is called a *residential mortgage*. Money is also frequently lent to construct buildings or make other improvements. Loans for this purpose are commonly called *construction* or *interim financing*. Construction loans are typically short-term notes. Upon completion of the construction the lender expects to be paid in full.

Another type of note that was popular during the 1970's is the wraparound mortgage. The wraparound mortgage involves the execution of a promissory note, the principal of which includes the balance due on the existing note and the difference between that note and the purchase price less the down payment. The wraparound note is secured by a second or additional mortgage. The wraparound mortgage became popular when interest rates were high and the supply of money was low.

CASE EXAMPLE

Al Borne owned property appraised at $250,000. The property was encumbered by a $125,000 first mortgage at nine percent interest with 12 years until maturity. Al wished to expand his plumbing business, but he needed additional funds. A friend agreed to lend him $100,000. As security Al was to give his friend a $225,000 second mortgage on the property. Al was to pay interest on this mortgage at 13 percent. The friend agreed to service the first mortgage interest of nine per cent out of the interest Al paid. Al's friend has a wraparound mortgage.

Typically, a wraparound mortgage has a higher rate of interest than the rate on the existing debt that it covers. The wraparound mortgagee collects interest exceeding that on the first mortgage, which the lender has agreed to service. This differential makes the loan attractive to the wraparound mortgagee, whose effective rate of return is increased. For example, Al's friend has advanced only $100,000 but he collects interest on $225,000. After paying the nine percent interest on the first mortgage, the friend retains the four percent difference on $125,000 as well as the 13 percent on the $100,000.

Wraparound mortgages can create a number of legal problems. Therefore, they should be used rarely and only by parties who completely understand the legal ramifications of the wraparound. For example, one hazard to the buyer is that the seller might fail to make the payments on the first mortgage and the lender may foreclose. Another problem is that the underlying mortgage may prohibit the transfer of title without permission by the lender. If it does, then a wraparound mortgage would violate that condition.

REGULATIONS AFFECTING MORTGAGE LOANS

Both state and federal regulations influence mortgage lending. Usually these regulations favor borrowers as legislators recognize that the borrower's bargaining position is weaker than the lender's. Usury statutes, the Truth-in-Lending Act and the Equal Credit Opportunity Act are examples of regulations with which lenders must contend. The Equal Credit Opportunity Act was discussed in Chapter 17. In this chapter usury laws and the Truth-in-Lending Act will be explained briefly.

Usury

Usury is the practice of charging interest on a loan in excess of a rate allowed by law. Religious disapproval of interest resulting in usury laws has influenced relationships between borrowers and lenders for centuries. The importance of usury laws depends to a large extent upon economic conditions. When money is scarce, lenders are able to charge higher rates for loans, and usury becomes a factor that they must consider. Almost every state has laws prohibiting lenders from charging excessive interest. These statutes vary appreciably from state to state. Not only do the permissible rates differ, but major differences exist in the transactions that are covered and the penalties levied against the usurious lender.

In the last twenty years the regulation of financial institutions has increasingly become the domain of federal laws and agencies. This trend has had an impact on state usury laws, particularly in the area of real estate financing. In Texas, the allowable interest rates for mortgage loans insured by the Federal Housing Administration or guaranteed by the Veterans Administration are established by those federal agencies. (Tex. Civ. Stat. art. 5069-1.09) Since 1980 the interest rate permitted on most mortgage loans secured by a first lien against residential real estate have been governed by the Depository Institutions Deregulation and Monetary Control Act, which is a federal law. However, the complex state law still limits the interest rate for such loans as home improvement loans, construction loans and business loans. Any of these loans can be secured by a lien against real estate.

There are several different usury laws in Texas. Their applicability is determined by the type of loan made and the purpose for which the loan was given. The complexity of the usury laws and the difficulty in calculating the rate of interest under conflicting court interpretations of the usury statutes would dictate a chapter or more on the topic. However, there are some general principles of usury laws that are readily understandable.

In order for a debtor to take advantage of the protection afforded by a usury statute, the transaction must involve the lending of money or its equivalent, an unqualified promise by the debtor to repay and a higher rate of interest than permitted by state law.

In calculating the rate of interest on a particular loan, all expenses of obtaining the financing with the exception of costs associated with servicing the loan are to be included. The ceilings on interest rates in Texas vary from six percent to 24 percent, depending upon the purpose of the loan, the type of borrower and the length of the loan.

A lender who violates one of the state's usury laws could be subjected to a forfeiture penalty of three times the amount of the usurious interest contracted for or charged. Usurious interest is the difference between the amount charged and the amount allowable by law. The winning borrower is also allowed to recover attorney fees and court costs. If the lender can prove that the usurious interest charge resulted from accident or a bona fide error in calculating the interest, then the lender can avoid the penalty and will merely forfeit the usurious interest charged the borrower. It should be noted that ignorance of the law or failure to understand the complexity of the state usury laws is not a bona fide error.

Truth-in-Lending Act

Truth-in-Lending is the popular name given to part of the Consumer Credit Protection Act of 1968. (15 U.S.C. §1601 et seq.) The ***Truth-in-Lending Act*** requires those who regularly lend or who regularly arrange for the extension of credit to disclose the cost of consumer credit so that users can better compare the terms available from different sources. The purpose is to foster the informed use of consumer credit, that is, credit extended to an individual to be used primarily for personal, family or household purposes. This legislation in no way fixes maximum or minimum charges for credit.

The key to understanding Truth-in-Lending is the *meaningful disclosure*. Provisions of both this act and of Regulation Z, the Federal Reserve Board's interpretations of the act, require that borrowers be furnished with the facts they need to make intelligent decisions on the use of credit. To accomplish this, information must be presented using terminology specified in the act and Regulation Z. This information must be clear, conspicuous and in writing. Generally, the information must cover all costs of credit, including in most cases the finance charge and the annual percentage rate.

Finance Charge

Prior to Truth-in-Lending, some lenders presented credit to borrowers in a manner that concealed or even misrepresented costs. Although institutions furnishing real estate credit were not generally as flagrant as other suppliers of consumer credit, some confusing practices did exist in the mortgage lending market. A relatively common practice was to charge a borrower for extras, loan fees, service charges or points that were not quoted with the interest rate. The 1968 act requires lenders to disclose the dollar total of *all costs* of credit. Extra charges cannot be tallied separately if they are a cost of credit but must be included in the finance charge.

Costs that a buyer would pay regardless of whether or not credit is extended need not be included in the finance charge. Items such as title examination fees, title insurance premiums, survey costs and legal fees fit into this category. These costs must be itemized and disclosed to the borrower separately if included in the total financed. One exception is a first purchase-money mortgage on residential property, for which the mortgage is not required to state the total dollar finance charge.

Annual Percentage Rate

The Truth-in-Lending Act defines the annual percentage rate as the relationship between the total finance charge and the amount to be financed. Disclosure of the annual percentage rate (APR) allows consumers to compare finance charges on a comparable basis, making the cost of credit more understandable. Based on a time period of a year, the APR is similar to simple annual interest, a concept with which many consumers are expected to be familiar.

Real estate credit is only one of many types of credit covered by the act. To come within the scope of the act, real estate credit must be extended to a natural person and be granted to finance acquisition or initial construction of the borrower's principal dwelling. Thus, mortgage loans to corporations and to individuals for business purposes are excluded. Credit extended to the owner of a dwelling containing more than four units is also exempt.

Three-Day Right of Rescission

Another important requirement of the Truth-in-Lending Act is the three-day right of rescission given to the borrower in certain transactions. If the loan is secured by a junior lien against the borrower's principal residence, then the borrower may have the right to rescind the loan agreement after it is signed. The lender is required to notify the consumer of this right of rescission, and the consumer must exercise his or her right within three business days after receipt of the notice or closing of the transaction, whichever is later. Residential first lien mortgages and refinancing of residential mortgages are specifically excluded. Residential mortgages are defined in the act as loans made for the purchase or initial construction of a residential dwelling. The area where the right of rescission is most important in Texas is loans made for home improvements. If the borrower elects to rescind a home improvement loan within the three days, the lien against the property becomes void, and the consumer is released from any liability for the finance charges. The consumer must return any money received to the creditor.

Advertisements

Finally, the Truth-In-Lending law regulates the contents of advertisements for credit. Credit advertising includes all commercial messages that either directly or indirectly promote a credit transaction. Developers, real estate brokers and lenders are subject to the act if their advertisement includes credit terms to be granted by the seller. Although the definition of advertising includes oral as well as written communication, the definition does not encompass a broker or developer responding to a buyer's inquiries about available financing.

Of the several advertising provisions of the Truth-in-Lending Act, two are generally applicable to real estate transactions. First, there is the fundamental principle that no advertisement contain terms that are not regularly granted by the creditor or seller. For example, an advertisement offering new homes at "$1.00 down" violates the act if the seller does not customarily accept this amount as a down payment. The second principle that applies to real estate transactions is referred to as "triggering." Triggering occurs when an advertisement provides certain credit information in the message. Regulation Z of the Truth-in-Lending Act mandates that additional information also be supplied along with that data. The four triggering terms are (1) amount or percentage of any down payment (2) the number of payments or time period for repayment, (3) the amount of any payment and (4) the amount of any finance charge. The inclusion of this information in the advertisement triggers a requirement that additional information also be included so that the consumer is not deceived or misled. The additional information is as follows: (1) the amount or percentage of the down payment, (2) the terms of repayment and (3) the annual percentage rate.

DEEDS OF TRUST

A mortgage in Texas is any type of agreement that pledges real property as security for repayment of a debt. The deed of trust is the most common way to create the mortgage, but it is not the only method.

The deed of trust is a written document in which the owner of the land, who is usually also the debtor, conveys title to the land to a trustee to secure repayment of the indebtedness for the benefit of the lender, who is the beneficiary of the trust. This conveyance of title is treated differently by the various states. In some states this conveyance is interpreted as an actual transfer of title from the mortgagor to the trustee for the mortgagee. This is called the *title theory*. However, even in states following the title theory, the mortgagee does not have the right to possession until there has been a default by the mortgagor.

Although the language used in the deed of trust could be interpreted as vesting legal title to the land in the trustee until the indebtedness has been repaid, the Texas courts have not chosen to accept this interpretation. In-

Figure 21.2: **DEED OF TRUST**

2402
Prepared by the State Bar of Texas for use by lawyers only.
Revised 10/85.
© 1985 by the State Bar of Texas

DEED OF TRUST

Date:

Grantor:

Grantor's Mailing Address (including county):

Trustee:

Trustee's Mailing Address (including county):

Beneficiary:

Beneficiary's Mailing Address (including county):

Note(s)
  Date:

  Amount:

  Maker:

  Payee:

  Final Maturity Date:

  Terms of Payment (optional):

Property (including any improvements):

Prior Lien(s) (including recording information):

Figure 21.2: (continued)

Other Exceptions to Conveyance and Warranty:

For value received and to secure payment of the note, Grantor conveys the property to Trustee in trust. Grantor warrants and agrees to defend the title to the property. If Grantor performs all the covenants and pays the note according to its terms, this deed of trust shall have no further effect, and Beneficiary shall release it at Grantor's expense.

Grantor's Obligations

Grantor agrees to:

1. keep the property in good repair and condition;
2. pay all taxes and assessments on the property when due;
3. preserve the lien's priority as it is established in this deed of trust;
4. maintain, in a form acceptable to Beneficiary, an insurance policy that:
   a. covers all improvements for their full insurable value as determined when the policy is issued and renewed, unless Beneficiary approves a smaller amount in writing;
   b. contains an 80% coinsurance clause;
   c. provides fire and extended coverage, including windstorm coverage;
   d. protects Beneficiary with a standard mortgage clause;
   e. provides flood insurance at any time the property is in a flood hazard area; and
   f. contains such other coverage as Beneficiary may reasonably require;
5. comply at all times with the requirements of the 80% coinsurance clause;
6. deliver the insurance policy to Beneficiary and deliver renewals to Beneficiary at least ten days before expiration;
7. keep any buildings occupied as required by the insurance policy; and
8. if this is not a first lien, pay all prior lien notes that Grantor is personally liable to pay and abide by all prior lien instruments.

Beneficiary's Rights

1. Beneficiary may appoint in writing a substitute or successor trustee, succeeding to all rights and responsibilities of Trustee.
2. If the proceeds of the note are used to pay any debt secured by prior liens, Beneficiary is subrogated to all of the rights and liens of the holders of any debt so paid.
3. Beneficiary may apply any proceeds received under the insurance policy either to reduce the note or to repair or replace damaged or destroyed improvements covered by the policy.
4. If Grantor fails to perform any of Grantor's obligations, Beneficiary may perform those obligations and be reimbursed by Grantor on demand at the place where the note is payable for any sums so paid, including attorney's fees, plus interest on those sums from the dates of payment at the rate stated in the note for matured, unpaid amounts. The sum to be reimbursed shall be secured by this deed of trust.
5. If Grantor defaults on the note or fails to perform any of Grantor's obligations or if default occurs on a prior lien note or other instrument, Beneficiary may:
   a. declare the unpaid principal balance and earned interest on the note immediately due;
   b. request Trustee to foreclose this lien, in which case Beneficiary or Beneficiary's agent shall give notice of the foreclosure sale as provided by the Texas Property Code as then amended; and
   c. purchase the property at any foreclosure sale by offering the highest bid and then have the bid credited on the note.

Figure 21.2: (continued)

Trustee's Duties

If requested by Beneficiary to foreclose this lien, Trustee shall:

1. either personally or by agent give notice of the foreclosure sale as required by the Texas Property Code as then amended;

2. sell and convey all or part of the property to the highest bidder for cash with a general warranty binding Grantor, subject to prior liens and to other exceptions to conveyance and warranty; and

3. from the proceeds of the sale, pay, in this order:

    a. expenses of foreclosure, including a commission to Trustee of 5% of the bid;

    b. to Beneficiary, the full amount of principal, interest, attorney's fees, and other charges due and unpaid;

    c. any amounts required by law to be paid before payment to Grantor; and

    d. to Grantor, any balance.

General Provisions

1. If any of the property is sold under this deed of trust, Grantor shall immediately surrender possession to the purchaser. If Grantor fails to do so, Grantor shall become a tenant at sufferance of the purchaser, subject to an action for forcible detainer.

2. Recitals in any Trustee's deed conveying the property will be presumed to be true.

3. Proceeding under this deed of trust, filing suit for foreclosure, or pursuing any other remedy will not constitute an election of remedies.

4. This lien shall remain superior to liens later created even if the time of payment of all or part of the note is extended or part of the property is released.

5. If any portion of the note cannot be lawfully secured by this deed of trust, payments shall be applied first to discharge that portion.

6. Grantor assigns to Beneficiary all sums payable to or received by Grantor from condemnation of all or part of the property, from private sale in lieu of condemnation, and from damages caused by public works or construction on or near the property. After deducting any expenses incurred, including attorney's fees, Beneficiary may release any remaining sums to Grantor or apply such sums to reduce the note. Beneficiary shall not be liable for failure to collect or to exercise diligence in collecting any such sums.

7. Grantor assigns to Beneficiary absolutely, not only as collateral, all present and future rent and other income and receipts from the property. Leases are not assigned. Grantor warrants the validity and enforceability of the assignment. Grantor may as Beneficiary's licensee collect rent and other income and receipts as long as Grantor is not in default under the note or this deed of trust. Grantor will apply all rent and other income and receipts to payment of the note and performance of this deed of trust, but if the rent and other income and receipts exceed the amount due under the note and deed of trust, Grantor may retain the excess. If Grantor defaults in payment of the note or performance of this deed of trust, Beneficiary may terminate Grantor's license to collect and then as Grantor's agent may rent the property if it is vacant and collect all rent and other income and receipts. Beneficiary neither has nor assumes any obligations as lessor or landlord with respect to any occupant of the property. Beneficiary may exercise Beneficiary's rights and remedies under this paragraph without taking possession of the property. Beneficiary shall apply all rent and other income and receipts collected under this paragraph first to expenses incurred in exercising Beneficiary's rights and remedies and then to Grantor's obligations under the note and this deed of trust in the order determined by Beneficiary. Beneficiary is not required to act under this paragraph, and acting under this paragraph does not waive any of Beneficiary's other rights or remedies. If Grantor becomes a voluntary or involuntary bankrupt, Beneficiary's filing a proof of claim in bankruptcy will be tantamount to the appointment of a receiver under Texas law.

8. Interest on the debt secured by this deed of trust shall not exceed the maximum amount of nonusurious interest that may be contracted for, taken, reserved, charged, or received under law; any interest in excess of that maximum amount shall be credited on the principal of the debt or, if that has been paid, refunded. On any acceleration or required or permitted prepayment, any such excess shall be canceled automatically as of the acceleration or prepayment or, if already paid, credited on the principal of the debt or, if the principal of the debt has been paid, refunded. This provision overrides other provisions in this and all other instruments concerning the debt.

9. When the context requires, singular nouns and pronouns include the plural.

10. The term *note* includes all sums secured by this deed of trust.

11. This deed of trust shall bind, inure to the benefit of, and be exercised by successors in interest of all parties.

12. If Grantor and Maker are not the same person, the term *Grantor* shall include Maker.

13. Grantor represents that this deed of trust and the note are given for the following purposes:

Figure 21.2: (continued)

(Acknowledgment)

STATE OF TEXAS
COUNTY OF

This instrument was acknowledged before me on the   day of   , 19
by

_____
Notary Public, State of Texas
Notary's name (printed)

Notary's commission expires

(Corporate Acknowledgment)

STATE OF TEXAS
COUNTY OF

This instrument was acknowledged before me on the   day of   , 19
by
of
a   corporation, on behalf of said corporation

_____
Notary Public, State of Texas
Notary's name (printed)

Notary's commission expires

AFTER RECORDING RETURN TO   PREPARED IN THE LAW OFFICE OF stead the courts have held that the language creates a lien with a power to foreclose in the trustee. This is called the *lien theory*, and most states, including Texas, follow this theory instead of the title theory. Typical language found in the deed of trust creating the lien is as follows:

> I, Bob Debtor, of Hudspeth County, Texas, hereinafter called Grantor, for the purpose of securing the indebtedness hereinafter described, and in consideration of the sum of TEN DOLLARS ($10.00) to us in hand paid by the Trustee hereinafter named, the receipt of which is hereby acknowledged, and for the further consideration of the uses, purposes and trusts hereinafter set forth, have granted, sold and conveyed, and by these presents do grant, sell and convey unto Tom Trustee, Trustee, of Hudspeth County, Texas, and his substitutes or successors, all of the following described property. . . .

The trustee named in the deed of trust is a special agent for both the debtor and the lender. The trustee has an obligation to act fairly and to follow the terms of the trust set out in the deed of trust. It is the deed of trust that gives the trustee his or her power to act. In Texas, the trustee is not required to be a neutral party. The lender can serve as his or her own trustee. However, if the lender chooses to act as the trustee, then he or she must act impartially.

The deed of trust recites and acknowledges the promissory note or debt for which the mortgage was created. The following language is common:

> This conveyance, however, is made in trust to secure payment of one certain promissory note of even date herewith in the principal sum of Sixty-two Thousand and no/100s Dollars ($62,000.00) executed by Grantors, payable to the order of First National Lender of Texas, in the City of Houston, Harris County, Texas as follows, to wit: bearing interest at the rate of 11.0% annually, payable in 360 equal monthly installments of $590.24 each, beginning April 1, 1986.

In addition to securing repayment of a particular promissory note, the deed of trust in Texas can secure repayment of other indebtedness. For example, the deed of trust can include a clause that expands the mortgage to include future advances made by the lender. The inclusion of the following language in the deed of trust would create a mortgage against the real property for future advances:

> Upon request of Borrower, Lender, at Lender's option prior to release of this mortgage, may make future advances to Borrower. Such future advances, with interest thereon, shall be secured by

this mortgage when evidenced by promissory notes stating that said notes are secured hereby.

In addition to creating the lien or mortgage, the deed of trust contains covenants and warranties made by the borrower to the lender. These covenants are important. They give the lender rights and impose duties on the borrower. Typical covenants found in a deed of trust in Texas are covenants of ownership; covenants to pay taxes on the real property, to insure the real property, and to maintain the real property; and an assignment of rents. These are just a few of the promises made by the borrower. Figure 21.3 contains typical deed of trust provisions and the effect of those clauses.

Figure 21.3: **TYPICAL DEED OF TRUST PROVISIONS**

Grantors covenant and agree as follows:

1. That they are lawfully seized of said property, and have the right to convey same; that said property is free from all liens and encumbrances, except as herein provided.

   [This covenant warrants ownership of the property and promises that there are no liens of any kind against the property except those specifically listed in the deed of trust.]

2. To protect the title and possession of said property and to pay when due all taxes and assessments now existing or hereafter levied or assessed upon said property, or the interest therein created by this Deed of Trust, and to preserve and maintain the lien hereby created as a first and prior lien on said property including any improvements hereafter made a part of the realty.

   [This covenant promises that the borrower will take whatever action is necessary to protect the title of the property. Further, the debtor promises to pay all taxes and protect the lender's lien against the property.]

3. To keep the improvements on said property in good repair and condition, and not to permit or commit any waste thereof; to keep buildings occupied so as not to impair the insurance carried thereon.

   [This covenant promises that the property will be maintained by the borrower and that any insurance provisions requiring occupancy of the building be honored.]

4. To insure and keep insured all improvements now or hereafter created upon said property against loss or damage by fire and windstorm, and any other hazard or hazards as may be reasonably required from time to time by Beneficiary during the term of the indebtedness hereby secured, to the extent of the original amount of the indebtedness hereby secured, or to the extent of the full insurable value of said improvements, whichever is lesser, in

such form and with such insurance company or companies as may be approved by said Beneficiary, and to deliver to Beneficiary the policies of such insurance having attached to said policies such mortgage indemnity clause as Beneficiary shall direct; to deliver renewals of such policies to Beneficiary at least ten days before any such insurance policies shall expire; any proceeds which Beneficiary shall receive under such policy or policies, may be applied by Beneficiary, at his option, to reduce the indebtedness hereby secured, whether then matured or to mature in the future, and in such manner as Beneficiary may elect, or Beneficiary may permit Grantors to use said proceeds to repair or replace all improvements damaged or destroyed and covered by said policy.

[This covenant requires that the property be insured to the extent possible and in a sum sufficient to protect the lender's interest. The policy must reflect the name of the lender and nature of his or her interest in the policy of insurance. Also important is the fact that this provision grants to the lender the right to choose how the insurance proceeds will be used. The lender can choose to take as much of the proceeds as he or she needs to satisfy the indebtedness. The lender is under no obligation to release to the debtor the money necessary to repair or rebuild.]

5. To pay to Lender on the day monthly installments of principal and interest are payable under the Note, until the Note is paid in full, a sum equal to one-twelfth (1/12) of the yearly taxes and assessments, and one-twelfth (1/12) of the yearly premium installments for hazard insurance, plus one-twelfth of yearly premium installments for mortgage insurance if any, all as reasonably estimated initially and from time to time by lender on the basis of assessments and bills and reasonable estimates thereof.

[This covenant allows the lender to escrow the amount necessary to pay taxes and insurance premiums on the property.]

6. Lender may make or cause to be made reasonable entries upon any inspections of the property, provided that lender shall give borrower notice prior to such inspection specifying reasonable cause therefor related to Lender's interest in the property.

[This covenant allows the lender to inspect the property.]

7. As further security for the payment of the hereinabove described indebtedness, Grantors hereby transfer, assign and convey unto Beneficiary all rents issuing or to hereafter issue from said real property, and in the event of any default in the payment of said note or hereunder, Beneficiary, his agent or representative, is hereby authorized, at his option, to collect said rents, or if such property is vacant to rent same and collect the rents, and

apply the same, less the reasonable costs and expenses of collection thereof, to the payment of said indebtedness, whether then matured or to mature in the future, and in such manner as Beneficiary may elect.

[This covenant assigns to the lender all rents from the property and the right to rent the property if it is vacant. Any rent collected by the lender will be applied to the indebtedness.]

8. Beneficiary shall be entitled to receive any and all sums which may become payable to Grantors for the condemnation of the hereinabove described real property, or any part thereof, for public or quasi-public use, or by virtue of private sale in lieu thereof, and any sums which may be awarded or become payable to Grantors for damages caused by public works or construction on or near the said property.

[This covenant grants to the lender the right to receive money received by the borrower as a result of the government's right of eminent domain. Any money received shall be applied to the amount due on the loan unless the lender chooses to pay all or a portion of it to the borrower.]

9. It is further agreed that if Grantors, their heirs or assigns, while the owner of the hereinabove described property should commit an act of bankruptcy, or authorize the filing of a voluntary petition in bankruptcy, or should an act of bankruptcy be committed and involuntary proceedings instituted or threatened, should the property hereinabove described be taken over by a Receiver for Grantors, their heirs or assigns, the note hereinabove described shall, at the option of Beneficiary, immediately become due and payable, and the acting Trustee may then proceed to sell the same under the provisions of this deed of trust.

[This covenant automatically accelerates payment of the note in the event the borrower is bankrupt and allows the lender to foreclose under the power of sale.]

Deeds of trust also have two clauses that are of particular importance to the borrower. These clauses allow the lender to demand that the borrower immediately repay the entire note. These are frequently called *acceleration clauses.*

The first type of acceleration clause allows the lender to accelerate payment of the indebtedness for failure to make the required payments on the note on a timely basis. It also allows for acceleration if any of the covenants set out in the deed of trust are breached, including such promises as the duty to keep the premises in good repair and to pay the taxes and insurance. An example of this type of acceleration clause is as follows:

Grantors covenant and agree as follows: That in the event of default in the payment of any installment, principal or interest, of the note hereby secured, in accordance with the terms thereof, or of a breach of any of the covenants herein contained to be performed by Grantors, then and in any of such events Beneficiary may elect, Grantors expressly waiving presentment and demand for payment, to declare the entire principal indebtedness hereby secured with all interest accrued thereon and all other sums hereby secured immediately due and payable.

The other type of acceleration clause allows the lender to demand that the debtor immediately repay the note in full when the property is sold. This is called a *due-on-sale* or *alienation clause.* The term is somewhat misleading because the clause usually allows the lender to call the note due if any type of transfer or assignment of any interest in the property is made. This provision is extremely important because it affects subsequent transfers and uses of the property by the debtor. Two clauses providing for acceleration of the note in the event of transfer follow. Compare and contrast these provisions.

A. Grantor covenants and agees that he will not convey, assign, otherwise transfer or hypothecate his interest, or any part of his interest, in the above described property, or any portion of the above described property, without first obtaining written consent of the lender. Any conveyance, assignment or other hypothecation without the prior written consent of the lender shall give the lender the right and option to mature said note and to declare the entire indebtedness, both principal and accrued interest, due and owing, and to demand prompt payment thereof, and if same is not paid within ten (10) days, foreclosure proceedings may be instituted hereunder. It is understood that the lender is under no obligation to give its consent to any such transfer or conveyance by the Grantor and may withhold its consent. The acceptance by the lender of any payment or payments subsequent to such sale, assignment, transfer or hypothecation shall not be deemed a waiver of the options set forth herein.

B. If all or any part of the property or an interest therein is sold or transferred by borrower without lender's prior written consent, excluding (a) the creation of a lien or encumbrance subordinate to this mortgage; (b) the creation of a purchase money security interest for household appliances; (c) a transfer by devise, descent, or operation of law upon the death of a joint tenant; or (d) the grant of any leasehold interest of three (3) years or less not containing an option to purchase, lender may, at lender's option, declare all the sums secured by this mortgage to be immediately due and payable. Lender shall have waived such option to accelerate if, prior to the sale or transfer, lender and the person to whom the property is to be sold or transferred reach agreement in writing that the credit of such person is satisfactory to lender and that the interest payable on the sums secured by this mortgage shall be at such rate as lender shall request. If lender has waived the option to accelerate provided in this paragraph and if borrower's successor in interest has executed a written assumption agreement accepted in writing by lender, lender shall release borrower from all obligations under this mortgage and the note. If lender exercises such option to accelerate, lender shall mail borrower notice of acceleration in accordance with the terms herein. Such notice shall provide a period of not less than thirty (30) days from the date the notice is mailed within which borrower may pay the sums declared due. If borrower fails to pay such sums prior to the expiration of such period, lender may, without further notice or demand on borrower, invoke any remedies permitted herein.

Neither of these clauses prohibits transfers of the property, nor do these provisions make acceleration of the note automatic. The lender has an option to demand full and final payment of the note immediately. The option rests solely with the lender. The exercise of the option must be reasonable, however, and notice must be given to the borrower.

Finally, deeds of trust in Texas contain a provision that allows the trustee to foreclose without a court order and apply the proceeds from the sale to the indebtedness. This provision and the procedure for foreclosure in Texas will be discussed in the next chapter.

Deeds of trust should be recorded in the real property records of the county in which the land is located. Failing to record the deed of trust does not affect the rights of the parties to the mortgage as to each other. Nor will failure to record invalidate a mortgage against someone who knew of the mortgage. However, recording does protect the mortgagee against other lienholders and subsequent purchasers for value. It preserves the lien against the property even if the owner sells it at a later date.

CASE EXAMPLE

Bank *A* has a mortgage against Blackacre that was never recorded. Sally buys Blackacre without notice of the lien held by Bank *A*. Sally owns Blackacre free and clear of any lien. If Bank *A* had recorded its lien, then Sally would own the land subject to the mortgage.

Recording can also affect the priority among competing lienholders. Priority is discussed in the next chapter.

Rights and Obligations of the Parties

Although the formal document called a *deed of trust* is usually executed when a mortgage is created, there are other ways to create a mortgage. There are only two requirements for the creation of a mortgage: the existence of a debt and a description of the property to be charged sufficient to identify it. In addition, the various covenants and clauses discussed in the previous section can be changed or deleted, and new terms can be added. No particular form is required. Consequently, a question can arise regarding the relative rights of the mortgagor and mortgagee that are not covered in the mortgage agreement. In the absence of a specific agreement to the contrary, the debtor and the lender each have rights that arise automatically. These rights can be waived, transferred or modified if the deed of trust specifically provides for it.

Because Texas is a lien theory state, the mortgagor (borrower) has the right to possession and use of the property. The right to possession remains in the mortgagor even if he or she has defaulted. The mortgagor has the right to remain in possession until the foreclosure sale is concluded. This right to use and possession of the property includes the right to rent the property and keep the rental.

The mortgagor also has the right to transfer the property. Of course the mortgagor should be aware that the lender may have the right to call the balance due on the note if there is a due-on-sale clause. Furthermore, the transfer of mortgaged property does not automatically release the seller from liability on the mortgage. Usually, the seller remains personally liable to repay the mortgage if the purchaser defaults. This is discussed in more detail below.

The mortgagee has the right to prevent the property from being destroyed or devalued. Further, the mortgagee can sue the person who caused the waste or destruction of the property for any damages the creditor suffered. The mortgagee can collect the indebtedness from the debtor personally, from the sale of the land or both.

RELATIONSHIP BETWEEN THE PROMISSORY NOTE AND THE DEED OF TRUST

The promissory note and the deed of trust perform two separate and distinct purposes. Both of these instruments are used when the purchase of land is financed. The example that follows illustrates the role of each document in financing.

CASE EXAMPLE

In 1983, Taylor, the purchaser, paid $75,000 for a house in San Antonio. State Bank lent Taylor $70,000 to make the purchase. At closing, Taylor signed a promissory note in the amount of $70,000, payable to State Bank, and a deed of trust that created a lien against the house to secure repayment of the note. Taylor defaults on the loan in 1986. Due to depressed economic conditions in the area, the house has actually decreased in value and is worth only $68,000 at the time of the default. State Bank has two remedies it can pursue. It can sue Taylor for breach of the promissory note, and it can foreclose under the lien created by the deed of trust. The amount due State Bank is $73,450, which includes the outstanding principal balance on the note, accrued unpaid interest and the costs of foreclosing. Since Taylor had signed a deed of trust giving State Bank a lien against the house, State Bank can foreclose its lien, sell the house and apply the proceeds to the loan.

At the foreclosure sale, the house is sold for $68,000. State Bank is owed $73,450; therefore, there remains a balance due of $5,450. State Bank has the right to sue Taylor to collect the deficiency of $5,450.

Alternatively, State Bank can sue Taylor for $73,450 and not foreclose. If State Bank chooses not to foreclose, then it is enforcing the promises made in the note.

OTHER FORMS OF MORTGAGES

Outside of Texas, the most commonly used mortgage in the United States is a two-party instrument. This two party instrument is called a *mortgage deed*. Mortgage deeds can be used in Texas but are uncommon. By its terms one of the parties, the mortgagor, creates a security interest in property for the other, the mortgagee. Because historically the mortgage was a conveyance, the mortgage often has many provisions similar to those of a deed.

Legislative bodies in a few states have adopted statutory mortgage forms. Although they contain all elements essential to a valid mortgage, use of the statutory form is not required.

In general for an instrument to be effective as a mortgage, it should at least include the following information:

- Names of the parties
- Description of the premises
- Language indicating that the instrument is given as security for a debt
- Statement of the debt secured
- Terms for repaying the debt

In addition, the mortgage must be signed by the mortgagor and executed according to the laws of the state in which the property is located. At least between the original parties, the law treats many instruments as mortgages even in the absence of such information. If the instrument is not in the proper form, however, the mortgagee often cannot assert it against other creditors, and it may not be recorded.

Most mortgages contain substantially more information than the minimal requirements. Because the parties insert many provisions designed to protect their rights, mortgage instruments may tend to be lengthy. The recording process is expensive and requires a great amount of storage space. A number of states have adopted statutes that allow mortgagees to record a *master mortgage* containing the desired covenants and clauses. This practice permits execution and recording of a mortgage that incorporates by reference the provisions of the master mortgage. What is stated is the recording date, file number, volume and page of the master mortgage.

Deed Absolute

Finally, in Texas and elsewhere it is possible for a warranty deed to be construed as a mortgage or deed of trust. Although this happens rarely, the court can look behind the language of the document and at the substance of the transaction. Usually there must be evidence of a debtor-creditor relationship and some evidence that there was an intent to reconvey the property when the debt was repaid.

• CASE BRIEF •

Gonzalez and Barrera were friends. Gonzalez lent Barrera some money to operate a garage and filling station. There was a note dated April 29, 1957. Gonzalez also cosigned a note for Barrera with a Mexican bank. On November 26, 1957, Barrera executed a general warranty deed conveying to Gonzalez the two lots on which the garage and filling station were located. On January 10, 1958, Barrera committed suicide. At the time of his death the notes had not been repaid. Mrs. Barrera claimed that she was the owner of the two lots. Gonzalez claimed ownership under the general warranty deed. The trial court held that Gonzalez was the owner of the property. On appeal the court held that there was evidence that Gonzalez was a creditor to Barrera and that the deed was given to Gonzalez to secure repayment of the debt. The existence of these two important facts would be grounds for interpreting the deed as a mortgage. *Barrera vs. Gonzalez*, 341 S.W.2d. 703 (Tex. Civ. App.—San Antonio 1961).

In trying to determine the intent of the parties when a claim exists that an absolute deed is in reality a security instrument, courts consider several factors. Although any single factor may be determinative, the following four are usually given weight:

1. Adequacy of consideration
2. Relationship of the parties
3. Possession of the property
4. Payment of taxes and improvements

If the consideration is much less than the value of the property, the conveyance is almost always declared a mortgage. The relationship of the parties is also important. Usually a discrepancy exists in the bargaining power of the parties, and the court protects the mortgagor as the weaker party and declares the instrument a mortgage. Conversely, courts often declare a deed absolute when it is clear that the grantor was using the device to defraud creditors.

Two additional factors courts often take into account are who is in possession of the property and who pays the ordinary expenses of ownership.

Allowing the grantor to retain possession is some evidence that the deed was given as security. A grantor's continued payment of taxes, insurance and maintenance is an indication that the instrument was not intended as a conveyance, but as a mortgage.

The use of the warranty deed as a mortgage instrument should be avoided. One significant problem that can arise for the mortgagor is sale of the property by the mortgagee while title is held in the mortgagee's name. If the deed was recorded and the purchaser did not know that the warranty deed was intended by the parties to be a mortgage, then the mortgagor could lose the property to the innocent purchaser.

Figure 21.4: **COMPARISON OF DOCUMENTS BY WHICH MORTGAGES ARE CREATED**

Document	Characteristics
1. Deed of Trust	most common in Texas; mortgagor conveys title to a trustee for protection of mortgagee; trustee has power to sell in the event of default
2. Mortgage Deed	common outside of Texas; mortgagor grants mortgagee a lien against the real property
3. Deed Absolute	document that on its face appears to convey absolute title to the lender, but there is evidence that the lender was to re-convey title upon repayment of some debt
4. Vendor's Lien	a lien that arises automatically in Texas when the seller is financing a portion of the purchase price; upon default the seller can rescind the sale or foreclose judicially

SALE OF MORTGAGED REAL ESTATE

CASE EXAMPLE

Hal Zenick owned a home encumbered with an $85,000 mortgage at nine percent interest. The mortgage was held by the Harper Hill Savings and Loan Association (Harper Hill.) Hal, who had purchased the property for $98,000, had lived there for about a year when he was transferred and forced to sell. During the year interest rates had risen considerably in Hal's area, and the broker with whom he listed the property suggested that Hal might make a better deal if the mortgage were retained. The buyer would have the advantage of a lower interest rate and might save in other ways.

The following discussion relates to potential problems in selling the property and the rights and duties of Hal, Harper Hill and the buyer. Hal has an interest in the property that he can sell. He cannot, however, escape personal liability for the mortgage debt unless Harper Hill, the mortgagee, releases him. In addition, the property remains subject to Harper Hill's lien. Nothing that Hal can do short of paying the underlying debt can elimi-

Figure 21.5: **DEED OF TRUST TO SECURE ASSUMPTION**

2255
Prepared by the State Bar of Texas for use by lawyers only.
Revised 10-85.
© 1985 by the State Bar of Texas

DEED OF TRUST TO SECURE ASSUMPTION

Date:

Grantor:

Grantor's Mailing Address (including county):

Trustee:

Trustee's Mailing Address (including county):

Beneficiary:

Beneficiary's Mailing Address (including county):

Note and Deed of Trust Assumed
   Date:

   Amount:

   Maker and Grantor:

   Payee and Beneficiary:

   Recording Information:

Property (including any improvements):

Prior Lien(s) (including recording information):

Other Exceptions to Conveyance and Warranty:

This form is reproduced here with the permission of the State Bar of Texas for informational purposes only. Further reproduction is not authorized without permission from the State Bar of Texas.

Figure 21.5: (continued)

By deed dated the same as this instrument, Beneficiary conveyed the property to Grantor, who as part of the consideration promised to pay the note assumed and to be bound by the deed of trust assumed. Beneficiary has retained a vendor's lien.

For value received and to secure Grantor's assumption, Grantor conveys the property to Trustee in trust. Grantor warrants and agrees to defend the title to the property. If Grantor performs all the covenants of the note and deed of trust assumed and if Beneficiary has not filed a notice of advancement, a release of the deed of trust assumed shall release this deed of trust to secure assumption and Beneficiary's vendor's lien.

Beneficiary's Rights

1. Beneficiary may appoint in writing a substitute or successor trustee, succeeding to all rights and responsibilities of Trustee.
2. If Grantor fails to perform any of Grantor's obligations under the note or deed of trust assumed, Beneficiary may perform those obligations, advance funds required, and then be reimbursed by Grantor on demand for any sums so advanced, including attorney's fees, plus interest on those sums from the dates of payment at the highest legal rate. The sum to be reimbursed shall be secured by this deed of trust to secure assumption.
3. Beneficiary may file a sworn notice of such advancement in the office of the county clerk where the property is located. The notice shall detail the dates, amounts, and purposes of the sums advanced and the legal description of the property.
4. If Grantor fails on demand to reimburse Beneficiary for the sums advanced, Beneficiary may:
    a. request Trustee to foreclose this lien, in which case Beneficiary or Beneficiary's agent shall give notice of the foreclosure sale as provided by the Texas Property Code as then amended; and
    b. purchase the property at any foreclosure sale by offering the highest bid and then have the bid credited to the reimbursement of Beneficiary.

Trustee's Duties

If requested by Beneficiary to foreclose this lien, Trustee shall:
1. either personally or by agent give notice of the foreclosure sale as required by the Texas Property Code as then amended;
2. sell and convey all or part of the property to the highest bidder for cash with a general warranty binding Grantor, subject to prior liens and to other exceptions to conveyance and warranty; and
3. from the proceeds of the sale, pay, in this order:
    a. expenses of foreclosure, including a commission to Trustee of 5% of the bid;
    b. to Beneficiary, the full amount advanced, attorney's fees, and other charges due and unpaid;
    c. any amounts required by law to be paid before payment to Grantor; and
    d. to Grantor, any balance.

General Provisions

1. If any of the property is sold under this deed of trust, Grantor shall immediately surrender possession to the purchaser. If Grantor fails to do so, Grantor shall become a tenant at sufferance of the purchaser, subject to an action for forcible detainer.
2. Recitals in any Trustee's deed conveying the property will be presumed to be true.
3. Proceeding under this deed of trust to secure assumption, filing suit for foreclosure, or pursuing any other remedy will not constitute an election of remedies.
4. This lien shall be superior to liens later created even if Beneficiary has made no advancements when later liens are created.
5. If any portion of the advancements cannot be lawfully secured by this deed of trust to secure assumption, payments shall be applied first to discharge that portion.
6. No sale under this deed of trust to secure assumption shall extinguish the lien created by this instrument.
7. Grantor assigns to Beneficiary absolutely, not only as collateral, all present and future rent and other income and receipts from the property. Leases are not assigned. Grantor warrants the validity and enforceability of the assignment. Grantor may as Beneficiary's licensee collect rent and other income and receipts as long as Grantor is not in default under the note or the deed of trust assumed. Grantor will apply all rent and other income and receipts to payment of the note and performance of the deed of trust assumed, but if the rent and other income and receipts exceed the amount due under the note and deed of trust assumed, Grantor may retain the excess. If Grantor defaults in payment of the note or performance of the deed of trust assumed, Beneficiary may terminate Grantor's license to collect and then as Grantor's agent may rent the property if it is vacant and collect all rent and other income and receipts. Beneficiary neither has nor assumes any obligations as lessor or landlord with respect to any occupant of the property. Beneficiary may exercise Beneficiary's rights and remedies under this paragraph without taking possession of the property. Beneficiary shall apply all rent and other income and receipts collected under this paragraph first to expenses incurred in exercising Beneficiary's rights and remedies and then to Grantor's obligations under the

Figure 21.5: (continued)

note and deed of trust assumed in the order determined by Beneficiary. Beneficiary is not required to act under this paragraph, and acting under this paragraph does not waive any of Beneficiary's other rights or remedies. If Grantor becomes a voluntary or involuntary bankrupt, Beneficiary's filing a proof of claim in bankruptcy will be tantamount to the appointment of a receiver under Texas law.

8.   Interest on the debt secured by this deed of trust to secure assumption shall not exceed the maximum amount of nonusurious interest that may be contracted for, taken, reserved, charged, or received under law; any interest in excess of that maximum amount shall be credited on the principal of the debt or, if that has been paid, refunded. On any acceleration or required or permitted prepayment, any such excess shall be canceled automatically as of the acceleration or prepayment or, if already paid, credited on the principal of the debt or, if the principal of the debt has been paid, refunded. This provision overrides other provisions in this and all other instruments concerning the debt.

9.   When the context requires, singular nouns and pronouns include the plural.

10.   This deed of trust to secure assumption shall bind, inure to the benefit of, and be exercised by successors in interest of all parties.

(Acknowledgment)

STATE OF TEXAS
COUNTY OF

This instrument was acknowledged before me on the   day of   , 19

by

_____
Notary Public, State of Texas
Notary's name (printed):

Notary's commission expires:

(Corporate Acknowledgment)

STATE OF TEXAS
COUNTY OF

This instrument was acknowledged before me on the   day of   19

by

of

a   corporation, on behalf of said corporation.

_____
Notary Public, State of Texas
Notary's name (printed):

Notary's commission expires:

AFTER RECORDING RETURN TO   PREPARED IN THE LAW OFFICE OF nate the lien so long as the mortgage is recorded properly. Hal's right to sell his interest without discharging the mortgage may be restricted by a due-on-sale provision in the deed of trust. This has become a common clause in many residential mortgages, and therefore the seller should read his deed of trust carefully. However, if Hal's mortgage does not contain a due-on-sale clause, he make take two major approaches to selling the property without discharging the mortgage. The property may be sold with the grantee agreeing to "assume and pay" the mortgage, or the property may be sold "subject to" the mortgage.

Assumption

Assumption is a contract between a grantor-mortgagor and a grantee in which the grantee agrees to assume responsibility for the mortgage debt. Hal's broker found a buyer who was willing to pay $100,000 for Hal's residence. The buyer had $15,000 in cash and was anxious to assume the mortgage. The purchase offer that the buyer submitted to Hal contained the following provision: "Buyer assumes and agrees to pay the obligation secured by mortgage to Harper Hill Savings and Loan Association recorded in . . . according to the terms of the mortgage and the note accompanying it." When Hal accepted this purchase offer, a contract was created, one provision of which was the buyer's promise to pay the mortgage debt. The agreement to assume and pay the mortgage debt must then be written specifically in the deed conveying title to the property to the buyer.

The land remains subject to the mortgage, and, if the debt is not paid, the mortgagee may foreclose. In addition, the mortgagee without foreclosing may sue the buyer on the assumption. The mortgagee's right exists in spite of the fact that it was not a party to the assumption agreement. Its right is based on the theory that the mortgagee was an intended third-party beneficiary.

A *third-party beneficiary* is one who is allowed to enforce a contract although not a party to the agreement. The third-party beneficiary's right is based upon the theory that the contract was made for its benefit. The following diagram (Figure 21.6) illustrates the relationship among Hal, Harper Hill and the buyer. Although the contract with assumption provision is between Hal and his buyer, Harper Hill, the third-party beneficiary, can sue the buyer if there is a breach.

Even when a loan has been assumed by a buyer who is personally liable on the note, the original borrower remains liable for repayment of the debt. In order for a seller to be discharged or released, the creditor must consent. In other words, Hal remains personally liable for the note even though he has sold the property. Consequently, the original borrower, in order to protect himself in the event of default by the subsequent purchaser, may require the purchaser to execute a mortgage in his favor. This is created by an instrument called a *deed of trust to secure assumption*. (See Figure 21.5.) It is similar to the deed of trust discussed above. It gives the original borrower

Figure 21.6: **THIRD-PARTY RIGHTS IN AN ASSUMPTION**

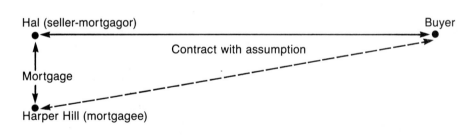

the option to pay the note if the purchaser defaults and then foreclose on the property to recover his or her loss. The deed of trust to secure assumption usually contains a provision such as the following:

> This conveyance, however, is made in trust for the following purposes:
>
> Whereas, Sam Seller, hereinafter called Beneficiary, by deed of even date herewith conveyed the herein described property to Grantors named herein, who, as part of the consideration therefor assumed and promised to pay, according to the terms thereof, all principal and interest remaining unpaid upon that one certain promissory note in the original principal sum of $62,000.00 dated March 2, 1980, executed by Sam Seller and payable to the order of First Lender of Texas which said note is secured by a Deed of Trust recorded in Volume 99, Page 99, Deed Records, of Travis County, Texas, the obligations and covenants of the grantors named in said Deed of Trust were also assumed by Grantors named herein and in said Deed the superior title and a vendor's lien were expressly reserved and retained by Beneficiary until said indebtedness and obligations so assumed are fully paid and satisfied.

The deed of trust to secure assumption has one possible disadvantage to the buyer. Occasionally, a lender will require a subordination agreement from the seller as a condition of extending new credit for a home improvement loan. Generally, sellers are more than willing to sign a subordination agreement. The problem arises only if the seller cannot be located or refuses to subordinate.

"Subject To"

Perhaps the buyer found by Hal's broker would not be willing to assume the mortgage debt. Under these circumstances, the buyer would pay Hal for his equity in the property. Any interest acquired by the buyer is "subject to" the lien of the mortgagee. If there is a default, the property will be foreclosed, but the buyer has not agreed to become personally liable.

Although the buyer has no personal liability for repayment of the note, he understands that he must pay the note according to its terms, in order to avoid foreclosure by the lender. However, if following the foreclosure sale there is a deficiency, the purchaser will not be liable. The original borrower does remain personally liable to the lender for the debt.

In recent years this particular type of sale of mortgaged property has been abused by unscrupulous purchasers in the Houston area. An economic recession in the area resulted in the loss of jobs and a depressed real estate market. Many homeowners could no longer meet their monthly house payments and at the same time found that the market value of their houses had fallen significantly. The result was that the houses could not be sold readily and, if sold, were sold at prices that did not cover the balance due on the loan. Unscrupulous investors "purchased" these homes by simply promising to take over the responsibility for the mortgage payments. Many of these investors bought the property "subject to" to the mortgage. Unfortunately, the investor did not make the monthly payments due to the mortgage company, and the mortgage company foreclosed. At the time of foreclosure the note was several months in arrears, and the proceeds from the sale of the house did not pay the balance due on the note. The seller was held to be personally liable for the deficiency and had no recourse against the investor who had promised to make the payments.

ASSIGNMENTS AND DISCHARGE

The mortgage and note are the essential instruments used when a loan is secured by real property. After the loan has been made, other developments involving it often occur. Time for repayment may be extended, the mortgagee may transfer ownership of the mortgage and note and in most cases the debt is repaid. The real estate professional should be familiar with these transactions and the documents used to accomplish them.

Assignment

One of the chief incidents of ownership is the right to assign, or to transfer to another, that which is owned. This principle applies to intangible as well as tangible property.

CASE EXAMPLE

South Central Savings financed the purchase of a residence for Marlene Jefferson. As a part of the transaction, Jefferson executed the customary note and mortgage in favor of South Central. South Central wished to obtain additional funds for lending and assigned the mortgage and note as part of a package to the Britan Insurance Company. The company discounted the notes and paid funds to South Central. Jefferson would be ob-

ligated to pay the insurance company because it now owned her obligation
to South Central Savings.

The example illustrates a common situation in which mortgages and
notes are assigned. South Central is the assignor, and Britan Insurance
Company is the *assignee*. The mortgagor, Marlene Jefferson, is referred to
as the *obligor*.

In addition to mortgages and notes, rights created by contracts, leases and
options also may be assigned. Sometimes, however, the document that creates the right may limit assignment unless the obligor agrees. This is unusual in a mortgage but more frequent in a contract for deed. The seller might
be concerned with the identity of the buyer. A mortgagor usually is not concerned with the identity of the person to whom the debt must be paid.

Understanding the mechanics of mortgage assignment is complicated by
the dual nature of the mortgage transaction. Remember that a mortgage
loan includes both a note, which is the borrower's personal promise to pay,
and the mortgage, which is security for the debt. An assignment that is
drafted properly transfers ownership of both the note and the mortgage. The
assignee becomes the owner of both the obligation and the security.

Sometimes an assignment will refer only to the note or the mortgage. In
these situations most courts have taken the position that the debt is of primary importance and the mortgage merely an incident of the debt. If an assignment transfers only the mortgage, courts rule that the assignee also
acquires the obligation, because a mortgage without a debt is meaningless.
Conversely, courts have generally ruled that any transfer of the obligation
also includes the mortgage, although the mortgage is not mentioned.

Discharge

Mortgages are commonly discharged by one of two methods: merger or payment of the mortgage debt. Merger is a combination of the interests of the
mortgagor and the mortgagee in the same person. Occasionally the mortgagee will voluntarily transfer his or her interest in the mortgaged property
to his or her creditor. For example, assume the mortgagor defaults in his
payments to the mortgagee and realizes that he will be unable to make up
the deficiency. The mortgagor offers to transfer title to the property to the
mortgagee if the mortgagee will agree not to hold him personally liable.
This type of transaction is referred to as a *deed in lieu of foreclosure*. (See
Chapter 22.) If the mortgagee accepts the offer of the mortgagor, then the
interest of the two parties has become merged in one person. This merger
results in a discharge of the deed of trust.

The more common method of discharging a deed of trust or mortgage is
by payment in full of the balance due on the note. Occasionally the borrower will have an agreement with the lender that allows for partial releases
of the mortgaged property as the balance due is reduced. For example, assume that the borrower is a developer who has borrowed funds from a com-

Figure 21.7: **RELEASE OF LIEN**

2259
Prepared by the State Bar of Texas for use by lawyers only.
Revised 10-85.
© 1985 by the State Bar of Texas

RELEASE OF LIEN

Date:

Note:
    Date:

    Original Amount:

    Maker:

    Payee:

    Date of Maturity:

Holder of Note and Lien:

Holder's Mailing Address (including county):

Note and Lien Are Described in the Following Documents, Recorded in:

Property (including any improvements) Subject to Lien:

Holder of the note acknowledges its payment and releases the property from the lien.

When the context requires, singular nouns and pronouns include the plural.

Figure 21.7: (continued)

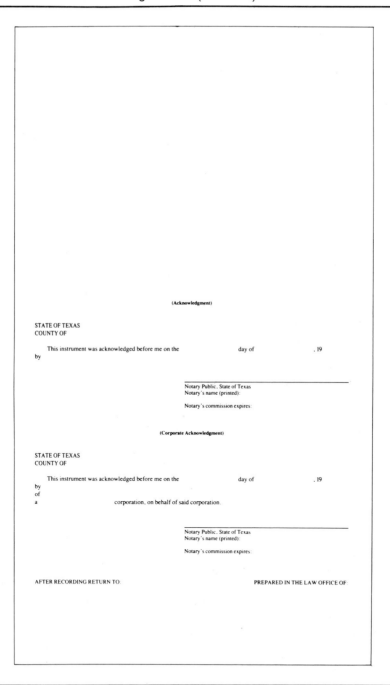

(Acknowledgment)

STATE OF TEXAS
COUNTY OF

This instrument was acknowledged before me on the   day of   , 19
by

_____
Notary Public, State of Texas
Notary's name (printed):

Notary's commission expires:

(Corporate Acknowledgment)

STATE OF TEXAS
COUNTY OF

This instrument was acknowledged before me on the   day of   , 19
by
of
a   corporation, on behalf of said corporation.

_____
Notary Public, State of Texas
Notary's name (printed):

Notary's commission expires:

AFTER RECORDING RETURN TO: PREPARED IN THE LAW OFFICE OF:

mercial lender for development of a 200-acre tract of land. The lender takes a lien against all 200 acres but agrees that as the borrower pays the note it will release portions of the property, usually on a lot-by-lot basis. This assists the developer by enabling him or her to sell lots and houses as they are developed without jeopardizing the security of the lender. Although partial releases are common in real estate development, in the ordinary residential mortgage the lien against the property will not be released until the loan has been paid in full. Upon payment in full of the mortgage, the borrower is entitled to a written release of lien from the lender. This release of lien is recorded by the borrower in the real property records in the county where the land is located. This clears the public record, serving as notice to all that the indebtedness has been paid.

VENDOR'S LIEN

A vendor's lien is a special type of mortgage arrangement that can be found in Texas. A vendor's lien is created whenever real property is sold by the owner but the purchase price has not been paid in full. The vendor's lien can be created expressly, or it can be implied from the fact that the property was sold on credit. The vendor's lien is usually reserved in the warranty deed that transfers title to the purchaser. However, it can be created in a separate instrument or in the promissory note. The following language creates a vendor's lien:

> But it is expressly agreed that the Vendor's Lien, as well as the Superior Title in and to the above described premises, is retained against the above described property, premises and improvements until the above described note and all interest thereon are fully paid according to the face, tenor, effect and reading thereof, when this Deed shall become absolute.

The vendor's lien is frequently used as additional security with a deed of trust. The vendor's lien can be claimed by the person or financial institution that provided the funds for the purchase of the property. Where this is the case, the seller usually retains a vendor's lien in the warranty deed as previously described and assigns that lien to the third-party lender in the same instrument.

A vendor's lien is a charge or encumbrance against the land that is enforceable against subsequent purchasers who knew of the debt. The vendor's lien does not contain the covenants and promises typically found in a deed of trust. The vendor's lien gives the seller or his or her assignee some security if the purchaser fails to pay the purchase price. The holder of the vendor's lien has two remedies if the debt is not paid. The first option is the right to sue the purchaser and ask the court to foreclose the vendor's lien and order the property sold to repay the debt. The other option, and more

Figure 21.8: **WARRANTY DEED WITH VENDOR'S LIEN**

2253
Prepared by the State Bar of Texas for use by lawyers only.
Revised 10-85.
© 1985 by the State Bar of Texas

WARRANTY DEED WITH VENDOR'S LIEN

Date:

Grantor:

Grantor's Mailing Address (including county):

Grantee:

Grantee's Mailing Address (including county):

Consideration:

Property (including any improvements):

Reservations from and Exceptions to Conveyance and Warranty:

Grantor, for the consideration and subject to the reservations from and exceptions to conveyance and warranty, grants, sells, and conveys to Grantee the property, together with all and singular the rights and appurtenances thereto in any wise belonging, to have and hold it to Grantee, Grantee's heirs, executors, administrators, successors, or assigns forever. Grantor hereby binds Grantor and Grantor's heirs, executors, administrators, and successors to warrant and forever defend all and singular the property to Grantee and Grantee's heirs, executors, administrators, successors, and assigns, against every person whomsoever lawfully claiming or to claim the same or any part thereof, except as to the reservations from and exceptions to warranty.

The vendor's lien against and superior title to the property are retained until each note described is fully paid according to its terms, at which time this deed shall become absolute.
When the context requires, singular nouns and pronouns include the plural.

Figure 21.8: (continued)

(Acknowledgment)

STATE OF TEXAS
COUNTY OF

This instrument was acknowledged before me on the   day of   , 19
by

———————————————————————————
Notary Public, State of Texas
Notary's name (printed):

Notary's commission expires:

(Corporate Acknowledgment)

STATE OF TEXAS
COUNTY OF

This instrument was acknowledged before me on the   day of   , 19
by
of
a   corporation, on behalf of said corporation.

———————————————————————————
Notary Public, State of Texas
Notary's name (printed):

Notary's commission expires:

AFTER RECORDING RETURN TO: PREPARED IN THE LAW OFFICE OF:

onerous to the purchaser, is the right of the seller to rescind the deed and take the property back.

Foreclosure requires court action and, consequently, can be time-consuming. Rescission does not require any court action but may be difficult to exercise unless the purchaser voluntarily relinquishes possession. If the purchaser refuses to vacate after the seller has rescinded, then the seller must file suit against the purchaser in order to have the purchaser removed.

Although the vendor's lien provides security to the mortgagee, the deed of trust is preferred. The vendor's lien cannot be quickly and easily enforced. The remedy of nonjudicial foreclosure granted in a deed of trust is the preferred method when the purchaser defaults.

Nevertheless, vendors' liens should not be overlooked. They can give the seller a different type of protection. They can cloud title to a piece of real estate. The following case illustrates the problems with land title that can be created by a vendor's lien.

• CASE BRIEF •

In 1916 Spann purchased from his seller approximately 104 acres of land. Spann signed a promissory note for a portion of the purchase price, and the seller retained a vendor's lien against the property. Later the seller assigned the note and vendor's lien to Webster. In 1919 Spann sold half of the mineral interest in the property to an unnamed party, and this was later resold to Whiteside. Spann defaulted in the payment of the note and in 1932 conveyed the 104 acres to Webster. Some time later Bell purchased the same property from Webster. The dispute between Whiteside and Bell concerns the ownership of the one-half mineral interest. Bell claims ownership through Webster and the 1932 deed. Whiteside claims ownership through the 1919 mineral deed.

The trial court found that Bell was the owner of the one-half mineral interest. The Supreme Court of Texas affirmed. The court held that the 1932 deed to Webster from Spann was a rescission of the 1916 deed. Webster exercised his option under the vendor's lien to rescind the 1916 deed, and Spann voluntarily agreed. The vendor's lien was recorded, and therefore Whiteside had notice of the terms of the lien. Whiteside took the mineral interest subject to the vendor's lien. Webster was under no obligation to notify Whiteside that the 1916 deed to Spann was being rescinded. *Whiteside v. Bell*, 347 S.W.2d 568 (Tex. 1961).

SUMMARY

The mortgage is one of two legal instruments used when real property is utilized as security for a debt. Its purpose is to reduce the risk inherent in lending by providing the lender with collateral in case the borrower defaults. The other instrument is the note, a written promise to repay a loan according to specific terms and conditions. If the borrower defaults, the lender may collect the debt by foreclosing against the property. As an alternative remedy, the lender may bring a personal action against the borrower on the note.

The mortgage loan starts with an application, which constitutes the borrower's offer to enter into a contract to borrow money. If the loan is approved, the lender issues a commitment, which constitutes acceptance, and a contract exists. In financing commercial real estate, a lender often proposes terms that differ from the loan for which the borrower applied. The commitment thus becomes a counteroffer. No contract exists unless the borrower accepts the new terms.

The promissory note is a contract between the debtor and the creditor that sets out the amount borrowed, the rate of interest and the time and method for repayment. The terms and conditions under which money will be lent are determined by the economic conditions of the money market at the time. Flexible-rate mortgages are one example of lenders' response to market conditions.

Mortgage lending practices are also influenced by state and federal laws. Two examples of legislation that regulate loan practices are state usury statutes and the Truth-in-Lending Act. The usury statutes set ceilings on the rate of interest that can be charged for a loan. In the residential real estate mortgage field the state usury statutes have been largely preempted by federal legislation. The Truth-in-Lending Act is a federal law that requires the disclosure of the cost of credit in a uniform manner so that borrowers can compare the loan offerings of various lenders. The act also regulates credit advertising and provides for a three-day right of rescission in home improvement loans.

In Texas the most common method for creating a mortgage to secure repayment of a debt is the execution of a deed of trust. By the deed of trust the borrower conditionally conveys title to the mortgaged real estate to a trustee who holds it for the benefit of the creditor.

The trustee is given certain powers under the deed of trust, and the borrower makes many promises to the lender. One of these promises is the covenant to keep the premises in good repair and condition. In the last ten years it has become a common practice for the deed of trust to include a due-on-sale or alienation clause. This is a type of provision that gives the lender the option to call the note due if the borrower transfers an interest in the property.

Mortgaged property can be sold or transferred even if there is an alienation clause. All that is necessary is to pay the lender in full at closing. In the absence of a due-on-sale clause, the mortgaged property can be sold without paying the mortgage.

A potential buyer may be able to assume the existing mortgage and continue to pay according to the same terms. Or, the owner may sell the property "subject to" the existing mortgage. In either of these cases, the mortgage continues as a lien on the property; the responsibilities of the buyer and seller differ, depending on whether the buyer "assumes" or purchases "subject to" the mortgage.

Mortgage lenders, when faced with the need to raise additional funds, often assign some of their mortgage loans to another institution. Payments on the loan so assigned must still be made according to the original terms.

The usual method of discharging a mortgage—that is, releasing property from the lien—is by payment of the debt. Upon payment, a release of lien is placed in the public record. Another method of terminating the lien is by merger of the interest of the mortgagor and the mortgagee.

QUESTIONS AND CASE PROBLEMS

1. Explain the differences in function and content between a promissory note and a deed of trust.

2. The terms *finance charge* and *annual percentage rate (APR)* are important in Truth-in-Lending legislation. Explain what each means.

3. What is a due-on-sale clause? Explain why this clause has become increasingly important in recent years.

4. On February 20, 1951, Rice and Shockley executed a promissory note and deed of trust as part of the consideration for the purchase of certain real property. Rice and Shockley sold the real property to Moore in 1953, and Moore expressly agreed to assume payment of the unpaid balance of the note. Moore defaulted in the payment of the note, the property was foreclosed and after applying the proceeds from the foreclosure sale to the indebtedness, there remained a deficiency of $14,949. The owner of the note sued Rice and Shockley for the deficiency. Rice and Shockley defended on the ground that they were released when they sold the property to Moore. Are Rice and Shockley liable for the deficiency?

5. A covenant in a deed of trust provided that the mortgagor insure the mortgaged property, and it further stated that all amounts recoverable under such policy shall be paid to the mortgagee. The deed of trust gave the mortgagee the option to apply any proceeds to the outstanding indebtedness. The Zidells suffered a fire loss on the property. They had the damage repaired at their own expense. The proceeds from the insurance coverage were paid to John Hancock Mutual Fire Insurance Co., which was the mortgagee. The Zidells demanded that Hancock release the insurance proceeds to them since they had had the fire damage repaired. Hancock refuses, citing the provision in the deed of trust giving it the option to apply the proceeds to the indebtedness. Who will prevail?

6. On September 21, 1972, Mintz sold 18.953 acres of land in Harris County to Lusk, reserving an express vendor's lien to secure the purchase money note. Lusk was declared incompetent in 1977. Default in payment of the note occurred in 1978. Mintz filed a claim with the guardian of Lusk in an attempt to collect on the note. Mintz was not able to collect on this claim, so he sought to rescind the deed and obtain the property. Can Mintz recover the property?

7. Taylor purchased a lot with two houses on it from the Reynoldses. The deed recited that title was subject to a prior outstanding lien held by Colonial Savings Association. Under the deed of trust Colonial had purchased fire insurance and had billed the Reynoldses for the premium. After the purchase by Taylor, Colonial notified Taylor that it had purchased coverage in the amount of $8,700 and sent Taylor a copy of the policy. The fire insurance policy covered only one of the houses. When the uninsured house was destroyed by fire, the Taylors sued Colonial for negligence in not insuring both structures. Did Colonial have a duty to Taylor to insure both structures?

8. In April 1980, Blankton borrowed $18,000 from his father to start a business. Blankton gave his father a promissory note to cover the loan. About $8,000 of the loan was used to purchase equipment for the business. The balance was used to help finance a building that was purchased in August 1980. In addition to the $10,000, the purchase was financed by the Hill National Bank, which took a mortgage on the property. When Blankton failed, his father claimed a lien on the property based upon the April loan. The father argued that as his loan preceded the purchase of the real estate and was used to pay part of the price he was entitled to a priority over the bank. Discuss the validity of this argument.

22

Default and Foreclosure

The climax of 19th-century melodramas frequently involves a mortgage. In return for not foreclosing, the villainous mortgagee demands the mortgagor's beautiful, young daughter. In the nick of time the hero enters, back from California where he struck it rich in the gold fields. Both property and heroine are saved. The villain is foiled again.

Although in the melodrama the villain curses his luck, few real-life mortgagees are anxious to foreclose. **Foreclosure** is the legal procedure by which a lender sells the real property that was pledged as security for the loan when the debtor has defaulted. The process is generally time-consuming, expensive and damaging to reputations. Most lending institutions turn to foreclosure as a last resort and will make every effort to prevent it. Their business is lending money, not managing property. Nevertheless, situations in which lenders must foreclose do arise.

This chapter explores the legal issues involved in foreclosure. The circumstances under which a lender can foreclose are explained. The procedure the lender must follow in foreclosing is described. The law establishing priority among creditors when a lien is foreclosed is discussed. Finally, the defenses or actions that the borrower can take when threatened with foreclosure are covered.

DEFAULT

Because foreclosure is a remedy available to the lender when a borrower has defaulted, the concept of default must be understood. As explained in Chapter 18, default is the nonperformance of a duty or an obligation. In a mortgage transaction the duties and obligations of the borrower and lender are established in the promissory note and the deed of trust. Consequently, the mortgage documents must be read to determine whether there has been a default. In the last chapter some of the common obligations created by the promissory note and deed of trust were explained. The covenants typically include a promise to repay the loan in a certain manner such as installments due on the first day of each month. The failure to pay the monthly installment on time is a default. Another common covenant is the promise to insure the premises against fire. The borrower's nonperformance of this promise is a default. The breach of any covenant, no matter how trivial, is a default.

Generally the mortgagee is not required to notify the mortgagor that he or she has defaulted. The law presumes that a mortgagee knows and understands the terms and conditions of the mortgage and therefore knows when he or she has defaulted. Even though formal notice is not required, most lenders will notify the borrower of default. This notice is usually given in the hope that the debtor will cure the default without necessitating more drastic action on the part of the lender. Occasionally, the promissory note or deed of trust will contain a provision requiring notice of default prior to foreclosure. If there is a contractual provision to that effect, then the lender must give the required notice.

The lender's rights following a default also are established by the mortgage documents. A lender has several possible options when there has been a breach of a covenant:

1. The lender can choose to ignore the default and waive his or her rights.
2. The lender can ask the borrower to comply or cure the default.
3. The lender can take direct action to cure the breach and charge the borrower for the cost of the cure.
4. The lender can sue the borrower for damages caused by the borrower's default.
5. The lender can foreclose his or her lien against the property.

The lender's choice with respect to these options depends in part on the mortgage documents. For example, the deed of trust may state that, if the borrower fails to insure the premises, then the lender can purchase an insurance policy and bill the borrower for the premium. The deed of trust provides the lender with a remedy for the borrower's breach of the promise to insure.

In most deeds of trust the borrower expressly gives to the lender the right to foreclose for any breach or default. This means that the lender has the same right to foreclose whether the default is the borrower's failure to repay the loan or the borrower's failure to keep the premises in good repair.

Acceleration

Deeds of trust frequently provide the lender with the option to demand full payment of the indebtedness immediately if the borrower defaults in any of his or her obligations. This is called the *right to accelerate*. Acceleration clauses were discussed in the last chapter. The right to accelerate the time for payment of the note can have significant repercussions for the borrower. For example, assume that the deed of trust provides that if the borrower fails to insure the premises then the lender can accelerate and demand full payment of the balance due on the note. The borrower neglects to insure the property, and the lender exercises the right to accelerate. The borrower is now required to obtain a large sum of money to pay the balance due on the note or risk foreclosure of the lien by the lender.

Another common provision in the deed of trust discussed in the last chapter is the due-on-sale clause, which requires prior approval by the lender when the property is sold and the loan is not repaid. This clause usually states that the failure to obtain prior approval gives the lender the right to accelerate the time for payment of the loan.

CASE EXAMPLE

Lance Subellte had executed a mortgage and note in favor of West End Savings and Loan. The mortgage contained a due-on-sale and an acceleration clause. Monthly payments of $298 were due on the note. When Subellte sold the property to a buyer who assumed the loan, West End demanded repayment of the entire debt. Subellte immediately tendered the next monthly installment, which West End refused to accept. Subellte and the new owner demanded that West End accept this amount. West End pointed out the mortgage default and that the acceleration clause entitled it to collect the entire debt.

Most of the litigation in Texas concerning the right to foreclose nonjudicially concerns acceleration of the note. The typical acceleration clause permits acceleration if the debtor defaults in the periodic payments required in the note, is tardy in the periodic payment or transfers any interest in the property without the written permission of the mortgagee, including a contract for deed.

Whether or not the balance due has been accelerated as a result of the default is significant for the borrower because it determines how much money the borrower must pay in order to cure the default and thereby prevent foreclosure. For example, if the mortgagor's default is his or her failure to make the last two payments due on the note, then the existence of an acceleration clause can make the difference between curing the default by paying the last two payments and curing it by paying the entire balance due. If the note has not been accelerated, then the debtor can redeem the property at any time prior to the date of foreclosure by paying the periodic payments due. If the note has been accelerated and notice of acceleration given, then the debtor can redeem the property only if he or she can pay the note in full prior to the date of foreclosure.

An acceleration clause can provide for automatic acceleration upon the happening of a certain event or can provide the mortgagee with the option to accelerate. If the clause states that the acceleration is automatic, then no notice need be given the debtor that the lender is expecting payment in full. However, if the clause contains simply an option to accelerate, the lender is required to notify the debtor that the lender is exercising that option. This notice must clearly state that the lender is accelerating the note and that the entire balance is now due and payable. A simple notice of foreclosure is not sufficient to notify the debtor of the lender's election to accelerate.

The right to receive notice of acceleration prior to foreclosure can be waived by the debtor. A waiver is the giving up or relinquishing of a known legal right. The waiver of notice must be in writing and typically appears in both the promissory note and the deed of trust. The following provision waives the debtor's right to notice of acceleration:

> On default in the payment of this note or in the performance of any obligation in any instrument securing or collateral to it, this note and all obligations in all instruments securing or collateral to it shall become immediately due at the election of Payee. Maker and each surety, endorser, and guarantor waive all demands for payment, presentations for payment, notices of intention to accelerate maturity, protests, and notices of protest.

The following case illustrates the effect of any express waiver of notice of acceleration of the note in the event the debtor fails to pay on time.

• CASE BRIEF •

On September 3, 1980, Grella purchased property from Berry. The consideration given for the sale included a promissory note in the amount of $112,000, payable to Berry. In addition to the promissory note, a deed of trust was executed to secure repayment of the note. The note and deed of trust contained acceleration provisions and a waiver of notice of acceleration. The payment due to Berry on February 1, 1981, was not made on time. On February 3, 1981, Berry notified Grella that he intended to accelerate and foreclose. On February 27, 1981, an agreement for reinstatement of the note was made by Berry and Grella. The reinstatement agreement restated the terms of the note and deed of trust. On July 1, 1982, the payment due on such date was not received by Berry. On July 5, 1982, Berry notified the trustee that Grella was in default and requested that the trustee foreclose. On July 6, 1982, Grella offered to pay the July payment to Berry. This tender was rejected, and Grella was given notice of foreclosure. Grella filed suit in court to stop the foreclosure proceeding. The trial court denied the request for injunction. The court of appeals affirmed. The court held that the note and deed of trust expressly waived notice of acceleration. Consequently, Berry could accelerate without sending Grella any notice of his action. After Berry elected to accelerate, he was not required to accept anything less than payment in full of the balance due on the note. The tender of the July payment was not sufficient. Grella had a right to redeem the property only upon payment in full of the balance due on the note. *Grella v. Berry*, 647 S.W.2d 15 (Tex. Civ. App.-Houston 1st Dist. 1982).

Although the notice of acceleration can be waived expressly, the Texas courts will require that the lender notify the debtor prior to foreclosure if the lender has been routinely accepting late payments from the debtor. The Texas courts have required the mortgagee to notify the debtor that late payments will no longer be accepted and that failure to pay on the due date will cause the lender to accelerate the balance due on the note.

• CASE BRIEF •

Brown owed Hewitt $8,500. The debt was evidenced by a note and mortgage containing an acceleration clause and a ten percent penalty for collection fees. Partial payments of $90 were due on the tenth of each month. Over a period of 14 consecutive months Hewitt had accepted overdue payments. In September Brown and Hewitt quarreled. When the October payment was late, Hewitt immediately accelerated the debt, demanding full payment plus the collection fee. Since Brown could not pay the entire debt, Hewitt commenced foreclosure proceedings. Brown's suit to enjoin these proceedings was successful. The court held that Hewitt could not accelerate without notifying Brown of Hewitt's intention to depart from the usual method of dealing between the parties. *Brown v. Hewitt*, 143 S.W. 2d 223 (Tex. 1940).

Ordinarily an extension of time given to a defaulting mortgagor to correct the default is not a waiver of the mortgagee's right to accelerate the debt. Similarly, a mortgagee who fails to accelerate because of one default is not precluded from accelerating upon a later default.

The right to accelerate upon transfer of the real property has been upheld in Texas. Usually, the right to accelerate under a due-on-sale clause requires that the lender notify the debtor that the lender is demanding the balance due on the note and that, if it is not paid within a stated period, the mortgagee will foreclose. This option to accelerate and foreclose must be exercised within a reasonable time after the lender learns of the transfer.

Default in Prior Mortgage Clause

Frequently property is encumbered with more than one mortgage. If the senior mortgage is in default and foreclosure occurs, the junior lien will be eliminated. Sometimes the senior mortgage will be in default but not the junior lien. This causes a problem for the junior mortgagee as it cannot foreclose, although the debt and security are endangered. For protection a junior mortgage should contain a clause providing that a default in a prior mortgage is a default in the junior obligation. If a clause of this nature exists, the junior mortgagee may commence its own foreclosure action. Of course, its lien does not become superior to the prior mortgage, but at least the junior mortgagee does not have to sit back and wait for the other to act.

REDEMPTION

Redemption is the right of the mortgagor to reclaim the property after default. It is the right to pay the mortgagee whatever amount is due and

thereby avoid foreclosure. The amount due will be the arrearage if the note
has not been accelerated. However, if the note has been accelerated, the
amount due is the balance due on the note. The time of redemption depends upon the manner in which the mortgage is foreclosed. If the foreclosure is under a power of sale, then redemption must occur prior to the date
of the sale. The right to redeem is extinguished at the sale. If the foreclosure
is by judicial decree, then the mortgagor has a reasonable time after the sale
in which to redeem the property.

In addition to the mortgagor, other parties having an interest in the property may redeem. Junior mortgagees, tenants under a lease, judgment creditors and grantees who have acquired through the mortgagor have this right.
The junior mortgagee who redeems acquires the rights of the senior mortgagee, not title to the premises. A mortgagor redeeming has a superior right.
Since the debt has been paid, he or she acquires the unencumbered fee.

Several states (not Texas) have passed statutes creating a right of redemption in favor of the mortgagor. Generally, the period is six months or a year.
In many of the states that have this statutory right to redeem, the mortgagor cannot waive this right by contract. In dealing with foreclosed property,
a purchaser should determine what redemption rights may exist.

POWER-OF-SALE FORECLOSURE

In Texas the right to foreclose without a court order must be created in writing and agreed to by the mortgagor and mortgagee. This nonjudicial foreclosure is called *foreclosure by power of sale* and is typically created in the
deed of trust. Nonjudicial foreclosures are more common in Texas than judicial foreclosures. Nonjudicial foreclosures are popular because the mortgagee can effect a sale of the property more quickly. Judicial foreclosures
require a trial before any sale can take place.

In the previous chapter several clauses that are common in deeds of trust
were discussed. The provision granting to the mortgagee the power of sale
or right to foreclose without court action is common in deeds of trust. This
provision creates an important remedy. In the absence of such a provision
the mortgagee does not have the right to foreclose nonjudicially and must
resort to a court action in order to foreclose. The following is the typical
clause found in Texas that grants to the mortgagee the power of sale:

> That in the event of default in the payment of any installment,
> principal or interest, of the note hereby secured, in accordance
> with the terms thereof, or of a breach of any of the covenants
> herein contained to be performed by Grantors, then and in any of
> such events Beneficiary may elect, Grantors hereby expressly
> waiving presentment and demand for payment, to declare the en-
> tire principal indebtedness hereby secured with all interest ac-

crued thereon and all other sums hereby secured immediately due and payable, and in the event of default in the payment of said indebtedness when due or declared due, it shall thereupon, or at any time thereafter, be the duty of the Trustee, or his successor or substitute as hereinafter provided, at the request of Beneficiary (which request is hereby conclusively presumed), to enforce this trust; and after advertising the time, place and terms of the sale of the above described and conveyed property, then subject to the lien hereof, for at least twenty-one (21) days preceding the date of sale by posting written or printed notice thereof at the courthouse door of the county where said real property is situated, which notice may be posted by the Trustee acting, or by any person acting for him, and the Beneficiary (the holder of the indebtedness secured hereby) has, at least twenty-one (21) days preceding the date of sale, served written or printed notice of the proposed sale by certified mail on each debtor obligated to pay the indebtedness secured by this Deed of Trust according to the records of Beneficiary, by the deposit of such notice, enclosed in postpaid wrapper, properly addressed to such debtor at debtor's most recent address as shown by the records of Beneficiary, in a post office or official depository under the care and custody of the United States Postal Service, the Trustee shall sell the above described property, then subject to the lien hereof, at public auction in accordance with such notice at the courthouse door of said county where such real property is situated (provided where said real property is situated in more than one county, the notice to be posted as herein provided shall be posted at the courthouse door of each of such counties where said real property is situated, and said above described and conveyed property may be sold at the courthouse door of any one of such counties, and the notices so posted shall designate the county where the property will be sold), on the first Tuesday in any month between the hours of ten o'clock A.M. and four o'clock P.M., to the highest bidder for cash, selling all of the property as an entirety or in such parcels as the Trustee acting may elect and make due conveyance to the Purchaser or Purchasers, with general warranty binding Grantors, their heirs and assigns; and out of the money arising from such sale, the Trustee acting shall pay first, all the expenses of advertising the sale and making the conveyance, including a commission of five percent (5%) to himself, which commission shall be due and owing in addition to the attorney's fees provided for in said note, and then to Beneficiary the full amount of principal, interest, attorney's fees and other charges due and unpaid on said note and all other indebtedness secured hereby, rendering the balance of the sales price, if any, to

Grantors, their heirs or assigns; and the recitals in the conveyance to the Purchaser or Purchasers shall be full and conclusive
evidence of the truth of the matters therein stated, and all prerequisites to said sale shall be presumed to have been performed,
and such sale and conveyance shall be conclusive against Grantors, their heirs and assigns.

In Texas it is the trustee named in the deed of trust who actually has the
power to sell the property belonging to the owner. The mortgagee or beneficiary requests that the trustee foreclose. The trustee by the terms of the
deed of trust is obligated to proceed if a request is made. If the trustee
refuses to act, then the mortgagee can remove the trustee named in the
deed of trust and substitute another person. Most deeds of trust specifically
permit substitute trustees. Typical language creating the right of a mortgagee to replace a trustee is as follows:

Beneficiary in any event is hereby authorized to appoint a substitute trustee, or a successor trustee, to act instead of the
trustee named herein without other formality than the designation in writing of a substitute or successor trustee; and the authority hereby conferred shall extend to the appointment of
other successor and substitute trustees successively until the indebtedness hereby secured has been paid in full, or until said
property is sold hereunder, and each substitute and successor
trustee shall succeed to all of the rights and powers of the original trustee named herein.

In foreclosing under a power of sale, the trustee must follow the terms of
the deed of trust verbatim. In Texas foreclosure is viewed as a necessary but
harsh remedy. Therefore, the right to foreclose and the procedure of foreclosure must be adhered to strictly.

Although the power-of-sale foreclosure is the most common method of
foreclosing in Texas, a few states have passed statutes that prohibit nonjudicial foreclosures. In other states potential title problems may arise because
the foreclosure was not officially sanctioned by a court order. Nevertheless,
most states, like Texas, do allow the power-of-sale foreclosure.

Statutory Procedure

In addition to complying with the notice requirements previously discussed and the express terms of the deed of trust, the foreclosure must follow the procedure established by law. The law that sets out the procedure
for foreclosure in Texas is found in §51.002 of the Texas Property Code. The
failure of the trustee to follow this procedure exactly is adequate reason to
set aside the trustee's sale.

First, the trustee must notify the debtor(s) of the foreclosure sale at least
21 days before the date of sale. The notice must be mailed to the debtor at

his or her last known address, certified and postage prepaid. The notice must also be posted at the courthouse door of each county in which the property is located and filed in the county clerk's office in the county where the sale is to be made.

Second, the sale must be by public auction to the highest bidder and held between 10:00 A.M. and 4:00 P.M. on the first Tuesday of the month.

Third, the sale must take place at the courthouse in the county where the land is located. If the property is located in more than one county, the trustee can choose the county where the sale will take place and state the selected county in the notices.

The Sale

At the foreclosure sale the trustee must act impartially and fairly in conducting the sale. The trustee cannot take any action that would discourage bidders. The mortgagee or his or her agent can bid at the foreclosure sale. The trustee can also bid on the mortgaged property. It is a public auction and open to all persons. The sale will be made to the highest bidder for cash. There is no requirement in Texas that the property be sold at fair market value. The courts in Texas repeatedly have held that inadequacy of the sale price is not sufficient to set aside a foreclosure sale.

The purchaser at the trustee's sale acquires only the title that the trustee had authority to sell. If the trustee had no authority, the purchaser acquires no title. If the trustee had authority to sell a life estate, then the purchaser acquired a life estate. Further, the purchaser takes the property without any covenants regarding title. The purchaser takes the property "as is" and subject to any claims or defenses of which the purchaser had notice at the time of the sale. This includes constructive or actual notice. The trustee conveys title by an instrument called a *trustee's deed*. This instrument recites the reasons for foreclosure and the procedure followed in foreclosing.

The proceeds from the sale are paid to those creditors who had liens against the land sold, and any surplus is paid to the debtor. The priority among creditors is established by the time of recording unless expressly subordinated. If the mortgagee who forecloses is a senior lienholder, the foreclosure sale terminates all junior lienholders unless the purchaser at the foreclosure sale is the debtor. If the mortgagee who forecloses is a junior lienholder, then the purchaser takes the property subject to the senior lien, but any other junior liens are extinguished.

DEBTOR'S DEFENSES AND OPTIONS

A debtor faced with a notice of foreclosure has several ways to prevent the sale of the mortgaged property and its accompanying economic loss. However, the debtor's options and defenses are limited, and the debtor's inability to pay the note is *not* a ground for delaying or enjoining the sale. If lack of funds is the debtor's only reason for default, then the debtor may consider filing for bankruptcy.

The first option that a debtor has is to exercise the right to redeem the property. This right was discussed earlier. It is important to remember that this right is extinguished when the property is sold at auction; therefore, the debtor must act quickly in asserting the right of redemption.

The second option of the debtor is to sell the property on his or her own prior to the foreclosure sale. This option may be desirable to the debtor who is concerned about losing his or her equity if the sale is made at public auction. This sale must be completed prior to the date of foreclosure and payment made to the mortgagee.

The third option of the debtor is to negotiate a settlement called *forbearance* with the mortgagee. The terms of the settlement are those agreeable to both parties. The agreement can include an extended time for paying the debt. If the lender is convinced that the mortgagor will be able to pay the debt if given more time, then they can enter into an extension agreement. The parties can also renegotiate the other terms of the note, such as the rate of interest or the pledging of additional security. These terms will usually be set forth in a contract called a *reinstatement agreement*. Typically, the debtor is given an opportunity to pay the arrearage, and the mortgagee halts the foreclosure but reserves the right to foreclose if the debtor defaults in the future.

Fourth, the debtor has the option to petition the court for an injunction. The debtor must prove that the attempted foreclosure is wrongful and that the mortgagee should be enjoined from foreclosing. There will be a hearing in court prior to the date of the scheduled foreclosure sale. The debtor must prove that either there is no ground or right to foreclose or that the mortgagee has not followed the proper procedure and given the required notices. The courts in Texas will not stop a foreclosure simply to allow the debtor more time to pay the debt.

Fifth, the debtor can file for bankruptcy. The filing of a petition in bankruptcy automatically stops the foreclosure sale. This is true even if the trustee is unaware that a bankruptcy petition has been filed. For example, assume the debtor files a petition in bankruptcy at 10:35 A.M. on the first Tuesday in June. At 10:45 A.M. the trustee auctions the property pursuant to the notices of foreclosure mailed to the debtor. The sale of the property is void even though the trustee was unaware that ten minutes prior to the sale the debtor had filed bankruptcy.

The filing of bankruptcy will give the debtor time to arrange for payment of the debt. The plan for payment is subject to court supervision. If the bankruptcy court finds that the debtor is unable to pay the mortgagee, then it can allow the trustee to foreclose. One benefit of filing bankruptcy is that the debtor can obtain a court order requiring the creditor to reinstate the original payment schedule even though the lender had accelerated payment. For example, assume that upon the debtor's default the lender notified the debtor that pursuant to the acceleration provision in the deed of trust the entire balance was now due and payable. The debtor offered to pay to the lender the amount of the arrearage but was unable to pay the note in full. The lender refused to accept the tender and posted the property for foreclosure. The bankruptcy court can require the lender to accept the delinquent payments and allow the debtor to continue making the monthly payments.

JUDICIAL FORECLOSURE

Foreclosure by court order is the mortgagee's alternative remedy in Texas. As required for nonjudicial foreclosure, the mortgagee must have a right to foreclose. The right to foreclose exists if the creditor has a lien against the property and the debtor has defaulted in his or her obligations to the creditor. In judicial foreclosure the mortgagee files suit against the debtor, asking the court to judge that the debtor is in default and owes the mortgagee a certain sum of money. The mortgagee also requests the court to order that the property be sold to satisfy the debt.

The debtor is served with notice of the lawsuit and must file an answer in court if he or she wishes to defend against the action. In addition, any other party who has an interest of any kind in the mortgaged property should be notified of the lawsuit and should file a response. This includes other lienholders, prior owners who are liable on the note, the present owner and any tenants.

The trial of the case can be either by judge or by jury. The debtor can raise as a defense any legal justification that he or she has for not paying the debt when due. After the trial of the case a judgment will be entered. If the mortgagee wins, then the property will be ordered sold by the court, usually at a public auction by a person appointed by the court. This person could be the trustee, the sheriff or a receiver. The proceeds will be paid to the parties named in the judgment.

Judicial foreclosure is the only remedy available if the deed of trust does not contain a power of sale. It is also the only foreclosure remedy available to foreclose a vendor's lien. Frequently, the judicial foreclosure suit will seek a monetary judgment against the debtor for any deficiency if the sale does not pay the debt in full.

There are two important differences between nonjudicial and judicial foreclosures. First, a junior lienholder's claim against the property is not automatically eliminated by the sale under a court order. A junior lienholder's interest in the property can be extinguished only if he or she was a party to the foreclosure suit. If the junior lienholder was not joined in the suit, the property will be sold subject to any junior liens. Second, foreclosure by court order does not automatically cut off the owner's right to redeem. The

Figure 22.1: **FLOWCHART OF FORECLOSURE ISSUES**

right to redeem the property continues for a reasonable time after the sale. Consequently, the purchaser at an auction held under court order purchases at a greater risk than does the purchaser at an auction held under a power of sale.

DEFICIENCY JUDGMENT

As explained in the previous chapter, the mortgagee usually has two remedies when there is default by the mortgagor. Foreclosure is one of those remedies. However, an equally important remedy is the right to sue the debtors individually. This includes a suit to recover from the debtor the difference between the amount due the creditor and the proceeds from the sale. If the foreclosure is by court order, then the judge will usually award the mortgagee damages against the debtors in the amount of any deficiency. If the foreclosure is under a power of sale, then the lender must file suit against the debtor to collect any deficiency. The decision of the mortgagee to pursue legal action against a debtor depends on many factors. Some of these are the amount of the deficiency and the likelihood that the debtor will be able to pay.

PRIORITIES

The general principles concerning priorities were discussed in Chapter 13, and the importance of recording interests in land to protect them was discussed in Chapter 12. Those rules are also applicable to mortgages. A mortgage is an interest in land and therefore must be recorded to preserve it against a subsequent lienholder or purchaser. This section will review briefly some of the fundamental principles regarding priority and examine the priority relationships between mortgages and leases and mortgages and mechanics' liens.

Mortgage priority problems generally occur when a debt is in default or probability of a default exists. Under these circumstances each secured creditor attempts to ensure that its lien has first claim to the proceeds if the security must be sold. Sometimes the rank of a creditor will be determined by a provision in the security document. At other times the creditor's position is established by case law or more often by some statute such as the recording acts.

The fundamental principle determining priority is "first in time, first in right," but modifications of this rule affect the mortgagee's position. Remember that as a result of the recording statutes the first in time priority can be lost if the lien is not recorded. If all liens are recorded, then usually the priority is determined by the date of recording.

Mortgages and Leases

In general, the "first in time" rule applies to the priority relationship between mortgages and leases. If a lease is executed before a mortgage, the lease has priority. In a foreclosure sale, the purchaser takes subject to the lease. A lease entered into after a mortgage is subordinate to the mortgage if the mortgage has been recorded. In the event of a foreclosure sale, the purchaser of the property takes it free of the lease.

In practice, most mortgages on commercial property contain agreements by the mortgagee authorizing the mortgagor to lease the premises. Under these circumstances, a lease made by the mortgagor is not subject to the mortgage lien. Unless a lease contains unfavorable terms, a mortgagee entitled to possession will often recognize a lease made after the mortgage. Although the mortgagee has a right to eject the tenant, the mortgagee will be more interested in continued rental income, which can be applied against the debt.

Mechanics' Liens and Mortgages

Litigation as to priority between mechanics' lienholders and mortgagees is widespread. Priority regarding a mechanic's lien is not determined by the date the lien was recorded. In Texas a mechanic's and materialman's lien is considered effective from the date the first work was done, regardless of when the actual lien affidavit was filed. Furthermore, the lien claimant can base his or her priority upon the first date that work was performed by anyone on the project. For this reason lenders will frequently make a physical inspection of the mortgaged property before making a construction loan. Occasionally a lender will require the borrower to have his or her subcontractors and suppliers sign a subordination agreement as a condition of the loan.

CASE EXAMPLE

Peter Thompson files his lien affidavit on June 20, 1987, for work performed in May 1987. Clearing of the tract site for development occurred on February 3, 1987. Thompson's lien relates back to February 3. The mortgagee must have filed its lien against the property prior to February 3 in order to have priority over Thompson.

Subordination Agreement

A *subordination agreement* is an agreement that alters priorities between parties with interests in or liens upon real property. Subordination agreements have become increasingly important in recent years to facilitate financing of many types of real estate transactions. A common use is the situation in which a purchase money mortgagee subordinates its lien to the later lien of a construction mortgagee.

CASE EXAMPLE

Randolph Enterprises wished to purchase and develop a 200-acre parcel of land near Ft. Worth, Texas. The property was purchased for $400,000 from Judson Boone. Randolph Enterprises paid Boone $150,000 in cash, and Boone took back a purchase-money mortgage for the balance. Both

> parties knew that Randolph Enterprises would have to obtain additional financing for construction. As a result, Boone agreed to a provision in his purchase-money mortgage subordinating it to a subsequent mortgage to be given by Randolph Enterprises to secure funds borrowed for development of the land.

A seller such as Judson Boone is often willing to accept a junior position for a purchase-money mortgage, since subordination enables the seller to obtain a higher price for the property. Sellers also know that the additional funds, if used properly, will increase the property's value. The loan, though now secured by a second mortgage, continues to be well protected. Because many state and federal regulations require loans of institutional lenders to be secured by first mortgages, the subordination agreement is frequently the key to selling undeveloped property.

Subordination agreements are used in a number of other transactions involving real estate. A tenant may agree that his or her lease will be junior to a mortgage or deed of trust subsequently executed by the landlord. On the other hand, it is also relatively common for a mortgagee to subordinate an existing interest to an interest arising out of a long-term lease that is created later.

The use of subordination agreements can create legal problems. Some subordination agreements are automatic, coming into existence when the interest or lien is created. Judson Boone's purchase-money mortgage might be an example. The provision in Boone's mortgage could be worded to subordinate his lien as soon as Randolph Enterprises obtained its additional financing. Other types of agreements are not automatic. Such a provision might be worded to require Boone to give a subordination agreement when particular conditions are met. Enforcement of this type of subordination presents potential difficulties.

If a lender refuses to subordinate as promised, the buyer can bring an action for specific performance. In order to be successful, the buyer must prove that all conditions precedent to the lender's promise to subordinate have been met. This necessitates that the provision upon which subordination is based be written clearly. Courts will not grant specific performance unless the standard against which performance is measured is clear.

Terms of a subordination provision are sometimes critical in foreclosure litigation involving the subordinated and subordinating lenders. The subordinated lender will not lose its "first in time" priority if the subordinating lender advances funds upon conditions that differ from the subordination provision. In one case a seller who had taken back a mortgage agreed to subordinate to a "construction loan for the purpose of constructing on each lot a dwelling house with the usual appurtenances." Partly on the basis of this provision, a construction mortgagee advanced the builder more than $2 million, but not all of the funds were used for construction. In litigation between the two lenders, the court refused the priority to the construction mortgagee because it knew the terms of subordination.

DEED IN LIEU OF FORECLOSURE

Judicial and power-of-sale foreclosures are not the only remedies by which a lender can recover the balance due on the note. Other steps can be taken when a loan is in default. Sometimes the mortgagee will accept a deed instead of foreclosing.

The use of a deed in lieu of foreclosure is a common practice in Texas. The *deed in lieu of foreclosure* is the procedure in which the mortgagor conveys the mortgaged real estate to the mortgagee, who promises in return not to foreclose or sue on the underlying debt. The mortgagee becomes the owner of the real estate.

CASE EXAMPLE

As security for a $50,000 loan, Naomi Tilson executed a mortgage to the Pike County National Bank. After making two payments on the loan, she defaulted. At the time of her default the market value of the property was slightly in excess of $50,000. Because Naomi and her family were valued customers, the bank offered to accept a deed to the property instead of foreclosing. After discussing the consequences of this action with her attorney, Naomi agreed to convey the property to the bank.

Potentially, the deed in lieu of foreclosure can benefit the mortgagor in a number of ways. Naomi Tilson's credit rating would be protected. The conveyance would be carried out in the same manner as any sale, and adverse publicity that might accompany foreclosure would not exist. Economically, she could anticipate three important benefits. First, any obligation for taxes and assessments would terminate. Foreclosure costs would also be saved. Probably most important of all, she would not be responsible for any deficiency.

The deed in lieu of foreclosure is also advantageous to the mortgagee. Long delays usually associated with foreclosure by judicial sale are avoided. In addition, the mortgagee escapes the poor public relations that are often the result of resorting to a judicial sale. On the other hand, the mortgagee faces the problem of disposing of the security. Until the property is sold, the mortgagee has to maintain it, and expenses of the sale must be borne by the mortgagee because it now owns the real estate.

A number of legal problems associated with the practice are of special concern to the mortgagee. First, the mortgagee must completely cancel the debt. If it does not, the courts treat the deed in lieu of foreclosure as a substitute for the original mortgage. The mortgagor under these conditions retains any redemption rights that exist. On the other hand, once the debt is canceled, the mortgagee loses the right to a deficiency judgment. If the market value of the property in the previous example were to be less than $50,000, the mortgagee would suffer the loss.

A second important legal consideration involves junior liens on the property. The purchaser at a foreclosure sale takes title free of such liens, but a mortgagee who acquires title to real estate by deed in lieu of foreclosure is subject to these interests. If Naomi Tilson had not paid for improvements on the property and a mechanic's lien existed, Pike County National Bank's deed would be subject to that lien. A deed in lieu of foreclosure is also subject to attack under the Bankruptcy Act. Were Naomi to file for bankruptcy within a period of, say, 90 days after delivery of the deed to the bank, the bank could be treated as a preferred creditor. The deed would be set aside as a preferential transfer.

MORTGAGE INSURANCE

Mortgage insurance is insurance provided by certain government agencies or private corporations that protect mortgage lenders against loss caused by a borrower's default. Mortgage insurance has increased in importance since the 1940s and is today an integral part of the real estate industry. Mortgage insurance is provided by the Federal Housing Administration (FHA) and by private mortgage carriers. Mortgage guarantees are provided by the Veterans Administration.

The FHA administers several programs providing insurance to lenders financing real estate transactions. Loans can be insured for the purchase, construction, repair and improvement of housing. Rental housing, cooperatives, condominiums, low-cost and moderate-income housing, housing for the elderly and nursing homes are among the many types of dwellings covered by FHA programs.

The loan guarantee program of the Veterans Administration provides protection to private lenders financing homes for veterans. As a result of the guarantee, veterans have been able to buy or build homes on long-term loans with no down payment. Loans may be guaranteed on one- to four-unit structures: the veteran must occupy one of the units. Most VA-guaranteed loans are for the purchase of single-family homes, mobile homes and units in condominium projects.

In addition to the insurance or guarantees given by FHA or VA, there are private insurance companies that sell mortgage insurance. Frequently, a lender will require the borrower to carry private mortgage insurance (PMI) as a condition of lending. Private mortgage insurance provides the lender with additional security that the loan will be repaid. PMI is most frequently required if the purchaser is not able to make a down payment equal to 20 percent of the purchase price.

Loans insured by the Federal Housing Administration or guaranteed by the Veterans Administration are subject to some special rules regarding foreclosure. First, a lender cannot begin foreclosure proceedings until the mortgagor is at least three full months in arrears. Second, the mortgagee must reinstate the loan if the mortgagor tenders the full amount due and all foreclosure costs prior to the trustee's sale. Third, the mortgagee may qualify for assignment of the note to the Department of Housing and Urban Development. If assignment is justified in the particular case, then HUD can allow the mortgagor a period of reduced payments or a complete moratorium on payments up to 36 months.

SUMMARY

Foreclosure is the legal procedure that the lender follows to sell the mortgaged real estate upon default by the debtor. There are two types of foreclosure actions: foreclosure under a power of sale and judicial foreclosure. In Texas the more common method is foreclosure under a power of sale because it is less expensive and quicker than judicial foreclosure.

The right to foreclose does not arise until the debtor has defaulted in one of his or her obligations to the mortgagee. The promissory note and the deed of trust will usually establish circumstances that constitute a default. It is common for the lender to have the right to accelerate payment of the note in the event of default. Acceleration provisions are important to the lender because they allow the lender to require payment in full as a condition of redeeming the property prior to the foreclosure sale. Usually if a lender intends to accelerate payment of the note, it must give notice to the debtor.

Redemption is the right of the mortgagor to reclaim the property after default but before foreclosure. If the debtor tenders full payment to the lender prior to the sale, then the lender is required to accept it. The right of redemption is usually cut off when the property is sold at the foreclosure sale.

The right to foreclose without a court order must be created in writing and agreed to by the borrower and the lender. The trustee is required to follow the procedure for foreclosing set out in the deed of trust and to comply with the notices and procedures required under state law. Even the slightest deviation from the required procedure is ground for enjoining the sale. At the foreclosure sale the mortgaged property is sold for cash to the highest bidder, who acquires title to the property without receiving any warranties as to title.

A debtor who has received notice of foreclosure can take several courses of action. The debtor can redeem the property, negotiate a settlement with the mortgagee or sell the property and pay the mortgage from the sale proceeds. If the debtor can assert any legal defenses against the foreclosure, the debtor can request a court to enjoin the sale. Finally, the debtor can file for bankruptcy. The filing of a petition in bankruptcy automatically stops all foreclosure action.

The less common method of foreclosing in Texas is by court order. The right to foreclose judicially arises automatically whenever a mortgage is created. It is important that notice of the court action be sent to all parties who have an interest in the real estate, including junior lienholders and tenants. If the sale of the mortgaged property does not bring enough money to pay the lender in full, the lender can sue the debtor for the deficiency.

The order of payment when there is more than one lienholder is very important. Frequently, funds from the sale are insufficient to pay all the lienholders in full. Generally, priority is determined by the "first in time" rule. However, an unrecorded lien loses its priority to a subsequent lienholder. Therefore, it is important that the deed of trust be recorded properly. Between subcontractors claiming a mechanic's lien and mortgagees the relation back doctrine applies. This means that the mechanic's lien is considered effective from the date on which any work was done on the real estate.

Frequently, a lender will require another lienholder or potential lienholder to execute a subordination agreement. A subordination agreement alters priorities among lienholders by establishing by contract which creditor will have the higher rank.

Occasionally a debtor who is in default will seek an agreement from the creditor to accept a transfer of title in exchange for the creditor's promise not to sue on the debt. This transaction is called a *deed in lieu of foreclosure* and requires the consent of both debtor and creditor.

Finally, in an effort to provide some additional protection to the lender in the event the debtor defaults, mortgage insurance can be required as one of the conditions for obtaining the loan. A loan insured by mortgage insurance or guarantees eliminates the necessity for a lender to foreclose in order to collect the balance due on a note. The lender can look to the insurer or guarantor for payment if the debtor defaults.

QUESTIONS AND CASE PROBLEMS

1. Explain why having an acceleration clause in a mortgage is important to the mortgagee.
2. Compare and contrast power of sale and judicial foreclosure.
3. Explain in detail the procedure that must be followed by the mortgagee to foreclose under a power of sale in Texas.
4. Dhanani Investments, Inc., purchased two apartment complexes and in connection with the purchase executed three promissory notes and deeds of trust to Second Master Bilt Homes, Inc. The notes contained a provision waiving notice of demand, presentment and acceleration. Between January 1982 and May 1982 all the payments on the note were late. The payment due on June 1, 1982, was not made, and on June 22, 1982, Second Master Bilt Homes, Inc. exercised its option to accelerate and posted the two apartment complexes for foreclosure. On June 28, 1982, Dhanani tendered the June payment, but Second Master refused to accept it. Dhanani sued to enjoin the foreclosure. Can Second Master Bilt Homes, Inc., foreclose?
5. Wallace purchased four tracts of land from Briers. Wallace executed three promissory notes; two notes were payable to Briers, and one

note was payable to Southern States Life Insurance Company. On three of the tracts, Southern was the first lienholder. On the fourth tract, Briers was the first lienholder and Southern was the junior lienholder. Deeds of trust to secure all three promissory notes were signed by Wallace on each tract. Wallace defaulted in the payment of all three notes, and Southern foreclosed its liens against all four tracts. After the foreclosure by Southern, what rights does Briers have with respect to collecting the balance due on the two promissory notes it held?

6. Lakeview Savings and Loan held a mortgage on property owned by Fisher. The mortgage secured a note of $40,000. Fisher defaulted and offered Lakeview a deed in lieu of foreclosure. Lakeview took the deed and shortly thereafter sold the property for $38,000. Lakeview then sued Fisher for $2,000. Would Lakeview be successful? Discuss.

7. Olaska purchased property at a foreclosure sale for $108,000. Shortly before the sale a large corporation had decided to build a plant in the area. This was not known to Olaska or to the public. Within a few days of Olaska's purchase, the company purchased the property from her for $200,000. The former owner sued to set the sale aside on grounds that the foreclosure price was inadequate. Would the owner be successful? Discuss.

23

★

Closing the Real Estate Transaction

The final stage of the real estate purchase transaction, when the deed and the purchase money are exchanged, is referred to as *closing* or *settlement*. Closing a real estate sale in Texas is similar to closings that take place elsewhere in the United States. In Texas, most residential closings take place in the office of a title insurance company and are handled by one of its employees called a *closer*. The title insurance company is typically specified in the earnest money contract as the escrow agent and the source for the title insurance policy. Attorneys are the other main category of persons who close real estate transactions.

After the buyer and the seller sign a real estate purchase contract, they need time to prepare for the closing. The buyer ordinarily must search for financing, while the seller needs time to prepare evidence of title. Other documents need preparation as directed by the purchase contract, laws and local customs. There is a deed to be drawn, inspection certificates to be obtained, expenses and income to be apportioned and other preparatory matters to be completed. The interval between the signing and the closing date is intended to provide the necessary time to accomplish these matters.

The date of closing is normally specified in the contract. The date may be as early as two weeks from the date of the contract or as long as two months and occasionally even longer. One difficulty with a long interval is that lending institutions normally do not extend a loan commitment for more than 30 days without some additional cost to the borrower.

A postponement of the closing date does not result in a breach of the purchase contract as long as the adjournment is reasonable. On the other hand, if the contract specifies that "time is of the essence," even a one-day postponement could be considered a breach for which the law would afford a remedy to the innocent party.

When the contract does not provide for a closing date, a reasonable time is implied. Since the purpose of the interval is to provide the necessary time to accomplish certain aims, a reasonable time would be a period within which these aims could reasonably be accomplished.

The rights and obligations of the parties are defined by the contract. To a large extent the contract governs the closing format. Local custom, to the extent that it does not contradict contractual provisions, also shapes the closing. Some localities, for example, customarily use the *escrow closing*, wherein the deed and purchase price are delivered to a third party, who is directed to close the transaction outside the presence of the parties. In other jurisdictions the parties meet each other face to face at the closing. Either method of closing is permissible in Texas.

The object of the closing is to complete the transaction so that the purchaser is vested with title to the realty and the seller receives the purchase price. Various persons who may be responsible for the closing proceedings (other than the buyer and seller) include the real estate broker, attorney and closer.

The Broker's Role

The broker has an economic interest in the closing because he or she is usually paid the commission at closing. For that reason the broker usually participates in the closing preparation and is present at the closing. Often the broker facilitates the closing by communicating with the lending institution, the purchaser, the seller and/or their representatives on last-minute details. The broker may hand-deliver closing documents to the parties or their legal representatives to minimize the risk of a breakdown in the critical last hours before closing. The broker may be responsible for reminding the parties of what documents they need to bring to the closing. To the extent permitted by law, the broker may even assist in the computation of prorations and preparation of closing statements. In the absence of an attorney representing the seller, the broker will explain to the seller the closing process as it unravels, thus reducing anxiety and confusion at the closing. In order to facilitate an orderly closing, the broker should review the documents for business details prior to closing.

The Attorney's Role

Every sale requires the services of an attorney to prepare the documents; however, not every closing involves attorney representation. When it does occur, purchasers are more apt to be represented than sellers. Perhaps this is because it is legally more difficult to ascertain whether a purchaser has received good marketable title to the real estate than whether the seller has received the full purchase price prescribed by the contract. In other words, the lay seller is in a better position to ensure receipt of the full purchase price than the lay buyer is to ensure receipt of marketable title to the real estate.

At the ordinary closing the attorney's role is routine, being confined to explaining the various documents to the client. Most of the attorney's preparation for the closing has occurred in advance, through examination of documents such as the title commitment, deed, promissory note, deed of trust and closing statements. If the attorney has prepared properly in advance, the routine closing is normally smooth and may seem anticlimactic. An attorney has a more important role, however, in the rare closing where a difficult legal problem arises. Since no one can determine beforehand whether the closing will present an extraordinary problem, it is best for all parties to be represented by counsel. When parties are represented by attorneys, closings are likely to be smoother and less confusing because each party generally has confidence in his or her legal representative.

The seller is responsible for delivering a deed in conformity with the contract. For this reason the seller must hire an attorney for the preparation of the deed or permit the title insurance company's attorney to prepare it, in which event the fee will be charged to the seller. The purchaser's attorney will examine the deed to ensure that the description of the property is accurate and that compliance with the necessary formalities for execution of the deed has occurred. The seller may be responsible, pursuant to the terms of the contract, for producing an abstract showing the history of the transactions that relate to the title of the property. An abstract may be prepared by the seller's attorney, an abstract company or a title insurance company. Based upon the abstract, the buyer's attorney may be called upon to render a certificate or letter of opinion regarding the marketability of the title. An attorney who negligently renders a wrong opinion to the buyer will be liable for damages. Of course, the buyer's attorney will not be liable for the inaccurate compilation of an abstract prepared by another attorney or abstractor. The attorney or abstractor who prepared the abstract is responsible to any damaged party for negligent preparation.

The Closer's Role

The person who supervises and coordinates the exchange of documents and money at the closing is called a *closer.* The closer is responsible for ensuring that all documents are signed and delivered properly to the appropriate party. The closer may be an attorney, real estate broker, employee of the lending institution or title insurance company or any other designated person. The deed and other documents may require acknowledgement before a notary. Hence, it is advisable that the closer be a notary public. Otherwise, a notary public must be present.

At the closing, a lot of paper changes hands. The closing is routine for the closer, who has undoubtedly performed numerous closings; for the buyers and sellers, however, it may be confusing. Unless the closer is sensitive to that fact, the closing may be less than successful. Each document and transaction should be explained to the parties, either by the closer or by the attorney representing the client. Most problems that emerge at the closing can be remedied by a calm spirit and thoughtful application, and many such problems can be avoided altogether if the broker carefully reviews the documents prior to the closing.

ANATOMY OF A RESIDENTIAL CLOSING

Figure 23.1 shows the transactions involved in a real estate closing. In Texas, after the earnest money contract is entered into by the buyer and the seller, a copy of the agreement will be sent to the title insurance company named in the earnest money contract. A well-drafted earnest money contract can serve as a guide to tasks that must be completed prior to closing. The title insurance company usually receives the contract and the earnest money from the broker. The title insurance company will open a file in its office and assign the file to an employee, who is designated a closer. The title insurance company will then begin an examination of the title of the property to determine whether it is willing to insure the title. The title insurance company makes the same type of examination that an abstracter would make in examining title. One of the steps in examining title is deter-

Figure 23.1: **TRANSACTIONS INVOLVED IN A REAL ESTATE CLOSING**

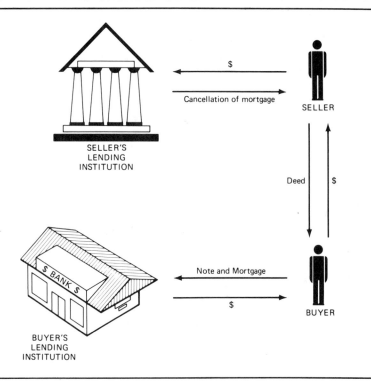

mining whether there are any uncollected taxes assessed against the property. This information may be obtained by the title company from private businesses that search the tax records and issue tax statements.

During the time that the closer is waiting for a report on the title to the property, the buyer and seller should be preparing for closing. The buyer should be completing the financial arrangements and performing any inspections authorized under the contract. The seller should be completing any required repairs, making arrangements to vacate the premises and obtaining any other information that will be necessary to complete the transaction. For example, in residential closings the seller may be required to obtain a termite inspection certificate signed by a termite inspector, certifying that the premises are free from termites and damage from those insects.

It is the responsibility of the broker to guide the buyer and seller in making the necessary preparations.

Typically, both parties rely upon the broker to communicate requests and answers among the closer, the seller and the buyer. A broker who provides accurate and quick communication provides an invaluable service to the parties and can make the consummation of the sale proceed smoothly.

When the buyer has chosen a lender, this information should be given to the closer. The closer will then gather the documents and information from the lender that it requires to be executed as a condition for making the loan. Documents generally required by the lender include the promissory note, deed of trust, surveyor's report and a hazard insurance policy. The lender may also require affidavits from either the buyer or the seller concerning encumbrances against the property or marital status. The lender will give the closer instructions regarding execution of these documents and any money to be collected at the time of closing for the lender's benefit. Typical costs that must be paid to the lender at the time of closing include the loan discount points and the funds for the escrow account, expenses and credit checks.

After the examination of the title has been made by the title insurance company, a report will be issued. The lender's copy of this report is called the *mortgagee's information letter*, and the buyer's copy is called the *owner's title commitment*. This report also contains instructions to the closer. It tells the closer the names of the present owners of the property, the taxes due on the property to date, the liens against the property, easements and any other special issues that may have arisen with respect to this property.

Usually the seller is required to deliver to the purchaser a marketable or indefeasible title. The title commitment reports any defects or encumbrances against the title that must be cured in order for the title to be marketable. For example, the title examination may reveal that the spouse of a grantor has failed to sign a release of his or her homestead rights. Encumbrances against the land such as a materialman's lien or a judgment lien may be found by the title examiner. These and other defects must be resolved prior to closing. The closer will contact the seller or his or her agent so that any problems with the title can be cured. The closer will also make this information available to the buyer. All title problems must be resolved prior to closing. Frequently, the removal of an encumbrance requires the payment of money. If the money is not paid and the encumbrance is not removed prior to closing, the closer can collect the money at the time of closing. In this case the closer will require the seller and creditor to agree on the amount due and how the encumbrance will be removed.

A date, place and time for closing the real estate sale are then set. The closing usually takes place at one of the offices of the title insurance company. Present at the closing are the closer, the buyer, the seller, the real estate agents and the attorneys of the parties. The parties can appear at the same time or at different times. In residential closings it is common for the parties to appear at the same time. The lender usually does not send a representative to the closing. The closer will have all the documents that must be executed by the parties, as well as a statement of the settlement charges and credits. (The settlement statement is discussed in detail in the next section, "Real Estate Settlement Procedures Act.") The closer usually calls the broker when the documents are ready for examination. The broker will then inform the buyer and seller that the documents can be reviewed. The broker also tells the buyer and seller the charges and costs that must be paid at closing. If the documents have not been reviewed previously, they will be reviewed at the time of closing. The closer will usually explain the settlement sheet charges and credits in detail. The closer will also briefly describe the documents and explain why each is being required in this closing. However, in most cases the closer is not a licensed attorney and will not answer any questions regarding the terms of the instrument or their legal significance. To a large extent the closer's duties are ministerial.

The closer collects any money that is due at the time of closing from either party. The closer is also an escrow agent. Because the closer does not represent either the buyer, the seller or the lender, he or she is required to act impartially and follow the instructions received. There are three sources for instructions. These are the earnest money contract, the lender's conditions of lending and the title report. If any problems arise that are not covered by these instruments, then the parties must resolve the problem. For example, if the lender sends to the title company a note bearing interest at the rate of 11 percent per annum, then the closer must have the buyer execute that note, or the sale cannot be closed. If the buyer thought that he or she had a commitment from the lender to lend at the rate of 10.5 percent per annum, then he or she will have to settle that issue with the lender.

After all documents have been executed properly and the money due has been paid, the closer will then disburse funds to the seller, the real estate agent and any other parties entitled to a portion of the sale proceeds. This disbursement may not take place until several days following the closing unless arrangements have been made with the lender in advance to do so at the closing. The delay is intended to provide time for the lender to check all papers executed at the closing. Disbursements are made by a check drawn on the escrow account of the title insurance company. The closer will also record necessary documents with the county clerk. The originals of those documents will then be sent to the proper party. The buyer will also receive his or her policy of title insurance after the title company knows that the deed has been recorded.

REAL ESTATE SETTLEMENT PROCEDURES ACT (RESPA)

The Real Estate Settlement Procedures Act (RESPA) is a federal law that requires lending institutions to disclose certain information to purchasers of residential real estate and prohibits those institutions from engaging in certain activities. (12 U.S.C. §2601 et seq.)

A borrower who seeks a mortgage loan needs full information from lending institutions in order to select a lender prudently. RESPA requires the lending institution to make certain disclosures designed to help the borrower make informed judgments. Generally, RESPA is applicable to first mortgage loans made for the purchase of residential real estate. Residential real estate includes one-family to four-family properties. Cooperatives, condominiums and mobile home lots can qualify as residential real estate. The act applies only to purchases where a lender (other than the seller) takes a purchase-money mortgage to secure the loan. A purchase-money mortgage in which the seller takes a mortgage back to secure the unpaid purchase price is not covered by RESPA. The requirements of RESPA are applicable only to lenders involved in a "federally related mortgage loan." The definition of *federally related* is very broad, including any lending institution whose deposits are federally insured or regulated.

However, if federal law is not applicable for some reason, the Texas Title Insurance Act requires that employees of title insurance companies follow the Uniform Settlement and Closing Statement created by the insurance board. (Tex. Ins. Code §§9.53–9.54) This state law also requires that the title insurance company disclose settlement costs in advance if a request for these costs is made in writing.

Settlement Costs Booklet

RESPA is administered by the Department of Housing and Urban Development (HUD). HUD has prepared a settlement costs booklet. Every lender is required to provide an applicant for a mortgage loan with the contents of this booklet on the day of the loan application, or, failing that, the lender must deposit it in the mail to the applicant within three business days after the application. The booklet contains information about the real estate purchase process, including negotiating a sales contract and home loan financing. Under the heading "Selecting a Lender," the booklet suggests certain inquiries a borrower should make in order to compare lenders. For example:

- Am I required to carry life or disability insurance? Must I obtain it from a particular company?
- Is there a late payment charge? How much? How late may the payment be before the charge is imposed?
- If I wish to pay off the loan in advance of maturity, must I pay a prepayment penalty? How much? If so, for how long a period will it apply?
- Will the lender release me from personal liability if my loan is assumed by someone else when I sell my house?
- If I sell the house and the buyer assumes the loan, will the lender have the right to charge an assumption fee, raise the rate of interest or require payment in full of the mortgage?
- Will I be required to pay monies into a special reserve account to cover taxes or insurance? If so, how large a deposit will be required at the closing of the sale?

Additionally, the booklet contains information regarding homebuyers' rights and obligations, settlement services and escrow accounts, as well as a sample work sheet to calculate the settlement costs.

Good-Faith Estimate

Another RESPA requirement is that the lender must provide the borrower with a good-faith estimate of settlement charges at the time of the application. These charges may be expressed as a range. A lender who fails to provide the required information on that date must deposit the information in the mail within three business days of the application. The good-faith estimates include the breakdown of the costs of settlement charges rendered by the mortgagee—for example, loan origination fee, credit report fee, appraisers' fees, title search charges, attorney fees, surveys and document preparation. The complete schedule of all settlement charges is contained in Section L of the Uniform Settlement Statement, discussed later in this chapter. The good-faith estimate does not have to include prepaid hazard insurance premiums or reserves deposited with the lender such as escrow for taxes and insurance (information not usually available to lenders at the application stage). Although the estimates must be made in good faith, they are subject to change as the market alters the costs of the various settlement charges.

Right To Inspect the Uniform Settlement Statement

A closing or settlement statement is normally prepared by the closer handling the closing. The settlement statement consists of a summary of the buyer's (borrower's) and the seller's transactions, broken down into various categories. For some items it may be necessary to prorate income and expenses between the parties. For example, assume that the seller has paid the insurance for six months in advance. Credit should be given to the seller for the portion paid that covers any period after closing. Apportionment or proration of the insurance ensures that each person bears the expense only for the months that person had use of the premises. Other expenses often apportioned include interests on loans assumed by the buyer and taxes. Rental income may also be prorated for unearned rentals received by the seller in advance.

RESPA requires that a lender permit the borrower a right to inspect the Uniform Settlement Statement (USS) one day before closing. The USS is a form settlement statement that contains a summary of the borrower's and seller's transactions and an itemization of the settlement charges as allocated to the borrower and seller. In the event that this information is unavailable the day before closing, the lender is relieved of the responsibility. In this case the completed statement must be given to the buyer no later than the closing. This requirement may be waived by the buyer, but in the event of such waiver, the USS must be mailed at the earliest practical date. Where there is a closing without an appearance of the buyer or the buyer's agent, the lender need only mail the statement to the buyer as soon as practical after the closing. The lender need not provide a USS to the buyer when there are no settlement charges to the buyer or when the settlement charges are a fixed amount communicated to the borrower at the time of the loan application. However, here the lender must provide the borrower with an itemized list of services provided within three days after closing.

In all transactions covered by RESPA the USS must be used. Otherwise, a statement resembling that form is normally used.

A Uniform Settlement Statement Example

A simple example of a residential closing is reflected in the settlement statement in Figure 23.2. Amounts in the statement are based upon the following information.

Jim Darrow has obtained a commitment for an 11 percent 30-year loan from the Poplar Savings and Loan for $80,000 to purchase Liz Nodler's home at 1984 Hatchback Center, Dearlake, Texas. The sales price, pursuant to the contract previously entered into by the parties, is $100,000. The closing is to take place at the offices of First American Title Company on May 15. In addition to the purchase price of the house, Darrow has arranged to purchase the curtains for $300. County and school taxes on the property are $1,200 per year, payable semiannually. The county and school are six months behind on billing and collecting taxes; Liz's last payment was made January 15, 1988. The seller prepaid $200 on January 1 for hazard insurance, which covers the calendar year. The house is heated by butane: 50 gallons of home butane costing $1.50 per gallon remain in the tank on the day of closing. Seller's tenant has paid $400 advance rent for the month of May.

Darrow is paying $20,000 down payment, which will be paid at the closing.

Figure 23.2: **EXAMPLE OF A UNIFORM SETTLEMENT STATEMENT**

A. Settlement Statement

First American Title Company

U.S. Department of Housing
and Urban Development

OMB No. 2502-0265 (Exp. 12-31-86)

B. Type of Loan

1. ☐ FHA 2. ☐ FmHA 3. ☐ Conv. Unins.
4. ☐ VA 5. ☒ Conv. Ins.

6. File Number | 7. Loan Number | 8. Mortgage Insurance Case Number

C. Note: This form is furnished to give you a statement of actual settlement costs. Amounts paid to and by the settlement agent are shown. Items marked "(p.o.c.)" were paid outside the closing; they are shown here for informational purposes and are not included in the totals.

D. Name and Address of Borrower	E. Name and Address of Seller	F. Name and Address of Lender
Jim Darrow	Liz Nodler	Poplar Savings and Loan

G. Property Location	H. Settlement Agent **First American Title Company**	
1984 Hatchback Center	Place of Settlement	I. Settlement Date
Dearlake, Texas	1234 Lake Lane Dearlake, Texas	5/15/88

J. Summary of Borrower's Transaction		K. Summary of Seller's Transaction	
100. Gross Amount Due From Borrower		**400. Gross Amount Due To Seller**	
101. Contract sales price	100,000.00	401. Contract sales price	100,000.00
102. Personal property	300.00	402. Personal property	300.00
103. Settlement charges to borrower (line 1400)	2,725.48	403.	
104.		404.	
105.		405.	
Adjustments for items paid by seller in advance		Adjustments for items paid by seller in advance	
106. City/town taxes to		406. City/town taxes to	
107. County taxes to		407. County taxes to	
108. Assessments to		408. Assessments to	
109. School taxes to		409. School taxes to	
110. Insurance 5/15 to 12/31	125.00	410. Insurance 5/15 to 12/31	125.00
111. Butane 50 gal. at $1.50/gal	75.00	411. Butane 50 gal. at $1.50/gal	75.00
112.		412.	
120. Gross Amount Due From Borrower	103,225.48	**420. Gross Amount Due To Seller**	100,500.00
200. Amounts Paid By Or In Behalf Of Borrower		**500. Reductions In Amount Due To Seller**	
201. Deposit or earnest money		501. Excess deposit (see instructions)	
202. Principal amount of new loan(s)	80,000.00	502. Settlement charges to seller (line 1400)	9,215.00
203. Existing loan(s) taken subject to		503. Existing loan(s) taken subject to	
204.		504. Payoff of first mortgage loan	37,120.00
205.		505. Payoff of second mortgage loan	
206.		506.	
207.		507.	
208.		508.	
209.		509.	
Adjustments for items unpaid by seller		Adjustments for items unpaid by seller	
210. City/town taxes to		510. City/town taxes to	
211. County taxes 7/15/87 to 5/15/88	1,000.00	511. County taxes 7/15/87 to 5/15/88	1,000.00
212. Assessments 4/1/88 to 5/15/88	37.50	512. Assessments 4/1/88 to 5/15/88	37.50
213. School taxes to		513. School taxes to	
214. Interest to		514. Interest to	
215. Rentals 5/15/88 to 5/31/88	200.00	515. Rentals 5/15/88 to 5/31/88	200.00
216.		516.	
217.		517.	
218.		518.	
219.		519.	
220. Total Paid By/For Borrower	81,237.50	**520. Total Reduction Amount Due Seller**	47,572.50
300. Cash At Settlement From/To Borrower		**600. Cash At Settlement To/From Seller**	
301. Gross Amount due from borrower (line 120)	103,225.48	601. Gross amount due to seller (line 420)	100,500.00
302. Less amounts paid by/for borrower (line 220)	(81,237.50)	602. Less reductions in amt. due seller (line 520)	(47,572.50)
303. Cash ☒ From ☐ To Borrower	21,987.98	**603. Cash** ☒ To ☐ From Seller	52,927.50

SELLER'S AND/OR PURCHASER'S STATEMENT

Seller's and Purchaser's signature hereon acknowledges his/their approval of tax prorations, and signifies their understanding that prorations were based on figures for preceding year, or estimates for current year, and in event of any change for current year, all necessary adjustments must be made between Seller and Purchaser direct; likewise any DEFICIT in delinquent taxes will be reimbursed to Title Company by the Seller.

Previous Edition Is Obsolete

HUD-1 (3-86)
RESPA, HB 4305.2

Figure 23.2: (continued).

L. Settlement Charges		Paid From Borrowers Funds at Settlement	Paid From Seller's Funds At Settlement
700. Total Sales/Broker's Commission based on a price $ 100,000.00 @ 6 %= 6,500.00			
Division of commission (line 700) as follows			
701. $ 6,500.00 to Decade Today Realtors			
702. $ to			
703. Commission paid at Settlement			6,500.00
704.			
800. Items Payable In Connection With Loan			
801. Loan Origination Fee 2 %		1,600.00	
802. Loan Discount 2 %			1,600.00
803. Appraisal Fee to			
804. Credit Report to			
805. Lender's Inspection Fee			
806. Mortgage Insurance Application Fee to			
807. Assumption Fee			
808.			
809.			
810.			
811.			
900. Items Required By Lender To Be Paid In Advance			
901. Interest from 5/15 to 5/31 @$ 24.44 /day		415.48	
902. Mortgage Insurance Premium for months to			
903. Hazard Insurance Premium for years to			
904. Flood Insurance years to			
905.			
1000. Reserves Deposited With Lender			
1001. Hazard insurance months@$ per month			
1002. Mortgage insurance months@$ per month			
1003. City property taxes months@$ per month			
1004. County property taxes 2 months@$ 100.00 per month		200.00	
1005. Annual assessments months@$ per month			
1006. School District month@$ per month			
1007. Water District months@$ per month			
1008. Flood Insurance months@$ per month			
1009. months@$ per month			
1010. months@$ per month			
1100. Title Charges			
1101. Settlement or closing fee to			
1102. Abstract or title search to			
1103. Title examination to			
1104. Title insurance binder to			
1105. Document preparation to Seller's Attorney			35.00
1106. Notary fees to			
1107. Attorney's fees to Lincoln Todd & Harrison		350.00	
(includes above items numbers:)			
1108. Title insurance to First American Title Co.			650.00
(includes above items number:			
1109. Lender's coverage $ 80,000			
1110. Owner's coverage $ 100,000			
1111. Escrow Fee to First American Title Co.			
1112. Restrictions to First American Title Co.			
1113. Messenger to First American Title Co.			
1114.			
1115.			
1200. Government Recording and Transfer Charges			
1201. Recording fees: Deed $ 5.00 ; Mortgage $ 5.00 ; Releases $ 5.00		10.00	5.00
1202. City/county tax/stamps: Deed $, Mortgage $			100.00
1203. State tax/stamps Deed $, Mortgage $			
1204. Tax Certificates to			
1205.			
1300. Additional Settlement Charges			
1301. Survey to Survey Plat, Inc.		150.00	
1302. Pest inspection to Exterm Pest			250.00
1303. Gas Line to City			75.00
1304.			
1305.			
1400. Total Settlement Charges (enter on lines 103, Section J and 502, Section K)		2,725.48	9,215.00

I have carefully reviewed the HUD-1 Settlement Statement and to the best of my knowledge and belief, it is a true and accurate statement of all receipts and disbursements made on my account or by me in this transaction. I further certify that I have received a copy of the HUD-1 Settlement Statement.

_____   _____

Borrowers   Sellers

The HUD-1 Settlement Statement which I have prepared is a true and accurate account of this transaction. I have caused or will cause the funds to be disbursed in accordance with this statement.

_____   _____

Settlement Agent   Date

WARNING: it is a crime to knowingly make false statements to the United States on this or any other similar form. Penalties upon conviction can include a fine and imprisonment. For details see: Title 18 U.S. Code Section 1001 and Section 1010.

Water and sewer assessments are payable quarterly at an even billing of $45 per quarter at the end of March, June, September and December. Nodler made the March 31 payment. Every six months a reading is taken to determine the actual usage for the six-month period, and adjustments are made at the end of the year. Average adjustments for the last five years have resulted in an additional assessment of $40 at the end of the year.

The payoff by the seller of the first mortgage on the home, as of the date of closing, is $37,120.

A listing agreement with Decade Today Realtors requires the seller to pay 6$^1/_2$ percent commission. The loan origination fee was two percent. Seller, pursuant to the terms of the contract, was to pay two mortgage discount points (two percent). The appraisal fee of $100 and $15 for a credit report was paid by Darrow at the time of the loan application. The survey fee of $150 to Survey Plat, Inc., is payable by the buyer at closing. Assume that simple interest based on a 360-day calendar year is to be paid at closing for the 17-day period encompassing May 15 to May 31. Darrow will be required to deposit two months' taxes at closing into escrow. Attorney fees for preparation of the deed, to be borne by the seller, are $35. The buyer's attorney fees for services connected with the closing are $350, payable to Lincoln, Todd and Harrison Law Firm at closing. The seller obtained a title insurance policy, as required per contract, to fully cover the lender and the owner. The cost to the seller, to be disbursed at closing to First American Title Company, is $650. The buyer's charge for recording fees for the deed and the mortgage amounts to $5 for each document. The seller must pay the recording fee for the release of the existing mortgage.

Additionally, a 0.1 percent county transfer conveyance fee is assessed against the seller. Seller, pursuant to the contract, agreed to pay for termite and gas line inspection costs. She employed Exterm Pest Control to do the termite inspection; the charge was $40 for the inspection and $210 for repair work. The seller employed the city to do the gas line inspection at a cost of $75.

Summary of Borrower's Transaction

Schedule J on the closing statement is a summary of the borrower's transactions. The total of amounts paid by the borrower is subtracted from the total of the amounts due from the borrower. From this calculation we derive the net amount the borrower needs to bring to the closing.

Line 101   The contract sales price of $100,000 is inserted on this line.

Line 102   The cost of curtains, which is $300, is inserted on this line.

Line 103   The settlement charges derived from Schedule L (explained later) are inserted on this line.

Line 110   The insurance is apportioned as of the date of closing. Nodler has paid $200 in advance on January 1 for the entire calendar year. She should get a credit for the amounts prepaid that extend beyond the closing. This amounts to $125 ($7^1/_2$ mos. × $16.66 per month).

Line 111   The seller should receive credit for the unused butane remaining in the tank on the day of closing. Since 50 gallons remain, the amount of $75 should be inserted on this line (50 × $1.50 per gallon).

Line 120   The total due from the borrower amounts to the sum total of lines 101–112, which is $103,225.48.

Line 202   The amount of the loan, $80,000, should be inserted on this line.

Line 211   The county taxes are apportioned as of the date of closing. The taxes are $100 per month ($1,200 ÷ 12). Nodler's last payment was on January 15, 1988. Because the county is six months behind on collecting tax, Nodler owes taxes from July 15, 1987, through January 15, 1988. In addition, she owes taxes from January 15 to May 15, the date of closing (10 × $100/month = $1,000).

Line 212   The water and sewer assessments need to be adjusted since Nodler has paid only through March. The buyer should be given a credit for the amounts unpaid from March 31 through May 15, or for $1^1/_2$ months. This amounts to $22.50 ($1/_2$ × $45.00). Additionally, the average adjustments at the end of the year must be taken into consideration. An additional $10 per quarter must be added to the figure or $15.00 ($1^1/_2$ quarters × $10). The total adjustment benefiting the borrower amounts to $37.50 ($22.50 + $15.00).

Line 215   The seller's tenant has paid $400 for rent covering the entire month of May. This amount must be apportioned as of May 15, the date of closing. Darrow should be given a credit for the period from May 15 through May 31. This amounts to $200 ($1/_2$ month × $400).

Line 220   The total paid by the borrower amounts to the sum total of lines 201–219 or $81,237.50.

Line 301   The total amount due from the borrower as derived from line 120 is inserted on this line.

Line 302   The total amount paid by the borrower as derived from line 220 is inserted on this line.

Line 303   The cash from the borrower at closing, amounting to $21,987.98, is derived by subtracting line 302 from line 301. In the event the amount of line 302 is greater than the amount on line 301, the borrower would receive cash at the closing.

Summary of Seller's Transaction

Schedule K on the closing statement is a summary of the seller's transactions. The total of the seller's reductions is subtracted from the total of the amounts due to the seller. From this calculation we derive the net amount the seller is to receive at closing.

Line 401   See explanation of line 101.
Line 402   See explanation of line 102.
Line 410   See explanation of line 110.
Line 411   See explanation of line 111.
Line 420   The total due to the seller amounts to the total of lines 401–412, which is $100,500.00.
Line 502   The settlement charges derived from Schedule L (explained later) are inserted on this line.
Line 504   The amount needed to pay off seller's mortgage, which is $37,120, is inserted on this line.
Line 511   See explanation of line 211.
Line 512   See explanation of line 212.
Line 515   See explanation of line 215.
Line 520   The total reduction from the seller amounts to the total of lines 501–519 or $47,572.50.
Line 601   The total amount due to seller as derived from line 420 is inserted on this line.
Line 602   The total reduction due seller as derived from line 520 is inserted on this line.
Line 603   The cash to the seller at closing, amounting to $52,927.50 is derived by subtracting line 602 from line 601. In the event the amount on line 602 is greater than the amount on line 601, the seller would owe cash at the closing.

Summary of Settlement Charges

Schedule L on the closing statement is a summary of the settlement charges that are paid from the borrower's funds and of those paid from the seller's funds at the settlement.

Paid from Borrower's Funds:

Line 801   The loan origination fee is $1,600 (2% × $80,000) and is payable to the mortgagee at settlement.
Line 901   The borrower is required to pay the interest on the loan for the 17-day period from May 15 to May 31. Assuming simple interest on the $80,000 loan, the daily rate amounts to $24.44/day (11% of $80,000 = $8,800 ÷ 360 = $24.44/day). For 17 days, the interest payable by the borrower amounts to $415.48 ($24.44 × 17 days).
Line 1003   The borrower is required to deposit two months of taxes in escrow, which amounts to $200 ($1,200 ÷ 12 × 2 = $200).
Line 1107   The borrower is required to pay attorney fees to Lincoln, Todd and Harrison in the amount of $350.00.

Line 1201 The borrower is required to pay the recording fees for the deed and the new mortgage, which amounts to $10.

Line 1301 The borrower is required to pay $150 to Survey Plat, Inc., for the survey.

Line 1400 The sum of the settlement charges to the seller, amounting to $2,725.48, is placed on this line and is also inserted at Section J on line 103.

Paid from Seller's Funds:

Line 700 The total sales/broker's commission is $6,500 (6¹/₂% of $100,000).

Line 701 The $6,500 is payable at the settlement to Decade Today Realtors.

Line 703 The $6,500 commission is listed on this line on the seller's side.

Line 802 The seller is required to pay mortgage loan discount points equal to $1,600 (2% × $80,000).

Line 1105 The seller is required to pay the attorney fee for preparing the deed, which amounts to $35.

Line 1108 The cost of the title insurance payable to First American Title Company appears on this line on the seller's side.

Line 1201 The cost of filing the release or satisfaction of mortgage in the amount of $5 is assessable against the seller.

Line 1202 The county transfer conveyance fee of $100 (0.001 × $100,000) is payable by the seller.

Line 1302 The seller is obligated to pay Exterm Pest $250 for the inspection and repair work.

Line 1303 The seller is obligated to pay the city $75 for the gas inspection.

Line 1400 The sum of the settlement charges to the seller, amounting to $9,215 is placed on this line and is also inserted at Section K on line 502.

Abusive Practices

One reason Congress passed RESPA was certain abusive practices that led to inflated closing costs. "Kickbacks" are one such practice expressly prohibited by RESPA. Kickbacks occur, for example, when a person or an entity gives a fee to another for business referrals.

CASE EXAMPLE

ABC Savings and Loan has an agreement with Alfred Hillman, attorney, whereby for every person ABC refers to Hillman for legal services in connection with real estate transactions, Hillman pays ABC ten percent of the fees generated. This is an illegal kickback under RESPA. Additionally, Hillman would be violating the attorney's code of ethics and would be subject to disciplinary measures.

There are similar prohibitions against the payment of a "phantom" charge, a fee that is given where no service has been performed. Both kickbacks and phantom fees may result in a violation for which criminal penalties may attach. Also, an aggrieved party may sue to recover three times the amount of the kickback or the phantom fee.

POSTCLOSING PROCEDURES

After the closing, the purchaser is the titleholder of the property as evidenced by the deed. The deed must now be recorded to give constructive notice to the world of the new ownership and thus protect the buyer against rival claimants. The purchaser, purchaser's attorney or, in most cases, the closer presents the deed for recording in the proper office in the county courthouse. After receiving the appropriate fees the clerk photocopies and records the deed and then returns the original deed to the purchaser. The release of lien for the preexisting mortgage should also be recorded. The new mortgage instrument that secures repayment of the loan is recorded by the mortgagee, the institution extending the loan to the purchaser. After the recording of these documents, the title insurer issues the title insurance policy in the name of the new owner and the mortgagee if title insurance was purchased. In the event an abstract is given as evidence of title, the search of the title should be updated or brought down to the moment of recording.

At the closing, a problem may have been remedied by setting up an escrow and charging an escrow agent with the obligation of holding a portion of the purchase price necessary to assure the resolution of the problem. For example, a last inspection by the buyer may have revealed a broken window. Instead of delaying the closing to await repair or an estimate of repair, the parties may have agreed to withhold $100 or some other sum pending the repair by the seller. In the event that the seller fails to repair the window, the buyer may use the escrow proceeds to have it repaired. Any unused portion of the escrow monies will be returned to the seller. Any escrow accounts that remain past the closing should be reconciled as soon thereafter as possible.

CASE EXAMPLE

At closing Fred Thomas, seller, is unable to produce any paid receipts for water bills for the last year. Frank Hander, purchaser, is wary of closing without an assurance that any unpaid bills will be borne by the seller. An escrow account is set up with $150 funded from the purchase price, an amount everyone agrees would be more than enough to pay any unpaid water bills for a year. After closing, contact with the water company reveals an unpaid water bill of $31. The escrow agent will pay the amount out of the escrow funds and send the remaining $119 to the seller.

In the event the property was sold subject to an existing lease, the purchaser should secure a "tenant's letter" from the seller, notifying the tenants of the sale and directing them to pay rent in the future to the purchaser. After closing, the purchaser should deliver that letter to the tenants.

SUMMARY

The closing, also called the *settlement*, is the final stage of a real estate purchase transaction. At the closing the deed and the purchase money are exchanged by the seller and buyer according to the terms of the contract.

In most cases the broker plays an active role in the preparation for closing by providing guidance to the parties in completing the different tasks necessary for a successful consummation of the earnest money contract.

Between the signing of the contract and the closing date, the buyer usually must obtain financing and secure hazard insurance and should inspect the premises, perform any required repairs, initiate a title search and examine any existing leases on the property. The seller also needs this interval to prepare by obtaining evidence of title, preparing a deed and satisfying any liens or other encumbrances.

The closing typically takes place at the office of the title insurance company named in the earnest money contract. It may also be closed at an attorney's office, the real estate broker's office or the lender's office. The closer, usually an employee of the title insurance company, is responsible for coordinating the paperwork. To aid in following the flow of funds at the closing, a settlement statement is prepared. The statement includes breakdowns for taxes, utilities, rents and any other payments that must be prorated. The settlement procedures are regulated by local custom, state law and a federal statute known as RESPA (Real Estate Settlement Procedures Act).

After the closing, the deed should be recorded to protect the purchaser. The old mortgage should be released and any new mortgage recorded.

QUESTIONS AND CASE PROBLEMS

1. What is the role of a broker in a real estate closing?
2. What is the role of the closer at closing? Who can act as a settlement clerk?
3. Upon whom does RESPA impose requirements? What are those requirements?
4. The Maple Ridge Construction Company and Kasten entered into an agreement for the purchase of lots in a subdivision owned by Kasten. Maple Ridge encountered problems in obtaining financing and requested postponement of the closing date. Kasten agreed to an extension of four months. Maple Ridge continued to try to ob-

tain a suitable financing arrangement without success. Repeated requests for additional extensions were turned down by Kasten. The closing date passed with neither party performing or demanding performance from the other. Five days after the expiration of the closing date Maple Ridge informed Kasten that it was ready to perform. Kasten refused Maple Ridge's tender, claiming that the contract had expired. Maple Ridge commenced an action in specific performance against Kasten in an attempt to force Kasten to comply with the terms of their contract. Who wins? Discuss.

5. Stephanie Andrew, seller, and John and Joan Lynch, purchasers, entered into a real estate purchase agreement that included the following mortgage financing contingency clause: "Buyer shall apply to a conventional bank or other mortgage loan institution for a loan of [$155,000] payable in not less than thirty...years at prevailing interest rates." The Lynches made one application to Bay Bank for a loan of $130,000. Bay Bank indicated that it was ready to lend the money to the Lynches if they would show where the remainder of the purchase money ($98,600) was coming from. The Lynches responded by informing the bank that the proceeds from the sale of their house would provide the balance. There was no agreement to sell their house at that date. The bank sought to accommodate the Lynches by offering them an additional loan for the $98,600 to be secured by a mortgage on the Lynches' existing house. The Lynches refused. The bank thereafter, pursuant to John Lynch's request, sent a letter rejecting the Lynches' application. Maintaining that the contingency was unfulfilled, the Lynches refused to close on the sale of Andrew's house. Is their refusal justified? Explain.

24

The Leasehold Estate and the Lease

LEASEHOLD ESTATE

The leasehold is an interest in land. The *leasehold estate* is created when the property owner, called the lessor, conveys a possessory interest in the real property to another, called the lessee, for a specified period of time in exchange for the lessee's payment of rent.

An unusual aspect of a lease is that it is rooted firmly in two distinct areas of law: contract law and real property law. As a contract, the lease must contain the essential elements of any contract—offer, acceptance, consideration capacity and legality—in order to be enforceable. Since it relates to real property, the lease involves a conveyance of an estate in land, or a leasehold estate. The landlord surrenders his or her possessory rights to the premises for the duration of the lease. The tenant must pay for that possession during the term of the lease. Because the tenant is getting an estate in land, he or she is required by law to pay the rent even if there is no specific agreement regarding rent. Possession is exchanged for rent.

The granting of a leasehold estate gives to a tenant the exclusive possession of the premises for an agreed-upon term with a reversion at the end of the term of possession to the landlord. This exclusive right of possession deprives the owner of the premises during the lease. Even where tenants fail to comply with the leasehold bargain, landlords can remove them from the premises only by bringing formal eviction proceedings.

Four different kinds of leasehold estates can be created. They are term tenancy, periodic tenancy, tenancy at will and tenancy at sufferance.

Term Tenancy

The term tenancy is also called an estate for years. The *term tenancy* is a leasehold estate that has a specific beginning date and a specific ending date. This tenancy terminates itself without any action by either party upon expiration of the term stated in the agreement. It should be noted that if the parties' lease stipulates notice or other conditions for termination of the tenancy, as written leases often do, then these conditions must be met.

If the parties fail to stipulate the amount of rent due, a reasonable rent is required. Under the common law, however, the rent is not due until the end of the tenancy. By way of contrast, most modern leases require the rent to be prepaid, since landlords are understandably unwilling to wait until the end of the term to receive payment of rent.

Periodic Tenancy

The *periodic tenancy* is a leasehold estate that continues from period to period until terminated by proper notice from one of the parties. This is sometimes also called a *tenancy from month to month.*

The periodic tenancy is normally from year to year or month to month but can be for any period up to a year. It can be created in several different ways. One way is by express agreement. If A leases her property to B "from month to month beginning April 1, 1987," a periodic tenancy is created. A periodic tenancy can also be implied from the rental period. For example, if rent is paid weekly, then it can be implied that the tenancy is from week to week.

This type of estate can also evolve from a term tenant who remains, or "holds over," after the expiration of the term tenancy. The holdover tenancy will be discussed in more detail later in this section.

The periodic tenancy can be terminated by either party upon giving adequate notice. The parties may contractually agree on what will constitute adequate notice. Absent such an agreement, adequate notice is determined by state law. In Texas the statute controlling notice of termination differentiates between the type and length of the tenancy. If the rent-paying period is at least one month, the leasehold is terminated by giving at least one month's notice. If the rent-paying period is less than a month, then the tenancy is terminated by giving at least the same number of days' notice as are in the rent-paying period. (Tex. Prop. Code §91.001)

CASE EXAMPLE

Karen Kaiser leases Greenacre to Franks "from year to year beginning April 1, 1986." To terminate the lease to Greenacre either Kaiser or Franks would have to give one month's notice, unless they had an agreement to the contrary. On the other hand, assume that Karen Kaiser leases space in her boarding house on a biweekly basis. Bill Boarder pays his rent every two weeks. To terminate the tenancy either Kaiser or Boarder would have to give two weeks' notice.

Tenancy At Will

The **tenancy at will** is a leasehold estate that exists so long as both lessor and lessee desire it to last. The tenant at will has taken possession with the landlord's permission and can remain there until the tenant chooses to leave or the landlord wants possession returned to him, whichever occurs first. This type of estate may arise by express agreement. For example, a lease may state "to Franks at the will of Kaiser." This wording creates a tenancy at will. Despite this restrictive language, tenancies at will can be terminated by either party.

As a practical matter the distinction between the periodic tenancy and the tenancy at will has become unimportant. At common law one of the chief distinctions between the two tenancies was the notice of termination difference. The tenancy at will under the common law required no notice to terminate the tenancy. However, by statute in Texas the parties are required to give the same notice whether it be a periodic tenancy or a tenancy at will.

Although the estate exists wholly by permission, all the rights and duties of the landlord-tenant relationship exist. Unlike the previously mentioned leasehold estates, however, a tenancy at will is terminated by the death of either party or by the sale of the property to a third party.

Tenancy at Sufferance

The last type of tenancy is the **tenancy at sufferance**. This leasehold estate is created when a tenant no longer has the landlord's permission to possess the premises. In other words, the tenant is wrongfully in possession. The tenant at sufferance is similar to a trespasser. The major difference is that the tenant at sufferance entered the property legally. Usually he or she is the holdover tenant from a term tenancy, the mortgagor who remains in possession following foreclosure of the mortgaged premises or the seller who refuses to vacate on the date for change in possession under an earnest money contract. The classification of a person as a tenant at sufferance, not as a trespasser actually works to the tenant's disadvantage. The tenant is unable to possess the property adversely against the landlord and eventually gain an ownership interest, as a trespasser could.

Holdover Tenant

Somewhat similar to the tenant at sufferance is the holdover tenant. The **holdover tenant** is one who failed to vacate or surrender possession of the premises at the termination of a term tenancy. The words *holdover tenant* are sometimes used in relation to a periodic tenancy, where the tenant stays on despite the landlord's adequate notice to vacate. Under these circumstances, a landlord who permits the tenant to remain has technically waived the notice and allowed the continuation of the periodic tenancy.

The term tenant who holds over after the expiration date of a lease temporarily becomes a tenant at sufferance. All options shift into the landlord's hands when the tenant holds over. The landlord has the option of evicting the tenant or of holding him or her for another term.

CASE EXAMPLE

Anton leases a house and lot to Glenn and Sarah Williams. The terms of the agreement stipulate that the lease commences on July 1, 1986, and terminates on June 30, 1987. On July 1, 1987, the couple is still living in the house. Anton has the option of beginning eviction proceedings against the Williamses, who are now tenants at sufferance, or of unilaterally extending their lease until June 30, 1988.

Once the landlord exercises the option to hold the tenant for an additional period, the estate becomes a periodic tenancy. The maximum length of the period will be one year, or more accurately year to year, even where the term tenancy was for a longer period. Most leases state that the tenancy shall be month to month.

The terms of the holdover tenant's new lease will be the same as those of the original lease except as to length of time, as noted above. One exception arises when the landlord notifies the tenant before the expiration of the lease that he or she is changing the terms (for example, raising the rent). The tenant is usually held to the altered terms.

If the holdover is involuntary and for a short period of time, courts will not hold the tenant for an additional term. For instance, if the holdover is caused by a tornado, a snowstorm, a death in the family, or a one-day delay of the moving van, the court is not likely to hold the tenant for an additional period.

LEASE

A *lease* is a contract, either written or oral, that transfers the right of possession of the premises to the lessee or tenant. The relationship of landlord and tenant usually arises from an express contract on the part of the parties. As previously stated, the lease is firmly rooted in the law of contracts. The lease or contract normally includes terms giving the tenant the right to possession and entitling the landlord to a certain amount of rent. To this extent these contractual components overlap the possession-rent aspects that arise inherently from the real property notion of a conveyance or an estate in land. The lease-contract is likely to specify the terms of the possession and the amount of the rent, as well as many other factors that together compose the essence of the landlord and tenant's agreement.

Essential Elements of the Lease

The purpose of the lease is to detail the rights and duties of each of the parties in the contract. It is incumbent upon the parties to take great care in drafting the lease, especially if the terms of the agreement are complex or

Figure 24.1: SUMMARY OF LEASEHOLD ESTATES

Name of Tenancy	Creation of Tenancy	Termination of Tenancy
1. Term Tenancy	by agreement between landlord and tenant specifying a beginning and ending date	automatically upon expiration of specified lease term unless there is a specific agreement to the contrary
2. Periodic Tenancy	by agreement between landlord and and tenant specifying that it will continue from one period to another	generally one full period's notice must be given except for periods of more than one month, which require one month's notice
3. Tenancy at Will	by agreement between landlord and tenant without specifying a lease term	at common law no notice was required; in Texas the same notice as required for a periodic tenancy must be given
4. Tenancy at Sufferance	permission to remain on the leased premises has been withdrawn by landlord, but tenant retains possession	terminates as soon as the landlord can evict tenant

the duration of the lease is long. Consequently, lease contracts are generally more complex than earnest money contracts.

A Valid Contract

Since a lease is a contract, it must contain the essential elements of a contract. There must be a mutual consent to enter the agreement, and the agreement must be supported by consideration (rent in exchange for possession). The lease agreement will not require the use of any particular prescribed words. Essentially it must be shown that it was mutually intended for the tenant to have possession and that the landlord retained a *reversionary* interest in the land (that is, the right to have the property back when the lease expired).

The consideration that supports the lease contract is usually the rent. Nevertheless, the periodic payment of rent is not necessary to have a valid contract. The requirement is merely that consideration, or something of value, be given at some time to the landlord.

The other elements of a valid contract, such as the capacity of the parties (both must be sane and of legal age) and legality of purpose, must be met as well.

Statute of Frauds

In Texas a leasehold of more than one year must be in writing and signed and delivered by the lessor. (Tex. Prop. Code §5.021) This requirement differs from the statute of fraud requirements in many states. The Texas statute does not require that the lease be signed by the lessee under any circumstances. The problem of fraud that could result from this difference is in part prevented by the requirement that the lessor deliver the lease to the lessee. The lease must be accepted by the lessee in order to be enforceable against him or her. However, if the lessee fails to accept the lease, the lessor may be unable to enforce the lease against the lessee unless the lessee has also signed the lease. Therefore, it is the better practice for both parties to sign the lease agreement.

Parties

The lease must identify the parties as lessor and lessee, and both parties should sign the document. The spouse of the lessor should sign the lease as well, if he or she has an outstanding interest or potential interest in the property. For example, if a married couple owns the premises jointly, both parties must sign the lease since the spouse is a concurrent owner. The wife should also sign the lease where the state recognizes a dower interest, inasmuch as her potential interest may come into effect during the term of the lease.

Under some contracts a lessee may have the power to sublease or to assign the property to a third party; the person signing as lessor of the property may not be the actual owner of the premises. For this reason a lessee should make certain that the nonowner lessor has the authority to sublet and convey all or part of the interest to another. Subleasing will be discussed in more detail in the following chapter.

If the lessor is an individual, he or she must have the *capacity* to contract—that is, be mentally competent and of legal age. If the lessor is a fiduciary, entering the lease for another, as guardian, executor or trustee, for example, the lessee must be assured that the authority to lease is within the fiduciary's powers. Similarly, if the lessor is a corporation that is not in the business of leasing real estate, the lessee must verify the authorization of the corporation's board of directors to be assured that it is entitled to lease the premises.

Description of the Premises

In order to avoid a future dispute the premises should be described clearly. If the landlord's entire conveyed premises are being leased, then the description as contained in the deed or deeds is satisfactory. A lot number or block number used for tax purposes may be used if it is complete and accurate. A street number may not be adequate in itself because it relates only to the building and not to the land that is probably part of the leasehold as well.

When the lessor is leasing something less than all that he or she has, the lease should state clearly and exactly what is to be leased. In the absence of an agreement to the contrary, the lease of a building will be construed to include the use of everything reasonably necessary for the enjoyment of the land. It is up to the lessor expressly to exclude a use, or exclusive possession may pass to the lessee.

CASE EXAMPLE

Arthur leases one-half of an apartment house to Melanie, who has three small children. Unless the lease specifically excludes use of the fenced-in backyard, Melanie can use it for ingress and egress and as a play area for the children.

It is also to the lessee's benefit to have the precise nature of his or her use or possession spelled out in the lease, rather than to rely on the uncertain notion that he or she is entitled to certain unstated uses.

Statement of a Lease Term

The term of the lease should be stipulated clearly. Stating the beginning and ending dates as well as the length of the term will reduce doubt as to date of entry and the like. The lease should state, for example, "for one year beginning January 1, 1988, and terminating December 31, 1988." Where the beginning date is not spelled out, some doubt may exist as to whether the tenant began the term on the date the lease was signed, the first of the following month or some other date. If the beginning date is not stated, the commencement of the lease should be related to some event or ascertainable time so that the beginning of the lease is clear.

CASE EXAMPLE

Sanchez leased to Williams for one year beginning upon the surrender of possession by the present tenant or April 1, 1987, whichever comes first.

The courts do not favor leases of unlimited duration. If the time of termination is not fixed, the courts may interpret the agreement to be a tenancy at will, which is probably not what the parties intended. In a periodic tenancy, of course, the time of termination is fixed, although the tenancy is subject to automatic renewal upon the existence of certain conditions, such as failure to give notice of termination.

Rent

Rent is the compensation paid by the lessee for the possession of the leased property. Normally, rent takes the form of a money payment. It could, however, take the form of a percentage of the crops harvested from the land or of relief for the lessor of an obligation owed to the lessee. A statement of the amount of rent is one of the essential terms of a lease; nevertheless, where it has been omitted, courts have declared that the landlord is entitled to a "reasonable rent."

The usual practice is to state in the lease that the rent will be paid in advance. If such a statement is lacking, the rent is due at the end of the period. The rationale behind this rule is that the lessee is paying for the possession that he or she has enjoyed, and nothing is due until he or she has had the enjoyment.

In addition to how much and when, the lease should indicate where the rent is to be paid. Absent such an indication, it is payable at the leasehold premises.

Unless stipulated to the contrary, the total rent is due on the date set for payment. The usual practice is to require in the lease monthly, quarterly or annual payments.

CASE EXAMPLE

Karen leases Greenacre to Frank for a rent of $2,400 annually, payable in advance and on the first of each month in installments of "$200, and presented at the residence of the lessor."

This wording covers each of the above considerations.

For short-term residential leases it is most common to have a straight rental fee, such as $200 per month. In commercial leases, however, a variety of methods are used for determining the rent. The net lease, percentage lease and ground lease will be discussed later. Another technique for assessing rent is on a *graduated* basis. A lease might stipulate a rent of $2,400 the first year, $3,600 per year for the following two years, and $4,800 per year for the last two years. If the lessee is operating a new business, under the graduated rental the amount of rent is smallest in the start-up period and increases as the business (theoretically) grows.

Other techniques include basing the rent on the consumer price index or on some other criterion that is particularly relevant to the parties, to the business or to the lease itself. In short, the days of the straight or flat rental fee as the sole method for calculating rent, especially in business leases, has long since passed.

Legal Use of the Premises

If the lease gives no indication as to the uses that can be made of the premises, the general rule is that the lessee can make any legal use of the land he or she wants. Some courts, however, would limit the lessee to "reasonable uses" where the agreement is silent on the matter. The question of reasonable use is a factual question that the court will examine in light of the type of premises involved and the prior uses of the property. If the building was constructed and has been used as a residence from its inception, it would be unreasonable to use it now as a cheese factory.

Although it is appropriate for the lessor to limit the lessee's use by the agreement, careful drafting is warranted.

CASE EXCERPT *Ferrari v. Bauerle*, 519 S.W.2d 144 (Tex. Civ. App.—Austin 1975). SHANNON, Justice. Robert Ferrari and Jacob Bauerle entered into a written agreement in August of 1970, in which Ferrari leased for seven years a parcel of land and improvements situated on South Lamar in Austin. The lease agreement was a printed one that was put in final form without the assistance of any attorney. The uses of the premises were stated in the second numbered paragraph of that agreement:

> **Second.** That the said premises shall be used for Bakery and associated purposes and traffic in foods and beverages. The Lessee shall have the right to cancel and terminate this lease on thirty days (30) written notice to the Lessor
> and for no other purpose.

At the beginning of his tenancy, Ferrari operated an Italian restaurant known as "Ferrari's Pizza." After the sale of mixed drinks became lawful, Ferrari obtained permission from Bauerle to sell mixed drinks on the premises. . . .

After Ferrari began serving mixed drinks, he changed the name of his business to "Ferrari Supper Club." In April of 1972, and in an effort to stimulate business, Ferrari initiated another change in his operation which was to provide, as entertainment, dancing girls who wore no clothing above the waist. Still searching for a more descriptive name for his business, Ferrari chose in June of 1972, the appellation, "Ferrari's 21 Club."

Ferrari complains that the court erred in holding that the lease prohibited the conducting of live entertainment on the premises [author's note: the dancing girls]....

As in other written instruments, the end sought in the construction of leases is the ascertainment of the intent of the parties as revealed by the language used in the lease. Words and phrases used in a lease contract will be accorded their ordinary and commonly accepted meanings.

Ferrari argues that the paragraph is "unclear" because of the positioning of the printed phrase, "and for no other purpose," with respect to the other part of that paragraph, and because a complete sentence is interposed between the first sentence and the printed phrase....

We would agree that the composition of the second numbered paragraph is neither choice nor grammatical. Still, in our opinion, the use of the phrase, "and for no other purpose," shows an intention by the parties to limit the uses of the premises to those listed in the first part of the paragraph.

The first use permitted by the second numbered paragraph is for a "bakery and associated purposes." A bakery may be described as any place used for the purpose of mixing or the baking of any food product of which flour or meal is a principal ingredient. "Associated purposes" of a bakery could well be the use of the premises for storage, display or sale of the bakery products.

The other permissible use of the premises is for "traffic in food and beverages." The words "traffic in" are synonymous with the words "deal" or "deal in." A business dealing in "foods and beverages" is most usually thought to be either a mercantile establishment such as a grocery store, or a public eating house, such as a restaurant....

We conclude that the common and ordinarily accepted meanings of the rather prosaic terms, "Bakery and associated purposes" and "traffic in food and beverages" do not encompass, and may not be so stretched to encompass the trooping of partially clad females....

The judgment is affirmed.

O'QUINN, Justice (dissenting).   Because I cannot agree with the majority that the trial court was correct in concluding that the lease "clearly prohibits" use of the premises "for live entertainment" I dissent and state my reasons.

The written lease, in broad terms, authorizes "traffic in food and beverages." By later agreement of the parties, the premises were converted, at Ferrari's considerable expense, from a pizza parlor to a supper club. It is common knowledge, which this Court can notice, that entertainment, live or mechanical, is frequently offered as an adjunct and as a customary part of the operation of a place where people eat. The custom was a firmly established part of the restaurant business prior to the making of the lease and must be considered within the contemplation of parties at the time, in the absence of an express prohibition in the writing.

If the lessor limits the use to a clearly designated purpose, courts will uphold that limitation. If the lessor indicates a *specific* purpose to which the premises can be put (for example, "...can be used for a beauty shop.") and nothing more, however, this wording will not prohibit the lessee from making other uses of the land than as a beauty shop. The rationale behind these rules is that the law favors unrestricted use of the land conveyed. In short, ambiguities will be construed against the lessor and toward maximizing the lessee's use. If the lessor's limitations on permitted uses are not designated clearly, the lease will be construed to favor the lessee. If the lessor by permitting use as a beauty shop has not clearly shown an intent to limit use to that purpose alone, the lessee will be able to make any other use as well. The careful drafter would have stated " . . . for use as a beauty shop only."

Where the lessee's use of the property has been made illegal by a change in the law, the lease is not usually invalidated. If the lease permits other legal uses, the lessee can change the type of use. If, however, the lease limits the lessee to the now illegal use, the change in the law will invalidate the lease. The fact that the lessee's business has become unprofitable or that the property no longer suits him or her for a residence will not excuse performance under the lease contract.

A tenant who leases only part of a building for commercial purposes should be careful to reach some agreement with the lessor regarding the leasing of other parts of the building to competitors and use by the lessor as a competitor with the lessee. Without such an agreement, the lessor is free to put the remainder of the property to a competitive use.

Besides the terms of the lease, the tenant also should be careful to check the public regulation restrictions on his or her use. The zoning code may well prohibit uses that the lessor has not prohibited.

Right of Possession

In a majority of jurisdictions, including Texas, the landlord covenants to give the right of possession and nothing more. If there is a wrongdoer in possession at the time the tenant's lease commences, the landlord has not violated his or her implied promise of giving the *right to possession.* The fact that the tenant may have to bring a lawsuit to obtain possession is an excellent reason why the tenant should be careful to see to it that the lease contains a provision ensuring that the landlord will give *possession* of the premises, not merely the right to possession. The possibility of the landlord's being unable to deliver actual possession is not terribly remote. Holding over by former tenants is not a rare incident.

In some jurisdictions, the landlord implicitly covenants to deliver the possession of the premises. The onus then falls on the landlord to take necessary action (for example, eviction proceedings) to recover possession for the tenant.

It should be remembered that normally the tenant's possession is exclusive. Even the landlord, who may be the owner of the premises in fee simple, is not permitted to invade that exclusive possession without authorization. The landlord would be a trespasser, and the tenant could bring the appropriate legal action against him or her.

Recording the Lease

The practice of recording leases is permitted in most states, including Texas, since a lease is a conveyance of an interest in land. It is uncommon to record residential and other short-term leases, however, because actual possession by the tenant is notice to everyone of the tenant's interest in the land. Upon finding a tenant in possession, a potential taker of an interest in the land would have actual notice of the possession and would have the duty to inquire as to the possessor's right to be there. Failing to inspect the premises, he or she would still have constructive notice of the possession.

TYPES OF LEASES

It was indicated earlier that several types of leases exist. Four of these will be discussed in more detail here. Most are used primarily in commercial applications.

Gross Lease

A *gross lease* is a lease in which a flat or fixed amount of rent is paid by the tenant. Generally under a gross lease the tenant pays the rent and the landlord is responsible for expenses incurred in operating the premises. The landlord pays the taxes, insurance, special assessments and the like. Responsibility for ordinary repairs may be bargained for separately. In residential leases the gross rental fee may or may not include utilities. It would seem to be to the benefit of both parties, and society as a whole, to exclude utilities from the fixed rent in order to encourage the tenant to minimize the costs by reducing the consumption of energy.

Where long-term leases are desired, gross leases have gradually fallen from favor because of inflation and the steady decrease in the value of the dollar. Unless there is some provision in the lease to compensate the lessor for the gradually diminishing value of the periodic rent check, rental property becomes a questionable investment.

Net Lease

A *net lease* is a type of lease in which the tenant agrees to pay the taxes, insurance, repairs and other operating expenses of the premises. This type of lease assures the lessor of a steady income from the property and relieves him or her of the responsibility of overseeing the operations on the property. In short, the lessor has a real estate investment without most of the problems that usually accompany this type of investment.

Like the gross lease, the net lease does not necessarily take into account the loss of purchasing power due to inflation. Net leases can be drawn up that tie the amount of periodic rent that is payable to some recognized indicator, such as the consumer price index. In this way the lessor will have the same purchasing power at the end of a long-term lease that existed at the beginning.

When the lessee agrees to assume payments for the principal and interest on the mortgage in addition to the operating expenses, the lease is called a net-net-lease. Such leases are considered appropriate for the rental of large office buildings and commercial industrial properties. The net-net-lease further removes responsibility for the premises from the lessor.

Ground Lease

A *ground lease* is a specialized type of net lease in which the lessor leases a piece of vacant land to the lessee, usually with the stipulation that the lessee at his or her own expense will construct a building. The ground lease is a type of net lease in that the lessee agrees to assume the operating expense of the property. Once the building is constructed, it becomes part of the realty and title passes to the lessor. In ground lease situations there are several provisions that are common. The term of the lease is either for the life expectancy of the building or, at least, for a long period. When the term of the lease is not tied to the building's life expectancy, provisions must be made for the building at the expiration of the lease. The parties may agree that the lessor will have to pay the lessee the appraised value of the building at the time the lease expires. Of course, the parties can write any agreement that suits them on this matter.

The rent agreement can be for a fixed rate but is often tied to the appraised value of the land. In this way the lessor retains the benefit of the land's appreciating value.

In most such leases the lessee needs financing to construct the building. If this is the case, provisions must be made to accommodate the mortgagee as well as the parties to the lease. The lessor will have to agree to permit the building to be mortgaged while excluding himself or herself from liability on that mortgage. Likewise, the mortgagee will insist upon the untrammeled right to sell the property in the case of a foreclosure. In addition, the mortgagee will usually insist that the term of the ground lease extend significantly beyond the duration of the mortgage so that the tenant does not lose the incentive to make mortgage payments during the latter years of the obligation.

Percentage Lease

A *percentage lease* is a lease whose rental is based in part on the gross sales made by the tenant on the premises. The lessee in such a lease is required to pay a fixed periodic rental, the amount of the rent to be less than the property's full rental value. In addition, the lessor is entitled to a percentage of the gross sales made by the lessee.

A common practice is to charge a flat minimum rent (perhaps $200 per month) plus a percentage of the gross sales over a stipulated figure (for example, $200 per month plus two percent of the gross sales over $30,000). If the lease has a long term, the percentage lease provides some hedge against inflation. As inflation grows, theoretically so do gross sales; once sales exceed $30,000, the rent increases proportionately. Since the flat minimum rent is usually lower than the maximum amount the landlord would expect, the percentage lease is a hedge for the commercial lessee against bad times.

Percentage leases have become very popular in leasing commercial property. The percentage may be very low (one or two percent) in the case of a supermarket or very high (70 to 80 percent) where a parking lot is involved. Regardless of the type of business or the percentage agreed upon, it is critical that the parties carefully draft their agreement. The lease should make clear exactly what is encompassed within the term *gross sales* and should establish the right of the lessor to examine records of the business. From the lessor's perspective, in addition to the protection of a carefully drafted lease, the lessee should be selected carefully based upon a sound credit rating and good business history.

Other Types of Leases

Leases are as variable as the parties are creative. Some types of leases, such as the variety that relates rent to the consumer price index or some other index, may come into vogue temporarily as a reaction to unstable economic conditions. Others, such as the graduated lease, are tailored to meet the needs of a new business. Here the rent rises over time as the anticipated growth of the business takes place. Still others, such as the sale and lease-back arrangement, are attractive for large firms, which sell their real estate and lease it back from the new owner in order to release investment capital for future expansion. Principals under this type of lease are investors who have capital to invest in order to ensure an agreeable rate of return from the rent on the leased-back property. These examples represent only a few types of leases that have been adapted to the special needs of the parties.

Finally, it is possible for an owner to lease only certain aspects of his or her property. For example, an owner of 1,000 acres of land might want to lease the land to different people for different uses. He could lease the grazing rights to Al, the hunting rights to Ben, the fishing rights to Calvin, the cultivation rights to David, the house to Ed and the barns to Frank.

LEASE RENEWAL

Depending on the type of leasehold estate that was conveyed by the landlord, or upon the terms of the parties' agreement, the lease will terminate on its own or upon appropriate notice by either party. It is not unusual, however, to include in the lease a term that provides for the renewal of the lease. The renewal provision may be one that requires the tenant to give notice of renewal either (a) within a specified period of time or (b) by a specified time prior to the termination of the lease. Alternatively, the renewal may be automatic, absent notice of nonrenewal by either party.

A renewal is a new lease. Unless otherwise stated, the renewal is under the same terms and conditions as the original lease. The parties may agree that the rent will be altered to reflect the present value of the land. For instance, each renewal may require a reappraisal of the land and a rent adjustment to reflect a specified percentage of the appraised value. Except where the agreement is for an automatic renewal of the lease, the parties should indicate whether the renewal clause will be operative in the second lease and in succeeding renewed leases.

Another method of renewal is by holding over. The legal implications for the holdover tenant have been discussed in a preceding section.

LEASE TERMS

Lease provisions in most commercial leases include restrictions on use of the property, identification of which party has an obligation to repair the premises, options for renewal and the grounds for default and termination of the lease. The courts in Texas will usually enforce the provisions of the lease according to its terms. Therefore, it is important to be familiar with the language used to create the rights and duties of the lessor and the lessee. The case that follows illustrates a Texas court's handling of a conflict regarding interpretation of a repair provision in a written lease.

• CASE BRIEF •

Perrone leased premises from Kline, which he used for retail business. The leased premises consisted of a store building and an adjoining parking area. A gas leak occurred under the asphalt paving of the parking area, and Perrone, deeming it an emergency situation endangering the premises and his customers, caused the leak to be repaired at his cost and sued Kline for reimbursement.

The pertinent repair provisions in the lease were:

3rd. That the Lessor shall at his expense maintain in good repair the roof, foundation and exterior walls of the building and parking area. The Lessee shall maintain all glass, including plate glass, and any special store front equipment.

Lessee agrees to give Lessor written notice of defects or need for repairs in roof, foundation or exterior walls of the building and parking area and Lessor shall not be liable to Lessee for any damage caused by same being or becoming out of repair until he has had reasonable opportunity to have same repaired after being notified of need of same by Lessee....

4th. That the Lessee shall at his expense keep the interior of the building, including the plumbing, closets, pipes and fixtures belonging thereto, in good repair; and shall take good care of the property and its fixtures and suffer no waste; and keep the water pipes and connections free from ice and other obstructions, to the satisfaction of the municipal or governmental authorities, during the term of the lease....

Perrone's position was that the language in the third section concerning the parking area obligated Kline to maintain in good repair the gas pipes lying beneath the paving of the parking area. The court disagreed, citing the following reasons:

We think that when the parties added "and parking area" to the portions of the building coming within the ambit of the lessor's responsibility they contemplated only the surface of that area, not conduits of gas, water or electric power that might lie beneath that surface. They did not speak of it as a lot or part of a lot; they did not describe it by metes and bounds; they merely described it as an area allocated to a certain use, that of parking, or temporarily storing vehicles on its surface. The presence or absence of gas pipes beneath the area was wholly immaterial to the contemplated use thereof. The lease did not specifically provide that the lessor should maintain those gas pipes in good repair, and we see nothing in the record before us to justify our implying such a covenant from the language used.

We think the leaking pipe was clearly within the definition of "plumbing" and "pipes and fixtures belonging thereto" as used in the 4th section of the lease. *Perrone v. Kline*, 425 S.W.2d 371 (Tex. Civ. App.—Dallas 1968).

Commercial Lease Terms

It is important to be able to read and understand legal documents; therefore, the balance of this chapter contains examples of commercial and residential lease terms. Following the sample clause is an explanation of its meaning.

Rent Provisions

Sample 1.

Lessee agrees to pay to Lessor the sum of $750 per month on or before the tenth day of each month as a fixed rent for the succeeding month. Rent for any fractional month at the beginning or end of the lease term shall be prorated on a per diem basis. This fixed rent will increase by $100 for each extended lease term, so that the fixed rent during the first extended term will be $850; the fixed rent during the second extended term will be $950 and so forth.

In addition to the fixed rent specified above, Lessee shall pay the full amount of all real property taxes, special assessments, and governmental charges of every character imposed on the leased premises during the term of this lease, including any special assessments imposed on or against the premises for the construction or improvement of public works. This additional rent shall be payable directly to the entity imposing the tax, assessment or charge. Lessee shall provide Lessor with a receipt or other evidence of payment upon request by Lessor.

This provision establishes a flat rental rate for the lease period with adjustment for renewals of the lease. It also passes through to the lessee the responsibility for the payment of taxes and assessments made on the property during the lease term by any governmental body. It requires the tenant to be informed of these debts and to make prompt payment to the appropriate governmental body. The lessor is not required to notify the tenant of these charges or make demand for payment.

Sample 2.

Lessee will pay to Lessor the sum of $600 per month, from the commencement of the term of this lease and continuing throughout the original lease term, in advance on the first day of each month. This will be known as the "basic rent."

If Lessor's cost, as determined by Lessor's auditors, of owning and maintaining the building, including the parking garage and other facilities maintained for the benefit of the building or its tenants, during any calendar month of the term of this lease, exceeds the average monthly cost for the first twelve (12 months) of the term, Lessee will pay to Lessor each month thereafter an amount representing Lessee's proportionate share of the increased cost. This amount will be known as "additional rent." Lessee's proportionate share of the increased costs of owning and maintaining the building will be determined by dividing the total rentable square footage of the building by the total square footage of the leased premises and multiplying the increase in the monthly operating expenses by the resulting percentage figure. The total rentable square footage shall be determined by determining the total square footage of the building and subtracting the square footage of all common areas, storage areas, areas required for heating or air conditioning, or other equipment required to service or maintain the building and the basement. It shall include any space occupied by Lessor as office space.

This provision provides for a fixed amount of rent for the first year. Thereafter the rent can be increased by the landlord if its operating expenses exceed the average of the previous 12 months. The tenants cover these increased expenses by paying additional rent based upon their proportionate share of the total rentable portion of the building.

Sample 3.

Lessee agrees to pay to Lessor the sum of $250 per month on or before the first day of each month as a minimum fixed rent for the succeeding month. If the lease term begins on a day other than the first day of a month or ends on a day other than the last of a month, then Lessee agrees to pay a pro-rata portion of the minimum fixed monthly rent described above for the partial initial and/or final months, prorated on a per diem basis, with payment for any partial month at the beginning of the term to be paid no later than the commencement date of the term.

In addition to the fixed minimum rent provided above, Lessee agrees to pay to Lessor, as additional rent for the use and occupancy of the lease premises, a sum equivalent to the amount, if any, by which four percent of Lessee's gross receipts for each month exceeds the fixed minimum rent payable for that month. This percentage rent must be paid monthly on or before the tenth day of each month succeeding the month for which the rent is paid.

This provision provides for a minimum monthly rent that is supplemented by a share of the gross receipts. This is typical for retail store and restaurant leases. The provision will also include a definition of gross receipts and the right of the landlord to inspect the books and records of the Lessee.

Repair Provisions

Sample 1.

Lessor shall, at its own expense and risk, maintain the roof, foundation, plumbing, heating and air conditioning systems, structural soundness of the exterior walls, parking lots, walkways surrounding the building, stairways, and elevators, including but not limited to repairs and all necessary replacements of these items. Lessor shall not, however, be liable for any damages to person or property resulting from Lessor's failure to make any repairs or perform any maintenance called for in this section unless, prior to the damages occurring, Lessee had given Lessor written notice of the need for the repair or maintenance and Lessor had failed to make the needed repair or to perform the needed maintenance within a reasonable time of receipt of the notice.

Except as provided above, Lessee shall maintain the leased premises and keep them free from waste or nuisance throughout the lease term and any extensions of that term. At the termination of the lease, Lessee shall surrender and deliver the leased premises to Lessor in as good a state of repair and condition as they were in at the time Lessor delivered possession to Lessee, reasonable wear and tear and damage by fire, tornado, or other casualty excepted.

This clause provides that the lessor shall maintain and repair the common areas of the structure. It then imposes on the tenant the responsibility to repair all other areas, which would include such work as replacement of broken windows, carpet and painting.

Sample 2.

Lessee shall, throughout the term of this lease and any extensions of that term, at its own expense and risk, maintain the leased premises and all improvements on the leased premises in good order and condition, including but not limited to making all repairs, and replacements necessary to keep the premises and improvements in such condition. All maintenance, repairs, and replacements required by this section must be performed promptly when required and in a manner that will not cause depreciation in the value of the premises.

This provision obligates the tenant to make all repairs and replacements. This is typical when the tenant is leasing the entire property for a commercial purpose. Failure to maintain the premises usually allows the lessor the option either to evict or to make repairs and charge them to the tenant. (See discussion of the implied warranty of habitability in Chapter 25.)

Residential Lease Terms

Lease Term

Sample 1.

The initial lease term shall begin on October 1, 1987, and end on March 31, 1988. This contract will be automatically renewed on a month-to-month basis unless written notice of termination is given by either party at least 30 days before the end of the above lease term or unless another lease is signed by both parties.

This provision establishes the initial term of the lease with the beginning and ending dates. It creates a term tenancy. However, it provides for an *automatic* renewal as a periodic tenancy unless written notice of termination is given at least 30 days before the ending date. The lease period is month-to-month and would require 30 days' notice of termination under state law. Vacating the premises at the end of the lease term without notice would be a violation of the lease agreement.

Move-out Notice

Sample 2.

At least 30 days written notice of intent to vacate must be given to owner's representative prior to move-out at the end of the above lease term and any renewal or extension period. In the event of automatic renewal or extension of the rental contract, rent shall be paid through the last day of the month following the expiration of the 30-day notice period, unless owner agrees otherwise in writing.

This provision restates that covered in Sample 1. The notice must be in writing. Verbal notice of intent to vacate is not sufficient to comply with the lease terms. This provision also illustrates a deviation from the common law notice requirements regarding term tenancies. Although this is a term tenancy, written notice of termination is required. The provision also establishes that rent will be due through the last day of the month following the month in which the 30-day notice is given *if* the tenant holds over beyond the original lease term.

Repairs

Sample 3.

Tenant agrees to request all repairs and services in writing to owner's designated representative, except in an emergency when verbal notice will be accepted. In case of malfunctions of equipment or utilities, or damage by fire, water, or other cause, tenant shall notify owner's representative immediately and owner shall act with due diligence in making repairs; and rent shall not abate during such periods. If the damaged premises are unfit for habitation and if owner decides not to repair the building, owner may terminate this contract by giving written notice to tenant. If it is so terminated, rent will be prorated and the balance refunded along with the deposit less any lawful deductions.

Although this provision does not specifically contain the landlord's covenant to make repairs, it does establish the tenant's duties regarding requests for repairs. Requests for repairs must be in writing unless there is a bona fide emergency. It also states that failure to make repairs is not grounds for withholding rent. Finally, this clause gives the owner an option not to repair if the damage makes the apartment uninhabitable. In that case the owner can terminate the lease.

Default by Landlord

Sample 4.

Owner agrees to (a) keep all areas of the apartment complex in a reasonably clean condition; (b) properly maintain hot water, heating and/or air conditioning equipment; (c) abide by applicable state and local laws regarding repairs; (d) make all reasonable repairs, subject to tenant's obligation to pay for damages caused by tenant, his family or guests. The tenant may terminate the lease only if the following has occurred: (1) owner has not attempted to make reasonable and necessary repairs to tenant's apartment within a reasonable time after written request, and (2) owner has not attempted to make such repairs for one week following written notice of tenant's intention to terminate this lease unless such repairs are made.

This clause establishes the landlord's duty to repair. Specifically, it establishes the tenant's rights if the landlord breaches its duty to repair. It establishes a two-step procedure that must be followed by the tenant in order to justify the tenant's early termination of the lease. First, the tenant gives written notice of the need for repairs to his or her apartment, and the landlord fails to make the repairs. Second, the tenant gives another notice to the landlord, requesting that the repairs be made and telling the landlord that the tenant intends to terminate the lease if the repairs are not made. (See discussion of the implied warranty of habitability in Chapter 25.)

Contractual Lien

Sample 5.

All personal property on the premises (except property exempt by statute) is hereby subjected to a contractual landlord lien to secure payment of delinquent rent and other sums due and unpaid under this contract. In order to exercise contractual lien rights, owner's representative may peacefully enter the premises and any storage facilities and remove and store all property therein owned by tenant, except exempt property; provided, however, tenant must be present or written notice of entry must be left afterward. Owner shall impose reasonable charges for storing the seized property and may sell same at public or private sale after 30 days' written notice of time and place of sale is sent certified mail return receipt requested to the tenant at the above apartment address. Sale shall be to the highest cash bidder; proceeds shall be first credited to cost of sale and then indebtedness; and surplus shall be mailed to tenant at the above apartment address. It is understood and agreed that none of the above procedures shall necessitate a court hearing or subject owner to any liability. Acceptance of rent or any other sum due is not a waiver of owner's right of eviction, damages, or past due rent if suit has been filed at the time of acceptance.

This provision establishes the contractual landlord's lien, which is discussed in the next chapter on the landlord-tenant relationship. It complies with state law regarding establishment of the lien. It also provides for nonjudicial foreclosure and sale of the tenant's property. In addition to compliance with the procedure set out in the lease for foreclosure, the landlord must comply with the state law. This is an important remedy for the landlord. For a list of exempt property, see the next chapter.

SUMMARY

A lease is both a contract and a conveyance. As a conveyance a lease creates a possessory interest in real property for a specified period of time. The owner of the real property conveys this estate to the tenant in exchange for rent. The tenant receives exclusive possession for the duration of the lease. As a lease is also contractual, it must contain the essential elements of any contract.

Four different types of leasehold estates may be created. They are the term tenancy, periodic tenancy, tenancy at will and tenancy at sufferance. The term tenancy and the periodic tenancy are the most common. They differ mainly in the manner in which they are terminated. A term tenancy ends automatically at the date specified in the lease. A tenant who fails to vacate upon termination of a term tenancy is a holdover tenant; this person may be held for an additional term. In a periodic tenancy, the party terminating the lease must notify the other party. The time of notification may be established in the lease. If no time is stated, the notice period is established by law.

Although an oral lease for a short term is valid, the Statute of Frauds requires leases for longer periods to be in writing. A written lease is required if the term exceeds one year. Regardless, parties should insist that the lease be in writing, especially if the terms are complex or the value of the leasehold estate is high.

Four kinds of leases are common for commercial use. In the gross lease, a fixed amount of rent is paid periodically. The landlord is responsible for taxes, insurance and utilities. Often, payment of extraordinary expenses is negotiable between landlord and tenant. This type is not popular for long-term leases. In the net lease, the tenant pays many of the operating expenses of the property such as taxes, utilities and insurance. The advantage to the landlord is obvious. The ground lease, another form, is a specialized type in which the lessee pays rent on vacant land, usually with the intent of constructing a building. This type of agreement can be very complex and is often of long duration. Finally, the percentage lease is another type widely used commercially. In a percentage lease, rental is based in part on the tenant's gross sales. Like all leases, the agreement should clearly stipulate the terms; in addition it should establish the lessor's rights to examine the tenant's accounting records.

Provisions for renewal of leases are sometimes included in the original agreement. Nevertheless, a renewal constitutes a new lease and should conform to contractual requirements. Finally, understanding the written terms of the lease is important. The court will enforce the written agreement of the parties.

QUESTIONS AND CASE PROBLEMS

1. Name and describe the application of the two areas of law relevant to a discussion of leases.
2. Match the following:

   (a) Tenancy at sufferance
   (b) Term tenancy
   (c) Tenancy at will
   (d) Periodic tenancy

   (1) has a specific beginning and ending date.
   (2) exists as long as neither party chooses to terminate it.
   (3) continues from period to period until terminated by one of the parties giving proper notice.
   (4) exists when a person is wrongfully in possession of another's land without a valid lease.

3. List and briefly describe four terms that should be specified in a lease contract.
4. Match the following:

   (a) net lease
   (b) gross lease
   (c) percentage lease
   (d) ground lease

   (1) The rent is based in part on the gross sales made by the lessee.
   (2) The lessor leases a piece of vacant land to the lessee, usually with the stipulation that the lessee at his or her own expense will construct a building.
   (3) The tenant agrees to pay taxes, insurance, repairs and other operating expenses of the premises.
   (4) The rent is a fixed or flat amount.

5. Describe the practical business situations in which the following types of leases would best satisfy the needs of the commercial lessor and lessee: (a) gross lease; (b) net lease; (c) percentage lease.
6. The written lease provided that Southern Warehouse Corporation would lease office space from Crain for a term of 36 months beginning July 1, 1976. In October 1976 Southern vacated the premises. In August 1978 Crain sued Southern for the accrued rental due under the lease for the period September 1976 to August 1978. Southern defended on the ground that the lease was unenforceable because there was an internal contradiction between a typed term and a printed term. Is the lease enforceable?
7. ABS Sherman Properties, Ltd., sued Ibrahim Abu Sarris, M.D., for breach of a lease. The lease provided that ABS was to construct cer-

tain improvements on the leased premises. These improvements were to be completed within 12 months. The lease further provided:

> In the event Landlord shall not have substantially completed the construction within the time period set forth above, Tenant may at its option, terminate this agreement by written notice to Landlord. Prior to exercising said option to terminate this lease, Tenant shall give Landlord sixty days advance notice of its intention to exercise said option. If the improvements are substantially completed prior to the end of said sixty day period or before notice of termination is actually received by Landlord, then this lease shall not be cancelled or terminated but shall be in full force and effect.

Prior to the expiration of the 12-month period, Sarris notified ABS that he intended to terminate the lease. The improvements were not completed within the 12-month period but were completed within 1 year and 60 days. Did Sarris have the right to terminate the lease?

8. American Eyewear, Inc., prepared a ten-year sublease and submitted it to Capital Bank. Capital Bank reviewed it, made several changes, signed it and delivered it to Eyewear. Eyewear made some additional changes, including a change in the beginning date and a release of liability upon assignment provision. Eyewear initialed these changes, signed it and returned the sublease to Bank. Bank never gave any written indication that it agreed to these changes. Is there a valid, enforceable sublease?

9. China Doll Restaurant, Inc., leased premises from Schweiger. China·Doll agreed to pay a base rent of $600 per month and an amount equal to five percent of the restaurant's first $288,000 of gross sales. The owners of China Doll had considerable experience in operating a Chinese restaurant.

The lease also contained a provision in which lessee agreed to use the premises "for conducting and operating a restaurant business." Before the expiration of the lease, China Doll moved to new and larger premises. At this time they stated that they intended to open a Mexican restaurant at the former China Doll location. Little was done to accomplish this, but they continued to pay the base rental of $600 per month. During this period the premises were unoccupied. Has China Doll violated the terms of the lease?

25

The Landlord-Tenant Relationship

The signing of a lease creates obligations on the part of both the lessor and the lessee. Failure by either party to comply with obligations imposed either by contract or by law gives rise to the availability of certain legal remedies. The remedies available depend upon the nature of the obligation breached and upon the present circumstances of the parties. For example, did the lessee remain in possession, or were the premises abandoned? Some problems result from actions taken by one of the parties to the transaction—the lessee may have sublet the premises, for example—or actions involving not the parties but other persons, such as when a visitor falls down the stairs of the leased premises. These occurrences lead to legal responsibilities on the part of the parties to the lease. Obligations imposed by the lease contract, by the relationship itself and by the law are the topics for this chapter.

LESSOR'S OBLIGATIONS

The lessor's obligations to the lessee are usually determined by the lease agreement. Consequently, it is important for the parties to consider and discuss their expectations regarding the leasehold. For example, if the tenant is expecting the landlord to repair potholes in the parking area promptly, then the lease should contain a provision regarding the obligation to repair. Unfortunately, the lessor and lessee do not always include lease provisions that clearly establish their respective obligations. In the absence of an agreement, the courts and the legislature have imposed a few obligations on the landlord. Some of these obligations can be waived expressly or assumed by the lessee. Others cannot be. When the law prohibits waiver by the tenant, a statement to that effect will be included in the discussion.

Covenant of Quiet Enjoyment

The *covenant of quiet enjoyment* is the landlord's warranty to the tenant that the tenant will have the premises free from interference by the landlord or his or her agent provided the tenant is not in default of the lease. There is no general guarantee by the landlord against wrongful intrusion by third persons. Should such an intrusion take place, the tenant will have satisfactory legal avenues to redress the interference. For centuries, however, the general common law rule has been that the tenant is protected from a wrongful intrusion by the landlord.

The covenant of quiet enjoyment is breached only upon eviction, either actual or constructive, by the landlord or his or her agent. Actual eviction consists of a physical removal of the tenant from the premises. Constructive eviction could occur when there is a substantial interference with the tenant's enjoyment of the premises.

Generally, in the case of either an actual or a constructive eviction the tenant must have vacated the premises before asserting a breach of the covenant of quiet enjoyment. The landlord also may have breached this covenant if he or she allows a neighboring tenant or employee to interfere with the lessee's use of the premises. For example, if the landlord refuses to evict a tenant who has routinely caused public disturbances in the apartment complex or threatened other tenants, then the landlord has breached the covenant of quiet enjoyment.

Covenant to Deliver Possession

The *covenant to deliver possession* is the landlord's promise to give to the tenant the *right* to possession at the beginning of the lease term. This covenant is quite limited. It does not warrant against a wrongdoer's being in possession of the premises at the time the lease commences, but only that the tenant will have the *right to possession*. If the lease does not contain language that obligates the landlord to deliver possession, the responsibility of taking possession from a trespasser or holdover tenant rests with the tenant. However, if the landlord agrees to deliver possession, then the responsibility for removing trespassers or holdover tenants rests with the landlord.

One aspect of this covenant that is sometimes misunderstood by residential landlords is that the tenant's right to possession is exclusive. Neither the landlord nor his or her agents have the right to enter the premises of the tenant without the tenant's permission except in an emergency. This also means that the landlord is prohibited from giving the keys to the leased premises to anyone except the tenant or the tenant's agent. Remember that the central characteristic of the leasehold estate is the transfer of the right of use and possession from the landowner to the tenant. In a lease that imposes on the landlord the duty to make repairs, there is also a right to go onto the leased premises for the purpose of making needed repairs. Even where the landlord has such a right, he or she is required to notify the tenant in advance of the date he or she intends to make repairs or perform routine maintenance, such as replacement of air-conditioning filters. Notice is excused in a bona fide emergency. This contractual modification of the covenant of possession is permissible.

Warranty of Habitability

In Chapter 20 the warranty of habitability as it applied to new home construction was explained. The warranty of habitability as it pertains to leasehold estates is defined differently. It is a warranty imposed by law on the landlord by which the landlord promises that *residential* property is safe, sanitary and fit for living during the lease term. The warranty of habitability was first imposed on landlords in 1978 by the Texas Supreme Court. Prior to that time, and consistent with common law, landlords had no duty of any kind to make repairs unless they contractually obligated themselves to do so. At common law the party who had possession of the property was solely responsible for its upkeep. The rule was created in an agrarian society in which the tenant was usually in the best position to recognize the need for repairs and to make those repairs. In an urban setting and particularly in multiple-unit apartment projects, this is no longer true. Furthermore, the tenant expects that the leased premises will provide reasonable shelter from the weather and will not pose a threat to his or her health. For these reasons and others, the Texas Supreme Court found that the common law doctrine needed modification. The landmark case that prompted the change in law follows.

CASE EXCERPT *Kamarath v. Bennett;* 568 S.W.2d 658 (Texas Supreme Court 1978) DENTON, Justice.   This case presents the question of whether in Texas an implied warranty of habitability arises as a consequence of a landlord-tenant relationship. Wilford Kamarath, a lessee of an apartment in Dallas, Texas, filed this suit against C. C. Bennett, for damages for breach of implied warranty of habitability of the urban residential rental property. The trial court, without a jury, rendered judgment against tenant Kamarath take nothing. . . .

On March 1, 1975, Kamarath entered into an oral, month to month, lease of a one-bedroom apartment from C. C. Bennett. The agreed rent was $110.00 per month with Bennett agreeing to pay all utilities. The apartment was one of four in a two story brick building owned by Bennett. Kamarath inspected the premises before accepting and occupying them with his family on March 1, 1975. . . . some of the defects—ancient plumbing that burst, depriving them of hot water; faulty electrical wiring; and structural defects causing the bricks of the building to fall—were not visible to him at the time of his inspection.

. . . Kamarath stopped paying rent in July 1975, claiming uninhabitability as an excuse. However, he did not vacate the premises until late September 1975. . . .

The law has regarded the relationship of landlord and tenant as one governed by the precepts and doctrines of property law. The lease was looked upon as a conveyance of an estate in land for a term which was based upon the mutual promises between the parties. The view was that the tenant's promise to pay was exchanged only for the bare right of possession. . . . Today the agrarian concept of landlord-tenant law has lost its credence, and has become less and less representative of the relationship existing between the lessor and lessee. The tenant is more concerned with habitability than the possibility of the landlord's interference with his possession. The present day dweller, in seeking the combination of living space, suitable facilities and tenant services, has changed the basic function of the lease. . . .

In our opinion the above considerations demonstrate that in a rental of a dwelling unit, whether for a specified time or at will, there is an implied warranty of habitability by the landlord that the apartment is habitable and fit for living. This means that at the inception of the rental lease there are no latent defects in the facilities that are vital to the use of the premises for residential purposes and that these essential facilities will remain in a condition which makes the property livable. . . .

In order to constitute a breach of implied warranty of habitability the defect must be of a nature which will render the premises unsafe, or unsanitary, or otherwise unfit for living therein.

In response to the above case, the Texas legislature enacted a law that also established a duty to repair when the condition materially affects the physical health or safety of an ordinary tenant. Although the statute does not specifically limit its application to residential tenancies, there has been no litigation involving commercial tenancies and the implied warranty of habitability. The statute requires the landlord to make a "diligent effort to repair or remedy a condition if: (1) the tenant specifies the condition in a notice to the person to whom or to the place where rent is normally paid; (2) the tenant is not delinquent in the payment of rent at the time notice is given; and (3) the condition materially affects the physical health or safety of an ordinary tenant." (Tex. Prop. Code §92.052)

Following receipt of notice of the need for repair, the landlord must act within eight days. If the landlord fails to make repairs within that time period, the tenant can terminate the lease or sue the landlord. Finally, the statute prohibits any type of retaliation by the landlord against the tenant who complains, such as eviction or an increase in rent.

An important exception to the duty to repair is set out in the statute concerning damage caused by the tenant. If the damage that rendered the premises uninhabitable was caused by the tenant, a member of the tenant's family or a guest of the tenant, then the landlord has no duty to make repairs. For example, if a window is broken by the tenant, the landlord is under no duty to replace it.

Duty to Pay Taxes

As the owner of the fee interest in the premises, the landlord is responsible for paying the taxes. If the property is sold at a tax sale for nonpayment, the sale is subject to the existing lease. Where the tenant makes improvements to the property that cause the taxes to rise, the tenant will probably be liable to pay for the increase.

Duty to Install Locks

The landlord is required to install, change or rekey the locking mechanism for the leased premises if a request is made by the tenant. (Tex. Prop. Code §92.153) The landlord's obligation to install locking mechanisms is limited to one window latch on each exterior window, one pin lock on each exterior sliding glass door and one deadbolt and night latch on each exterior door. When a request for installation or change of the locking mechanism is made, the landlord must comply within 15 days. There is no limit to the number of requests for change that a tenant can make. Although the landlord has a duty to change the locks, the cost of the change must be paid by the tenant. If the tenant fails to pay the total cost in advance, then the landlord will be excused from performance. A tenant is not required to pay for the initial installation of the locks. This cost is borne by the landlord.

Duty to Install Smoke Detectors

Landlords in Texas are required to install smoke detectors in all leased residences, including apartments and houses. The location and procedure for the installation are set out in the statute. This requirement is found in §§92.255–92.256 of the Texas Property Code. Periodically, the smoke detector should be checked by the landlord to determine if it is still operational. A landlord who fails to install or maintain a smoke detector can be liable for damages suffered by the tenant as a result of this breach of duty. However, a landlord has no liability if the tenant damages the detector or removes the batteries.

LESSOR'S REMEDIES AND SECURITY

Having discussed the landlords' obligations to the tenants, in this section the methods by which landlords can protect themselves from breaches of the lease by tenants will be discussed. Several techniques and remedies have developed over time that offer the landlord some protection from economic loss caused by a tenant's failure to perform his or her obligations under the lease. Some of these remedies should be included in the lease agreement if the landlord desires to avail himself or herself of the remedy at a later date. Others arise automatically as a result of the landlord-tenant relationship.

Rent Paid in Advance

Under common law where it is not otherwise specified, rent is due at the end of the rental period. The modern practice of requiring advance payment of the rent in the lease gives the landlord some additional assurance of stability. Where the rent is not forthcoming from the tenant by the first of the month *in advance*, the landlord is given some lead time in pursuing remedies for nonpayment. If the rent were not due until the end of the rental period, the landlord would lose additional time pursuing the remedies.

Landlord's Lien

Four statutes in Texas address landlords' liens. The oldest statute creates a preference lien against farm crops of an agricultural tenant. (Tex. Prop. Code §54.001) Another statute creates a preference lien against a tenant's property in the commercial building that is leased. (Tex. Prop. Code §54.021) Both of these liens give the landlord priority against the proceeds from the sale of this property in the event the tenant has not paid the rent. These liens terminate shortly after removal of the property from the building by the tenant. The liens are enforceable only through court action. This means that the landlord cannot foreclose the lien without filing a lawsuit, presenting evidence to a judge of the tenant's default and obtaining the court's permission. This type of lawsuit is sometimes referred to as a *distress warrant*.

A distress warrant can be obtained when the tenant owes rent, is about to abandon the premises or is about to remove its property from the premises. This court action allows the landlord to take possession of the property and later sell it with court permission. Petitions for distress warrants are filed with the justice of the peace for the county where the leased premises are located. (Tex. Code Civ. Proc. Rule 610)

The *residential* landlord's lien attaches to nonexempt property that is in the residence or a storage area of the facility. (Tex. Prop. Code §54.041) It applies to all types of residential leases and secures the payment of the rent. The statute establishes several items which are exempt from the lien. The exemptions are:

1. wearing apparel;
2. tools, apparatus and books of a trade or profession;
3. school books;
4. a family library;
5. family portraits and pictures;
6. one couch, two living room chairs and a dining table and chairs;
7. beds and bedding;
8. kitchen furniture and utensils;
9. food and foodstuffs;
10. medicine and medical supplies;
11. one automobile;
12. one truck;
13. agricultural implements;
14. children's toys not commonly used by adults;
15. goods that the landlord knows are owned by a person other than the tenant and
16. goods that the landlord knows are subject to a recorded financing agreement.

Seizure and enforcement of the statutory landlord's lien is only by court order.

All of the previous liens require court action for enforcement and consequently provide a limited amount of protection to the landlord because of the time that can elapse between the filing of the lawsuit to enforce the lien and the trial. Too often the landlord may find that the tenant has removed all of the nonexempt property prior to court action and therefore has nothing to seize and sell for the delinquent rent. The lessor and lessee can contractually agree in the lease agreement to the creation of a lien in favor of the landlord. This is called a *contractual landlord's lien*. A *contractual* landlord's lien is created in writing in the lease agreement by consent of the parties. (Tex. Prop. Code §54.043) It cannot include any exempt property and is enforceable only if it is underlined or printed in conspicuous bold print. One of the major benefits of the contractual lien is that it can provide for nonjudicial foreclosure, thereby affording the landlord a more effective method of collecting the past-due rent. An example of a lease provision creating a contractual lien and a method for nonjudicial foreclosure was included in the last chapter.

If the contractual lien authorizes seizure of the nonexempt property, the landlord can take possession of the tenant's property, provided it can be accomplished without a breach of the peace. After seizure of the property, the landlord must give the tenant written notice itemizing the things taken, the amount of delinquent rent and the name, address and telephone number of the person to contact regarding payment. The landlord is not allowed to charge a fee for packing or storing the seized property. If the landlord is not paid in full the amount of the delinquent rent, he or she can then proceed to sell the property.

Before selling the seized property the landlord must give the tenant notice of the sale at least 30 days before the scheduled date. Again the notice must state the amount of rent due; the name, address and telephone number of the person to contact regarding payment and the date, time and place of the sale. The tenant has until the date of sale to redeem the property by paying the delinquent rent and any other charges authorized by the lease agreement. Sale is to the highest cash bidder and proceeds are applied to the delinquent rent and other authorized charges due by the tenant to the landlord. If there is any excess, it is paid to the tenant.

Security Deposits

By statute in Texas, a *security deposit* is any advance of money, other than an advance payment of rent, that is intended primarily to secure performance under a lease of a dwelling. Security deposits serve a slightly broader function than the landlord's lien. As stated, the landlord's lien protects only the landlord's right to receive rent from the tenant. The security deposit can also provide rent protection if the clause creating the deposit provides for it. However, its main purpose is to protect the landlord against the tenant's damage of the leased property during the lease period. The security deposit serves a more general purpose than a special deposit, such as a damage deposit or a cleaning deposit. The amount of the security deposit is established by the parties to the lease. Frequently, it is the equivalent of one month's rent. The security deposit also provides protection against a tenant who wrongfully abandons the premises. As a practical matter, it induces tenants to honor their lease agreement, maintain the premises more carefully during occupancy and clean the premises thoroughly upon leaving.

As a result of much controversy regarding retention of all or a portion of the security deposit by the landlord at the termination of the lease, the Texas Legislature passed a law in 1973 that governs the landlord's rights with respect to retention of the deposit and the time for return. (Tex. Prop. Code §92.101) The landlord is allowed to deduct from the deposit any damages and charges for which the tenant is legally liable under the lease or as a result of breach of the lease. The balance must be returned to the tenant within 30 days after the tenant surrenders the premises. If the landlord is retaining all or a part of the deposit, he or she must give the tenant a written description and an itemized list of all deductions. The landlord cannot retain any portion of the security deposit to cover normal wear and tear. It is the tenant's responsibility to notify the landlord of the tenant's forwarding address. If no address is provided, the landlord is relieved of his or her obligation to refund within the 30-day period. In addition, the landlord is excused from accounting to the tenant regarding the security deposit if the tenant and landlord agreed that the tenant was delinquent in the rent at the time the tenant vacated the premises.

Over the last few years there have been many cases litigating the return of security deposits in Texas courts. One of the reasons for the large number of cases is the fact that the statute provides for substantial economic penalties against a landlord who acts in bad faith in either not refunding the deposit or not providing a written description of why he or she is not refunding the deposit. The statute provides that the tenant, if he or she proves that the retention of deposit was wrongful and the landlord was acting in bad faith, can recover (1) three times the amount of the deposit wrongfully withheld, (2) $100 and (3) reasonable attorney fees incurred in bringing the suit. The burden of proving that the deductions were reasonable is on the landlord. The case that follows illustrates the application of this statute.

• CASE BRIEF •

Jaeckle, Kohlmeyer, Dodd, Moore and Schermerhorn rented a house from Hogg under a written lease agreement. Each made a $100 deposit to her. On May 15, 1975, following the tenants' vacation of the house, Jaeckle and Dodd along with Hogg inspected the premises. Hogg made notes of the items of damage in their presence and wrote down Jaeckle's name and forwarding address. There was conflicting testimony as to whether an itemized list of damages had been sent to Jaeckle within the 30-day period. However, the court found that no list had been mailed. Jaeckle sued Hogg for return of the deposit plus statutory damages and attorney fees. Hogg was ordered to pay to Jaeckle $2,500, which included three times the deposit, $1,500, $100 penalty and $900 attorney fees. The court of appeals upheld the trial court's findings and judgment. The court agreed that Hogg had acted in bad faith in failing to send Jaeckle a written list of deductions within the 30-day period. Hogg having failed to comply forfeited her right to retain any portion of the security deposit or to bring suit against Jaeckle for damages to the premises. *Hogg v. Jaeckle*, 561 S.W.2d 568 (Tex. Civ. App.—Tyler, 1978).

Lastly, the statute requires landlords to maintain records of security deposits. In the event the leased premises are sold, the former landlord remains liable unless the new landlord has delivered to the tenant a signed letter stating that the new landlord has received and is responsible for the security deposit.

Third-Person Guaranty of Rent

The landlord who has doubts about the capacity or reliability of the tenant in meeting the conditions of the lease may require a third person to guarantee performance. In a commercial or industrial lease where the tenant is thinly capitalized, a personal guaranty by the individuals actually running the business under the corporate veil may be required. Also, where the tenant has a poor credit rating, the landlord may insist on the assurance of a more reliable third person. The guaranty would have to be in writing and signed by the guarantor. The guaranty agreement may be a part of the lease or a separate agreement usually appended to the lease.

Eviction by the Landlord

The legal proceeding to evict a tenant is called *forceable entry and detainer* in Texas and is filed in the justice of the peace courts. (Tex. Code Civ. Proc. Rule 738 et seq.) Prior to filing the suit, the landlord must give the tenant at least three days' written notice to vacate the leased premises. If the tenant fails to surrender the leased premises, then the landlord files suit, requesting the court to find that he or she is entitled to possession. The right to possession may be based upon the termination of the lease or a default by the tenant in the terms of the lease. If the landlord convinces the court that he or she is entitled to possession of the property, then the court will enter an order awarding possession to the landlord and recovery of reasonable attorney fees. On the sixth day after the judgment is entered, the judge orders a writ of possession. The writ of possession is an order to the sheriff or constable to go out to the leased premises and remove the tenant and his or her belongings. The personal property of the tenant must be removed to a secure storage warehouse and notice of its location given to the tenant.

A suit for eviction can also include a request that the tenant pay whatever rent may be due to the date of eviction. However, the jurisdictional limits of the justice of the peace courts is $1,000 in the larger counties and $500 in the less populous counties. Therefore, the court cannot award the landlord for rent in excess of that limit. If additional rent is owed, the land-lord can sue for damages in one of the other Texas courts.

Action For Rent or Damages

The usual action by the landlord for damages involves the recovery of un-paid rent. If no agreement exists to the contrary, the landlord will have to wait until the end of the lease to begin action for unpaid rent. However, most leases provide terms permitting an action for rent prior to termina-tion, though these generally include the right to evict as discussed above.

Should the tenant cause damage to the premises or otherwise violate the covenants of the lease over and above the value of the rent, the landlord has the right to sue for damages.

Statutory Limitations on Landlord Remedies

Most of the remedies discussed require court action by the landlord. Court proceedings take time and money, and occasionally the landlord seeking to avoid these disadvantages will try other tactics to collect the rent or remove the tenant. Due to some excesses on the part of both landlords and tenants, the Texas Legislature has specifically prohibited certain self-help remedies. These include the interruption of utility service to the unit and the exclu-sion of the tenant from the leased premises either forcibly or by changing the locks. (Tex. Prop. Code §91.002)

LESSEE'S OBLIGATIONS

Generally, the tenant will be obligated to comply faithfully and fully with the terms of the lease agreement. There are only two implied covenants: the implied covenant against waste and the implied covenant to surrender the premises at the end of the lease in good condition.

Covenant Against Waste

Absent an agreement to the contrary, the tenant has no law-imposed duty to make substantial repairs to the premises. However, the tenant is obli-gated to maintain the property so as to protect it from the weather. This ob-ligation is referred to as the *tenant's responsibility to avoid waste*. **Waste** is damage caused by the tenant, including failure to protect the premises from decay and ruin caused by the natural elements.

CASE EXAMPLE

During a period of severe cold weather a tenant allowed the furnace to go out. The water pipes then froze, causing serious injury to the premises. The tenant failed in his responsibility to avoid waste.

The notion of waste can take two different forms. Voluntary waste results from the positive actions of the tenant, such as willfully breaking the windows or destroying the landscaping. It also includes any unauthorized changes to the premises, even those that the tenant claims improved the value of the property. Permissive waste results from an act of omission such as the failure to repair an accidentally broken window, thereby permitting injury to the premises from the weather.

The tenant may agree to perform repairs, just as the landlord might. Whether or not the tenant agrees to repair, he or she will be liable in damages to the landlord for any injury, beyond normal wear and tear, caused to the premises. Fire caused by the tenant's negligence is also a breach of the covenant, and the tenant will be liable to the landlord for damages.

Covenant to Return Premises in Same Condition

The landlord can expect that at the termination of the lease the premises will be in the same condition they were in at the beginning of the lease. There is an allowance for *ordinary wear and tear.* Ordinary wear and tear includes that depreciation or diminution in value resulting from normal use. For example, with age and use carpet will become dirty and thin. This is ordinary wear and tear. However, with normal aging and usage carpet does not become stained with paint or oil. If the carpet is stained as described above, then the tenant will be responsible to the landlord for the cost of returning the carpet to its former condition.

This covenant also requires the tenant to remove any unauthorized alterations to the leased premises. For example, if the tenant without permission builds a bookshelf in the bedroom of the unit, the landlord can require removal by the tenant at the expiration of the lease and repair to the wall to which it was attached. If the alterations were approved by the landlord prior to the tenant's erection of them, then removal is determined by the parties' agreement.

The law regarding fixtures was discussed in Chapter 4 and will not be repeated here; however, the concept of fixtures is important in leases. It is good practice for the tenant and landlord to include a lease provision that deals with the installation and removal of fixtures. As explained in Chapter 4, the tenant may lose the installed item to the landlord at the termination of the lease. There is, of course, the exception for trade fixtures, which are generally removable at the end of the lease unless there is an agreement with the landlord to the contrary. If removal causes damage to the property, the tenant is responsible for repairs.

LESSEE'S REMEDIES

The lessee's remedy for breach of the lease by the landlord is usually damages. The measure of damages is the difference between the value of the tenant's bargain and the value of the premises with the breach. In some circumstances the tenant can sue for specific performance or injunctive relief, particularly with respect to the enforcement of a restrictive covenant in the lease.

Tenant's Lien

Texas does recognize a tenant's lien against the landlord's nonexempt property in the tenant's possession and on the rent due to the landlord to secure the payment of damages caused by the landlord's breach of the lease. (Tex. Prop. Code §91.004)

Wrongful Eviction

Wrongful eviction occurs when the landlord without justification deprives the tenant of the possession of the premises. A tenant who has been wrongfully evicted (also referred to as an *actual eviction*) can sue for recovery of the possession of the premises or for damages caused by the breach of covenant of quiet enjoyment. In a somewhat punitive aspect to this area of the law, if the landlord wrongfully evicts the tenant from only part of the premises, the tenant may retain the remainder of the property but will have no obligation to pay any rent until the partial wrongful eviction ceases.

A wrongful eviction and breach of the covenant of quiet enjoyment will exist also where the tenant is ousted because a third person has proved rights superior to those of the landlord. In such a case the tenant will have an action for money damages.

Constructive Eviction

Constructive eviction occurs when the actions of the landlord so materially interfere with the tenant's enjoyment as to make the premises untenable. Theoretically at least, the right to assert a constructive eviction occurs when the tenant is forced by the condition of the premises to vacate. The tenant must notify the landlord of the conditions, where appropriate, and give the landlord a reasonable time to remedy the situation. Finally, the tenant must actually vacate the premises to be able to allege constructive eviction.

The concept of constructive eviction is a judicial construction. It is used to offset the fact that the landlord normally inserts in the lease a provision permitting the eviction of the tenant for failure to comply with the terms of the lease. Leases do not normally provide for comparable rights for the tenant.

The case that follows illustrates when constructive eviction occurs.

CASE EXCERPT *Briargrove Shopping Center Joint Venture v. Vilar, Inc.,* 647 S.W. 2d 329 (Tex. Civ. App.—1st Dist. 1982) DYESS, Justice. In September 1975 Briargrove Shopping Center, leased a warehouse at the back of the shopping center to Vilar, Inc., d/b/a Swedish Auto Repair, for a period of three years. There were two aspects of the property that were appealing to Rolf Larsson, the President of Vilar, Inc: (1) the cost of renting the building, which was only $0.10 per square foot and (2) a vacant concrete area in front of the building that would hold a number of cars. Larsson testified that it would be impossible for an auto repair shop to profitably exist without the use of a parking lot near the garage on which cars could be parked when they were not being worked on.

In July, Larsson learned that the Shopping Center planned to build a theatre in front of his shop. . . .

The construction began around September or October of 1976 and continued at least through December 31, 1976, when Larsson moved to a new location. There was testimony that the construction consumed all but a strip of ten feet in front of the shop. One of the two accessways to the repair shop was completely cut off, except for a shell driveway built around the construction site, and even the shell driveway was often impassable for cars because it was so muddy. . . .

Not only did Larsson receive complaints from customers, but also from his mechanics, who were forced to walk much farther to reach the cars and to wash their feet before getting into the cars because of the muddy conditions around the construction. . . . Larsson decided that he could no longer continue a profitable business at Briargrove Shopping Center without sufficient parking near the shop. He was also afraid of losing some of his mechanics so he rented a new shop, and moved there as of January 1, 1977. Thus, December 1976 was the last month for which he paid rent on his three year lease at Briargrove. . . .

Constructive eviction was defined. . . as being a composite of four distinct elements: 1) an intention on the landlord's part that the tenant no longer enjoy the premises, 2) a material act by the landlord substantially interfering with the use and enjoyment of the premises for the purposes for which they are let, 3) an act that permanently deprives the tenant of the use and enjoyment of the premises, and 4) an abandonment of the premises by the tenant within a reasonable time after the commission of the act. . . . When the construction started in November, the entire parking area in front of the repair shop was destroyed. No longer being able to use the parking area, the mechanics had to resort to parking cars along the side of buildings along the concrete alleyway, and to parking them in lots that were farther from the shop than the lot they had been using. Larsson and one of his employees testified that the conditions made operations extremely difficult. In fact, one of the employees testified that he would not have stayed with Swedish Auto Repair Shop if conditions had continued for much longer. . . .

There is, in the above evidence, support for the proposition that the acts of Briargrove substantially interfered with Swedish Auto Repairs' use and enjoyment of the premises, the second of the four criteria. . . . There is also support for the inferred intention on the part of the landlord that Larsson no longer enjoy the premises based on the shopping center's actions. . . . Neither is there doubt that Larsson moved out within a reasonable time after the commission of the act.

The closest question notedly appears when one attempts to determine if the landlord's actions permanently deprived Larsson of the use and enjoyment of the premises. . . .

We conclude that the deprivation of the use and enjoyment of the premises encountered by Larsson was substantial enough to constitute a permanent deprivation within the meaning of the constructive eviction rule.

Damages, Reformation and Rescission

The remedies made available to the tenant when the implied warranty of habitability is breached are of a complementary nature. That is, the tenant is afforded relief short of vacating the premises or withholding rent, both of which may be risky remedies.

The tenant may sue for damages measured by expenses incurred as a result of the landlord's refusal to perform the covenants in the lease. The tenant may seek reformation of the contract due to the conduct of the landlord in refusing to perform repairs. The reformation could take the form of reducing the amount of rent due in order to conform to the lessened value of the unrepaired premises. If the breach of covenant has reduced the value of the lease to the tenant significantly, prior to the tenant's entry, he or she may seek to have a court rescind or negate the entire agreement.

CASE EXAMPLE

Laferty, the landlord, has agreed to provide repairs in his lease with Manne. The roof leaks into a small bedroom. Despite requests by Manne to Laferty to repair the roof prior to moving in, the roof remains unrepaired. Manne *needs* the bedroom for a child and seeks rescission of the lease. The tenant's attorney chooses this as a safer, albeit more time-consuming, remedy for the tenant than vacating after entry and contending constructive eviction. Under constructive eviction Manne would run the risk of the court's disagreeing with his contention that the premises are "untenable" and charging him for unpaid rent.

Rent Withholding

A few states allow the tenant to withhold rent as an inducement to force the landlord to perform repairs. This is *not* a remedy available to tenants in Texas. Generally, the tenant's duty to pay rent is independent of the landlord's duties under the lease. Because the covenants are independent, the tenant does not have the right to withhold the rent to offset his or her damages caused by the landlord's breach.

THIRD-PARTY-RELATED TRANSACTIONS

On occasion a person other than the landlord or tenant becomes involved with the leasehold agreement. Because of a job change, for example, a tenant may seek a substitute to complete the tenancy. Or a person visiting the tenant may fall down the hall stairway in the apartment due to poor lighting or a faulty railing. These and other third-party incidents affecting the lease are the topics discussed next.

Subleases and Assignments

A *sublease* is the transfer of a part of the leasehold interest of the tenant, with the tenant retaining a reversionary interest.

CASE EXAMPLE

Granville leases Hilltop Acres to Tomas under a term lease beginning January 1 and ending December 31 of the same year. On March 1, Tomas trans-

fers her interest in Hilltop Acres to Nantes until December 30. This
agreement is a sublease because Tomas has retained a one-day reversionary interest.

By contrast, an ***assignment*** is a transfer in which the tenant gives the entire interest in the leasehold estate without retaining a reversionary interest. Using the example above, if Tomas had transferred her interest until
December 31, the agreement would have been an assignment; Tomas transferred her entire interest in the land.

In most states subleases and assignments are valid unless there is an express contractual prohibition against them. However, in Texas the tenant is
forbidden to rent the leasehold to any other person without the prior consent of the landlord. (Tex. Prop. Code §91.005) The consent to assign or sublet can be written into the lease or obtained after the lease is executed. This
approach is different from that taken in most jurisdictions. The law requires consent prior to subletting or assigning. Court interpretation of the
statute has focused on when the landlord is required to consent. The general rule is that the landlord cannot be unreasonable in withholding consent. For example, if the proposed substitute tenant will be using the
premises in the same manner as the present tenant and the financial ability
of the two tenants is similar, then the landlord must consent to the sublease or assignment. However, the court will not require a landlord to accept a substitute tenant that increases the landlord's liability or risk of loss.
As a result of this interpretation, assignments and subleases are quite common in Texas.

The difference between an assignment and a sublease is more than defi-
nitional. It also affects the liability of the various parties involved.

Impact of an Assignment

At the beginning of the preceding chapter some care was taken to describe a
lease as a conveyance of an estate in land as well as a contractual obligation.
In the area of assignment the dichotomy is important. The tenant upon
taking a transfer by lease enters into a dual relationship. Under the estate-
in-land aspect of the agreement, the parties are said to have *privity of estate*. Under the contractual side of the agreement, the parties have created
privity of contract. As explained earlier, privity connotes the mutuality
that binds parties to their agreement.

A tenant who assigns the lease to a third person surrenders possession
and transfers the *privity of estate* to the assignee. The assignee literally
stands in the legal shoes of the tenant, since he or she received all that the
tenant has, and privity of estate now exists between the landlord and the assignee. The assignee's right to possession makes him or her liable directly
to the landlord for payment of rent. Possession automatically gives rise to
the obligation to pay rent.

By way of contrast, there is no *privity of contract* between the landlord
and the assignee. No contract, or mutual agreement to be bound, is created

by the assignment. An outgrowth of this is that the tenant-assignor continues to be bound by the terms of the lease-contract to the landlord.

As the result of privity of estate existing between the landlord and the assignee, the landlord can sue the assignee for nonpayment of rent. If, when the assignment takes place, the assignee agrees to assume the obligations of the lease and to be bound to the lessor for rent, he or she will have privity of contract with the lessor as well as the privity of estate previously discussed.

Impact of a Sublease

When the tenant creates a sublease by conveying less than the entire interest in the land to a sublessee, there is no privity of estate or contract between the landlord and the sublessee. In short, the sublease does not alter in any respect the original landlord-tenant agreement. The sublessee will have an obligation to pay rent to the tenant, and the tenant will continue to have the obligation to pay rent to the landlord. Likewise, any restriction on limitations included in the original landlord-tenant agreement will pertain to the tenant-sublessee contract as well, since the tenant cannot give greater rights than he or she has. The tenant, despite not being in possession, will still have all the obligations arising from the initial landlord-tenant contract.

TORT LIABILITY

A *tort* is a breach of a noncontractual duty imposed by general law. The duty arises from the relationship between two parties. For example, a common tort is the violation of the duty imposed on drivers to yield to oncoming traffic when making a left turn. If the driver breaches this duty and as a result someone is injured, then the driver will be liable to compensate the injured party. Property owners generally have a duty arising out of their ownership of the land to avoid the creation of dangerous conditions on the land that could result in injury. For example, a merchant has an obligation to replace the rotten stairs leading into his store. If a customer falls through the stairs, then the merchant will be liable to compensate the customer for his injuries.

Generally, the duty to maintain leased premises from unreasonable risks of injury rest with the person who has control over the premises. A tenant who has exclusive possession of the leased premises and the duty to make repairs to the leased premises has control. Therefore, if a guest is injured because the tenant did not properly maintain the premises, the tenant would be liable to the injured guest. This general rule does not necessarily preclude the landlord from liability if the injury was caused by a defective condition which made the premises uninhabitable.

In many modern multifamily residential leases the landlord maintains control over the common areas. The common areas include the parking lot, courtyards, elevators, lobbies and any other area generally open for use by all the tenants. If a tenant or a tenant's guest is injured because the landlord breached his or her duty to maintain the common area, then the landlord is liable in tort.

Exculpatory Clauses

In an effort to avoid tort liability, a landlord will frequently include in the lease an exculpatory clause. An *exculpatory clause* is a provision by which the landlord excuses himself or herself from liability for negligence in maintaining the leased premises. At the present time there is a sharp split among the courts as to the enforceability of these clauses. Some courts permit the enforcement of the clause because of the notion that the parties have the right to contract freely. The incongruity in this conclusion is the erroneous assumption that the usual leasehold agreement involves equality of bargaining position. At least in residential leasing, the tenant seldom has the freedom to negotiate the terms of the lease.

Conversely, other courts have held that the position of the landlord in exculpating himself or herself from liability for negligence, in a typically unbargained-for lease, defies sound public policy. Sanctioning of these clauses would also lead to the demise of the warranty of habitability, since all form leases would incorporate a waiver clause. The trend is to prohibit the landlord from exculpating himself or herself from responsibility.

Landlord Tort Liability for Third-Party Acts

An area of increasing interest and change in tort liability for leased premises is whether the landlord should be liable for torts committed by third parties against the tenant. The present law holds that where a third person actually causes the injury the landlord is not liable. However, in 1985 the Texas Supreme Court held that the intervention of an outsider does not necessarily preclude the landlord from liability if the landlord's acts or omissions may have contributed to the circumstances in which the injury occurred. This issue is far from being resolved in Texas and other jurisdictions. Should the landlord in the case that follows be liable to the tenant for the injuries caused by the criminal?

• CASE BRIEF •

At about 7:00 P.M. on August 7, 1981 while it was still light, a young man abducted R.M.V., age ten, from a sidewalk outside the Landmark Apartments and dragged her to the Chalmette Apartments, located diagonally across the street from the Landmark Apartments. The assailant took R.M.V. directly to a vacant apartment at Chalmette Apartments and there he raped her, put her in the closet, told her not to leave and disappeared. R.M.V. sued Mr. Property Management Company, Inc., and Brett Davis. Davis was the owner of the Chalmette Apartments, and Mr. Property was the manager. R.M.V. claimed that Davis and Mr. Property in violation of a city ordinance had an open and vacant apartment and that the violation of this city ordinance was a breach of its duty to her and was a cause of her injuries. The trial court dismissed the suit against Davis and Mr. Property on the basis that the landlord had no duty to R.M.V. The Texas Supreme Court reversed and remanded this case for a trial on the merits. The court held that the violation of the city ordinance could support R.M.V.'s claim of negligence against Davis and Mr. Property. It stated that a trial was necessary to determine whether the negligence of the landlord contributed to the happening of this assault. The two concurring opinions in the case suggested that the landlord could be liable even if there had not been a breach of the city ordinance. *Nixon v. Mr. Property Management Co., Inc. 690 S.W.2d 546* (Tex. 1985)

SUMMARY

A lease creates obligations for both parties. These obligations arise both from the contract itself and from the law. Legal remedies vary according to the obligation breached and the relationships of the parties.

Among the obligations the landlord owes the tenant are the covenant to deliver possession (that is, to make the right of possession available to the tenant at the start of the lease period), the covenant of quiet enjoyment (protection from intrusion by someone claiming better rights than the landlord) and the warranty of habitability (that is, the leased premises are fit for habitation). In addition, state law requires that the landlord install smoke detectors in residential dwellings and install certain safety locks when so requested by a tenant.

If the tenant fails to meet the contractual terms of the lease, the landlord has several remedies. Eviction of the tenant, one example, is the legal procedure whereby the tenant is forced to vacate the leased premises. The landlord may also seek damages for unpaid rent or injury to the property. In addition to these remedies, a landlord has several methods by which he or she can reduce the potential of economic loss from a defaulting tenant. By statute in Texas the landlord may have a lien against the tenant's nonexempt property. This allows the landlord to take possession of and sell the tenant's property, provided the landlord has obtained a distress warrant. A more powerful lien, though, is the contractual landlord lien, which can provide for nonjudicial foreclosure. Another effective incentive to encouraging tenant compliance with the lease is the requirement that the tenant deposit a sum of money to secure performance. This is called a *security deposit*. State law has established rules regarding the return of security deposits by the landlord on a timely basis.

Along with the duty to pay rent, the tenant's obligations include the promise not to damage the premises during the lease term. This is called the *covenant against waste*. The tenant also impliedly promises to return the leased premises in the same condition as they were in at the inception of the lease. The only exception is for depreciation of the leased premises resulting from ordinary wear and tear.

If the landlord violates the provisions of the lease, several remedies are available to the tenant. The tenant has recourse to the law when he or she is wrongfully evicted—that is, put out by the landlord without justification. On the other hand, a tenant may claim constructive eviction and thus be released from the lease if forced to vacate because of the condition of the property. Since this remedy, as well as withholding of the rent, may be risky and inconvenient for the tenant, other legal actions are available whereby the tenant may sue for correction of conditions.

The addition of a third party, either by a sublease arrangement or through an accident resulting in injury to a guest, further complicates the landlord-tenant relationship. A tenant can sublease or assign the lease only with the consent of the landlord, which cannot be unreasonably withheld. In a sublease there is no privity between the lessor and the sublessee; therefore, the landlord cannot sue a sublessee for breach of the lease. However, in an assignment, there is privity between the lessor and the assignee, which means that the assignee is responsible directly to the landlord.

Finally, a tenant or guest can be injured on the premises. The extent of the landlord's financial responsibility depends upon many factors, including whether negligence can be proved and the nature and extent of the injury.

QUESTIONS AND CASE PROBLEMS

1. What is the warranty of habitability as it applies to leasehold estates? If the landlord fails to make repairs, what remedies does the tenant have?

2. Explain the differences between the statutory landlord's lien and the contractual landlord's lien in residential tenancies.

3. What are the legal requirements for the refund of security deposits?

4. What is an exculpatory clause?

5. In dispute is a lease provision that read that the tenant shall pay "a non-refundable painting and cleaning fee in the sum of $40.00." The tenant claims that this is a security deposit under Texas law, which should have been refunded. The landlord denies that it is a security deposit. Is this a security deposit?

6. Catlett, the landlord, seized a freezer owned by Causey, the tenant. Causey had agreed to the creation of the statutory landlord's lien and was in arrears in the payment of the rent at the time Catlett seized the freezer. The statutory lien exempts from seizure all "kitchen furniture and utensils." Could Catlett legally seize Causey's freezer?

7. The lease provided that the tenant will "make no alterations or additions in or to said premises without the written consent of said Landlord, which consent shall not be unreasonably withheld; such changes which neither reduce the value of the building nor impair its structural strength shall not require consent of the Landlord." The tenant seeks to install gasoline pumps and sales facilities in

the parking area 150 feet from the building. Is the landlord's consent required?

8. Lubin owns an apartment in a college town. Many units in the building are rented to college students. Lubin retains keys to these apartments. From time to time she visits the tenants. Although she always phones first, if the tenants are not available she will use her duplicate key to enter. The main purpose of Lubin's visit is to ensure that the utilities, appliances and plumbing are functioning properly. If she does not interfere with the tenant's occupancy, is Lubin's conduct legally proper? Discuss.

9. Lubin leases two separate apartments on the second floor to Stearns and Forrest. The apartments are reached by a common stairway and hall. The plumbing in Forrest's apartment becomes inoperative, and a riser on the stair splits. Who is responsible for these repairs?

Glossary

Abstract of judgment A document prepared by a court clerk containing information about a judgment. This document is filed in the county records to perfect a judgment lien.

Abstract of title A summary of all the recorded transactions, including deeds, mortgages, judgments and the like, that affect the title to a specific parcel of land.

Acceleration clause A provision in a mortgage giving the mortgagee the right to declare the entire debt due and payable upon default.

Acceptance Assent to the terms of an offer.

Accord An agreement to substitute a different kind of performance for that originally contracted for.

Accretion Gradual increase in the size of riparian or littoral property as a result of deposits of sediment made by a body of water.

Acknowledgement In conveyancing, the act by which a person who has executed an instrument goes before an authorized officer, usually a notary public, and declares that the instrument is genuine and executed voluntarily.

Actual notice Information that is acquired personally by the interest holder.

Adaptation test A test used by a court when the intent of the party(ies) is not expressed to determine whether an item is a fixture. The inquiry by the court is whether the item was specially adapted for use with the land or improvements to the land.

Administrative remedies Remedies provided by the administrative agencies based on power granted in their enabling act.

Administrator (Administratrix) A person charged with administering the estate of an intestate decedent.

Adverse possession Acquisition of title to real estate by means of wrongful occupancy for a period of time established by statute.

Agency A legal relationship in which one party, called the *principal*, authorizes another, called the *agent*, to act in the principal's behalf.

Alienable The right of a landowner to transfer all or any portion of his or her rights in land during his or her lifetime.

Alienation Transferring ownership, title or interest in real estate from one person to another.

Alluvion Land created by sediment left by a body of water.

Amortization Repayment of a debt in periodic installments of interest and principal over a period of time.

Annexation test   A test used by a court when the intent of the party(ies) is not expressed to determine if an item is a fixture. The inquiry by the court is whether the item is physically attached to the land or an improvement to the land.

Annual percentage rate (APR)   As defined in the "Truth-in-Lending" Act, the percentage that the total finance charge calculated on an annual basis bears to the amount of the loan or credit.

Anticipatory breach   A breach of contract that occurs as a result of repudiating a contract before the date due for performance.

Appeal   Process in which a higher court reviews alleged legal errors made by a lower court or an administrative agency.

Appropriation rights   A water rights doctrine that gives primary rights to the first users of the water.

Assignee   A party to whom a right is transferred.

Assignment   Transfer of property right from one person (the assignor) to another (the assignee).

Assignor   A party who transfers a right.

Assumption   A contract between a grantor/mortgagor and a grantee in which the grantee agrees to assume responsibility for the mortgage debt.

Attachment   In a secured transaction, this refers to the process of creating the security interest.

Attestation   The act of witnessing the execution of an instrument and subscribing as a witness.

Attorney's title opinion   The professional judgment of a lawyer as to the condition of the title based on facts revealed in the abstract.

Authority   Term used in the law of agency denoting the agent's power to perform acts authorized by the principal. (See also Express authority and Implied authority.)

Bargain and sale deed   A deed that conveys title but makes no warranties.

Bilateral contract   A contract involving a promise in exchange for a promise.

Blockbusting   Inducing (for profit) the sale or rental of any dwelling by indicating that a particular class of person (for example, nonwhite) has entered or will enter the neighborhood.

Board of adjustment   A quasijudicial body that hears and decides requests for variances, permits and exceptions to a zoning code.

Bonus   In mineral leases, a sum of money paid to the mineral owner at the time the mineral lease is executed.

Breach of contract   The unexcused failure to perform an obligation under a contract.

Call   Term used to refer to the different monuments, courses and distances that make up a metes-and-bounds description.

Capacity   The legal ability to enter into a contract.

Caveat emptor   Let the buyer beware.

Caveat venditor   Let the seller beware.

Chain of title   The recorded history of events that affect the title to a specific parcel of land, usually beginning with the original patent or grant.

Closing   The final stage of the real estate purchase transaction, when the deed and the purchase money are exchanged.

Codification   Collection and organization of law into a code or statute.

Color of title   A consecutive chain of land transfers that may contain some defects.

Commitment   Used in mortgage financing to designate the lender's promise to loan a specified amount of money at an agreed-upon rate of interest.

Common elements   In condominium ownership, those areas of the project that are co-owned with all other unit owners.

Common law   (1) Law based upon written opinions of appellate courts; (2) the traditional nonstatutory law of England and the United States.

Community property A form of co-ownership between husband and wife in Texas in which each spouse has a one-half interest in property acquired during marriage and that is not separate property.

Concurrent ownership See Co-ownership.

Condemnation Legal action by which government acquires private property for a public use. Based upon the right of eminent domain.

Condition precedent In contracts, a condition or contingency that must exist before a party is bound to perform.

Condition subsequent In contracts, a condition or contingency that terminates a party's obligation to perform.

Conditional sales contract See Security agreement.

Condominium The fee simple ownership of one unit in a multiple-unit structure, combined with an ownership of an undivided interest in the land and all other parts of the structure held in common with the owners of the other individual units in the structure.

Condominium assessments The regular monthly payments for upkeep of the common elements, as well as payments required for special expenses or improvements to those common elements.

Condominium association The organization stipulated by statute to administer the operation of the common elements of the condominium.

Condominium bylaws The rules governing the internal operation of the condominium development.

Condominium declaration A document required by state law, which must accompany and be recorded with the master deed for the condominium development.

Condominium individual unit deed The deed for each individual condominium unit in the development.

Consideration A promise, act or forbearance bargained for and given in exchange for a promise, act or forbearance.

Constructive eviction An occurrence that results when the actions of the landlord so materially interfere with the tenant's enjoyment as to make the premises untenable.

Constructive notice The knowledge of certain facts that might be discovered through careful inspection of public records, provided that such information is within the history of title, or discovered through an inspection of the premises.

Contingency clause A provision within a contract that makes performance under the contract conditional upon the occurrence of a stated event.

Contract A promise or an agreement that the law will enforce.

Contract for deed A contract in which the buyer pays the purchase price on an installment basis. The seller/owner retains title until the purchase price is paid; also called *land installment contract*.

Contractual lien In written leases, a provision that gives the landlord a lien against the tenant's property to secure payment of the rent.

Cooperative A form of ownership in which the land and buildings are (usually) owned by a corporation; individual unit residents own stock in the corporation and have a proprietary lease in a specific unit or apartment.

Co-ownership Ownership of real estate in which two or more people have undivided interests.

Cotenancy See Co-ownership.

Counteroffer A new offer made as a response to a person who has made an offer.

Covenant of quiet enjoyment A warranty by the landlord that the tenant will have the premises free from interference by the landlord or anyone claiming better right to the premises than the landlord.

Covenant to deliver possession The landlord promises to deliver the right of possession to the tenant at the time the lease is scheduled to start.

Curtesy   A common law estate that provided a husband with a life interest in all his wife's real property at the time a child was born of the marriage.

Damages   Money recoverable by one suffering a loss or an injury due to breach of the contract.

Dedication   The grant of real property such as a public street to a governmental unit for public use.

Deed   A legal instrument that conveys title to real property upon delivery and acceptance by the grantee.

Deed absolute   An instrument in the form of a deed that the courts construe as a mortgage.

Deed in lieu of foreclosure   A deed in which a mortgagor conveys mortgaged real estate to the mortgagee, who promises in return not to foreclose on the mortgage debt, which is in default.

Deed of trust   A legal instrument in which a borrower transfers real property to a trustee as security for a debt. The lender is the beneficiary of the trust.

Deed of trust to secure assumption   A deed of trust creating a lien in favor of the seller in order to secure the buyer's promise to pay the existing mortgage debt on the land.

Deed without warranty   A deed that purports to convey title but contains no warranties or promises.

Defeasible fee   A fee simple estate that terminates upon the occurrence of a specified condition; also called a *qualified fee.*

Deficiency judgment   A money judgment awarded to the mortgagee when funds obtained as a result of a foreclosure sale are insufficient to pay the debt.

Delay rental   In mineral leases, a sum of money paid to the lessor by the lessee for the right to continue the lease when the lessee has failed to commence drilling operations within the original lease period.

Delivery   Surrender of possession and control of a document to a third party.

Descendible   The right of landowners to have their land pass to their heirs-at-law upon death.

Devisable   The right of a landowner to dispose of the land by will.

Discharge   The release of contractual obligations.

Diversity jurisdiction   Power of federal courts to hear cases involving citizens of different states.

Dominant estate   The parcel of land that benefits from an easement appurtenant; also called *dominant tenement.*

Dower   Life estate of a widow in one-third of any real estate to which her husband had legal title during marriage.

Due-on-sale-clause   A provision found in some mortgages requiring the mortgagor to pay off the mortgage debt if he or she sells or transfers the property.

Earnest money   A cash deposit evidencing a good-faith intention to complete a transaction.

Earnest money contract   A real estate purchase contract in which the buyer deposits a sum of money upon acceptance of the contract to show good faith.

Easement   A nonpossessory interest in real property; the right to use another's real property for a particular purpose.

Easement appurtenant   The right of an owner of a specific piece of land to benefit from the use of another's land. (See also Dominent estate and Servient estate.)

Easement by necessity   An easement that permits the owner of a landlocked parcel to cross a parcel of land of which the landlocked parcel formerly was a part.

Easement in gross   An easement that exists as a personal right apart from a dominant estate.

Eminent domain   Right of the state to take private property for public use. Just compensation must be paid the owner.

Equal protection The constitutional mandate that all people be treated equally under the law.

Equitable lien A lien arising from a transaction that shows an intention of the parties to use some particular real estate as security for a debt.

Equitable title The buyer's right to obtain ownership of real property upon payment of the purchase price.

Equity of redemption The right of a mortgagor or another person with an interest in real estate to reclaim it after default but before foreclosure.

Escheat Reversion to the state of title to property of a person dying without heirs or a will.

Escrow A process by which money and/or documents are held by a third party until the terms and conditions of an agreement are satisfied.

Escrow agent The third party who is the depository in an escrow transaction.

Escrow agreement An agreement that directs the escrow agent regarding terms and conditions under which the deed or other instruments are to be delivered to the parties and the disposition of the deed or other instruments on default.

Estate The extent and character of a person's ownership interest in real property. (See also Future estate and Life estate.)

Estoppel A doctrine that prevents a person from denying the consequences of facts or actions that lead another person to rely on them and suffer loss.

Eviction by the landlord The term usually associated with the legal procedure by which a landlord has the tenant removed from the premises because the tenant had breached the lease agreement.

Exceptions in zoning Permitted uses provided for in the ordinance that are inconsistent with the designated zone.

Exclusive agency A listing agreement in which the seller gives a single broker authority to procure a buyer for the property. The broker is entitled to a commission if he or she provides the buyer, but no commission is due if the seller procures the buyer.

Exclusive right to sell A listing agreement in which the seller gives a single broker authority to procure a buyer for the property. The broker is entitled to receive a commission regardless of who sells the property.

Exculpatory clause A lease by which the landlord attempts to excuse himself or herself from liability for negligence in maintaining the leasehold premises.

Executed A promise that has been performed.

Executor (Executrix) Person appointed to administer the estate of a decedent who died testate.

Executory An unperformed promise.

Executory interest A future estate that follows a fee simple subject to an executory limitation.

Exemplary damages Damages awarded to the injured party in excess of his or her actual loss for the purpose of punishing the wrongdoer.

Express authority Authority a principal confers upon an agent explicitly and distinctly. May be conferred orally or in writing.

Extension agreement Agreement by a mortgagee to extend the time that a debt is due.

Fair housing The term used to express a national policy against most types of discrimination in housing.

Fee simple The most extensive estate in real property that an owner can possess.

Fee simple on a condition subsequent A defeasible fee that may terminate upon the happening of a stated event or condition if the owner of the future interest asserts his or her rights.

Fee simple determinable A defeasible fee that terminates automatically if a stated act or event occurs.

Fee simple subject to an executory limitation See Fee simple on a condition subsequent.

Fiduciary   A person who acts primarily for another in a relationship based on trust and confidence. A fiduciary is held to a high standard of conduct.

Finance charge   Defined in the "Truth-in-Lending" Act as the monetary total of all charges a borrower must pay the lender for credit or a loan.

Financing statement   A document that, properly recorded, perfects a security interest.

Fixture   An item that was personal property but has become part of the real property.

Floodplains   Areas near waterways that are prone to flooding.

Foreclosure   A procedure in which property used as security for a debt is sold in the event of default to satisfy the debt. (See also Judicial foreclosure and Power-of-sale foreclosure.)

Forfeiture   The loss of the right to a down payment or real estate as a result of a breach of contract.

Fraud   A deceptive act or statement intentionally done in an attempt to gain an unfair financial advantage over another.

Freehold estate   An interest in real property that is created to last for an uncertain period of time.

Future estate   An interest in real property that will become possessory in the future.

General warranty deed   See Warranty deed.

Good title   See Marketable title.

Grantee   Person who acquires title to real property by deed.

Grantor   Person who transfers title to real property by deed.

Gross lease   A lease in which a flat or fixed amount of rent is paid by the tenant.

Ground lease   A specialized type of net lease in which the lessor leases a piece of vacant land to the lessee, usually with the stipulation that the lessee at his or her own expense will construct a building thereon.

Holdover tenant   One who failed to vacate or surrender possession of the premises on the ending date of a term tenancy.

Holographic will   A will completely in the handwriting of the decedent.

Homestead   The dwelling that is the family residence together with the land on which it is located. The land can be either urban or rural.

Implied authority   An agent's authority to do those acts necessary and proper to accomplish the express terms of the agency.

Implied notice   Legal notice that is imposed by law when conditions exist that would lead a reasonable person to inquire further.

Implied warranty of habitability   See Warranty of habitability.

In pari delicto   At equal fault.

In terrorem clause   A clause in an installment contract that prohibits recording at the expense of forfeiture.

Inception of title rule   A rule that holds that property is characterized as separate or community by reference to the date of acquisition.

Indefeasible title   See Marketable title.

Indemnification   The act of compensating another in the event of loss.

Independent contractor   A person who is retained to do a job, using his or her own judgment as to how the work will be done.

Injunction   An equitable remedy that orders a party to stop or refrain from some specific activity or conduct.

Innocent misrepresentation   An unintentional misstatement of a material fact that induces justifiable reliance to the detriment of a party.

Inter vivos trust   A trust that takes effect during the life of the creator.

Interpleader   A legal procedure whereby a third party can be joined or can intervene in a lawsuit.

Intestate   A person who dies without leaving a will.

Installment land contract   See Contract for deed.

Joint tenancy Co-ownership in which the entire estate passes to the survivor upon the death of the other joint tenant or tenants.

Joint venture A business entity in which two or more persons agree to carry out a single undertaking for profit.

Judgment creditor A plaintiff who has won a monetary judgment that has not yet been paid.

Judgment lien A lien that attaches to real property of a defendant when a plaintiff wins a judgment in the jurisdiction in which the property is located.

Judicial foreclosure A foreclosure ordered by a court.

Judicial remedies Remedies provided by the courts.

Jurisdiction The power of a court to hear a case.

Laches An equitable principle that requires a person to enforce his or her rights diligently and timely.

Landlord's lien Under common law, the lien known as the *right of distress* provided the landlord with a lien on the personal property of the tenant where there was a failure to pay rent.

Lease A contract, either written or oral, that transfers the right of possession of the premises to the lessee or tenant.

Leasehold estate An estate created when the owner of property, known as the *lessor* or *landlord*, conveys a possessory interest in the real property to another, known as the *lessee* or *tenant*, for a specific period of time in exchange for the tenant's payment of rent.

Legal description A description of land in a written document that will be accepted by a court as complete enough to locate and identify the land.

Legal notice A knowledge of another's interest in real property sufficient to make the adverse interest legally binding to the prospective purchaser or any other party acquiring interest in the property.

Letters of administration A document issued by a probate court that is evidence of an administrator's authority to settle an estate.

Letters testamentary A documentary issued by a probate court that is evidence of the executor's authority to settle an estate.

License A personal privilege to enter another's property for a specific purpose.

Lien A claim against another's property securing either payment of a debt or fulfillment of some other monetary charge or obligation.

Life estate An ownership interest in real property created to last for a person's life.

Limited common elements In condominium ownership, that portion of the common elements that is restricted to use by one or more but less than all unit owners.

Limited partnership A partnership formed according to the provisions of a state limited partnership act. The liability of a limited partner is limited to the amount he or she has invested.

Liquidated damages Damages that the parties to a contract have agreed are reasonable compensation in the event of a breach.

Lis pendens, notice of A notice filed for the purpose of warning people that legal action has been taken that might affect title or possession of specified real property.

Listing agreement A contract between a seller and a broker authorizing the broker to find a buyer for real property upon specified terms in return for a fee if the broker is successful. (See also Exclusive agency, Exclusive right to sell and Open listing.)

Littoral lands Lands that border on an ocean, a sea or a lake.

Marketable title Title that is free of liens or other encumbrances that interfere with the peaceful enjoyment of the property.

Materialman's lien or **Mechanic's lien** The right of one who renders services or supplies materials in connection with improvements to real property to seek a judicial sale of the realty to satisfy unpaid claims.

Metes and bounds   A method of describing land using compass directions, monuments or landmarks and linear measurements.

Mineral deed   A deed used to convey title to minerals.

Misrepresentation   A false statement or act negligently or innocently done that was a material factor in the victim's decision to act.

Mistake   Unintentional error.

Mortgage   A document that uses real property to secure payment of a debt.

Mortgage insurance   Insurance that protects mortgage lenders against loss caused by a borrower's default.

Mortgagee   A lender who acquires an interest in a borrower's real property as security for repayment of the loan.

Mortgagor   A borrower who gives a lender an interest in the borrower's real property to secure payment of a loan.

Multiple listing   A contract among brokers who as members of a multiple-listing exchange agree to share listings with each other.

Negative amortization   When periodic payments on an amortized loan do not cover all the interest that is due, the unpaid amount is added to the principal. This is referred to as *negative amortization.*

Net lease   As contrasted with the gross lease, a type of lease in which the tenant agrees to pay the taxes, insurance, repairs and other operating expenses of the premises.

Net listing   A listing agreement in which the broker's commission is the difference between the seller's asking price and that price for which the property is actually sold.

Nonconforming use   A legal use that was established prior to zoning or prior to the present zoning classification and is permitted to continue despite its nonconformance with the zoning code.

Nonfreehold estate   Estates in land created for a fixed period of time.

Nonjudicial foreclosure   See Power-of-sale foreclosure.

Notary public   A person authorized by the state to take acknowledgments.

Note   The borrower's written promise to repay a loan according to its terms.

Notice statutes   Statutes that provide that the subsequent buyer prevails over all interested parties who have not recorded their interest at the time the buyer accepts the conveyance and pays consideration for the land without notice of the preexisting conveyance.

Novation   An agreement in which a party agrees to discharge the other party to the contract and to substitute a new obligation and a new party in its place.

Nuisance   An unreasonable interference by one party with another's use or enjoyment of his or her land.

Offer   A proposal intended to create a contract upon acceptance by the person to whom it is made.

Open listing   A brokerage agreement that entitles the broker to a fee only if his or her activities bring about the sale. The property may be listed with several brokers.

Open mine doctrine   A legal doctrine that permits the holder of a life estate to receive the royalties from mineral extraction that had begun prior to acquiring the life estate.

Option   A contract that gives a person a designated period of time to buy or lease real property at a specified price.

Optionee   One who is the recipient of an option.

Optionor   One who grants an option.

Parol evidence   Oral or other evidence extraneous to a written contract.

Partition   A legal action in which a co-owner obtains a division of real property, terminating any interest of other co-owners in the divided portion. Each former co-owner's share is now owned individually.

Party wall   A single wall on the boundary of adjoining properties; it serves as a common support for buildings on each of two parcels.

Per capita Distribution of an intestate's property in equal shares to persons who have the same relationship to the decedent without reference to the share an ancestor would have taken.

Per stirpes Distribution of an intestate's property to persons who take only the share that an ancestor would have taken.

Percentage lease A lease whose rental is based in part on the gross sales made by the tenant on the premises.

Percolating water Water that passes through the ground, not flowing in a clearly defined underground stream or supplied by streams flowing on the surface.

Perfection The process by which public notice of a lien or security interest is given.

Periodic tenancy An estate from period to period, continuing from period to period until terminated by proper notice from one of the parties.

Personal property Property that is not real property, generally characterized as having substance and being movable.

Planned unit development (PUD) A concept involving a development larger than a traditional subdivision, generally permitting mixed uses within the development and attempting to provide a maximum amount of land for open space.

Plat A map of a subdivision showing boundaries of individual properties. Includes details such as lot numbers, blocks, streets, public easements and monuments.

Pooling agreement An oil or gas contract that allocates to various mineral owners a proportion of the production from a reservoir.

Possibility of reverter A possibility that an estate based upon a condition may revert to the grantor if the grantee or those who take through the grantee breach the condition.

Post-nuptial agreement A contract made by a married couple concerning their property.

Power of attorney A document authorizing a person, the attorney-in-fact, to act as agent on behalf of another as indicated in the instrument.

Power-of-sale foreclosure Foreclosure based on terms in a mortgage giving a mortgagee or third party the power to sell the security without a court order if the borrower defaults.

Precedent A published opinion of an appellate court that serves as authority for determining a legal question in a later case that has similar facts.

Pre-nuptial agreement A contract made by a couple prior to marriage concerning property that each owns or may acquire in the future.

Privity of contract The relationship between the parties to a contract.

Probate The legal proceeding that establishes the validity of a will.

Procuring cause Acts on the part of the broker that result in the location of a buyer who is ready, willing and able to purchase the property on terms satisfactory to the seller.

Profit A nonpossessory interest in real property permitting the holder to remove part of the soil or produce of the land.

Promissory estoppel A doctrine that prevents a party from denying that a promise is supported by consideration.

Promissory note See Note.

Property Legal rights that a person possesses with respect to a thing; rights that have economic value.

Prorate To divide or allocate proportionately.

Puffing Statements of opinion made by a seller to induce the purchaser to buy.

Punitive damages See Exemplary damages.

Purchase-money mortgage A mortgage given to a buyer to secure part of the purchase price of real property and delivered contemporaneously with the transfer of title to the buyer.

Pure race statutes Statutes that provide that the first person who records an instrument prevails over all other takers from the same source. It is not relevant that the first recorder and prevailing party had notice of the prior transactions.

Quitclaim deed An instrument that conveys whatever title the grantor has.

Race-notice statutes Statutes that provide that a subsequent buyer will prevail only if he or she has no notice of the prior transaction at the time of conveyance and records first.

Ratify Approve as in a contract.

Real estate investment trust (REIT) A tax shelter that exempts certain qualified real estate investment syndications from corporate taxes where 95 percent or more of the ordinary income is distributed annually to the beneficiaries or investors.

Real estate purchase contract An agreement whereby a seller promises to sell an interest in realty by conveying a deed to the designated estate for which a buyer promises to pay a specified purchase price. (See also Earnest money contract.)

Real Estate Recovery Fund A fund of money administered by the Texas Real Estate Commission that can be used to compensate victims who have been injured by a real estate licensee's dishonesty or fraud.

Real estate syndicate Generally refers to a group of investors who combine funds and managerial resources to develop, manage or purchase real estate.

Real property Land, buildings and other improvements permanently affixed to land.

Receivership Appointment by a court of a disinterested party to manage or operate mortgaged property during foreclosure.

Recording statutes Laws requiring that written instruments affecting the title to real property be entered into public records.

Rectangular survey system A system of land description used in many midwestern and western states. It divides land into townships and then subdivides a township into sections. This method of describing land is not used in Texas.

Redemption The process of reacquiring property lost to a lienholder because of default in paying the underlying obligation.

Redlining Denial of a loan by a lending institution or the exacting of harsher terms for loans in certain parts of a city.

Rejection An offeree's refusal or failure to accept an offer.

Relation back A legal doctrine whereby the title acquired by a deed relates back to the moment of the first delivery to an escrow agent.

Release of mortgage A written statement signed by the mortgagee that the debt secured by the mortgage has been paid or satisfied.

Reliction Land created when water recedes.

Remainder See Reversion.

Rent withholding The practice, allowed in a few states under limited circumstances, in which the tenant withholds rent as an inducement to force the landlord to perform repairs. Generally, this is not allowed in Texas.

Rescission A cancellation of a contract that results in the parties being restored to the position they were in before the contract was made.

Residuary clause A will provision that disposes of property not specifically devised.

Respondeat superior, doctine of The legal doctrine that an employer is liable for the wrongful acts of employees done within the scope of their employment.

Restitution An equitable remedy that returns or restores a party to his or her position before the transaction.

Restrictive covenant A provision in a deed limiting the uses that may be made of the property.

Retainage fund A fund of money that state law requires the property owner to retain for 30 days following completion of construction. The purpose of this fund is to pay subcontractors and laborers who were not paid by the general contractor.

Reversion The future estate that follows a life estate.

Revocation An offeror's act of withdrawing an offer.

Right of possession   In all jurisdictions the right of possession implicitly resides in the tenant; that is, no one will have possessory rights inconsistent with those granted to the tenant.

Right of re-entry   The future interest that follows a fee simple on a condition subsequent.

Right of survivorship   A characteristic of some forms of co-ownership by which the surviving cotenant acquires the entire estate.

Riparian lands   Lands that border on a stream or watercourse.

Riparian rights   Water rights doctrine based on the idea that all owners of riparian lands are entitled to share equally in the use of water.

Royalty   A percentage of the minerals extracted paid by the lessee to the lessor. It can be paid in kind or in cash.

Rule of capture   A legal principle of oil and gas law allowing a landowner the right to all oil and gas from wells on his or her land, including oil and gas migrating from the land of others.

Run with the land   Rights in real property that pass to successive owners are said to run with the land.

S corporation   A corporation that has elected to be treated as a partnership for tax purposes and under subchapter S of the Internal Revenue Code.

Satisfaction   The performance of an agreement to substitute a different kind of performance for that originally contracted for.

Scienter   In fraud action, knowingly making a false statement or asserting that something is true without actual knowledge.

Section   An area of land approximately one mile square, containing as nearly as possible 640 acres.

Secured transaction   A transaction in which a party agrees that personal property or a fixture will secure repayment of a debt.

Security   An investment of money in a common enterprise with profits to come primarily from the efforts of others.

Security agreement   A document that creates a security interest.

Security deposit   Money deposited by the tenant, usually at the inception of the lease, over and above the advance payment of rent for the security of the landlord.

Security interest   A lien against personal property or a fixture to secure repayment of a debt.

Seisin   Ownership of real property.

Self-proving affidavit   An affidavit attached to a will that makes the will easier to probate. It is signed by the testator and the witnesses in the presence of a notary public.

Separate property   In community property jurisdictions, property owned by either spouse prior to marriage and property acquired during marriage by gift, inheritance or will.

Servient estate   The parcel of land that is subject to an easement appurtenant; also called *servient tenement*.

Sheriff's deed   A deed used to convey title to property by a sheriff at a forced auction.

Special use permit   A system whereby special exceptions to the zoning ordinance are granted by the land-use administrator under a permit arrangement.

Special warranty deed   A deed in which the seller warrants against acts that he or she has done that might affect title.

Specific performance   A court decree mandating a party to perform according to the contract.

Spot zoning   A zone change permitted by the local governing body that is not in harmony with the comprehensive plan for that area.

Statute of frauds   A statute that necessitates that certain contracts, in order to be enforceable, be supported by a written memorandum and signed by the party against whom enforcement is sought.

Statute of limitations   A statute that limits the period of time a person has to file a lawsuit.

Statutory law   Law enacted by local and state legislative bodies and by Congress.

Strict foreclosure   A judicial procedure that terminates the mortgagor's equity of redemption and establishes the mortgagee's absolute title to mortgaged real property.

Subject to   As used in financing the purchase of real property, a sale in which an existing mortgage on the property is not paid off. The buyer paying only for the seller's equity.

Sublease   A transfer of part of the leasehold interest of the tenant, with the tenant retaining a reversionary interest.

Subordination agreement   As used in mortgage financing, an agreement in which a mortgagee surrenders a priority lien and accepts a junior position in relation to other liens or claims.

Substantial performance   The amount of compliance under the terms of a contract that discharges a party from further obligation although failing to perform totally under the contract.

Taking   A regulation that deprives the owner of all reasonable use of the land constitutes a de facto taking of the property without due process of law under the Fifth and Fourteenth Amendments to the United States Constitution.

Tenancy at sufferance   Created when a person is wrongfully in possession of another's land without a valid lease.

Tenancy at will   A tenancy that exists until either party chooses to terminate it.

Tenancy by the entirety   Co-ownership of real property by husband and wife recognized in some states but not in Texas. The right of survivorship is characteristic of it.

Tenancy in common   A form of co-ownership in which each owner possesses an undivided right to the entire property. Shares of co-owners need not be equal, and no right of survivorship exists.

Tenancy in partnership   A form of co-ownership in which each partner owns partnership property along with all other partners.

Tender   An offer of money or property as required by the contract.

Tenure   An historic system of holding lands, a characteristic of which was the possessor's subordination to some superior to whom the possessor owed certain duties.

Term tenancy   A leasehold estate for a specified period of time that has a specific beginning date and a specific ending date. When the ending date arrives, the estate is terminated without notice by either party.

Testamentary trust   A trust that does not take effect until the death of the creator.

Testator   A person who dies leaving a will.

Third-party beneficiary   A person who is allowed to enforce a contract although not a party to it.

Third-person guaranty of rent   The landlord who has doubts about the capacity or reliability of the tenant in meeting the conditions of the lease may require a third person to guarantee performance.

Time-shares   A device by which use or ownership of land is divided by time.

Title   The totality of rights and obligations possessed by an owner; also, evidence of ownership.

Title insurance   The comprehensive indemnity contract that insures the titleholder against title defects and encumbrances that may exist at the time the policy is issued.

Title opinion   See Attorney's title opinion.

Torrens certificate   A document issued under the Torrens system, a type of land title registration.

Tort   A noncontractual civil wrong.

Trade fixtures   Items added to land or buildings by a tenant to be used in the tenant's trade or business.

Trespass   A wrongful, physical invasion of the property of another.

Trust   A legal relationship in which a person transfers legal title to property to a trustee who manages it for the benefit of third parties, the beneficiaries of the trust. (See also Inter vivos trust and Testamentary trust.)

Trustee's deed   A deed frequently used to convey title to property sold at a nonjudicial foreclosure.

Unconscionable contract   A contract that a court may render unenforceable because it is grossly unfair.

Underground streams   Subterranean waters that flow in clearly defined channels discoverable from the earth's surface.

Undivided interest   Interest of a co-owner that gives him or her the right to possession of the entire property along with other co-owners. (See also Co-ownership.)

Undue influence   The exertion of dominion over another person that destroys that person's ability to exercise independent judgment.

Uniform settlement statement   A closing statement required for all federal related residential first mortgages by the Real Estate Settlement Procedures Act.

Unilateral contract   A contract involving a promise in exchange for an act.

Usufruct   The right to use, enjoy or receive some benefit from property that belongs to another.

Usury   The practice of charging interest on a loan in excess of a rate allowed by law.

Vara   A measurement found in land grants and deeds that is equivalent to 33-$\frac{1}{3}$ inches.

Variance   Permission obtained from the appropriate governmental authorities to deviate somewhat from the designations under the zoning code.

Vendor's lien   A lien in favor of the seller that is automatically created when the seller conveys land for which he or she is not paid fully.

Voidable   A contract that may be voided or validated at the option of a party.

Waiver   The releasing or giving up of a legal right.

Warranty deed   A deed that conveys title and warrants that title is good and free of liens and encumbrances. (See also Special warranty deed.)

Warranty of habitability   In leaseholds, the implied promise by the landlord that the leased premises are safe, sanitary and fit for living. In new home construction, the implied warranty by the builder-seller that the house was constructed in a good and workmanlike manner.

Will   A document made by the decedent that distributes the decedent's estate upon his or her death.

Wrongful abandonment   The tenant's vacating of the premises without justification and with the intention of no longer performing under the terms of the lease.

Wrongful eviction   An act that occurs when the landlord without justification deprives the tenant of the possession of the premises.

Zone change   A zoning amendment made by the legislative body that created the zoning code.

Zoning   The regulation by the public, usually a municipality, of structures and uses of land within designated zones.

Zoning commission   An investigative body that makes recommendations to the city or town concerning the need for zoning or rezoning.

Appendices

APPENDIX A: TEXAS REAL ESTATE LICENSE ACT

The Texas Real Estate License Act is known as Article 6573a as included in Vernon's Texas Civil Statutes. Texas has had a real estate license law in effect since 1939. This law was extensively revised in August 1967 and again in May 1975, with an increase of educational requirements, removal of surety bond provisions and the establishment of a recovery fund. Further amendments were made by the 1977, 1979, 1981, 1983 and 1985 sessions of the Texas Legislature.

The Texas Real Estate License Act is reproduced in full on the following pages. To help you study the act, which you must read through completely, headings have been added by the authors, and some parts are emphasized in boldface type. An aid to understanding the act is *Rules of the Texas Real Estate Commission*, which serves to interpret and define the provisions set forth in the real estate license act. In any case, this act must be interpreted as applied for each person or case by his or her legal counsel. It may be changed or amended by action of the state legislature.

THE REAL ESTATE LICENSE ACT

General Provisions

Section 1. (a)This Act shall be known and may be cited as "The Real Estate License Act."

(b) **It is unlawful for a person to act in the capacity of, engage in the business of, or advertise** or hold himself out as engaging in or conducting the business of **a real estate broker or a real estate salesman within this state without first obtaining** a real estate license from the Texas Real Estate Commission. It is unlawful for a person licensed as a real estate salesman to act or attempt to act as a real estate agent unless he is, at such time, associated with a licensed Texas real estate broker and acting for the licensed real estate broker.

(c) Each real estate broker licensed pursuant to this Act is responsible to the commission, members of the public, and his clients for all acts and conduct performed under this Act by himself or by a real estate salesman associated with or acting for the broker.

(d) No real estate salesman shall accept compensation for real estate sales and transactions from any person other than the broker under whom he is at the time licensed or under whom he was licensed when he earned the right to compensation.

(e) No real estate salesman shall pay a commission to any person except through the broker under whom he is at the time licensed.

Definitions

Section 2. As used in this Act:

(1) **"Real estate"** means a leasehold, as well as any other interest or estate in land, whether corporeal, incorporeal, freehold, or nonfreehold, and whether the real estate is situated in this state or elsewhere.

(2) **"Real estate broker"** means a person who, for another person and for a fee, commission, or other valuable consideration, or with the intention or in the expectation or on the promise of receiving or collecting a fee, commission, or other valuable consideration from another person:

(A) sells, exchanges, purchases, rents, or leases real estate;

(B) offers to sell, exchange, purchase, rent, or lease real estate;

(C) negotiates or attempts to negotiate the listing, sale, exchange, purchase, rental, or leasing of real estate;

(D) lists or offers or attempts or agrees to list real estate for sale, rental, lease, exchange, or trade;

(E) appraises or offers or attempts or agrees to appraise real estate;

(F) auctions, or offers or attempts or agrees to auction, real estate;

(G) buys or sells or offers to buy or sell, or otherwise deals in options on real estate;

(H) aids, attempts, or offers to aid in locating or obtaining for purchase, rent, or lease any real estate;

(I) procures or assists in the procuring of prospects for the purpose of effecting the sale, exchange, lease, or rental of real estate; or

(J) procures or assists in the procuring of properties for the purpose of effecting the sale, exchange, lease, or rental of real estate.

(3) **"Broker"** also includes a person employed by or on behalf of the owner or owners of lots or other parcels of real estate, at a salary, fee, commission, or any other valuable consideration, to sell the real estate or any part thereof, in lots or parcels or other disposition thereof. It also includes a person who engages in the business of charging an advance fee or contracting for collection of a fee in connection with a contract whereby he undertakes primarily to promote the sale of real estate either through its listing in a publication issued primarily for such purpose, or for referral of information concerning the real estate to brokers, or both.

(4) **"Real estate salesman"** means a person associated with a Texas-licensed real estate broker for the purposes of performing acts or transactions comprehended by the definition of "real estate broker" as defined in this Act.

(5) **"Person"** means an individual, a partnership, or a corporation, foreign or domestic.

(6) **"Commission"** means the Texas Real Estate Commission.

(7) If the sense requires it, words in the present tense include the future tense; in the masculine gender, include the feminine or neuter gender; in the singular number, include the plural number; in the plural number, include the singular number; the word "and" may be read "or"; and the word "or" may be read "and." This Act is substantive in character and is intended to be applied prospectively only.

Exemptions

Section 3.   The provisions of this Act shall not apply to any of the following persons and transactions, and each and all of the following persons and transactions are hereby exempted from the provisions of this Act, to wit:

(a) **an attorney at law** licensed in this state or in any other state;

(b) **an attorney in fact under a duly-executed power of attorney** authorizing the consummation of a real estate transaction;

(c) **a public official** in the conduct of his official duties;

(d) a person acting officially as a **receiver, trustee, administrator, executor, or guardian;**

(e) **a person acting under a court order or under the authority of a will or a written trust instrument;**

(f) **a salesperson employed by an owner** in the sale of structures and land on which said structures are situated, provided such structures are erected by the owner in the due course of his business;

(g) **an on-site manager of an apartment complex;**

(h) transactions involving the sale, lease, or transfer of any **mineral or mining interest** in real property;

(i) **an owner or his employees in renting or leasing his own real estate** whether improved or unimproved;

(j) transactions involving the sale, lease, or transfer of **cemetery lots.**

A Single Act Is a Violation

Section 4.   A person who, directly or indirectly for another, **with the intention or on the promise of receiving any valuable consideration,** offers, attempts, or agrees to perform, or **performs, a single act defined in Subdivisions 2 and 3, Section 2 of this Act,** whether as a part of a transaction, or as an entire transaction, **is deemed to be acting as a real estate broker or salesman** within the meaning of this Act. The commission of a single such act by a person required to be licensed under this Act and not so licensed **shall constitute a violation of this Act.**

Administration

Section 5. (a) The administration of the provisions of this Act is vested in a commission, to be known as the **"Texas Real Estate Commission,"** consisting of **nine members** to be appointed by the governor with the advice and consent of two-thirds of the senate present. **The commissioners hold office for staggered terms of six years** with the terms of three members expiring every two years. Each member holds office until his successor is appointed and has qualified. Within 15 days after his appointment, each member shall qualify by taking the constitutional oath of office and furnishing a bond payable to the Governor of

Texas in the penal sum of $10,000, conditional on the faithful performance of his duties as prescribed by law. A vacancy for any cause shall be filled by the governor for the unexpired term. Notwithstanding any other provisions in this subsection, the six members of the commission in office on September 1, 1979, shall continue in office until the 5th day of October of the years in which their respective terms expire, or until their successors are appointed and have qualified. The terms of office of the appointees who fill the offices of incumbent members whose terms expire October 5, 1979, 1981, and 1983, expire on January 31, 1985, 1987, and 1989, respectively. Each succeeding term of office expires on January 31 of odd-numbered years. For the three public members initially appointed under this Act, the governor shall designate one member for a term expiring January 31, 1981, one member for a term expiring January 31, 1983, and one member for a term expiring January 31, 1985. At a regular meeting in February of each year, **the commission shall elect from its own membership a chairman, vice-chairman, and secretary.** Each member of the commission shall be present for at least one-half of the regularly scheduled meetings held each year by the commission. The failure of a member to meet this requirement automatically removes the member from the commission and creates a vacancy on the commission. A quorum of the commission consists of five members.

(b) All members, officers, employees, and agents of the commission are subject to the code of ethics and standards of conduct imposed by Chapter 421, Acts of the 63rd Legislature, Regular Session, 1973 (Article 6252-9b, Vernon's Texas Civil Statutes).

(c) Appointments to the commission shall be made without regard to the race, creed, sex, religion, or national origin of the appointees. **Each member of the commission shall be a citizen of Texas and a qualified voter.** Six members shall have been engaged in the real estate brokerage business as **licensed real estate brokers** as their major occupations for at least five years next preceding their appointments. **Three members** must be representatives of the **general public** who are not licensed under this Act and who do not have, other than as consumers, a financial interest in the practice of a real estate broker or real estate salesman. It is grounds for removal from the commission if:

(1) a broker-member of the commission ceases to be a licensed real estate broker; or

(2) a person is required to register as a lobbyist under Chapter 422, Acts of the 63rd Legislature, Regular Session, 1973, as amended (Article 6252-9c, Vernon's Texas Civil Statutes), by virtue of his activities for compensation in or on behalf of a profession related to the operation of the commission.

(d) Each member of the commission shall receive as compensation for each day actually spent on his official duties the sum of $75 and his actual and necessary expenses incurred in the performance of his official duties.

(e) **The commission shall have the authority and power to make and enforce all rules and regulations necessary for the performance of its duties, to establish standards of conduct and ethics for its licensees** in keeping with the purposes and intent of this Act or to ensure compliance with the provisions of this Act. If the appropriate standing committees of both houses of the legislature acting under Subsection (g), Section 5, Administrative Procedure and Texas Register Act, as added (Article 6252-13a, Vernon's Texas Civil Statutes), transmit to the commission statements opposing adoption of a rule under that section, the rule may not take effect, or if the rule has already taken effect, the rule is repealed effective on the date the commission receives the committees' statements. In addition to any other action, proceeding, or remedy authorized by law, **the commission shall have the right to institute an action in its own name to enjoin any violation of any provision of this Act** or any rule or regulation of the commission and in order for the commission to sustain such action it shall not be necessary to allege or prove, either that an adequate remedy at law does not exist, or that substantial or irreparable damage would result from the continued violation thereof. Either party to such action may appeal to the appellate court having jurisdiction of said cause. The commission shall not be required to give any appeal bond in any action or proceeding to enforce the provisions of this Act.

(f) **The commission is empowered to select and name an administrator, who shall also act as executive secretary,** and to select and employ such other subordinate officers and employees as are necessary to administer this Act. The salaries of the administrator and the officers and employees shall be fixed by the commission not to exceed such amounts as are fixed by the applicable general appropriations bill. The commission may designate a subordinate officer as assistant administrator, who shall be authorized to act for the administrator in his absence. A person who is required to register as a lobbyist under Chapter 422, Acts of the 63rd Legislature, Regular Session, 1973, as amended (Article 6252-9c, Vernon's Texas Civil Statutes), may not act as the general counsel to the commission or serve as a member of the commission.

(g) The commission shall adopt a seal of a design which it shall prescribe. Copies of all records and papers in the office of the commission, duly certified and authenticated by the seal of the commission, shall be received in evidence in all courts with like efforts as the original.

(h) Except as provided in Subsections (i) and (j) of this section, all money derived from fees, assessments, or charges under this Act, shall be paid by the commission into the State Treasury for safekeeping, and shall be placed by the State Treasurer in a separate fund to be available for use of the commission in the administration of this Act on requisition by the commission. A necessary amount of the money so paid into the State Treasury is hereby specifically appropriated to the commission for the purpose of paying the salaries and expenses necessary and proper for the administration of this Act, including equipment and maintenance of supplies for the offices or quarters occupied by the commission, and necessary travel expenses for the commission or persons authorized to act for it when performing duties under this Act. At the end of the state fiscal year, any unused portion of the funds in the special account, except such funds as may be appropriated to administer this Act pending receipt of additional revenues available for that purpose, shall be paid into the General Revenue Fund. The comptroller shall, on requisition of the commission, draw warrants from time to time on the State Treasurer for the amount specified in the requisition, not exceeding, however, the amount in the fund at the time of making a requisition. However, all money expended in the administration of this Act shall be specified and determined by itemized appropriation in the general departmental appropriation bill for the Texas Real Estate Commission, and not otherwise.

(i) In the event that fees collected under the Residential Service Company Act (Article 6573b, Vernon's Texas Civil Statutes), are insufficient to fund the legislative appropriation for that activity, funds from the real estate license fund are hereby authorized to be used for the administration of that Act. In no event, however, will the total expenditures for that activity exceed the legislative appropriation therefore.

(j) **Fifteen dollars received by the commission from fees received from real estate brokers and $7.50 received by the commission from fees received from real estate salesmen for licensure status shall be transmitted annually to Texas A&M University for deposit in the separate banking account. The money in the separate account shall be expended for the support and maintenance of the Texas Real Estate Research Center** and for carrying out the purposes, objectives, and duties of the center. However, all money expended from the separate account shall be as determined by legislative appropriation.

(k) The Texas Real Estate Commission is subject to the **Texas Sunset Act,** as amended (Article 5429k, Vernon's Texas Civil Statutes); and unless continued in existence as provided by that Act the commission is abolished, and this Act expires effective September 1, 1991.

(1) The commission is subject to the open meetings law, Chapter 271, Acts of the 60th Legislature, Regular Session, 1967, as amended (Article 6252-17, Vernon's Texas Civil Statutes), and the Administrative Procedure and Texas Register Act, as amended (Article 6252-13a, Vernon's Texas Civil Statutes).

General Requirements for Licensure

Section 6. (a) A person desiring to act as a real estate broker in this state shall file an application for a license with the commission on a form prescribed by the commission. **A broker desiring to engage a person to participate in real estate brokerage activity shall join the person in filing an application for a salesman license** on a form prescribed by the commission.

(b) **To be eligible for a license, an individual must be a citizen of the United States or a lawfully admitted alien, be at least 18 years of age, and be a legal resident of Texas** for at least 60 days immediately preceding the filing of an application, and must **satisfy the commission as to his honesty, trustworthiness, integrity, and competency.** However, the competency of the individual, for the purpose of qualifying for the granting of licensure privileges, **shall be judged solely on the basis of the examination referred to in Section 7 of this Act.**

(c) To be eligible for a license, **a corporation must designate one of its officers to act for it.** The designated person must be a citizen of the United States or a lawfully admitted alien, be at least 18 years of age, and be a resident of Texas for at least 60 days immediately preceding the filing of an application, and must be qualified to be licensed individually as a real estate broker. However, the competency of the person shall be judged solely on the basis of the examination referred to in Section 7 of this Act.

Moral Character Determination

Section 6A. (a) If, at any time before a person applies for a license under this Act, the person requests the commission to determine whether his moral character complies with the commission's moral character requirements for licensing under this Act and the person pays a $10 fee for the moral character determination, the commission shall make its determination of the person's moral character.

(b) Not later than the 30th day after the day on which the commission makes its determination, the commission shall give the person notice of the determination.

(c) If the person later applies for a license under this Act, the commission may conduct a supplemental moral character check of the person. The supplemental check may cover only the time since the day on which the person requested the original moral character determination.

Requirements for Licensing

Section 7. (a) Competency as referred to in Section 6 of this Act shall be established by an examination prepared by or contracted for by the commission. The examination shall be given at such times and at such places within the state as the commission shall prescribe. The examination shall be of scope sufficient in the judgment of the commission to determine that a person is competent to act as a real estate broker or salesman in a manner to protect the interest of the public. The examination for a salesman license shall be less exacting and less stringent than the examination for a broker license. The commission shall furnish each applicant with study material and references on which his examination shall be based. When an applicant for real estate license fails a qualifying examination, he may apply for reexamination by filing a request therefore together with the proper fee. The examination requirement shall be satisfied within one year from the date the application for a license is filed. **Courses of study required for licensure shall include but not be limited to the following,** which shall be considered core real estate courses for all purposes of this Act:

(1) **Principles of Real Estate** (or equivalent) shall include but not be limited to an overview of licensing as a real estate broker and salesman, ethics of practice, titles to and conveyancing of real estate, legal descriptions, law of agency, deeds, encumbrances and liens, distinctions between personal and real property, contracts, appraisal, finance and regulations, closing procedures, and real estate mathematics.

(2) **Real Estate Appraisal** (or equivalent) shall include but not be limited to the central purposes and functions of an appraisal, social and economic determinant of value, appraisal case studies, cost, market data and income approaches to value estimates, final correlations, and reporting.

(3) **Real Estate Law** (or equivalent) shall include but not be limited to legal concepts of real estate, land description, real property rights and estates in land, contracts, conveyances, encumbrances, foreclosures, recording procedures, and evidence of titles.

(4) **Real Estate Finance** (or equivalent) shall include but not be limited to monetary systems, primary and secondary money markets, sources of mortgage loans, federal government programs, loan applications, processes and procedures, closing costs, alternative financial instruments, equal credit opportunity acts, community reinvestment act, and state housing agency.

(5) **Real Estate Marketing** (or equivalent) shall include but not be limited to real estate professionalism and ethics, characteristics of successful salesmen, time management, psychology of marketing, listing procedures, advertising, negotiating and closing, financing, and the Deceptive Trade Practices-Consumer Protection Act, as amended, Section 17.01 et seq., Business & Commerce Code.

(6) **Real Estate Mathematics** (or equivalent) shall include but not be limited to basic arithmetic skills and review of mathematical logic, percentages, interest, time-valued money, depreciation, amortization, proration, and estimation of closing statements.

(7) **Real Estate Brokerage** (or equivalent) shall include but not be limited to law of agency, planning and organization, operational policies and procedures, recruiting, selection and training of personnel, records and control, and real estate firm analysis and expansion criteria.

(8) **Property Management** (or equivalent) shall include but not be limited to role of property manager, landlord policies; operational guidelines, leases, lease negotiations, tenant relations, maintenance, reports, habitability laws, and the Fair Housing Act.

(9) **Real Estate Investments** (or equivalent) shall include but not be limited to real estate investment characteristics, techniques of investment analysis, time-valued money, discounted and nondiscounted investment criteria, leverage, tax shelters, depreciation, and applications to property tax.

(b) **The commission shall waive the examination of an applicant for broker licensure** who has, within one year previous to the filing of his application, been licensed in this state as a broker, and shall waive the examination of an applicant **for salesman licensure who has, within one year previous to the filing of his application, been licensed in this state as either a broker or salesman.**

(c) From and after the effective date of this Act, each applicant for broker licensure shall furnish the commission **satisfactory evidence that he has had not less than two years' active experience in this state as a licensed real estate**

salesman practitioner during the 36-month period immediately preceding the filing of the application; and, in addition, shall furnish the commission satisfactory evidence of having completed successfully 36 semester hours of core real estate courses or related courses accepted by the commission. On January 1, 1983, the number of required semester hours shall be increased to 48. On or after January 1, 1985, the required semester hours shall be increased to 60. These qualifications for broker licensure shall not be required of an applicant who, at the time of making the application, is duly licensed as a real estate broker by any other state in the United States if that state's requirements for licensure are comparable to those of Texas. As a prerequisite for applying for broker licensure, those persons licensed as salesmen subject to the annual education requirements provided by Subsection (d) of this section shall, as part of the semester hours required by this subsection, furnish the commission satisfactory evidence of having completed all the requirements of Subsection (d) of this section.

(d) **From and after the effective date of this Act, as a prerequisite for applying for salesman licensure, each applicant shall furnish the commission satisfactory evidence of having completed 12 semester hours of postsecondary education, six semester hours of which must be completed in core real estate courses, of which a minimum of two semester hours must be completed in Principles of Real Estate as described in Subdivision (1) of Subsection (a) of Section 7. The remaining six semester hours shall be completed in core real estate courses or related courses.** As a condition for the first annual certification of salesman licensure privileges, the applicant shall furnish the commission satisfactory evidence of having completed a minimum of 14 semester hours, 8 semester hours of which must be completed in core real estate courses. As a condition for the second annual certification of salesman licensure privileges, the applicant shall furnish the commission satisfactory evidence of having completed a minimum of 16 semester hours, 10 semester hours of which must be completed in core real estate courses. As a condition for the third annual certification of salesman licensure privileges, the applicant shall furnish the commission satisfactory evidence of having completed a minimum of 18 semester hours, 12 semester hours of which must be completed in core real estate courses.

Section 7. (e) Repealed.

(f) Insofar as is necessary for the administration of this Act, **the commission is authorized to inspect and accredit educational programs or courses of study in real estate and to establish standards of accreditation for such programs conducted in the State of Texas, other than accredited colleges and universities.** Schools, other than accredited colleges and universities which are authorized to offer real estate educational courses pursuant to provisions of this section shall be required to maintain a corporate surety bond in the sum of $10,000 payable to the commission, for the benefit of a party who may suffer damages resulting from failure of a commission-approved school or course to fulfill obligations attendant to the approval.

(g) A person licensed as a salesman on May 19, 1975, is not subject to the educational requirements or prerequisites of this Act as a condition for holding salesman licensure privileges. A person licensed as a broker on May 19, 1975, is not subject to the educational requirements or prerequisites of this Act as a condition for holding broker licensure privileges.

(h) Notwithstanding any other provision of this Act, from and after the effective date of this Act each applicant for broker licensure shall furnish the commission with satisfactory evidence:

(1) that he has satisfied the requirements of Subsection (c) of this section; or

(2) that he is a licensed real estate broker in another state, that he has had not less than two years' active experience in the other state as a licensed real es-

tate salesman or broker during the 36-month period immediately preceding the filing of the application, and that he has satisfied the educational requirements for broker licensure as provided by Subsection (c) of this section; or

(3) that he has, within one year previous to the filing of his application, been licensed in this state as a broker.

(i) Notwithstanding any other provision of this Act, the commission shall waive the requirements of Subsection (d) of Section 7 of this Act for an applicant for salesman licensure who has, within one year previous to the filing of his application, been licensed in this state as a broker or salesman. However, with respect to an applicant for salesman licensure who was licensed as a salesman within one year previous to the filing of the application but whose original licensure privileges were issued under the provisions that second and third annual certification of the licensure privileges would be conditioned upon furnishing satisfactory evidence of successful completion of additional education, the commission shall require the applicant to furnish satisfactory evidence of successful completion of any additional education that would have been required if the licensure privileges had been maintained without interruption during the previous year.

(j) Not later than the 30th day after the day on which a person completes an examination administered by the commission, the commission shall send to the person his or her examination results. If requested in writing by a person who fails the examination, the commission shall send to the person not later than the 30th day after the day on which the request is received by the commission an analysis of the person's performance on the examination.

(k) All applicants for licensure must complete at least three classroom hours of coursework on federal, state, and local laws governing housing discrimination, housing credit discrimination, and community reinvestment or at least three semester hours of coursework on constitutional law.

Real Estate Recovery Fund

Section 8. Part 1. (a) The commission shall establish a **real estate recovery fund** which shall be set apart and maintained by the commission as provided in this section. The fund shall be used in the manner provided in this section **for reimbursing aggrieved persons who suffer actual damages by reason of certain acts committed by a duly licensed real estate broker or salesman, or by an unlicensed employee or agent of a broker or salesman,** provided the broker or salesman was licensed by the State of Texas at the time the act was committed and provided recovery is ordered by a court of competent jurisdiction against the broker or salesman. **The use of the fund as provided in Part 1 of this section is limited to an act that is either a violation of Section 15(3) or (4) of this Act.**

(b) On the effective date of this Act, **the commission shall collect from each real estate broker and salesman licensed by this state a fee of $10** which shall be deposited in the real estate recovery fund. The commission shall suspend a license issued under the provisions of this Act for failure to pay this fee. After the effective date of this Act, **when a person makes application for an original license pursuant to this Act he shall pay, in addition to his original license application fee, a fee of $10,** which shall be deposited in the real estate recovery fund. If the commission does not issue the license, this fee shall be returned to the applicant.

Replenishment

Part 2. **If on December 31 of any year the balance remaining in the real estate recovery fund is less than $300,000, each real estate broker and each real estate salesman, on recertification of his license during the following calendar year, shall pay,** in addition to his license recertification fee, **a fee of $10,** which shall be deposited in the real estate recovery fund, **or a pro rata share of the amount necessary to bring the fund to $1 million,** whichever is less.

Judgment Against Fund

Part 3. (a) No action for a judgment which subsequently results in an order for collection from the real estate recovery fund shall be started later than two years from the accrual of the cause of action. When an aggrieved person commences action for a judgment which may result in collection from the real estate recovery fund, the real estate broker or real estate salesman shall notify the commission in writing to this effect at the time of the commencement of the action.

(b) When an aggrieved person recovers a valid judgment in a court of competent jurisdiction against a real estate broker, or real estate salesman, on the grounds described in Part 1(a) of this section that occurred on or after May 19, 1975, the aggrieved person may, after final judgment has been entered, execution returned nulla bona, and a judgment lien perfected, file a verified claim in the court in which the judgment was entered and, on 20 days' written notice to the commission, and to the judgment debtor, may apply to the court for an order directing payment out of the real estate recovery fund of the amount unpaid on the judgment, subject to the limitations stated in Part 8 of this section.

(c) The court shall proceed on the application forthwith. On the hearing on the application, the aggrieved person is required to show that:

(1) the judgment is based on facts allowing recovery under Part 1(a) of this section;

(2) he is not a spouse of the debtor, or the personal representative of the spouse; and he is not a real estate broker or salesman, as defined by this Act, who is seeking to recover a real estate commission in the transaction or transactions for which the application for payment is made;

(3) he has obtained a judgment as set out in Part 3(b) of this section, stating the amount of the judgment and the amount owing on the judgment at the date of the application;

(4) the judgment debtor lacks sufficient attachable assets to satisfy the judgment; and

(5) the amount that may be realized from the sale of real or personal property or other assets liable to be sold or applied in satisfaction of the judgment and the balance remaining due on the judgment after application of the amount that may be realized.

(d) The court shall make an order directed to the commission requiring payment from the real estate recovery fund of whatever sum it finds to be payable on the claim, pursuant to and in accordance with the limitations contained in this section, if the court is satisfied, on the hearing, of the truth of all matters required to be shown by the aggrieved person by Part 3(c) of this section and that the aggrieved person has satisfied all of the requirements of Parts 3(b) and (c) of this section.

(e) A license granted under the provisions of this Act shall be revoked by the commission on proof that the commission has made a payment from the real estate recovery fund of any amount toward satisfaction of a judgment against a licensed real estate broker or salesman. **No broker or salesman is eligible to receive a new license until he has repaid in full, plus interest at the current legal rate, the amount paid from the real estate recovery fund on his account.** A discharge in bankruptcy shall not relieve a person from the penalties and disabilities provided in this Act.

Investment of Fund

Part 4. The sums received by the real estate commission for deposit in the real estate recovery fund shall be held by the commission in trust for carrying out the purposes of the real estate recovery fund. These funds may be invested and reinvested in the same manner as funds of the Texas State Employees Retirement System, and the interest from these investments shall be deposited to the credit of the real estate recovery fund, provided, however, that no investments shall be made which will impair the necessary liquidity required to satisfy judgment payments awarded pursuant to this section.

Protect Claims from Unjust Claims

Part 5. When the real estate commission receives notice of entry of a final judgment and a hearing is scheduled under Part 3(d) of this section, the commission may notify the attorney general of Texas of its desire to enter an appearance, file a response, appear at the court hearing, defend the action, or take whatever other action it deems appropriate on behalf of, and in the name of, the defendant, and take recourse through any appropriate method of review on behalf of, and in the name of, the defendant. In taking such action the real estate commission and the attorney general shall act only to protect the fund from spurious or unjust claims or to ensure compliance with the requirements for recovery under this section.

Subrogation

Part 6. When, on the order of the court, the commission has paid from the real estate recovery fund any sum to the judgment creditor, the commission shall be subrogated to all of the rights of the judgment creditor to the extent of the amount paid. The judgment creditor shall assign all his right, title, and interest in the judgment up to the amount paid by the commission which amount shall have priority for repayment in the event of any subsequent recovery on the judgment. Any amount and interest recovered by the commission on the judgment shall be deposited to the fund.

Waiver of Rights

Part 7. The failure of an aggrieved person to comply with the provisions of this section relating to the real estate recovery fund shall constitute a waiver of any rights under this section.

Payments from Fund

Part 8. (a) Notwithstanding any provision, payments from the real estate recovery fund are subject to the conditions and limitations in Subsections (b) through (d) of this part.

(b) Payments may be made only pursuant to an order of a court of competent jurisdiction, as provided in Part 3, and in the manner prescribed by this section.

(c) Payments for claims, including attorneys' fees, interest, and court costs, arising out of the same transaction shall be limited in the aggregate to $20,000 regardless of the number of claimants.

(d) Payments for claims based on judgments against any one licensed real estate broker or salesman may not exceed in the aggregate $50,000 until the fund has been reimbursed by the licensee for all amounts paid.

Disciplinary Action Against Licensee

Part 9. Nothing contained in this section shall limit the authority of the commission to take disciplinary action against a licensee for a violation of this Act or the rules and regulations of the commission; nor shall the repayment in full of all obligations to the real estate recovery fund by a licensee nullify or modify the effect of any other disciplinary proceeding brought pursuant to this Act.

Attorney's Fees

Part 10. Any person receiving payment out of the real estate recovery fund pursuant to Section 8 of this Act shall be entitled to receive reasonable attorney fees as determined by the court, subject to the limitations stated in Part 8 of this section.

License and Renewal

Section 9. (a) When an applicant has satisfactorily met all requirements and conditions of this Act, a license shall be issued which may remain in force and effect so long as the holder of the license remains in compliance with the obligations of this Act, which include payment of the annual certification fee as provided in Section 11 of this Act. **Each salesman license issued shall be delivered or mailed to the broker with whom the salesman is associated and shall be kept under this custody and control.**

(b) **An applicant is not permitted to engage in the real estate business either as a broker or salesman until a license evidencing his authority to engage in the real estate business has been received.**

(c) The commission by rule may adopt a system under which licenses expire on various dates during the year. Dates for payment of the annual certification fee shall be adjusted accordingly. For the year in which the certification date is changed, annual certification fees payable shall be prorated on a monthly basis so each licensee shall pay only that portion of the license fee which is allocable to the number of months during which the license is valid. On certification of the license on the new certification date, the total annual certification fee is payable.

(d) Any other provision of this Act notwithstanding, the commission may issue licenses valid for a period not to exceed 24 months and may charge and collect certification fees for such period; provided, however, that such certification fees shall not, calculated on an annual basis, exceed the amounts established in Section 11 of this Act, and further provided that the educational conditions for annual certification established in Subsection (d) of Section 7 of this Act shall not be waived by the commission.

Failure or Refusal to License

Section 10. If the commission declines or fails to license an applicant, it shall immediately give written notice of the refusal to the applicant. Before the applicant may appeal to a district court as provided in Section 18 of this Act, he must file within 10 days after the receipt of the notice an appeal from the ruling, requesting a time and place for a hearing before the commission. The commission shall set a time and place for the hearing within 30 days from the receipt of the appeal, giving 10 days' notice of the hearing to the applicant. The time of the hearing may be continued from time to time with the consent of the applicant. Following the hearing, the commission shall enter an order which is, in its opinion, appropriate in the matter concerned.

If an applicant fails to request a hearing as provided in this section, the commission's ruling shall become final and not subject to review by the courts.

Fees

Section 11. The commission shall charge and collect the following fees:

(1) a fee not to exceed $100 for the filing of an original application for real estate broker licensure;

(2) a fee not to exceed $100 for annual certification of real estate broker licensure status;

(3) a fee not to exceed $50 for the filing of an original application for salesman licensure;

(4) a fee not to exceed $50 for annual certification of real estate salesman licensure status;

(5) a fee not to exceed $25 for taking a license examination;

(6) a fee not to exceed $10 for filing a request for a license for each additional office or place of business;

(7) a fee not to exceed $20 for filing a request for a license for a change of place of business or change of sponsoring broker;

(8) a fee not to exceed $10 for filing a request to replace a license lost or destroyed.

(9) a fee not to exceed $400 for filing an application for approval of a real estate course pursuant to the provisions of Subsection (f) of Section 7 of this Act; and

(10) a fee not to exceed $200 per annum for and in each year of operation of a real estate course, established pursuant to the provisions of Subsection (f) of Section 7 of this Act.

(11) a fee of $15 for transcript evaluation.

Broker Office Requirements

Section 12. (a) Each resident broker shall maintain a fixed office within this state. The address of the office shall be designated on the broker's license. Within 10 days after a move from a previously designated address, the broker shall submit an application for a new license, designating the new location of his office, together with the required fee, whereupon the commission shall issue a license, reflecting the new location, provided the new location complies with the terms of this section.

(b) If a broker maintains more than one place of business within this state, he shall apply for, pay the required fee for, and obtain an additional license to be known as a branch office license for each additional office he maintains.

(c) The license or licenses of the broker shall at all times be prominently displayed in the licensee's place or places of business.

(d) Each broker shall also prominently display in his place or in one of his places of business the license of each real estate salesman associated with him.

Salesman Change of Employment

Section 13. (a) When the association of a salesman with his sponsoring broker is terminated, the broker shall immediately return the salesman license to the commission. The salesman license then becomes inactive.

(b) The salesman license may be activated if, before the license expires, a request, accompanied by the required fee, is filed with the commission by a licensed broker advising that he assumes sponsorship of the salesman.

Broker—Nonresident

Section 14. (a) It is unlawful for a licensed broker to employ or compensate directly or indirectly a person for performing an act enumerated in the definition of real estate broker in Section 2 of this Act if the person is not a licensed broker or licensed salesman in this state or an attorney at law licensed in this state or in any other state. However, a licensed broker may pay a commission to a licensed broker of another state if the foreign broker does not conduct in this state any of the negotiations for which the fee, compensation, or commission is paid.

(b) A resident broker of another state who furnishes the evidence required in Subsection (h) of Section 7 of this Act may apply for a license as a broker in this state. A nonresident licensee need not maintain a place of business in this state. The commission may in its discretion refuse to issue a broker license to an applicant who is not a resident of this state for the same reasons that it may refuse to license a resident of this state.

(c) **Each nonresident applicant shall file an irrevocable consent that legal actions may be commenced against him in the proper court of any county of this state in which a cause of action may arise,** or in which the plaintiff may reside, by service of process or pleading authorized by the laws of this state, or by serving the administrator or assistant administrator of the commission. The consent shall stipulate that the service of process or pleading shall be valid and binding in all courts as if personal service had been made on the nonresident broker in this state. The consent shall be duly acknowledged, and if made by a corporation, shall be authenticated by its seal. A service of process or pleading served on the commission shall be by duplicate copies, one of which shall be filed in the office of the commission and the other forwarded by registered mail to the last known principal address which the commission has for the nonresident broker against whom the process or pleading is directed. No default in an action may be taken except on certification by the commission that a copy of the process or pleading was mailed to the defendant as provided in this section, and no default judgment may be taken in an action or proceeding until 20 days after the day of mailing of the process or pleading to the defendant.

Notwithstanding any other provision of this subsection, a nonresident of this state who resides in a city whose boundaries are contiguous at any point to the boundaries of a city of this state, and who has been an actual bona fide resident of that city for at least 60 days immediately preceding the filing of his application, is eligible to be licensed as a real estate broker or salesman under this Act in the same manner as a resident of this state. If he is licensed in this manner, he shall at all times maintain a place of business either in the city in which he resides or in the city in this state which is contiguous to the city in which he resides, and he may not maintain a place of business at another location in this state unless he also complies with the requirements of Section 14(b) of this Act. The place of business must satisfy the requirements of Subsection (a) of Section 12 of this Act, but the place of business shall be deemed a definite place of business in this state within the meaning of Subsection (a) of Section 12.

Suspension and Revocation of Licenses

Section 15. **The commission may, on its own motion, and shall, on the verified complaint in writing of any person, provided the complaint, or the complaint together with evidence, documentary or otherwise, presented in connection with the complaint, provides reasonable cause, investigate the actions and records of a real estate broker or real estate salesman. The commission may suspend or revoke a license** issued under the provisions of this Act at any time when it has been determined that:

(1) (A) **the licensee has entered a plea of guilty or nolo contendere to, or been found guilty of, or been convicted of, a felony, in which fraud is an essential element,** and the time for appeal has elapsed or the judgment or conviction has been affirmed on appeal, irrespective of an order granting probation following such conviction, suspending the imposition of sentence; or

(B) **a final money judgment has been rendered against the licensee** resulting from contractual obligations of the licensee incurred in the pursuit of his business, and such judgment remains unsatisfied for a period of more than six months after becoming final; or

(2) the licensee has procured, or attempted to procure, a real estate license, for himself or a salesman, by fraud, misrepresentation or deceit, or by making a material misstatement of fact in an application for a real estate license; or

(3) the licensee, when selling, buying, trading, or renting real property in his own name, engaged in misrepresentation or dishonest or fraudulent action; or

(4) the licensee has failed within a reasonable time to make good a check issued to the commission after the commission has mailed a request for payment by certified mail to the licensee's last known business address as reflected by the commission's records; or

(5) the licensee has disregarded or violated a provision of the Act; or

(6) the licensee, while performing an act constituting an act of a broker or a salesman, as defined by this Act, has been guilty of:

(A) making a material misrepresentation, or failing to disclosure to a potential purchaser any latent structural defect or any other defect known to the broker or salesman. Latent structural defects and other defects do not refer to trivial or insignificant defects but refer to those defects that would be a significant factor to a reasonable and prudent purchaser in making a decision to purchase; or

(B) making a false promise of a character likely to influence, persuade, or induce any person to enter into a contract or agreement when the licensee could not or did not intend to keep such promise; or

(C) pursuing a continued and flagrant course of misrepresentation or making of false promises through agents, salesmen, advertising, or otherwise; or

(D) failing to make clear, to all parties to a transaction, which party he is acting for, or receiving compensation from more than one party except with the full knowledge and consent of all parties; or

(E) failing within a reasonable time properly to account for or remit money coming into his possession which belongs to others, or commingling money belonging to others with his own funds; or

(F) paying a commission or fees to or dividing a commission or fees with anyone not licensed as a real estate broker or salesman in this state or in any other state, or not an attorney at law licensed in this state or any other state, for compensation for services as a real estate agent; or

(G) failing to specify in a listing contract a definite termination date which is not subject to prior notice; or

(H) accepting, receiving, or charging an undisclosed commission, rebate, or direct profit on expenditures made for a principal; or

(I) soliciting, selling, or offering for sale real property under a scheme or program that constitutes a lottery or deceptive practice; or

(J) acting in the dual capacity of broker and undisclosed principal in a transaction; or

(K) guaranteeing, authorizing, or permitting a person to guarantee that future profits will result from a resale of real property; or

(L) placing a sign on real property offering it for sale, lease, or rent without the written consent of the owner or his authorized agent; or

(M) inducing or attempting to induce a party to a contract of sale or lease to break the contract for the purpose of substituting in lieu thereof a new contract; or

(N) negotiating or attempting to negotiate the sale, exchange, lease, or rental of real property with an owner or lessor, knowing that the owner or lessor had a written outstanding contract, granting exclusive agency in connection with the property to another real estate broker; or

(O) offering real property for sale or for lease without the knowledge and consent of the owner or his authorized agent, or on terms other than those authorized by the owner or his authorized agent; or

(P) publishing, or causing to be published, an advertisement including, but not limited to, advertising by newspaper, radio, television, or display which is misleading, or which is likely to deceive the public, or which in any manner tends to create a misleading impression, or which fails to identify the person causing the advertisement to be published as a licensed real estate broker or agent; or

(Q) having knowingly withheld from or inserted in a statement of account or invoice, a statement that made it inaccurate in a material particular; or

(R) publishing or circulating an unjustified or unwarranted threat of legal proceedings, or other action; or

(S) establishing an association, by employment or otherwise, with an unlicensed person who is expected or required to act as a real estate licensee, or aiding or abetting or conspiring with a person to circumvent the requirements of this Act; or

(T) failing or refusing on demand to furnish copies of a document pertaining to a transaction dealing with real estate to a person whose signature is affixed to the document; or

(U) failing to advise a purchaser in writing before the closing of a transaction that the purchaser should either have the abstract covering the real estate which is the subject of the contract examined by an attorney of the purchaser's own selection, or be furnished with or obtain a policy of title insurance; or

(V) conduct which constitutes dishonest dealings, bad faith, or untrustworthiness; or

(W) acting negligently or incompetently in performing an act for which a person is required to hold a real estate license; or

(X) disregarding or violating a provision of this Act; or

(Y) failing within a reasonable time to deposit money received as escrow agent in a real estate transaction, either in trust with a title company authorized to do business in this state, or in a custodial, trust, or escrow account maintained for that purpose in a banking institution authorized to do business in this state; or

(Z) disbursing money deposited in a custodial, trust, or escrow account, as provided in Subsection (Y) before the transaction concerned has been consummated or finally otherwise terminated; or

(AA) discriminating against an owner, potential purchaser, lessor, or potential lessee on the basis of race, color, religion, sex, national origin, or ancestry. Prohibited discrimination shall include but not be limited to directing prospective home buyers or lessees interested in equivalent properties to different areas according to the race, color, religion, sex, national origin, or ancestry of the potential owner or lessee, or

(7) the licensee has failed or refused on demand to produce a document, book, or record in his possession concerning a real estate transaction conducted by him for inspection by the Real Estate Commission or its authorized personnel or representative; or

(8) the licensee has failed within a reasonable time to provide information requested by the commission as a result of a formal or informal complaint to the commission which would indicate a violation of this Act; or

(9) the licensee has **failed without cause to surrender to the rightful owner,** on demand, a document or instrument coming into his possession.

The provisions of this section do not relieve a person from civil liability or from criminal prosecution under this Act or under the laws of this state.

Section 15A. If the commission revokes a person's license issued under this Act, the commission may not issue another license to the person for one year after the revocation.

Section 15B. It is the intent of the legislature that **the commission only is vested with the authority and responsibility for the administration, implementation, and enforcement of this Act.** Duties, functions, and responsibilities of the commission's administrative assistants, agents, investigators, and all other employees shall be those assigned and determined by the commission. Notwithstanding any other provision of the Act, there shall be no undercover or covert investigations conducted by authority of this Act unless expressly authorized by the commission after due consideration of the circumstances and determination by the commission that such measures are necessary to carry out the purposes of this Act. No investigations of licensees or any other actions against licensees shall be initiated on the basis of anonymous complaints whether in writing or otherwise but shall be initiated only upon the commission's own motion or a verified written complaint. Upon the adoption of such motion by the commission or upon receipt of such complaint, the licensee shall be notified promptly and in writing unless the commission itself, after due consideration, determines otherwise. Provided, however, that the commission shall have the right and may, upon majority vote, rule that an order revoking, cancelling, or suspending a license be probated upon reasonable terms and conditions determined by the commission.

Licensees Not to Practice Law

Section 16. (a) **A license granted under the provisions of this Act shall be suspended or revoked by the commission on proof that the licensee, not being licensed and authorized to practice law in this state, for a consideration,** reward, pecuniary benefit, present or anticipated, direct or indirect, or in connection with or as a part of his employment, agency, or fiduciary relationship as a licensee, drew a deed, note, deed of trust, will, or other written instrument that may transfer or anywise affect the title to or an interest in land, except as provided in the subsections below, or advised or counseled a person as to the validity or legal sufficiency of an instrument or as to the validity of title to real estate.

(b) Notwithstanding the provisions of this Act or any other law, **the completion of contract forms** which bind the sale, exchange, option, lease, or rental of any interest in real property **by a real estate broker or salesman incident to the performance of the acts of a broker** as defined by this article **does not constitute the unauthorized or illegal practice of law in this state, provided the forms have been promulgated for use by the Texas Real Estate Commission** for the particular kind of transaction involved, or the forms have been prepared by an attorney at law licensed by this state and approved by said attorney for the particular kind of transaction involved, or the forms have been prepared by the property owner or prepared by an attorney and required by the property owner.

Broker-Lawyer Committee

(c) A Texas Real Estate Broker-Lawyer Committee is hereby created which, in addition to other powers and duties delegated to it, shall draft and revise contract forms capable of standardization for use by real estate licenses and which will expedite real estate transactions and reduce controversies to a minimum while containing safeguards adequate to protect the interests of the principals to the transaction.

(d) **The Texas Real Estate Broker-Lawyer Committee shall have 12 members including six members appointed by the Texas Real Estate Commission and six members of the State Bar of Texas** appointed by the President of the State Bar of Texas. The members of the committee shall hold office for staggered terms of six years with the terms of two commission appointees and two State Bar appointees expiring every two years. Each member shall hold office until his successor is appointed. A vacancy for any cause shall be filled for the expired term by the agency making the original appointment. Appointments to the committee shall be made without regard to race, creed, sex, religion, or national origin.

(e) In the best interest of the public the commission may adopt rules and regulations requiring real estate brokers and salesmen to use contract forms which have been prepared by the Texas Real Estate Broker-Lawyer Committee and promulgated by the Texas Real Estate Commission; provided, however, that **the Texas Real Estate Commission shall not prohibit a real estate broker or salesman from using a contract form or forms binding the sale, exchange, option, lease, or rental of any interest in real property which have been prepared by the property owner or prepared by an attorney and required by the property owner.** For the purpose of this section, contract forms prepared by the Texas Real Estate Broker-Lawyer Committee appointed by the commission and the State Bar of Texas and promulgated by the commission prior to the effective date of this Act shall be deemed to have been prepared by the Texas Real Estate Broker-Lawyer Committee. **The commission may suspend or revoke a license issued under the provisions of this article when it has determined that the licensee failed to use a contract form as required by the commission pursuant to this section.**

Hearings before Suspensions

Section 17. (a) **Before a license is suspended or revoked, the licensee is entitled to a public hearing.** The commission shall prescribe the time and place of the hearing. However, the hearing shall be held, if the licensee so desires, within the county where the licensee has his principal place of business, or if the licensee is a nonresident, the hearing may be called for and held in any county within this state. **The notice calling the hearing shall recite the allegations** against the licensee and the notice may be served personally or by mailing it by certified mail to the licensee's last known business address, as reflected by the commission's records, **at least 10 days prior to the date set for the hearing. In the hearing, all witnesses shall be duly sworn and stenographic notes of the proceedings shall be taken and filed as a part of the records in the case.** A party to the proceeding desiring it shall be furnished with a copy of the stenographic notes on the payment to the commission of a fee of $1.50 per page plus applicable sales tax and postage. After a hearing, the commission shall enter an order based on its findings of fact adduced from the evidence presented.

(b) The commission may issue subpoenas for the attendance of witnesses and the production of records or documents. The process issued by the commission may extend to all parts of the state, and the process may be served by any person designated by the commission. The person serving the process shall receive compensation to be allowed by the commission, not to exceed the fee prescribed by law for similar services. A witness subpoenaed who appears in a proceeding before the commission shall receive the same fees and mileage allowances as allowed by law, and the fees and allowances shall be taxed as part of the cost of the proceedings.

(c) If, in a proceeding before the commission, a witness fails or refuses to attend on subpoena issued by the commission, or refuses to testify, or refuses to produce a record or document, the production of which is called for by the subpoena, the attendance of the witness and the giving of his testimony and the production of the documents and records shall be enforced by a court of competent jurisdiction of this state in the same manner as the attendance, testimony of witnesses, and production of records are enforced in civil cases in the courts of this state.

(d) If a hearing relating to the denial, suspension, or revocation of a license under this Act is conducted by the administrator or assistant administrator, the applicant for the license or the licensee who is adversely affected by the decision of the administrator or assistant administrator is entitled to request a rehearing by the commission itself on making a timely motion for the rehearing.

Appeal to Courts

Section 18. (a) A person aggrieved by a ruling, order, or decision of the commission has the right to appeal to a district court in the county where the hearing was held within 30 days from the service of notice of the action of the commission.

(b) The appeal having been properly filed, the court may request of the commission, and the commission on receiving the request shall within 30 days prepare and transmit to the court, a certified copy of its entire record in the matter in which the appeal has been taken. The appeal shall be tried in accordance with Texas Rules of Civil Procedure.

(c) In the event an appeal is taken by a licensee or applicant, the appeal does not act as a supersedeas unless the court so directs, and the court shall dispose of the appeal and enter its decision promptly.

(d) If an aggrieved person fails to perfect an appeal as provided in this section, the commission's ruling becomes final.

Listing Forms

Section 18A. (a) Any listing contract form adopted by the commission relating to the contractual obligations between a seller of real estate and a real estate broker or salesman acting as an agent for the seller shall include a section that informs the parties to the contract that real estate commissions are negotiable.

(b) When appropriate to the form, it shall include a section explaining the availability of Texas coastal natural hazards information important to coastal residents.

Complaint Procedures

Section 18B. (a) If a person files a complaint with the commission relating to a real estate broker or salesman, the commission shall furnish to the person an explanation of the remedies that are available to the person under this Act and information about appropriate state or local agencies or officials with which the person may file a complaint. The commission shall furnish the same explanation and information to the person against whom the complaint is filed.

(b) The commission shall keep an information file about each complaint filed with the commission.

(c) If a written complaint is filed with the commission relating to a real estate broker or salesman, the commission, at least as frequently as quarterly and until the complaint is finally resolved, shall inform the complainant and the person against whom the complaint is filed of the status of the complaint.

Licensed Real Estate Inspectors

Section 18C. (a) For purposes of this section, the following definitions shall apply:

(1) **"Real Estate Inspector"** means a person or persons who hold themselves out to the public as being trained and qualified to inspect improvements to real property, including structural items and/or equipment and systems, and who

accept employment for the purpose of performing such an inspection for a buyer or seller of real property.

(2) **"Real Estate Inspection"** means a written or oral opinion as to the condition of improvements to real property, including structural items and/or equipment and systems.

(3) **"Commission"** means the Texas Real Estate Commission.

(4) **"Core Real Estate Inspection Courses"** means educational courses approved by the commission, including, but not limited to, electrical, mechanical, plumbing, roofing, and structural courses of study.

(b) The commission shall promulgate and prescribe the following rules and regulations:

(1) the application forms and requirements for original and renewal licenses;

(2) the method and content of examinations administered under this section; and

(3) the fees for original and renewal license application as provided by Subsection (f) of this section and a fee for each licensing examination as provided by Subsection (f) of this section.

(c) **A person may not act or attempt to act as a real estate inspector in this state for a buyer or seller of real property unless the person possesses a real estate inspector license issued under this section.** To be eligible for a license, an applicant must be an individual, a citizen of the United States or a lawfully admitted alien and a resident of this state for at least 60 days immediately preceding the filing of an application. The applicant must be at least 18 years old and must satisfy the commission as to the applicant's honesty, trustworthiness, integrity, and competency. **An applicant for an original real estate inspector license must submit satisfactory evidence to the commission of successful completion of not less than ninety classroom hours of core real estate inspection courses.** The commission shall determine the competency of an applicant solely on the basis of the examination required by Subsection (g) of this section. An applicant must file an application for a license with the commission on a form prescribed by the commission.

(d) The commission shall issue a real estate inspector license to an applicant who possesses the required qualifications, passes the appropriate licensing examination, pays the examination fee and original license application fee required by this section, and pays the fee required by Subdivision (2) of Subsection (1) of this section.

(e) **A license issued under this section expires one year after the date it is issued.** To renew a license, the licensee must submit a renewal application to the commission before the expiration date of the license. The renewal application must be on a form prescribed by the commission, and must be accompanied by the renewal fee. The commission shall notify the licensee of the expiration date of the license and the amount of the renewal fee. The notice shall be mailed not later than the 30th day before the expiration date. A licensee shall notify the commission within 30 days after a change of place of business and pay the applicable fee provided by subsection (f) of this section.

(f) The commission shall charge and collect reasonable and necessary fees to administer this section as follows:

(1) a fee not to exceed $150 for the filing of an original application for a license as a real estate inspector.

(2) a fee not to exceed $200 for the annual license renewal of a real estate inspector.

(3) a fee not to exceed $50 for taking a license examination;

(4) a fee not to exceed $20 for a request for a change of place of business

or to replace a lost or destroyed license. All fees paid to the commission shall be by cashier's check or money order.

(g) The commission shall prescribe the licensing examination, which shall be prepared by or contracted for by the commission. A licensing examination shall evaluate competency in the subject matter of all required core real estate inspection courses. **The licensing examination shall be offered not less often than once every two months in Austin.** If a license applicant fails the examination, the applicant may apply for reexamination by filing a request with the commission and paying the examination fee. **Each license applicant must satisfy the examination requirement not later than six months after the date on which the license application is filed.** A license applicant who fails to satisfy the examination requirement within six months after the date on which the license application is filed must submit a new license application with the commission and pay the examination fee to be eligible for examination.

Revocation, Suspension or Denial of Real Estate Inspector License

(h) **A violation of this section or a rule adopted under this section is a ground for denial, suspension, or revocation of a license** under this section. Proceedings for the denial, suspension, or revocation of a license and appeals from those proceedings are governed by the Administrative Procedure and Texas Register Act (Article 6252-13a, Vernon's Texas Civil Statutes.)

(i) **A real estate inspector licensed under this section may not:**

(1) **accept an assignment for real estate inspection if the employment or fee is contingent on the reporting of a specific, predetermined condition of the improvements to real property or is contingent on the reporting of specific findings** other than those known by the inspector to be facts at the time of accepting such **assignment;** or

(2) **act in a manner or engage in a practice that is dishonest or fraudulent or that involves deceit or misrepresentation;** or

(3) **perform a real estate inspection in a negligent or incompetent manner;** or

(4) **act in the dual capacity of real estate inspector and undisclosed principal in a transaction;** or

(5) **act in the dual capacity of real estate inspector and real estate broker or salesman;** or

(6) perform or agree to **perform any repairs or maintenance in connection with a real estate inspection pursuant to the provisions of any earnest money contract, lease agreement, or exchange of real estate;** or

(7) **perform a real estate inspection pursuant to a written contract for inspection which does not contain the following statement in the contract** for inspection in at least 10-point bold type above or adjacent to the signature of the purchaser of the real estate inspection, to wit:

> "NOTICE: YOU THE BUYER HAVE OTHER RIGHTS AND REMEDIES UNDER THE TEXAS DECEPTIVE TRADE PRACTICES-CONSUMER PROTECTION ACT WHICH ARE IN ADDITION TO ANY REMEDY WHICH MAY BE AVAILABLE UNDER THIS CONTRACT. FOR MORE INFORMATION CONCERNING YOUR RIGHTS, CONTACT THE CONSUMER PROTECTION DIVISION OF THE ATTORNEY GENERAL'S OFFICE, YOUR LOCAL DISTRICT OR COUNTY ATTORNEY, OR THE ATTORNEY OF YOUR CHOICE."

(8) **violate the rules adopted by the commission, or any provisions of this section.**

(j) **A person commits an offense if the person knowingly or intentionally engages in the business of real estate inspecting without a license** under this section or performs an inspection during a period in which the inspector's license is revoked or suspended. An offense under this subsection is a Class B misdemeanor.

(k) This section does not apply to any electrician, plumber, carpenter, any person engaged in the business of structural pest control in compliance with the Texas Structural Pest Control Act (Article 135b-6, Vernon's Texas Civil Statutes), or any other person who repairs, maintains, or inspects improvements to real property and who does not hold himself or herself out to the public through personal solicitation or public advertising as being in the business of inspecting such improvements. It is further provided that the provisions of this section shall not be construed so as to prevent any person from performing any and all acts which said person is authorized to perform pursuant to a license issued by the State of Texas or any governmental Subdivision thereof.

Real Estate Inspection Recovery Fund

(1)(1) The commission shall establish a **real estate inspection recovery fund** which shall be set apart and maintained by the commission as provided in this subsection. The fund shall be used in the manner provided in this subsection for **reimbursing aggrieved persons who suffer actual damages by reason of certain acts committed by a duly licensed real estate inspector,** provided the real estate inspector was licensed by the State of Texas at the time the act was committed and provided recovery is ordered by a court of competent jurisdiction against the real estate inspector. The use of the fund as provided in Subdivision (1) of this subsection is limited to an act that is a violation of either Subsection (i) (3), (4), (5), (6), or (7), of this section.

(2) After the effective date of this section, when a person receives notice that he has successfully completed the licensing examination provided by Subsection (g) of this section, he shall pay, in addition to any other fees required by this section, **a fee of $250,** which shall be deposited in the real estate inspection recovery fund prior to the commission issuing such person a real estate inspector license.

(3) If on December 31 of any year the balance remaining in the real estate inspection recovery fund is less than $50,000, each real estate inspector, on renewal of his license during the following calendar year, shall pay, in addition to his license renewal fee, a fee of $100, which shall be deposited in the real estate inspection recovery fund, or a pro rata share of the amount necessary to bring the fund to $75,000, whichever is less.

(4)(A) No action for a judgment which subsequently results in an order for collection from the real estate inspection recovery fund shall be started later than two years from the accrual of the cause of action. When an aggrieved person commences action for a judgment which may result in collection from the real estate inspection recovery fund, the real estate inspector shall notify the commission in writing to this effect at the time of the commencement of the action.

(B) When an aggrieved person recovers a valid judgment in a court of competent jurisdiction against a real estate inspector, on the grounds described in Subdivision (1) of this subsection that occurred on or after January 1, 1986, the aggrieved person may, after final judgment has been entered, execution returned nulla bona, and a judgment lien perfected, file a verified claim in the court in which the judgment was entered and, on twenty days written notice to the commission, and to the judgment debtor, may apply to the court where the judgment was rendered for an order directing payment out of the real estate inspection recovery fund of the amount unpaid on the judgment, subject to the limitation stated in Subdivision (9) of this subsection.

(C) The court shall proceed on the application forthwith. On the hearing on the application, the aggrieved person is required to show:

(i) that the judgment is based on the facts allowing recovery under Subdivision (1) of this subsection;

(ii) that he is not a spouse of the debtor, or the personal representative of the spouse, and he is not a real estate inspector as defined by this section;

(iii) that he has obtained a judgment as set out in Subdivision (4)(B) of this subsection, stating the amount of the judgment and the amount owing on the judgment at the date of the application;

(iv) that based on the best information available, the judgment debtor lacks sufficient attachable assets to satisfy the judgment; and

(v) the amount that may be realized from the sale of real or personal property or other assets liable to be sold or applied in satisfaction of the judgment and the balance remaining due on the judgment after application of the amount that may be realized.

(D) The court shall make an order to the commission requiring payment out of the real estate inspection recovery fund of whatever sum it finds to be payable on the claim, pursuant to and in accordance with the limitations contained in this subsection, if the court is satisfied, on the hearing, of the truth of all matters required to be shown by the aggrieved person by Subdivision (4)(C) of this subsection and that the aggrieved person has satisfied all of the requirements of Subdivisions (4)(B) and (C) of this subsection.

(E) A license granted under the provisions of this section shall be revoked by the commission on proof that the commission has made a payment from the real estate inspection recovery fund of any amount toward satisfaction of a judgment against a licensed real estate inspector. **No real estate inspector is eligible to receive a new license until he has repaid in full, plus interest at the current legal rate, the amount paid from the real estate recovery fund on his account.** A discharge in bankruptcy shall not relieve a person from the penalties and disabilities provided in this subsection.

(5) The sums received by the real estate commission for deposit in the real estate inspection recovery fund shall be held by the commission in trust for carrying out the purpose of the real estate inspection fund. These funds may be invested and reinvested in the same manner as funds of the Employees Retirement System of Texas, and the interest from these investments shall be deposited to the credit of the real estate inspection recovery fund, provided, however, that no investments shall be made which will impair the necessary liquidity required to satisfy judgment payments awarded pursuant to this subsection.

(6) When the commission receives notice of entry of a final judgment in a hearing as scheduled under Subdivision (4)(C) of this subsection, the commission may notify the attorney general of Texas of its desire to enter an appearance, file a response, appear at the court hearing, defend the action, or take whatever other action it deems appropriate on behalf of, and in the name of, the defendant, and take recourse through any appropriate method of review on behalf of, and in the name of, the defendant. In taking such action the commission and the attorney general shall act only to protect the fund from spurious or unjust claims or to ensure compliance with the requirements for recovery under this subsection.

(7) When, on the order of the court, the commission has paid from the real estate inspection recovery fund any sum to the judgment creditor, the commission shall be subrogated to all of the rights of the judgment creditor to the extent of the amount paid. The judgment creditor shall assign all his right, title, and interest in the judgment up to the amount paid by the commission which amount shall have priority for repayment in the event of any subsequent recovery on the judgment. Any amount in interest recovered by the commission on the judgment shall be deposited to the fund.

(8) The failure of an aggrieved person to comply with the provisions of this subsection relating to the real estate inspection recovery fund shall constitute a waiver of any rights under this subsection.

(9)(A) Notwithstanding any other provision, payments from the real estate inspection recovery fund are subject to the conditions and limitations in paragraphs (B) through (D) of this Subdivision.

(B) Payments may be made only pursuant to an order of a court of competent jurisdiction, as provided in Subdivision (4) of this subsection, and in the manner prescribed by this subsection.

(C) Payments for claims, including attorneys' fees, interest, and court costs, arising out of the same transaction shall be limited in the aggregate to $7,500 regardless of the number of claimants.

(D) Payments for claims based on judgments against any one licensed real estate inspector may not exceed in the aggregate $15,000 until the fund has been reimbursed by the licensee for all amounts paid.

(10) Nothing contained in this subsection shall limit the authority of the commission to take disciplinary action against a licensee for a violation of this section or the rules and regulations of the commission nor shall the repayment in full of all obligations to the real estate inspection recovery fund by a licensee nulify or modify the effect of any other disciplinary proceeding brought pursuant to this section.

(11) Any person receiving payment out of the real estate inspection recovery fund pursuant to Subdivision (9) of this subsection shall be entitled to receive reasonable attorney's fees as determined by the court, subject to the limitations stated in Subdivision (9) of this subsection.

(m) A person is not required to be licensed under this section to engage in the business of real estate inspecting until January 1, 1986. During the interim period between the effective date of this section and January 1, 1986, registration of real estate inspectors is covered by the law in effect on August 31, 1985, and that law is continued in effect for that purpose until midnight on December 31, 1985, at which time it shall cease to be operative.

Unlicensed Activity

Section 19. (a) A person acting as a real estate broker or real estate salesman without first obtaining a license is guilty of a misdemeanor and on conviction shall be punishable by a fine of not less than $100 nor more than $500, or by imprisonment in the county jail for a term not to exceed one year, or both; and if a corporation, shall be punishable by a fine of not less than $1,000 nor more than $2,000. A person, on conviction of a second or subsequent offense, shall be punishable by a fine of not less than $500 nor more than $1,000, or by imprisonment for a term not to exceed two years, or both; and if a corporation, shall be punishable by a fine of not less than $2,000 nor more than $5,000.

(b) In case a person received money, or the equivalent thereof, as a fee, commission, compensation, or profit by or in consequence of a violation of Subsection (a) of this section, he shall, in addition, be liable to a penalty of not less than the amount of the sum of money so received and not more than three times the sum so received, as may be determined by the court, which penalty may be recovered in a court of competent jurisdiction by an aggrieved person.

(c) When in the judgment of the Commission a person has engaged, or is about to engage, in an act or practice which constitutes or will constitute a violation of a provision of this Act, the county attorney or district attorney in the county in which the violation has occurred or is about to occur, or in the county of the defendant's residence, or the attorney general may **maintain an action in the name** of the State of Texas in the district court of such county to abate and temporarily and permanently enjoin the acts and practices and to enforce compliance with this Act. The plaintiff in an action under this subsection is not required to give a bond, and court costs may not be adjudged against the plaintiff.

Requirements for Compensation

Section 20. (a) A person may not bring or maintain an action for the collection of compensation for the performance in this state of an act set forth in Section 2 of this Act without alleging and proving that the person performing the brokerage services was a duly-licensed real estate broker or salesman at the time the alleged services were commenced, or was a duly-licensed attorney at law in this state or in any other state.

(b) An action may not be brought in a court in this state for the recovery of a commission for the sale or purchase of real estate unless the promise or agreement on which the action is brought, or some memorandum thereof, is in writing and signed by the party to be charged or signed by a person lawfully authorized by him to sign it.

(c) When an offer to purchase real estate in this state is signed, the real estate broker or salesman shall advise the purchaser or purchasers, in writing, that the purchaser or purchasers should have the abstract covering the real estate which is the subject of the contract examined by an attorney of the purchaser's own selection, or that the purchaser or purchasers should be furnished with or obtain a policy of title insurance. Failure to advise the purchaser as provided in this subsection precludes the payment of or recovery of any commission agreed to be paid on the sale.

APPENDIX B: §537.11 OF TREC REGULATIONS

This regulation of the Texas Real Estate Commission was created to help licensees avoid the unauthorized practice of law. With the assistance of the State Bar of Texas (the agency that monitors the activities of lawyers in Texas) TREC defines some of the parameters of permissible law-related brokerage activities. This rule should be read carefully and the licensee should check periodically with TREC to determine if the rule has been amended.

(a) Standard Contract Form TREC 2-2 is promulgated for use as an addendum only to another promulgated standard contract form. Standard Contract Form TREC 9-1 is promulgated for use in the sale of unimproved property where intended use is for one to four family residences. Standard Contract Form TREC 10-1 [10-0] is promulgated for use as an addendum concerning sale of other property by a buyer to be attached to promulgated forms of contracts. Standard Contract Form TREC 11-1 [11-0] is promulgated for use as an addendum to be attached to promulgated forms of contracts which are second or back-up contracts. Standard Contract Form TREC 12-0 is promulgated for use as an addendum to be attached to promulgated forms of contracts where there is a Veterans Administration release of liability or restoration entitlement. Standard Contract Form TREC 13-0 is promulgated for use as an addendum concerning new home insulation to be attached to promulgated forms of contracts. Standard Contract Form TREC 14-0 is promulgated for use as an addendum concerning financing conditions to be attached to promulgated contracts where there is a conventional loan. Standard Contract Form TREC 15-1 is promulgated for use as a residential lease when a seller temporarily occupies property after closing. Standard Contract Form TREC 16-1 is promulgated for use as a residential lease when a buyer temporarily occupies property prior to closing. Standard Contract Form TREC 20-0 is promulgated for use in the resale of residential real estate where there is all cash or owner financing, an assumption of an existing loan or a conventional loan. Standard Contract Form TREC 21-0 is promulgated for use in the resale of residential real property where there is a Veterans Administration guaranteed loan or a Federal Housing Administration insured loan. Standard Contract Form TREC 23-0 is promulgated for use in the sale of a new home where construction is incomplete. Standard Contract Form 24-0 is promulgated for use in the sale of a new home where construction is completed. Standard Contract Form 25-0 is promulgated for use in the sale of a farm or ranch. Standard Contract Form 26-0 is promulgated for use as an addendum concerning seller financing. Forms approved or promulgated by the commission shall be reproduced from numbered proofs obtained from the commission from printed copies made from proofs obtained from the commission, or from legible photocopies made from such proofs or printed copies. The control number of each proof must appear on all forms reproduced from the proof. Forms shall not be reproduced by means of word processors, computers, optical scanners, or other similar devices or machines. When reproducing a form, additions or changes are prohibited, except that brokers, organizations, or printing services may add their name and/or logo at the top of the form itself. Also, the real estate broker's name may be inserted on the front page of the form in the blank space provided after the words "broker's fee" and the broker's name and license number may be printed in the signature section on the back page.

(b) When negotiating contracts binding the sale, exchange, option, lease, or rental or any interest in real property, a real estate licensee shall use only those contract forms promulgated by the Texas Real Estate Commission for that kind of transaction with the following exceptions:

(1) transactions in which the licensee is functioning solely as a principal, not as an agent;

(2) transactions in which an agency of the United States government requires a different form to be used.

(3) transactions for which a contract form has been prepared by the property owner or prepared by an attorney and required by the property owner.

(4) transactions for which no standard contract form has been promulgated by the Texas Real Estate Commission, and the licensee uses a form prepared by an attorney at law licensed by this state and approved by the attorney for the particular kind of transactions involved or prepared by the Texas Real Estate Broker-Lawyer Committee and made available for trial use by licensees with the consent of the Texas Real Estate Commission.

(c) A licensee shall not practice law, offer, give nor attempt to give advice, directly, or indirectly; he shall not act as a public conveyancer nor give advice or opinions as to the legal effect of any contracts or other such instruments which may affect the title to real estate; he shall not give opinions concerning the status or validity of title to real estate; and he shall not attempt to prevent nor in any manner whatsoever discourage any principal to a real estate transaction from employing a lawyer. However, nothing herein shall be deemed to limit the licensee's fiduciary obligation to disclose to his principals all pertinent facts which are within the knowledge of the licensee, including such facts which might affect the status of or title to real estate.

(d) A licensee shall not undertake to draw or prepare documents fixing and defining the legal rights of the principals to a transaction. However, in negotiating real estate transactions, the licensee may fill in forms for such transactions using, except as otherwise permitted by these rules exclusively, those printed forms which have been approved and promulgated by the Texas Real Estate Commission as the required standard forms to be used by all real estate licensees. When filling in such a form, the licensee may only fill in the blanks provided and may not add to or strike matter from such form, except that licensees shall add factual statements and business details desired by the principals and shall strike only such matter as is desired by the principals and as is necessary to conform the instrument to the intent of the principals. Nothing herein shall be deemed to prevent the licensee from explaining to the principals the meaning of the factual statements and business details contained in the said instrument so long as the licensee does not offer or give legal advice. It is not the practice of law as defined in this Act for a real estate licensee to complete a contract form which is either promulgated by the Texas Real Estate Commission or prepared by the Texas Real Estate Broker-Lawyer Committee and made available for trial use by licensees with the consent of the Texas Real Estate Commission. Contract forms prepared by the Texas Real Estate Broker-Lawyer Committee for trial use may be used on a voluntary basis after being approved by the commission. Contract forms prepared by the Texas Real Estate Broker-Lawyer Committee and approved by the commission to replace previously promulgated forms may be used by licensees on a voluntary basis prior to the effective date of rules requiring use of the replacement forms.

(e) Where it appears that, prior to the execution of any such instrument, there are unusual matters involved in the transaction which should be resolved by legal counsel before the instrument is executed or that the instrument is to be acknowledged and filed for record, the licensee shall advise the principals that each should consult a lawyer of his choice before executing same.

(f) A licensee shall not employ, directly or indirectly, a lawyer nor pay for the services of a lawyer to represent any principal to a real estate transaction in which he, the licensee, is acting as an agent. The licensee may also employ and pay for the services of a lawyer to represent only the licensee in a real estate transaction, including preparation of the contract, agreement, or other legal instruments to be executed by the principals to the transaction.

(g) A broker shall advise the principals that the instrument they are about to execute is binding on them.

APPENDIX C: ADDITIONAL FORMS APPROVED BY TREC

02-08-85

RESIDENTIAL EARNEST MONEY CONTRACT (RESALE)
FHA INSURED OR VA GUARANTEED FINANCING

PROMULGATED BY TEXAS REAL ESTATE COMMISSION

NOTICE: Not For Use For Condominium Transactions

1. PARTIES: _____ (Seller) agrees to sell
and convey to _____ (Buyer) and Buyer
agrees to buy from Seller the property described below.

2. PROPERTY: Lot _____, Block _____, _____
Addition, City of _____, _____ County, Texas, known as
_____(Address); or as described on attached exhibit, together
with the following items, if any: curtains and rods, draperies and rods, valances, blinds, window shades, screens, shutters, awnings, wall-to-wall carpeting, mirrors
fixed in place, ceiling fans, attic fans, mail boxes, television antennas, permanently installed heating and air conditioning units and equipment, built-in security
and fire detection equipment, lighting and plumbing fixtures, water softener, trash compactor, garage door openers with controls, shrubbery and all other property
owned by Seller and attached to the above described real property. All property sold by this contract is called the "Property".

3. CONTRACT SALES PRICE:
   A. Cash payable at closing .... $_____
   B. Sum of all financing described below excluding any VA Funding Fee or FHA Mortgage Insurance Premium (MIP) .... $_____
   C. Sales Price payable to Seller on Loan funding after closing (Sum of A and B) .... $_____

4. FINANCING: (Check applicable boxes below)
   ☐ A. FHA INSURED FINANCING:
   This contract is subject to approval for Buyer of a Section _____ FHA Insured Loan (the Loan) of not less than $_____,
   amortizable monthly for not less than _____ years, with interest not to exceed _____% per annum for the first _____ year(s) of
   the Loan.
   As required by HUD-FHA, if FHA valuation is unknown, "It is expressly agreed that, notwithstanding any other provisions of this contract, the Purchaser
   (Buyer) shall not be obligated to complete the purchase of the Property described herein or to incur any penalty by forfeiture of Earnest Money deposits
   or otherwise unless the Seller has delivered to the Purchaser (Buyer) a written statement issued by the Federal Housing Commissioner setting forth the
   appraised value of the Property (excluding closing costs and MIP) of not less than $_____, which statement the Seller hereby agrees
   to deliver to the Purchaser (Buyer) promptly after such appraised value statement is made available to the Seller. The Purchaser (Buyer) shall, however,
   have the privilege and option of proceeding with the consummation of this contract without regard to the amount of the appraised valuation made by the
   Federal Housing Commissioner. The appraised valuation is arrived at to determine the maximum mortgage the Department of Housing and Urban
   Development will insure. HUD does not warrant the value or the condition of the property. The purchaser should satisfy himself/herself that the price and
   the condition of the property are acceptable."
   If the FHA appraised value of the Property (excluding closing costs and MIP) is less than the Sales Price (3C above), Seller may reduce the Sales Price
   to an amount equal to the FHA appraised value (excluding closing costs and MIP) and the parties to the sale shall close the sale at such lower Sales Price
   with appropriate adjustments to 3A and 3B above.

   ☐ B. VA GUARANTEED FINANCING:
   This contract is subject to approval for Buyer of a _____
   (type loan) VA guaranteed loan (the Loan) of not less than $_____, amortizable monthly for not less than _____ years,
      ☐ 1. with interest at maximum rate allowable at time of loan funding if the Loan is a fixed rate loan or
      ☐ 2. with interest not to exceed _____% per annum for the first _____ year(s) of the Loan if such loan is not fixed rate.
   VA NOTICE TO BUYER: "It is expressly agreed that, notwithstanding any other provisions of this contract, the Buyer shall not incur any penalty by
   forfeiture of earnest money or otherwise or be obligated to complete the purchase of the Property described herein, if the contract purchase price or cost
   exceeds the reasonable value of the Property established by the Veterans Administration. The Buyer shall, however, have the privilege and option of
   proceeding with the consummation of this contract without regard to the amount of the reasonable value established by the Veterans Administration."
   If Buyer elects to complete the purchase at an amount in excess of the reasonable value established by VA, Buyer shall pay such excess amount in cash
   from a source which Buyer agrees to disclose to the VA and which Buyer represents will not be from borrowed funds except as approved by VA. If VA
   reasonable value of the Property is less than the Sales Price (3C above), Seller may reduce the Sales Price to an amount equal to the VA reasonable value
   and the parties to the sale shall close at such lower Sales Price with appropriate adjustments to 3A and 3B above.

   ☐ C. TEXAS VETERANS' HOUSING ASSISTANCE PROGRAM LOAN:
   This contract is also subject to approval for Buyer of a Texas Veterans' Housing Assistance Program Loan (the Program Loan) in an amount of
   $_____ for a period of at least _____ years at the interest rate established by the Texas Veterans' Land Board at the time
   of closing.
   NOTE: Describe special terms of any non-fixed rate loan in Paragraph 11.

   Buyer shall apply for all loan(s) within _____ days from the effective date of this contract and shall make every reasonable effort to obtain approval.
   Such financing shall have been approved when Buyer has satisfied all of lender's financial conditions. e.g., sale of other property, requirements of a co-signer or
   financial verification. If all loan approvals have not been secured by the Closing Date, this contract shall terminate and Earnest Money shall be refunded to Buyer.

5. EARNEST MONEY: $_____ is herewith tendered by Buyer and is to be deposited as Earnest Money with _____
   _____ at _____ (Address) as Escrow Agent, upon execution
   of the contract by both parties. ☐ Additional Earnest Money of $_____ shall be deposited by Buyer with the Escrow Agent on or
   before _____, 19____.

6. TITLE: Seller shall furnish to Buyer at Seller's expense either:
   ☐ A. Owner's Policy of Title Insurance (the Title Policy) issued by _____in
   the amount of the Sales Price and dated at or after closing: OR

   ☐ B. Abstracts of Title certified by an abstract company (1) from the sovereignty to the effective date of this contract (Complete Abstract) and (2) supplemented
   to the Closing Date (Supplemental Abstract).

   NOTICE TO SELLER AND BUYER: AS REQUIRED BY LAW, Broker advises Buyer that Buyer should have the Abstract covering the Property examined by an
   attorney of Buyer's selection, or Buyer should be furnished with or obtain a Title Policy. If a Title Policy is to be obtained, Buyer should obtain a Commitment for
   Title Insurance (the Commitment) which should be examined by an attorney of Buyer's choice at or prior to closing. If the Property is situated in a Utility District,
   Section 50.301 Texas Water Code requires the Buyer to sign and acknowledge the statutory notice from Seller relating to the tax rate and bonded indebtedness of
   the District.

001

FHA or VA Residential Earnest Money Contract — Page Two   02-08-85

7. PROPERTY CONDITION: (Check A or B)

☐ A. Buyer accepts the Property in its present condition, subject only to FHA or VA required repairs and _____
_____

☐ B. Buyer requires inspections and repairs required by the FHA or VA and the Property Condition Addendum attached hereto.

On Seller's receipt of all loan approvals and inspection reports, Seller shall commence repairs and termite treatment required of Seller by the contract, any lender and the Property Condition Addendum, if any, and complete such repairs prior to closing. Seller's responsibility for the repairs, termite treatment and repairs to termite damage shall not exceed $_____. If Seller fails to complete such repairs, Buyer may do so and Seller shall be liable up to the amount specified and the same paid from the proceeds of the sale. If the repair costs will exceed the stated amount and Seller refuses to pay such excess, Buyer may (1) pay the additional cost or (2) accept the Property with the limited repairs unless such repairs are required by FHA/VA or (3) Buyer may terminate this contract and the Earnest Money shall be refunded to Buyer. Buyer shall make his election within three (3) days after Seller notifies Buyer of Seller's refusal to pay such excess. Failure of Buyer to make such election within the time provided shall be deemed to be Buyer's election to accept the Property with the limited repairs as permitted by FHA/VA, and the sale shall be closed as scheduled. (NOTE: If VA Buyer pays additional costs of repairs, Buyer may be paying in excess of the VA Certificate of Reasonable Value.)

If the repair costs will exceed five (5) percent of the Sales Price of the Property and Seller agrees to pay the cost of such repairs, Buyer shall have the option of closing the sale with the completed repairs, or terminating the sale and the Earnest Money shall be refunded to Buyer. Buyer shall make this election within three (3) days after Seller notifies Buyer of Seller's willingness to pay the cost of such repairs that exceed five (5) percent of the Sales Price. Failure of Buyer to make such election within the time provided shall be deemed to be Buyer's election to close the sale with the completed repairs.

Broker(s) and sales associates have no responsibility or liability for inspections or repairs made pursuant to this contract.

8. BROKER'S FEE: _____, Listing Broker, and any Co-Broker represent Seller unless otherwise specified herein. Seller agrees to pay Listing Broker the fee specified by separate agreement between Listing Broker and Seller. Escrow Agent is authorized and directed to pay Listing Broker's fee from the sale proceeds at closing.

9. CLOSING: The closing of the sale shall be on or before _____, 19_____, or within seven (7) days after objections to title have been cured, whichever date is later (the Closing Date); however, if financing approval has been obtained pursuant to Paragraph 4, the Closing Date shall be extended daily up to fifteen (15) days if necessary to complete loan requirements. If either party fails to close this sale by the Closing Date, the non-defaulting party shall be entitled to execute the remedies contained in Paragraph 16 immediately and without notice.

10. POSSESSION: The possession of the Property shall be delivered to Buyer on _____ in its present or required improved condition, ordinary wear and tear excepted. Any possession by Buyer prior to or Seller after closing that is not authorized by the Buyer's Temporary Residential Lease or Seller's Temporary Residential Lease forms promulgated by the Texas Real Estate Commission shall establish a landlord-tenant at sufferance relationship between the parties.

11. SPECIAL PROVISIONS: (Insert factual statements and business details applicable to this sale.)

12. SALES EXPENSES TO BE PAID AT OR PRIOR TO CLOSING:

A. Loan appraisal fee shall be paid by _____

B. (1) FHA Sale: The total of the loan discount and any buydown fees shall not exceed $_____ of which Buyer shall pay the first $_____ and Seller shall pay the remainder.

(2) VA Sale: The total of the loan discount and buydown fees shall not exceed $_____ which shall be paid by Seller.

C. Seller's Expenses: (1) FHA or VA required repairs and any other inspections, reports or repairs required of Seller herein and in the Property Condition Addendum (2) releases of existing loans, including prepayment penalties and recordation; tax statements; preparation of deed; ½ of escrow fee (3) expenses VA prohibits Buyer to pay (e.g., preparation of loan documents, copies of restrictions, photos, excess cost of survey, remaining ½ of escrow fee) (4) any Texas Veterans' Housing Assistance Program Participation Fee (5) other expenses stipulated to be paid by Seller under other provisions of this contract.

D. Buyer's Expenses: Interest on the note(s) from date of disbursement to one (1) month prior to date of first monthly payment, expenses stipulated to be paid by Buyer under other provisions of this contract and any customary Texas Veterans' Housing Assistance Program Loan costs for Buyers.

(1) FHA Buyer: (a) All prepaid items required by applicable HUD-FHA or other regulations (e.g., required premiums for flood and hazard insurance, reserve deposits for other insurance, ad valorem taxes and special governmental assessments) (b) expenses incident to any loan (e.g., ½ of escrow fee, preparation of loan documents, survey, recording fees, copies of restrictions and easements, amortization schedule, Mortgagee's Title Policy, loan origination fee, credit reports, photos) (c) loan related inspection fees.

(2) VA Buyer: (a) All prepaid items (e.g., required premiums for flood and hazard insurance, reserve deposits for other insurance, ad valorem taxes and special governmental assessments) (b) expenses incident to any loan (e.g., credit reports, recording fees, Mortgagee's Title Policy, loan origination fee, that portion of survey cost VA Buyer may pay by VA Regulation) (c) loan related inspection fees.

E. The VA Loan Funding Fee or FHA Mortgage Insurance Premium (MIP) in the amount of $_____ is to be paid by _____.

If paid by Buyer, it is to be [   ] paid in cash at closing [   ] added to the amount of the loan to the extent permitted by lender. If financed, the amount is to be added to the loan amount in Paragraph 3-B by lender but is not part of the Contract Sales Price.

F. If any sales expenses exceed the maximum amount herein stipulated to be paid by either party, either party may terminate this contract unless the other party agrees to pay such excess. In no event shall Buyer pay charges and fees expressly prohibited by FHA/VA Regulations.

13. PRORATIONS: Taxes, flood and hazard insurance (at Buyer's option), any rents and maintenance fees shall be prorated through the Closing Date. If Buyer elects to continue Seller's insurance policy, it shall be transferred at closing.

14. TITLE APPROVAL:

A. If abstract is furnished, Seller shall deliver Complete Abstract to Buyer within twenty (20) days from the effective date hereof. Buyer shall have twenty (20) days from date of receipt of Complete Abstract to deliver a copy of the examining attorney's title opinion to Seller, stating any objections to title, and only objections so stated shall be considered.

B. If Title Policy is furnished, the Title Policy shall guarantee Buyer's title to be good and indefeasible subject only to (1) restrictive covenants affecting the Property (2) any discrepancies, conflicts or shortages in area or boundary lines, or any encroachments, or any overlapping of improvements (3) taxes for the current and subsequent years and subsequent assessments for prior years due to a change in land usage or ownership (4) existing building and zoning ordinances (5) rights of parties in possession (6) liens created as security for the sale consideration (7) utility easements common to the platted subdivision of which this Property is a part and (8) reservations or other exceptions contained in the Deed or permitted by the terms of this contract. Exceptions permitted in the Deed and zoning ordinances shall not be valid objections to title. If the Title Policy will be subject to exceptions other than those recited above in sub-paragraphs (1) through (7) inclusive, Seller shall deliver to Buyer the Commitment and legible copies of any documents creating such exceptions that are not recited in sub-paragraphs (1) through (7) above at least five (5) days prior to closing. If Buyer has objection to any such previously undisclosed exceptions, Buyer shall have five (5) days after receipt of such Commitment and copies to make written objections to Seller. If no Title Commitment is provided to Buyer at or prior to closing, it will be conclusively presumed that Seller represented at closing that the Title Policy would not be subject to exceptions other than those recited above in sub-paragraphs (1) through (7).

C. In either instance if title objections are raised, Seller shall have fifteen (15) days from the date such objections are disclosed to cure the same, and the Closing Date shall be extended accordingly. If the objections are not satisfied by the extended closing date, this contract shall terminate and the Earnest Money shall be refunded to Buyer, unless Buyer elects to waive the unsatisfied objections and complete the purchase.

D. Seller shall furnish tax statements showing no delinquent taxes, a Supplemental Abstract when applicable, showing no additional title exceptions and a General Warranty Deed conveying title subject only to liens securing payment of debt created as part of the consideration, taxes for the current year, restrictive covenants and utility easements common to the platted subdivision of which the Property is a part, and reservations and conditions permitted by this contract or otherwise acceptable to Buyer. Each note shall be secured by vendor's and deed of trust liens. In case of dispute as to the form of the deed, forms prepared by the State Bar of Texas shall be used.

001

TREC NO. 21-0

FHA or VA Residential Earnest Money Contract concerning _____ Page Three 02-08-85
(Address of Property)

15. CASUALTY LOSS: If any part of Property is damaged or destroyed by fire or other casualty loss, Seller shall restore the same to its previous condition as soon as reasonably possible, but in any event by Closing Date. If Seller is unable to do so without fault, Buyer may terminate this contract and the Earnest Money shall be refunded to Buyer.

16. DEFAULT: If Buyer fails to comply herewith, Seller may either (a) enforce specific performance and seek such other relief as may be provided by law or (b) terminate this contract and receive the Earnest Money as liquidated damages. If Seller is unable without fault, within the time herein required, to (a) make any non-casualty repairs or (b) deliver the Commitment or (3) deliver the Complete Abstract, Buyer may either terminate this contract and receive the Earnest Money as the sole remedy or extend the time for performance up to fifteen (15) days and the Closing Date shall be extended pursuant to other provisions of this contract. If Seller fails to comply herewith for any other reason, Buyer may either (a) enforce specific performance hereof and seek such other relief as may be provided by law or (b) terminate this contract and receive the Earnest Money, thereby releasing Seller from this contract.

17. ATTORNEY'S FEES: Any signatory of this contract, Broker or Escrow Agent who is the prevailing party in any legal proceeding brought under or with relation to this contract or transaction shall be additionally entitled to recover court costs and reasonable attorney fees from the nonprevailing party.

18. ESCROW: The Earnest Money is deposited with Escrow Agent with the understanding that Escrow Agent (a) is not a party to this contract and does not assume or have any liability for performance or non-performance of any signatory (b) has the right to require from all signatories a written release of liability of the Escrow Agent which authorizes the disbursement of the Earnest Money (c) is not liable for interest or other charge on the funds held and (d) is not liable for any losses of escrow funds caused by the failure of any banking institution in which such funds have been deposited, unless such banking institution is acting as Escrow Agent. If any signatory unreasonably fails to deliver promptly the document described in (b) above, then such signatory shall be liable to the other signatories as provided in Paragraph 17. At closing, the Earnest Money shall be applied first to any cash down payment required, then to Buyer's closing costs and any excess refunded to Buyer. Any refund or payment of the Earnest Money under this contract shall be reduced by the amount of any actual expenses incurred on behalf of the party receiving the Earnest Money, and Escrow Agent will pay the same to the creditors entitled thereto.

19. REPRESENTATIONS: Seller represents that as of the Closing Date there will be no unrecorded liens, assessments or Uniform Commercial Code Security Interests against any of the Property which will not be satisfied out of the Sales Price. If any representation in this contract is untrue on the Closing Date, this contract may be terminated by Buyer and the Earnest Money shall be refunded to Buyer. All representations contained in this contract shall survive closing.

20. AGREEMENT OF PARTIES: This contract contains the entire agreement of the parties and cannot be changed except by their written consent. Texas Real Estate Commission promulgated addenda which are part of this contract are: (list) _____

_____

21. NOTICES: All notices shall be in writing and effective when delivered at the addresses shown below.

22. CONSULT YOUR ATTORNEY: The Broker cannot give you legal advice. This is intended to be a legally binding contract. READ IT CAREFULLY. Federal law may impose certain duties upon Brokers or Signatories to this contract when any of the signatories is a foreign party, or when any of the signatories receives certain amounts of U.S. currency in connection with a real estate closing. If you do not understand the effect of any part of this contract, consult your attorney BEFORE signing.

SELLER'S   BUYER'S
ATTORNEY: _____   ATTORNEY: _____

EXECUTED in multiple originals effective the _____ day of _____, 19____ (**BROKER: FILL IN THE DATE OF FINAL ACCEPTANCE.**)

_____   _____
Buyer   Seller

_____   _____
Buyer   Seller

_____   _____
Buyer's Address   Phone No.   Seller's Address   Phone No.

AGREEMENT BETWEEN BROKERS

Listing Broker agrees to pay _____. Co-Broker,
a fee of _____ of the total sales price when the Broker's fee described in Paragraph 8 is received. Escrow Agent is authorized and directed to pay Co-Broker from Listing Broker's fee at closing.

_____   _____
Co-Broker   License No.   Listing Broker   License No.

By: _____   By: _____

_____   _____
Co-Broker's Address   Phone No.   Listing Broker's Address   Phone No.

EARNEST MONEY RECEIPT

Receipt of $_____ Earnest Money is acknowledged in the form of _____

_____

Escrow Agent _____   By: _____

Date: _____, 19____

The form of this contract has been approved by the Texas Real Estate Commission. Such approval relates to this contract form only. No representation is made as to the legal validity or adequacy of any provision in any specific transaction. It is not suitable for complex transactions. Extensive riders or additions are not to be used. (02-85) TREC NO. 21-0. This form replaces TREC NO. 2-0 and NO. 3-0.   001

02-08-85

UNIMPROVED PROPERTY EARNEST MONEY CONTRACT

This Contract Is Limited To Transactions Where Intended Use Is For One To Four Family Residences

PROMULGATED BY TEXAS REAL ESTATE COMMISSION

1. PARTIES: _____ (Seller) agrees to
    sell and convey to _____ (Buyer) and Buyer
    agrees to buy from Seller the property described below.

2. PROPERTY: Lot _____, Block _____, _____ Addition,
    City of _____, _____, County, Texas, or as described on attached exhibit (the Property).

3. CONTRACT SALES PRICE:

    A. Cash payable at closing .... $_____
    B. Sum of all financing described in Paragraph 4 below .... $_____
    C. Sales Price (Sum of A and B) .... $_____

4. FINANCING: (Check applicable boxes below)

    ☐ A. ALL CASH: This is an all cash sale; no financing is involved.
    ☐ B. ASSUMPTION:

        (1) Buyer's assumption of the unpaid principal balance of a first lien promissory note payable to _____
             in present monthly installments of $_____, including principal, interest and any reserve deposits, with Buyer's first installment payment
             being payable on the first installment payment date after closing, the assumed principal balance of which at closing will be $_____.
        (2) Buyer's assumption of the unpaid principal balance of a second lien promissory note payable to _____
             in present monthly installments of $_____, including principal, interest and any reserve deposits, with Buyer's first installment payment
             being payable on the first installment payment date after closing, the assumed principal balance of which at closing will be $_____.
        Buyer's assumption of an existing note includes all obligations imposed by the deed of trust securing the note.
        If the total principal balance of all assumed loans varies in an amount greater than $350.00 at closing either party may terminate this contract and the Earnest
        Money shall be refunded to Buyer. If the noteholder on assumption (a) requires Buyer to pay an assumption fee in excess of $_____ in
        B(1) above or $_____ in B(2) above and Seller declines to pay such excess or (b) raises the existing interest rate above _____ %
        in B(1) above or _____ % in B(2) above, Buyer may terminate this contract and the Earnest Money shall be refunded to Buyer. The cash payable at
        closing shall be adjusted by the amount of any variance in the loan balance(s) shown above.
        NOTICE TO BUYER: Monthly payments, interest rates or other terms of some loans may be adjusted after closing. Before signing the contract, examine the
        notes and deeds of trust to determine the possibility of future adjustments.

    ☐ C. THIRD PARTY FINANCED:
        ☐ 1. A third party first lien note of $_____, due in full in _____ year(s), payable in initial monthly payments of principal
              and interest not exceeding $_____ for the first _____ year(s) of the loan.
        ☐ 2. A third party second lien note of $_____, due in full in _____ year(s), payable in initial monthly payments of principal
              and interest not exceeding $_____ for the first _____ year(s) of the loan.
        NOTICE TO PARTIES: Before signing this contract Buyer is advised to determine the financing options from lenders. Certain loans have variable rates of
        interest, some have monthly payments which may not be sufficient to pay the accruing interest, and some have interest rate "buydowns" which reduce the
        rate of interest for part or all of the loan term at the expense of one or more of the parties to the contract.

    ☐ D. SELLER FINANCED: A promissory note from Buyer to Seller in the amount of $_____, bearing _____ % interest per annum,
          and payable:
        ☐ 1. In one payment due _____ after the date of the note with interest payable _____.
        ☐ 2. In installments of $_____ [   ] including interest [   ] plus interest beginning _____
              after the date of the note and continuing at _____ intervals thereafter for _____ year(s) when the entire balance of the
              note shall be due and payable.
        ☐ 3. Interest only in _____ installments for the first _____ year(s) and thereafter in installments of $_____
              [   ] including interest [   ] plus interest beginning _____ after the date of the note and continuing at _____
              intervals thereafter for _____ year(s) when the entire balance of the note is due and payable.
        ☐ 4. This contract is subject to Buyer furnishing Seller evidence of good credit within _____ days from the effective date of this contract. If notice
              of disapproval of Buyer's credit is not given within five (5) days thereafter, Seller shall be deemed to have approved Buyer's credit. Buyer hereby
              authorizes Buyer's credit report to be furnished to Seller.
              Any Seller financed note may be prepaid in whole or in part at any time, without penalty. The lien securing payment of such note will be inferior to any
              lien securing any loan assumed or given in connection with third party financing. If an Owner's Policy of Title Insurance is furnished, Buyer shall furnish
              Seller with a Mortgagee's Title Policy.
        Buyer shall apply for all third party financing or noteholder's approval of Buyer for assumption and waiver of the right to accelerate the note within _____
        days from the effective date of this contract and shall make every reasonable effort to obtain the same. Such financing or assumption shall have been approved when
        Buyer has satisfied all of lender's financial conditions, e.g., sale of other property, requirement of co-signer or financial verifications. If such financing
        or noteholder's approval and waiver is not obtained within _____ days from the effective date hereof, this contract shall terminate and the Earnest Money
        shall be refunded to Buyer.

5. EARNEST MONEY: $_____ is herewith tendered by Buyer and is to be deposited as Earnest Money with
    _____, at _____ (Address),
    as Escrow Agent, upon execution of the contract by both parties. ☐ Additional Earnest Money of $_____ shall be deposited by Buyer with
    the Escrow Agent on or before _____, 19____.

6. TITLE: Seller shall furnish to Buyer at Seller's expense either:
    ☐ A. Owner's Policy of Title Insurance (the Title Policy) issued by _____
          in the amount of the Sales Price and dated at or after closing: OR
    ☐ B. Abstracts of Title certified by an abstract company (1) from the sovereignty to the effective date of this contract (Complete Abstract) and (2) supplemented
          to the Closing Date (Supplemental Abstract).
    NOTICE TO SELLER AND BUYER: AS REQUIRED BY LAW, Broker advises Buyer that Buyer should have an Abstract covering the Property examined by an
    attorney of Buyer's selection, or Buyer should be furnished with or obtain a Title Policy. If a Title Policy is to be obtained, Buyer should obtain a Commitment for
    Title Insurance (the Commitment) which should be examined by an attorney of Buyer's choice at or prior to closing. If the Property is situated in a Utility District,

Farm and Ranch Earnest Money Contract — Page Two 05-22-87

4. FINANCING: (Check applicable boxes below)

☐ A: ALL CASH: This is an all cash sale; no financing is involved.

☐ B. ASSUMPTION:

☐ (1) Buyer's assumption of the unpaid balance of a first lien promissory note payable to ______ ______ dated ______, the unpaid principal balance of which at closing will be $ ______ (including the face amount of any lender required stock), and those obligations imposed by the Deed of Trust recorded in Volume ______, Page ______ of the Real Property Records in the county where the Property is situated. Buyer's initial payment shall be the first payment due after closing.

☐ (2) Buyer's assumption of the unpaid balance of a second lien promissory note payable to ______ ______ dated ______, the unpaid principal balance of which at closing will be $______ (including the face amount of any lender required stock), and those obligations imposed by the Deed of Trust recorded in Volume ______, Page ______ of the Real Property Records in the county where the Property is situated. Buyer's initial payment shall be the first payment due after closing.

If any assumed loan initially required the purchase of lender's stock, the sale of the Property shall include such stock.

If the total unpaid principal balance of all assumed loans varies in an amount greater than $500.00 at closing, either party may terminate this contract and the Earnest Money shall be refunded to Buyer. If the noteholder on assumption (a) requires Buyer to pay an assumption fee in excess of $ ______ in B(1) above or $ ______ in B(2) above and Seller declines to pay such excess or (b) raises the existing interest rate above ______% in B(1) above or ______% in B(2) above, Buyer may terminate this contract and the Earnest Money shall be refunded to Buyer. The cash payable at closing shall be adjusted by the amount of any variance in the loan balance(s) shown above.

☐ C. THIRD PARTY FINANCING:

☐ (1) A third party first lien note of $______ (including the face amount of any lender required stock) payable at ______ intervals for not less than ______ years with the initial interest rate not to exceed ______% per annum.

☐ (2) A third party second lien note of $______ (including the face amount of any lender required stock) payable at ______ intervals for not less than ______ years with the initial interest rate not to exceed ______% per annum.

☐ D. SELLER FINANCING: A promissory note from Buyer to Seller of $ ______, bearing ______% interest per annum, and payable:

☐ (1) In one payment due ______ after the date of the note with interest payable ______.

☐ (2) In installments of $ ______ ☐ including interest ☐ plus interest beginning ______ ______ after the date of the note and continuing at ______ intervals thereafter for ______ years when the entire balance of the note shall be due and payable.

☐ (3) Interest only in ______ installments for the first ______ years and thereafter in installments of $______ ☐ including interest ☐ plus interest beginning ______ after the date of the note and continuing at ______ intervals thereafter for ______ year(s) when the entire balance of the note shall be due and payable.

☐ (4) This contract is subject to Buyer furnishing Seller evidence of good credit within ______ days from the effective date of this contract. If notice of disapproval of Buyer's credit is not given within five (5) days thereafter, Seller shall be deemed to have approved Buyer's credit. Buyer hereby authorizes Buyer's credit report to be furnished to Seller.

Any Seller financed note may be prepaid in whole or in part at any time without penalty. The lien securing payment of such note will be inferior to any lien securing any loan assumed or given in connection with third party financing described above. If an Owner's Policy of Title Insurance is furnished, Buyer shall furnish Seller with a Mortgagee's Title Policy.

Buyer shall apply for all third party financing or noteholder's approval of Buyer for assumption and waiver of the right to accelerate the note within ______ days from the effective date of this contract and shall make every reasonable effort to obtain the same. Such financing or assumption shall have been approved when Buyer has satisfied all of lender's financial conditions, e.g., requirement of sale of other property, co-signer or financial verifications. If such financing or noteholder's approval and waiver is not obtained within ______ days from the effective date hereof, this contract shall terminate and the Earnest Money shall be refunded to Buyer.

NOTICE TO BUYER: Loan payments, interest rates or other terms of some loans may be adjusted after closing. Before signing the contract, examine the notes and deeds of trust to determine the possibility of future adjustments.

5. EARNEST MONEY: Buyer shall deposit the sum of $______ as Earnest Money with ______ at ______ (location), as Escrow Agent, upon execution of the contract by both parties. If Buyer fails to deposit the Earnest Money, Seller may terminate this contract.

6. TITLE: Seller shall furnish to Buyer at Seller's expense either:

☐ A. Owner's Policy of Title Insurance (the Title Policy) issued by ______ in the amount of the Sales Price and dated at or after closing; OR

☐ B. Abstracts of Title certified by an abstract company (1) from the sovereignty to the effective date of this contract (Complete Abstract) and (2) supplemented to the closing date (Supplemental Abstract).

NOTICE TO SELLER AND BUYER: AS REQUIRED BY LAW. Broker advises Buyer that Buyer should have an Abstract covering the Property examined by an attorney of Buyer's selection, or Buyer should be furnished with or obtain a Title Policy. If a Title Policy is to be obtained, Buyer should obtain a Commitment for Title Insurance (the Commitment) which should be examined by an attorney of Buyer's choice at or prior to closing. If the Property is situated in a Utility District, Section 50.301, Texas Water Code requires the Buyer to sign and acknowledge the statutory notice from Seller relating to the tax rate and bonded indebtedness of the District. If the Property is situated seaward of the Gulf Intracoastal Waterway, attach an addendum containing the statement required by Section 61.025, Texas Natural Resources Code.

7. PROPERTY CONDITION: (Check A or B)

☐ A. Buyer accepts the Property in its present condition, subject only to any lender required repairs and ______ ______.

☐ B. Buyer requires inspections and repairs required by any lender and the Property Condition Addendum attached hereto.

On Seller's receipt of all loan approvals and inspection reports, Seller shall commence repairs and termite treatment required of Seller in A or B above (including the Property Condition Addendum, if any) and complete such repairs prior to closing. Seller's responsibility for the repairs, termite treatment and repairs to termite damage shall not exceed $______. If Seller fails to complete such repairs, Buyer may do so and Seller shall be liable up to the amount specified and the same paid from the proceeds of the sale. If the repair costs will exceed the stated amount and Seller refuses to pay such excess, Buyer may (1) pay the additional cost (if permitted by lender) or (2) accept the Property with the limited repairs (if permitted by lender) or (3) Buyer may terminate this contract and the Earnest Money shall be refunded to Buyer. Buyer shall make his election within three (3) days after Seller notifies Buyer of Seller's refusal to pay such excess. Failure of Buyer to make such election within the time provided shall be deemed to be Buyer's election to accept the Property with the limited repairs, and the sale shall be closed as scheduled; however, if lender prohibits Buyer's payment of additional cost or acceptance with the limited repairs, this contract shall terminate and the Earnest Money shall be refunded to Buyer.

If all the repair costs will exceed two (2) percent of the Sales Price of the Property and Seller agrees to pay the cost of such repairs, Buyer shall have the option of closing the sale with the completed repairs, or terminating this contract and the Earnest Money shall be refunded to Buyer. Buyer shall make this election within three (3) days after Seller notifies Buyer of Seller's willingness to pay the cost of such repairs. Failure of Buyer to make such election within the time provided shall be deemed to be Buyer's election to close the sale with the completed repairs.

Broker(s) and sales associates have no responsiblity or liability for inspections or repairs made pursuant to this contract.

INITIALED FOR IDENTIFICATION BY BUYER ______ ______ AND SELLER ______

007 TREC No. 25-0

Unimproved Property Earnest Money Contract — Page Two 02-08-85

Section 50.301 Texas Water Code requires the Buyer to sign and acknowledge the statutory notice from Seller relating to the tax rate and bonded indebtedness of the District.

7. PROPERTY CONDITION: Buyer accepts the Property in its present condition, subject only to ______ ______.

8. BROKER'S FEE: ______, Listing Broker, and any Co-Broker represent Seller unless otherwise specified herein. Seller agrees to pay Listing Broker the fee specified by separate agreement between Listing Broker and Seller. If there is no separate agreement, Seller agrees to pay Listing Broker in ______ County, Texas, on consummation of this sale or on Seller's default a total cash fee of ______ of the Total Sales Price or upon Buyer's default, one half of the Earnest Money paid to Seller not to exceed the amount of cash fee. Escrow Agent is authorized and directed to pay Listing Broker said fee from the sale proceeds.

9. CLOSING: The closing of the sale shall be on or before ______, 19____, or within seven (7) days after objections to title have been cured, whichever date is later (the Closing Date); however, if financing or assumption approval has been obtained pursuant to Paragraph 4, the Closing Date shall be extended daily up to fifteen (15) days if necessary to complete loan requirements. If either party fails to close this sale by the Closing Date, the non-defaulting party shall be entitled to exercise the remedies contained in Paragraph 15 immediately and without notice.

10. POSSESSION: The possession of the Property shall be delivered to Buyer at closing.

11. SPECIAL PROVISIONS: (Insert factual statements and business details applicable to this sale.)

12. SALES EXPENSES TO BE PAID IN CASH AT OR PRIOR TO CLOSING:

A. Loan appraisal fees shall be paid by ______.

B. The total of the loan discount and buydown fees shall not exceed $ ______ of which Buyer shall pay the first $ ______ and Seller shall pay the remainder.

C. Seller's Expenses: Prepayment penalties on any existing loans paid at closing, plus cost of releasing such loans and recording releases; tax statements; ½ of any escrow fee; preparation of deed; preparation and recording of any deed of trust to secure assumption; other expenses stipulated to be paid by Seller under other provisions of this contract.

D. Buyer's Expenses: Application, origination and commitment fees; private mortgage insurance premiums and any loan assumption fee; expenses incident to new loan(s) (e.g., preparation of any note, deed of trust and other loan documents, survey [unless stipulated to be paid by Seller in Paragraph 20], recording fees, copies of restrictions and easements, Mortgagee's Title Policies, credit reports, photos); ½ of any escrow fee; any required reserve deposits for ad valorem taxes and special governmental assessments; interest on all monthly installment payment notes from date of disbursements to one (1) month prior to dates of first monthly payments; expenses stipulated to be paid by Buyer under other provisions of this contract.

E. If any sales expenses exceed the maximum amount herein stipulated to be paid by either party, either party may terminate this contract unless the other party agrees to pay such excess.

13. PRORATIONS AND TAXES: Interest on any assumed loan, current taxes, any rents and maintenance fees shall be prorated through the Closing Date. If ad valorem taxes for the year in which the sale is closed are not available on the Closing Date, proration of taxes shall be made on the basis of taxes assessed in the previous year.

If this sale or Buyer's use of the Property after closing results in the assessment of additional taxes for periods prior to closing, such additional taxes shall be the obligation of the Buyer and such obligation shall survive closing. If Seller's change in use of the Property prior to closing or denial of a special use valuation claimed by Seller results in the assessment of additional taxes for periods prior to closing, such additional taxes shall be the obligation of Seller, and such obligation shall survive closing.

14. TITLE APPROVAL:

A. If abstract is furnished, Seller shall deliver Complete Abstract to Buyer within twenty (20) days from the effective date hereof. Buyer shall have twenty (20) days from date of receipt of Complete Abstract to deliver a copy of the examining attorney's title opinion to Seller, stating any objections to title, and only objections so stated shall be considered.

B. If Title Policy is furnished, the Title Policy shall guarantee Buyer's title to be good and indefeasible subject only to (1) restrictive covenants affecting the Property (2) any discrepancies, conflicts or shortages in area or boundary lines, or any encroachments, or any overlapping of improvements (3) taxes for the current and subsequent years and subsequent assessments for prior years due to a change in land usage or ownership (4) existing building and zoning ordinances (5) rights of parties in possession (6) liens created or assumed as security for the sale consideration (7) utility easements common to the platted subdivision of which this Property is a part and (8) reservations or other exceptions permitted by the terms of this contract. Exceptions permitted in the Deed and zoning ordinances shall not be valid objections to title. If the Title Policy will be subject to exceptions other than those recited above in sub-paragraphs (1) through (7) inclusive, Seller shall deliver to Buyer the Commitment and legible copies of any documents creating such exceptions that are not recited in sub-paragraphs (1) through (7) above at least five (5) days prior to closing. If Buyer has objection to any such previously undisclosed exceptions, Buyer shall have five (5) days after receipt of such Commitment and copies to make written objections to Seller. If no Title Commitment is provided to Buyer at or prior to closing, it will be conclusively presumed that Seller represented at closing that the Title Policy would not be subject to exceptions other than those recited above in sub-paragraphs (1) through (7).

C. In either instance if title objections are raised, Seller shall have fifteen (15) days from the date such objections are disclosed to cure the same, and the Closing Date shall be extended accordingly. If the objections are not satisfied by the extended closing date, this contract shall terminate and the Earnest Money shall be refunded to Buyer, unless Buyer elects to waive the unsatisfied objections and complete the purchase.

D. Seller shall furnish tax statements showing no delinquent taxes, a Supplemental Abstract when applicable, showing no additional title exceptions and a General Warranty Deed conveying title subject only to liens securing payment of debt created or assumed as part of the consideration, taxes for the current year, restrictive covenants and utility easements common to the platted subdivision of which the Property is a part and reservations and conditions permitted by this contract or otherwise acceptable to Buyer. Each note shall be secured by vendor's and deed of trust liens. A vendor's lien and deed of trust to secure assumption shall be required, which shall automatically be released on execution and delivery of a release by noteholder. If Seller is released from liability on any assumed note, the vendor's lien and deed of trust to secure assumption shall not be required. In case of dispute as to the form of the Deed, note(s), deed of trust or deed of trust to secure assumption, forms prepared by the State Bar of Texas shall be used.

15. DEFAULT: If Buyer fails to comply herewith, Seller may either (a) enforce specific performance and seek such other relief as may be provided by law or (b) terminate this contract and receive the Earnest Money as liquidated damages. If Seller is unable without fault, within the time herein required, to (a) deliver the Commitment or (b) deliver the Complete Abstract, Buyer may either terminate this contract and receive the Earnest Money as the sole remedy or extend the time for performance up to fifteen (15) days and the Closing Date shall be extended pursuant to other provisions of this contract. If Seller fails to comply herewith for any other reason, Buyer may either (a) enforce specific performance hereof and seek such other relief as may be provided by law or (b) terminate this contract and receive the Earnest Money, thereby releasing Seller from this contract.

16. ATTORNEY'S FEES: Any signatory to this contract, Broker or Escrow Agent who is the prevailing party in any legal proceeding brought under or with relation to this contract or transaction shall be additionally entitled to recover court costs and reasonable attorney fees from the non-prevailing party.

17. ESCROW: The Earnest Money is deposited with Escrow Agent with the understanding that Escrow Agent (a) is not a party to this contract and does not assume or have any liability for performance or non-performance of any signatory (b) has the right to require from all signatories a written release of liability of the Escrow Agent which authorizes the disbursement of the Earnest Money (c) is not liable for interest or other charge on the funds held and (d) is not liable for any losses of escrow funds caused by the failure of any banking institution in which such funds have been deposited, unless such banking institution is acting as Escrow Agent. If any signatory unreasonably fails to deliver promptly the documents described in (b) above, then such signatory shall be liable to the other signatories as provided in Paragraph 16. At closing, the Earnest Money shall be applied first to any cash down payment required, then to Buyer's closing costs and any excess refunded to Buyer. Any refund or payment of the Earnest Money under this contract shall be reduced by the amount of any actual expenses incurred on behalf of the party receiving the Earnest Money, and Escrow Agent will pay the same to the creditors entitled thereto.

18. REPRESENTATIONS: Seller represents that as of the Closing Date (a) there will be no unrecorded liens, assessments or Uniform Commercial Code Security Interests against any of the Property which will not be satisfied out of the Sales Price, unless securing payment of any loans assumed by Buyer and (b) that assumed loan(s) will be without default. If any representation above is untrue on the Closing Date this contract may be terminated by Buyer and the Earnest Money shall be refunded to Buyer. All representations contained in this contract shall survive closing.

001

TREC No. 9-1

Unimproved Property Earnest Money Contract concerning _____ Page Three 02-08-85
                                        (Address of Property)

19. USE AND UTILITIES: The intended use of the Property by Buyer is | | single family dwelling | | multiple family dwelling of _____units
| | mobile home. Utilities required at the Property for such use are | | water | | sanitary sewer | | gas | | electricity | | telephone
| | _____. If Buyer ascertains that applicable zoning ordinances, restrictions or governmental laws, rules or regula-
tions prevent such intended use or that such required utilities are not available, or that the Property is located within the 100 year flood plain as designated by the

appropriate governmental authority, and Buyer so notifies Seller within _____days from the effective date of this contract, then the same shall terminate
and the Earnest Money shall be refunded to Buyer; failure on the part of Buyer to give the notice within the required time shall constitute Buyer's acceptance of
the Property for Buyer's intended use.

20. SURVEY: | | required | | not required. If required, then within _____days from the effective date of this contract a current survey of the Property
shall be furnished by and at the expense of | | Seller | | Buyer by a mutually acceptable Registered Public Surveyor licensed by the State of Texas. A plat of
the survey together with any appropriate field notes shall be furnished to Seller and Buyer. The survey shall locate all improvements, encroachments and overlapping
of improvements on the Property, together with all easements and roadways adjoining or crossing the Property.

21. AGREEMENT OF PARTIES: This contract contains the entire agreement of the parties and cannot be changed except by their written agreement. Texas Real Estate
Commission promulgated addenda which are a part of this contract are (list): _____

22. NOTICES: All notices shall be in writing and effective when delivered at the addresses shown below.

23. CONSULT YOUR ATTORNEY: The Broker cannot give you legal advice. This is intended to be a legally binding contract. READ IT CAREFULLY. Federal law
may impose certain duties upon Brokers or Signatories to this contract when any of the signatories is a foreign party, or when any of the signatories receives certain
amounts of U.S. currency in connection with a real estate closing. If you do not understand the effect of any part of this contract, consult your attorney BEFORE
signing.

SELLER'S
ATTORNEY: _____   BUYER'S
                                               ATTORNEY: _____

EXECUTED in multiple originals effective the _____day of _____, 19_____ (BROKER: FILL IN THE DATE OF FINAL ACCEPTANCE.)

Buyer _____   Seller _____

Buyer _____   Seller _____

Buyer's Address _____ Phone No.   Seller's Address _____ Phone No.

AGREEMENT BETWEEN BROKERS

Listing Broker agrees to pay _____, Co-Broker,
a fee of _____of the total sales price when the Broker's fee described in Paragraph 8 is received. Escrow Agent is authorized and directed to pay
Co-Broker from Listing Broker's fee at closing.

Co-Broker _____ License No.   Listing Broker _____ License No.

By: _____   By: _____

Co-Broker's Address _____ Phone No.   Listing Broker's Address _____ Phone No.

EARNEST MONEY RECEIPT

Receipt of $_____ Earnest Money is acknowledged in the form of _____

Escrow Agent: _____   By: _____

Date: _____, 19_____.

The form of this contract has been approved by the Texas Real Estate Commission. Such approval relates to this contract
form only. No representation is made as to the legal validity or adequacy of any provision in any specific transactions. It is
not suitable for complex transactions. Extensive riders or additions are not to be used. (Rev. 02-85) TREC No. 9-1. This
form replaces TREC No. 9-0.

001

TREC No. 9-0.

05-22-87

FARM AND RANCH EARNEST MONEY CONTRACT
PROMULGATED BY TEXAS REAL ESTATE COMMISSION

1. PARTIES: _____ (Seller) agrees to sell
and convey to _____ (Buyer) and Buyer
agrees to buy from Seller the property described below.

2. PROPERTY: The land situated in _____ County, Texas, described as follows:

or as described on attached Exhibit, together with all improvements thereon and all rights, privileges and appurtenances pertaining thereto; including but not limited to,
water rights, claims and permits, easements, all rights, and obligations of applicable government programs and cooperative or association memberships; and the following
items, if any: curtains and rods, draperies and rods, valances, blinds, window shades, screens, shutters, awnings, wall-to-wall carpeting, mirrors fixed in place, ceiling fans,
attic fans, mail boxes, television antennas, permanently installed heating and air conditioning units and equipment, built-in security and fire detection equipment, lighting
and plumbing fixtures, water softener, trash compactor, garage door openers with controls, shrubbery and all other property owned by Seller and attached to the above
described real property. All property sold by this contract is called the "Property." The Property shall be subject, however, to the following exceptions, reservations,
conditions and restrictions (if none, insert "none"; insert recording data for recorded documents):

A. Minerals, royalties, and timber interests:
    (i) Presently outstanding in third parties:

    (ii) To be additionally retained by Seller:

B. Mineral Leases:

C. Surface Leases:

D. Easements:

E. Restrictions, Zoning Ordinances or Exceptions:

together with the following crops and equipment _____

3. CONTRACT SALES PRICE:
    A. Cash payable at closing. . . . . $_____
    B. 1. Sum of all financing described in Paragraph 4 below . . . . $_____
        2. Less: Face amount of any Lender required stock . . . . (_____)
        3. Difference between B1 and B2 . . . . $_____
    C. Sales Price (sum of A and B3) . . . . $_____
□   D. The Sales Price shall be adjusted, based on the survey required by Paragraph 20, and the number of acres over or under _____ acres
        shall be multiplied by $_____ per acre, and the product thereof shall be added to or subtracted from the Sales Price, and the cash amount set out in
        subparagraph 3A shall be adjusted accordingly; however, if the amount set out in subparagraph 3A is to be adjusted by more than 10%, either party may terminate this
        contract and the Earnest Money shall be refunded to Buyer.

INITIALED FOR IDENTIFICATION BY BUYER _____ AND SELLER _____

007   TREC No. 25-0

Farm and Ranch Earnest Money Contract — Page Three   05-22-87

8.   BROKER'S FEE: _____ (Broker) and any co-broker represent Seller unless otherwise specified herein. Seller agrees to pay Broker the fee specified by separate agreement between Broker and Seller. If there is no separate agreement,

Seller agrees to pay Broker in _____ County, Texas, on closing of this sale, or on termination of this contract by

agreement of the parties (except as permitted by the terms of this contract), or on Seller's default a total cash fee of _____ of the Total Sales Price or upon Buyer's default, one-half of any Earnest Money to which Seller is entitled under Paragraph 16 not to exceed the amount of the cash fee. Escrow Agent is authorized and directed to pay Broker said fee from the sales proceeds.

9.   CLOSING: The closing of the sale shall be on or before _____, 19 _____, or within seven (7) days after objections to title have been cured, whichever date is later (the Closing Date). If financing or assumption approval has been obtained pursuant to Paragraph 4, the Closing Date shall be extended daily up to fifteen (15) days if necessary to complete loan requirements. If either party fails to close this sale by the Closing Date, the non-defaulting party shall be entitled to exercise the remedies contained in Paragraph 16 immediately and without notice.

10. POSSESSION: The possession of the Property shall be delivered to Buyer on _____ in its present or required improved condition, ordinary wear and tear excepted. In the absence of a written lease, any possession by Buyer prior to closing or by Seller after closing, shall establish a landlord-tenant at sufferance relationship between the parties.

11. SPECIAL PROVISIONS: Insert factual statements and business details applicable to this sale. A licensee shall not add to a promulgated earnest money contract form factual statements or business details for which a contract addendum, lease or other form has been promulgated by TREC for mandatory use: 22 TAC §537.11(d).

12. SALES EXPENSES TO BE PAID IN CASH AT OR PRIOR TO CLOSING:

     A.   Loan appraisal fee shall be paid by _____

     B.   SELLER'S EXPENSES: Prepayment penalties on any existing loans paid at closing, plus cost of releasing such loans and recording releases; tax statements; ½ of any escrow fee; preparation of deed; preparation and recording of any deed of trust to secure assumption; other expenses stipulated to be paid by Seller under other provisions of this contract.

     C.   BUYER'S EXPENSES: Application, origination, processing, commitment and loan discount fees; private mortgage insurance premiums and any loan assumption fee; expenses incident to new loan(s) (e.g., preparation of any note, deed of trust and other loan documents, recording fees, copies of restrictions and easements, amortization schedule, Mortgagee's Title Policies, credit reports, photos and any lender's required stock); ½ of any escrow fee; any required reserve deposits for insurance premiums, ad valorem taxes and special governmental assessments; any prepaid interest required by lender to be paid at closing; expenses stipulated to be paid by Buyer under other provisions of this contract.

13. PRORATIONS AND ROLLBACK TAXES:

     A.   PRORATIONS: Insurance (at Buyer's option), interest on any assumed loan, current taxes, and any rents shall be prorated through the Closing Date. If ad valorem taxes for the year in which the sale is closed are not available on the Closing Date, proration of taxes shall be made on the basis of taxes assessed in the previous year.

     B.   ROLLBACK TAXES: If this sale or Buyer's use of the Property after closing results in the assessment of additional taxes for periods prior to closing, such additional taxes shall be the obligation of Buyer. If Seller's change in use of the Property prior to closing or denial of a special use valuation on the Property claimed by Seller results in the assessment of additional taxes for periods prior to closing, such additional taxes shall be the obligation of the Seller, and such obligation shall survive closing.

14. TITLE APPROVAL:

     A.   If abstract is furnished, Seller shall deliver Complete Abstract to Buyer within twenty (20) days from the effective date hereof. Buyer shall have twenty (20) days from date of receipt of Complete Abstract to deliver a copy of the examining attorney's title opinion to Seller stating any objections to title and only objections so stated shall be considered. However, the exceptions, reservations, conditions or restrictions set out and described in Paragraph 2 of this contract shall not be recited by Buyer as objections to title.

     B.   If Title Policy is furnished, the Title Policy shall guarantee Buyer's title to be as good and indefeasible subject only to (1) restrictive covenants affecting the Property (2) any discrepancies, conflicts or shortages in area or boundary lines, or any encroachments, or any overlapping of improvements (3) taxes for the current and subsequent years and subsequent assessments for prior years due to a change in land usage or ownership (4) existing building and zoning ordinances (5) rights of parties in possession (6) liens created as security for the sale consideration (7) utility easements common to the platted subdivision of which this Property is a part (8) exceptions, reservations, conditions or restrictions set out and described in Paragraph 2 of this contract and (9) any other reservations or exceptions permitted by the terms of this contract. If the Title Policy will be subject to exceptions other than those recited above in items (1) through (8) inclusive, Seller shall deliver to Buyer the Commitment and legible copies of any documents creating exceptions that are not recited in items (1) through (8) above at least five (5) days prior to closing. If Buyer has objection to any such previously undisclosed exceptions, or to any unrecorded easement or adverse condition with respect to the boundaries which are revealed by any survey of the Property, Buyer shall have five (5) days after receipt of such Commitment, copies, and survey to make written objections to Seller. If no Commitment is provided to Buyer at or prior to closing, it will be conclusively presumed that Seller represented at closing that the Title Policy would not be subject to exceptions other than those recited above in items (1) through (8).

     C.   In either instance if title objections are raised by Buyer or Title Company named in Paragraph 6A, Seller shall have fifteen (15) days from the date such objections are disclosed to cure the same, and the Closing Date shall be extended accordingly. If the objections are not timely cured, this contract shall terminate and the Earnest Money shall be refunded to Buyer, unless Buyer elects to waive the unsatisfied objections and complete the purchase.

     D.   Seller shall furnish tax statements showing no delinquent taxes; a Supplemental Abstract, when applicable, showing no additional title objections; and a General Warranty Deed conveying title subject only to liens securing payment of debt created or assumed as part of the consideration, taxes for the current year, restrictive covenants, easements, reservations and conditions set out in Paragraph 2 and any exceptions or reservations acceptable to Buyer. Each note shall be secured by vendor's and deed of trust liens. A vendor's lien and deed of trust to secure any assumption shall be required, which shall automatically be released on execution and delivery of a release by noteholder. If Seller is released from liability on any assumed note, the vendor's lien and deed of trust to secure assumption shall not be required. In case of dispute as to the form of the Deed, (and in Seller financed transactions, the note(s) and deed of trust to secure assumption), forms prepared by the State Bar of Texas shall be used.

15. CASUALTY LOSS: If any part of the Property is damaged or destroyed by fire or other casualty loss, Seller shall restore the same to its previous condition as soon as reasonably possible, but in any event by Closing Date. If Seller is unable to do so without fault, Buyer may terminate this contract and the Earnest Money shall be refunded to Buyer.

16. DEFAULT: If Buyer fails to comply herewith, Seller may either enforce specific performance and seek such other relief as may be provided by law or terminate this contract and receive the Earnest Money as liquidated damages, thereby releasing Buyer from this contract. If Seller is unable without fault, within the time herein required, to (a) make any non-casualty repairs or (b) deliver the Commitment or (c) deliver the Complete Abstract, Buyer may either terminate this contract and receive the Earnest Money as the sole remedy or extend the time for performance up to fifteen (15) days and the Closing Date shall be extended pursuant to other provisions of this contract. If Seller fails to comply herewith for any other reason, Buyer may either enforce specific performance hereof and seek such other relief as may be provided by law or terminate this contract and receive the Earnest Money, thereby releasing Seller from this contract.

INITIALED FOR IDENTIFICATION BY BUYER _____ AND SELLER _____

   TREC No. 25-0

Farm and Ranch Earnest Money Contract — Page Four

17. ATTORNEY'S FEES: Any party to this contract, Broker, co-broker or Escrow Agent who prevails in any legal proceeding brought under or with relation to this contract or transaction shall be additionally entitled to recover court costs and reasonable attorney's fees.

18. ESCROW: The Earnest Money is deposited with Escrow Agent with the understanding that Escrow Agent (a) is not a party to this contract and does not assume or have any liability for performance or non-performance of any party to this contract (b) has the right to require from all parties and brokers a written release of liability of the Escrow Agent which authorizes the disbursement of the Earnest Money (c) is not liable for interest or other charge on the funds held and (d) is not liable for any losses of escrow funds caused by the failure of any banking institution in which such funds have been deposited, unless such banking institution is acting as Escrow Agent. If any party or broker unreasonably fails to deliver promptly the document described in (b) above, then such party or broker shall be liable as provided in Paragraph 17. At closing, the Earnest Money shall be applied first to any cash down payment required, then to Buyer's closing costs and any excess refunded to Buyer. Any refund or payment of the Earnest Money under this contract shall be reduced by the amount of any actual expenses incurred on behalf of the party receiving the Earnest Money, and Escrow Agent shall pay the same to the creditors entitled thereto.

19. REPRESENTATIONS: Seller represents that as of the Closing Date (a) there will be no unrecorded liens, assessments or Uniform Commercial Code Security Interests against any of the Property which will not be satisfied out of the Sales Price, unless securing payment of any loans assumed by Buyer and (b) that assumed loan(s) will be without default. If any representation above is untrue on the Closing Date this contract may be terminated by Buyer and the Earnest Money shall be refunded to Buyer. All representations contained in this contract shall survive closing.

20. PROPERTY SURVEY:
    - ☐ A. No survey is required.
    - ☐ B. Seller shall furnish to Buyer Seller's existing survey of the Property dated _____, 19____.
      Such survey ☐ shall ☐ shall not be recertified to a date subsequent to the effective date of this contract at the expense of ☐ Seller ☐ Buyer within _____ days from the effective date of this contract.
    - ☐ C. A survey of the Property dated subsequent to the effective date of this contract which shall be furnished within _____ days from the effective date of this contract showing the location of the Property with respect to the original survey lines and showing the boundaries and visible conditions along the boundaries, perimeter fences, easements, rights of way, roadways, and computation of area, which shall be furnished by and at the expense of ☐ Seller ☐ Buyer by a mutually acceptable Registered Public Surveyor licensed by the State of Texas.

21. AGREEMENT OF PARTIES: This contract contains the entire agreement of the parties and cannot be changed except by their written agreement. Texas Real Estate Commission promulgated addenda which are part of this contract are: (list) _____
    _____
    _____

22. NOTICES: All notices shall be in writing and effective when delivered at the addresses shown below.

23. CONSULT YOUR ATTORNEY: The Broker cannot give you legal advice. This is intended to be a legally binding contract. READ IT CAREFULLY. If you do not understand the effect of any part of this contract, consult your attorney BEFORE signing. Federal law may impose certain duties upon brokers or parties to this contract when any party is a foreign party or when any party receives certain amounts of U.S. currency in connection with a real estate closing.

BUYER'S ATTORNEY: _____   SELLER'S ATTORNEY: _____

EXECUTED in multiple originals effective the _____ day of _____, 19____ **(BROKER: FILL IN THE DATE OF FINAL ACCEPTANCE.)**

_____   _____
Buyer   Seller

_____   _____
Buyer   Seller

Buyer's Address   Phone No.   Seller's Address   Phone No.

AGREEMENT BETWEEN BROKERS

Broker agrees to pay _____ (Co-Broker) a fee of _____ of the total sales price when the Broker's fee described in Paragraph 8 is received. Escrow Agent is authorized and directed to pay Co-Broker from Broker's fee at closing.

_____   _____
Co-Broker   License No.   Broker   License No.

By: _____   By: _____

Co-Broker's Address   Phone No.   Broker's Address   Phone No.

EARNEST MONEY RECEIPT

Receipt of $ _____ Earnest Money in the form of _____
is acknowledged and is accepted subject to the terms of the contract.

Escrow Agent: _____   By: _____

Date: _____, 19____.

The form of this contract has been approved by the Texas Real Estate Commission. Such approval relates to this contract form only. No representation is made as to the legal validity or adequacy of any provision in any specific transaction. It is not suitable for complex transactions. Extensive riders or additions are not to be used. (05-87)
TREC NO. 25-0.

007

2-16-84

NOTICE: Not For Use Where Seller Owns Fee Simple Title To Land Beneath Unit

RESIDENTIAL CONDOMINIUM EARNEST MONEY CONTRACT (RESALE)
ALL CASH, ASSUMPTION, THIRD PARTY CONVENTIONAL OR SELLER FINANCING

1. PARTIES: _____(Seller) agrees to sell
    and convey to _____(Buyer) and Buyer
    agrees to buy from Seller the property described below.

2. PROPERTY AND CONDOMINIUM DOCUMENTS:

    A. Condominium Unit _____, in Building _____, of _____
        a condominium project, located at _____(Address),
        City of _____ , _____County, Texas, described in the Condominium Declaration and Plat
        and any amendments thereto of record in said County; together with such Unit's undivided interest in the Common Elements designated by the Declaration,
        including those areas reserved as Limited Common Elements appurtenant to the Unit and such other rights to use the Common Elements which have been
        specifically assigned to the Unit in any other manner.
        The property shall include the following items, if any: curtains and rods, draperies and rods, valances, blinds, window shades, screens, shutters, awnings,
        wall-to-wall carpeting, mirrors fixed in place, ceiling fans, mail boxes, television antenna, permanently installed heating and air conditioning units and
        equipment, built-in security and fire detection equipment, lighting and plumbing fixtures, water softener, stove, trash compactor, garage door openers and all
        other personal property owned by Seller and attached to the Unit, or located in the Unit and given as collateral for any indebtedness which will remain in
        effect after closing. All property, interests and rights sold herein are called the "Property".
    B. The Declaration and Plat, Articles of Association or Incorporation, By-Laws, Restrictions, any Rules and Regulations and amendments thereto are called
        "Condominium Documents". (Check 1, 2 or 3):

        ☐ 1. Prior to signing this contract Buyer has received and approved a copy of the Condominium Documents and agrees to be bound thereby.

        ☐ 2. Buyer has received but not approved a copy of the Condominium Documents prior to signing this contract. Buyer shall have five (5) days after the
              effective date hereof to terminate this contract for any reason and the Earnest Money shall be refunded to Buyer.

        ☐ 3. Buyer has not received the Condominium Documents. Seller shall have five (5) days after the effective date hereof to deliver the Condominium
              Documents to Buyer or Buyer may terminate this contract and the Earnest Money shall be refunded to Buyer. Buyer shall have five (5) days after
              receipt of such documents to terminate this contract for any reason and the Earnest Money shall be refunded to Buyer.
        If Buyer does not give notice of termination as provided above, Buyer shall be deemed to have approved the Condominium Documents.
    C. The Certificate from the condominium owners association (the Association) described in Paragraph 20 herein is called the "Certificate". (Check 1, 2 or 3):

        ☐ 1. Buyer has received and approved a copy of the Certificate prior to signing this contract.

        ☐ 2. Buyer has received but not approved a copy of the Certificate prior to signing this contract. Buyer shall have five (5) days after the effective date hereof
              to terminate this contract for any reason and the Earnest Money shall be refunded to Buyer.

        ☐ 3. Buyer has not received the Certificate. Seller shall have five (5) days after the effective date hereof to deliver the Certificate to Buyer or Buyer may
              terminate this contract and the Earnest Money shall be refunded to Buyer. Buyer shall have five (5) days after receipt of such Certificate to terminate
              this contract for any reason and the Earnest Money shall be refunded to Buyer.
        If Buyer does not give notice of termination as provided above, Buyer shall be deemed to have approved the Certificate.

3. CONTRACT SALES PRICE:
    A. Cash payable at closing ....$_____
    B. Sum of all financing described in Paragraph 4 below ....$_____
    C. Sales Price payable to Seller (Sum of A and B) ....$_____

4. FINANCING CONDITIONS: (Check applicable box below)
    ☐ A. ALL CASH: This is an all cash sale; no financing is involved.
    ☐ B. ASSUMPTION:
          (1) Buyer's assumption of the unpaid principal balance of a first lien promissory note payable to _____
          _____in present monthly installments of $_____ , including principal,
          interest and any reserve deposits, with Buyer's first installment payment being payable on the first installment payment date after closing, the
          assumed principal balance of which at closing will be $_____
          (2) Buyer's assumption of the unpaid principal balance of a second lien promissory note payable to _____
          _____in present monthly installments of $_____ , including principal,
          interest and any reserve deposits, with Buyer's first installment payment being payable on the first installment payment date after closing, the assumed
          principal balance of which at closing will be $_____
          Buyer's assumption of an existing note includes all obligations imposed by the deed of trust securing the note. If the principal balance of all assumed
          loans varies in an amount greater than $350.00 at closing from the total of the amount stated above, or if noteholders on assumption (i) require Buyer to
          pay an assumption fee in excess of $_____ in B(1) above and $_____ in B(2) above and Seller declines to pay
          such excess or (ii) raise the existing interest rate above _____% in B(1) or _____% in B(2) above, Buyer may terminate this contract and the
          Earnest Money shall be refunded to Buyer. The cash payable at closing shall be adjusted by the amount of the variance from the loan balance(s) shown
          above.
          NOTICE TO BUYER: Monthly payments, interest rates or other terms of some loans may be adjusted after closing. Before signing the contract, examine
          the note and deed of trust to determine the possibility of future adjustments.
    ☐ C. THIRD PARTY FINANCED: A conventional third party fixed rate loan to Buyer in the amount of $_____ , payable in
          _____intervals for not less than _____years with the interest rate not to exceed _____% per annum, ☐ with
          ☐ without private mortgage insurance.
    ☐ D. SELLER FINANCED: A promissory note from Buyer to Seller in the amount of $_____ , bearing _____% interest per annum,
          principal and interest payable (Check 1 or 2):
          ☐ 1. In one payment due _____after the date of the note with
                interest payable _____ .
          ☐ 2. In installments of $_____ ☐ including interest ☐ plus interest beginning _____after the date
                of the note and continuing at _____ intervals thereafter for _____years when the entire balance of the note
                shall be due and payable.
          ☐ 3. This contract is subject to Buyer furnishing Seller evidence of good credit within _____days from the effective date of this contract. If notice
                of disapproval of Buyer's credit is not given within three (3) days thereafter, Seller shall be deemed to have approved Buyer's credit. Buyer hereby
                authorizes Buyer's credit report to be furnished to Seller.
          Any Seller financed note may be prepaid in whole or in part at any time without penalty. The lien securing payment of such note will be inferior to any
          lien securing any loan assumed or given in connection with third party financing. Buyer shall furnish Seller with a Mortgagee's Title Policy.
          NOTICE: If the term, interest rate or payment of a note is subject to change or additional assumptions are required, use Paragraph 11.

019

Buyer shall apply for all third party financing or noteholder's approval of Buyer for assumption and waiver of the right to accelerate the note within _____ days from the effective date of this contract and shall make every reasonable effort to obtain the same. Such financing or assumption shall have been approved when Buyer has satisfied all of lender's or noteholder's financial requirements, including sale of other property, requirement of co-signature or financial verifications. If such financing or assumption approval and waiver of acceleration is not obtained within _____ days from the effective date hereof, this contract shall terminate and the Earnest Money shall be refunded to Buyer.

5.   EARNEST MONEY: $_____ is herewith tendered and is to be deposited as Earnest Money with _____
_____ at _____ (location) as Escrow Agent, upon execution
of the contract by both parties. Additional Earnest Money in the amount of $_____ shall be deposited with the Escrow Agent on or
before _____, 19_____.

6.   TITLE: Seller at Seller's expense shall furnish to Buyer an Owner's Policy of Title Insurance (the Title Policy) issued by _____
_____ in the amount of the Sales Price and dated at or after closing.
NOTICE TO BUYER: AS REQUIRED BY LAW, Broker advises that YOU should have the Abstract covering the Property examined by an attorney of YOUR
selection, or YOU should be furnished with or obtain a Title Policy. If the Property is situated in a Utility District, Section 50.301 Texas Water Code requires the
Buyer to sign and acknowledge a statutory notice relating to the tax rate and bonded indebtedness of the District.

7.   PROPERTY CONDITION (Check A or B):
☐ A.   Buyer accepts the Property in its present condition, subject to lender required repairs and _____

☐ B.   Buyer requires inspections and repairs required by the Property Condition Addendum (attached hereto) and any lender.
On Seller's receipt of all loan approvals and inspection reports, Seller shall commence repairs required of Seller by the contract and the Property
Condition Addendum, if any, and complete such repairs prior to closing. Seller's responsibility for the repairs shall not exceed
$_____. If Seller fails to commence or complete such repairs, Buyer may do so and Seller shall be liable up to the amount specified and the
same paid from the proceeds of the sale. If the repair costs will exceed the stated amount and Seller refuses to pay such excess, Buyer may pay the additional cost
or accept the Property with the limited repairs and this sale shall be closed as scheduled, or Buyer may terminate this contract and the Earnest Money shall be
refunded to Buyer. If the repair costs will exceed five (5) percent of the Sales Price of the Property and Seller agrees to pay the cost of such repairs, Buyer shall
have the option of closing the sale with the completed repairs, or terminating the sale and the Earnest Money shall be refunded to Buyer. Seller's obligation to make
repairs required by this contract and Property Condition Addendum shall be limited to those items which Seller has the sole obligation to maintain and repair under
the terms of the Declaration. After Buyer receives all reports of needed common element repairs that are not the responsibility of Seller, Buyer shall have five (5)
days to give written notice to Seller that Buyer will terminate this contract unless Buyer receives written confirmation from the Association that such repairs will
be made in a reasonable time. If Buyer does give such notice, Seller shall have five (5) days after receipt of such notice to cause to be delivered to Buyer written
confirmation of the Association's commitment to repair. If Buyer does not give such notice to Seller, Buyer will be deemed to have accepted the Property without
such repairs. If required by Buyer and written confirmation of repairs is not delivered to Buyer as required above, Buyer may terminate this contract and the Earnest
Money shall be refunded to Buyer.
Broker(s) and sales associates have no responsibility or liability for inspections or repairs made pursuant to this contract.

8.   BROKER'S FEE: _____, Listing Broker, and any Co-Broker represent
Seller. Seller agrees to pay Listing Broker the fee specified by separate agreement between Listing Broker and Seller. Escrow Agent is authorized and directed to
pay Listing Broker's fee from the sale proceeds at closing.

9.   CLOSING: The closing of the sale shall be on or before _____, 19_____, or within seven (7) days after objections to title
have been cured, whichever date is later (the Closing Date); however, if financing or assumption approval has been obtained pursuant to Paragraph 4, the Closing
Date shall be extended daily up to fifteen (15) days if necessary to complete other loan requirements.

10. POSSESSION: The possession of the Property shall be delivered to Buyer on _____
in its present or required improved condition, ordinary wear and tear excepted.

11. SPECIAL PROVISIONS: (BROKER: List addenda and insert factual statements and business details applicable to this sale.)

12. SALES EXPENSES TO BE PAID IN CASH AT OR PRIOR TO CLOSING:
A.   Loan appraisal fees shall be paid by _____
B.   Any Condominium Association transfer or processing fee shall be paid by _____
C.   The total loan discount points shall not exceed _____ points (not including origination fee) of which Buyer shall pay
_____ points and Seller shall pay the remainder.
D.   Seller's Expenses: Prepayment penalties on any existing loans paid at closing, plus cost of releasing such loans and recording releases; tax statements; 1/2 of
any escrow fee; preparation of deed; preparation and recording of any deed of trust to secure assumption; other expenses stipulated to be paid by Seller under
other provisions of this contract.
E.   Buyer's Expenses: Application, origination and commitment fees; private mortgage insurance premiums and any loan assumption fee; expenses incident to
loan(s) (e.g., preparation of any note, deed of trust and other loan documents, survey, recording fees, copies of restrictions and easements, Mortgagee's Title
Policies, credit reports, photos); 1/2 of any escrow fee; any required premiums for flood and hazard insurance; any required reserve deposits for insurance
premiums, and valorem taxes and special governmental assessments; interest on all monthly installment payment notes from date of disbursements to one (1)
month prior to dates of first monthly payments; expenses stipulated to be paid by Buyer under other provisions of this contract.
F.   If any sales expenses exceed the maximum amount herein stipulated to be paid by either party, either party may terminate this contract unless the other party
agrees to pay such excess.

13. PRORATIONS: Ad valorem taxes, rents, insurance premiums, interest and any current regular condominium assessments shall be prorated to Closing Date. Cash
reserves from regular condominium assessments for deferred maintenance or capital improvements established by the Association shall not be credited to Seller
except as otherwise provided by the Declaration. Any unpaid special assessments due the Association shall be the obligation of Seller except as otherwise provided
by the Condominium Documents.

14. TITLE APPROVAL: The Title Policy shall guarantee Buyer's title to be good and indefeasible subject only to (i) restrictive covenants affecting the Property (ii)
any discrepancies, conflicts or shortages in area or boundary lines, or any encroachments, or any overlapping of improvements (iii) taxes for the current and
subsequent years, and subsequent assessments for prior years due to change in land usage or ownership (iv) existing building and zoning ordinances (v) rights of
parties in possession (vi) liens created or assumed as security for the sale consideration (vii) terms and provisions of the Condominium Documents including the
platted easements and assessments set out therein and (viii) other exceptions permitted by the terms of this contract. Exceptions permitted in the deed and zoning
ordinances shall not be valid objections to title. If the Title Policy will be subject to exceptions other than those recited above in sub-paragraph (i) through (vii)
inclusive, Seller shall deliver to Buyer a Commitment for Title Insurance (the Commitment) and legible copies of any documents creating such exceptions that are
not recited in sub-paragraph (i) through (vii) above. If Buyer has objection to any such previously undisclosed exceptions, Buyer shall have five (5) days after
receipt of such Commitment and copies to make written objections to Seller. If Buyer makes such objections, Seller shall have fifteen (15) days from the date such
objections are disclosed to cure the same, and the Closing Date shall be extended accordingly. If the objections are not satisfied by the extended closing date, this
contract shall terminate and the Earnest Money shall be refunded to Buyer, unless Buyer elects to waive the unsatisfied objections and complete the purchase. Seller
shall furnish tax statements showing no delinquent taxes and a General Warranty Deed conveying title subject only to liens securing payment of debt created or
assumed as part of the consideration, taxes for the current year and easements, restrictions, reservations and conditions permitted by this contract or otherwise
acceptable to Buyer. Each note herein provided shall be secured by vendor's and deed of trust liens. A vendor's lien and deed of trust to secure any assumption
shall be required, which shall be automatically released on execution and delivery of a release by noteholder. If Seller is released from liability on an assumed note
the vendor's lien and deed of trust to secure assumption shall not be required. In case of dispute as to the form of the deed, note(s), deed of trust or deed of trust
to secure assumption, forms prepared by the State Bar of Texas shall be used.

Third page — Residential Condominium Earnest Money Contract   2-16-84

15. CASUALTY LOSS: If any part of the Unit is damaged or destroyed by fire or other casualty loss, Seller shall restore the same to its previous condition as soon as reasonably possible, but in any event by Closing Date. If Seller is unable to do so without fault, Buyer may terminate this contract and the Earnest Money shall be refunded to Buyer. If any part of the Common Elements or any Unit adjoining the Unit described in Paragraph 2A is damaged or destroyed by fire or other casualty loss, Buyer shall have five (5) days from receipt of notice of such casualty loss within which to notify Seller in writing that the contract will be terminated unless Buyer receives written confirmation from the Association that the damaged condition will be restored to its previous condition within a reasonable time at no cost to Buyer. Unless Buyer gives such notice within such time, Buyer will be deemed to have accepted the Property without confirmation of such restoration. Seller shall have five (5) days from the date of receipt of Buyer's notice within which to cause to be delivered to Buyer such confirmation. If required by Buyer and written confirmation is not delivered to Buyer as required above, Buyer may terminate this contract and the Earnest Money will be refunded to Buyer. NOTICE TO BUYER: CONSULT YOUR INSURANCE AGENT PRIOR TO THE CLOSING DATE DUE TO THE UNIQUE REQUIREMENTS OF THIS TYPE OF PROPERTY.

16. DEFAULT: If Buyer fails to comply herewith, Seller may either (i) enforce specific performance and seek such other relief as may be provided by law or (ii) terminate this contract and receive the Earnest Money as liquidated damages. If Seller is unable without fault to deliver the Title Policy Commitment required herein, Buyer may either terminate this contract and receive the Earnest Money as the sole remedy or extend the Closing Date up to fifteen (15) days. If Seller is unable without fault to deliver the Certificate described in Paragraph 20 within the time herein specified, Buyer may either terminate this contract and receive the Earnest Money as the sole remedy or extend the time for delivery up to fifteen (15) days. If Seller fails to comply herewith for any other reason, Buyer may either (i) enforce specific performance hereof and seek such other relief as may be provided by law or (ii) terminate this contract and receive the Earnest Money, thereby releasing Seller from this contract.

17. ATTORNEY'S FEES: Any signatory of this contract who is the prevailing party in any legal proceeding against any other signatory brought under or with relation to this contract or transaction shall be additionally entitled to recover costs and reasonable attorney fees from the nonprevailing party.

18. ESCROW: The Earnest Money is deposited with Escrow Agent with the understanding that Escrow Agent (i) is not a party to this contract and does not assume or have any liability for performance or non-performance of any party or other signatory (ii) has the right to require from all signatories a written release of liability of the Escrow Agent, which terminates this contract and authorizes the disbursement of the Earnest Money and (iii) is not liable for interest or other charge on the funds held. If any signatory unreasonably fails to deliver promptly the document described in (ii) above, then such signatory shall be liable to the other signatories as provided in Paragraph 17. At closing, the Earnest Money shall be applied first to any cash down payment required, then to Buyer's closing costs and any excess refunded to Buyer. Any refund or payment of the Earnest Money under this contract shall be reduced by the amount of any actual expenses incurred on behalf of the party receiving the Earnest Money, and Escrow Agent may pay the same to the creditors entitled thereto.

19. REPRESENTATIONS: Seller represents that as of the Closing Date (i) there will be no unrecorded liens, assessments or Uniform Commercial Code Liens against any of the Property which will not be satisfied out of the Sales Price, unless securing payment of any deferred consideration (ii) loan(s) will be without default (iii) any reserve deposits held by the lender will not be deficient (iv) the present amount of the regular condominium assessment is $_____ which will be current and (v) Seller has no knowledge of any misrepresentation or errors in the Condominium Certificate or any material changes in the information contained therein. If any representation in this contract or the Certificate is untrue on the Closing Date, this contract may be terminated by Buyer and the Earnest Money shall be refunded to Buyer. All representations contained in this contract shall survive closing.

20. CERTIFICATE BY THE ASSOCIATION: The Certificate shall state or have attached thereto:
    A. Any right of first refusal held by the Association on the Unit;
    B. The amount of the monthly common expense assessment and the amount and effective date of any increase in such assessment;
    C. Any unpaid common expense or special assessment due and unpaid by the Seller to the Association;
    D. Any other unpaid amounts payable by Seller to the Association;
    E. Future capital expenditures approved by the Association;
    F. The amount of reserves for capital expenditures and any portion of those reserves allocated by the Association for specified projects;
    G. The most recent regularly prepared balance sheet and income and expense statement;
    H. The current operating budget of the Association;
    I. Any judgments against the Association and the nature of pending suits to which the Association is a party;
    J. A description of any insurance coverage provided for the benefit of Unit owners;
    K. The remaining term of any leasehold estate on which the condominium project is situated;
    L. Any knowledge by the governing body of the Association (the Board) of alterations or improvements to the Unit or to any other portions of the project which violate any provision of the Declaration;
    M. Any knowledge by the Board of violations of the Health or Building Codes with respect to the Unit or any other portion of the project; and
    N. Any knowledge of a condition which, in the good faith opinion of the Board, is a material physical defect in the Unit or in the common elements of the project.
    The Certificate may be in a form approved by the Texas Real Estate Commission for use with this contract.

21. AGREEMENT OF PARTIES: This contract contains the entire agreement of the parties and cannot be changed except by their written consent.

22. NOTICES: All notices shall be in writing and effective when delivered at the addresses shown below.

23. CONSULT YOUR ATTORNEY: The Broker cannot give you legal advice. This is intended to be a legally binding contract. READ IT CAREFULLY. If you do not understand the effect of any part, consult your attorney BEFORE signing.

Seller's Atty: _____ Buyer's Atty: _____

EXECUTED in multiple originals effective the _____ day of _____, 19____ **(BROKER: FILL IN THE DATE OF FINAL ACCEPTANCE.)**

Buyer _____ Seller _____

Buyer _____ Seller _____

Buyer's Address _____ Phone No. _____ Seller's Address _____ Phone No. _____

Listing Broker agrees to pay _____, Co-Broker.
a fee of _____ of the total sales price when the Broker's fee described in Paragraph 8 is received. Escrow Agent is authorized and directed to pay Co-Broker from Listing Broker's fee at closing.

Co-Broker _____ License No. _____ Listing Broker _____ License No. _____

By _____ By _____

Co-Broker's Address _____ Phone No. _____ Listing Broker's Address _____ Phone No. _____

Receipt of $_____ Earnest Money is acknowledged in the form of _____

Escrow Agent _____ By _____

Date _____, 19____

This form has been approved by the Texas Real Estate Commission For Voluntary Use.

019

2-16-84

CONDOMINIUM RESALE CERTIFICATE
Approved by Texas Real Estate Commission for Voluntary Use

Condominium Certificate concerning Condominium Unit _____, in Building _____, of _____

_____, a condominium project, located at _____ (Address),

City of _____, _____ County, Texas, on behalf of the condominium owners association (the Association) by the Association's governing body (the Board).

A. The Association ☐ does ☐ does not have a right of first refusal on the Unit. If a right of first refusal exists, see Section _____ of Declaration.

B. The monthly common expense assessment for the Unit is $_____ per month. The Association ☐ has ☐ has not approved an

increase in such assessment. If an increase has been approved, the new assessment will be $_____ per month and the effective date will be

_____, 19_____.

C. There ☐ is ☐ is not a common expense or special assessment due and unpaid by the Seller to the Association. If so, the amount is

$_____ and is for _____.

D. Other amounts ☐ are ☐ are not payable by Seller to the Association. If so, the amount is $_____ and is for _____

_____.

E. There ☐ are ☐ are not any future capital expenditures that have been approved by the Association. If so, the amount is $_____

and is for _____.

F. The amount of reserves for capital expenditures are $_____ as of _____, 19_____,

and $_____ of the reserves has been allocated by the Association for specified projects.

G. The most recent regularly prepared balance sheet and income and expense statement are attached.

H. The current operating budget of the Association is attached.

I. There ☐ are ☐ are no judgments against the Association. The nature and amount of the judgments are _____

_____

_____

and the nature of any pending suit is _____

_____

J. The Association ☐ has ☐ has not purchased a blanket policy of fire and extended coverage insurance on the common elements and specified portions of the Unit as per the attached summary from the condominium project's insurance agent.

K. The condominium project ☐ is ☐ is not on leased land. If so, the remaining term is _____ years. A portion of the common element facilities ☐ is ☐ is not leased to others.

L. The Board ☐ has ☐ has no knowledge of alterations or improvements to the Unit or any other portion of the project which violate any provisions of the Declaration. If so, they are _____

_____

M. The Board ☐ has ☐ has no knowledge of any violations of the Health or Building Codes with respect to the Unit or any other portion of the condominium project. If so, they are _____

_____

N. The Board ☐ has ☐ has no knowledge of any condition which is, in the good faith opinion of the Board, a material physical defect in the Unit or in the common elements of the condominium project. If so, they are _____

_____

_____

REQUIRED ATTACHMENTS:
1. Balance Sheet
2. Income and Expense Statement
3. Operating Budget
4. Insurance Summary

_____
(Name of condominium owners association)

Received: _____ 19_____

By: _____ (Signed)

_____
Buyer

_____
Title

_____
Mailing Address

_____
Buyer

_____
Date

_____
Phone No.

019

02-08-85

(NOTICE: For use only when BUYER occupies property PRIOR to closing)

BUYER'S TEMPORARY RESIDENTIAL LEASE

PROMULGATED BY TEXAS REAL ESTATE COMMISSION

1. PARTIES: The parties to this Lease are _____

(Landlord) and _____ (Tenant).

2. LEASE: Landlord leases to Tenant the property (the Property) described in the Earnest Money Contract (the Contract) between Landlord as Seller

and Tenant as Buyer dated _____, 19___, and known as _____

_____ (address).

3. TERM: The term of this Lease commences on _____
and terminates on the Contract Closing Date, unless terminated earlier by reason of other provisions hereof.

4. CONSIDERATION: A. Tenant shall pay as rental the sum of $_____ per day, payable ( ) monthly ( ) weekly in advance, or ( ) upon termination of this Lease. No portion of the rental paid shall be applied to payment of any items covered by the Contract. The rental shall be paid to Landlord or Landlord's agent at the address which appears by Landlord's signature below.

B. Tenant shall pay to the Escrow Agent in the Contract the sum of $_____ as additional Earnest Money prior to taking possession of the Property. This fund is deposited with Escrow Agent with the understanding that Escrow Agent (1) is not a party to this contract and does not assume or have any liability for performance or non-performance of any party or other signatory (2) has the right to require from all signatories a written release of liability of the Escrow Agent which authorizes the disbursement of the fund (3) is not liable for interest or other charge on the funds held and (4) is not liable for any losses of escrow funds caused by the failure of any banking institution in which such funds have been deposited, unless such banking institution is acting as Escrow Agent. If any signatory unreasonably fails to deliver promptly the documents described in (2) above, then such signatory shall be liable to the other signatories as provided in Paragraph 19.

5. SECURITY DEPOSIT: Tenant has paid to Landlord or his agent, _____

_____, as a deposit the sum of $_____ to secure performance of this Lease by Tenant. If this Lease is terminated before closing of the sale of the Property, the deposit shall be used by the Landlord to the extent necessary to satisfy Tenant's obligations under this Lease, and the unused portion of the deposit will be refunded to Tenant, together with an itemized list of all deductions from the deposit, within thirty (30) days after Tenant surrenders possession of the Property. If this Lease is terminated by the closing of the sale of the Property, the deposit will be refunded to Tenant at the closing. NOTICE: The security deposit must be in addition to the Earnest Money deposit under the terms of the Contract.

6. UTILITIES: The Tenant shall be responsible for all utility company connections and payment of all deposits and charges to utility companies,

except _____

_____ , which shall be paid by Landlord.

7. USE OF PROPERTY: The Property shall be used and occupied by Tenant for single family dwelling purposes only. The Tenant shall not assign this Lease or sublet any part of the Property.

8. PETS: No pets shall be kept on the Property except _____

_____

9. CONDITION OF PROPERTY: Tenant accepts the Property in its present condition and state of repair, but Landlord shall be obligated to make all repairs and improvements required by the Contract. If this Lease is terminated other than by the closing of the sale under the Contract, Tenant shall surrender the Property to Landlord in its present condition, or as may have been improved by Landlord, normal wear and tear and loss by fire or other casualty only excepted.

10. ALTERATIONS: No holes may be made or nails driven into the woodwork, floors, walls, or ceilings of the improvements, nor may Tenant alter, paint or decorate the Property or install improvements or fixtures thereon without prior written consent of Landlord. Any additional improvements or fixtures placed on the Property shall become the property of Landlord if this Lease is terminated other than by closing of the sale under the Contract. Such improvements or fixtures shall remain upon and be surrendered with the Property.

11. INSPECTIONS: Landlord may enter the Property at all reasonable times to inspect, complete, replace or repair the improvements.

12. LAWS: Tenant shall obey all applicable laws, restrictions, ordinances, rules and regulations with respect to the Property.

13. REPAIRS AND MAINTENANCE: Tenant shall bear all expense of repairing and maintaining the Property, including but not limited to yard, trees and shrubs, unless otherwise stipulated in the Contract. Notwithstanding the provision of the Contract relating to Casualty Loss, Tenant shall replace or repair at the expense of Tenant any damage to the Property caused directly or indirectly by the acts or omissions of the Tenant or any other person therein or thereon by the consent, invitation or sufferance of the Tenant. The repair or replacement of such damage shall be commenced and prosecuted to completion with reasonable dispatch. Tenant hereby knowingly, voluntarily, specifically and for a valuable consideration waives all duties imposed on the Landlord that can be waived pursuant to Section 92.006 of the Texas Property Code.

001   TREC No 16-1

14.   INDEMNITY: Tenant shall indemnify Landlord from the claims of all third parties for injury or damage to the person or property of such third party arising from the use or occupancy of the Property by Tenant. This indemnification shall include all costs and expenses incurred by Landlord, including attorney's fees.

15.   INSURANCE: Landlord and Tenant shall each maintain such insurance on the improvements and Property as each party may deem appropriate during the term of this Lease. NOTE: Possession of the Property by the Tenant changes policy rights. CONSULT YOUR INSURANCE AGENT prior to change of possession.

16.   DEFAULT: If Tenant fails to perform or observe any provision of this Lease and fails to remedy same within three (3) days after notice by Landlord, or if bankruptcy proceedings are commenced by or against Tenant, or an assignment for the benefit of creditors is made by Tenant, the same shall constitute a default under this Lease.

17.   TERMINATION: This Lease shall terminate upon (a) expiration of the term, (b) closing of the sale under the Contract, (c) termination of the Contract prior to closing, (d) Tenant's default under this Lease, (e) Tenant's failure to close the sale after all conditions of the Contract necessary for the closing of the sale have been satisfied and the Landlord has given five (5) days notice of a date and time of closing, whichever occurs first. Upon termination other than by closing of the sale, Tenant shall vacate the Property within five (5) days after notice for possession.

18.   HOLDING OVER: Any possession by Tenant after termination shall not operate or renew or extend the term but shall be construed as a tenancy at sufferance of the Landlord. Tenant shall pay rental at a rate of two (2) times the rental stipulated in Paragraph 4 above during the period of any possession after termination.

19.   ATTORNEY'S FEES: Any signatory of this Lease, Broker or Escrow Agent who is the prevailing party in any legal proceeding brought under or with relation to this Lease or transaction shall be additionally entitled to recover court costs and reasonable attorney's fees from the non-prevailing party.

20.   NOTICES: All notices by Landlord shall be in writing and effective when delivered to the Property. All notices by Tenants submitted as required by law shall be in writing and effective when delivered to the designated address for payment of rent.

21.   NOTICE TO LANDLORD: You are hereby advised that Section 92.051 of the Texas Property Code requires the installation of smoke detectors in all rental property.

22.   CONSULT YOUR ATTORNEY: This is intended to be a legally binding contract. READ IT CAREFULLY. If you do not understand the exact effect of any part consult your attorney before signing.

23.   SPECIAL PROVISIONS:

DATED this _____ day of _____, 19_____.

LANDLORD _____

Designated name and address
for payment of rent:

LANDLORD _____

_____
Name

TENANT _____

_____
Street

TENANT _____

_____
City   State   Zip

Receipt of additional Earnest Money is acknowledged in the form of

_____

Escrow Agent   Date

By _____

02-08-85

(NOTICE: For use only when SELLER occupies property AFTER the closing)

SELLER'S TEMPORARY RESIDENTIAL LEASE

PROMULGATED BY TEXAS REAL ESTATE COMMISSION

1. PARTIES: The parties to this Lease are _____

(Landlord) and _____ (Tenant).

2. LEASE: Landlord leases to Tenant the property (the Property) described in the Earnest Money Contract (the Contract) between Landlord as Buyer

and Tenant as Seller dated _____, 19____, and known as _____

_____ (address).

3. TERM: The term of this Lease commences on the date the sale covered by the Contract is closed and terminates on _____,

19____, unless terminated earlier by reason of other provisions hereof.

4. RENTAL: Tenant shall pay as rental the sum of $_____ per day, payable ( ) monthly ( ) weekly in advance,
or ( ) upon termination of this Lease. The rental shall be paid to Landlord or Landlord's agent at the address which appears by Landlord's signature
below.

5. SECURITY DEPOSIT: Tenant will pay to Landlord at closing as a deposit the sum of $_____ to secure performance of this Lease
by Tenant. The deposit shall be used by Landlord to the extent necessary to satisfy Tenant's obligations under this Lease, and the unused portion of
the deposit shall be refunded to Tenant, together with an itemized list of all deductions from the deposit, within thirty (30) days after Tenant surrenders
possession of the Property.

6. UTILITIES: Tenant shall pay all utility charges except _____

_____, which shall be paid by Landlord.

7. USE OF PROPERTY: The Property shall be used and occupied by Tenant for single family dwelling purposes only. The Tenant shall not assign
this Lease or sublet any part of the Property.

8. PETS: No pets shall be kept on the Property except _____

_____.

9. CONDITION OF PROPERTY: Tenant accepts the Property in its condition and state of repair at the commencement of the lease term, and
Landlord shall not be obligated to make any repairs or improvements. Upon termination Tenant shall surrender the Property to the Landlord in its

required condition under the Contract at the time of closing, except normal wear and tear and loss by fire or other casualty and _____

_____

10. ALTERATIONS: No holes may be made or nails driven into the woodwork, floors, walls, or ceilings of the improvements, nor may Tenant alter,
paint or decorate the Property or install improvements or fixtures thereon without prior written consent of Landlord. Any additional improvements or
fixtures placed on the Property shall become the property of Landlord.

11. INSPECTIONS: During the lease term Landlord may enter the Property at all reasonable times to inspect the improvements.

12. LAWS: Tenant shall obey all applicable laws, restrictions, ordinances, rules and regulations with respect to the Property.

13. REPAIRS AND MAINTENANCE: Tenant shall bear all expense of repairing and maintaining the Property, including but not limited to yard,
trees and shrubs. Tenant shall replace or repair at the expense of Tenant any damage to the Property caused directly or indirectly by the acts or
omissions of the Tenant or any other person therein or thereon by the consent, invitation or sufferance of Tenant. The repair or replacement of such
damage shall be commenced and prosecuted to completion with reasonable dispatch. Tenant hereby knowingly, voluntarily, specifically and for a
valuable consideration waives all duties imposed on the Landlord that can be waived pursuant to Section 92.006 of the Texas Property Code.

14. INDEMNITY: Tenant shall indemnify Landlord from the claims of all third parties for injury or damage to the person or property of such third
party arising from the use or occupancy of the Property by Tenant. This indemnification shall include all costs and expenses incurred by Landlord,
including attorney's fees.

15. INSURANCE: Landlord and Tenant shall each maintain such insurance on the improvements and Property as each party may deem appropriate
during the term of this Lease. NOTE: Possession of the Property by the Tenant changes policy rights. CONSULT YOUR INSURANCE AGENT prior
to closing the Contract.

16. DEFAULT: If Tenant fails to perform or observe any provision of this Lease and fails to remedy same within three (3) days after notice by
Landlord, or if bankruptcy proceedings are commenced by or against Tenant, or an assignment for the benefit of creditors is made by Tenant, the same
shall constitute a default under this Lease.

17.   TERMINATION: This Lease shall terminate upon expiration of the term or upon Tenant's default under this Lease. Upon termination, and after notice for possession by Landlord, Tenant shall vacate the Property within five (5) days.

18.   HOLDING OVER: A. Any possession by Tenant after termination shall not operate to renew or extend the term but shall be construed as a

tenancy at sufferance of the Landlord. Tenant shall pay rental at a rate of $_____ per day during the period of any possession after termination.

B. As an advance on any such hold over rental the Escrow Agent under the Contract shall retain from the sale proceeds under the Contract the

sum of $_____. When Tenant delivers possession of the Property to Landlord, the Escrow Agent shall pay to the Landlord the amount of any accrued and unpaid hold over rental and the balance shall be paid to Tenant. This fund is deposited with Escrow Agent with the understanding that Escrow Agent (1) is not a party to this contract and does not assume or have any liability for performance or non-performance of any party or other signatory (2) has the right to require from all signatories a written release of liability of the Escrow Agent which authorizes the dispersement of the fund (3) is not liable for interest or other charge on the funds held and (4) is not liable for any losses of escrow funds caused by the failure of any banking institution in which such funds have been deposited, unless such banking institution is acting as Escrow Agent. If any signatory unreasonably fails to deliver promptly the documents described in (2) above, then such signatory shall be liable to the other signatories as provided in Paragraph 19.

19.   ATTORNEY'S FEES: Any signatory to this Lease, Broker or Escrow Agent who is the prevailing party in any legal proceeding brought under or with relation to this Lease or transaction shall be additionally entitled to recover court costs and reasonable attorney's fees from the non-prevailing party.

20.   NOTICES: All notices by Landlord shall be in writing and effective when delivered to the Property. All notices by Tenants submitted as required by law shall be in writing and effective when delivered to the designated address for payment of rent.

21.   NOTICE TO LANDLORD: You are hereby advised that Section 92.051 of the Texas Property Code requires the installation of smoke detectors in all rental property.

22.   CONSULT YOUR ATTORNEY: This is intended to be a legally binding contract. READ IT CAREFULLY. If you do not understand the exact effect of any part consult your attorney before signing.

23.   SPECIAL PROVISIONS:

DATED this _____ day of ___ _____, 19_____ .

Designated name and address
for payment of rent:

_____
Name

_____
Street

_____
City   State   Zip

_____
LANDLORD

_____
LANDLORD

_____
TENANT

_____
TENANT

Receipt of advance hold over rental is acknowledged in the form of

_____

_____

Escrow Agent   Date
By _____

05-22-87

NEW HOME RESIDENTIAL EARNEST MONEY CONTRACT
(Completed Construction)

PROMULGATED BY TEXAS REAL ESTATE COMMISSION

Notice: Not For Use In Condominium Transactions

1. **PARTIES:** _____ (Seller) agrees to sell
and convey to _____ (Buyer) and Buyer
agrees to buy from Seller the property described below.

2. **PROPERTY:** Lot _____ , Block _____ , _____
Addition, City of _____ , _____ County, Texas, known as
_____ (Address); or as described on attached exhibit, together
with the improvements, fixtures and all other property located thereon or placed thereon pursuant to Paragraph 7 below. All property sold by this contract
is called the "Property".

3. **CONTRACT SALES PRICE:**

   A.   Cash payable at closing . . . . **$**_____

   B.   Sum of all financing described below excluding any FHA Mortgage Insurance Premium (MIP) or VA funding fee . . . . **$**_____

   C.   Sales Price (sum of A and B) . . . . **$**_____

4. **FINANCING:** (Check applicable boxes below)

   ☐ A.   ALL CASH: This is an all cash sale; no financing is involved.

   ☐ B.   THIRD PARTY CONVENTIONAL FINANCING:

       ☐ 1.   A third party first lien note of not less than **$**_____ , due in full in _____ years, payable in initial monthly payments of
   principal and interest not exceeding **$**_____ for the first _____ year(s) of the loan.

       ☐ 2.   A third party second lien note of not less than **$**_____ , due in full in _____ years, payable in initial monthly payments of
   principal and interest not exceeding **$**_____ for the first _____ year(s) of the loan.

   ☐ C.   FHA INSURED FINANCING:

       A Section _____ FHA insured loan of not less than **$**_____ , due in full in
   _____ years, payable in initial monthly payments of principal and interest not exceeding **$**_____
   for the first _____ year(s) of the Loan.

   As required by HUD-FHA, if FHA valuation is unknown, "It is expressly agreed that, notwithstanding any other provisions of this contract, the
   Purchaser (Buyer) shall not be obligated to complete the purchase of the Property described herein or to incur any penalty by forfeiture of Earnest
   Money deposits or otherwise unless the Seller has delivered to the Purchaser (Buyer) a written statement issued by the Federal Housing
   Commissioner setting forth the appraised value of the Property (excluding closing costs and MIP) of not less than **$**_____ ,
   which statement the Seller hereby agrees to deliver to the Purchaser (Buyer) promptly after such appraised value statement is made available to the
   Seller. The Purchaser (Buyer) shall, however, have the privilege and option of proceeding with the consummation of this contract without regard to
   the amount of the appraised valuation made by the Federal Housing Commissioner. The appraised valuation is arrived at to determine the
   maximum mortgage the Department of Housing and Urban Development will insure. HUD does not warrant the value or the condition of the
   Property. The Purchaser (Buyer) should satisfy himself/herself that the price and the condition of the Property are acceptable."
   If the FHA appraised value of the Property (excluding closing costs and MIP) is less than the Sales Price (3C above), Seller may reduce the Sales Price
   to an amount equal to the FHA appraised value (excluding closing costs and MIP) and the parties to the sale shall close the sale at such lower Sales
   Price with appropriate adjustments to 3A and 3B above.

   ☐ D.   VA GUARANTEED FINANCING:

       A VA guaranteed loan of not less than **$**_____ , due in full in _____ years,

       ☐ 1.   with interest at maximum rate allowable at time of loan funding if the loan is a fixed rate loan or

       ☐ 2.   with interest not to exceed _____ % per annum for the first _____ year(s) of the loan if such loan is not fixed rate.

   VA NOTICE TO BUYER: "It is expressly agreed that, notwithstanding any other provisions of this contract, the Buyer shall not incur any penalty by
   forfeiture of earnest money or otherwise or be obligated to complete the purchase of the Property described herein, if the contract purchase price or cost
   exceeds the reasonable value of the Property established by the Veterans Administration. The Buyer shall, however, have the privilege and option of
   proceeding with the consummation of this contract without regard to the amount of the reasonable value established by the Veterans Administration."
   If Buyer elects to complete the purchase at an amount in excess of the reasonable value established by VA, Buyer shall pay such excess amount in cash from
   a source which Buyer agrees to disclose to the VA and which Buyer represents will not be from borrowed funds except as approved by VA. If VA reasonable
   value of the Property is less than the Sales Price (3C above), Seller may reduce the Sales Price to an amount equal to the VA reasonable value and the parties
   to the sale shall close the sale at such lower Sales Price with appropriate adjustments to 3A and 3B above.

   ☐ E.   TEXAS VETERANS' HOUSING ASSISTANCE PROGRAM LOAN:

       A Texas Veterans' Housing Assistance Program loan of **$**_____ due in full in _____ years at the interest rate established by the
   Texas Veterans' Land Board at the time of closing.

   ☐ F.   SELLER FINANCING: A promissory note from Buyer to Seller of **$**_____ , bearing _____ % interest per annum, and
   payable:

       ☐ 1.   In one payment due _____ after the date of the note with interest pay-
   able _____ .

       ☐ 2.   In installments of **$**_____ ☐ including interest ☐ plus interest beginning _____ after the date
   of the note and continuing at _____ intervals thereafter for _____ year(s) when the entire balance of the note
   shall be due and payable.

       ☐ 3.   Interest only in _____ installments for the first _____ year(s) and thereafter in installments of

INITIALED FOR IDENTIFICATION BY BUYER _____ AND SELLER _____

006   TREC No. 24-0

New Home (Completed Construction)—Page Two   05-22-87

$ _____ □ including interest □ plus interest beginning _____ after the date of the note and continuing at _____ intervals thereafter for _____ year(s) when the entire balance of the note shall be due and payable.

□ 4. This contract is subject to Buyer furnishing Seller evidence of good credit within _____ days from the effective date of this contract. If notice of disapproval of Buyer's credit is not given within five (5) days after receipt by Seller, Seller shall be deemed to have approved Buyer's credit. Buyer hereby authorizes Buyer's credit report to be furnished to Seller.

Any Seller financed note may be prepaid in whole or in part at any time without penalty. The lien securing payment of such note will be inferior to any lien securing any loan given in connection with third party financing described above. If an Owner's Policy of Title Insurance is furnished, Buyer shall furnish Seller with a Mortgagee's Title Policy.

Buyer shall apply for all third party financing within _____ days from the effective date of this contract and shall make every reasonable effort to obtain the same from _____, as lender, or any lender that will make the loan at no greater loan expense (including but not limited to discounts or other charges however designated) to Seller than charged by the designated lender. Such financing shall have been approved when Buyer has satisfied all of lender's financial conditions; e.g., requirements of sale of other property, co-signer, or financial verifications. If such financing is not approved within _____ days from the effective date hereof, this contract shall terminate and the Earnest Money shall be refunded to Buyer.

NOTICE TO PARTIES: Before signing this contract Buyer is advised to determine the financing options available from lenders. Certain loans have variable rates of interest, some have monthly payments which may not be sufficient to pay the accruing interest, and some have interest rate "buydowns" which reduce the rate of interest for part or all of the loan term at the expense of one or more of the parties to this contract.

5. EARNEST MONEY: Buyer shall deposit the sum of $ _____ as Earnest Money with _____ at _____ (Address), as Escrow Agent, upon execution of the contract by both parties. □ Additional Earnest Money of $ _____ shall be deposited by Buyer with the Escrow Agent on or before _____, 19 ___. If Buyer fails to deposit the Earnest Money or any additional Earnest Money, Seller may terminate this contract.

NOTICE: Escrow Agent should be a disinterested third party. Review Paragraph 18 before selecting Escrow Agent.

6. TITLE: Seller shall furnish to Buyer at _____'s expense either:

□ A. Owner's Policy of Title Insurance (the Title Policy) issued by _____ in the amount of the Sales Price and dated at or after closing; OR

□ B. Abstracts of Title certified by an abstract company (1) from the sovereignty to the effective date of this contract (Complete Abstract) and (2) supplemented to the closing date (Supplemental Abstract).

NOTICE TO SELLER AND BUYER: AS REQUIRED BY LAW, Broker advises Buyer that Buyer should have the Abstract covering the Property examined by an attorney of Buyer's selection, or Buyer should be furnished with or obtain a Title Policy. If a Title Policy is to be obtained, Buyer should obtain a Commitment for Title Insurance (the Commitment) which should be examined by an attorney of Buyer's choice at or prior to closing. If the Property is situated in a Utility District, Section 50.301, Texas Water Code require the Buyer to sign and acknowledge the statutory notice from Seller relating to the tax rate and bonded indebtedness of the District. If the Property is situated seaward of the Gulf Intracoastal Waterway, attach an addendum containing the statement required by Section 61.025, Texas Natural Resources Code.

7. PROPERTY CONDITION:

A. CONDITION OF THE PROPERTY: (Check 1 or 2)

□ 1. Buyer accepts the Property in its present condition, subject only to any FHA, VA or lender requirements and _____

_____

□ 2. Buyer requires inspections and repairs required by FHA, VA or any lender and the Property Condition Addendum attached hereto.

On Seller's receipt of all loan approvals and inspection reports, Seller shall commence repairs and termite treatment required of Seller in A 1 or A 2 above (including the Property Condition Addendum, if any) and complete such repairs prior to closing. Seller's responsibility for the repairs, termite treatment and repairs to termite damage shall not exceed $ _____. If Seller fails to complete such repairs, Buyer may do so and Seller shall be liable up to the amount specified and the same paid from the proceeds of the sale. If the repair costs will exceed the stated amount and Seller refuses to pay such excess, Buyer may (1) pay the additional cost if permitted by lender or (2) accept the Property with the limited repairs (if permitted by lender) or (3) Buyer may terminate this contract and the Earnest Money shall be refunded to Buyer. Buyer shall make his election within three (3) days after Seller notifies Buyer of Seller's refusal to pay such excess. Failure of Buyer to make such election within the time provided shall be deemed to be Buyer's election to accept the Property with the limited repairs, and the sale shall be closed as scheduled; however, if lender prohibits Buyer's payment of additional costs or acceptance with the limited repairs, this contract shall terminate and Earnest Money shall be refunded to Buyer.

If all the repair costs will exceed five (5) percent of the Sales Price of the Property and Seller agrees to pay the cost of such repairs, Buyer shall have the option of closing the sale with the completed repairs, or terminating this contract and the Earnest Money shall be refunded to Buyer. Buyer shall make this election within three days after Seller notifies Buyer of Seller's willingness to pay the cost of such repairs. Failure of Buyer to make such election within the time provided shall be deemed to be Buyer's election to close the sale with the completed repairs.

B. WARRANTIES: In connection with all improvements, fixtures and all other property located on or made a part of the Property: □ Seller makes no express warranties, OR □ Seller makes the express warranties stated in Paragraph 11 or attached. Seller agrees to assign to Buyer at closing all assignable manufacturer warranties.

C. INSULATION: Insulation information required under Federal Trade Commission Regulations is included in an attached addendum unless previously disclosed to Buyer in writing.

8. BROKER'S FEE: _____ (Broker) and any co-broker represent Seller unless otherwise specified herein. Seller agrees to pay Broker the fee specified by separate agreement between Broker and Seller. If there is no separate agreement, Seller agrees to pay Broker in _____ County, Texas, on closing of this sale, or on termination of this contract by agreement of the parties (except as permitted by the terms of this contract), or on Seller's default a total cash fee of _____ of the total Sales Price or upon Buyer's default, one half of any Earnest Money to which Seller is entitled under Paragraph 16 not to exceed the amount of the cash fee. Escrow Agent is authorized and directed to pay Broker said fee from the sale proceeds.

9. CLOSING: The closing of the sale shall be on or before _____, 19 ___, or within seven (7) days after objections to title have been cured, whichever date is later (the Closing Date). If financing approval has been obtained pursuant to Paragraph 4, the Closing Date shall be extended daily up to fifteen (15) days if necessary to complete loan requirements. If either party fails to close this sale by the Closing Date, the non defaulting party shall be entitled to exercise the remedies contained in Paragraph 16 immediately and without notice. Seller's obligation to complete all improvements and required repairs shall survive closing.

10. POSSESSION: The possession of the Property shall be delivered to Buyer on _____ in its present or required improved condition, ordinary wear and tear excepted. The parties agree to use the Buyer's Temporary Residential Lease Form promulgated by the Texas Real Estate Commission (TREC), if Buyer takes possession prior to closing. In the absence of such written lease, any possession by Buyer prior to closing shall establish a landlord-tenant at sufferance relationship between the parties.

INITIALED FOR IDENTIFICATION BY BUYER _____ AND SELLER _____

TREC No. 24-0

006

New Home (Completed Construction)—Page Three   05-22-87

11. **SPECIAL PROVISIONS:** Insert factual statements and business details applicable to this sale. A licensee shall not add to a promulgated earnest money contract form factual statements or business details for which a contract addendum, lease or other form has been promulgated by TREC for mandatory use. 22 TAC §537.11(d).

12. **SALES EXPENSES TO BE PAID IN CASH AT OR PRIOR TO CLOSING:**

   A. Loan appraisal fee shall be paid by _____.

   B. (1) Conventional or FHA Sale: The total of the loan discount and any buydown fees (excluding any Texas Veterans' Housing Assistance Program Participation Fee) shall not exceed $ _____ of which Buyer shall pay the first $ _____ and Seller shall pay the remainder.

   (2) VA Sale: The total of the loan discount and buydown fees (excluding any Texas Veterans' Housing Assistance Program Participation Fee) shall not exceed $ _____ which shall be paid by Seller.

   C. Seller's Expenses: (1) Lender, FHA or VA completion requirements, and any other inspections, reports or repairs required of Seller; (2) releases of existing loans, including prepayment penalties and recordation; tax statements; preparation of deed; one-half of escrow fee; (3) for VA loans, expenses VA prohibits Buyer from paying (e.g., preparation of loan documents, copies of restrictions, photos, excess cost of survey, remaining one-half of escrow fee); (4) any Texas Veterans' Housing Assistance Program Participation Fee not exceeding $ _____ ; (5) other expenses stipulated to be paid by Seller under other provisions of this contract.

   D. Buyer's Expenses: (1) Application and origination fees; (2) interest on the notes from dates of disbursements to one (1) month prior to date of first monthly payments; (3) all prepaid items (e.g. required premiums for flood and hazard insurance, reserve deposits for insurance, ad valorem taxes and special governmental assessments); (4) loan related inspection fees; (5) any customary Texas Veterans' Housing Assistance Program loan costs; (6) expenses stipulated to be paid by Buyer under other provisions of this contract and

   (a) FHA Buyer: (1) expenses incident to any loan (e.g., preparation of loan documents, survey, recording fees, copies of restrictions and easements, amortization schedule, Mortgagee's Title Policies, credit reports, photos); one-half of escrow fee.

   (b) VA Buyer: (a) expenses incident to any loan (e.g., that portion of survey costs VA Buyer may pay by VA Regulation; recording fees, Mortgagee's Title Policies, credit reports).

   (c) Conventional Buyer: (1) private mortgage insurance premiums; (2) expenses incident to any new loan (e.g., preparation of loan documents, survey, recording fees, copies of restrictions and easements, Mortgagee's Title Policies, credit reports, photos); (3) one-half of escrow fee.

   (d) Cash Buyer: (1) recording fees; (2) one-half of escrow fee.

   E. The VA Loan funding fee or FHA MIP in the amount of $ _____ is to be paid by _____. If paid by Buyer, it is to be □ paid in cash at closing □ added to the amount of the loan to the extent permitted by lender. If financed, the amount is to be added to the loan amount in Paragraph 3B by lender in the loan documents but is not part of the Contract Sales Price.

   F. If any expenses exceed the amount herein stipulated to be paid by either party, either party may terminate this contract unless the other party agrees to pay such excess. In no event shall Buyer pay charges and fees expressly prohibited by FHA, VA or Texas Veterans' Housing Assistance Program Regulations.

13. **PRORATIONS AND TAXES:** Current taxes, any rents and subdivision dues and assessments shall be prorated through the Closing Date. If Seller's change in use of the Property prior to closing or denial of a special use valuation claimed by Seller results in the assessment of additional taxes for periods prior to closing, such additional taxes shall be the obligation of Seller, and such obligation shall survive closing.

14. **TITLE APPROVAL:**

   A. If abstract is furnished, Seller shall deliver Complete Abstract to Buyer within twenty (20) days from the effective date hereof. Buyer shall have twenty (20) days from date of receipt of Complete Abstract to deliver a copy of the examining attorney's title opinion to Seller stating any objections and only objections so stated shall be considered. However, the following items shall not be recited as objections to title by Buyer: liens securing payment of debt created as part of the consideration, taxes for the current year, restrictive covenants and utility easements common to the platted subdivision of which the Property is a part, existing building and zoning ordinances, and any exceptions permitted by the terms of this contract.

   B. If Title Policy is furnished, the Title Policy shall guarantee Buyer's title to be good and indefeasible subject only to (1) restrictive covenants affecting the Property (2) any discrepancies, conflicts or shortages in area or boundary lines, or any encroachments, or any overlapping of improvements (3) taxes for the current and subsequent years and subsequent assessments for prior years due to a change in land usage or ownership (4) existing building and zoning ordinances (5) rights of parties in possession (6) liens created as security for the sale consideration (7) utility easements common to the platted subdivision of which this Property is a part and (8) reservations or other exceptions permitted by the terms of this contract. If the Title Policy will be subject to exceptions other than those recited above in items (1) through (7) inclusive, Seller shall deliver to Buyer the Commitment and legible copies of any documents creating exceptions that are not recited in items (1) through (7) above at least five (5) days prior to closing. If Buyer has objection to any such previously undisclosed exceptions, or to any unrecorded easement or adverse condition with respect to the boundaries which are revealed by any survey of the Property, Buyer shall have five (5) days after receipt of such Commitment, copies, and survey to make written objections to Seller. If no Commitment is provided to Buyer at or prior to closing, it will be conclusively presumed that Seller represented at closing that the Title Policy would not be subject to exceptions other than those recited above in items (1) through (7).

   C. In either instance if title objections are raised by Buyer or Title Company named in Paragraph 6A, Seller shall have fifteen (15) days from the date such objections are disclosed to cure the same, and the Closing Date shall be extended accordingly. If the objections are not timely cured, this contract shall terminate and the Earnest Money shall be refunded to Buyer, unless Buyer elects to waive the unsatisfied objections and complete the purchase.

   D. Seller shall furnish tax statements showing no delinquent taxes; a Supplemental Abstract, when applicable, showing no additional title objections; and a General Warranty Deed conveying title subject only to liens securing payment of debt created as part of the consideration, taxes for the current year, restrictive covenants and utility easements common to the platted subdivision of which the Property is a part, existing building and zoning ordinances, and any exceptions or reservations acceptable to Buyer. Each note shall be secured by vendor's and deed of trust liens. In case of dispute as to the form of the deed (and in Seller financed transactions, the note and deed of trust), forms prepared by the State Bar of Texas shall be used.

15. **CASUALTY LOSS:** If any part of the Property is damaged or destroyed by fire or other casualty loss, Seller shall restore the same to its previous condition, the Closing Date shall be extended for a maximum of fifteen (15) days if necessary for Seller to do so. If Seller is unable to do so without fault, this contract shall terminate and the Earnest Money shall be refunded to Buyer.

16. **DEFAULT:** If Buyer fails to comply herewith, Seller may either seek such relief as may be provided by law or terminate this contract and receive the Earnest Money as liquidated damages, thereby releasing Buyer from this contract. If Seller is unable without fault, within the time herein required to (a) make any noncasualty repairs or (b) deliver the Commitment or (c) deliver the Complete Abstract, Buyer may either terminate this contract and receive the Earnest Money as the sole remedy or extend the time for performance up to fifteen (15) days and the Closing Date shall be extended pursuant to other provisions of this contract. If Seller fails to comply herewith for any other reason, Buyer may either seek such relief as may be provided by law or terminate this contract and receive the Earnest Money, thereby releasing Seller from this contract.

17. **ATTORNEY'S FEES:** Any party to this contract, Broker, Co-broker or Escrow Agent who prevails in any legal proceeding brought under or with relation to this contract or transaction shall be additionally entitled to recover court costs and reasonable attorney's fees.

INITIALED FOR IDENTIFICATION BY BUYER _____ AND SELLER _____

006 TREC No. 24-0

New Home (Completed Construction)—Page Four

18. **ESCROW:** The Earnest Money is deposited with Escrow Agent with the understanding that Escrow Agent (a) is not a party to this contract and does not assume or have any liability for performance or non-performance of any party to this contract (b) has the right to require from all parties and brokers a written release of liability of the Escrow Agent which authorizes the disbursement of the Earnest Money (c) is not liable for interest or other charge on the funds held and (d) is not liable for any losses of escrow funds caused by the failure of any banking institution in which such funds have been deposited, unless such banking institution is acting as Escrow Agent. If any party or broker unreasonably fails to deliver promptly the document described in (b) above, then such party or broker shall be liable as provided in Paragraph 17. At closing, the Earnest Money shall be applied first to any cash down payment required, then to Buyer's closing costs and any excess refunded to Buyer. Any refund or payment of the Earnest Money under this contract shall be reduced by the amount of any actual expenses incurred on behalf of the party receiving the Earnest Money, and Escrow Agent shall pay the same to the creditors entitled thereto. If the Earnest Money is deposited with the Seller, this paragraph is not applicable.

19. **REPRESENTATIONS:** Seller represents that as of the Closing Date there will no unrecorded liens, assessments or Uniform Commercial Code Security Interests against any of the Property which will not be satisfied out of the Sales Price. If any representation in this contract is untrue on the Closing Date, this contract may be terminated by Buyer and the Earnest Money shall be refunded to Buyer. All representations contained in this contract shall survive closing.

20. **AGREEMENT OF PARTIES:** This contract contains the entire agreement of the parties and cannot be changed except by their written agreement. Texas Real Estate Commission promulgated addenda which are part of this contract are: (list) _____

_____

21. **NOTICES:** All notices shall be in writing and effective when delivered at the addresses shown below.

22. **CONSULT YOUR ATTORNEY:** The Broker cannot give you legal advice. This is intended to be a legally binding contract. READ IT CAREFULLY. If you do not understand the effect of any part of this contract, consult your attorney BEFORE signing. Federal law may impose certain duties upon brokers or parties to this contract when any party is a foreign party or when any party receives certain amounts of U.S. currency in connection with a real estate closing.

BUYER'S　　　　　　　　　　　　　　　　　　　SELLER'S
ATTORNEY: _____　　ATTORNEY: _____

EXECUTED in multiple originals effective the _____ day of _____, 19 _____ . **(BROKER: FILL IN THE DATE OF FINAL ACCEPTANCE.)**

_____　　　　　_____
Buyer　　　　　　　　　　　　　　　　　Seller

_____　　　　　_____
Buyer　　　　　　　　　　　　　　　　　Seller

_____　　　　　_____
Buyer's Address　　　　Phone No.　　　Seller's Address　　　　Phone No.

- -

AGREEMENT BETWEEN BROKERS

Broker agrees to pay _____ (Co-Broker) a fee
of _____ of the total sales price when the Broker's fee described in Paragraph 8 is received. Escrow Agent is authorized and directed to pay Co-Broker from Broker's fee at closing.

_____　　　　　_____
Co-Broker　　　　　License No.　　　Broker　　　　　　License No.

By: _____　　By: _____

_____　　　　　_____
Co-Broker's Address　　　Phone No.　　Broker's Address　　　　Phone No.

- -

EARNEST MONEY RECEIPT

Receipt of $ _____ Earnest Money in the form of _____
is acknowledged and is accepted subject to the terms of the contract.

Escrow Agent: _____　　By: _____

Date: _____ , 19 _____ .

The form of this contract has been approved by the Texas Real Estate Commission. Such approval relates to this contract form only. No representation is made as to the legal validity or adequacy of any provision in any specific transaction. It is not suitable for complex transactions. Extensive riders or additions are not to be used. (05-87) TREC NO. 24-0.　　　　　　　　　　　　　　　　　　　　　006

Alphabetical Index of Cases

Subject Index of Cases

Index